Sixth Edition

CompTIA ®

SECURITY+ GUIDE TO NETWORK SECURITY FUNDAMENTALS

D0203610

Mark Ciampa, Ph.D.

CENGAGE

Australia • Brazil • Mexico • Singapore • United Kingdom • United States

Security+ Guide to Network Security Fundamentals, Sixth Edition

Mark Ciampa

SVP, GM Skills: Jonathan Lau

Product Team Manager: Kristin McNary

Associate Product Manager: Amy Savino

Executive Director of Development: Marah Bellegarde

Senior Product Development Manager: Leigh Hefferon

Senior Content Developer: Michelle Ruelos Cannistraci

Product Assistant: Jake Toth

Marketing Director: Michelle McTighe

Production Director: Patty Stephan

Senior Content Project Manager: Brooke Greenhouse

Art Director: Diana Graham

Cover image(s): iStockPhoto.com/ supernitram

For product information and technology assistance, contact us at **Cengage Customer & Sales Support, 1-800-354-9706.**

For permission to use material from this text or product, submit all requests online at **www.cengage.com/permissions.** Further permissions questions can be e-mailed to **permissionrequest@cengage.com.**

Library of Congress Control Number: 2017950178

ISBN: 978-1-337-28878-1

LLF ISBN: 978-1-337-68585-6

Cengage

20 Channel Center Street

Boston, MA 02210

USA

Cengage is a leading provider of customized learning solutions with employees residing in nearly 40 different countries and sales in more than 125 countries around the world. Find your local representative at **www.cengage.com.**

Cengage products are represented in Canada by Nelson Education, Ltd.

To learn more about Cengage platforms and services, register or access your online learning solution, or purchase materials for your course, visit **www.cengage.com.**

Printed at CLDPC, USA, 02-19

Brief Contents

Table of Contents

PART 3

NETWORK ATTACKS AND DEFENSES

CHAPTER 5

Networking and Server Attacks

CHAPTER 12

Access Management 521

Table of Contents

INTRODUCTION

The number one concern of computer professionals today continues to be information security, and with good reason. Consider the evidence: over 1.5 billion Yahoo user accounts were compromised in just two separate attacks.[1] A ransom of $1 million dollars was paid to unlock files that had been encrypted by ransomware.[2] A global payment system used to transfer money between countries was compromised by attackers who stole $81 billion from the central bank of Bangladesh.[3] It is estimated that global spending on products and services to prevent these attacks will exceed $1 trillion cumulatively between 2017 and 2021. But despite the huge sum spent on protection, cybercrime will still cost businesses over $6 trillion by 2021.[4]

As attacks continue to escalate, the need for trained security personnel also increases. It is estimated that there are currently over 1.5 million unfilled security jobs worldwide and this will grow by 20 percent to 1.8 million by the year 2022.[5] According to the U.S. Bureau of Labor Statistics (BLS) "Occupational Outlook Handbook," the job outlook for information security analysts through 2024 is expected to grow by 18 percent, faster than the average growth rate.[6]

To verify security competency, most organizations use the Computing Technology Industry Association (CompTIA) Security+ certification, a vendor-neutral credential. Security+ is one of the most widely recognized security certifications and has become the security foundation for today's IT professionals. It is internationally recognized as validating a foundation level of security skills and knowledge. A successful Security+ candidate has the knowledge and skills required to identify threats, attacks and vulnerabilities; use security technologies and tools; understand security architecture and design; perform identity and access management; know about risk management; and use cryptography.

Security+ Guide to Network Security Fundamentals, Sixth Edition is designed to equip learners with the knowledge and skills needed to be information security professionals. Yet it is more than an "exam prep" book. While teaching the fundamentals of information security by using the CompTIA Security+ exam objectives as its framework, it takes a comprehensive view of security by examining in-depth the attacks against networks and computer systems and the necessary defense mechanisms. *Security+ Guide to Network Security Fundamentals, Sixth Edition* is a valuable tool for those who want to learn about security and who desire to enter the field of information security. It also provides the foundation that will help prepare for the CompTIA Security+ certification exam.

Intended Audience

This book is designed to meet the needs of students and professionals who want to master basic information security. A fundamental knowledge of computers and networks is all that is required to use this book. Those seeking to pass the CompTIA Security+ certification exam will find the text's approach and content especially helpful; all Security+ SY0-501 exam objectives are covered in the text (see Appendix A). *Security+ Guide to Network Security Fundamentals, Sixth Edition* covers all aspects of network and computer security while satisfying the Security+ objectives.

The book's pedagogical features are designed to provide a truly interactive learning experience to help prepare you for the challenges of network and computer security. In addition to the information presented in the text, each chapter includes Hands-On Projects that guide you through implementing practical hardware, software, network, and Internet security configurations step by step. Each chapter also contains case studies that place you in the role of problem solver, requiring you to apply concepts presented in the chapter to achieve successful solutions.

Chapter Descriptions

Here is a summary of the topics covered in each chapter of this book:

Chapter 1, "Introduction to Security," introduces the network security fundamentals that form the basis of the Security+ certification. It begins by examining the current challenges in computer security and why security is so difficult to achieve. It then defines information security in detail and explores why it is important. Finally, the chapter looks at the fundamental attacks, including who is responsible for them, and defenses.

Chapter 2, "Malware and Social Engineering Attacks," examines attacks that use different types of malware, such as viruses, worms, Trojans, and botnets. It also looks at the different types of social engineering attacks.

Chapter 3, "Basic Cryptography," explores how encryption can be used to protect data. It covers what cryptography is and how it can be used for protection, and then examines how to protect data using three common types of encryption algorithms: hashing, symmetric encryption, and asymmetric encryption. It also covers how to use cryptography on files and disks to keep data secure.

Chapter 4, "Advanced Cryptography and PKI," examines how to implement cryptography and use digital certificates. It also looks at public key infrastructure and key management. This chapter covers different transport cryptographic algorithms to see how cryptography is used on data that is being transported.

Chapter 5, "Networking and Server Attacks," explores the different attacks that are directed at enterprises. It includes networking-based attacks as well as server attacks.

Chapter 6, "Network Security Devices, Design, and Technology," examines how to protect networks through standard network devices and network security hardware. It also covers implementing security through network architectures and network technologies.

Chapter 7, "Administering a Secure Network," looks at the techniques for administering a network. This includes understanding common network protocols and the proper placement of security devices and technologies. It also looks at analyzing security data and securing network platforms such as virtualization, cloud computing, and software defined networks.

Chapter 8, "Wireless Network Security," investigates the attacks on wireless devices that are common today and explores different wireless security mechanisms that have proven to be vulnerable. It also covers several secure wireless protections.

Chapter 9, "Client and Application Security," examines securing the client through hardware and peripherals through hardware and the operating system. It also looks at physical security to create external perimeter defenses and internal physical access security. This chapter also covers application security vulnerabilities and the development of secure apps.

Chapter 10, "Mobile and Embedded Device Security," looks at the different types of mobile devices and the risks associated with these devices. It also explores how to secure these devices and the applications running on them. Finally, it examines how embedded systems and the Internet of Things devices can be secured.

Chapter 11, "Authentication and Account Management," looks at authentication and the secure management of user accounts to enforce authentication. It covers the different types of authentication credentials that can be used to verify a user's identity and how a single sign-on might be used. It also examines the techniques and technology used to manage user accounts in a secure fashion.

Chapter 12, "Access Management," introduces the principles and practices of access control by examining access control terminology, the standard control models, and managing access through account management. It also covers best practices, implementing access control, and identity and access services.

Chapter 13, "Vulnerability Assessment and Data Security," explains what vulnerability assessment is and examines the tools and techniques associated with it. It also explores the differences between vulnerability scanning and penetration testing. The chapter concludes with an examination of data privacy.

Chapter 14, "Business Continuity," covers the importance of keeping business processes and communications operating normally in the face of threats and disruptions. It explores business continuity, fault tolerance, environmental controls, and incident response.

Chapter 15, "Risk Mitigation," looks at how organizations can establish and maintain security in the face of risk. It defines risk and the strategies to control it. This chapter also covers practices for reducing risk and troubleshooting common security issues.

Appendix A, "CompTIA SY0-501 Certification Examination Objectives," provides a complete listing of the latest CompTIA Security+ certification exam objectives and shows the chapters and headings in the book that cover material associated with each objective, as well as the Bloom's Taxonomy level of that coverage.

Features

To aid you in fully understanding computer and network security, this book includes many features designed to enhance your learning experience.

- **Maps to CompTIA Objectives.** The material in this text covers all the CompTIA Security+ SY0-501 exam objectives.
- **Chapter Objectives.** Each chapter begins with a detailed list of the concepts to be mastered in that chapter. This list provides you with both a quick reference to the chapter's contents and a useful study aid.
- **Today's Attacks and Defenses.** Each chapter opens with a vignette of an actual security attack or defense mechanism that helps to introduce the material covered in that chapter.
- **Illustrations and Tables.** Numerous illustrations of security vulnerabilities, attacks, and defenses help you visualize security elements, theories, and concepts. In addition, the many tables provide details and comparisons of practical and theoretical information.
- **Chapter Summaries.** Each chapter's text is followed by a summary of the concepts introduced in that chapter. These summaries provide a helpful way to review the ideas covered in each chapter.
- **Key Terms.** All the terms in each chapter that were introduced with bold text are gathered in a Key Terms list, providing additional review and highlighting key concepts. Key Term definitions are included in the Glossary at the end of the text.
- **Review Questions.** The end-of-chapter assessment begins with a set of review questions that reinforce the ideas introduced in each chapter. These questions help you evaluate and apply the material you have learned. Answering these questions will ensure that you have mastered the important concepts and provide valuable practice for taking CompTIA's Security+ exam.
- **Hands-On Projects.** Although it is important to understand the theory behind network security, nothing can improve on real-world experience. To this end, each chapter provides several Hands-On Projects aimed at providing you with practical security software and hardware implementation experience. These projects use the Windows 10 operating system, as well as software downloaded from the Internet.
- **Case Projects.** Located at the end of each chapter are several Case Projects. In these extensive exercises, you implement the skills and knowledge gained in the chapter through real design and implementation scenarios.

New to This Edition

- Maps fully to the latest CompTIA Security+ exam SY0-501
- Completely revised and updated with expanded coverage on attacks and defenses
- New chapter units: Security and Its Threats, Cryptography, Network Attacks and Defenses, Device Security, Identity and Access Management, and Risk Management
- Earlier coverage of cryptography and advanced cryptography
- All new "Today's Attacks and Defenses" opener in each chapter
- New and updated Hands-On Projects in each chapter covering some of the latest security software
- More Case Projects in each chapter
- Expanded Information Security Community Site activity in each chapter allows learners to interact with other learners and security professionals from around the world
- All SY0-501 exam topics fully defined
- Linking of each exam sub-domain to Bloom's Taxonomy (see Appendix A)

Text and Graphic Conventions

Wherever appropriate, additional information and exercises have been added to this book to help you better understand the topic at hand. Icons throughout the text alert you to additional materials. The following icons areo used in this textbook:

The Note icon draws your attention to additional helpful material related to the subject being described.

Tips based on the author's experience provide extra information about how to attack a problem or what to do in real-world situations.

Caution

The Caution icons warn you about potential mistakes or problems, and explain how to avoid them.

Hands-On Projects help you understand the theory behind network security with activities using the latest security software and hardware.

Case Projects

The Case Projects icon marks Case Projects, which are scenario-based assignments. In these extensive case examples, you are asked to implement independently what you have learned.

Certification icons indicate CompTIA Security+ objectives covered under major chapter headings.

Instructor's Materials

Everything you need for your course in one place. This collection of book-specific lecture and class tools is available online. Please visit *login.cengage.com* and log in to access instructor-specific resources on the Instructor Companion Site, which includes the Instructor's Manual, Solutions Manual, test creation tools, PowerPoint Presentations, Syllabus, and figure files.

- **Electronic Instructor's Manual**. The Instructor's Manual that accompanies this textbook includes the following items: additional instructional material to assist in class preparation, including suggestions for lecture topics.
- **Solutions Manual**. The instructor's resources include solutions to all end-of-chapter material, including review questions and case projects.
- **Cengage Testing Powered by Cognero**. This flexible, online system allows you to do the following:
  - Author, edit, and manage test bank content from multiple Cengage solutions.
  - Create multiple test versions in an instant.
  - Deliver tests from your LMS, your classroom, or wherever you want.
- **PowerPoint Presentations**. This book comes with a set of Microsoft PowerPoint slides for each chapter. These slides are meant to be used as a teaching aid for classroom presentations, to be made available to students on the network for chapter review, or to be printed for classroom distribution. Instructors are also at liberty to add their own slides for other topics introduced.
- **Figure Files**. All the figures and tables in the book are reproduced. Similar to PowerPoint presentations, these are included as a teaching aid for classroom presentation, to make available to students for review, or to be printed for classroom distribution.

Total Solutions For Security

To access additional course materials, please visit *www.cengagebrain.com*. At the *cengagebrain.com* home page, search for the ISBN of your title (from the back cover of your book) using the search box at the top of the page. This will take you to the product page where these resources can be found.

MindTap

MindTap for *Security+ Guide to Network Security Fundamentals, Sixth Edition* is a personalized, fully online digital learning platform of content, assignments, and services that engages students and encourages them to think critically, while allowing you to easily set your course through simple customization options.

MindTap is designed to help students master the skills they need in today's workforce. Research shows employers need critical thinkers, troubleshooters, and creative problem solvers to stay relevant in our fast paced, technology-driven world. MindTap helps you achieve this with assignments and activities that provide hands-on practice, real-life relevance, and certification test prep. Students are guided through assignments that help them master basic knowledge and understanding before moving on to more challenging problems.

The live virtual machine labs provide real-life application and practice as well as more advanced learning. Students work in a live environment via the Cloud with real servers and networks that they can explore. The IQ certification test preparation engine allows students to quiz themselves on specific exam domains, and the pre- and post-course assessments measure exactly how much they have learned. Readings, lab simulations, capstone projects, and videos support the lecture, while "In the News" assignments encourage students to stay current.

MindTap is designed around learning objectives and provides the analytics and reporting to easily see where the class stands in terms of progress, engagement, and completion rates.

Students can access eBook content in the MindTap Reader, which offers highlighting, note-taking, search and audio, as well as mobile access. Learn more at *www.cengage.com/mindtap/*.

Instant Access Code: (ISBN: 9781337289306)
Printed Access Code: (ISBN: 9781337289313)

Lab Manual

Hands-on learning is necessary to master the security skills needed for both CompTIA's Security+ Exam and for a career in network security. *Security+ Guide to Network Security Fundamentals Lab Manual, 6th Edition* contains hands-on exercises that use fundamental networking security concepts as they are applied in the real world. Each chapter offers review questions to reinforce your mastery of network security topics and to sharpen your critical thinking and problem-solving skills. (ISBN: 9781337288798)

Bloom's Taxonomy

Bloom's Taxonomy is an industry-standard classification system used to help identify the level of ability that learners need to demonstrate proficiency. It is often used to classify educational learning objectives into different levels of complexity. Bloom's Taxonomy reflects the "cognitive process dimension." This represents a continuum of increasing cognitive complexity, from remember (lowest level) to create (highest level). There are six categories in Bloom's Taxonomy as seen in Figure A.

In all instances, the level of coverage the domains in *Security+ Guide to Network Security Fundamentals, Sixth Edition* meets or exceeds the Bloom's Taxonomy level indicated by CompTIA for that objective. See Appendix A for more detail.

Information Security Community Site

Stay secure with the Information Security Community Site. Connect with students, professors, and professionals from around the world, and stay on top of this ever-changing field.

Visit *http://community.cengage.com/Infosec2/* to:

- **Download** resources such as instructional videos and labs.
- **Ask** authors, professors, and students the questions that are on your mind in the Discussion Forums.
- **See** up-to-date news, videos, and articles.

Bloom's Taxonomy

create	Produce new or original work *Design, assemble, construct, conjecture, develop, formulate, author, investigate*
evaluate	Justify a stand or decision *appraise, argue, defend, judge, select, support, value, critique, weigh*
analyze	Draw connections among ideas *differentiate, organize, relate, compare, contrast, distinguish, examine, experiment, question, test*
apply	Use information in new situations *execute, implement, solve, use, demonstrate, interpret, operate, schedule, sketch*
understand	Explain ideas or concepts *classify, describe, discuss, explain, identify, locate, recognize, report, select, translate*
remember	Recall facts and basic concepts *define, duplicate, list, memorize, repeat, state*

Figure A   Bloom's taxonomy

- **Read** regular blogs from author Mark Ciampa.
- **Listen** to podcasts on the latest Information Security topics.
- **Review** textbook updates and errata.

Each chapter's Case Projects include information on a current security topic and ask the learner to post reactions and comments to the Information Security Community Site. This allows users from around the world to interact and learn from other users as well as security professionals and researchers.

What's New With Comptia Security+ Certification

The CompTIA Security+ SY0-501 exam was updated in October 2017. Several significant changes have been made to the exam objectives. The exam objectives have been significantly expanded to more accurately reflect current security issues and knowledge requirements. These exam objectives place importance on knowing "how to" rather than just knowing or recognizing security concepts.

Here are the domains covered on the new Security+ exam:

Domain	% of Examination
1.0 Threats, Attacks & Vulnerabilities	21%
2.0 Technologies & Tools	22%
3.0 Architecture & Design	15%
4.0 Identity & Access Management	16%
5.0 Risk Management	14%
6.0 Cryptography & PKI	12%
Total	100%

CompTIA.

Becoming a CompTIA Certified IT Professional is Easy

It's also the best way to reach greater professional opportunities and rewards.

Why Get CompTIA Certified?

Growing Demand

Labor estimates predict some technology fields will experience growth of over 20% by the year 2020.* CompTIA certification qualifies the skills required to join this workforce.

Higher Salaries

IT professionals with certifications on their resume command better jobs, earn higher salaries and have more doors open to new multi-industry opportunities.

Verified Strengths

91% of hiring managers indicate CompTIA certifications are valuable in validating IT expertise, making certification the best way to demonstrate your competency and knowledge to employers.**

Universal Skills

CompTIA certifications are vendor neutral—which means that certified professionals can proficiently work with an extensive variety of hardware and software found in most organizations.

Learn more about what the exam covers by reviewing the following:

- Exam objectives for key study points.
- Sample questions for a general overview of what to expect on the exam and examples of question format.
- Visit online forums, like LinkedIn, to see what other IT professionals say about CompTIA exams.

Purchase a voucher at a Pearson VUE testing center or at CompTIAstore.com.

- Register for your exam at a Pearson VUE testing center:
- Visit pearsonvue.com/CompTIA to find the closest testing center to you.
- Schedule the exam online. You will be required to enter your voucher number or provide payment information at registration.
- Take your certification exam.

Congratulations on your CompTIA certification!

- Make sure to add your certification to your resume.
- Check out the CompTIA Certification Roadmap to plan your next career move.

Learn more: Certification.CompTIA.org/securityplus

* Source: CompTIA 9th Annual Information Security Trends study: 500 U.S. IT and Business Executives Responsible for Security
** Source: CompTIA Employer Perceptions of IT Training and Certification

About The Author

Dr. Mark Ciampa is an Associate Professor of Information Systems in the Gordon Ford College of Business at Western Kentucky University in Bowling Green, Kentucky. Prior to this, he was an Associate Professor and served as the Director of Academic Computing at Volunteer State Community College in Gallatin, Tennessee for 20 years. Mark has worked in the IT industry as a computer consultant for businesses, government agencies, and educational institutions. He has published over 20 articles in peer-reviewed journals and is also the author of 25 technology textbooks, including *Security+ Guide to Network Security Fundamentals 6e*, *CWNA Guide to Wireless LANs 3e*, *Guide to Wireless Communications*, *Security Awareness: Applying Practical Security in Your World 5e*, and *Networking BASICS*. Dr. Ciampa holds a PhD in technology management with a specialization in digital communication systems from Indiana State University and has certifications in Security+ and HIT.

Acknowledgments

A large team of dedicated professionals all contributed to the creation of this book. I am honored to be part of such an outstanding group of professionals. First, thanks go to Product Manager Kristin McNary for giving me the opportunity to work on this project and for providing her continual support, and to Associate Product Manager Amy Savino for answering all my questions. Also thanks to Senior Content Developer Michelle Ruelos Cannistraci who was very supportive, to Senior Content Product Manager Brooke Greenhouse who helped keep this fast-moving project on track, and to Dr. Andy Hurd who performed the technical reviews. To everyone on the team I extend my sincere thanks.

Special recognition again goes to the very best developmental editor, Deb Kaufmann, who is a true professional in every sense of the word. She made many helpful suggestions, found all my errors, watched every small detail, and even took on additional responsibilities so that this project could accelerate to be completed even before its deadlines. Without question, Deb is simply the very best there is.

And finally, I want to thank my wonderful wife, Susan. Her love, interest, support, and patience gave me what I needed to complete this project. I could not have written this book without her.

Dedication
To Braden, Mia, Abby, Gabe, Cora, and Will.

To The User

This book should be read in sequence, from beginning to end. Each chapter builds on those that precede it to provide a solid understanding of networking security fundamentals. The book may also be used to prepare for CompTIA's Security+ certification exam. Appendix A pinpoints the chapters and sections in which specific Security+ exam objectives are covered.

Hardware and Software Requirements
Following are the hardware and software requirements needed to perform the end-of-chapter Hands-On Projects.

- Microsoft Windows 10
- An Internet connection and web browser
- Microsoft Office

Free Downloadable Software Requirements

Free, downloadable software is required for the Hands-On Projects in the following chapters.

Chapter 1:
- Microsoft Safety Scanner
- Oracle VirtualBox

Chapter 2:
- Irongeek Thumbscrew
- Refog Keylogger

Chapter 3:
- OpenPuff Steganography
- HashCalc
- Jetico BestCrypt

Chapter 4:
- Comodo Secure Email Certificate

Chapter 5:
- Qualys Browser Check
- GRC Securable

Chapter 6:
- GlassWire
- K9 Web Protection

Chapter 7:
- VMware vCenter Converter
- VMware Workstation Player

Chapter 8:
- Xirrus Wi-Fi Inspector
- Vistumbler

Chapter 9:
- EICAR AntiVirus Test File

Chapter 10:
- Prey Project
- Bluestacks
- Andy Android emulator
- Lookout Security & Antivirus

Chapter 11:
- Hashcat
- HashcatGUI
- BioID Facial Recognition Authenticator
- GreyC-Keystroke
- KeePass

Chapter 13:
- Flexera Personal Software Inspector
- Macrium Reflect
- Nmap

Chapter 14:
- Directory Snoop
- Nmap

Chapter 15:
- Browzar
- UNetbootin
- Linux Mint

References

1. Newman, Lilly, "Hack brief: Hackers breach a billion Yahoo accounts," *Wired*, Dec. 14, 2016, retrieved Jul. 3, 2017, https://www.wired.com/2016/12/yahoo-hack-billion-users/.
2. Chang, Ziv, Sison, Gilbert, Jocson, Jeanne, "Erebus resurfaces as Linux ransomware," *TrendLabs Security Intelligence Blog*, Jun. 19, 2017, retrieved Jul. 3, 2017, http://blog.trendmicro.com/trendlabs-security-intelligence/erebus-resurfaces-as-linux-ransomware/.
3. Corkery, Michael, and Goldstein, Matthew, "North Korea said to be target of inquiry over $81 million cyberheist," *New York Times*, Mar. 22, 2017, retrieved Jul. 3, 2017, https://www.nytimes.com/2017/03/22/business/dealbook/north-korea-said-to-be-target-of-inquiry-over-81-million-cyberheist.html.
4. "Cybersecurity market report," *Cybersecurity Ventures*, Q2 2017, retrieved Jul. 3, 2017, http://cybersecurityventures.com/cybersecurity-market-report/.
5. Nash, Kim, "Firms vie in hiring of cyber experts," *Wall Street Journal*, May 15, 2017, retrieved Jul. 10, 2017, https://www.wsj.com/articles/for-many-companies-a-good-cyber-chief-is-hard-to-find-1494849600.
6. "Information security analysts: Occupational outlook handbook," *Bureau of Labor Statistics*, Dec. 17, 2015, retrieved Jul. 3, 2017, https://www.bls.gov/ooh/computer-and-information-technology/information-security-analysts.htm.

SECURITY AND ITS THREATS

The security of the data and information contained on computers and digital devices today is threatened more than ever before, and the attacks are escalating every day. The chapters in this part introduce security and outline many of these threats. The chapters in later parts will give you the understanding and tools you need to defend against these attacks.

PART I

SECURITY AND ITS THREATS

Chapter 1 Introduction to Security

Chapter 2 Malware and Social Engineering Attacks

The security of the data and information contained on computers and digital devices today is threatened more than ever before, and the attacks are escalating every day. The chapters in this part introduce security and outline many of these threats. The chapters in later parts will give you the understanding and tools you need to defend against these attacks.

CHAPTER 1

INTRODUCTION TO SECURITY

After completing this chapter you should be able to do the following:

Explain the challenges of securing information

Define information security and explain why it is important

Identify the types of threat actors that are common today

Describe how to defend against attacks

Today's Attacks and Defenses

Almost everyone would assume that the director of the Central Intelligence Agency (CIA) would be well-versed in security procedures and would practice these to the letter of the law. This is because of the extreme danger that would result from a compromise or theft of highly classified information about active CIA agents or sensitive activities that are underway. The exposure of this information could result in a serious international incident or even the capture and torture of secret agents. However, a former CIA director who failed to follow basic security procedures put sensitive CIA information at risk.

Former CIA Director John Brennan had recently completed a sensitive 47-page SF-86 application to update his own top-secret government security clearance. These applications are used by the federal government for conducting a background check on individuals requesting such a security clearance. The forms contain a wealth of sensitive data about the person—criminal history, psychological records, any past drug use, information about the applicant's interactions with foreign nationals—as well as information on their spouses, family members, and even friends. In the wrong hands this information could easily be used as blackmail material. Despite government restrictions Brennan routinely forwarded classified emails from his CIA email account to his less-secure personal AOL email account. One of the emails contained his own SF-86 application as an attachment, a serious breach of CIA security protocol.

An attacker who claimed to be under the age of 20 along with two friends decided to see if they could uncover classified CIA documents. The attacker first did a reverse lookup of Brennan's public phone number to reveal that the phone was served by the carrier Verizon Wireless. The attacker called Verizon's customer service number and pretended to be a Verizon technician. He said he had a customer lined up on a scheduled callback but was unable to access Verizon's customer database on his own because "our tools were down." So, could Verizon customer service give him the email address that was linked to Brennan's phone number? The friendly and helpful Verizon customer service representative said, "Sure, no problem." The pretender then asked if the Verizon representative would also give him the last four digits of the customer's bank card that was on file. Once again, the representative was glad to help. By the time the call was over the pretender had Brennan's Verizon account number, his four-digit personal identification number, the backup private mobile cellphone number on the account, his AOL email address, and the last four digits on his bank card.

The attacker now had the information that he needed. Knowing that Brennan had an AOL email account he next called AOL and said he was locked out of that account. The AOL representative asked him to verify his identity by answering two questions: the name and phone number associated with the account and the last four digits of the bank card on file—all of which had been provided by Verizon. The AOL representative then reset the password on the email account to a new password for the attacker.

The attacker then logged into Brennan's AOL email account, where he read several dozen emails, some of which the director had forwarded from his government work email and that contained attachments. Among the attachments was Brennan's own SF-86 application and a spreadsheet containing names and Social Security numbers of several U.S. intelligence officials. It is speculated that the spreadsheet might have been a list of guests who were visiting the White House when Brennan was the President's counter-terrorism adviser. Another attachment was a letter from the U.S. Senate asking the CIA to halt its controversial use of torture tactics as interrogation techniques. The hacker posted screenshots of some of the documents on a Twitter account along with portions of the director's AOL email contact list.

When Brennan realized that this information came from his AOL email account and that it had been compromised, he reset his AOL password. However, he failed to change the cell phone number and bank card number on file that was used to reset the password. Once the attacker discovered the password had been changed, he simply reset the password again, locking out Brennan. This back-and-forth of password resets was repeated three times between the attacker and the CIA director until he finally deleted the email account.

In one last act, the attacker called Brennan's private mobile phone number that he had received from Verizon and told the former director of the CIA that he had been hacked. According to the attacker, the conversation was brief.[1]

Today our world is one in which citizens from all nations are compelled to continually protect themselves and their property from attacks by adversaries. Random shootings, suicide bombings, assassinations, and other types of physical violence occur almost daily around the world with no end in sight. To counteract this violence, new types of security defenses have been implemented. Passengers using public transportation are routinely searched. Borders are closely watched. Telephone calls are secretly monitored. These attacks and security defenses have significantly impacted how all of us work, play, and live.

These attacks are not just physical. One area that has also been an especially frequent target of attacks is information technology (IT). A seemingly endless array of attacks is directed at individuals, schools, businesses, and governments through desktop computers, laptops, and smartphones. Internet web servers must resist thousands of attacks every day. Identity theft using stolen electronic data has skyrocketed. An unprotected computer connected to the Internet may be infected in fewer than 60 seconds. Viruses, phishing, worms, and botnets—virtually unheard of just a few years ago—are now part of our everyday technology vocabulary.

The need to defend against these attacks directed toward our technology devices has created an element of IT that is now at the very core of the industry. Known as *information security*, it is focused on protecting the electronic information of enterprises and users.

Two broad categories of information security personnel are responsible for providing protection for an enterprise like a business or nonprofit organization. Information security *managerial personnel* administer and manage plans, policies, and people, while information security *technical personnel* are concerned with designing, configuring, installing, and maintaining technical security equipment. Within these two broad categories are four generally recognized security positions:

- *Chief Information Security Officer (CISO)*. This person reports directly to the CIO (large enterprises may have more layers of management between this person and the CIO). This person is responsible for assessing, managing, and implementing security.

- *Security manager*. The security manager reports to the CISO and supervises technicians, administrators, and security staff. Typically, a security manager works on tasks identified by the CISO and resolves issues identified by technicians. This position requires an understanding of configuration and operation but not necessarily technical mastery.
- *Security administrator*. The security administrator has both technical knowledge and managerial skills. A security administrator manages daily operations of security technology, and may analyze and design security solutions within a specific entity as well as identifying users' needs.
- *Security technician*. This position is generally an entry-level position for a person who has the necessary technical skills. Technicians provide technical support to configure security hardware, implement security software, and diagnose and troubleshoot problems.

Note 📎

Individuals in these positions provide protection but are not the only employees responsible for security. It is the job of every employee—both IT and non-IT—to know and practice basic security defenses.

As attacks continue to escalate, the need for trained security personnel also increases. Unlike some IT positions, security is rarely offshored or outsourced: because security is such a critical element, security positions generally remain within the enterprise. In addition, security jobs typically do not involve "on-the-job training" where employees can learn as they go; the risk is simply too great.

Note 📎

The job outlook for security professionals is exceptionally strong. According to the U.S. Bureau of Labor Statistics (BLS) "Occupational Outlook Handbook," the job outlook for information security analysts through 2024 is expected to grow by 18 percent, much faster than the average growth rate.[2] One report states that by the end of the decade demand for security professionals worldwide will rise to 6 million, with a projected shortfall of 1.5 million unfilled positions.[3]

Employment trends indicate that security personnel who also have a certification in security are in high demand. IT employers want and pay a premium for certified security personnel. An overwhelming majority of enterprises use the Computing

Technology Industry Association (CompTIA) Security+ certification to verify security competency. Of the hundreds of security certifications currently available, Security+ is one of the most widely acclaimed. Because it is internationally recognized as validating a foundation level of security skills and knowledge, the Security+ certification has become the security baseline for today's IT professionals.

> **Note** 📎
>
> The value for an IT professional who holds a security certification is significant. The extra pay awarded to IT professions who hold an IT certification is 3.5 percent over someone who does not hold that certification. However, those who hold a security certification earn 8.7 percent more than their counterparts who do not have a security certification.[4]

The CompTIA Security+ certification is a vendor-neutral credential that requires passing the current certification exam SY0-501. A successful candidate has the knowledge and skills required to identify risks and participate in risk mitigation activities; provide infrastructure, application, operational and information security; apply security controls to maintain confidentiality, integrity, and availability; identify appropriate technologies and products; troubleshoot security events and incidents; and operate with an awareness of applicable policies, laws, and regulations. The CompTIA Security+ certification is aimed at an IT security professional who has a recommended background of a minimum of two years' experience in IT administration with a focus on security.

> **Note** 📎
>
> CompTIA Security+ meets the ISO 17024 standard and is approved by U.S. Department of Defense to fulfill Directive 8570.01-M requirements. It is also compliant with government regulations under the Federal Information Security Management Act (FISMA).

This chapter introduces the security fundamentals that form the basis of the Security+ certification. It begins by examining the current challenges in computer security. It then defines information security in detail and explores why it is important. Finally, the chapter looks at who is responsible for these attacks and the fundamental defenses against such attacks.

Challenges of Securing Information

1.6 Explain the impact associated with types of vulnerabilities.

A *silver bullet* refers to an action that provides an immediate solution to a problem by cutting through the complexity that surrounds it. Why shouldn't there be such a silver bullet for securing computers? Why can't users just install an improved hardware device or use a more secure version of software to stop attacks? Unfortunately, no single and simple solution exists for securing devices. This can be illustrated by looking at the different types of attacks that users face today as well as the reasons why these attacks are successful and the difficulties in defending against attacks.

Today's Security Attacks

Even though information security continues to rank as the number one concern of IT managers and tens of billions of dollars are spent annually on computer security, the number of successful attacks continues to increase. Consider the following examples of recent attacks:

- In order to demonstrate how easy it is to remotely control a car, a reporter drove a Jeep Cherokee outside St. Louis while two security researchers 10 miles away remotely connected to it and started manipulating its controls. The air conditioning on the Jeep suddenly switched to its maximum setting. Next, the car's radio changed stations and the volume increased, even though the driver repeatedly tried to turn the volume down and change the station to no avail. Then the windshield wipers suddenly turned on and wiper fluid squirted out. While on an Interstate highway the driver pressed the accelerator but the Jeep instead started slowing down so that is was almost rammed from behind by a large truck. The researchers even remotely disabled the brakes so that the Jeep finally ended up in a ditch. The security researchers had taken advantage of the car's Internet-connection feature that controls its entertainment and navigation systems, enables phone calls, and can be used to create a Wi-Fi hot spot. Due to a vulnerability, anyone could gain access remotely to the car's control systems from virtually anywhere. This demonstration immediately caused the National Highway Traffic Safety Administration (NHTSA) to recall 1.4 million vehicles to patch this vulnerability. This was the first time a car was recalled because of a security vulnerability.[5]
- A security researcher boarded a United Airlines flight from Denver to Syracuse with a stop in Chicago. On the second leg of the trip the researcher tweeted that he was probing the aircraft systems of his flight. The United Airlines'

Cyber Security Intelligence Department, which monitors social media, saw the tweet, and alerted the FBI. According to the FBI, a special agent later examined the first-class cabin seat where the researcher was seated and found that he had tampered with the Seat Electronic Box (SEB), which is located under some passenger seats. This allowed him to connect his laptop to the in-flight entertainment (IFE) system via the SEB. Once he accessed the IFE he could then access other systems on the plane. The researcher claimed that he could have caused the airplane to change altitude after manipulating its software. United Airlines has permanently banned him from any future flights.[6]

- Yahoo announced that a then-record half a billion Yahoo accounts were compromised by attackers who gained unauthorized access to its web servers. Information stolen included names, email addresses, phone numbers, birth dates, answers to security questions, and passwords. Yahoo believed the breach occurred two years prior but had only recently discovered it. Two months later Yahoo announced that after an investigation into data provided by law enforcement officials and outside experts they determined that yet another previously undetected data breach compromised over 1 billion Yahoo user accounts three years earlier. It was not known how law enforcement officials came across this evidence, but security researchers speculate that it was discovered by someone who was watching for data on underground "dark web" markets that attackers use to buy and sell stolen data. If that was the case, then this data had been for sale for several years, and likely had been used by attackers in targeted attacks to gain access to other web accounts. Yahoo's response to the attacks was, "We continuously enhance our safeguards and systems that detect and prevent unauthorized access to user accounts."[7]

- It is not uncommon for attackers to install their malware onto a USB flash drive and then leave it in a parking lot, cafeteria, or another public place. An unsuspecting victim finds the drive and inserts it into her computer, either to discover the rightful owner or to snoop around its contents, suddenly finds her computer infected. Now the results can be even worse if the drive is a device called the USB Killer. Resembling a regular flash drive, the USB Killer, if inserted into any USB port, starts drawing power from the computer using a DC-to-DC converter. The flash drive stores the electricity in its capacitors, and when those reach a certain voltage level then USB Killer sends all the stored electricity back to the computer in a single burst. The result is that the computer is destroyed, typically burning up the motherboard. And if the computer is not destroyed on the first attempt, USB Killer will keep charging and sending the electricity over and over until the computer is "fried."[8]

- The AVS WINVote voting machine passed state voting system standards and has been used in Virginia, Pennsylvania, and Mississippi. However, the security on the machine was alarmingly weak. Easily guessed passwords like *admin*, *abcde*, and *shoup* were used to lock down its administrator account and wireless network settings, as well as the voting results database. Because these passwords were hard-coded into the machines they could not be changed. The wireless network settings used to transmit results relied upon a configuration that could easily be broken in fewer than 10 minutes. These tabulating machines lacked even basic security like a firewall and exposed several Internet openings to attackers. In addition, WINVote ran a version of an operating system that had not received a security update since 2004.[9]

- The educational toy maker VTech revealed that millions of accounts containing information on children were stolen. Approximately 11.6 million accounts were compromised in an attack that included information on 6.4 million children. The data on children that was stolen included name, gender, birth date, profile photo, and progress log. As with many recent breaches, VTech did not know that it had been a victim until it was approached by a security research firm that had discovered the attack.[10]

- The European Space Agency (ESA) is an intergovernmental organization made up of 22 countries and states that explores space. They are involved in the International Space Station and launch unmanned space exploration missions to different planets through their spaceport in French Guiana. A group of attackers stole data from the ESA, including information on 8107 of its users, and then posted it online. Even though the ESA information regarding space exploration needed to be kept secure so that it was not altered, the passwords used by ESA scientists were alarmingly weak. Of the passwords exposed, 39 percent (or 3191) were only three characters long, such as *410, 832, 808,* and *281.* Only 22 total users had a strong password of a recommended length of 20 characters.[11]

- The Internal Revenue Service (IRS) reported that through its online *Get Transcript* program, used by taxpayers who need a transcript to view tax account transactions or line-by-line tax return information for a specific tax year, attackers were able to steal 104,000 tax transcripts while an additional 100,000 attempts were unsuccessful. The attacks were made possible because in order to access the information online the inquirer had only to prove their identity by entering personal information (Social Security number, date of birth, tax filing status, and street address) and out-of-wallet information (such as the amount of a current car payment). Both types of information can be easily obtained online from a variety of sources. Once attackers had the information they began filing fake tax returns under the victim's name and stealing their tax refund. The IRS later revealed that the situation was much worse than first reported: up to 390,000 individuals had their tax information stolen out of 600,000 attempts.[12]

- Hyatt Hotels Corporation reported that cybercriminals successfully attacked restaurants, front desks, spas, and parking facilities at 250 of their hotels worldwide over a four-month period. The attacker's software was installed on the Hyatt computers and could capture payment card details like cardholder names, card numbers, expiration dates, and verification codes when the cards were swiped. Other hotel chains have likewise been compromised. Security researchers speculate that attackers are keenly interested in attacking the hospitality industry. Hotels today are rarely owned by the big companies themselves, but instead the hotels are owned by separate investors with the hotel chains simply collecting management and franchise fees. This creates uneven security at the different hotels, and even within the hotels: hotel-based restaurants, spas, and gift shops are often owned and managed by third-party companies. While the hotel brands may require property owners to follow specific standards—such as using pillowcases of 100 percent Egyptian cotton with a 1500 thread count—they often do not have the same requirements for security. There is even speculation that the hotel brands are hesitant to mandate strict security guidelines, because if a hotel is attacked then the hotel brand may be legally liable. Another reason for the popularity of hacking hotels is that hotel brands cater to high-end, frequent business travelers. These customers often make charges on their trips using a corporate credit card and can be slower to spot unusual transactions compared to using their personal card. And many hotels keep multiple cards on file for their frequent guests. This makes it easy to not only check in and out, but also allows guests to use their door key card to make purchases instead of giving a specific credit card. Having multiple instances of credit card data scattered throughout the hotel makes for multiple targets for attackers.[13]

- Apple recently announced in one month a long list of security update patches. One of its operating systems patched 11 security vulnerabilities, most of them rated as *critical* while several vulnerabilities were ranked as *serious*. Another of its operating systems fixed 18 security flaws, with 13 of them related to its web browser. Apple also announced that it will pay those who uncover critical vulnerabilities found in the latest version of iOS and the newest iPhones. The rewards range up to $200,000 for critical flaws discovered in its hardware and software.[14]

Note 🖉

Like many software and hardware vendors, Apple maintains a lengthy online list of security vulnerabilities that have been corrected. Apple's list going back to 2003 and earlier is at *support.apple.com/en-us/HT201222*.

The number of security breaches that have exposed users' digital data to attackers continues to rise. From 2005 through early 2017, over 907 million electronic data records in the United States had been breached, exposing to attackers a range of personal electronic data, such as addresses, Social Security numbers, health records, and credit card numbers. Table 1-1 lists some recent major security breaches, according to the Privacy Rights Clearinghouse.[15]

Table 1-1	Selected security breaches involving personal information in a one-month period	
Organization	Description of security breach	Number of identities exposed
Michigan State University, MI	A database was compromised that contained names, Social Security numbers, MSU identification numbers, and date of birth of current and former students and employees.	Potentially 400,000
Poway Unified School District, CA	The district inadvertently sent information to unauthorized recipients that included children's names, nicknames, addresses, phone numbers, hearing and vision exam results, dates of birth, language fluency, academic test results, and occupation of parents.	70,000
University of Central Florida, FL	Unauthorized access to the university's system exposed financial records, medical records, grades, and Social Security numbers.	63,000
Southern New Hampshire University, NH	Due to a third-party vendor's configuration error a database that contained student information—student names, email addresses, and IDs, course name, course selection, assignment details and assignment score, instructor names and email addresses—was exposed.	140,000
Quest Diagnostics, NJ	An unknown error resulted in the exposure of the name, date of birth, lab results, and telephone numbers of customers.	34,000
Anchor Loans, CA	A publicly exposed database revealed customers' name, address, email address, Social Security number, check routing number, bank account number, bank statement data, birth date, and birth place.	Unknown
United States Navy Career Waypoints Database, DC	A re-enlistment approval database was stolen from a contractor's laptop, which included the names and Social Security numbers of 134,386 current and former sailors.	134,000
Internal Revenue Service, DC	IRS employees sent unencrypted emails that contained different taxpayers' personally identifiable information.	Potentially 28 million

Reasons for Successful Attacks

Why do attacks like these continue to be successful, despite all the efforts to stop them? There are several reasons:

- *Widespread vulnerabilities*. Because vulnerabilities are so common in hardware and software, attackers can virtually choose which vulnerability to exploit for an attack. And because of the sheer number of vulnerabilities it is difficult to identify and correct all of them. This is made even worse by the fact that not all hardware and software can be corrected once a vulnerability is uncovered. Some devices, particularly consumer devices, have no support from the company that made the device (called **lack of vendor support**). This means that no effort is made to fix any vulnerabilities that are found. Other systems have no capabilities to receive security updates when a vulnerability is found. And some systems are so old (called **end-of-life systems**) that vendors have dropped all support for security updates, or else charge an exorbitant fee to provide updates.

Note

Microsoft provides two types of security support for its software. It offers *mainstream support* for a minimum of five years from the date of a product's general availability and *extended support* for an additional five years. For example, Windows 10, which was released in July 2015, will have mainstream support until October 2020 and extended support until October 2025. After this time, Microsoft will no longer provide security updates, automatic fixes, updates, or online technical assistance.

- *Configuration issues*. Hardware and software that does have security features often are not properly configured, thus allowing attacks to be successful. Almost all devices come with *out-of-the-box* configuration settings, or **default configurations**. These are generally simple configurations that are intended to be changed by the user; however, often they are left in place. Some devices have **weak configuration** options that provide limited security choices. Users who incorrectly configure devices, known as a **misconfiguration**, find that these errors allow the device to be compromised. Misconfiguration is commonly seen in **improperly configured accounts** that are set up for a user that provide more access than is necessary, such as providing total access over the entire device when the access should be more limited.
- *Poorly designed software*. Successful attacks are often the result of software that is poorly designed and has **architecture/design weaknesses**. Software that allows the user to enter data but has **improper input handling** features does not filter or validate user input to prevent a malicious action. For example, a webpage on a web server with improper input handling that asks for the user's email address could allow an attacker to instead enter a direct command that the server would then execute. Other software may not properly trap an error condition and thus provide an attacker with underlying access to the system. This is known as **improper error handling**. Suppose an attacker enters a string of characters that is much longer than expected. Because the software has not been designed for this event the program

could crash or suddenly halt its execution and then display an underlying operating system prompt, giving an attacker access to the computer. A **race condition** in software occurs when two concurrent threads of execution access a shared resource simultaneously, resulting in unintended consequences. For example, in a program with two threads that have access to the same location in memory, Thread #1 stores the value A in that memory location. But since Thread #2 is also executing it may overwrite the same memory location with the value Z. When Thread #1 retrieves the value stored it is then given Thread #2's Z instead of its own A.

- *Hardware limitations*. Hardware with limited resources (CPU, memory, file system storage, etc.) could be exploited by an attacker who intentionally tries to consume more resources than intended. This might cause the system to become slow or even unable to respond to other users, thus prevent valid users from accessing the device. This is called **resource exhaustion**.

- *Enterprise-based issues*. Often attacks are successful not because of compromised technology but because of the manipulation of processes that an enterprise performs. **Vulnerable business processes**, also called *business process compromise (BPC)*, occurs when an attacker manipulates commonplace actions that are routinely performed. For example, late on a Friday afternoon an attacker in India could make a request to New York to have money transferred to Taiwan. Because these transactions are in different countries, time zones, and even on different days, it can be difficult for this process to be quickly verified. Another problem in the enterprise is the rapid acquisition and deployment of technology devices without proper documentation. This results in **undocumented assets**, or devices that are not formally identified, and results in **system sprawl**, or the widespread proliferation of devices across the enterprise. Often servers, computers, and other devices are purchased and quickly installed without adequate forethought regarding how they can be protected.

Difficulties in Defending Against Attacks

The challenge of keeping computers secure has never been greater, not only because of continual attacks but also because of the difficulties faced in defending against these attacks. These difficulties include the following:

- *Universally connected devices*. Today virtually every technology device—not only traditional computers but even programmable thermostats and light bulbs—is connected to the Internet. Although this provides enormous benefits, it also makes it easy for an attacker halfway around world to silently launch an attack against a connected device.

- *Increased speed of attacks*. With modern tools at their disposal, attackers can quickly scan millions of devices to find weaknesses and launch attacks with unprecedented speed. Most attack tools initiate new attacks without any human participation, thus increasing the speed at which systems are attacked.

- *Greater sophistication of attacks.* Attacks are becoming more complex, making it more difficult to detect and defend against them. Many attackers use common protocols to distribute their attacks, making it more difficult to distinguish an attack from legitimate traffic. Other attack tools vary their behavior so the same attack appears differently each time, further complicating detection.
- *Availability and simplicity of attack tools.* At one time an attacker needed to have an extensive technical knowledge of networks and computers as well as the ability to write a program to generate an attack. Today that is no longer the case. Modern software attack tools do not require sophisticated knowledge on the part of the attacker. In fact, many of the tools, such as the Kali Linux interface shown in Figure 1-1, have a graphical user interface (GUI) that allows the user to easily select options from a menu. These tools are generally freely available.

Figure 1-1   Menu of attack tools

Source: Kali Linux

In addition, attackers who create attacks tools will often then sell these tools to other attackers.

- *Faster detection of vulnerabilities.* Weaknesses in hardware and software can be more quickly uncovered and exploited with new software tools and techniques. Often an attacker may find a vulnerability and initiate an attack taking advantage of it even before users or security professionals are aware of the vulnerability. This is called a **zero day** attack, since there are no days of warning ahead of this **new threat**.

- *Delays in security updating.* Hardware and software vendors are overwhelmed trying to keep pace with updating their products against attacks. One antivirus software security institute receives more than 390,000 submissions of potential malware *each day*.[16] At this rate the antivirus vendors would have to create and distribute updates *every few seconds* to keep users fully protected. This delay in distributing security updates adds to the difficulties in defending against attacks.

- *Weak security update distribution.* Vendors of mainstream products, such as Microsoft, Apple, and Adobe, have a system for notifying users of security updates for their products and distributing them on a regular basis, but few other software vendors have invested in these costly distribution systems. Users are generally unaware that a security update even exists for a product because there is no reliable means for the vendor to alert the user. Also, these vendors often do not create small security updates that *patch* the existing software; instead, they fix the problem in an entirely new version of the software—and then require the user to pay for the updated version that contains the patch.

> **Note** 📎
>
> Smartphones, unlike computers and laptops, do not give the owner of the device the ability to download security updates. Instead, these must be sent out from the wireless carriers. Many carriers do not provide security updates on a timely basis, if at all.

- *Distributed attacks.* Attackers can use millions of computers or devices under their control in an attack against a single server or network. This "many against one" approach makes it virtually impossible to stop an attack by identifying and blocking a single source.

- *Use of personal devices.* Many enterprises allow employees to use and connect their personal devices to the company's network. This has made it difficult for IT departments to provide adequate security for an almost endless array of devices that they do not own.

- *User confusion.* Increasingly, users are called upon to make difficult security decisions regarding their computer systems, sometimes with little or no information to guide them. It is not uncommon for a user to be asked security questions such as *Do you want to view only the content that was delivered securely?* or *Is it safe to quarantine this attachment?* or *Do you want to install this add-on?* With little or no direction, these **untrained users** are inclined to provide answers to questions without understanding the security risks.

Table 1-2 summarizes the reasons why it is difficult to defend against today's attacks.

Table 1-2   Difficulties in defending against attacks

Reason	Description
Universally connected devices	Attackers from anywhere in the world can send attacks.
Increased speed of attacks	Attackers can launch attacks against millions of computers within minutes.
Greater sophistication of attacks	Attack tools vary their behavior so the same attack appears differently each time.
Availability and simplicity of attack tools	Attacks are no longer limited to highly skilled attackers.
Faster detection of vulnerabilities	Attackers can discover security holes in hardware or software more quickly.
Delays in security updating	Vendors are overwhelmed trying to keep pace updating their products against the latest attacks.
Weak security update distribution	Many software products lack a means to distribute security updates in a timely fashion.
Distributed attacks	Attackers use thousands of computers in an attack against a single computer or network.
Use of personal devices	Enterprises are having difficulty providing security for a wide array of personal devices.
User confusion	Users are required to make difficult security decisions with little or no instruction.

What Is Information Security?

 **Certification**

5.3 Explain risk management processes and concepts.

Before it is possible to defend against attacks, it is necessary to understand exactly what security is and how it relates to information security. Also, knowing the terminology used can be helpful when creating defenses for computers. Understanding the importance of information security is also critical.

Understanding Security

What is *security*? The word comes from the Latin, meaning *free from care*. Sometimes security is defined as *the state of being free from danger*, which is the *goal* of security. It is also defined as the *measures taken to ensure safety*, which is the *process* of security. Since complete security can never be fully achieved, the focus of security is more often on the process instead of the goal. In this light, security can be defined as the *necessary steps to protect from harm*.

It is important to understand the relationship between *security* and *convenience*. As security is increased, convenience is often decreased. That is, the more secure something is, the less convenient it may become to use (security is said to be *inversely proportional* to convenience). This is illustrated in Figure 1-2. Consider a typical house. A homeowner might install an automated alarm system that requires a code to be entered on a keypad within 30 seconds of entering the house. Although the alarm system makes the house more secure, it is less convenient than just walking into the house. Thus, security may be understood as *sacrificing convenience for safety*.

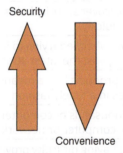

Security

Convenience

Figure 1-2   **Relationship of security to convenience**

Defining Information Security

Several terms are used when describing security in an IT environment: *computer security, IT security, cybersecurity,* and *information assurance,* to name just a few. Whereas each has its share of proponents and slight variations of meanings, the term *information security* may be the most appropriate because it is the broadest: protecting information from harm. Information security is often used to describe the tasks of securing information that is in a digital format, whether it be manipulated by a microprocessor (such as on a personal computer), preserved on a storage device (like a hard drive or USB flash drive), or transmitted over a network (such as a local area network or the Internet).

Information security cannot completely prevent successful attacks or guarantee that a system is totally secure, just as the security measures taken for a house can

> **Note** 📎
>
> Information security should not be viewed as a war to be won or lost. Just as crimes such as burglary can never be completely eradicated, neither can attacks against technology devices. The goal is not a complete victory but instead maintaining equilibrium: as attackers take advantage of a weakness in a defense, defenders must respond with an improved defense. Information security is an endless cycle between attacker and defender.

never guarantee complete safety from a burglar. The goal of information security is to ensure that protective measures are properly implemented to ward off attacks and prevent the total collapse of the system when a successful attack does occur. Thus, information security is first *protection*.

Second, information security is intended to protect *information* that provides value to people and enterprises. There are three protections that must be extended over information: *confidentiality, integrity, and availability*—or *CIA*:

1. *Confidentiality*. It is important that only approved individuals can access important information. For example, the credit card number used to make an online purchase must be kept secure and not made available to other parties. **Confidentiality** ensures that only authorized parties can view the information. Providing confidentiality can involve several different security tools, ranging from software to scramble the credit card number stored on the web server to door locks to prevent access to those servers.

2. *Integrity*. **Integrity** ensures that the information is correct and no unauthorized person or malicious software has altered the data. In the example of the online purchase, an attacker who could change the amount of a purchase from $10,000.00 to $1.00 would violate the integrity of the information.

3. *Availability*. Information has value if the authorized parties who are assured of its integrity can access the information. **Availability** ensures that data is accessible to authorized users. This means that the information cannot be "locked up" so tight that no one can access it. It also means that attackers have not performed an attack so that the data cannot be reached. In this example the total number of items ordered as the result of an online purchase must be made available to an employee in a warehouse so that the correct items can be shipped to the customer.

Because this information is stored on computer hardware, manipulated by software, and transmitted by communications, each of these areas must be protected. The third objective of information security is to protect the integrity, confidentiality, and availability of information *on the devices that store, manipulate, and transmit the information*.

This protection is achieved through a process that is a combination of three entities. As shown in Figure 1-3 and Table 1-3, information and the hardware, software,

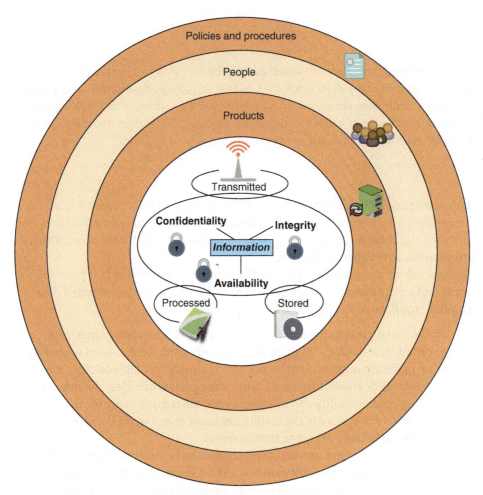

Figure 1-3   Information security layers

Layer	Description
Products	Form the security around the data. May be as basic as door locks or as complicated as network security equipment.
People	Those who implement and properly use security products to protect data.
Policies and procedures	Plans and policies established by an enterprise to ensure that people correctly use the products.

Table 1-3   Information security layers

and communications are protected in three layers: *products, people, and policies and procedures*. The procedures enable people to understand how to use products to protect information.

Thus, information security may be defined as *that which protects the integrity, confidentiality, and availability of information through products, people, and procedures on the devices that store, manipulate, and transmit the information.*

Information Security Terminology

As with many advanced subjects, information security has its own set of terminology. The following scenario helps to illustrate information security terms and how they are used.

Suppose that Ellie wants to purchase a new motorized Italian scooter to ride from her apartment to school and work. However, because several scooters have been stolen near her apartment she is concerned about its protection. Although she parks the scooter in the gated parking lot in front of her apartment, a hole in the fence surrounding the apartment complex makes it possible for someone to access the parking lot without restriction. The threat to Ellie's scooter is illustrated in Figure 1-4.

Ellie's new scooter is an **asset**, which is defined as an item that has value. In an enterprise, assets have the following qualities: they provide value to the enterprise; they cannot easily be replaced without a significant investment in expense, time, worker skill, and/or resources; and they can form part of the enterprise's corporate identity. Based on these qualities not all elements of an enterprise's information technology infrastructure may be classified as an asset. For example, a faulty desktop computer that can easily be replaced would generally not be considered an asset, yet the information contained on that computer can be an asset. Table 1-4 lists a description of the elements of an enterprise's information technology infrastructure and whether they would normally be considered as an asset.

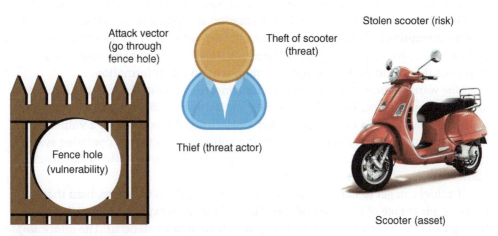

Figure 1-4   Information security components analogy

Table 1-4   Information technology assets

Element name	Description	Example	Critical asset?
Information	Data that has been collected, classified, organized, and stored in various forms	Customer, personnel, production, sales, marketing, and finance databases	Yes: Extremely difficult to replace
Customized business software	Software that supports the business processes of the enterprise	Customized order transaction application	Yes: Unique and customized for the enterprise
System software	Software that provides the foundation for application software	Operating system	No: Can be easily replaced
Physical items	Computers equipment, communications equipment, storage media, furniture, and fixtures	Servers, routers, DVDs, and power supplies	No: Can be easily replaced
Services	Outsourced computing services	Voice and data communications	No: Can be easily replaced

What Ellie is trying to protect her scooter from is a **threat**, which is a type of action that has the potential to cause harm. Information security threats are events or actions that represent a danger to information assets. A threat by itself does not mean that security has been compromised; rather, it simply means that the potential for creating a loss is real. For Ellie, the threat could result in the theft of her scooter; in information security, a threat can result in the corruption or theft of information, a delay in information being transmitted, or even the loss of good will or reputation.

A **threat actor** is a person or element that has the power to carry out a threat. For Ellie, the threat actor is a thief. In information security, a threat actor could be a person attempting to break into a secure computer network. It could also be malicious software that attacks the computer network, or even a force of nature such as a hurricane that could destroy computer equipment and its information.

Ellie wants to protect her scooter and is concerned about a hole in the fencing around her apartment. The hole in the fencing is a **vulnerability**, which is a flaw or weakness that allows a threat actor to bypass security. An example of a vulnerability that information security must deal with is a software defect in an operating system that allows an unauthorized user to gain control of a computer without the user's knowledge or permission.

If a thief can get to Ellie's scooter because of the hole in the fence, then that thief is taking advantage of the vulnerability. This is known as exploiting the vulnerability through an *attack vector*, or the means by which an attack can occur. The *attack surface* is the sum of all the different attack vectors. An attacker, knowing that a flaw in a web server's operating system has not been patched, is using the attack vector (exploiting the vulnerability) to steal user passwords.

Ellie must decide: what is the *likelihood* that the threat will come to fruition and her scooter stolen? This can be understood in terms of risk. A **risk** is a situation that involves exposure to some type of danger. There are different options available when dealing with risks, called **risk response techniques**:

- *Accept*. To **accept** risk simply means that the risk is acknowledged but no steps are taken to address it. In Ellie's case, she could accept the risk and buy the new scooter, knowing there is the chance of it being stolen by a thief entering through a hole in the fence.
- *Transfer*. Ellie could transfer the risk to a third party. She can do this by purchasing insurance so that the insurance company absorbs the loss and pays if the scooter is stolen. This is known as risk **transfer**.
- *Avoid*. To **avoid** risk involves identifying the risk but making the decision to not engage in the activity. Ellie could decide based on the risk of the scooter being stolen that she will not purchase the new scooter.
- *Mitigate*. To **mitigate** risk is the attempt to address risk by making the risk less serious. Ellie could complain to the apartment manager about the hole in the fence to have it repaired.

Note

If the apartment manager posted signs in the area that said "Trespassers will be punished to the full extent of the law" this would be called *risk deterrence*. Risk deterrence involves understanding something about attackers and then informing them of the harm that could come their way if they attack an asset.

Table 1-5 summarizes these information security terms.

Table 1-5   Information security terminology

Term	Example in Ellie's scenario	Example in information security
Asset	Scooter	Employee database
Threat	Steal scooter	Steal data
Threat actor	Thief	Attacker, hurricane
Vulnerability	Hole in fence	Software defect
Attack vector	Climb through hole in fence	Access web server passwords through flaw in operating system
Likelihood	Probability of scooter stolen	Likelihood of virus infection
Risk	Stolen scooter	Virus infection or stolen data

Understanding the Importance of Information Security

Information security is important to enterprises as well as to individuals. That is because information security can be helpful in preventing data theft, thwarting identity theft, avoiding the legal consequences of not securing information, maintaining productivity, and foiling cyberterrorism.

Preventing Data Theft

Security is often associated with theft prevention: Ellie could park her scooter in a locked garage to prevent it from being stolen. The same is true with information security: preventing data from being stolen is often cited by enterprises as a primary objective of their information security. Enterprise data theft involves stealing proprietary business information, such as research for a new drug or a list of customers that competitors would be eager to acquire. Stealing user personal data such as credit card numbers is also a prime action of attackers. This data can then be used to purchase thousands of dollars of merchandise online before the victim is even aware the number has been stolen.

> **Note**
>
> There are different types of fraud associated with credit card theft. Creating counterfeit debit and credit cards is called *existing-card fraud*, while *new-account fraud* occurs when new card accounts are opened in the name of the victim without their knowledge. *Card-not-present fraud* occurs when a thief uses stolen card information in an online purchase and does not actually have the card in hand.

Thwarting Identity Theft

Identity theft involves stealing another person's personal information, such as a Social Security number, and then using the information to impersonate the victim, generally for financial gain. The thieves often create new bank or credit card accounts under the victim's name and then large purchases are charged to these accounts, leaving the victim responsible for the debts and ruining his credit rating.

> **Note**
>
> In some instances, thieves have bought cars and even houses by taking out loans in someone else's name.

One of the areas of identity theft that is growing most rapidly involves identity thieves filing fictitious income tax returns with the U.S. Internal Revenue Service (IRS). Identity thieves who steal a filer's Social Security number will then file a fake income tax return claiming a large refund—often larger than the victim is entitled to—that is sent to the attacker. Because the IRS has been sending refunds more quickly than in the past, thieves can receive the refund and then disappear before the victim files a legitimate return and the fraud is detected. The IRS delivered over $5.8 billion in refund checks to identity thieves who filed fraudulent tax returns in one year, even though it stopped about 3 million fraudulent returns for that year.[17] Tax identity thieves are also known to set up fake tax preparation service centers to steal tax information from victims. One group filed $3.4 million worth of fraudulent returns through a sham tax preparation business.[18]

Note 📎

There have also been instances of identity thieves filing fake tax returns while using the victims' actual mailing addresses, then bribing postal workers to intercept the refund checks before they are delivered. One postal employee was convicted of stealing over 100 refund envelopes sent to addresses along his route.[19]

Avoiding Legal Consequences

Several federal and state laws have been enacted to protect the privacy of electronic data. Businesses that fail to protect data they possess may face serious financial penalties. Some of these laws include the following:

- *The Health Insurance Portability and Accountability Act of 1996 (HIPAA)*. Under the Health Insurance Portability and Accountability Act (HIPAA), healthcare enterprises must guard protected healthcare information and implement policies and procedures to safeguard it, whether it be in paper or electronic format. Those who wrongfully disclose individually identifiable health information can be fined up to $50,000 for each violation up to a maximum of $1.5 million per calendar year and sentenced up to 10 years in prison.

Note 📎

HIPAA regulations have been expanded to include all third-party business associate organizations that handle protected healthcare information. Business associates are defined as any subcontractor that creates, receives, maintains, or transmits protected health information on behalf of a covered HIPAA entity. These associates must now comply with the same HIPAA security and privacy procedures.

- *The Sarbanes-Oxley Act of 2002 (Sarbox).* As a reaction to a rash of corporate fraud, the Sarbanes-Oxley Act (Sarbox) is an attempt to fight corporate corruption. Sarbox covers the corporate officers, auditors, and attorneys of publicly traded companies. Stringent reporting requirements and internal controls on electronic financial reporting systems are required. Corporate officers who willfully and knowingly certify a false financial report can be fined up to $5 million and serve 20 years in prison.
- *The Gramm-Leach-Bliley Act (GLBA).* Like HIPAA, the Gramm-Leach-Bliley Act (GLBA) passed in 1999 protects private data. GLBA requires banks and financial institutions to alert customers of their policies and practices in disclosing customer information. All electronic and paper data containing personally identifiable financial information must be protected. The penalty for noncompliance for a class of individuals is up to $500,000.
- *Payment Card Industry Data Security Standard (PCI DSS).* The *Payment Card Industry Data Security Standard (PCI DSS)* is a set of security standards that all companies that process, store, or transmit credit or debit card information must follow. PCI applies to any enterprise or merchant, regardless of its size or number of card transactions, that processes transactions either online or in person. The maximum penalty for not complying is $100,000 per month.
- *State notification and security laws.* Since the passage of California's Database Security Breach Notification Act in 2003, all other states (except for Alabama, New Mexico, and South Dakota) have passed similar notification laws. These laws typically require businesses to inform residents within a specific period (typically 48 hours) if a breach of personal information has or is believed to have occurred. In addition, several states are strengthening their information security laws. For example, Connecticut requires any enterprise doing business in the state to scramble (encrypt) all sensitive personal data that is being transmitted over a public Internet connection or stored on portable devices like a USB flash drive, and companies must notify any potential victims of a data breach within 90 days of the attack and offer at least one year of identity theft prevention services. Oregon's law includes protection of an individual's healthcare information while New Hampshire requires the state's education department to notify students and teachers if their personal data was possibly stolen.

The penalties for violating these laws can be sizeable. Enterprises must make every effort to keep electronic data secure from hostile outside forces to ensure compliance with these laws and avoid serious legal consequences.

Maintaining Productivity

Cleaning up after an attack diverts time, money, and other resources away from normal activities. Employees cannot be productive and complete important tasks during or after an attack because computers and networks cannot function properly. Table 1-6

Table 1-6   Cost of attacks

Number of total employees	Average hourly salary	Number of employees to combat attack	Hours required to stop attack and clean up	Total lost salaries	Total lost hours of productivity
100	$25	1	48	$4066	81
250	$25	3	72	$17,050	300
500	$30	5	80	$28,333	483
1000	$30	10	96	$220,000	1293

provides a sample estimate of the lost wages and productivity during an attack and the subsequent cleanup.

Note

The single most expensive malicious attack was the Love Bug in 2000, which cost an estimated $8.7 billion.[20]

Foiling Cyberterrorism

The FBI defines *cyberterrorism* as any "premeditated, politically motivated attack against information, computer systems, computer programs, and data which results in violence against noncombatant targets by subnational groups or clandestine agents."[21] Unlike an attack that is designed to steal information or erase a user's hard disk drive, cyberterrorism attacks are intended to cause panic or provoke violence among citizens. Attacks are directed at targets such as the banking industry, military installations, power plants, air traffic control centers, and water systems. These are desirable targets because they can significantly disrupt the normal activities of a large population. For example, disabling an electrical power plant could cripple businesses, homes, transportation services, and communications over a wide area.

Note

One of the challenges in combatting cyberterrorism is that many of the prime targets are not owned and managed by the federal government. Because these are not centrally controlled, it is difficult to coordinate and maintain security.

Who Are the Threat Actors?

1.3 Explain threat actor types and attributes.

Threat actor is a generic term used to describe individuals who launch attacks against other users and their computers (another generic word is simply *attackers*). Many threat actors belong to organized gangs of young attackers, often clustered in Eastern European, Asian, and Third World regions, who meet in hidden online dark web forums to trade information, buy and sell stolen data and attacker tools, and even coordinate attacks.

Whereas at one time the reason for attacking a computer was to show off their technology skills (*fame*), today threat actors have a more focused goal of financial gain: to exploit vulnerabilities that can generate income (*fortune*). This financial cybercrime is often divided into two categories. The first category focuses on individuals as the victims. The threat actors steal and use stolen data, credit card numbers, online financial account information, or Social Security numbers to profit from its victims or send millions of spam emails to peddle counterfeit drugs, pirated software, fake watches, and pornography. The second category focuses on enterprises and governments. Threat actors attempt to steal research on a new product from an enterprise so that they can sell it to an unscrupulous foreign supplier who will then build an imitation model of the product to sell worldwide. This deprives the legitimate business of profits after investing hundreds of millions of dollars in product development, and because these foreign suppliers are in a different country they are beyond the reach of domestic enforcement agencies and courts. Governments are also the targets of threat actors: if the latest information on a new missile defense system can be stolen it can be sold—at a high price—to that government's enemies.

Note 📎

Some security experts maintain that East European threat actors are mostly focused on activities to steal money from individuals, whereas cybercriminals from East Asia are more interested in stealing data from governments or enterprises. This results in different approaches to their attacks. East European cybercriminals tend to use custom-built, highly complex malware while East Asian attackers use off-the-shelf malware and simpler techniques. Also, East European attackers work in small, tightly knit teams that directly profit from their attacks. East Asian threat actors usually are part of a larger group of attackers who work at the direction of large institutions from which they receive instructions and financial backing.

The **attributes**, or characteristic features, of the different groups of threat actors can vary widely. Some groups are very **sophisticated** (have developed a high degree of complexity) and have created a massive network of resources, while others are simply individuals just seeing what they can do. In addition, some groups have deep **funding and resources** while others have none. And whereas some groups of threat actors may work within the enterprise (**internal**) others are strictly **external**. Finally, the **intent and motivation**—the reason "why" behind the attacks—of the threat actors vary widely.

In the past, the term *hacker* referred to a person who used advanced computer skills to attack computers, and variations of that term were also introduced (*black hat hackers, white hat hackers, gray hat hackers*). However, that term did not accurately reflect the different motives and goals of the attackers. Today threat actors are recognized in more distinct categories, such as script kiddies, hactivists, nation state actors, insiders, and others.

Script Kiddies

Script kiddies are individuals who want to attack computers yet they lack the knowledge of computers and networks needed to do so. Script kiddies instead do their work by downloading freely available automated attack software (called **open-source intelligence** or *scripts*) from websites and using it to perform malicious acts. Figure 1-5 illustrates the skills needed for creating attacks. Over 40 percent of attacks require low or no skills and are frequently conducted by script kiddies.

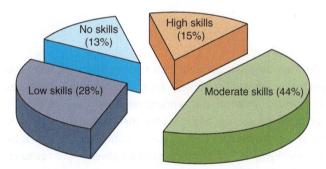

Figure 1-5   **Skills needed for creating attacks**

Hactivists

A group that is strongly motivated by ideology (for the sake of their principles or beliefs) is **hactivists**. Hactivists (a combination of the words *hack* and *activism*) are generally not considered to be a well-defined and well-organized group of threat actors. Attacks by hactivists can involve breaking into a website and changing the contents on the site as a means of making a political statement (one hactivist group changed the website of the U.S. Department of Justice to read *Department of Injustice*). In addition to attacks as a means of protest or to promote a political agenda, other attacks can be retaliatory. For example, hactivists may disable the website belonging to a bank because that bank stopped accepting online payments that were deposited into accounts belonging to the hactivists.

> **Note** 📎
>
> Most hactivists do not explicitly call themselves *hacktivists*. The term is more commonly used by security researchers and journalists to distinguish them from other types of threat actors.

It is estimated that there are thousands of hacktivist groups worldwide supporting a wide variety of causes. Some groups are opposing a specific government, country, or other entity, while others express no particular allegiances.

Nation State Actors

Instead of using an army to march across the battlefield to strike an adversary, governments are increasingly employing their own using state-sponsored attackers for launching computer attacks against their foes. These are known as **nation state actors**. Their foes may be foreign governments or even citizens of its own nation that the government considers hostile or threatening. A growing number of attacks from nation states actors are directed toward businesses in foreign countries with the goal of causing financial harm or damage to the enterprise's reputation.

> **Note** 📎
>
> Many security researchers believe that nation state actors might be the deadliest of any threat actors. When fortune motivates a threat actor but the target's defenses are too strong, the attacker simply moves on to another promising target with less-effective defenses. With nation state actors, however, the target is very specific and the attackers keep working until they are successful, showing both deep resources and tenacity. This is because state-sponsored attackers are highly skilled and have enough government resources to breach almost any security defense.

Nation state actors are known for being well-resourced and highly trained attackers. They often are involved in multiyear intrusion campaigns targeting highly sensitive economic, proprietary, or national security information. This has created a new class of attacks called **Advanced Persistent Threat (APT)**. These attacks use innovative attack tools (*advanced*) and once a system is infected it silently extracts data over an extended period (*persistent*). APTs are most commonly associated with nation state actors.

Insiders

Another serious threat to an enterprise comes from its own employees, contractors, and business partners, called **insiders**. For example, a healthcare worker disgruntled about being passed over for a promotion might illegally gather health records on celebrities and sell them to the media, or a securities trader who loses billions of dollars on bad stock bets could use her knowledge of the bank's computer security system to conceal the losses through fake transactions. In one study, it was determined that 58 percent of the breaches of an enterprise were attributed to insiders who abused their right to access corporate information.[22] These attacks are harder to recognize because they come from within the enterprise yet may be costlier than attacks from the outside.

Although some insider attacks consist of sabotage (from employees who have been formally reprimanded or demoted) or the result of bribery or blackmail, most insider attackers involve the theft of data. Because most of these thefts occur within 30 days of an employee resigning, the offenders may actually believe that the accumulated data is owned by them and not the enterprise.

Note

In recent years insiders have stolen large volumes of sensitive information and then published it. The purpose is to alert citizens about clandestine governmental actions and to pressure the government to change its policies.

Other Threat Actors

In addition, there are other categories of threat actors. These are summarized in Table 1-7.

Table 1-7   Descriptions of other attackers

Threat Actor	Description	Explanation
Competitors	Launch attack against an opponents' system to steal classified information.	Competitors may steal new product research or a list of current customers to gain a competitive advantage.
Organized crime	Moving from traditional criminal activities to more rewarding and less risky online attacks.	Criminal networks are usually run by a small number of experienced online criminal networks who do not commit crimes themselves but act as entrepreneurs.
Brokers	Sell their knowledge of a vulnerability to other attackers or governments.	Individuals who uncover vulnerabilities do not report it to the software vendor but instead sell them to the highest bidder, who are willing to pay a high price for the unknown vulnerability.
Cyberterrorists	Attack a nation's network and computer infrastructure to cause disruption and panic among citizens.	Targets may include a small group of computers or networks that can affect the largest number of users, such as the computers that control the electrical power grid of a state or region.

Defending Against Attacks

3.1 Explain use cases and purpose for frameworks, best practices and secure configuration guides.

How can a computer or network be defended against the many attacks from a variety of threat actors? Protection calls for following five fundamental security principles. In addition, following established frameworks and architectures is important.

Fundamental Security Principles

Although multiple defenses may be necessary to withstand an attack, these defenses should be based on five fundamental security principles: layering, limiting, diversity, obscurity, and simplicity. These principles provide a foundation for building a secure system.

Layering

The Crown Jewels of England, which are worn during coronations and important state functions, have a dollar value of over $32 million yet are virtually priceless as symbols of English culture. How are precious stones like the Crown Jewels protected from theft? They are not openly displayed on a table for anyone to pick up. Instead, they are enclosed in protective cases with 2-inch thick glass that is bullet-proof, smash-proof, and resistant to almost any outside force. The cases are in a special room with massive walls and sensors that can detect slight movements or vibrations. The doors to the room are monitored around the clock by remote security cameras, and the video images from each camera are recorded. The room itself is in the Tower of London, surrounded by roaming guards and fences. In short, these precious stones are protected by *layers* of security. If one layer is penetrated—such as the thief getting into the building—several more layers must still be breached, and each layer is often more difficult or complicated than the previous. A layered approach has the advantage of creating a barrier of multiple defenses that can be coordinated to thwart a variety of attacks.

> **Note** 🖉
>
> The Jewel House, which holds the Crown Jewels in the Tower of London, is actually located inside an Army barracks that is staffed with soldiers.

Likewise, information security must be created in layers. If only one defense mechanism is in place, an attacker only has to circumvent that single defense. Instead, a security system must have layers, making it unlikely that an attacker has the tools and skills to break through *all* the layers of defenses. A **layered security** approach, also called **defense-in-depth**, can be useful in resisting a variety of attacks. Layered security provides the most comprehensive protection.

Limiting

Consider again protecting the Crown Jewels of England. Although the jewels may be on display for the general public to view, permitting anyone to touch them increases the chances that they will be stolen. Only approved personnel should be authorized to handle the jewels. Limiting who can access the jewels reduces the threat against them.

The same is true with information security. Limiting access to information reduces the threat against it. This means that only those personnel who must use the data should have access to it. In addition, the type of access they have should be limited to what those people need to perform their jobs. For example, access to the human resource database for an enterprise should be limited to only employees who have a genuine need to access it, such as human resource personnel or vice presidents. And, the type of access also should be restricted: human resource employees may be able to view employee salaries but not change them.

Note What level of access should users have? The correct answer is the *least amount necessary* to do their jobs, and no more.

Some ways to limit access are technology-based, such as assigning file permissions so that a user can only read but not modify a file, while others are procedural, such as prohibiting an employee from removing a sensitive document from the premises. The key is that access must be restricted to the bare minimum. And although some personnel may balk at not being able to freely access any file or resource that they may choose, it is important that **user training** help instruct the employees as to the security reasons behind the restrictions.

Diversity

Diversity is closely related to layering. Just as it is important to protect data with layers of security, the layers also must be different (diverse). This means that if attackers penetrate one layer, they cannot use the *same* techniques to break through all other layers. A jewel thief, for instance, might be able to foil the security camera by dressing in black clothing but should not be able to use the same technique to trick the motion detection system. Using diverse layers of defense means that breaching one security layer does not compromise the whole system.

Information security diversity may be achieved in several ways. For example, some enterprises use security products provided by different manufacturers (**vendor diversity**).

An attacker who can circumvent a security device from Manufacturer A could then use those same skills and knowledge to defeat all of the same devices used by the enterprise. However, if devices from Manufacturer A and similar devices from Manufacturer B were both used by the same enterprise, the attacker would have more difficulty trying to break through both types of devices because they would be different. Or, the groups who are responsible for regulating access to a system (**control diversity**) are also different, so that those who perform **technical controls** (using technology as a basis for controlling the access and usage of sensitive data) are different from those personnel who administer the broad **administrative controls** (regulating the human factors of security).

Obscurity

Suppose a thief plans to steal the Crown Jewels during a shift change of the security guards. When the thief observes the guards, however, she finds that the guards do not change shifts at the same time each night. On a given Monday they rotate shifts at 2:13 AM, while on Tuesday they rotate at 1:51 AM, and the following Monday at 2:24 AM. Because the shift changes cannot be known for certain in advance, the planned attack cannot be carried out. This technique is sometimes called *security by obscurity*: obscuring to the outside world what is on the inside makes attacks that much more difficult.

An example of obscurity in information security would be not revealing the type of computer, version of operating system, or brand of software that is used. An attacker who knows that information could use it to determine the vulnerabilities of the system to attack it. However, if this information is concealed it is more difficult to attack the system, since nothing is known about it and it is hidden from the outside. Obscuring information can be an important means of protection.

> **Note** 📎
>
> Although obscurity is an important element of defense, it is not the only element. Sometimes the design or implementation of a device is kept secret with the thinking that if attackers do not know how it works, then it is secure. This attempt at *security through obscurity* is flawed because it depends solely on secrecy as a defense.

Simplicity

Because attacks can come from a variety of sources and in many ways, information security is by its very nature complex. Yet the more complex it becomes, the more difficult it is to understand. A security guard who does not understand how motion detectors interact with infrared trip lights may not know what to do when one system alarm shows an intruder but the other does not. In addition, complex systems allow many opportunities for something to go wrong. In short, complex systems can be a thief's ally.

The same is true with information security. Complex security systems can be hard to understand, troubleshoot, and even feel secure about. As much as possible, a secure system should be simple for those on the inside to understand and use. Complex security schemes are often compromised to make them easier for trusted users to work with, yet this can also make it easier for the attackers. In short, keeping a system simple from the inside, but complex on the outside, can sometimes be difficult but reaps a major benefit.

Frameworks and Reference Architectures

The field of information security contains various supporting structures for implementing security. Known as **industry-standard frameworks** and **reference architectures**, these provide a resource of how to create a secure IT environment. Some frameworks/architectures give an overall program structure and security management guidance to implement and maintain an effective security program, while others contain in-depth technical guidelines. Various frameworks/architectures are specific to a particular sector (**industry-specific frameworks**) such as the financial industry and may be required by external agencies that regulate the industry (**regulatory**), others are not required (**non-regulatory**). Finally, some of the framework/architectures are domestic while others are world wide (**national** vs. **international**).

Note

Common security frameworks include ISO, NIST, COBIT, ETSI, RFC, and ISA/IEC.

Chapter Summary

- Attacks against information security have grown exponentially in recent years, even though billions of dollars are spent annually on security. No computer system is immune from attacks or can be considered completely secure.
- There are many reasons for the high number of successful attacks. One reason is the number of widespread vulnerabilities that exist today. Because

of the sheer number of vulnerabilities, it is difficult to identify and correct all of them. And not all hardware and software can even be corrected once a vulnerability is uncovered. Another reason is that hardware and software are not always properly configured, either because the default configurations are not strengthened or there is a misconfiguration, allowing the device to be compromised. Successful attacks are often the result of software that is poorly designed and has architecture/design weaknesses. These weaknesses include not properly handling input or handling errors. Hardware limitations can be exploited by attackers who consume more resources than intended, causing the system to become slow or even unable to respond to other users. There are also enterprise-based issues, such as vulnerable business processes that an attacker can exploit or the widespread "sprawl" of devices that have not been properly protected.

- It is difficult to defend against today's attacks for several reasons. These reasons include the fact that virtually all devices are connected to the Internet, the speed of the attacks, greater sophistication of attacks, the availability and simplicity of attack tools, faster detection of vulnerabilities by attackers, delays in security updating, weak security update distribution, distributed attacks coming from multiple sources, and user confusion.

- Information security can be defined as that which protects the integrity, confidentiality, and availability of information through products, people, and procedures on the devices that store, manipulate, and transmit the information. As with many advanced subjects, information security has its own set of terminology. A threat is an event or action that represents a danger to information assets, which is something that has value. A threat actor is a person or element that has the power to carry out a threat, usually by exploiting a vulnerability, which is a flaw or weakness, through a threat vector. A risk is the likelihood that a threat actor will exploit a vulnerability.

- The main goals of information security are to prevent data theft, thwart identify theft, avoid the legal consequences of not securing information, maintain productivity, and foil cyberterrorism.

- The threat actors, or individuals behind computer attacks, fall into several categories and exhibit different attributes. Script kiddies do their work by downloading automated attack software from websites and then using it to break into computers. Hactivists are strongly motivated by their ideology and often attack to make a political statement. Nation state actors are employed by governments as state-sponsored attackers for launching computer attacks against foes. One serious threat to an enterprise comes from its employees, contractors, and business partners, known as insiders. Other threat actors include competitors, organized crime, brokers, and cyberterrorists.

- Although multiple defenses may be necessary to withstand the steps of an attack, these defenses should be based on five fundamental security principles: layering, limiting, diversity, obscurity, and simplicity. In addition, there are various industry-standard frameworks and reference architectures that provide resources for how to create a secure IT environment.

Key Terms

accept

administrative controls

Advanced Persistent
   Threat (APT)

architecture/design
   weaknesses

asset

attributes

availability

avoid

competitors

confidentiality

control diversity

default configurations

defense-in-depth

end-of-life system

external

funding and resources

hactivists

improper error
   handling

improper input handling

improperly configured
   accounts

industry-specific
   frameworks

industry-standard
   frameworks

insiders

integrity

intent and motivation

internal

international

lack of vendor support

layered security

misconfiguration

mitigate

nation state actors

national

new threat

non-regulatory

open-source intelligence

organized crime

race condition

reference architectures

regulatory

resource exhaustion

risk

risk response
   techniques

script kiddies

sophisticated

system sprawl

technical controls

threat

threat actor

transfer

undocumented assets

untrained users

user training

vendor diversity

vulnerability

vulnerable business
   processes

weak configuration

zero day

Review Questions

1. Ian recently earned his security
   certification and has been offered a
   promotion to a position that requires
   him to analyze and design security
   solutions as well as identifying users'
   needs. Which of these generally
   recognized security positions has Ian
   been offered?
   a. Security administrator
   b. Security technician
   c. Security officer
   d. Security manager

2. Alyona has been asked by her
   supervisor to give a presentation
   regarding reasons why security
   attacks continue to be successful. She
   has decided to focus on the issue of
   widespread vulnerabilities. Which of the
   following would Alyona NOT include in
   her presentation?
   a. Large number of vulnerabilities
   b. End-of-life systems
   c. Lack of vendor support
   d. Misconfigurations

3. Tatyana is discussing with her supervisor potential reasons why a recent attack was successful against one of their systems. Which of the following configuration issues would NOT covered?
   a. Default configurations
   b. Weak configurations
   c. Vulnerable business processes
   d. Misconfigurations

4. What is a race condition?
   a. When a vulnerability is discovered and there is a race to see if it can be patched before it is exploited by attackers.
   b. When two concurrent threads of execution access a shared resource simultaneously, resulting in unintended consequences.
   c. When an attack finishes its operation before antivirus can complete its work.
   d. When a software update is distributed prior to a vulnerability being discovered.

5. Which the following is NOT a reason why it is difficult to defend against today's attackers?
   a. Delays in security updating
   b. Greater sophistication of defense tools
   c. Increased speed of attacks
   d. Simplicity of attack tools

6. Which of the following is NOT true regarding security?
   a. Security is a goal.
   b. Security includes the necessary steps to protect from harm.
   c. Security is a process.
   d. Security is a war that must be won at all costs.

7. Adone is attempting to explain to his friend the relationship between security and convenience. Which of the following statements would he use?
   a. "Security and convenience are not related."
   b. "Convenience always outweighs security."
   c. "Security and convenience are inversely proportional."
   d. "Whenever security and convenience intersect, security always wins."

8. Which of the following ensures that only authorized parties can view protected information?
   a. Authorization
   b. Confidentiality
   c. Availability
   d. Integrity

9. Which of the following is NOT a successive layer in which information security is achieved?
   a. Products
   b. People
   c. Procedures
   d. Purposes

10. Complete this definition of information security: *That which protects the integrity, confidentiality, and availability of information_____.*
   a. *on electronic digital devices and limited analog devices that can connect via the Internet or through a local area network*
   b. *through a long-term process that results in ultimate security*
   c. *using both open-sourced as well as supplier-sourced hardware and software that interacts appropriately with limited resources*
   d. *through products, people, and procedures on the devices that store, manipulate, and transmit the information*

11. Which of the following is an enterprise critical asset?
    a. System software
    b. Information
    c. Outsourced computing services
    d. Servers, routers, and power supplies
12. Gunnar is creating a document that explains risk response techniques. Which of the following would he NOT list and explain in his document?
    a. Extinguish risk
    b. Transfer risk
    c. Mitigate risk
    d. Avoid risk
13. Which act requires banks and financial institutions to alert their customers of their policies in disclosing customer information?
    a. Sarbanes-Oxley Act (Sarbox)
    b. Financial and Personal Services Disclosure Act
    c. Health Insurance Portability and Accountability Act (HIPAA)
    d. Gramm-Leach-Bliley Act (GLBA)
14. Why do cyberterrorists target power plants, air traffic control centers, and water systems?
    a. These targets are government-regulated and any successful attack would be considered a major victory.
    b. These targets have notoriously weak security and are easy to penetrate.
    c. They can cause significant disruption by destroying only a few targets.
    d. The targets are privately owned and cannot afford high levels of security.
15. Which tool is most commonly associated with nation state threat actors?
    a. Closed-Source Resistant and Recurrent Malware (CSRRM)
    b. Advanced Persistent Threat (APT)
    c. Unlimited Harvest and Secure Attack (UHSA)
    d. Network Spider and Worm Threat (NSAWT)
16. An organization that practices purchasing products from different vendors is demonstrating which security principle?
    a. Obscurity
    b. Diversity
    c. Limiting
    d. Layering
17. What is an objective of state-sponsored attackers?
    a. To right a perceived wrong
    b. To amass fortune over of fame
    c. To spy on citizens
    d. To sell vulnerabilities to the highest bidder
18. Signe wants to improve the security of the small business where she serves as a security manager. She determines that the business needs to do a better job of not revealing the type of computer, operating system, software, and network connections they use. What security principle does Signe want to use?
    a. Obscurity
    b. Layering
    c. Diversity
    d. Limiting
19. What are industry-standard frameworks and reference architectures that are required by external agencies known as?
    a. Compulsory
    b. Mandatory
    c. Required
    d. Regulatory
20. What is the category of threat actors that sell their knowledge of vulnerabilities to other attackers or governments?
    a. Cyberterrorists
    b. Competitors
    c. Brokers
    d. Resource managers

Hands-On Projects

Project 1-1: Examining Data Breaches—Textual

The Privacy Rights Clearinghouse (PRC) is a nonprofit organization whose goals are to raise consumers' awareness of how technology affects personal privacy and empower consumers to take action to control their own personal information. The PRC maintains a searchable database of security breaches that impact consumer's privacy. In this project, you gather information from the PRC website.

1. Open a web browser and enter the URL **www.privacyrights.org** (if you are no longer able to access the site through the web address, use a search engine to search for "Privacy Rights Clearinghouse data breach."

2. First spend time reading about the PRC by clicking **LEARN MORE**.

3. Click **Data Breaches** at the top of the page.

4. In the search bar enter a school, organization, or business with which you are familiar to determine if it has been the victim of an attack in which your data has been compromised.

5. Click **Data Breaches** to return to the main Data Breaches page.

6. Now create a customized list of the data that will only list data breaches of educational institutions. Under **Select organization type(s)**, check only **EDU- Educational Institutions**.

7. Click **Search Data Breaches**.

8. Read the **Breach Subtotal** information. How many breaches that were made public pertain to educational institutions? How many total records were stolen?

9. Scroll down and observe the breaches for educational institutions.

10. Scroll back to the top of the page. Click **New Data Breach Search**.

11. Now search for breaches that were a result of lost, discarded, or stolen equipment that belonged to the government and military. Under **Choose the type of breaches to display**, check **Portable device (PORT) - Lost, discarded or stolen laptop, PDA, smartphone, portable memory device, CD, hard drive, data tape, etc**.

12. Under **Select organization type(s)**, check **GOV - Government & Military**.

13. Click **Search Data Breaches**.

14. Read the **Breach Subtotal** by clicking the **Download Results (CSV)** file.

15. Open the file and then scroll down the different breaches. What should the government be doing to limit these breaches?

16. Scroll back to the top of the page. Click **New Data Breach Search**.

17. Now create a search based on criteria that you are interested in, such as the Payment Card Fraud against Retail/Merchants during the current year.

18. When finished, close all windows.

Project 1-2: Examining Data Breaches—Visual

In this project, you view the biggest data breaches resulting in stolen information through a visual format.

1. Open your web browser and enter the URL **http://www.informationisbeautiful.net /visualizations/worlds-biggest-data-breaches-hacks/** (if you are no longer able to access the site through this web address, use a search engine to search for "Information Is Beautiful World's Biggest Data Breaches."

2. Click **Hide Filter** to display a visual graphic of the data breaches, as shown in Figure 1-6.

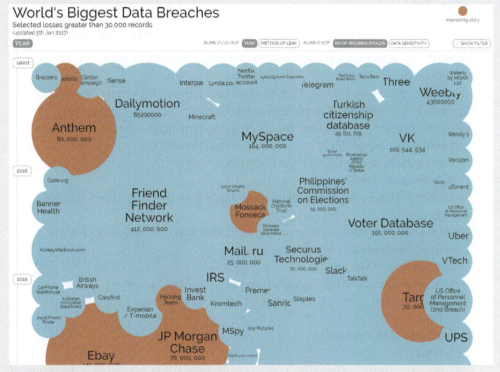

Figure 1-6   World's biggest data breaches

Source: Information is Beautiful

3. Scroll down the page to view the data breaches. Note that the size of the breach is indicated by the size of the bubble.

4. Scroll back up to the top and note the color of the bubbles that have an "Interesting Story." Click one of the bubbles and read the story.

5. Click **Read a bit more**.

6. Click **Click to see the original report**.

7. Read about the data breach. When finished, close only this tab in your browser.

8. Click **Show Filter** to display the filter menu.

9. Under Organisation, click **Government**.

10. Under Method of Leak, click **All**.

11. Click one of the bubbles and read the story.

12. Uncheck **Government**. Under Organisation, now click **Tech** to see the breaches that have targeted the technology industry. Click one of the bubbles and read the story.

13. At the top of the graphic, click **Method of Leak** so that the bubbles display how the leak occurred. Which type of leak is the most common? Why do you think this is the case?

14. Create your own filters to view different types of breaches. Does this graphic convey a better story than the textual data in the previous project?

15. How does this visualization help you with the understanding of threats?

16. Close all windows.

Project 1-3: Scanning for Malware Using the Microsoft Safety Scanner

In this project, you download and run the Microsoft Safety Scanner to determine if there is any malware on the computer.

1. Determine which system type of Windows you are running. Click **Start, Settings, System,** and then **About this PC**. Look under System type for the description.
   Open your web browser and enter the URL **www.microsoft.com/security/scanner /en-us/default.asp** (if you are no longer able to access the site through the URL, use a search engine to search for "Microsoft Safety Scanner").

2. Click **Download Now**.

3. Select either **32-bit** or **64-bit**, depending upon which system type of Windows you are running.

4. When the program finishes downloading, right-click **Start** and click **File Explorer**.

5. Click the **Downloads** icon in the left pane.

6. Double-click the **msert.exe** file.

7. If the **User Account Control** dialog box appears, click **Yes**. Click **Run**.

8. Click the check box to accept the license terms for this software. Click **Next**.

9. Click **Next**.

10. Select **Quick scan** if necessary.

11. Click **Next**.

12. Depending on your computer this scan may take several minutes. Analyze the results of the scan to determine if there is any malicious software found in your computer.

13. If you have problems, you can click **View detailed results of the scan**. After reviewing the results, click **OK**. If you do not find any problems, click **Finish**.

14. If any malicious software was found on your computer run the scan again and select **Full scan**. After the scan is complete, click **Finish** to close the dialog box.

15. Close all windows.

Project 1-4: Creating a Virtual Machine of Windows 10 for Security Testing—Part 1

Installing and running new security applications may not always be desirable on a normal production computer or in an environment in which the security configuration settings of a computer should not be changed. As an alternative, a virtual machine can be created in which new applications can be installed or configuration settings changed without impacting the regular computer. In a virtual machine environment, the host computer runs a guest operating system. Security programs and testing can be conducted within this guest operating system without any impact on the regular host operating system. In this project, you create a virtual machine using Oracle VirtualBox software.

> **Notes** ✐
>
> The operating system of the host computer can be the same or different from that of the guest operating system. That is, a computer that already has installed Windows 10 as its host operating system can still create a virtual machine of Windows 10 that is used for testing.

1. Open a web browser and enter the URL **www.virtualbox.org** (if you are no longer able to access the site through this web address, use a search engine to search for "Oracle VirtualBox download").
2. Click **Downloads**.
3. Under **VirtualBox binaries** select the latest version of VirtualBox to download for your specific host operating system. For example, if you are running Windows, select the version for "Windows hosts."
4. Under **VirtualBox x.x.x Oracle VM VirtualBox Extension Pack** click **All supported platforms** to download the extension package.
5. Navigate to the folder that contains the downloads and launch the VirtualBox installation program **VirtualBox-xxx-nnnnn-hhh.exe**.
6. Accept the default configurations from the installation Wizard to install the program.
7. If you are asked "Would you like to install this device software?" on one or more occasions, click **Install**.
8. When completed click **Finish** to launch VirtualBox, as seen in Figure 1-7.
9. Now install the VirtualBox extensions. Click **File** and **Preferences**.
10. Click **Extensions**.
11. Click the **Add a package** icon on the right side of the screen.
12. Navigate to the folder that contains the extension pack downloaded earlier to select that file. Click **Open**.
13. Click **Install**. Follow the necessary steps to complete the default installation.
14. Remain in VirtualBox for the next project to configure VirtualBox and install the guest operating system.

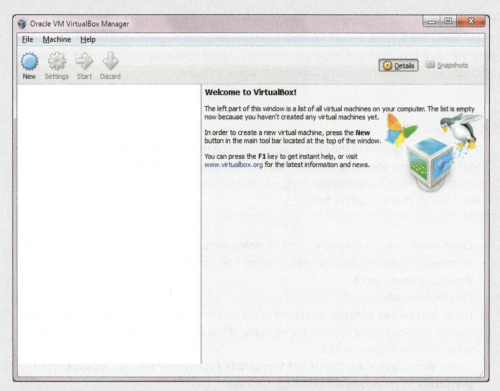

Figure 1-7 **VirtualBox**

Source: VirtualBox software developed by Oracle Corporation

Project 1-5: Creating a Virtual Machine of Windows 10 for Security Testing—Part 2

After installing VirtualBox the next step is to create the guest operating system. For this project Windows 10 will be installed. Different options are available for obtaining a copy of Windows 8.1:

- A retail version of the software can be purchased.
- If your school is a member of the Microsoft Imagine the operating system software and a license can be downloaded (www.imagine.microsoft.com). See your instructor or lab supervisor for more information.
- A 90-day evaluation copy can be downloaded and installed from the Microsoft TechNet Evaluation Center (www.microsoft.com/en-US/evalcenter/evaluate-windows-10 -enterprise).

1. Obtain the ISO image of Windows 10 using one of the options above and save it on the hard drive of the computer.
2. Launch VirtualBox.
3. Click **New**.
4. In **Name**: enter **Windows 10** as the name of the virtual machine.
5. Be sure that **Type**: says **Microsoft Windows** and **Version**: changes to **Windows 10 (xx-bit)**. Click **Next**.
6. Under **Memory size** accept the recommended size or increase the allocation if you have sufficient RAM on your computer. Click **Next**.
7. Under **Hard disk** accept **Create a virtual hard drive now**. Click **Create**.

Figure 1-8   VirtualBox virtual machine settings

Source: VirtualBox software developed by Oracle Corporation

8. Under **Hard drive file type** accept the default **VID (VirtualBox Disk Image)**. Click **Next**.
9. Under **Storage on physical hard drive** accept the default **Dynamically allocated**. Click **Next**.
10. Under **File location and size** accept **Windows 10**. Click **Create**.
11. Now the configuration settings for the virtual machine are set, as seen in Figure 1-8.
12. Next you will load the Windows 10 ISO image. Click **Settings**.
13. In the left pane click **Storage**.
14. Under **Controller**: click **Empty**.
15. In the right page under **Attributes** click the icon of the optical disc.
16. Click **Choose Virtual Optical Disk File . . .**
17. Navigate to the location of the Windows 10 ISO file and click **Open**.
18. Click **OK**.
19. Click **Start** to launch the Windows 10 ISO.
20. Follow the Windows 10 installation wizard to complete the installation.
21. To close the Windows 10 guest operating system in VirtualBox click **File** and then **Exit**.
22. Close all windows.

Case Projects

Case Project 1-1: Personal Attack Experiences

What type of computer attack have you (or a friend or another student) experienced? When did it happen? What type of computer or device was involved? What type of damage did it inflict? What had to be done to clean up following the attack? How was the computer fixed after the attack? What could have prevented it? Using the information in Table 1-2, list the reason or reasons you think that the attack was successful. Write a one-page paper about these experiences.

Case Project 1-2: Personal Information Security Terminology

The scenario of Ellie protecting her scooter was used in this chapter to introduce important key terms used in information security: asset, threat, threat actor, vulnerability, attack vector, attack surface, likelihood, and risk. Create your own one-paragraph scenario with those key terms using a situation with which you are familiar. Also, create a table similar to Table 1-5 that lists these terms and how they are used in your scenario.

Case Project 1-3: Security Podcasts or Video Series

Many different security vendors and security researchers now post weekly audio podcasts or video series on YouTube on security topics. Locate two different podcasts and two different video series about computer security. Listen and view one episode of each. Then, write a summary of what was discussed and a critique of the podcasts and videos. Were they beneficial to you? Were they accurate? Would you recommend them to someone else? Write a one-page paper on your research.

Case Project 1-4: What Are Your Layers?

Security defenses should be based on five fundamental security principles: layering, limiting, diversity, obscurity, and simplicity. Analyze these principles for the computers that you use. Create a table that lists the five fundamental security principles across the top, and then list down the side at least three computers that you commonly use at school, your place of employment, home, a friend's house, etc. Then enter the security element of each principle for each of the computers (such as, for *Limiting* you may indicate the number of people who have keys to the door of the office or apartment that contains the computer). Leave blank any box for which that security layer does not exist. Based on your analysis, what can you say regarding the security of these computers? Finally, for each of the elements that you think is inadequate or missing, add what you believe would improve security. Write a one-paragraph analysis of your findings.

Case Project 1-5: Sources of Security Information

The following is a partial overall list of some of the sources for security information:

- Security content (online or printed articles that deal specifically with unbiased security content)
- Consumer content (general consumer-based magazines or broadcasts not devoted to security but occasionally carry end-user security tips)

- Vendor content (material from security vendors who sell security services, hardware, or software)
- Security experts (IT staff recommendations or newsletters)
- Direct instruction (college classes or a workshop conducted by a local computer vendor)
- Friends and family
- Personal experience

Create a table with each of these sources and columns listed Advantages, Disadvantages, Example, and Rating. Use the Internet to complete the entire table. The Rating column is a listing from 1-7 (with 1 being the highest) of how useful each of these sources is in your opinion. Compare your table with other learners.

Case Project 1-6: Preventing Attacks

Select one of the recent attacks listed under *Today's Security Attacks* earlier in the chapter. How could the attack been prevented if the five fundamental security principles—layering, limiting, diversity, obscurity, and simplicity—had been applied? Create a table that lists each of these security principles and how they could have been used to mitigate the attack. You may need to be creative in your thinking.

Case Project 1-7: Security Frameworks and Architectures

There are several security frameworks and architectures available to use as templates for creating a secure environment. These include ISO, NIST, COBIT, ETSI, RFC, and ISA/IEC. Select three security frameworks/architectures and use the Internet to research each of them. How are they predominately used? What are their strengths? What are their weaknesses? Are they general or specific? What is a setting (small business, school, home office, etc.) that you would recommend for each of these? Write a one-page paper on your comparison and analysis.

Case Project 1-8: Lake Point Consulting Services

Lake Point Consulting Services (LPCS) provides security consulting and assurance services to over 500 clients across a wide range of enterprises in more than 20 states. A new initiative at LPCS is for each of its seven regional offices to provide internships to students who are in their final year of the security degree program at the local college.

As part of National Cybersecurity Awareness Month LPCS has been conducting a series of "Lunch-and-Learn" meetings each Monday and Friday for local citizens and small business owners to learn more about security. LPCS has asked you to present an introductory session on the fundamentals of security: what it is, why it is important today, who are the attackers, what types of attacks do they launch, etc.

1. Create a PowerPoint presentation that explains what IT security is and why it is important today. Include who is responsible for attacks and their attack techniques. Your presentation should be seven to ten slides in length.
2. As a follow-up to your presentation, create a Frequently Asked Questions (FAQ) sheet that outlines general principles that can be used to protect valuable assets. Write a one-page FAQ about security protections.

Case Project 1-9: Information Security Community Site Activity

The Information Security Community Site is an online companion to this textbook. It contains a wide variety of tools, information, discussion boards, and other features to assist learners. To gain the most benefit from the site you will need to set up a free account.

Go to **community.cengage.com/Infosec2**. Click **Join the Community**. On the Join the Community page, enter the requested information to create your account.

> **Caution** ⚠
>
> Your instructor may have a specific naming convention that you should use, such as the name of your course followed by your initials. Check with your instructor before creating your sign-in name.

Explore the various features of the Information Security Community Site and become familiar with it. Visit the blog section and read the blog postings to learn about some of the latest events in IT security.

References

1. Zetter, Kim, "Teen who hacked CIA director's email tells how he did it," *Wired,* Oct. 19, 2015, accessed Feb. 16, 2017, www.wired.com/2015/10/hacker-who-broke-into -cia-director-john-brennan-email-tells-how-he-did-it/.
2. "Information security analysts," *Bureau of Labor Statistics,* Dec. 17, 2015, accessed Feb. 16, 2017, www.bls.gov/ooh/computer-and-information-technology/information-security- analysts.htm
3. Morgan, Steve, "One million cybersecurity job openings in 2016," *Forbes,* Jan. 2, 2016, accessed Feb. 16, 2017, www.forbes.com/sites/stevemorgan/2016/01/02/one-million -cybersecurity-job-openings-in-2016/#1118fc737d27.
4. "2017 IT skills demand and pay trends report," *Foote Partners,* accessed Feb. 16, 2017, footepartners.com/fp_pdf/FooteNewsrelease_2Q16ITSkillsTrends_09182016.pdf.
5. Greenberg, Andy, "Hackers remotely kill a jeep on the highway—with me in it," *Wired,* Jul. 21, 2015, accessed Feb. 16, 2017, www.wired.com/2015/07/hackers-remotely-kill-jeep-highway/.
6. Zetter, Kim, "Feds say that banned researcher commandeered a plane," *Wired,* May 15, 2015, accessed Mar. 6, 2017, www.wired.com/2015/05/feds-say-banned -researcher-commandeered-plane/.
7. Goodin, Dan, "Yahoo says half a billion accounts breached by nation-sponsored hackers," *ArsTechnica*, Sep. 22, 2016, accessed Sep. 23, 2016, arstechnica.com/security/2016/09 /yahoo-says-half-a-billion-accounts-breached-by-nation-sponsored-hackers/.

8. "USB Killer v3," *USB Kill*, accessed Dec. 2, 2016, www.usbkill.com/usb-killer
/13-usb-killer-v3.html.

9. "Security assessment of WINVvote voting equipment for Department of Elections," *Virginia Information Technologies Agency*, Apr. 14, 2015, accessed Sep. 16, 2016, www.elections
.virginia.gov/WebDocs/VotingEquipReport/WINVote-final.pdf.

10. "FAQ about cyber attack on VTech Learning Lodge," *VTech*, updated
Dec. 16, 2016, accessed Feb. 17, 2017, www.vtech.com/en/press_release/2016/
faq-about-cyber-attack-on-vtech-learning-lodge/#9

11. Storm, Darlene, "Attackers hack European Space Agency, leak thousands of credentials 'for the lulz'," *Computerworld*, Dec. 14, 2015, accessed Feb. 17, 2017, www.computerworld.com
/article/3014539/cybercrime-hacking/attackers-hack-european-space-agency-leak
-thousands-of-credentials-for-the-lulz.html.

12. "IRS statement on 'Get Transcript,'" *IRS*, Feb. 26, 2016, accessed Mar. 6, 2017, www.irs.gov
/uac/newsroom/irs-statement-on-get-transcript.

13. Constantin, Lucian, "Hyatt hackers hit payment processing systems, scooped cards used at 250 locations," *PC World*, Jan. 15, 2016, accessed Jan. 20, 2016, www.pcworld.com
/article/3023204/security/hyatt-hackers-hit-payment-processing-systems-scooped-cards-
used-at-250-locations.html.

14. Cluley, Grahan, "Apple issues security patches for . . . just about everything," *We Live Security*, Jan. 24, 2017, accessed. Mar. 6, 2017, www.welivesecurity.com/2017/01/24/
apple-issues-security-patches-just-everything/.

15. "Data Breaches," *Privacy Rights Clearinghouse*, updated Feb. 16, 2017, accessed Feb. 16, 2017, www.privacyrights.org/data-breaches.

16. "Malware," *AVTest*, Feb. 8, 2017, accessed Feb. 17, 2017, www.av-test.org/en/statistics
/malware/.

17. Ohlemacher, Stephen, "IRS to delay tax refunds for millions of low-income families," The Seattle Times, Jan. 10, 2017, retrieved May 4, 2017, http://www.seattletimes.com/business
/irs-to-delay-tax-refunds-for-millions-of-low-income-families/

18. Rubin, Richard and Gambrell, Dorothy, Ripping off Uncle Sam," *Bloomberg Business*,
retrieved Aug. 5, 2015, http://www.bloomberg.com/graphics/2015-web-comic-irs-tax-fraud/

19. "Ripping off Uncle Sam," *Bloomberg BusinessWeek*, Apr. 13, 2015, accessed Jun. 9, 2015,
http://www.ritholtz.com/blog/2015/04/ripping-off-uncle-sam/.

20. "The cost of 'Code Red': $1.2 billion," *USA Today*, Aug. 1, 2001, accessed Feb. 28, 2011,
www.usatoday.com/tech/news/2001-08-01-code-red-costs.htm.

21. Reed, John, "Cyber terrorism now at the top of the list of security concerns,"
Defensetech, accessed Jan. 27, 2013, http://defensetech.org/2011/09/12/cyber-terrorism
-now-at-the-top-of-the-list-of-security-concerns/.

22. "58% Information Security Incidents Attributed to Insider Threat," *Infosecurity*, May 3,
2013, accessed Feb. 18, 2017, www.infosecurity-magazine.com/news/58-information
-security-incidents-attributed-to/.

CHAPTER 2

MALWARE AND SOCIAL ENGINEERING ATTACKS

After completing this chapter, you should be able to do the following:

Define malware

List the different types of malware

Identify payloads of malware

Describe the types of psychological social engineering attacks

Explain physical social engineering attacks

Today's Attacks and Defenses

The term *customer service* would lead one to think that *service* is what is being provided to customers. However, with increasing frequency, customer service is turning into the latest new security vulnerability.

Kevin, a journalist, wanted to determine how difficult it would be to have his information stolen. He sat down with Jessica, a security researcher, and laid out the challenge: could Jessica find Kevin's personal email address just by having his cell phone number?

Jessica started her attack in an unconventional way. Instead of searching the Internet for hints of Kevin's email address or using sophisticated hacking techniques to uncover a link to his email address from his cell phone number, Jessica determined who Kevin's wireless cell phone provider was by using a simple Internet lookup. Then she used software on her laptop computer to "spoof" Kevin's cell phone number from her device, so that to the recipient of a call it looked like it was coming from Kevin's phone. Finally, Jessica pulled out her ace: she accessed a website of sounds of a baby crying, and turned up the volume.

Now she was ready. Jessica dialed Kevin's cell phone provider and started a dialog with a customer service representative that went something like this:

Jessica: "Hello? I'm sorry, can you hear me OK? My baby is crying. I'm so sorry."

Customer Service Rep: "Yes, I can barely hear you. What can I do for you today?"

Jessica: "We're about to apply for a loan, and we've just had a new baby—that's who's crying!—and my husband told me that I need to get this done today. I'm so sorry, I can't call you back later. I'm just trying to log into our account for our user information. I don't seem to remember the email we use to log in, and now the baby's crying more, and—can you please help me?"

Customer Service Rep: "Sure. I have your phone number showing up on my screen. Let me look up the email address we have on file for this account. Here it is."

Jessica: "Thank you so much. Oh, and we need to add an older daughter on this account so she can call in and make changes to it."

Customer Service Rep: "I will need to send you a secure PIN to this cell phone number to verify that you have the phone."

Jessica: "But I can't receive a text while I'm talking on this phone. And there goes the baby again. Can you please help me just this once?"

Customer Service Rep: "OK. Oh, it looks like you're not on the account either. Would you like for me to also add you to this account?"

Jessica: "My husband was supposed to add me but I guess he forgot. Yes, if you could add me that would be great! But what's the password on the account so I can get to it?"

Customer Service Rep: "Since I just added you to this account I'll reset the account password to 'Jess' for you."

Jessica: "Thank you so much! You've been a big help."

Customer Service Rep: "My pleasure. Anything else I can do for you today?"

Starting with just Kevin's cell phone number, Jessica was able to not only get his email address but also reset his entire account with a new password, locking Kevin out of his own account. And she did it all in less than two minutes.

Most successful attacks on computers today fall into one of two categories. The first category is malicious software programs that are created by threat actors to infiltrate the victim's computers silently and without their knowledge. Once onboard, this software can intercept data, steal information, launch other attacks, or even damage the computer so that it no longer properly functions.

The other category may be overlooked but is equally deadly: tricking users into performing a compromising action or providing sensitive information. These attacks take advantage of user confusion about good security practices and deceive them into opening the door for the attacks. Defeating security through a person instead of technology is the most cost-effective approach and can generate some of the highest success rates.

This chapter examines attacks that fall into these two categories of malicious software programs and tricking users. It begins by looking at attacks that utilize malicious software. Then it explores how attacks through users are being conducted today. Later chapters detail the defenses against these attacks.

Attacks Using Malware

 Certification

1.1 Given a scenario, analyze indicators of compromise and determine the type of malware.

Malware (*mal*icious soft*ware*) is software that enters a computer system without the user's knowledge or consent and then performs an unwanted and harmful action. Malware is most often used as the general term that refers to a wide variety of damaging software programs.

Note

Many jurisdictions use the legal term *computer contaminant* instead of malware to be as encompassing and precise as possible so that offenders cannot find a loophole to escape prosecution. A typical definition is: "Computer contaminant means any data, information, image, program, signal or sound that is designed or has the capability to: (a) Contaminate, corrupt, consume, damage, destroy, disrupt, modify, record or transmit; or (b) Cause to be contaminated, corrupted, consumed, damaged, destroyed, disrupted, modified, recorded or transmitted, any other data, information, image, program, signal or sound contained in a computer, system or network without the knowledge or consent of the person who owns the other data, information, image, program, signal or sound or the computer, system or network."[1]

As security defenses have continued to evolve in order to repel malware, so too has malware continued to become more complex, with new malware being written and distributed. This has resulted in an enormous number of different *instances* of malware that have emerged (an example is the malware *ZeuS*). Yet there has been no standard established for the classification of these different instances of malware; many malware classifications are simply lists of different *types* of malware (*virus*) instead of broader categories in which like instances can be grouped together. As a result, the attempts to classify malware can be confusing.

> **Note** 📎
>
> Because threat actors often tweak their malware so that it evades the latest security defenses, many instances of malware are similar. These similar instances of malware are sometimes referred to as malware *families*.

One method of classifying the various instances of malware is by using the primary trait that the malware possesses. These traits are circulation, infection, concealment, and payload capabilities.

- *Circulation*. Some malware has as its primary trait spreading rapidly to other systems to impact a large number of users. Malware can circulate through a variety of means: by using the network to which all the devices are connected, through USB flash drives that are shared among users, or by sending the malware as an email attachment. Malware can be circulated automatically or it may require an action by the user.
- *Infection*. Once the malware reaches a system through circulation, then it must "infect" or embed itself into that system. The malware might run only one time, or it might remain on the system and be launched an infinite number of times. Some malware attaches itself to a benign program while other malware functions as a stand-alone process.
- *Concealment*. Some malware has as its primary trait avoiding detection by concealing its presence from software scanners that are looking for malware. Some malware attempts to avoid detection by changing itself, while other malware can embed itself within existing processes or modify the underlying host operating system.
- *Payload capabilities*. When payload capabilities are the primary trait of malware, the goal is the nefarious actions the malware performs. Does it steal passwords and other valuable data from the user's system? Does it delete programs so the computer can no longer function properly? Does the malware modify the system's security settings? In some cases, the purpose of the malware is to use the infected system to launch attacks against other computers.

The sections that follow give more details and examples of malware classified by circulation, infection, concealment, and payload capabilities.

Some types of malware have more than one of these traits: that is, the malware both circulates and carries a payload. However, in terms of classification the *primary* trait of the malware is used here.

Circulation

Two types of malware have the primary trait of circulation. These are viruses and worms.

Virus

A *biological virus* is an agent that reproduces inside a cell. When a cell is infected by a virus, the virus takes over the operation of that cell, converting it into a virtual factory to make more copies of it. The cell is forced to produce thousands or hundreds of thousands of identical copies of the original virus very rapidly (the polio virus can make more than *one million* copies of itself inside one single infected human cell). Biologists often say that viruses exist only to make more viruses. A computer **virus** is malicious computer code that, like its biological counterpart, reproduces itself on the same computer. Strictly speaking a computer virus replicates itself (or an evolved copy of itself) without any human intervention.

Strictly speaking, *virus* and *malware* are not interchangeable terms. A virus is only one type of malware.

Almost all viruses infect by inserting themselves into a computer file, either an executable program file or a user-created data file. A virus that infects an executable program file is called a *program virus*. When the program is launched, the virus is activated. A virus can also be part of a data file. One of the most common is a *macro virus*. A *macro* is a series of instructions that can be grouped together as a single command. Often macros are used to automate a complex set of tasks or a repeated series of tasks. Macros can be written by using a macro scripting language, such as Visual Basic for Applications (VBA), and are stored within the user document (such as in an Excel .xlsx worksheet or Word .docx file). Once the document is opened, the macro instructions execute, whether those instructions are benign or a macro virus.

Note 📎

The first macro virus appeared in 1995. Macro viruses infecting Microsoft Word documents became the dominant type of virus until 2000 when Microsoft disabled macros by default in its Office products. However, a macro virus is not a relic of the past; it has recently made a resurgence as threat actors have discovered new ways to trick their victims into enabling macros that will then allow the macro virus to run.

A very large number of different file types can contain a virus. Table 2-1 lists some of the 50 different Microsoft Windows file types that can be infected with a virus.

Table 2-1   Windows file types that can be infected

File extension	Description
.docx or .xlsx	Microsoft Office user documents
.exe	Executable program file
.msi	Microsoft installer file
.msp	Windows installer patch file
.scr	Windows screen saver
.cpl	Windows Control Panel file
.msc	Microsoft Management Console file
.wsf	Windows script file
.ps1	Windows PowerShell script

Note 📎

One of the first viruses found on a microcomputer was written for the Apple II in 1982. Rich Skrenta, a ninth-grade student in Pittsburgh, wrote "Elk Cloner," which displayed his poem on the screen after every 50th use of the infected floppy disk. Unfortunately, the virus leaked out and found its way onto the computer used by Skrenta's math teacher.[2] In 1984, the mathematician Dr. Frederick Cohen introduced the term *virus* based on a recommendation from his advisor, who came up with the name from reading science fiction novels.

Early viruses were relatively straightforward in how they infected files. One basic type of infection is the *appender infection*. The virus first attaches or appends itself to the end of the infected file. It then inserts at the beginning of the file a *jump* instruction that points to the end of the file, which is the beginning of the virus code. When the program is launched, the jump instruction redirects control to the virus. Figure 2-1 shows how an appender infection works.

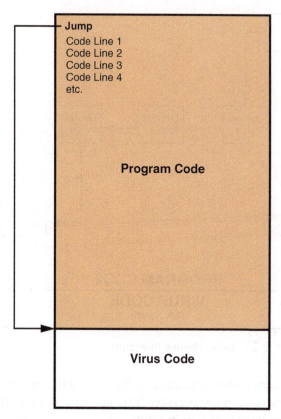

Jump
Code Line 1
Code Line 2
Code Line 3
Code Line 4
etc.

Program Code

Virus Code

Figure 2-1   Appender infection

However, these types of viruses could be detected by virus scanners relatively easily. Most viruses today go to great lengths to avoid detection; this type of virus is called an *armored virus*. Some of the armored virus infection techniques include:

- *Swiss cheese infection*. Instead of having a single *jump* instruction to the "plain" virus code, some armored viruses perform two actions to make detection more difficult. First, they scramble (encrypt) the virus code to make it more difficult to detect. Then they divide the engine to unscramble (decrypt) the virus code into different pieces and inject these pieces throughout the infected program code. When the program is launched, the different pieces are then tied together and unscramble the virus code. A Swiss cheese infection is shown in Figure 2-2.
- *Split infection*. Instead of inserting pieces of the decryption engine throughout the program code, some viruses split the malicious code itself into several parts (along with one main body of code), and then these parts are placed at random

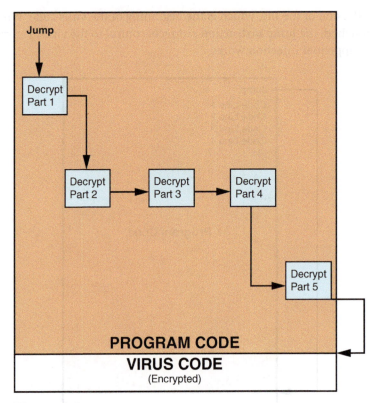

Figure 2-2   Swiss cheese infection

positions throughout the program code. To make detection even more difficult these parts may contain unnecessary "garbage" code to mask their true purpose. A split infection virus is shown in Figure 2-3.

- *Mutation*. Instead of just hiding itself within a fire, some viruses can *mutate* or change. An *oligomorphic virus* changes its internal code to one of a set number of predefined mutations whenever it is executed, while a *polymorphic virus* completely changes from its original form whenever it is executed. A *metamorphic virus* can actually rewrite its own code and thus appears different each time it is executed by creating a logical equivalent of its code whenever it is run.

Note 📎

Some armored viruses scan for the presence of files that security researchers typically use. If those files are present, then it is assumed that the virus is being examined for weaknesses and the virus will then automatically self-destruct by deleting itself.

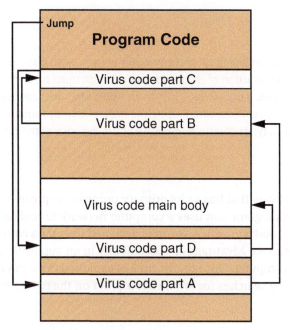

Figure 2-3   Split infection

Each time the infected program is launched or the data file is opened—either by the user or the computer's operating system—the virus performs two actions. First, it unloads a payload to perform a malicious action. Although early viruses often did nothing more than display an annoying message, viruses today are much more harmful. Viruses can corrupt or delete files, prevent programs from launching, steal data to be sent to another computer, cause a computer to crash repeatedly, and even turn off the computer's security settings.

 Note

Sometimes a virus will remain dormant for a period before unleashing its payload.

The second action a virus takes when executed is to reproduce itself by inserting its code into another file, but only on the same computer. A virus can only replicate itself on the host computer on which it is located; it cannot automatically spread to another computer by itself. Instead, it must rely on the actions of users to spread to other computers. Because viruses are attached to files they are spread when a user transfers those files to other devices. For example, a user might send an infected file as an email attachment or copy an infected file to a USB flash drive and give the drive to another user. Once the virus reaches a new computer it begins to infect it. Thus, a virus must have two carriers: a file to which it attaches and a human to transport it to other computers.

> **Note** 📎
>
> Several similarities between biological and computer viruses exist: both must enter their host passively (by relying on the action of an outside agent), both must be on the correct host (a horse virus cannot make a human sick, just as an Apple Mac virus cannot infect a Windows computer), both can only replicate when inside the host, both may remain dormant for a period of time, and both types of viruses replicate at the expense of the host.

Worm

A second type of malware that has as its primary purpose to spread is a worm. A **worm** is a malicious program that uses a computer network to replicate (worms are sometimes called *network viruses*). A worm is designed to enter a computer through the network and then take advantage of vulnerability in an application or an operating system on the host computer. Once the worm has exploited the vulnerability on one system, it immediately searches for another computer on the network that has the same vulnerability.

> **Note** 📎
>
> One of the first wide-scale worms occurred in 1988. This worm exploited a misconfiguration in a program that allowed commands emailed to a remote system to be executed on that system, and it also carried a payload that contained a program that attempted to determine user passwords. Almost 6000 computers, or 10 percent of the devices connected to the Internet at that time, were affected. The threat actor who was responsible was later convicted of federal crimes in connection with this incident.

Early worms were relatively benign and designed simply to spread quickly but not corrupt the systems they infected. These worms slowed down the network through which they were transmitted by replicating so quickly that they consumed all network resources. Today's worms can leave behind a payload on the systems they infect and cause harm, much like a virus. Actions that worms have performed include deleting files on the computer or allowing the computer to be remotely controlled by an attacker.

> **Note** 📎
>
> Although viruses and worms are said to be automatically self-replicating, *where* they replicate is different. A virus self-replicates *on* the host computer but does not spread to other computers by itself. A worm self-replicates *between* computers (from one computer to another).

Table 2-2 lists the differences between viruses and worms.

Table 2-2	Differences between viruses and worms	
Action	Virus	Worm
What does it do?	Inserts malicious code into a program or data file	Exploits a vulnerability in an application or operating system
How does it spread to other computers?	User transfers infected files to other devices	Uses a network to travel from one computer to another
Does it infect a file?	Yes	No
Does there need to be user action for it to spread?	Yes	No

Infection

There are three examples of malware that have the primary trait of infection. These are Trojans, ransomware, and crypto-malware.

Trojans

According to ancient legend, the Greeks won the Trojan War by hiding soldiers in a large hollow wooden horse that was presented as a gift to the city of Troy. Once the horse was wheeled into the fortified city, the soldiers crept out of the horse during the night and attacked the unsuspecting defenders.

A computer **Trojan** is an executable program that masquerades as performing a benign activity but also does something malicious. For example, a user might download what is advertised as a calendar program, yet when it is installed, in addition to installing the calendar it also installs malware that scans the system for credit card numbers and passwords, connects through the network to a remote system, and then transmits that information to the attacker.

A special type of Trojan is a **remote access Trojan (RAT)**. A RAT has the basic functionality of a Trojan but also gives the threat actor unauthorized remote access to the victim's computer by using specially configured communication protocols. This creates an opening into the victim's computer, allowing the threat actor unrestricted access. The attacker can not only monitor what the user is doing but also can change computer settings, browse and copy files, and even use the computer to access other computers connected on the network.

Ransomware

One of the fastest-growing types of malware is ransomware. **Ransomware** prevents a user's device from properly and fully functioning until a fee is paid. The ransomware embeds itself onto the computer in such a way that it cannot be bypassed, and even rebooting causes the ransomware to launch again.

Although it existed earlier, ransomware became widespread around 2010. This earliest ransomware displays a screen and prevents the user from accessing the computer's resources (called *blocker ransomware*). The screen contains instructions that pretend to be from a reputable third party, giving a "valid" reason for blocking the user's computer. One example is ransomware that purports to come from a law enforcement agency. This message, using official-looking imagery, states that the user had performed an illegal action such as downloading pornography and must immediately pay a fine online by entering a credit card number. Figure 2-4 shows a ransomware message.

Figure 2-4   Ransomware message

Source: Symantec Security Response

Another variation of this type of ransomware pretends to come from a software vendor and displays a fictitious warning that a software license has expired or there is a problem with the computer such as imminent hard drive failure or—in a touch of irony—a malware infection. This ransomware variation tells users that they must immediately renew their license or purchase additional software online to fix a non-existent problem. The ransomware example in Figure 2-5 uses color schemes and icons like those found on legitimate Windows software.

Note

Users who provide a credit card number to pay the online fine or make the required purchase usually find that the threat actors simply steal the card information and then make purchases using it.

Figure 2-5   **Ransomware computer infection**
Source: Microsoft Security Intelligence Report

As ransomware became more widespread the threat actors dropped the pretense that the ransomware was from a reputable third party requiring a fine or a purchase. Instead, they simply blocked the user's computer and demanded a fee for its release. Ransomware attackers have determined what they consider the optimal price point for payment to unblock a computer: the amount must be small enough that most victims will begrudgingly pay to have their systems unblocked, but large enough that when thousands of victims pay up the attackers can garner a handsome sum.

Note 📎

Initially for individuals the price was around $500 while for enterprises the range was between $8000 to $17,000. However, the demanded ransoms have been significantly increasing. For example, recent well-publicized ransomware attacks demanding higher ransoms were against Hollywood Presbyterian Medical Center ($17,000), Los Angeles Valley College ($28,000), and San Francisco's Municipal Transportation Agency ($73,000).[3]

Ransomware continues to be a serious threat to users. One recent report estimated that $1 billion was paid in ransom in one year, yet only 42 percent of those who paid the ransom could then retrieve their data. Enterprises are also prime targets. A recent survey revealed that almost half of all enterprises have been a victim of a ransomware attack.[4]

Note 📎

The FBI does not support paying a ransom in response to a ransomware attack. It states, "Paying a ransom doesn't guarantee an organization that it will get its data back—we've seen cases where organizations never got a decryption key after having paid the ransom. Paying a ransom not only emboldens current cyber criminals to target more organizations, it also offers an incentive for other criminals to get involved in this type of illegal activity. And finally, by paying a ransom, an organization might inadvertently be funding other illicit activity associated with criminals."[5]

Crypto-malware

Blocker ransomware, the earliest form of ransomware, displayed a screen and prevented the user from accessing the computer. However, there were limitations to blocker ransomware's continued success. Due to the way in which blocker ransomware functions, security researchers were able to develop automated technologies that help to fight against it, even after infection. And in a worst-case scenario, the user of an infected computer could reinstall the operating system to gain control again of her computer and files.

Threat actors then developed a more malicious form of ransomware: instead of just blocking the user from accessing the computer, they encrypted all the files on the device so that none of them could be opened. This is called **crypto-malware**. A screen appears telling the victim that his files are now encrypted and a fee must be paid to receive a key to unlock them. In addition, threat actors increased the urgency for payment: the cost for the key to unlock the crypto-malware increases every few hours or several of the encrypted user files are deleted every few hours, with the number continually increasing. And if the ransom is not paid promptly (often within 36 to 96 hours) the key can never be retrieved. Figure 2-6 shows a crypto-ransomware message.

Once infected with crypto-malware, the software connects to the threat actor's *command and control (C&C)* server to receive instructions or updated data. Crypto-malware first generates a locking key for the encrypted files and then encrypts the locking key with another key that has been downloaded from the C&C. This second key, which remains on the C&C server, is what is sent to the victims once they pay the ransom. However, this process poses problems for attackers. If the address of the C&C server is known it can be blocked by the network so that once the computer is infected the malware could not communicate back with the C&C, thus preventing the encryption process from even starting. To circumvent this problem some crypto-malware started using locking encryption keys that were hard-coded into the malware itself. But once one victim paid for the unlocking key, it could be distributed to other victims to unlock their files. Now new forms of crypto-malware have circumvented these limitations by adding a second round of encryption.

Figure 2-6 Crypto-malware message
Source: PC Risk

Two additional recent enhancements to crypto-malware are causing increasing concern. First, instead of encrypting files only on the user's local hard drive, now crypto-malware encrypts all files on *any* network or attached device that is connected to that computer. This includes secondary hard disk drives, USB hard drives, network-attached storage devices, network servers, and even cloud-based data repositories. This means if a user's computer in an enterprise is infected with crypto-malware potentially *all* files for the enterprise—and not just those on one computer—can be locked. In addition, threat actors are also using crypto-malware to infect mobile devices such as smartphones and tablets.

Note 📎

The specific techniques for using multiple keys for crypto-malware encryption and decryption are covered in Chapter 3, while the defenses for protecting against crypto-malware from encrypting all files are covered in Chapter 9.

Concealment

Some types of malware have as a primary trait avoiding detection. One example of this type of malware is a rootkit. A **rootkit** can hide its presence or the presence of other malware (like a virus) on the computer by accessing lower layers of the operating system or even using undocumented functions to make alterations. This enables the rootkit and its accompanying software to become undetectable by the operating system and common antimalware scanning software that is designed to seek and find malware.

Consider the following example. A rootkit infects a computer and hides its presence from the operating system so that the rootkit files are not visible to the operating system, as illustrated in Figure 2-7. Scanning software looking for malicious files is installed on the computer, and it then requests from the operating system a list of all files. However, because the rootkit files are hidden from the operating system, those files are not provided to the scanning software, thus eluding detection.

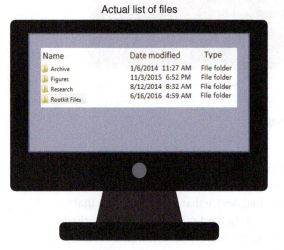
Actual list of files

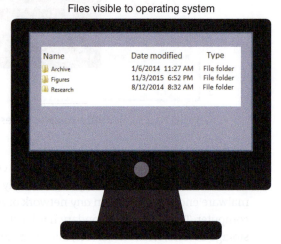
Files visible to operating system

Figure 2-7   **Computer infected with rootkit**

Payload Capabilities

The true destructive power of malware is to be found in its payload capabilities. The primary payload capabilities are to collect data, delete data, modify system security settings, and launch attacks.

Collect Data

Different types of malware are designed to collect important data from the user's computer and make it available to the threat actor. This malware includes spyware and adware.

Spyware

Spyware is tracking software that is deployed without the consent or control of the user. Spyware typically secretly monitors users by collecting information without their approval by using the computer's resources, including programs already installed on the computer, to collect and distribute personal or sensitive information. Table 2-3 lists different technologies used by spyware.

Table 2-3   Technologies used by spyware

Technology	Description	Impact
Automatic download software	Used to download and install software without the user's interaction	Could install unauthorized applications
Passive tracking technologies	Used to gather information about user activities without installing any software	Could collect private information such as websites a user has visited
System modifying software	Modifies or changes user configurations, such as the web browser home page or search page, default media player, or lower-level system functions	Changes configurations to settings that the user did not approve
Tracking software	Used to monitor user behavior or gather information about the user, sometimes including personally identifiable or other sensitive information	Could collect personal information that can be shared widely or stolen, resulting in fraud or identity theft

Note 📎

Not all spyware is necessarily malicious. For example, spyware monitoring tools can help parents keep track of the online activities of their children.

One type of nefarious spyware is a **keylogger** that silently captures and stores each keystroke that a user types on the computer's keyboard. The threat actor can then search the captured text for any useful information such as passwords, credit card numbers, or personal information.

A keylogger can be a software program or a small hardware device. The most common are software keyloggers, which are programs installed on the computer that silently capture sensitive information. Today software keyloggers go far beyond just capturing a user's keystrokes. These programs can also make screen captures of everything that is on the user's screen and silently turn on the computer's web camera to record images of the user. A software keylogger is illustrated in Figure 2-8. Software keylogger programs generally conceal themselves so that the user cannot detect them. An advantages of software keyloggers is that they do not require physical access to the user's computer and can often be installed remotely as a Trojan or by a virus, and they can routinely send captured information back to the attacker through the computer's Internet connection.

Figure 2-8   Software keylogger
Source: Ecodsoft

The original keyloggers were hardware devices inserted between the computer keyboard connection and USB port, as shown in Figure 2-9. Because the device resembles an ordinary keyboard plug and the computer keyboard USB port is often on the back of the computer, a hardware keylogger can easily go undetected. In addition, the device is beyond the reach of the computer's antimalware scanning software and thus raises no alarms. But because the attacker who installed the hardware keylogger must return later and physically remove the device in order to access the information it has gathered, hardware keyloggers are rarely used today.

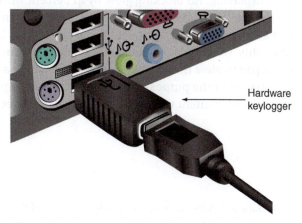

Figure 2-9   Hardware keylogger

Adware

Adware delivers advertising content in a manner that is unexpected and unwanted by the user. Once the adware malware becomes installed, it typically displays advertising banners, popup ads, or opens new web browser windows at random intervals. Users generally disapprove of adware because:

- Adware can display objectionable content, such as gambling sites or pornography.
- Frequent popup ads can interfere with a user's productivity.
- Popup ads can slow a computer or even cause crashes and the loss of data.
- Unwanted advertisements can be a nuisance.

Note 🖉

Some adware goes beyond affecting the user's computer experience. This is because adware programs can also perform a tracking function, which monitors and tracks a user's online activities and then sends a log of these activities to third parties without the user's authorization or knowledge. For example, a user who visits online automobile sites to view specific types of cars can be tracked by adware and classified as someone interested in buying a new car. Based on the sequence and type of websites visited, the adware can also determine whether the surfers' behavior suggests they are close to making a purchase or are also looking at competitors' cars. This information is gathered by adware and then sold to automobile advertisers, who send the users regular mail advertisements about their cars or even call the user on the telephone.

As the volume of ads has steadily increased on many websites, it has resulted in user backlash. More users are installing ad blocking software in their web browsers to prevent the ads from displaying. Ad blocking grew by 41 percent worldwide in one year (198 million users), while U.S. ad blocking grew by 48 percent (45 million users), and it is estimated that ad blocking cost website publishers nearly $22 billion each year.[6] In order to combat this, web marketers are increasingly including adding pay walls (forcing the user to pay to view the content instead of watching ads), displaying friendly reminders to users about the purpose of ads (that ads are the price to pay for free content), or notices that content will be blocked if the site detects ad blockers being used.

> **Note** 📎
>
> One of the popular ad blocking software packages recently announced that it is launching an online advertising service to help marketers place "acceptable" ads on a website. Advertisers must pay a fee to have their ads tagged as "acceptable" and these ads must be of a certain size, placement, and labeling. If a user has ad blocking software, these "acceptable" ads will not be blocked.

Delete Data

Whereas spyware and adware are designed to collect data, the payload of other types of malware are designed to do just the opposite: delete data. This may involve deleting important user data files, such as documents or photos, or erasing vital operating system files so that the computer will no longer function properly.

One type of malware that is frequently used to delete data is a logic bomb. A **logic bomb** is computer code that is typically added to a legitimate program but lies dormant until a specific logical event triggers it. Once it is triggered, the program then deletes data or performs other malicious activities. In one example, a Maryland government employee tried to destroy the contents of more than 4000 servers by planting a logic bomb script that was scheduled to activate 90 days after he was terminated.[7]

One of the recent high-profile attacks based on a logic bomb simultaneously erased the hard drives of computers belonging to three banks and two media broadcasting companies in South Korea. The malware consisted of four files, including *AgentBase.exe* that triggered the attack. Contained within the file was a hexadecimal string (*4DAD4678*) that was the date and time the attack was to begin: *2013-3-20 14:00:00* (March 20, 2013 at 2:00 PM). As soon as the internal clock on the computers reached 2:01 PM the logic bomb was triggered to overwrite the hard drive and master boot record on Microsoft Windows computers and then reboot the system, rendering them useless. The malware also included a module for deleting data from remote Linux machines. Other famous logic bombs are listed in Table 2-4.

Table 2-4	Famous logic bombs	
Description	**Reason for attack**	**Results**
A logic bomb was planted in a financial services computer network that caused 1000 computers to delete critical data.	A disgruntled employee had counted on this to cause the company's stock price to drop; he planned to use that event to earn money.	The logic bomb detonated but the employee was caught and sentenced to eight years in prison and ordered to pay $3.1 million in restitution.[8]
A logic bomb at a defense contractor was designed to delete important rocket project data.	The employee's plan was to be hired as a highly paid consultant to fix the problem.	The logic bomb was discovered and disabled before it triggered. The employee was charged with computer tampering and attempted fraud and was fined $5000.[9]
A logic bomb at a health services firm was set to go off on the employee's birthday.	The employee was angered that he might be laid off (although he was not).	The employee was sentenced to 30 months in a federal prison and paid $81,200 in restitution to the company.[10]

Logic bombs are difficult to detect before they are triggered. This is because logic bombs are often embedded in very large computer programs, some containing tens of thousands of lines of code, and a trusted employee can easily insert a few lines of computer code into a long program without anyone detecting it. In addition, these programs are not routinely scanned for containing malicious actions.

Note 📎

Logic bombs should not be confused with an *Easter egg*, which refers to an undocumented, yet benign hidden feature that launches by entering a set of special commands, key combinations, or mouse clicks. Usually programmers insert Easter eggs for their own recreation or notoriety during the software's development. For example, in a Google search engine entering the phrase *do a barrel roll* will cause the screen to rotate 360 degrees. A previous version of Microsoft Excel contained an entire Easter egg game called "The Hall of Tortured Souls."

Modify System Security

The payload of some types of malware attempts to modify the system's security settings so that more insidious attacks can be made. One type of malware in this category is called a backdoor. A **backdoor** gives access to a computer, program, or service that circumvents any normal security protections. Backdoors that are installed on a computer allow the attacker to return later and bypass security settings.

Note

Creating a legitimate backdoor is a common practice by developers, who may need to access a program or device on a regular basis, yet do not want to be hindered by continual requests for passwords or other security approvals. The intent is for the backdoor to be removed once the application is finalized. However, in some instances backdoors have been left installed, and attackers have used them to bypass security.

Launch Attacks

One of the more popular payloads of malware today is software that will allow the infected computer to be placed under the remote control of an attacker for the purpose of launching attacks. This infected robot computer is known as a **bot** or *zombie*. When hundreds, thousands, or even millions of bot computers are gathered into a logical computer network, they create a *botnet* under the control of a *bot herder*.

Note

Due to the multitasking capabilities of modern computers, a computer can act as a bot while at the same time carrying out the tasks of its regular user. The user is completely unaware that his or her computer is being used for malicious activities.

Table 2-5 lists some of the attacks that can be generated through botnets.

Table 2-5 Uses of botnets

Type of attack	Description
Spamming	Botnets are widely recognized as the primary source of spam email. A botnet consisting of thousands of bots enables an attacker to send massive amounts of spam.
Spreading malware	Botnets can be used to spread malware and create new bots and botnets. Bots can download and execute a file sent by the attacker.
Manipulating online polls	Because each bot has a unique Internet Protocol (IP) address, each "vote" by a bot will have the same credibility as a vote cast by a real person. Online games can be manipulated in a similar way.
Denying services	Botnets can flood a web server with thousands of requests and overwhelm it to the point that it cannot respond to legitimate requests.

Infected bot computers receive instructions through a C&C structure from the bot herders regarding which computers to attack and how. There are a variety of ways for this communication to occur, including:

- A bot can receive its instructions by automatically signing in to a website that the bot herder operates on which information has been placed that the bot knows how to interpret as commands.
- Bots can sign in to a third-party website; this has an advantage in that the bot herder does not need to have a direct affiliation with that website.
- Commands can be sent via blogs, specially coded attack commands through posts on Twitter, or notes posted in Facebook.
- Bot herders are increasing using a *dead drop* C&C mechanism by creating a Google Gmail email account and then creating a draft email message that is never sent but contains commands that the bot receives when it logs in to Gmail and reads the draft. Because the email message is never sent there is no record of it and all Gmail transmissions are protected so that outsiders cannot view them.

The number of bots and botnets worldwide is staggering. According to the FBI's cyber division, every second 18 computers worldwide are being infected and added to a botnet, which amounts to hundreds of millions of compromised computers each year.[11] One single botnet had under its control between 3 and 4 million bots. Another botnet that was used primarily to send email spam was sending upwards of 60 billion emails *daily*.[12]

Note

When the hosting service was taken offline that was supporting the bot sending the billions of spam emails, the worldwide spam volume immediately dropped by 75 percent.[13]

Social Engineering Attacks

 Certification

1.2 Compare and contrast types of attacks.

One morning a small group of strangers walked into the corporate office of a large shipping firm and soon walked out with access to the firm's entire computer network, which contained valuable and highly sensitive information. Here is how they could accomplish this feat with no technical tools or skills:

1. Before entering the building, one person of the group called the company's Human Resource (HR) office and asked for the names of key employees. The office willingly gave out the information without asking any questions.

2. As the group walked up to the building, one of them pretended to have lost the key code to the door, so a friendly employee let them in. When they entered a secured area on the third floor, they claimed to have misplaced their identity badges, so another smiling employee opened the door for them.

3. Because these strangers knew that the chief financial officer (CFO) was out of town because of his voicemail greeting message, they walked unchallenged into his office and gathered information from his unprotected computer. They also dug through trash receptacles and retrieved useful documents. A custodian was even stopped and asked for a box in which to place these documents so they could be carried out of the building.

4. One of the group's members then called the company's help desk from the CFO's office and pretended to be the CFO (they had listened to his voice from his voicemail greeting message and knew how he spoke). The imposter CFO claimed that he desperately needed his password because he had forgotten it and was on his way to an important meeting. The help desk gave out the password, and the group left the building with complete access to the network.

This true story illustrates that technology is not always needed for attacks on IT.[14] **Social engineering** is a means of gathering information for an attack by relying on the weaknesses of individuals. Social engineering attacks can involve psychological approaches as well as physical procedures.

Psychological Approaches

Many social engineering attacks rely on psychology, which is the mental and emotional approach rather than the physical. At its core, social engineering relies on an attacker's clever manipulation of human nature to persuade the victim to provide information or take actions. Several basic principles make psychological social engineering highly effective. These are listed in Table 2-6 with the example of an attacker pretending to be the chief executive officer (CEO) calling the organization's help desk to have a password reset.

Because many of the psychological approaches involve person-to-person contact, attackers use a variety of techniques to gain trust. For example:

- *Provide a reason.* Many social engineering threat actors are careful to add a reason along with their request. By giving a rationalization and using the word *because* it is much more likely for the victim to provide the information. For example, "I was asked to call you because the director's office manager is out sick today."
- *Project confidence.* A threat actor is unlikely to generate suspicion if she enters a restricted area but calmly walks through the building as if she knows exactly where she going (without looking at signs, down hallways, or reading door labels) and even greets people she sees with a friendly "Hi, how are you doing?"
- *Use evasion and diversion.* When challenged, a threat actor might evade a question by giving a vague or irrelevant answer. They could also feign innocence or confusion, or just keep denying any allegations, until the victim eventually

Table 2-6	Social engineering effectiveness	
Principle	**Description**	**Example**
Authority	Directed by someone impersonating an authority figure or falsely citing their authority	"I'm the CEO calling."
Intimidation	To frighten and coerce by threat	"If you don't reset my password, I will call your supervisor."
Consensus	Influenced by what others do	"I called last week and your colleague reset my password."
Scarcity	Something is in short supply	"I can't waste time here."
Urgency	Immediate action is needed	"My meeting with the board starts in 5 minutes."
Familiarity	Victim is well-known and well-received	"I remember reading a good evaluation on you."
Trust	Confidence	"You know who I am."

believes his suspicions are wrong. Sometimes a threat actor can resort to anger and cause the victim to drop the challenge. "Who are you to ask that? Connect me with your supervisor immediately!"

- *Make them laugh.* Humor is an excellent tool to put people at ease and to develop a sense of trust. "I can't believe I left my badge in my office again! You know, some mistakes are too much fun to only make once!"

Social engineering psychological approaches often involve impersonation, phishing, spam, hoaxes, and watering hole attacks.

Impersonation

Social engineering **impersonation** means to masquerade as a real or fictitious character and then play out the role of that person on a victim. For example, an attacker could impersonate a help desk support technician who calls the victim, pretends that there is a problem with the network, and asks her for her user name and password to reset the account.

Common roles that are often impersonated include a repairperson, IT support, a manager, a trusted third party, or a fellow employee. Often attackers will impersonate individuals whose roles are authoritative because victims generally resist saying "no" to anyone in power.

Phishing

One of the most common forms of social engineering is phishing. **Phishing** is sending an email or displaying a web announcement that falsely claims to be from a legitimate enterprise in an attempt to trick the user into surrendering private information. Users are asked to respond to an email or are directed to a website where they are requested to update personal information, such as passwords, credit card numbers, Social Security numbers, bank account numbers, or other information. However, the email or website is actually an imposter and is set up to steal what information the user enters.

Note

The word *phishing* is a variation on the word *fishing*, with the idea being that bait is thrown out knowing that while most will ignore it, some will "bite."

Whereas at one time phishing messages were easy to spot with misspelled words and obvious counterfeit images, that is no longer the case. In fact, one of the reasons that phishing is so successful today is that the emails and the fake websites are difficult to distinguish from those that are legitimate: logos, color schemes, and wording seems to be almost identical. Figure 2-10 illustrates an actual phishing email message that looks like it came from a genuine source.

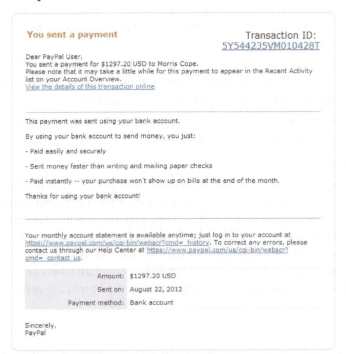

Figure 2-10   **Phishing email message**
Source: Email sent to Dr. Mark Revels

> **Note** 📎
>
> Phishing is also used to validate email addresses. A phishing email can display an image retrieved from a website that is requested when the user opens the email message. A unique code is used to link the image to the recipient's email address, which then tells the phisher that the email address is active and valid. This is the reason most email today does not automatically display images that are received in emails.

Several variations on phishing attacks are:

- *Spear phishing*. Whereas phishing involves sending millions of generic email messages to users, **spear phishing** targets specific users. The emails used in spear phishing are customized to the recipients, including their names and personal information, to make the message appear legitimate.
- *Whaling*. One type of spear phishing is **whaling**. Instead of going after the "smaller fish," whaling targets the "big fish," namely, wealthy individuals or senior executives within a business who typically would have larger sums of money in a bank account that an attacker could access if the attack is successful. By focusing upon this smaller group, the attacker can invest more time in the attack and finely tune the message to achieve the highest likelihood of success.
- *Vishing*. Instead of using email to contact the potential victim, a telephone call can be used instead. Known as **vishing** (*voice phishing*), an attacker calls a victim who, upon answering, hears a recorded message that pretends to be from the user's bank stating that her credit card has experienced fraudulent activity or that her bank account has had unusual activity. The victim is instructed to call a specific phone number immediately (which has been set up by the attacker). When the victim calls, it is answered by automated instructions telling her to enter her credit card number, bank account number, Social Security number, or other information on the telephone's key pad.

> **Note** 📎
>
> A new variation on vishing now uses short message service (SMS) text messages in conjunction with callback recorded phone messages. The threat actors first send a text message to a user's cellphone that pretends to come from their bank saying that their account has been broken into or their credit card number has been stolen. Along with the text message is a callback telephone number the customer is instructed to call immediately. That phone number plays a recording telling the customer to enter their Social Security number or credit card number for verification. The attackers then simply capture the information that is entered.

Phishing continues to be a primary weapon used by threat actors. About 97 percent of all attacks start with phishing, and with 5000 new phishing sites appearing daily, the number of phishing incidents exceeds 58 million annually.[15] Approximately 30 percent of all phishing emails are opened by unsuspecting users. About 84 percent of all enterprises reported that they have been the victims of a successful spear phishing attack,[16] and the average cost of a successful spear phishing campaign against an enterprise is $1.6 million.[17]

> **Note** 📎
>
> Although most web browsers automatically block known phishing websites, because so many sites are appearing so rapidly it is difficult for the browsers to stay up-to-date.

Spam

Spam is unsolicited email that is sent to a large number of recipients. Spam continues to flood the email inboxes of Internet users. Statistics about spam that bear this out include the following:[18]

- *Volume of total email.* Worldwide the volume of spam as a percentage of all email traffic peaked in 2008, when 92 percent of all email was spam. Since that time, due to aggressive efforts to take down botnets, the percentage is around 61 percent, which is still a staggering amount.
- *Daily spam emails.* The number of spam messages sent each day is about 28 billion emails.
- *Content categories.* The most common category of spam content is healthcare products (38 percent), followed by dating solicitations (18 percent), adult products (12 percent), and advertisements for stocks (6 percent).
- *User actions.* When frustrated about receiving spam, about 60 percent of users attempt to unsubscribe from future emails, while 45 percent simply ignore any future emails. More extreme user actions are to stop using the product being advertised (14 percent), completely boycott the company doing the advertising (13 percent), tell their friends (9 percent), or hit the computer or mobile device in frustration (4 percent).

The reason users receive so many spam messages is because sending spam is lucrative. It costs spammers very little to send millions of spam email messages. Almost all spam is sent from botnets, and a spammer who does not own his own botnet can lease time from other attackers ($40 per hour) to use a botnet of up to 100,000 infected computers to launch a spam attack. And even if spammers receive only a very small percentage of responses, they still make a large profit. For example, if a spammer sent spam to 6 million users for a product with a sale price of $50 that cost only $5 to make, and if only 0.001 percent of the recipients responded and bought the product (a typical response rate), the spammer would still make more than $270,000 in profit.

Text-based spam messages that include words such as *Viagra* or *investments* can easily be trapped by filters that look for these words and block the email. Because of the increased use of these filters, spammers have turned to *image spam*, which uses graphical images of text to circumvent text-based filters. Image spam cannot be filtered based on the textual content of the message because it appears as an image instead of text. These spam messages often include nonsense text so that it appears the email message is legitimate (an email with no text can prompt the spam filter to block it). Figure 2-11 shows an example of an image spam.

Figure 2-11   Image spam

Beyond being annoying and interfering with work productivity as users spend time reading and deleting spam messages, spam can be a security vulnerability. This is because spam can be used to distribute malware. Spam sent with attachments that contain malware is one of the most common means by which threat actors distribute their malware today.[19]

Hoaxes

Threat actors can use hoaxes as a first step in an attack. A **hoax** is a false warning, often contained in an email message claiming to come from the IT department. The hoax purports that there is a "deadly virus" circulating through the Internet and that the recipient should erase specific files or change security configurations, and then forward the message to other users. However, changing configurations allows an attacker to compromise the system. Or, erasing files may make the computer unstable, prompting the victim to call the telephone number in the hoax email message for help, which is actually the phone number of the attacker.

Watering Hole Attack

In the natural world, similar types of animals are known to congregate around a pool of water for refreshment. In a similar manner, a **watering hole attack** is directed toward a smaller group of specific individuals, such as the major executives working for a manufacturing company. These executives all tend to visit a common website, such as that of a parts supplier to the manufacturer. An attacker who wants to target this group of executives will attempt to determine the common website that they frequent and then infect it with malware that will make its way onto the group's computers.

Physical Procedures

Just as some social engineering attacks rely on psychological manipulation, other attacks rely on physical acts. These attacks take advantage of user actions that can result in compromised security. Two of the most common physical procedures are dumpster diving and tailgating.

Dumpster Diving

Dumpster diving involves digging through trash receptacles to find information that can be useful in an attack. Table 2-7 lists the different items that can be retrieved—many of which appear to be useless—and how they can be used.

An electronic variation of physical dumpster diving is to use Google's search engine to look for documents and data posted online that can be used in an attack. This is called *Google dorking* and it uses advanced Google search techniques to look for information that unsuspecting victims have carelessly posted on the web.

> **Note**
>
> *Google dorking* is from a slang term that originally was used to refer to someone who is not considered intelligent (a *dork*) and later came to refer to uncovering security vulnerabilities that are the result of the actions of such a person.

For example, to find on the web any Microsoft Excel spreadsheets (.xlsx) that contain the column heading "SSN" (Social Security number) the Google search term *intext:"SSN" filetype:xlsx* can be used, or to find any Microsoft Word documents (.docx) that contained the word "passwords" as part of the title the Google search term *allintitle: "passwords" filetype:docx* is used.

Table 2-7   Dumpster diving items and their usefulness

Item retrieved	Why useful
Calendars	A calendar can reveal which employees are out of town at a particular time.
Inexpensive computer hardware, such as USB flash drives or portal hard drives	These devices are often improperly disposed of and might contain valuable information.
Memos	Seemingly unimportant memos can often provide small bits of useful information for an attacker who is building an impersonation.
Organizational charts	These identify individuals within the organization who are in positions of authority.
Phone directories	A phone directory can provide the names and telephone numbers of individuals in the organization to target or impersonate.
Policy manuals	These may reveal the true level of security within the organization.
System manuals	A system manual can tell an attacker the type of computer system that is being used so that other research can be conducted to pinpoint vulnerabilities.

Tailgating

Organizations can invest tens of thousands of dollars to install specialized doors that permit access only to authorized users who possess a special card or who can enter a specific code. These automated access control systems are designed to restrict entry into an area. However, a weakness of these systems is that they cannot always control *how many* people enter the building when access is allowed; once an authorized person opens the door, one or more individuals can follow behind and also enter. This is known as **tailgating**.

Several ways in which tailgating can occur are:

- A tailgater waits at the end of the sidewalk until an authorized user opens the door. She then calls out to him to "Please hold the door!" as she hurries up to the door. In most cases, good etiquette wins out over good security practices, and the door is held open for the tailgater.
- A tailgater waits near the outside of the door and then quickly enters once the authorized employee leaves the area. This technique is used most commonly during weekends and at nights, where the actions of the more overt tailgater would be suspicious.
- A tailgater stands outside the door and waits until an employee exits the building. He then slips behind the person as he is walking away and grabs the door just before it closes to gain access to the building.

- An employee conspires with an unauthorized person to allow him to walk in with him through the open door (called *piggybacking*).

If an attacker cannot enter a building as a tailgater without raising suspicion, an alternative is to watch an individual entering the security code on a keypad. Known as **shoulder surfing**, it can be used in any setting in which a user casually observes someone entering secret information, such as the security code on a door keypad. Attackers are also using webcams and smartphone cameras to "shoulder surf" users of ATM machines to record keypad entries.

> **Note** 📎
>
> A defense against shoulder surfing is an application that uses the computer's web cam to watch if anyone nearby is looking at the computer screen. If someone is detected, the user can be alerted with a popup window message or the screen will automatically blur so that it cannot be read.

Chapter Summary

- Malware is malicious software that enters a computer system without the user's knowledge or consent and includes an unwanted and harmful action. One method of classifying the various types of malware is by using the primary trait that the malware possesses. These traits are circulation, infection, concealment, and payload capabilities.

- One of the types of malware that has the primary trait of circulation is a computer virus. A virus is malicious computer code that reproduces itself on the same computer. A virus inserts itself into a computer file (a data file or program) and then looks to reproduce itself on the same computer as well as unload its malicious payload. Most viruses go to

great lengths to avoid detection. Another type of such malware is a worm, which travels through a network and is designed to take advantage of vulnerability in an application or an operating system to enter a user's computer. Once the worm has exploited the vulnerability on one system, it immediately searches for another computer that has the same vulnerability.

- Another category of malware has infection as its primary trait. A Trojan is a program advertised as performing one activity but in addition does something malicious. A special type of Trojan is a remote access Trojan (RAT), which has the basic functionality of a Trojan but also gives the threat actor unauthorized remote access to the victim's computer by using specially configured communication protocols. Ransomware prevents a user's device from properly and fully functioning until a fee is paid. Ransomware embeds itself onto the computer in such a way that the it cannot be bypassed, and even rebooting still causes the ransomware to launch again. Crypto-malware encrypted all the files on the device so that none of them could be opened until a ransom is paid.

- Some malware has as its primary trait avoiding detection. A rootkit can hide its presence or the presence of other malware (like a virus) on the computer by accessing lower layers of the operating system or even using undocumented functions to make alterations.

- The destructive power of malware is to be found in its payload capabilities. Different types of malware are designed to collect important data from the user's computer and make it available at the attacker. Spyware is tracking software that is deployed without the consent or control of the user. One type of spyware is a keylogger, which silently captures and stores each keystroke that a user types on the computer's keyboard. A keylogger can be a software program or a small hardware device. Adware is a software program that delivers advertising content in a manner that is unexpected and unwanted by the user.

- The payload of other types of malware deletes data on the computer. A logic bomb is computer code that is typically added to a legitimate program but lies dormant until it is triggered by a specific logical event. Once it is triggered, the program then deletes data or performs other malicious activities. The payload of some types of

malware attempts to modify the system's security settings so that more insidious attacks can be made. One type of malware in this category is called a backdoor. A backdoor gives access to a computer, program, or service that circumvents any normal security protections.

- One of the most popular payloads of malware is software that will allow the infected computer to be placed under the remote control of an attacker. This infected robot computer is known as a bot. When multiple bot computers are gathered into a logical computer network, they create a botnet.

- Social engineering is a means of gathering information for an attack by relying on the weaknesses of individuals. Many social engineering attacks rely on psychology, which is the mental and emotional approach rather than the physical. At its core, social engineering relies on an attacker's clever manipulation of human nature to persuade the victim to provide information or take actions. Several basic principles make psychological social engineering highly effective. These include authority, intimidation, consensus, scarcity, urgency, familiarity, and trust. Impersonation means to masquerade as a real or fictitious character and then play out the role of that person on a victim. Phishing is sending an email or displaying a web announcement that falsely claims to be from a legitimate enterprise in an attempt to trick the user into surrendering private information. Several variations on phishing attacks exist, such as spear phishing, whaling, and vishing. Spam, or unsolicited email that is sent to a large number of recipients, is annoying, interferes with work productivity, and can be a security vulnerability.

- Attackers can use hoaxes (false warnings) as a first step in an attack, often contained in an email message claiming to come from the IT department. Recipients are told that they should erase specific files or change security configurations, and then forward the message to other users. A watering hole attack is directed toward a smaller group of specific individuals, such as the major executives working for a manufacturing company.

- Some social engineering attacks rely on physical acts. Dumpster diving involves digging through trash receptacles to find information that can be useful in an attack. Organizations invest large sums of money to install specialized doors that only permit access to authorized users who possess a special card or who can enter a specific code, yet they do not always control how many people enter the building when access is allowed. Following an authorized person through an open door is known as tailgating. If an attacker cannot enter a building as a tailgater without raising suspicion, an alternative is to watch an individual entering secret information, such as the security code on a keypad. This is known as shoulder surfing.

Key Terms

adware	keylogger	spear phishing
authority	logic bomb	spyware
backdoor	malware	tailgating
bot	phishing	Trojan
consensus	ransomware	trust
crypto-malware	remote access	urgency
dumpster diving	Trojan (RAT)	virus
familiarity	rootkit	vishing
hoax	scarcity	watering hole attack
impersonation	shoulder surfing	whaling
intimidation	social engineering	worm

Review Questions

1. Which of the following is NOT a primary trait of malware?
   a. Diffusion
   b. Circulation
   c. Infection
   d. Concealment

2. Which type of malware requires a user to transport it from one computer to another?
   a. Worm
   b. Rootkit
   c. Adware
   d. Virus

3. Which type of mutation completely changes a virus from its original form by rewriting its own code whenever it is executed?
   a. Betamorphic
   b. Oligomorphic
   c. Polymorphic
   d. Metamorphic
4. Ebba received a message from one of her tech support employees. In violation of company policy, a user had downloaded a free program to receive weather reports, but the program had also installed malware on the computer that gave the threat actor unrestricted access to the computer. What type of malware had been downloaded?
   a. Virus
   b. Ransomware
   c. RAT
   d. Trojan
5. Linnea's father called her to say that a message suddenly appeared on his screen that says his software license has expired and he must immediately pay $500 to have it renewed before control of the computer will be returned to him. What type of malware is this?
   a. Persistent virusware
   b. Trojanware
   c. Blocking ransomware
   d. Lockoutware
6. Astrid's computer screen suddenly says that all files are now locked until money is transferred to a specific account, at which time she will receive a means to unlock the files. What type of malware has infected her computer?
   a. Bitcoin malware
   b. Crypto-malware

c. Blocking virus
   d. Networked worm
7. What is the name of the threat actor's computer that gives instructions to an infected computer?
   a. Command and control (C&C) server
   b. Resource server
   c. Regulating Net Server (RNS)
   d. Monitoring and Infecting (M&I) server
8. Which of these could NOT be defined as a logic bomb?
   a. If the company's stock price drops below $100, then credit Juni's account with 10 additional years of retirement credit.
   b. Erase all data if Matilda's name is removed from the list of employees.
   c. Reformat the hard drive three months after Sigrid left the company.
   d. Send spam email to Moa's inbox on Tuesday.
9. Which of the following is NOT correct about a rootkit?
   a. A rootkit is able to hide its presence or the presence of other malware.
   b. A rootkit accesses "lower layers" of the operating system.
   c. A rootkit is always the payload of a Trojan.
   d. The risk of a rootkit is less today than previously.
10. Which of these is a general term used for describing software that gathers information without the user's consent?
   a. Gatherware
   b. Adware
   c. Spyware
   d. Scrapeware

11. Which statement regarding a keylogger is NOT true?
    a. Keyloggers can be used to capture passwords, credit card numbers, or personal information.
    b. Software keyloggers are generally easy to detect.
    c. Hardware keyloggers are installed between the keyboard connector and computer keyboard USB port.
    d. Software keyloggers can be designed to send captured information automatically back to the attacker through the Internet.

12. A watering hole attack is directed against____ .
    a. wealthy individuals
    b. a smaller group of specific users
    c. all users of a large corporation
    d. attackers who send spam

13. ____ sends phishing messages only to wealthy individuals.
    a. Whaling
    b. Spear phishing
    c. Target phishing
    d. Microing

14. Lykke receives a call while working at the helpdesk from someone who needs his account reset immediately. When Lykke questions the caller, he says, "If you don't reset my account immediately, I will call your supervisor!" What psychological approach is the caller attempting to use on Lykke?
    a. Familiarity
    b. Scarcity
    c. Intimidation
    d. Consensus

15. Hedda pretends to be the help desk manager and calls Steve to trick him into giving her his password. What social engineering attack has Hedda performed?
    a. Aliasing
    b. Duplicity
    c. Impersonation
    d. Luring

16. How can an attacker use a hoax?
    a. A hoax could convince a user that a bad Trojan is circulating and that he should change his security settings.
    b. By sending out a hoax, an attacker can convince a user to read his email more often.
    c. A user who receives multiple hoaxes could contact his supervisor for help.
    d. Hoaxes are not used by attackers today.

17. Which of these items retrieved through dumpster diving would NOT provide useful information?
    a. Calendars
    b. Organizational charts
    c. Memos
    d. Books

18. ____ is following an authorized person through a secure door.
    a. Tagging
    b. Tailgating
    c. Backpacking
    d. Caboosing

19. Each of these is a reason why adware is scorned EXCEPT____ .
    a. it displays objectionable content
    b. it displays the attacker's programming skills
    c. it can interfere with a user's productivity
    d. it can cause a computer to crash or slow down

20. What is the term used for a threat actor who controls multiple bots in a botnet?
    a. Bot herder
    b. Zombie shepherd
    c. Rogue IRC
    d. Cyber-robot

Hands-On Projects

Note 📎

If you are concerned about installing any of the software in these projects on your regular computer, you can instead install the software in the Windows virtual machine created in the Chapter 1 Hands-On Projects 1-3 and 1-4. Software installed within the virtual machine will not impact the host computer.

Project 2-1: Analyzing Files and URLs for Viruses Using VirusTotal

VirusTotal, a subsidiary of Google, is a free online service that analyzes files and URLs to identify potential malware. VirusTotal scans and detects any type of binary content, including a Windows executable program, Android, PDFs, and images. VirusTotal is designed to provide a "second opinion" on a file or URL that may have been flagged as suspicious by other scanning software. In this project, you use VirusTotal to scan a file and a URL.

1. First view several viruses from 20 years ago and observe their benign but annoying impact. Open your web browser and enter the URL **archive.org/details /malwaremuseum&tab=collection** (if you are no longer able to access the site through the web address, use a search engine to search for "Malware Museum").
2. Click several of the viruses and notice what they do (all of the viruses have been rendered ineffective and will not harm a computer).
3. When finished close your web browser.
4. Use Microsoft Word to create a document that contains the above paragraph about VirusTotal. Save the document as **VirusTotal.docx**.
5. Now save this document as a PDF. Click **File** and **Save As**.
6. Under **Save as type:** select **PDF (*.pdf)**.
7. Save this file as **YourName-VirusTotal.pdf**.
8. Exit Word.
9. Open your web browser and enter the URL **www.virustotal.com** (if you are no longer able to access the site through the web address, use a search engine to search for "Virus Total").
10. If necessary, click the **File** tab.
11. Click **Choose File**.
12. Navigate to the location of **YourName-VirusTotal.pdf** and click **Open**.
13. Click **Scan it!**
14. If the **File already analysed** dialog box opens, click **Reanalyse**.
15. Wait until the analysis is completed.
16. Scroll through the list of AV vendors that have been polled regarding this file. A green checkmark means no malware was detected.

17. Click the **File detail** tab and read through the analysis.
18. Use your browser's back button to return to the VirusTotal home page.
19. Click **URL**.
20. Enter the URL of your school, place of employment, or another site with which you are familiar.
21. Click **Scan it!** If the **URL already analysed** dialog box opens, click **Reanalyse**.
22. Wait until the analysis is completed.
23. Scroll through the list of vendor analysis. Do any of these sites indicate **Unrate site** or **Malware site**?
24. Click **Additional information**.
25. How could VirusTotal be useful to users? How could it be useful to security researchers? Could it also be used by attackers to test their own malware before distributing it to ensure that it does not trigger an AV alert? What should be the protections against this?
26. Close all windows.

Project 2-2: Write-Protecting a USB Flash Drive and Disabling a USB Port

Viruses and other malware are often spread from one computer to another by infected USB flash drives. This can be controlled by either disabling the USB port or by write-protecting the drive so that no malware can be copied to it. Disabling the port can be accomplished through changing a Windows registry setting, while write-protecting the drive can be done through third-party software that can control USB device permissions. In this project, you download and install a software-based USB write blocker to prevent data from being written to a USB device and disable the USB port. You will need a USB flash drive for this project.

1. Open your web browser and enter the URL **www.irongeek.com/i.php?page=security /thumbscrew-software-usb-write-blocker** (if you are no longer able to access the program through the URL, use a search engine to search for "Irongeek Thumbscrew").
2. Click **Download Thumbscrew**.
3. If the File Download dialog box appears, click **Save** and follow the instructions to save this file in a location such as your desktop or a folder designated by your instructor.
4. When the file finishes downloading, extract the files in a location such as your desktop or a folder designated by your instructor. Navigate to that location and double-click **thumbscrew.exe** and follow the default installation procedures.
5. After installation, notice that a new icon appears in the system tray in the lower right corner of the screen.
6. Insert a USB flash drive into the computer.
7. Navigate to a document on the computer.
8. Right-click the document and then select **Send to**.
9. Click the appropriate **Removable Disk** icon of the USB flash drive to copy the file to the flash drive.
10. Now make the USB flash drive write protected so it cannot be written to. Click the icon in the system tray.

11. Click **Make USB Read Only**. Notice that a red circle now appears over the icon to indicate that the flash drive is write protected.

12. Navigate to a document on the computer.

13. Right-click the document and then select **Send to**.

14. Click the appropriate **Removable Disk** icon of the USB flash drive to copy the file to the flash drive. What happens?

15. Click the icon in the system tray to change the permissions so that the USB drive is no longer read only.

16. Now disable the USB port entirely. First remove the flash drive from the USB port.

17. In the Windows **Run** dialog box enter **regedit**.

18. In the left pane double-click **HKEY_LOCAL_MACHINE** to expand it.

19. Double-click **SYSTEM**.

20. Double-click **ControlSet001**.

21. Double-click **Services**.

22. Double-click **USBSTOR** as shown in Figure 2-12.

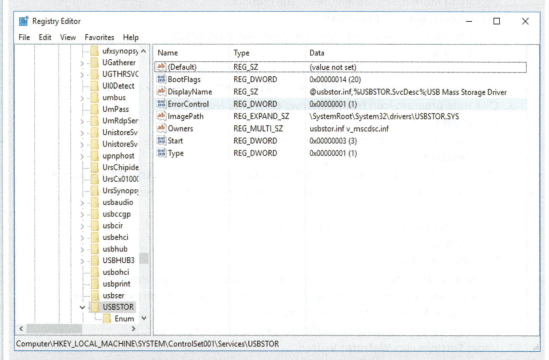

Figure 2-12   Windows Registry Editor

23. In the right pane double-click **Start**.

24. In **Value data**: change the number of **3** to **4**. Be sure that **Hexadecimal** under **Base** is selected.

25. Click **OK**.

26. Now insert a USB flash drive into the USB port. What happens?

27. To reactivate the port, change the **Value data**: back to **3** and click **OK**.
28. Close all windows.

Project 2-3: Using a Software Keylogger

A keylogger program captures everything that a user enters on a computer keyboard. In this project, you download and use a software keylogger.

> ### Caution ⚠
>
> The purpose of this activity is to provide information regarding how these programs function in order that adequate defenses can be designed and implemented. These programs should never be used in a malicious fashion against another user.

1. Open your web browser and enter the URL **refog.com** (if you are no longer able to access the program through the URL, use a search engine to search for "Refog Keylogger").
2. Click **Read More** to see the features of the product.
3. Under **Keylogger** click **Download**.
4. Click **Create an account** and enter the requested information.
5. Click **Download**.
6. When the file finishes downloading, run the installation program.
7. When asked **I'm going to use this software to monitor:** select **My own computer**.
8. Click **Hide program icon from Windows tray**. Click **Next**.
9. Click **I Agree**.
10. Enter the Windows account password. Click **Install**.
11. Click **Restart Now**.
12. After the computer has restarted use the keystroke combination **Ctrl + Alt + Shift + K** to launch Refog Keylogger. The Refog Keylogger screen appears as seen in Figure 2-13.
13. Click **Tools** and then click **Settings**.
14. Note the default settings regarding what is captured.
15. Click **Back to log**.
16. Minimize Refog Keylogger.
17. Use your computer normally by opening a web browser to surf to a website. Open Microsoft Word and type several sentences. Open and close several programs on the computer.
18. Maximize Keylogger and note the information that was captured.
19. In the left pane click through the different items that were captured.
20. Under **Settings** click **Websites Visited**.
21. Under **Websites Visited** click **Make website screenshots**.
22. Click **Apply**.
23. Open a web browser to surf to multiple websites.
24. Under **Users** click **Websites visited**. Note the screen captures of the different sites.
25. What type of information would a software keylogger provide to a threat actor? How could it be used against the victim?
26. Click **File** and then **Exit** to close Keylogger.
27. Close all windows.

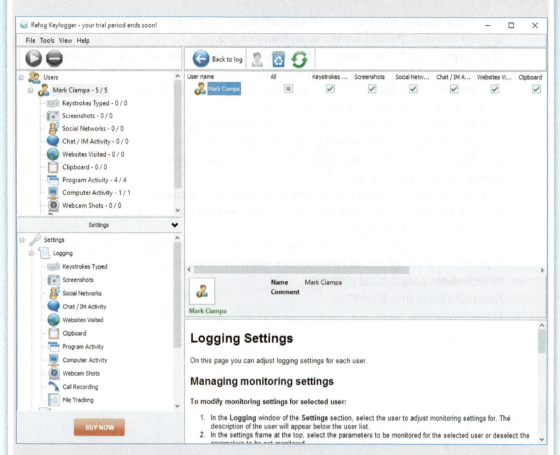

Figure 2-13   Refog Keylogger

Source: Refog

Project 2-4: Exploring Ransomware Sites

There are a variety of sites that provide information about ransomware along with tools for counteracting some types of infection. In this project, you explore different ransomware sites.

1. Open your web browser and enter the URL **ransomwaretracker.abuse.ch** (if you are no longer able to access the program through the URL, use a search engine to search for "Ransomware Tracker").
2. Read about the features of Ransomware Tracker on the home page.
3. Click **Tracker**.
4. Scroll through the list of ransomware malware.
5. Under **Filter by threat:** click **Payment Sites** to display those payment sites.
6. Under **Filter by malware:** click **Locky** or another of the ransomware families.
7. Select one of the instances of malware and click it to view the details. What can you tell from it?

8. Now visit a site that provides user information about ransomware. Open your web browser and enter the URL **www.nomoreransom.org**.

9. Click **Crypto Sheriff**. How could this be useful to a user who has suffered a ransomware infection?

10. Click **Ransomware: Q&A**. Read through the information. Which statements would you agree with? Which statements would you disagree with?

11. Click **Decryption Tools.** This contains a list of different tools that may help restore a computer that has been infected by a specific type of ransomware. Click **Download** to download one of the tools. Note that these tools change frequently based on the latest types of ransomware that is circulating.

12. Run the program to understand how these decryption tools function. Note that you will not be able to complete the process because there are no encrypted files on the computer. Close the program.

13. Now visit another site that provides ransomware information and tools. Open your web browser and enter the URL **id-ransomware.malwarehunterteam.com**

14. What features does this site provide?

15. How could these sites be useful?

16. Close all windows.

Case Projects

Case Project 2-1: Preventing Vishing Attacks

Vishing, or voice phishing, continues to increase as an attack against users. What would you do to help prevent users from becoming victims? First, access the online SoundCloud repository by NumberCop that contains several different recordings of vishing attacks (*soundcloud.com/numbercop*). After listening to several of the recordings to understand what attackers typically ask and how they craft their attacks, create guidelines for not falling prey to these attacks. What messages do the attackers commonly use? How do they trick users into entering their information? What social engineering effectiveness reasons do they use? Then write a series of steps that would help users resist these attacks. Write a one-page paper on your research.

Case Project 2-2: Social Engineering Psychological Approaches

Several basic principles or reasons make psychological social engineering effective. These include authority, intimidation, consensus, scarcity, urgency, familiarity, and trust. Table 2-6 uses these principles in a scenario of an attacker pretending to be the chief executive officer (CEO) calling the organization's help desk to have a password reset. Create two additional scenarios, such as an attacker impersonating a help desk employee who wants access to an employee's protected information, and create a dialog example for each of the seven principles.

Case Project 2-3: Your Social Engineering Attack

Today's Attacks and Defenses at the beginning of this chapter illustrated how a security researcher could manipulate a help desk support technician into compromising security. If you were to create your own social engineering attack, what would it be? Using your place of employment or school, first determine exactly what your goal would be in the attack, and then craft a detailed description of how you would carry out the attack using only social engineering to achieve your goal. You might want to search the Internet for examples of previously successful attacks that used social engineering. Why do you think your attack would be successful? Who would be involved? What would be the problems in achieving your goal? Why? Write a one-page paper on your research.

Case Project 2-4: Google Dorking

Google dorking, or using advanced Google search techniques to find sensitive information, has been likened to "online dumpster diving." Use the Internet to research Google dorking. First, use the Internet to determine how the following advanced Google search engine operators are used: *allintext, allintitle, allinurl, cache, filetype, inanchor, intest, intitle, link, site,* +, |, and *. Then, use at least five of the operators to create potential Google dorking searches. Finally, try out your searches to see if they are effective. How easy is it for a threat actor to use Google dorking? How can users and organizations combat this? List your Google dorking searches, the results, and the defenses that should be used against it. Write a one-page paper on your activity.

Case Project 2-5: Crypto-malware Attacks

Use the Internet to research some of the recent different crypto-malware ransomware attacks. What do they do? Why are they so successful? How are they being spread? What can users do to protect themselves? Write a one-page summary of your research.

Case Project 2-6: Online Phishing Tests

Detecting phishing emails can often be difficult. Point your web browser to the following three online phishing tests: *www.sonicwall.com/phishing/, www.opendns.com/phishing-quiz/,* and *www.komando.com/tips/361345/can-you-spot-a-fake-email-take-our-phishing-iq-test* (or search the Internet for others). What did you learn from these tests? Were they helpful? What do you think general users would think about these tests? Write a one-paragraph summary on what you learned about phishing from these tests.

Case Project 2-7 Lake Point Consulting Services

Lake Point Consulting Services (LPCS) provides security consulting and assurance services to over 500 clients across a wide range of enterprises in more than 20 states. A new initiative at LPCS is for each of its seven regional offices to provide internships to students who are in their final year of the information security degree program at the local college.

Manna is a regional bakery and café. Although Manna has used an outside security consultant to help their small IT team with security they nevertheless have been the victims of several attacks over the last two quarters. Manna decided not to renew the consultant's contract and has now turned to LPCS for assistance. While LPCS is performing an audit and evaluating the enterprise's current security position, LPCS has asked you to conduct a presentation about malware to the staff of three of Manna's retail sites during their annual regional meeting.

1. Create a PowerPoint presentation that lists 15 different types of malware and defines each type in detail regarding what the malware can do, how it spreads, its dangers, etc. Your presentation should contain at least 10 slides.

2. After your presentation, it is apparent that some of the attacks were the result of social engineering. Manna has asked you to create a one-page "cheat sheet" that describes social engineering attacks and how they may be performed, including a list of practical tips to resist these attacks. This sheet paper will be posted in the stores in which employees can make quick reference to when necessary. Create the paper for Manna, using a format that is easy to reference.

Case Project 2-8: Information Security Community Site Activity

The Information Security Community Site is an online companion to this textbook. It contains a wide variety of tools, information, discussion boards, and other features to assist learners. Go to *community.cengage.com/Infosec2* and click the *Join or Sign in* icon to log in, using your login name and password that you created in Chapter 1. Click **Forums (Discussion)** and click on **Security+ Case Projects (6**th **edition)**. Read the following case study.

Eric received an email from Amazon Customer Service that said "Thank you for contacting us." But Eric did not contact them. Instead, an attacker had contacted them and pretended to be Eric. When Amazon Customer Service asked the attacker to identify himself all he had to do was give Eric's name, email address, and mailing address—which the attacker got from Whois, which contains Eric's registration information for his website. However, Eric knew to protect his actual mailing address so the registration information on Whois was actually a hotel close to Eric's house. Because the information matched what was on file, Customer Service told the attacker the mailing address of Eric's order, which was his real home address. Eric contacted Amazon, found out these details, and told them not to release any of his information to anyone who contacted Customer Service, to which Amazon agreed.

Fast forward two months. Eric again received another "Thank you for contacting us" email. After contacting Amazon again, he found that this time the attacker had tried to get the last four digits of Eric's credit card number on file through more social engineering tricks. Fortunately, this time Amazon did not surrender that specific piece of information (although they had ignored his previous instruction not to give out any information). Had they provided the credit card number the attacker would have had enough information to pass the "I'm-the-real-Eric" test on almost any of Eric's online accounts (using his name, email address, mailing address, and last four digits of his credit card) and trick their Customer Service into resetting Eric's password. This would then allow the attacker to get into Eric's online accounts and purchase a virtually unlimited number of items charged to Eric's credit card.

What went wrong? Should the first Amazon Customer Service representative have been reprimanded? What policies should Amazon have had in place to prevent this? What technologies should there be in place to prevent this? As a customer, what should you do to protect your online accounts? Enter your answers on the InfoSec Community Server discussion board.

References

1. "2010 Nevada Code, Title 15 Crimes and punishments, Chapter 205 Crimes against property, NRS 205.4737 "Computer contaminant" defined," *Justia US Law*, accessed Feb. 24, 2017, law.justia.com/codes/nevada/2010/title15/chapter205/nrs205-4737.html.
2. "The first computer virus," accessed Mar. 3, 2011, www.worldhistorysite.com/virus.html.
3. Storm, Darlene, "LA college pays $28,000 ransom demand; new sophisticated Spora ransomware," *Computerworld*, Jan. 11, 2017, accessed Jan. 14, 2017, www.computerworld.com/article/3156829/security/la-college-pays-28-000-ransom-demand-new-sophisticated-spora-ransomware.html.
4. Crowe, Jonathan, "Ransomeware by the numbers: Must-know ransomware statistics for 2016," *Barkly*, Nov. 15, 2016, accessed Feb. 25, 2017, blog.barkly.com/ransomware-statistics-2016.
5. "Incidents of ransomware on the rise: Protect yourself and your organization," *FBI News*, Apr. 29, 2016, accessed Feb. 25, 2017, www.fbi.gov/news/stories/incidents -of-ransomware-on-the-rise.
6. "The 2015 ad blocking report," *PageFair*, Aug. 10, 2015, accessed Dec. 4, 2015, pagefair.com/blog/2015/ad-blocking-report/.
7. Cluley, Graham, "Fannie Mae worker accused of planting malware timebomb," *Naked Security Sophos Blog*, accessed Mar. 3, 2011, http://nakedsecurity.sophos.com/2009/01/29/fannie-mae-worker-accused-planting-malware-timebomb/.
8. "History and milestones," *About RSA Conference*, accessed Mar. 3, 2011, www.rsaconference.com/about-rsa-conference/history-and-milestones.htm.
9. "Logic bombs," *Computer Knowledge*, accessed Mar. 3, 2011, www.cknow.com/cms/vtutor/logic-bombs.html.
10. Vijayan, Jaikumar, "Unix admin pleads guilty to planting logic bomb," *Computerworld*, Sep. 21, 2007, accessed Mar. 3, 2011, www.pcworld.com/article/137479/unix_admin_pleads_guilty_to_planting_logic_bomb.html.
11. Khandelwal, Swati. "FBI: Botnets Infecting 18 Computers per Second. But How Many of Them NSA Holds?" *The Hacker News*, Jul. 17, 2014, accessed Feb. 27, 2017, thehackernews.com/2014/07/fbi-botnets-infecting-18-computers-per.html
12. Thomas, Karl, "Nine bad botnets and the damage they did," *Welivesecurity*, Feb. 25, 2015, retrieved Feb. 27, 2017, www.welivesecurity.com/2015/02/25/nine-bad-botnets-damage/.
13. Ibid.
14. Granger, Sarah, "Social engineering fundamentals, part 1: Hacker tactics," *Symantec*, Dec. 18, 2001, accessed Mar. 3, 2011, www.symantec.com/connect/articles/social-engineering -fundamentals-part-i-hacker-tactics.
15. Fowler, Geoffrey, "Phishing: You're still at risk," *Wall Street Journal*, Feb. 23, 2017.

16. "The year in phishing," *RSA Online Fraud Report*, Jan. 2013, accessed Jan. 7, 2014, www.emc.com/collateral/fraud-report/online-rsa-fraud-report-012013.pdf.

17. Crowe, Jonathan, "Phishing by the numbers: Must-known phishing statistics 2016," *Barkly*, accessed Feb. 27, 2017, blog.barkly.com/phishing-statistics-2016.

18. "Global spam," *Statista*, accessed Feb. 27, 2017, www.statista.com/statistics/420391 /spam-email-traffic-share/.

19. Crowe, Jonathan, "Phishing by the numbers: Must-known phishing statistics 2016," *Barkly*, accessed Feb. 27, 2017, blog.barkly.com/phishing-statistics-2016.

PART II

CRYPTOGRAPHY

Chapter 3: Basic Cryptography
Chapter 4: Advanced Cryptography and PKI

This part introduces you to an essential element of modern security, that of cryptography. The importance of cryptography has increased over time to become a key defense in securing data from threat actors. Chapter 3 defines cryptography, explains different cryptographic algorithms, looks at attacks on cryptography, and shows how cryptography is implemented. Chapter 4 continues with more advanced cryptography topics such as digital certificates, public key infrastructure (PKI), and transport encryption algorithms.

CRYPTOGRAPHY

Chapter 3 Cryptography

Chapter 4 Advanced Cryptography and PKI

This part introduces you to an essential element of modern security, that of cryptography. The importance of cryptography has increased over time to become a key defense in securing data from threat actors. Chapter 3 defines cryptography, explains different cryptosystems and algorithms, looks at attacks on cryptography, and shows how cryptography is implemented. Chapter 4 continues with more advanced cryptography topics such as digital certificates, public key infrastructure (PKI), and transport encryption algorithms.

CHAPTER 3

BASIC CRYPTOGRAPHY

After completing this chapter, you should be able to do the following:

Define cryptography

Describe hash, symmetric, and asymmetric cryptographic algorithms

Explain different cryptographic attacks

List the various ways in which cryptography is used

Today's Attacks and Defenses

One of the most highly publicized recent events involving cryptography pitted the federal government against a major computer vendor. A terrorist attack in San Bernardino, California in December, 2015 resulted in the death of 14 individuals and the two terrorists and the injury of 24 more. One of the attackers used an Apple iPhone 5C owned by his employer that was recovered by police. About six weeks prior to the attack the terrorists had turned off the online backup feature so that the phone's contents were no longer copied to Apple's iCloud online servers; the data was stored only on the iPhone itself. The FBI was given permission from the employer who owned the device to examine the phone's contents to determine if this attacker was connected to other terrorists at home or abroad.

However, the iPhone had protections that prevented the FBI from easily viewing its contents. Access to this iPhone was protected by a passcode, which serves two functions: it is used as authentication to access the phone and is used to create a decryption key that allows data on the phone to be viewed. To prevent anyone from randomly guessing passcodes, there were more security protections on the phone. In addition to delays incorporated between incorrect passcode attempts, to prevent someone from randomly guessing passwords indefinitely until the right code was entered, the iPhone was configured to make it permanently inaccessible after 10 failed passcode attempts.

The FBI asked a court to compel Apple to create custom iPhone firmware that would remove the delays and prevent device lockup after 10 incorrect attempts. Apple's CEO said the government's legal position was setting "a dangerous precedent" and refused to comply. He went on to say that building this capability to bypass security would undeniably create a "backdoor," and while the government might argue that its use would be limited to this case, there was no way to guarantee such control. Once created, the CEO said, the technique could be used over and over, on any number of devices. He concluded, "No reasonable person would find that acceptable." Apple said it would appeal the court order, all the way to the Supreme Court if necessary.

After several weeks of contentious back-and-forth drama played out in the courts between Apple and the FBI, an unexpected turn of events occurred. The FBI suddenly asked a judge to postpone a court hearing scheduled that same day. After several more days the FBI said in a court filing that an "outside party demonstrated to the FBI a possible method" for unlocking the iPhone, but it did not indicate what the method was. There was much speculation by security researchers of what it could be. The most likely method involves a cloning technique called *NAND mirroring*. The memory chip on the iPhone is removed (by de-soldering it), put into a chip reader/programmer device, and then its contents are copied. This would allow multiple copies to be made of the iPhone's memory so that the FBI could make multiple attempts on the phone by guessing passcodes. When one copy locks up (because it only allows 10 attempts of a passcode) then they simply move on to the next copy. After several days, the FBI asked the courts to completely drop the order by stating, "It no longer requires the assistance from Apple."

Did the FBI break into the iPhone and view its contents? Who was the "outside party" who was responsible for assisting the FBI? Was it a broker who knew a zero-day vulnerability? Has this outside party broken into other iPhones so that these devices are no longer secure? The FBI provided no detailed information.

And in another twist Apple, who refused to give the FBI the help it wanted, then decided it might need the FBI's help. Attorneys for Apple starting researching legal tactics to compel the FBI to turn over the specifics of how the phone was compromised so that Apple would know how to build better defenses on its iPhone. Legal experts agreed that because the government faces no legal obligation to provide any information to Apple, it was unlikely the FBI would share this information with Apple or the public. Besides, if the government gave Apple the information and Apple built stronger devices, it could be that much more difficult to break into an iPhone the next time. Apple ultimately decided not to sue the FBI to try to gain access to the solution.[1]

Information security **can be defined as that which protects the integrity, confidentiality,** and availability of information through products, people, and procedures on the devices that store, manipulate, and transmit the information. In most instances the focus of that protection is keeping the threat actors as far away as possible from the information by building barriers around it. This may include technology barriers (like firewalls) or physical defenses (such as erecting a fence that surrounds the property) to keep threat actors at bay.

Whereas these technology and physical defenses are critical, what if another element was added so that if the attackers were able to get to the information it would nevertheless be useless to them? What if the information was scrambled in such a way that while authorized individuals could read it the attackers still could not?

This is the protection that cryptography affords: it masks the data so that if a threat actor could access it they still cannot read it. As such, cryptography provides an even deeper level of protection, and this has made it a critical element in protecting data. Yet there is still significant room for growth: if more of our information were properly encrypted it would significantly reduce the impact of any data loss.

In this chapter, you learn how cryptography can be used to protect data. You first learn what cryptography is and how it can be used for protection. Then you examine how to protect data using different types of cryptography algorithms. After that, the chapter details the attacks on cryptography, followed by how to use cryptography on files and disks to keep data secure.

Defining Cryptography

 **Certification**

6.1 Compare and contrast basic concepts of cryptography.

6.2 Explain cryptography algorithms and their basic characteristics.

Defining cryptography involves understanding what it is and what it can do. It also involves understanding how cryptography can be used as a security tool to protect data as well as knowing its limitations.

What Is Cryptography?

Cryptography (from Greek words meaning *hidden writing*) is the practice of transforming information so that it is secure and cannot be accessed by unauthorized parties. This is accomplished through *scrambling* the information in such a way that only approved recipients can access it.

Whereas cryptography scrambles a message so that it cannot be understood, **steganography** hides the existence of the data. What appears to be a harmless image can contain hidden data, usually some type of message, embedded within the image. Steganography typically takes the data, divides it into smaller pieces, and hides these in unused portions of the file, as shown in Figure 3-1. Steganography may hide data in the file header fields that describe the file, between sections of the *metadata* (data that is used to describe the content or structure of the actual data), or in the areas of a file that contain the content itself. Steganography can use a wide variety of file types—image files, audio files, video files, etc.—to hide messages and data.

Message to
be hidden

Message in
binary form

Metadata Header 1		
Header size	00110011	00000000
File size	00110001	01011001
Reserved space 1	01101111	01110101
Reserved space 2	00100000	01110011
Offset address for start data	00110111	00000000

Message hidden
in metadata

01110101
01101100

Metadata Header 2		
Image width	00111001	00000000
Image height	00110000	01100100
Number of graphic planes	00110101	00000000
Number of bits per pixel	00110101	01101100
Compression type	00110101	00100000
Number of colors	00110101	00000000

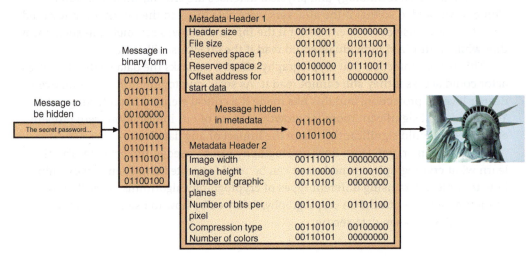

Figure 3-1 **Data hidden by steganography**

Photo: Chris Parypa Photography/Shutterstock.com

Note 📎

Steganography is sometimes used together with cryptography so that the information is doubly protected. By using cryptography to first encrypt the data and then steganography to hide it this requires someone seeking the information to first find the data and then decrypt it.

When using cryptography, the process of changing the original text into a scrambled message is known as **encryption** (the reverse process is *decryption*, or changing the message back to its original form). In addition, there is other terminology that applies to cryptography:

- *Plaintext*. Unencrypted data that is input for encryption or is the output of decryption is called *plaintext*.
- *Ciphertext*. *Ciphertext* is the scrambled and unreadable output of encryption.
- *Cleartext*. Readable (unencrypted) data that is transmitted or stored in "the clear" and is not intended to be encrypted is called *cleartext*.

Plaintext data is input into a cryptographic **algorithm** (also called a **cipher**), which consists of procedures based on a mathematical formula to encrypt and decrypt the data. A *key* is a mathematical value entered into the algorithm to produce the ciphertext. Just as a key is inserted into a door lock to lock the door, in cryptography a unique mathematical key is input into the encryption algorithm to "lock down" the data by creating the ciphertext. When the ciphertext is to be returned to plaintext, the reverse process occurs with a decryption algorithm and key. The cryptographic process is illustrated in Figure 3-2.

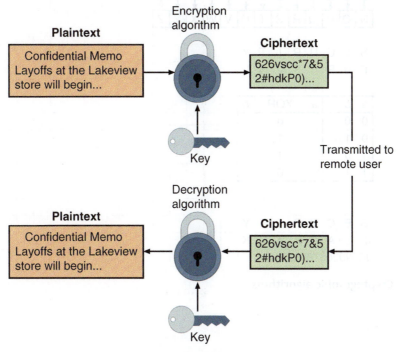

Figure 3-2 Cryptographic process

There are different categories of algorithms and within those different types. One category is a **substitution cipher** that substitutes one character for another. By substituting 1 for the letter *A*, 2 for the letter *B*, etc., the word *security* becomes *1804022017081924*. One type of substitution cipher is a **ROT13**, in which the entire alphabet is rotated 13 steps: $A = N$, $B = O$, etc., so that the word *security* becomes *frphevgl*. Another common algorithm is the **XOR cipher**. This is based on the binary operation e*X*clusive *OR* that compares two bits: if the bits are different a *1* is returned, but if they are identical then a *0* is returned. For example, to encrypt the word *security* by "XOR-ing" it with the word *flapjack* the binary equivalent of the first letter *s* (*01110011*) is compared with that of the letter *f* (*01100110*) to return *00010101*. Then the letter *e* is compared with the *l*, etc., followed by a comparison of each remaining letter. These algorithms are illustrated in Figure 3-3.

Substitution Cipher																										
	A	B	C	D	E	F	G	H	I	J	K	L	M	N	O	P	Q	R	S	T	U	V	W	X	Y	Z
	1	2	3	4	5	6	7	8	9	10	11	12	13	14	15	16	17	18	19	20	21	22	23	24	25	26

Example	S	E	C	U	R	I	T	Y
Result	19	5	3	21	18	9	20	25

ROT13	A	B	C	D	E	F	G	H	I	J	K	L	M
	N	O	P	Q	R	S	T	U	V	W	X	Y	Z

Example	S	E	C	U	R	I	T	Y
Result	F	R	P	H	E	V	G	L

XOR Cipher	a	b		a	XOR	b
	0	0			0	
	0	1			1	
	1	0			1	
	1	1			0	

Example	S	E	C	U	R	I	T	Y
Combinator	F	L	A	P	J	A	C	K
Result	*1509020518081712*							

Figure 3-3 Cryptographic algorithms

Note

The entire result of *security* XOR *flapjack* is 00010101 00001001 00000010 00000101 00011000 00001000 00010111 00010010.

The strength of a cryptographic algorithm depends upon several factors. Modern cryptographic algorithms rely upon underlying mathematical formulas. For these formulas to provide strong security they depend upon the quality of **random numbers**, or numbers for which there is no identifiable pattern or sequence. The primary property of a truly random number is that the probability of it being selected is the same as any other number being selected, so that it is not possible to predict a future number based on a previous number. However, the fundamental nature of computer software is to always be predictable (a mouse click on an icon today will achieve the same results as a mouse click on an icon tomorrow) so that they cannot produce numbers that are truly random. Software instead relies upon a **pseudorandom number generator (PRNG)**, which is an algorithm for creating a sequence of numbers whose properties approximate those of a random number.

> **Note**
>
> PRNGs attempt to create numbers that are as random as possible.

Threat actors often use sophisticated statistical analysis on the ciphertext (*cryptoanalysis*) to try to discover the underlying key to the cryptographic algorithm. There are two factors that can thwart statistical analysis to make a strong algorithm. One factor is **diffusion**. Diffusion means that if a *single* character of plaintext is changed then it should result in *multiple* characters of the ciphertext changing. Eliminating a one-to-one correspondence between the plaintext and the ciphertext makes it more difficult for a threat actor to perform cryptoanalysis, since the plaintext is *diffused* across several characters of the ciphertext. Another factor is **confusion**, which means that the key does not relate in a simple way to the ciphertext. Each character of the ciphertext should depend upon several different parts of the key. This forces the threat actor to create the entire key simultaneously, a difficult task, rather than trying to recreate the key piece by piece.

Cryptography and Security

Cryptography can provide a range of security protections. Cryptography can support the following basic protections:

- *Confidentiality*. Cryptography can protect the confidentiality of information by ensuring that only authorized parties can view it. When private information, such as a list of employees to be laid off, is transmitted across the network or stored on a file server, its contents can be encrypted, which allows only authorized individuals who have the key to see it.
- *Integrity*. Cryptography can protect the integrity of information. Integrity ensures that the information is correct and no unauthorized person or malicious software has altered that data. Because ciphertext requires that a key must be used to open the data before it can be changed, cryptography can ensure its integrity. The list of employees to be laid off, for example, can be protected so that no names can be added or deleted by unauthorized personnel.
- *Authentication*. The authentication of the sender can be verified through cryptography. Specific types of cryptography, for example, can prevent a situation such as circulation of a list of employees to be laid off that appears to come from a manager, but in reality, was sent by an imposter.
- *Non-repudiation*. Cryptography can enforce non-repudiation. *Repudiation* is defined as denial; non-repudiation is the inability to deny. In information technology, **non-repudiation** is the process of proving that a user performed

an action, such as sending an email message. Non-repudiation prevents an individual from fraudulently reneging on an action. The non-repudiation features of cryptography can prevent a manager from claiming he never sent the list of employees to be laid off to an unauthorized third party.

Note 📎

A practical example of non-repudiation is Astrid taking her car into a repair shop for service and signing an estimate form of the cost of repairs and authorizing the work. If Astrid later returns and claims she never approved a specific repair, the signed form can be used as non-repudiation.

- *Obfuscation*. **Obfuscation** is making something obscure or unclear. One example may be disguising the operational details of software so that a threat actor cannot "reverse engineer" the program to determine how it is functioning to bypass its security protections. Cryptography can help ensure obfuscation by hiding the details so that the original code cannot be determined in order that an unauthorized user cannot see the list of employees to be laid off.

The concept of obfuscation has led to an approach in security called **security through obscurity**, or the notion that virtually any system can be made secure so long as outsiders are unware of it or how it functions. However, this is a flawed approach since it is essentially impossible to keep "secrets" from everyone.

The security protections afforded by cryptography are summarized in Table 3-1.

Table 3-1	Information protections by cryptography	
Characteristic	**Description**	**Protection**
Confidentiality	Ensures that only authorized parties can view the information	Encrypted information can only be viewed by those who have been provided the key.
Integrity	Ensures that the information is correct and no unauthorized person or malicious software has altered that data	Encrypted information cannot be changed except by authorized users who have the key.
Authentication	Provides proof of the genuineness of the user	Proof that the sender was legitimate and not an imposter can be obtained.
Non-repudiation	Proves that a user performed an action	Individuals are prevented from fraudulently denying that they were involved in a transaction.
Obfuscation	Makes something obscure or unclear	By hiding the details the original cannot be determined.

Cryptography can provide protection to data as that data resides in any of three states:

- *Data in-use.* **Data-in-use** is data actions being performed by "endpoint devices," such as printing a report from a desktop computer.
- *Data in-transit.* Actions that transmit the data across a network, like an email sent across the Internet, are called **data-in-transit**.
- *Data at-rest.* **Data-at-rest** is data that is stored on electronic media.

Because cryptography can provide protection to data in these three states and not in just one single state this make cryptography a key defense against threat actors.

Cryptography Constraints

Despite providing widespread protections cryptography faces constraints (limitations) that can impact its effectiveness. In recent years, the number of small electronic devices that consume very small amounts of power (**low-power devices**) has grown significantly. These devices range from tiny sensors that control office heating and lighting to consumer devices such as wireless security cameras and even lightbulbs. Increasingly, these devices need to be protected from threat actors who could use data accumulated from these devices in nefarious ways, such as intercepting the signal from a wireless security camera to determine if an individual is home alone. Cryptography is viewed as a necessary feature to be added to these devices to enable them to provide a higher level of security.

> **Note** 🔗
>
> Compared with the average energy requirements of a laptop computer (60 watts) the typical wireless sensor draws only .001 watt.

In addition, many applications require extremely fast response times. These include communication applications (like collecting car toll road payments), high-speed optical networking links, and secure storage devices such as solid-state disks. Again, cryptography is a very important feature of these applications.

However, adding cryptography to low-power devices or those that have near instantaneous response times can be a problem. To perform their computations, cryptographic algorithms require both time and energy, which are typically in short supply for low-power devices and applications needing ultra-fast response times. This results in a **resource vs. security constraint**, or a limitation in providing strong cryptography due to the tug-of-war between the available resources (time and energy) and the security provided by cryptography. Ideally, for a cryptographic algorithm there should be **low latency**, or a small amount of time that occurs between when something is input into a cryptographic algorithm and the time the output is obtained. However, some algorithms require multiple (even 10 or higher) "cycles" on sections of the plaintext, each of which draws power and delays the output. One way to decrease latency is to make the cryptographic algorithm run faster. But this increases power consumption, which is either not available to low-power devices or would slow down the normal operations of the device. The resource vs. security constraint is illustrated in Figure 3-4.

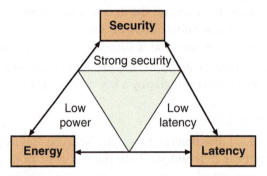

Figure 3-4   Resource vs. security constraint

It is important that there be **high resiliency** in cryptography, or the ability to quickly recover from these resource vs. security constraints. Due to the importance of incorporating cryptography in low-power devices, a new subfield of cryptography is being developed called *lightweight cryptography*. This has the goal of providing cryptographic solutions that are uniquely tailored for low-power devices that need to manage resource vs. security constraints. Lightweight cryptography is not a weakened cryptography but may have fewer features and be less robust than "normal" cryptography.

Note

One of the techniques proposed in lightweight cryptography is to include simpler operations like XOR instead of more complex operations.

Cryptographic Algorithms

 **Certification**

6.1 Compare and contrast basic concepts of cryptography.

6.2 Explain cryptography algorithms and their basic characteristics.

6.4 Given a scenario, implement public key infrastructure.

There are many variations of cryptographic algorithms. One variation is based on the device—if any—that is used in the cryptographic process. During the last half of the 20th century all cryptography has become computer-based, whereas for the first half of that century calculating machines were being used. Prior to this, cryptographic algorithms were entirely hand-calculated. An example is a *one-time pad (OTP)* that combines plaintext with a random key. A *pad* is a long sequence of random letters. These letters are combined with the plaintext message to produce the ciphertext. To decipher the message, the recipient must have a copy of the pad to reverse the process.

To encipher a message, the position in the alphabet of the first letter in the plaintext message is added to the position in the alphabet of the first random letter from the pad. For example, if *SECRET* is to be encrypted using the pad *CBYFEA*, the first letter *S* (#19 of the alphabet) is added to the first letter of the pad *C* (#3 of the alphabet) and then 1 is subtracted (19 + 3 − 1 = 21). This results in *U* (#21 of the alphabet). Each letter is similarly encrypted (any number larger than 26 is wrapped around to the start of the alphabet). To decipher a message, the recipient takes the first letter of the ciphertext and subtracts the first random letter from the pad (any negative numbers are wrapped around to the end of the alphabet). An OTP is illustrated in Table 3-2.

Table 3-2   OTP

Plaintext	Position in alphabet	Pad	Position in alphabet	Calculation	Result
S	19	C	3	19 + 3 − 1 = 21	U
E	5	B	2	5 + 2 − 1 = 6	F
C	3	Y	25	3 + 25 − 1 = 1	A
R	18	F	6	18 + 6 − 1 = 23	W
E	5	E	5	5 + 5 − 1 = 9	I
T	20	A	1	20 + 1 − 1 = 20	T

Note

As its name implies, the pad should be used only one time and then destroyed. Because OTP can be hand-calculated and is the only known method to perform encryption that cannot be broken mathematically, OTPs were used by special operations teams and resistance groups during World War II as well as by intelligence agencies and spies during the Cold War.

Another variation in cryptographic algorithms is the amount of data that is processed at a time. Some algorithms use a **stream cipher** that takes one character and replaces it with one character. Other algorithms make use of a **block cipher**. Whereas a stream cipher works on one character at a time, a block cipher manipulates an entire block of plaintext at one time. The plaintext message is divided into separate blocks of 8 to 16 bytes, and then each block is encrypted independently. For additional security, the blocks can be randomized. Recently a third type has been introduced called a *sponge function*. A sponge function takes as input a string of any length, and returns a string of any requested variable length. This function repeatedly applies a process on the input that has been *padded* with additional characters until all characters are used (*absorbed* in the *sponge*).

> **Note** 📎
>
> Stream ciphers are less secure because the engine that generates the stream does not vary; the only change is the plaintext itself. Block ciphers are considered more secure because the output is more random, particularly because the cipher is reset to its original state after each block is processed.

There are three broad categories of cryptographic algorithms. These are hash algorithms, symmetric cryptographic algorithms, and asymmetric cryptographic algorithms.

Hash Algorithms

One type of cryptographic algorithm is a one-way hash algorithm. A **hash** algorithm creates a unique "digital fingerprint" of a set of data. This process is called *hashing*, and the resulting fingerprint is a *digest* (sometimes called a *message digest* or *hash*) that represents the contents. Hashing is used primarily for comparison purposes.

Although hashing is a cryptographic algorithm, its purpose is *not* to create ciphertext that can later be decrypted. Instead, hashing is intended to be oneway in that its digest cannot be reversed to reveal the original set of data. For example, when 12 is multiplied by 34 the result is 408. If a user were asked to determine the two numbers used to create the number 408, it would not be possible to work backward and derive the original numbers with absolute certainty because there are too many mathematical possibilities (204+204, 407+1, 999−591, 361+47, etc.). Hashing is similar in that it is not possible to determine the plaintext from the digest.

> **Note** 📎
>
> Although hashing and checksums are similar in that they both create a value based on the contents of a file, hashing is not the same as creating a checksum. A checksum is intended to verify (*check*) the integrity of data and identify data-transmission errors, while a hash is designed to create a unique digital fingerprint of the data.

A hashing algorithm is considered secure if it has these characteristics:

- *Fixed size.* A digest of a short set of data should produce the same size as a digest of a long set of data. For example, a digest of the single letter *a* is 86be7afa339d0fc7cfc785e72f578d33, while a digest of 1 million occurrences of the letter *a* is 4a7f5723f954eba1216c9d8f6320431f, the same length.
- *Unique.* Two different sets of data cannot produce the same digest. Changing a single letter in one data set should produce an entirely different digest. For example, a digest of *Sunday* is 0d716e73a2a7910bd4ae63407056d79b while a digest of *sunday* (lowercase s) is 3464eb71bd7a4377967a30da798a1b54.
- *Original.* It should not be possible to produce a data set that has a desired or predefined hash.
- *Secure.* The resulting hash cannot be reversed to determine the original plaintext.

Hashing is often used as a check to verify that the original contents of an item has not been changed. For example, digests are often calculated and then posted on websites for files that can be downloaded. After downloading the file a user can create her own digest on the file and then compare it with the digest value posted on the website. A match indicates that there has been no change to the original file. This is shown in Figure 3-5.

Image Name	Direct	Torrent	Size	Version	SHA1Sum
Kali Linux 64 bit	ISO	Torrent	2.9G	2016.2	25cc6d53a8bd8886fcb468eb4fbb4cdfac895c65
Kali Linux 32 bit	ISO	Torrent	2.9G	2016.2	9b4e167b0677bb0ca14099c379e0413262eefc8c
Kali Linux 64 bit Light	ISO	Torrent	1.1G	2016.2	f7bdc3a50f177226b3badc3d3eafcf1d59b9a5e6

Figure 3-5   Verifying file integrity with digests

Source: https://www.kali.org/downloads/

The most common hash algorithms are Message Digest 5, Secure Hash Algorithm, RACE Integrity Primitives Evaluation Message Digest, and Hashed Message Authentication Code.

Message Digest 5 (MD5)

One of the earliest hash algorithms is actually a family of algorithms known as *Message Digest (MD)*. Four different versions of MD hashes were introduced over almost 20 years: MD2 (1989), MD4 (1990), MD5 (1992), and MD6 (2008). The most well-known of these algorithms is **Message Digest 5 (MD5)**. A revision of MD4, MD5 was designed to address MD4's weaknesses. Like MD4, the length of a message is padded to 512 bits in length. The hash algorithm then uses four variables of 32 bits each in a round-robin fashion to create a value that is compressed to generate the digest. Serious weaknesses have been identified in MD5 and is no longer considered suitable for use.

Secure Hash Algorithm (SHA)

Another family of hashes is the **Secure Hash Algorithm (SHA)**. The first version was *SHA-0*, which due to a flaw was withdrawn shortly after it was first released. Its successor, *SHA-1*, was developed in 1993 by the U.S. National Security Agency (NSA) and the National Institute of Standards and Technology (NIST). It is patterned after MD4 and MD5, but creates a digest that is 160 bits instead of 128 bits in length. SHA pads messages of less than 512 bits with zeros and an integer that describes the original length of the message. The padded message is then processed through the SHA algorithm to produce the digest.

Note

In early 2017 security researchers decisively demonstrated that SHA-1 could create the same digest from two different plaintexts, although this weakness had been theorized for over 10 years. The compromise of SHA-1 has rendered it no longer suitable for use.

Another family of SHA hashes is known as *SHA-2*. SHA-2 is comprised of six variations: SHA-224, SHA-256, SHA-384, SHA-512, SHA-512/224, and SHA-512/256 (the last number indicates the length in bits of the digest that is generated). SHA-2 is currently considered to be a secure hash.

In 2015, after eight years of competition between 51 original entries, *SHA-3* was announced as a new standard. One of the design goals of SHA-3 was for it to be dissimilar to previous hash algorithms to prevent threat actors from building upon any previous work of compromising these algorithms. Because SHA-3 is relatively compact, it may be suitable for some low-power devices.

RACE Integrity Primitives Evaluation Message Digest (RIPEMD)

Another hash was developed by the Research and Development in Advanced Communications Technologies (RACE), an organization that is affiliated with the European Union (EU). **RIPEMD** stands for **RACE Integrity Primitives Evaluation Message Digest**, which was designed after MD4.

The primary design feature of RIPEMD is two different and independent parallel chains of computation, the results of which are then combined at the end of the process. There are several versions of RIPEMD, all based on the length of the digest created. RIPEMD-128 is a replacement for the original RIPEMD and is faster than RIPEMD-160. RIPEMD-256 and RIPEMD-320 reduce the risk of collisions but do not provide any higher levels of security.

Hashed Message Authentication Code (HMAC)

As its name implies, a **Hashed Message Authentication Code (HMAC)** uses hashing to authenticate the sender. It does this by using both a hash function and a secret cryptographic key. A *message authentication code (MAC)* combines the original message with a shared secret key that only the sender and receiver know. A hash function is then applied to both the key and the message, and for added security they are hashed in separate steps. When the receiver gets the HMAC it then creates its own HMAC to compare with what was sent: if they match then it knows that the MAC came from the sender (because only the sender has the secret key), thus authenticating the sender of the message.

> **Note**
>
> Any cryptographic hash function can be used in the calculation of an HMAC. For example, if SHA-2 is used, the result would be called HMAC-SHA2.

Table 3-3 illustrates the digests generated from several different one-way hash algorithms using the original phrase *CengageLearning*.

Table 3-3   Digests generated from one-way hash algorithms

Hash	Digest
MD2	c4b4c4568a42895c68e5d507d7f0a6ca
MD4	9a5b5cec21dd77d611e04e10f902e283
MD5	0e41799d87f1179c1b8c38c318132236
RIPEMD-160	d4ec909f7b0f7dfb6fa45c4c91a92962649001ef
SHA-1	299b20adfec43b1e8fade03c0e0c61fc51b55420
SHA-256	133380e0ebfc19e91589c2feaa346d3e679a7529fa8d03617fcd661c997d7287
SHA-512	867f14c0ae57b960ba22539b0f321660e08bc6f298846cae8e10f71e57e0c2b27d d344c577bfab1ddbd3517e0e1d0da9393fbd04a467a270744ff2e78da4b08b
SHA3-512	e7e2ca148c6b40d191d6e8e414d3db9e4c10191547a86fbee810b00a7530ff83ef 43321f00ec4c9ee15d8292b68a0b77bb42b6cbbd5c889d52856e9a08695574

Symmetric Cryptographic Algorithms

The original cryptographic algorithms for encrypting and decrypting data are symmetric cryptographic algorithms. **Symmetric cryptographic algorithms** use the same single key to encrypt and decrypt a document. Unlike hashing, in which the hash is not intended to be decrypted, symmetric algorithms are designed to encrypt and decrypt the ciphertext. Data encrypted with a symmetric cryptographic algorithm by

Alice will be decrypted when received by Bob. It is therefore essential that the key be kept private (confidential), because if an attacker obtained the key he could read all the encrypted documents. For this reason, symmetric encryption is also called *private key cryptography*. Symmetric encryption is illustrated in Figure 3-6 where identical keys are used to encrypt and decrypt a document.

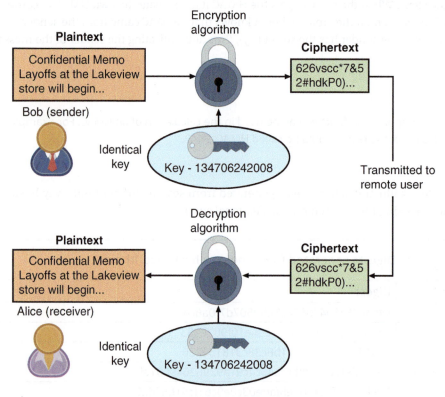

Figure 3-6   Symmetric (private key) cryptography

Symmetric cryptography can provide strong protections against attacks if the key is kept secure. Common symmetric cryptographic algorithms include the Data Encryption Standard, Triple Data Encryption Standard, Advanced Encryption Standard, and several other algorithms.

Data Encryption Standard (DES)

One of the first widely popular symmetric cryptography algorithms was the **Data Encryption Standard (DES)**. The predecessor of DES was a product originally designed in the early 1970s by IBM called Lucifer that had a key length of 128 bits. The key was later shortened to 56 bits and renamed DES. The U.S. government officially adopted DES as the standard for encrypting non-classified information.

Note 📎

DES effectively catapulted the study of cryptography into the public arena. Until the deployment of DES, cryptography was studied almost exclusively by military personnel. The popularity of DES helped move cryptography implementation and research to academic and commercial organizations.

Although DES was once widely implemented, its 56-bit key is no longer considered secure and has been broken several times. It is no longer considered suitable for use.

Triple Data Encryption Standard (3DES)

Triple Data Encryption Standard (3DES) is designed to replace DES. As its name implies, 3DES uses three rounds of encryption instead of just one. The ciphertext of one round becomes the entire input for the second iteration. 3DES employs a total of 48 iterations in its encryption (3 iterations times 16 rounds). The most secure versions of 3DES use different keys for each round, as shown in Figure 3-7. By design 3DES performs better in hardware than as software.

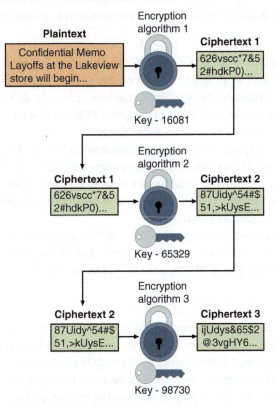

Figure 3-7   **3DES**

> **Note**
>
> In some versions of 3DES, only two keys are used, but the first key is repeated for the third round of encryption. The version of 3DES that uses three keys is estimated to be 2 to the power of 56 times stronger than DES.

Although 3DES addresses several of the key weaknesses of DES, it is no longer considered the most secure symmetric cryptographic algorithm.

Advanced Encryption Standard (AES)

The **Advanced Encryption Standard (AES)** is a symmetric cipher that was approved by the NIST in late 2000 as a replacement for DES. AES performs three steps on every block (128 bits) of plaintext. Within step 2, multiple rounds are performed depending upon the key size: a 128-bit key performs 9 rounds, a 192-bit key performs 11 rounds, and a 256-bit key, known as AES-256, uses 13 rounds. Within each round, bytes are substituted and rearranged, and then special multiplication is performed based on the new arrangement. To date, no attacks have been successful against AES.

Other Algorithms

Rivest Cipher (RC) is a family of six algorithms, ranging from RC1 to RC6 (however there was no release of RC1 and RC3). *RC2* is a block cipher that processes blocks of 64 bits. **RC4** is a stream cipher that accepts keys up to 128 bits in length. *RC5* is a block cipher that can accept blocks and keys of different lengths. *RC6* has three key sizes (128, 192, and 256 bits) and performs 20 rounds on each block.

Blowfish is a block cipher algorithm that operates on 64-bit blocks and can have a key length from 32 to 448 bits. Blowfish was designed to run efficiently on 32-bit computers. To date, no significant weaknesses have been identified. A later derivation of Blowfish known as **Twofish** is also considered to be a strong algorithm, although it has not been used as widely as Blowfish.

The *International Data Encryption Algorithm (IDEA)* dates back to the early 1990s and is used in European nations. It is a block cipher that processes 64 bits with a 128-bit key with 8 rounds. It is generally considered to be secure.

Asymmetric Cryptographic Algorithms

If Bob wants to send an encrypted message to Alice using symmetric encryption, he must be sure that she has the key to decrypt the message. Yet how should Bob get the key to Alice? He cannot send it electronically through the Internet, because that would make it vulnerable to interception by attackers. Nor can he encrypt the key and send it, because Alice would not have a way to decrypt the encrypted key. This example illustrates the primary weakness of symmetric encryption algorithms: distributing and maintaining a secure single key among multiple users, who are often scattered geographically, poses significant challenges.

A completely different approach from symmetric cryptography is **asymmetric cryptographic algorithms**, also known as *public key cryptography*. Asymmetric encryption uses two keys instead of only one. These keys are mathematically related and are called the public key and the private key. The **public key** is known to everyone and can be freely distributed, while the **private key** is known only to the individual to whom it belongs. When Bob wants to send a secure message to Alice, he uses Alice's public key to encrypt the message. Alice then uses her private key to decrypt it. Asymmetric cryptography is illustrated in Figure 3-8.

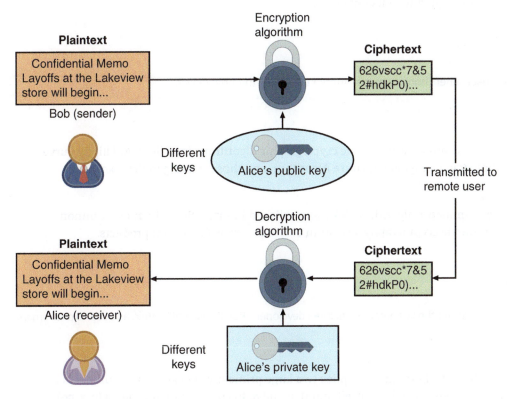

Figure 3-8   Asymmetric (public key) cryptography

Note 🔗

Different cryptographers were working on the idea of asymmetric encryption in the early 1970s. The development is often credited to Whitfield Diffie and Martin Hellman based on a publication of their paper *New Directions in Cryptography* in November 1976.

Several important principles regarding asymmetric cryptography are:

- *Key pairs.* Unlike symmetric cryptography that uses only one key, asymmetric cryptography requires a pair of keys.
- *Public key.* Public keys by their nature are designed to be public and do not need to be protected. They can be freely given to anyone or even posted on the Internet.
- *Private key.* The private key should be kept confidential and never shared.
- *Both directions.* Asymmetric cryptography keys can work in both directions. A document encrypted with a public key can be decrypted with the corresponding private key. In the same way, a document encrypted with a private key can be decrypted with its public key.

Note

No user other than the owner should ever have the private key.

The common asymmetric cryptographic algorithms include RSA, Elliptic Curve Cryptography, Digital Signature Algorithm, and those relating to Key Exchange.

RSA

The asymmetric algorithm **RSA** was published in 1977. RSA is the most common asymmetric cryptography algorithm and is the basis for several products.

Note

RSA stands for the last names of its three developers, Ron Rivest, Adi Shamir, and Leonard Adleman.

The RSA algorithm multiplies two large prime numbers (a prime number is a number divisible only by itself and 1), p and q, to compute their product ($n = pq$). Next, a number e is chosen that is less than n and a prime factor to $(p-1)(q-1)$. Another number d is determined, so that $(ed-1)$ is divisible by $(p-1)(q-1)$. The values of e and d are the public and private exponents. The public key is the pair (n,e) while the private key is (n,d). The numbers p and q can be discarded.

An illustration of the RSA algorithm using very small numbers is as follows:

1. Select two prime numbers, p and q (in this example $p = 7$ and $q = 19$)
2. Multiply p and q together to create $n (7 * 19 = 133)$
3. Calculate m as $p-1 * q-1$ ([7−1]*[19−1] or $6 * 18 = 108$)

4. Find a number e so that it and m have no common positive divisor other than 1 ($e=5$)

5. Find a number d so that $d = (1 + n*m)/e$ or ([1 + 133*108]/5 or 14,364/5 = 2875)

For this example, the public key n is 133 and e is 5, while for the private key n is 133 and d is 2873.

Note

RSA is slower than other algorithms. DES is approximately 100 times faster than RSA in software and between 1000 and 10,000 times as fast in hardware.

Elliptic Curve Cryptography (ECC)

Elliptic curve cryptography (ECC) was first proposed in the mid-1980s. Instead of using large prime numbers as with RSA, elliptic curve cryptography uses sloping curves. An elliptic curve is a function drawn on an X-Y axis as a gently curved line. By adding the values of two points on the curve, a third point on the curve can be derived, of which the inverse is used as illustrated in Figure 3-9. With ECC, users share one elliptic curve and one point on the curve. One user chooses a secret random number and computes a public key based on a point on the curve; the other user does the same. They can now exchange messages because the shared public keys can generate a private key on an elliptic curve.

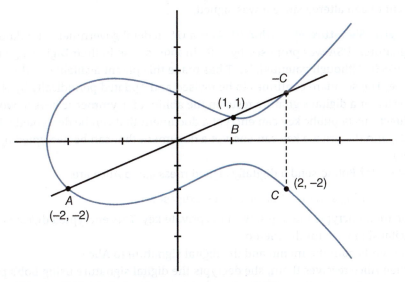

Figure 3-9   Elliptic curve cryptography (ECC)

ECC is considered as an alternative for prime-number-based asymmetric cryptography for mobile and wireless devices. Because mobile devices are limited in terms of computing power due to their smaller size, ECC offers security that is comparable to other asymmetric cryptography but with smaller key sizes. This can result in faster computations and lower power consumption.

Digital Signature Algorithm (DSA)

Asymmetric cryptography also can be used to provide proofs. Suppose that Alice receives an encrypted document that says it came from Bob. Although Alice can be sure that the encrypted message was not viewed or altered by someone else while being transmitted, how can she know for certain that Bob was the sender? Because Alice's public key is widely available, anyone could use it to encrypt the document. Another individual could have created a fictitious document, encrypted it with Alice's public key, and then sent it to Alice while pretending to be Bob. Alice's key can verify that no one read or changed the document in transport, but it cannot verify the sender.

Proof can be provided with asymmetric cryptography, however, by creating a **digital signature**, which is an electronic verification of the sender. A handwritten signature on a paper document serves as proof that the signer has read and agreed to the document. A digital signature is much the same, but can provide additional benefits. A digital signature can:

- *Verify the sender*. A digital signature serves to confirm the identity of the person from whom the electronic message originated.
- *Prevent the sender from disowning the message*. The signer cannot later attempt to disown it by claiming the signature was forged (nonrepudiation).
- *Prove the integrity of the message*. A digital signature can prove that the message has not been altered since it was signed.

The **Digital Signature Algorithm (DSA)** is a U.S. federal government standard for digital signatures. DSA was proposed by NIST in 1991 for use in their Digital Signature Standard (DSS). Although patented, NIST has made this patent available world wide royalty-free. The standard continues to be revised and updated periodically by NIST.

The basis for a digital signature rests on the ability of asymmetric keys to work in both directions (a public key can encrypt a document that can be decrypted with a private key, and the private key can encrypt a document that can be decrypted by the public key).

The steps for Bob to send a digitally signed message to Alice are:

1. After creating a memo, Bob generates a digest on it.
2. Bob then encrypts the digest with his private key. This encrypted digest is the digital signature for the memo.
3. Bob sends both the memo and the digital signature to Alice.
4. When Alice receives them, she decrypts the digital signature using Bob's public key, revealing the digest. If she cannot decrypt the digital signature, then she

knows that it did not come from Bob (because only Bob's public key can decrypt the digest generated with his private key).

5. Alice then hashes the memo with the same hash algorithm Bob used and compares the result to the digest she received from Bob. If they are equal, Alice can be confident that the message has not changed since he signed it. If the digests are not equal, Alice will know the message has changed since it was signed.

These steps are illustrated in Figure 3-10.

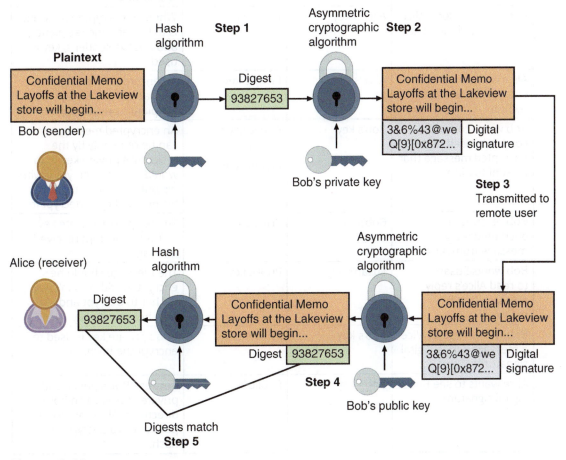

Figure 3-10   Digital signature

Note

Using a digital signature does not encrypt the message itself. In the example, if Bob wanted to ensure the privacy of the message, he also would have to encrypt it using Alice's public key.

Public and private keys may result in confusion regarding whose key to use and which key should be used. Table 3-4 lists the practices to be followed when using asymmetric cryptography.

Table 3-4 Asymmetric cryptography practices

Action	Whose key to use	Which key to use	Explanation
Bob wants to send Alice an encrypted message	Alice's key	Public key	When an encrypted message is to be sent, the recipient's, and not the sender's, key is used.
Alice wants to read an encrypted message sent by Bob	Alice's key	Private key	An encrypted message can be read only by using the recipient's private key.
Bob wants to send a copy to himself of the encrypted message that he sent to Alice	Bob's key	Public key to encrypt Private key to decrypt	An encrypted message can be read only by the recipient's private key. Bob would need to encrypt it with his public key and then use his private key to decrypt it.
Bob receives an encrypted reply message from Alice	Bob's key	Private key	The recipient's private key is used to decrypt received messages.
Bob wants Susan to read Alice's reply message that he received	Susan's key	Public key	The message should be encrypted with Susan's key for her to decrypt and read with her private key.
Bob wants to send Alice a message with a digital signature	Bob's key	Private key	Bob's private key is used to encrypt the hash.
Alice wants to see Bob's digital signature	Bob's key	Public key	Because Bob's public and private keys work in both directions, Alice can use his public key to decrypt the hash.

Key Exchange

Even though asymmetric cryptography allows two users to send encrypted messages using separate public and private keys, it does not completely solve the problem of sending and receiving keys (**key exchange**), such as exchanging a symmetric private key. One solution is to make the exchange outside of the normal communication channels (for example, Alice could hire Charlie to carry a USB flash drive containing the key directly to Bob).

There are different solutions for a key exchange that occurs within the normal communications channel of cryptography, including:

- *Diffie-Hellman (DH)*. The **Diffie-Hellman (DH)** key exchange requires Alice and Bob to each agree upon a large prime number and related integer. Those two numbers can be made public, yet Alice and Bob, through mathematical computations and exchanges of intermediate values, can separately create the same key.
- *Diffie-Hellman Ephemeral (DHE)*. Whereas DH uses the same keys each time, **Diffie-Hellman Ephemeral (DHE)** uses different keys. **Ephemeral keys** are temporary keys that are used only once and then discarded.
- *Elliptic Curve Diffie-Hellman (ECDH)*. **Elliptic Curve Diffie–Hellman (ECDH)** uses elliptic curve cryptography instead of prime numbers in its computation.
- *Perfect forward secrecy*. Public key systems that generate random public keys that are different for each session are called **perfect forward secrecy**. The value of perfect forward secrecy is that if the secret key is compromised, it cannot reveal the contents of more than one message.

Cryptographic Attacks

 **Certification**

1.2 Compare and contrast types of attacks.

1.6 Explain the impact associated with types of vulnerabilities.

6.1 Compare and contrast basic concepts of cryptography.

Because cryptography provides a high degree of protection, it is a defense that remains under attack by threat actors for any vulnerabilities. Several of the more common cryptographic attacks include those that target algorithm weaknesses or implementations and those that exploit collisions.

Algorithm Attacks

Modern cryptographic algorithms are typically reviewed, tested, and vetted by specialists in cryptography over several years before they are released to the public for use. And very few threat actors have the advanced skills needed to even attempt to break an algorithm. However, there are other methods by which attackers can focus on circumventing strong algorithms. These include known ciphertext attacks, downgrade attacks, using deprecated algorithms, and taking advantage of improperly implemented algorithms.

Known Ciphertext Attack

When properly implemented, cryptography prevents the threat actor from knowing the plaintext or the key; the only item that she can see is the ciphertext itself. Yet there are statistical tools that can be used to attempt to discover a pattern in the ciphertexts, which then may be useful in revealing the plaintext text or key. This is called a **known ciphertext attack** (sometimes called a *ciphertext-only attack*), because all that is known is the ciphertext—but this can still reveal clues that may be mined.

> **Note** 📎
>
> Wireless data networks are particularly susceptible to known ciphertext attacks. This is because threat actors can capture large sets of ciphertexts to be analyzed, and the attackers may be able to inject their own frames into the wireless transmissions.

The type of information that can be used in a known ciphertext attack is listed in Table 3-5.

Table 3-5   Known ciphertext analysis

Statistic	Example	How Used
Underlying language of plaintext	English	By knowing which language is used for the plaintext message inferences can be made regarding statistical values of that language.
Distribution of characters	In English *E* is most commonly used letter, *Q* is least commonly used	Patterns can emerge when more common letters are used more frequently.
Null ciphertexts	Distinguishing between actual ciphertexts and injected null messages	Attacks may inject a frame that contains null values to compare it with the frames containing ciphertext.
Management frames	Analyze content of network management information	Because network management frames typically contain information that remains constant this can help establish patterns.

Downgrade Attack

Because of the frequent introduction of new hardware and software often they include *backwards compatibility* so that a newer version can still function with the older version. However, in most instances this means that the newer version must revert to the older and less secure version. In a **downgrade attack** a threat actor forces the system to abandon the current higher security mode of operation and instead "fall back" to implementing an older and less secure mode. This then allows the threat actor to attack the weaker mode.

Using Deprecated Algorithms

Deprecated means something that is disapproved of. Using **deprecated algorithms** means to use a cryptographic algorithm that, although still available, should not be used because of known vulnerabilities. Selecting weak algorithms, like DES or SHA-1, should be avoided since these could be broken by a threat actor.

> **Note**
>
> It is the duty of all security professionals to stay current on the status of the viability of cryptographic algorithms.

Improper Implementation

Many breaches of cryptography are the result not of weak algorithms but instead of incorrect configurations or uses of the cryptography, known as **misconfiguration implementation**. Many cryptographic algorithms have several configuration options, and unless careful consideration is given to these options the cryptography may be improperly implemented. Also, careless users who, for example, choose SHA-224 when a much stronger SHA-512/256 can instead be used by a simple menu choice or those who expose their asymmetric private key can also seriously weaken cryptography.

Collision Attacks

One of the foundations of a hash algorithm is that each digest must be unique. If it were not unique then a threat actor could trick users into performing an action that was assumed to be safe but in reality, was not. For example, digests are often calculated and then posted on websites for files that can be downloaded. After downloading the file a user can create her own digest on the file and then compare it with the digest value posted on the website, assuring that there has been no change to the original file. Suppose an attacker could infiltrate that website and post her own malicious file for download, but when the digest was generated for this malicious file it created the same as that posted for the legitimate file. When two files have the same hash this is known as a **collision**. A **collision attack** is an attempt to find two input strings of a hash function that produce the same hash result.

A hash digest of a short set of data will produce the same size as a digest of a long set of data (a digest of the single letter *a* is the same length as a digest of 1 million occurrences of the letter *a*). This means that there is a possibility that there could be a collision of hash digests. While for hash algorithms that produce long digests, like

SHA3-512, the odds of such a collision are very low, yet for hash algorithms that produce shorter digests, such as MD5, the odds increase, although it would still be difficult.

Note

Table 3-3 shows a comparison of the lengths of various digests.

Typically, a threat actor would be forced to try all possible combinations until a collision was found. However, there is a statistical phenomenon that makes it easier. This is called the **birthday attack**. It is based on the *birthday paradox*, which says that for there to be a 50 percent chance that someone in a given room shares your birthday, 253 people would need to be in the room. If, however, you are looking for a greater than 50 percent chance that any two people in the room have the same birthday, you only need 23 people. That's because the matches are based on pairs. If you choose yourself as one side of the pair, then you will need 253 people to have 253 pairs (in other words, it is you combined with 253 other people to make up all 253 sets). But if you are only concerned with matches and not concerned with matching someone with you specifically, then you only need 23 people in the room, because it only takes 23 people to form 253 pairs when cross-matched with each other. This applies to hashing collisions in that it is much harder to find something that collides with a specific hash than it is to find any two inputs that hash to the same value.

Note

With the birthday paradox, the question is whether each person must link with every other person. If so, only 23 people are needed; if not, comparing only your single birthday to everyone else's, 253 people are needed.

Using Cryptography

Certification

3.3 Given a scenario, implement secure systems design.

Ideally cryptography should be used to secure data-in-transit, data-at-rest, and when possible data-in-use. This includes individual files, databases, removable media, or data on mobile devices. Cryptography can be applied through either software or hardware.

Encryption through Software

Encryption can be implemented through cryptographic software running on a system so that it can be applied to individual files by using the software to encrypt and decrypt each file. The encryption also can be performed on a larger scale through the file system or by encrypting the entire disk drive itself.

File and File System Cryptography

Encryption software can be used to encrypt or decrypt files one by one. However, this can be a cumbersome process. Instead, protecting groups of files, such as all files in a specific folder, can take advantage of the operating system's file system. A *file system* is a method used by operating systems to store, retrieve, and organize files.

Protecting individual files or multiple files through file system cryptography can be performed using software such as Pretty Good Privacy and operating system encryption features.

Pretty Good Privacy (PGP)

One widely used asymmetric cryptography software for encrypting files and email messages is a commercial product called **Pretty Good Privacy (PGP)**. It uses both asymmetric and symmetric cryptography. PGP generates a random symmetric key and uses it to encrypt the message. The symmetric key is then encrypted using the receiver's public key and sent along with the message. When the recipient receives a message, PGP first decrypts the symmetric key with the recipient's private key. The decrypted symmetric key is then used to decrypt the rest of the message.

Note

PGP uses symmetric cryptography because it is faster than asymmetric cryptography.

There are similar programs to PGP that are available. **GNU Privacy Guard** (which was originally abbreviated *GPG* but is now **GNuPG**) is an open-source product that runs on different operating systems. *OpenPGP* is another open-source alternative that is based on PGP.

Operating System Encryption

Modern operating systems provide encryption support natively. Microsoft's *Encrypting File System (EFS)* is a cryptography system for Windows operating systems that use the Windows NTFS file system, while Apple's *FileVault* performs a similar function. Because these are tightly integrated with the file system, file encryption and decryption are transparent to the user. Any file created in an encrypted folder or added to an encrypted folder is automatically encrypted. When an authorized user opens a file, it is decrypted by as data is read from a disk; when a file is saved, the operating system encrypts the data as it is written to a disk.

Full Disk Encryption

Cryptography can also be applied to entire disks instead of individual files or groups of files. This is known as **full disk encryption (FDE)** and protects all data on a hard drive. One example of full disk encryption software is that included in Microsoft Windows known as *BitLocker* drive encryption software. BitLocker encrypts the entire system volume, including the Windows Registry and any temporary files that might hold confidential information. BitLocker prevents attackers from accessing data by booting from another operating system or placing the hard drive in another computer.

Note

A fundamental difference between FDE and software products like PGP and operating system encryption is that FDE is a "set it and forget it" system: it automatically encrypts everything. PGP and operating system encryption require the user to select and then encrypt individual files and directories one by one.

Hardware Encryption

Software encryption suffers from the same fate as any application program: it can be subject to attacks to exploit its vulnerabilities. As a more secure option, cryptography can be embedded in hardware. Hardware encryption cannot be exploited like software encryption. Hardware encryption can be applied to USB devices and standard hard drives. More sophisticated hardware encryption options include self-encrypting drives, the trusted platform module, and the hardware security model.

USB Device Encryption

Many instances of data leakage are the result of USB flash drives being lost or stolen. Although this data can be secured with software-based cryptographic application programs, vulnerabilities in these programs can open the door for attackers to access the data.

As an alternative, encrypted hardware-based USB devices like flash drives can be used to prevent these types of attacks. These drives resemble standard USB flash drives, with several significant differences:

- Encrypted hardware-based USB drives will not connect to a computer until the correct password has been provided.
- All data copied to the USB flash drive is automatically encrypted.
- The external cases are designed to be tamper-resistant so attackers cannot disassemble the drives.

- Administrators can remotely control and track activity on the devices.
- Compromised or stolen drives can be remotely disabled.

Note

One hardware-based USB encrypted drive allows administrators to remotely prohibit accessing the data on a device until it can verify its status, to lock out the user completely the next time the device connects, or even to instruct the drive to initiate a self-destruct sequence to destroy all data.

Self-Encrypting Drives (SEDs)

Just as an encrypted hardware-based USB flash drive will automatically encrypt any data stored on it, **self-encrypting drives (SEDs)** can protect all files stored on them. When the computer or other device with an SED is initially powered up, the drive and the host device perform an authentication process. If the authentication process fails, the drive can be configured to simply deny any access to the drive or even perform a *cryptographic erase* on specified blocks of data (a cryptographic erase deletes the decryption keys so that no data can be recovered). This also makes it impossible to install the drive on another computer to read its contents.

Note

SEDs are commonly found in copiers and multifunction printers as well as point-of-sale systems used in government, financial, and medical environments.

Trusted Platform Module (TPM)

The **Trusted Platform Module (TPM)** is essentially a chip on the motherboard of the computer that provides cryptographic services. For example, TPM includes a true random number generator instead of a PRNG as well as full support for asymmetric encryption (TPM can also generate public and private keys). Because all of this is done in hardware and not through the software of the operating system, malicious software cannot attack it. Also, TPM can measure and test key components as the computer is starting up. It will prevent the computer from booting if system files or data have been altered. With TPM, if the hard drive is moved to a different computer, the user must enter a recovery password before gaining access to the system volume.

> **Note** 📎
>
> Apple's Secure Enclave is a coprocessor that uses encrypted memory, contains a hardware-based random number generator, and provides all cryptographic operations. Because it is critical for cryptographic functions Apple will pay up to $100,000 to anyone for exposing exploits that can extract confidential material from its Secure Enclave processor. And Apple is willing to double the payout for researchers who donate their reward to a charity.

Hardware Security Module (HSM)

A **Hardware Security Module (HSM)** is a secure cryptographic processor. An HSM includes an onboard key generator and key storage facility, as well as accelerated symmetric and asymmetric encryption, and can even back up sensitive material in encrypted form. Most HSMs are local area network (LAN)-based appliances that can provide services to multiple devices.

Chapter Summary

- Cryptography is the practice of transforming information into a secure form so that unauthorized persons cannot access it. Unlike steganography, which hides the existence of data, cryptography masks the content of documents or messages so that they cannot be read or altered. The original data, called plaintext, is input into a cryptographic encryption algorithm that has a mathematical value (a key) used to create ciphertext. There are different categories and types of algorithms. A substitution cipher exchanges one character for another. One type of substitution cipher is a ROT13, in which the entire alphabet is rotated 13 steps. Another common algorithm is the XOR cipher, which uses the binary operation eXclusive OR that compares two bits.

- The strength of a cryptographic algorithm depends upon several factors. Because modern cryptographic algorithms rely upon underlying mathematical formulas using random numbers, a strong random number generator is critical. A method used by threat actors to break a cryptographic algorithm is to uncover the underlying key is to use sophisticated statistical analysis on the ciphertext (*cryptoanalysis*). This can be thwarted by diffusion, which means that if a single character of plaintext is changed then it should result in multiple characters of the ciphertext changing and by confusion, which means that the key does not relate in a simple way to the ciphertext.

- Cryptography can provide confidentiality, integrity, authentication, non-repudiation, and obfuscation. It can also protect data as it resides in any of three states: data-in-use, data-in-transit, and data-in-rest. Yet despite providing these protections cryptography faces constraints that can impact its effectiveness. Adding cryptography to low-power devices or those that have near instantaneous response times can be a problem because the algorithms require both time and energy, which are typically in short supply for low-power devices and applications needing ultra-fast response times. This results in a resource vs. security constraint. Due to the importance of incorporating cryptography in low-power devices, a new subfield of cryptography is being developed called lightweight cryptography.

- There are many variations of cryptographic algorithms. One variation is based on the device (if any) that is used in the cryptographic process. Another variation is the amount of data that is processed at a time. A stream cipher takes one character and replaces it with another character while a block cipher manipulates an entire block of plaintext at one time.

- Hashing creates a unique digital fingerprint called a digest that represents the contents of the original material. Hashing is not designed for encrypting material that will be later decrypted. If a hash algorithm produces a fixed-size hash that is unique, and the original contents of the material cannot be determined from the hash, the hash is considered secure. Common hashing algorithms are Message Digest 5, Secure Hash Algorithm, RACE Integrity Primitives Evaluation Message Digest, and Hashed Message Authentication Code.

- Symmetric cryptography, also called private key cryptography, uses a single key to encrypt and decrypt a message. Symmetric cryptographic algorithms are designed to decrypt the ciphertext. Symmetric cryptography can provide strong protections against attacks if the key is kept secure. Common symmetric cryptographic algorithms include Data Encryption Standard, Triple Data Encryption Standard, Advanced Encryption Standard, and several other algorithms.

- Asymmetric cryptography, also known as public key cryptography, uses two keys instead of one. These keys are mathematically related and are known as the public key and the private key. The public key is widely available and can be freely distributed, while the private key is known only to the recipient of the message and must be kept secure. Asymmetric cryptography also can be used to create a digital signature, which verifies the sender, proves the integrity of the message, and prevents the sender from disowning the message. Common asymmetric cryptographic algorithms include RSA, Elliptic Curve Cryptography, Digital Signature Algorithm, and those relating to Key Exchange.

- Because cryptography provides a high degree of protection, it remains under attack. A known ciphertext attack uses statistical tools to attempt to discover a pattern in the ciphertexts, which then may be useful in revealing the plaintext text or key. In a downgrade attack, a threat actor forces the system to abandon the current higher security mode of operation and instead fall back to implementing an older and less secure mode. Using deprecated algorithms means to use a cryptographic algorithm that, although still available, should not be used because of known vulnerabilities. Many breaches of cryptography are the result not of weak algorithms but instead of incorrect configuration or uses of the cryptography, known as misconfiguration implementation.

- Cryptography can be applied through either software or hardware. Software-based cryptography can protect large numbers of files on a system or an entire disk. One of the most widely used asymmetric cryptography systems is a commercial product called Pretty Good Privacy (PGP); similar open-source programs are GNU Privacy Guard (GNuPG) and OpenPGP. Modern operating systems provide encryption support natively.

Cryptography also can be applied to entire disks, known as full disk encryption (FDE).

- Hardware encryption cannot be exploited like software cryptography. Hardware encryption devices can protect USB devices and standard hard drives. More sophisticated hardware encryption options include self-encrypting drives, the Trusted Platform Module, and the Hardware Security Model.

Key Terms

Advanced Encryption Standard (AES)

algorithm

asymmetric cryptographic algorithm

birthday attack

block cipher

Blowfish

cipher

collision

collision attack

confusion

cryptography

Data Encryption Standard (DES)

data-at-rest

data-in-transit

data-in-use

deprecated algorithm

Diffie-Hellman (DH)

Diffie-Hellman Ephemeral (DHE)

diffusion

digital signature

Digital Signature Algorithm (DSA)

downgrade attack

elliptic curve cryptography (ECC)

Elliptic Curve Diffie–Hellman (ECDH)

encryption

ephemeral key

full disk encryption (FDE)

GNU Privacy Guard (GNuPG)

Hardware Security Module (HSM)

hash

Hashed Message Authentication Code (HMAC)

high resiliency

key exchange

known ciphertext attack

low latency

low-power devices

Message Digest 5 (MD5)

misconfiguration implementation

non-repudiation

obfuscation

perfect forward secrecy

Pretty Good Privacy (PGP)

private key

pseudorandom number generator (PRNG)

public key

RACE Integrity Primitives Evaluation Message Digest (RIPEMD)

random numbers

RC4

resource vs. security constraint

ROT13

RSA

Secure Hash Algorithm (SHA)

security through obscurity

self-encrypting drives (SEDs)

steganography

stream cipher

substitution cipher

symmetric cryptographic algorithm

Triple Data Encryption Standard (3DES)

Trusted Platform Module (TPM)

Twofish

XOR cipher

Review Questions

1. The Hashed Message Authentication Code (HMAC) _____.
   a. encrypts only the message
   b. encrypts only the key
   c. encrypts the key and the message
   d. encrypts the DHE key only

2. What is the latest version of the Secure Hash Algorithm?
   a. SHA-2
   b. SHA-3
   c. SHA-4
   d. SHA-5

3. Alexei was given a key to a substitution cipher. The key showed that the entire alphabet was rotated 13 steps. What type of cipher is this?
   a. AES
   b. XAND13
   c. ROT13
   d. Alphabetic

4. Abram was asked to explain to one of his coworkers the XOR cipher. He showed his coworker an example of adding two bits, 1 and 1. What is the result of this sum?
   a. 2
   b. 1
   c. 0
   d. 16

5. Which of the following key exchanges uses the same keys each time?
   a. Diffie-Hellman-RSA (DHRSA)
   b. Diffie-Hellman Ephemeral (DHE)
   c. Diffie-Hellman (DH)
   d. Elliptic Curve Diffie-Hellman (ECDH)

6. Public key systems that generate random public keys that are different for each session are called _____.
   a. Public Key Exchange (PKE)
   b. perfect forward secrecy
   c. Elliptic Curve Diffie-Hellman (ECDH)
   d. Diffie-Hellman (DH)

7. What is data called that is to be encrypted by inputting it into a cryptographic algorithm?
   a. Opentext
   b. Plaintext
   c. Cleartext
   d. Ciphertext

8. Which of these is NOT a basic security protection for information that cryptography can provide?
   a. Authenticity
   b. Risk loss
   c. Integrity
   d. Confidentiality

9. Which areas of a file *cannot* be used by steganography to hide data?
   a. In areas that contain the content data itself
   b. In the file header fields that describe the file
   c. In data that is used to describe the content or structure of the actual data
   d. In the directory structure of the file system

10. Proving that a user sent an email message is known as _____.
    a. Non-repudiation
    b. Repudiation
    c. Integrity
    d. Availability

11. A(n) _____ is not decrypted but is only used for comparison purposes.
    a. Key
    b. Stream
    c. Digest
    d. Algorithm

12. Which of these is NOT a characteristic of a secure hash algorithm?
    a. Collisions should be rare.
    b. A message cannot be produced from a predefined hash.
    c. The results of a hash function should not be reversed.
    d. The hash should always be the same fixed size.

13. Alyosha was explaining to a friend the importance of protecting a cryptographic key from cryptoanalysis. He said that the key should not relate in a simple way to the cipher text. Which protection is Alyosha describing?
    a. Diffusion
    b. Confusion
    c. Integrity
    d. Chaos

14. Which of these is the strongest symmetric cryptographic algorithm?
    a. Data Encryption Standard
    b. Triple Data Encryption Standard
    c. Advanced Encryption Standard
    d. RC 1

15. If Bob wants to send a secure message to Alice using an asymmetric cryptographic algorithm, which key does he use to encrypt the message?
    a. Alice's private key
    b. Bob's public key
    c. Alice's public key
    d. Bob's private key

16. Egor wanted to use a digital signature. Which of the following benefits will the digital signature not provide?
    a. Verify the sender
    b. Prove the integrity of the message
    c. Verify the receiver
    d. Enforce nonrepudiation

17. Illya was asked to recommend the most secure asymmetric cryptographic algorithm to his supervisor. Which of the following did he choose?
    a. SHA-2
    b. ME-312
    c. BTC-2
    d. RSA

18. At a staff meeting one of the technicians suggested that the enterprise protect its new web server by hiding it and not telling anyone where it is located. Iosif raised his hand and said that security through obscurity was a poor idea. Why did he say that?
    a. It is an unproven approach and has never been tested.
    b. It would be too costly to have one isolated server by itself.
    c. It would be essentially impossible to keep its location a secret from everyone.
    d. It depends too heavily upon non-repudiation in order for it to succeed.

19. What is a characteristic of the Trusted Platform Module (TPM)?
    a. It provides cryptographic services in hardware instead of software.
    b. It allows the user to boot a corrupted disk and repair it.
    c. It is available only on Windows computers running BitLocker.
    d. It includes a pseudorandom number generator (PRNG).

20. Which of these has an onboard key generator and key storage facility, as well as accelerated symmetric and asymmetric encryption, and can back up sensitive material in encrypted form?
    a. Trusted Platform Module (TPM)
    b. Hardware Security Module (HSM)
    c. Self-encrypting hard disk drives (SED)
    d. Encrypted hardware-based USB devices

Hands-On Projects

> **Note** 📎
>
> If you are concerned about installing any of the software in these projects on your regular computer, you can instead install the software in the Windows virtual machine created in the Chapter 1 Hands-On Projects 1-3 and 1-4. Software installed within the virtual machine will not impact the host computer.

Project 3-1: Using OpenPuff Steganography

Unlike cryptography that scrambles a message so that it cannot be viewed, steganography hides the existence of the data. In this project, you use OpenPuff to create a hidden message.

1. Use your web browser to go to **embeddedsw.net/OpenPuff_Steganography_Home .html**.

> **Note** 📎
>
> It is not unusual for websites to change the location of where files are stored. If the URL above no longer functions, open a search engine and search for "OpenPuff".

2. Click **Manual** to open the OpenPuff manual. Save this file to your computer. Read through the manual to see the different features available.
3. Click **OpenPuff** to download the program.
4. Click **Screenshot** to view a screen capture of OpenPuff. Right-click on this image and save this image **OpenPuff_Screenshot.jpg** to your computer. This will be the carrier file that will contain the secret message.

> **Note** 📎
>
> For added security OpenPuff allows a message to be spread across several carrier files.

5. Navigate to the location of the download and uncompress the Zip file on your computer.
6. Now create the secret message to be hidden. Open Notepad and enter **This is a secret message**.
7. Save this file as **Message.txt** and close Notepad.
8. Create a Zip file from the **Message** file. Navigate to the location of this file through Windows Explorer and click the right mouse button.
9. Click **Send to** and select **Compressed (zipped) folder** to create the Zip file.

10. Navigate to the OpenPuff directory and double-click **OpenPuff.exe**.
11. Click **Hide**.

> **Note** 📎
>
> Under Bit selection options, note the wide variety of file types that can be used to hide a message.

12. Under **(1)** create three unrelated passwords and enter them into **Cryptography (A)**, **(B)**, and **(C)**. Be sure that the **Scrambling (C)** password is long enough to turn the **Password check** bar from red to green.
13. Under **(2)** locate the message to be hidden. Click **Browse** and navigate to the file **Message.zip**. Click **Open**.
14. Under **(3)** select the carrier file. Click **Add** and navigate to **OpenPuff_Screenshot.jpg** as shown in Figure 3-11.

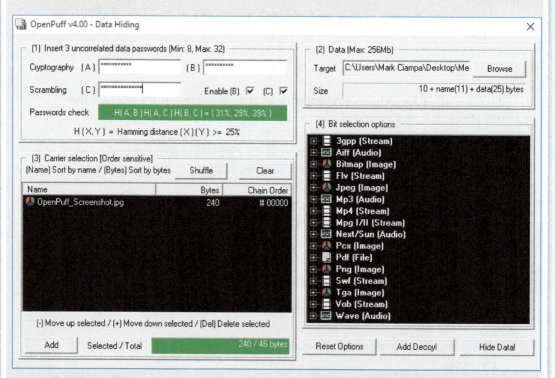

Figure 3-11 OpenPuff

Source: EmbeddedSW.net

15. Click **Hide Data!**
16. Navigate to a different location than that of the carrier files and click **OK**.
17. After the processing has completed, navigate to the location of the carrier file that contains the message and open the file. Can you detect anything different with the file now that it contains the message?

18. Now uncover the message. Close the OpenPuff Data Hiding screen to return to the main menu.
19. Click **Unhide**.
20. Enter the three passwords.
21. Click **Add Carriers** and navigate to the location of **Carrier1** that contains the hidden message.
22. Click **Unhide!** and navigate to a location to deposit the hidden message. When it has finished processing click **OK**.
23. Click **Done** after reading the report.
24. Go to that location and you will see **Message.zip**.
25. Close OpenPuff and close all windows.

Project 3-2: Running an RSA Cipher Demonstration

The steps for encryption using RSA can be illustrated in a Java applet on a website. In this project, you observe how RSA encrypts and decrypts.

> **Note** 📎
>
> It is recommended that you review the section earlier in this chapter regarding the steps in the RSA function.

1. Use your web browser to go to **people.cs.pitt.edu/~kirk/cs1501/notes/rsademo/**.

> **Note** 📎
>
> It is not unusual for websites to change the location of where files are stored. If the URL above no longer functions, open a search engine and search for "RSA Cipher Demonstration".

2. Read the information about the demonstration.
3. Click **key generation page**.
4. Change the first prime number (P) to **7**.
5. Change the second prime number (Q) to **5**.
6. Click **Proceed**.
7. Read the information in the popup screen and record the necessary numbers. Close the screen when finished.
8. Click **Encryption Page**.
9. Next to **Enter Alice's Exponent key, E:** enter **5** as the key value from the previous screen.
10. Under **Enter Alice's N Value:** enter **35**.
11. Click **Encrypt**. Read the message and record the values. Close the screen when finished.
12. Click **Decryption Page**.

13. Next to **Enter the encrypted message** enter **1**.
14. Next to **Enter your N value:** enter **35**.
15. Next to **Enter your private key, D:** enter **5**.
16. Click **Proceed**. Note that **1** has been decrypted to **A**.
17. Close all windows.

Project 3-3: Installing GUI Hash Generator and Comparing Digests

In this project, you download a GUI hash generator and compare the results of various hash algorithms.

1. Create a Microsoft Word document with the contents **Now is the time for all good men to come to the aid of their country.**
2. Save the document as **Country1.docx** on the desktop or in a directory specified by your instructor.
3. Now make a single change to **Country1.docx** by removing the period at the end of the sentence so it says **Now is the time for all good men to come to the aid of their country** and then save the document as **Country2.docx** in the same directory.
4. Close the document and Microsoft Word.
5. Use your web browser to go to **hashcalc.soft112.com**.

> **Note** 🖇
>
> It is not unusual for websites to change the location of where files are stored. If the URL above no longer functions, open a search engine and search for "HashCalc".

6. Click **Download**.
7. Click **Download** 1.
8. Click **External Download Link** 1.
9. Follow the default instructions to install HashCalc.
10. Launch HashCalc to display the HashCalc window as seen in Figure 3-12.
11. In addition to the hash algorithms selected by default check the box next to the following hash algorithms to add them: **MD5**, **SHA256**, **SHA384**, **SHA512**, and **MD2**.
12. Click the file explore button next to **Data:**.
13. Navigate to the document **Country1.docx**.
14. Click **Open**.
15. In the HashCalc window click **Calculate**.
16. Review the different digests generated. If necessary, expand the size of the window. What can you say about these digests? Compare MD2 with SHA512. What makes SHA512 better than MD2? Why?
17. Click the file explore button next to **Data:**.
18. Navigate to the document **Country2.docx**.
19. Click **Open**.
20. In the HashCalc window click **Calculate**.

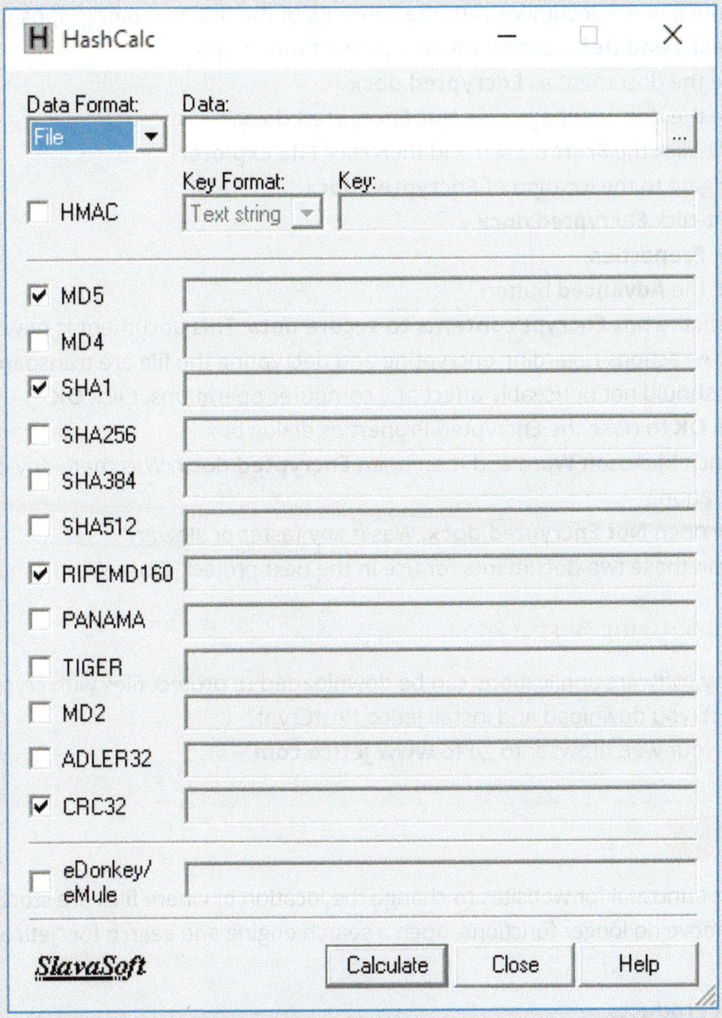

Figure 3-12   HashCalc

Source: SlavaSoft

21. This file is the same as the previous except a single period was removed. Are the digests different? What does this tell you about hashing digests?

22. Close all windows.

Project 3-4: Using Microsoft's Encrypting File System (EFS)

Microsoft's Encrypting File System (EFS) is a cryptography system for Windows operating systems that uses the Windows NTFS file system. Because EFS is tightly integrated with the file system, file encryption and decryption are transparent to the user. In this project, you turn on and use EFS.

1. Create a Word document with the contents of the first two paragraphs under **Today's Attacks and Defenses** on the first page of this chapter.
2. Save the document as **Encrypted.docx**.
3. Save the document again as **Not Encrypted.docx**.
4. Right-click the **Start** button and then click **File Explorer**.
5. Navigate to the location of **Encrypted.docx**.
6. Right-click **Encrypted.docx**.
7. Click **Properties**.
8. Click the **Advanced** button.
9. Check the box **Encrypt contents to secure data**. This document is now protected with EFS. All actions regarding encrypting and decrypting the file are transparent to the user and should not noticeably affect any computer operations. Click **OK**.
10. Click **OK** to close the Encrypted Properties dialog box.
11. Launch Microsoft Word and then open **Encrypted.docx**. Was there any delay in the operation?
12. Now open **Not Encrypted.docx**. Was it any faster or slower?
13. Retain these two documents for use in the next project. Close Word.

Project 3-5: Using BestCrypt

Third-party software applications can be downloaded to protect files with cryptography. In this project, you download and install Jetico BestCrypt.

1. Use your web browser to go to **www.jetico.com**.

> **Note** 📎
>
> It is not unusual for websites to change the location of where files are stored. If the URL above no longer functions, open a search engine and search for "Jetico BestCrypt".

2. Click **Products**.
3. Click **Personal Privacy**.
4. Click **BestCrypt Container Encryption**.
5. Click **Download**.
6. Click the **Encryption** tab.
7. Under **BestCrypt Container Encryption** click **Download**.
8. Follow the default installation procedures to install BestCrypt. A computer restart will be necessary.

> **Note** 📎
>
> Note that this is a limited-time evaluation copy. Any files that are encrypted will only be available as read-only after the time limit expires.

9. Launch BestCrypt to display the BestCrypt control panel, as seen in Figure 3-13.

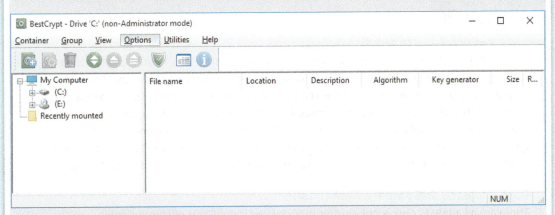

Figure 3-13   BestCrypt control panel

Source: Jetico Software

10. Files to be automatically encrypted are placed in a BestCrypt container. To create a container in the left pane right-click on the drive in which you want the container to be created, then click **Container** and **New**.

11. Note the default file path for this container. Click **Show Advanced Settings**.

12. In the **Security Options** tab click the arrow next to **Algorithm:** to display the different cryptographic algorithms. Change to **Blowfish-448**.

13. Click **Create**.

14. The **Enter password** dialog box appears. Enter a strong password and confirm it. Click **OK**.

15. The **Seed value generation** window appears. Read carefully the instructions. What is the purpose of this? Follow the instructions by pressing random keys or moving your cursor.

16. The **Format Local Disk** dialog box appears. This is to format the virtual drive that will contain your files. Click **Start** and then **OK**. When completed click **Close**.

17. Note that you now have a new drive letter added to your computer, which is where you will place the files you want to encrypt. This container is entirely encrypted, including file names and free space, and functions like a real disk. You can copy, save, or move files to this container disk and they will be encrypted as they are being written.

18. Right-click **Start** and then **File Explorer**.

19. Click on the drive letter of the drive that BestCrypt created.

20. Now drag a file into this drive (BestCrypt container). The file is automatically encrypted.

21. Open the document from your BestCrypt container. Did it take any longer to open now that it is encrypted? Close the document again.

22. Maximize the BestCrypt window and then click **Container** and **Dismount** to stop your container. A container will also be unmounted when you log off.

23. Based on your experiences with BestCrypt and EFS, which do you prefer? Why? What advantages and disadvantages do you see for both applications?

24. Close all windows.

Case Projects

Case Project 3-1: Broken SHA-1

In early 2017 security researchers decisively demonstrated that SHA-1 could create the same digest from two different plaintexts, although this weakness had been theorized for over 10 years. The compromise of SHA-1 has rendered it no longer suitable for use. How did they do it? Visit the website Shattered (**shattered.io**) that provides information about how it was breached. Read the Q&A section and view the Infographic. Try dragging one of your files to the File Tester to see if it is part of the collision attack. What did you learn? How serious is a collision? What is the impact? Write a one to two paragraph explanation of what you learned.

Case Project 3-2: Compare Cipher Tools

There are a variety of online cipher tools that demonstrate different cryptographic algorithms. Visit the website Cipher Tools (**rumkin.com/tools/cipher/**) and explore the different tools. Select three tools, one of which is mentioned in this chapter (ROT13, One-Time Pad, etc.). Experiment with the three different tools. Which is easy to use? Which is more difficult? Which tool would you justify to be more secure than the others? Why? Write a one-page paper on your analysis of the tools.

Case Project 3-3: Lightweight Cryptography

Due to the importance of incorporating cryptography in low-power devices, a new "subfield" of cryptography is being developed called *lightweight cryptography*. This has the goal of providing cryptographic solutions that are uniquely tailored for low-power devices that need to manage resource vs. security constraints. Research lightweight cryptography. What are its goals? How will it work? Who is behind it? Will it be standardized? When will it appear? Write a one-page paper on your findings.

Case Project 3-4: Twofish and Blowfish

Research Twofish and Blowfish. How secure are they? What are their features? What are their strengths and weaknesses? How are they currently being used? How would you compare them? Write a one-page paper on your findings.

Case Project 3-5: Hash Algorithm Comparison

Research the different hash algorithms (Message Digest, Secure Hash Algorithm, and RIPEMD) and then create a table that compares them. Include the size of the digest, the number of rounds needed to create the hash, block size, who created it, what previous hash it was derived from, its strengths, and its weaknesses.

Case Project 3-6: One-Time Pad (OTP) Research

Use the Internet to research OTPs: who was behind the initial idea, when they were first used, in what applications they were found, how they are used today, etc. Then visit an online OTP creation site such as **www.braingle.com/brainteasers/codes/onetimepad.php** and practice creating your own ciphertext with OTP. If possible exchange your OTPs with other students to see how you might try to break them. Would it be practical to use OTPs? Why or why not? Write a one-page paper on your findings.

Case Project 3-7: Diffie-Hellman Research

How does Diffie-Hellman work? Use the Internet to research this this key-sharing function. Then visit the website **dkerr.home.mindspring.com/diffie_hellman_calc.html** to see how values are created. Write a one-page paper on Diffie-Hellman.

Case Project 3-8: USB Device Encryption

Use the Internet to select four USB flash drives that support hardware encryption. Create a table that compares all four and their features. Be sure to include any unique features that the drives may have along with their costs. Which would you recommend? Why? Write a one-page paper on your research.

Case Project 3-9: Lake Point Consulting Services

Lake Point Consulting Services (LPCS) provides security consulting and assurance services to over 500 clients across a wide range of enterprises in more than 20 states. A new initiative at LPCS is for each of its seven regional offices to provide internships to students who are in their final year of the security degree program at the local college.

National Meteorological Services (NMS) offers in-depth weather forecasting services to airlines, trucking firms, event planners, and other organizations that need the latest and most accurate weather forecasting services. NMS has discovered that their forecast information, which was being sent out as email attachments to its customers, was being freely distributed without NMS's permission, and in some instances, was being resold by their competitors. NMS wants to look into encrypting these weather forecast documents, but is concerned that its customers may find decrypting the documents cumbersome. The company also wants to provide to their customers a level of assurance that these documents originate from NMS and have not been tampered with. NMS has asked LPSC to make a presentation about different solutions, and BPSC has asked you to help them prepare it.

1. Create a PowerPoint presentation about encryption and the different types of encryption. Include the advantages and disadvantages of each. Your presentation should contain at least 10 slides.
2. After the presentation, an NMS officer asks for your recommendation regarding meeting their needs for encryption. Create a memo communicating the actions you believe would be best for the company to take.

Case Project 3-10: Information Security Community Site Activity

The Information Security Community Site is an online companion to this textbook. It contains a wide variety of tools, information, discussion boards, and other features to assist learners. Go to **community.cengage.com/Infosec2** and click the *Join or Sign in* icon to log in, using your login name and password that you created in Chapter 1. Click **Forums (Discussion)** and click on **Security+ Case Projects (6th edition)**. Read the following case study.

This is a true story (with minor details changed). Microsoft had uncovered several licensing discrepancies in its software that clients were using while claiming they had purchased it from an authorized software retailer. The sale of one software package to a company in Tampa was traced back to a retailer in Pennsylvania, and yet the retailer had no record of any sales to the Tampa company. A private security consulting agency was called in, and they discovered that the network system administrator "Ed" in Pennsylvania was downloading pirated software from the Internet and selling it to customers as legitimate software behind the company's back. Ed had sold almost a half-million dollars in illegal software. The security firm also noticed a high network bandwidth usage. Upon further investigation, they found that Ed was using one of the company's servers as a pornographic website with more than 50,000 images and 2500 videos. In addition, a search of Ed's desktop computer uncovered a spreadsheet with hundreds of credit card numbers from the company's e-commerce site. The security firm speculated that Ed was either selling these card numbers to attackers or using them himself.

The situation was complicated by the fact that Ed was the only person who knew certain administrative passwords for the core network router and firewall, network switches, the corporate virtual private network (VPN), the entire Human Resources system, the email server, and the Windows Active Directory. In addition, the company had recently installed a Hardware Security Module (HSM) to which only Ed had the password. The security consultant and the Pennsylvania company were worried about what Ed might do if he was confronted with the evidence, since essentially he could hold the entire organization hostage or destroy virtually every piece of useful information.

A plan was devised. The company invented a fictitious emergency at one of their offices in California that required Ed to fly there overnight. The long flight gave the security team a window of about five and a half hours during which Ed could not access the system (the flight that was booked for Ed did not have wireless access). Working as fast as they could, the team mapped out the network and reset all the passwords. When Ed landed in California, the chief operating officer was there to meet him and Ed was fired on the spot.

Now it's your turn to think outside of the box. What would you have done to keep Ed away so you could reconfigure the network? Or how could you have tricked Ed into giving up the passwords without revealing to him that he was under suspicion? Record your answers on the Community Site discussion board.

References

1. Nakashima, Ellen, "FBI paid professional hackers one-time fee to crack San Bernardino iPhone," *The Washington Post*, Apr. 12, 2016, accessed Mar. 6, 2017, www.washingtonpost.com/world/national-security/fbi-paid-professional-hackers-one-time-fee-to-crack-san-bernardino-iphone/2016/04/12/5397814a-00de-11e6-9d36-33d198ea26c5_story.html?utm_term=.5ee2e09d6415.

CHAPTER 4

ADVANCED CRYPTOGRAPHY AND PKI

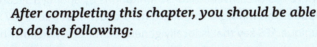

After completing this chapter, you should be able to do the following:

Explain how to implement cryptography

Define digital certificates

Describe the components of Public Key Infrastructure (PKI)

Describe the different transport encryption algorithms

Today's Attacks and Defenses

Although encryption can help safeguard users' data, it is also being used by threat actors in a new and more malicious form of ransomware. Recall that ransomware embeds itself on a user's device, prevents the user from accessing the device's files and resources, and continues to deny access unless a fee is paid. Now, instead of just blocking the user from accessing the computer or device, threat actors have developed ransomware that encrypts all the files on the device—or any attached removable storage device or server—so that no files can be opened. This is called *crypto-malware*.

The crypto-malware Spora truly stands out from the crowd. Most ransomware generates an Advanced Encryption Standard (AES) key for each encrypted file and then encrypts these keys with an RSA public key that has been generated by a command and control (C&C) server and then downloaded to the local computer. The private key stays on the server, and this is what is sent to the victims once they pay the ransom. However, this process posed a problem for attackers. If the C&C server is known and blocked by a firewall, the encryption process could not begin. To get around this, some ransomware used encryption with the same RSA public key that was hard-coded into the malware. However, once one victim paid for the decryptor tool, it could be distributed to other victims to unlock their files.

Spora ransomware has circumvented these limitations by adding a second round of AES and RSA encryption. This malware contains a hard-coded RSA public key, but this is used to encrypt a unique AES key that is locally generated for every victim. This AES key in turn is used to encrypt the private key from a public-private RSA key pair that is also unique and locally created for each victim. Then the victim's public RSA key is used to encrypt the AES keys that are used to encrypt the victim's files. When victims want to pay the ransom, they must upload their encrypted AES keys to the attackers' payment website. The attackers then use their master RSA private key to decrypt it and return it to the victim with a decryptor tool. The decryptor uses this AES key to decrypt the victim's unique RSA private key (that was generated locally) and that key is then used to decrypt the AES keys needed to recover the files.

So, what defenses are there for crypto-malware? The No More Ransom project[1] is a coalition of law enforcement and security companies and has 32 new decryption tools for various ransomware variants (of course, these are no defense against Spora). As of 2017 the delivery of ransomware is now illegal in California (previous lawsuits were brought under existing extortion statutes). The maximum penalty for ransomware usage is four years in state prison. California is the second state to outlaw computer ransomware, with Wyoming passing a similar statute in 2014.

For end users, cryptography has clear benefits for safeguarding sensitive data. Users can generate a digest on a downloaded file to compare it with that displayed on a website to ensure that the downloaded file has not been altered. Users can also take advantage of symmetric encryption software to encrypt sensitive documents stored on their computers. And they can also use asymmetric encryption to send and receive confidential email messages.

However, when cryptography is utilized in the enterprise, a new level of complexity is added. What happens if an employee has encrypted an important proposal but suddenly falls ill and cannot return to work? Where is her key stored?

Who can have access to it? And how can the encryption keys of hundreds or even thousands of employees be managed?

These and other issues relating to using cryptography in the enterprise move the discussion from the basics of cryptography to a higher level of cryptographic procedures. In this chapter, you are introduced to advanced cryptography. First you learn about how cryptography is implemented. Next, you explore digital certificates along with public key infrastructure. Finally, you look at different transport cryptographic algorithms to see how cryptography is used on data-in-transit.

Implementing Cryptography

 Certification

6.1 Compare and contrast basic concepts of cryptography.

6.2 Explain cryptography algorithms and their basic characteristics.

Cryptography that is improperly applied can lead to vulnerabilities that threat actors will exploit. Thus, it is essential to understand the different options that relate to cryptography so that it can be implemented correctly. Implementing cryptography includes understanding key strength, secret algorithms, block cipher modes of operation, cryptographic service providers, and the use of algorithm input values.

Key Strength

A cryptographic key is a value that serves as input to an algorithm, which then transforms plaintext into ciphertext (and vice versa for decryption). A key, which is essentially a random string of bits, serves as an input parameter for symmetric and asymmetric crytographic algorithms and selected hash algorithms.

> **Note** 📎
>
> A key is different from a password. Passwords are designed to be created and remembered by humans so that the passwords can be reproduced when necessary. A key is used by hardware or software that is running the cryptographic algorithm; as such, human readability is not required.

There are three primary characteristics that determine the resiliency of the key to attacks (called **key strength**). The first is its randomness. For a key to be considered strong, it must be random with no predictable pattern. This thwarts an attacker from attempting to uncover the key.

The second characteristic is the length of the key. Shorter keys can be more easily broken than longer keys. All the possible values for a specific key make up its *key space*. The formula for determining a given key space for symmetric algorithms is *character-set$^{key\text{-}length}$*. For example, suppose a key has a length of 3 and is using a 26-character alphabet. The list of possible keys (*aaa, aab, aac*, etc.) would be 26^3 or 17,576 possible outcomes. Thus, the key length in this example is *3* and the key space is *17,576*.

On average, half the key space must be searched to discover the key. In the example, a key with a length of only 3 that has a key space of 17,576 requires only 8788 keys to be searched (on average) until the correct key is discovered. This number of searches is very small and can easily be compromised by a threat actor.

However, if the key length of 3 was increased by just 1 character to 4, the key space increases to *456,976* requiring on average *228,488* attempts. Table 4-1 illustrates the key strength for different key lengths, the key space, and average attempts necessary to break the key for a 26-character alphabet.

Table 4-1   Key strength

Key length	Key space	Average number of attempts needed to break
3	17,576	8788
4	456,976	228,488
5	11,881,376	5,940,688
6	308,915,776	154,457,888
7	8,031,810,176	4,015,905,088
8	208,827,064,576	104,413,532,288

A third characteristic that determines key strength is its *cryptoperiod*, or the length of time for which a key is authorized for use. Having a limited cryptoperiod helps protect the ciphertext from extended cryptanalysis and limits the exposure time if a key is compromised.

Note

Different cryptoperiods are recommended for different types of keys.

Secret Algorithms

Although keys need to be kept secret (except for public keys), does the same apply to algorithms? That is, should an enterprise invest in hiring a cryptographer to create a new cryptographic algorithm and then hide the existence of that algorithm from everyone? Wouldn't such a **secret algorithm** enhance security in the same way as keeping a key or password secret?

The answer is no. In the past, cryptographers have often attempted to keep their algorithms or the workings of devices that encrypted and decrypted documents a secret. However, this approach has always failed. One reason is because for cryptography to be useful it needs to be widespread: a military force that uses cryptography must by nature allow many users to know of its existence to use it. And the more users who know about it, the more difficult it is to keep it a secret. In contrast, a password only requires one person—the user—to keep it confidential.

> **Note**
>
> In 1883, Auguste Kerckhoffs, a Dutch linguist and cryptographer, published what is known as the *Kerchhoff Principles*, which were six design standards for military ciphers. One of his principles stated that systems should not require secrecy so that it should not be a problem if it falls into enemy hands. This principle is still applied today by splitting algorithms from keys: algorithms are public while keys are private.

Block Cipher Modes of Operation

One variation in cryptographic algorithms is the amount of data that is processed at a time. Some algorithms use a *stream cipher* while other algorithms make use of a *block cipher*. Whereas a stream cipher works on one character at a time, a block cipher manipulates an entire block of plaintext at one time. Because the size of the plaintext is usually larger than the block size itself, the plaintext is divided into separate blocks of specific lengths, and then each block is encrypted independently.

> **Note**
>
> Stream and block ciphers are covered in Chapter 3.

A **block cipher mode of operation** specifies how block ciphers should handle these blocks. Some of the most common modes are:

- *Electronic Code Book (ECB)*. The **Electronic Code Book (ECB)** mode is the most basic approach: the plaintext is divided into blocks, and each block is then encrypted separately. However, this can result in two identical plaintext blocks being encrypted into two identical ciphertext blocks. Attackers can use this repetition to their advantage. They could modify the encrypted message by modifying a block or even reshuffle the order of the blocks of ciphertext. ECB is not considered suitable for use.

Note

Using ECB is like assigning code words from a codebook to create an encrypted message, and was the basis for naming this process Electronic Code Book.

- *Cipher Block Chaining (CBC)*. **Cipher Block Chaining (CBC)** is a common cipher mode. After being encrypted, each ciphertext block gets "fed back" into the encryption process to encrypt the next plaintext block. Using CBC, each block of plaintext is XORed with the previous block of ciphertext before being encrypted. Unlike ECB in which the ciphertext depends only upon the plaintext and the key, CBC is also dependent on the previous ciphertext block, making it much more difficult to break.

Note

XOR ciphers are covered in Chapter 3.

- *Counter (CTR)*. **Counter (CTR)** mode requires that both the message sender and receiver access a counter, which computes a new value each time a ciphertext block is exchanged. The weakness of CTR is that it requires a synchronous counter for both the sender and receiver.
- *Galois/Counter (GCM)*. The **Galois/Counter (GCM)** mode both encrypts plaintext and computes a message authentication code (MAC) to ensure that the message was created by the sender and that it was not tampered with during transmission. Like CTR, GCM uses a counter. It adds a plaintext string called *additional authentication data (AAD)* to the transmission. The AAD may contain the addresses and parameters of a network protocol that is being used.

Note

There are a variety of block cipher modes, with specific modes specializing in encryption, data integrity, privacy and integrity, and hard drive encryption. There are even specialized modes that gracefully recover from errors in transmission while other modes are designed to stop upon encountering transmission errors.

Crypto Service Providers

A **crypto service provider** allows an application to implement an encryption algorithm for execution. Typically, crypto service providers implement cryptographic algorithms, generate keys, provide key storage, and authenticate users by calling various **crypto modules** to perform the specific tasks. Crypto service providers can be implemented in software, hardware, or both, and are often part of the operating system. Figure 4-1 shows the cryptographic services enabled on a Microsoft Windows 10 computer. Providers may also be created and distributed by third parties, allowing for a broader algorithm selection.

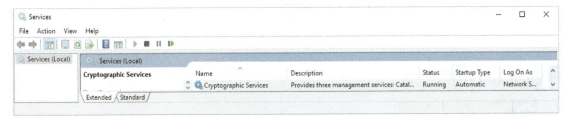

Figure 4-1   Microsoft Windows 10 cryptographic services

Note

Applications cannot manipulate the keys created by crypto service providers or alter the cryptographic algorithm itself.

Algorithm Input Values

Some cryptographic algorithms require that in addition to a key another value can or must be input. These may be called *algorithm input values*. A unique characteristic of these input values is that even though it is often possible to hide them, they do not need to be kept secret; in fact, it is generally assumed that these values are visible to attackers. As such, the strength of the cryptographic algorithms should not depend on the secrecy of these values.

A **salt** is a value that can be used to ensure that plaintext, when hashed, will not consistently result in the same digest. Salt is most often used in password-based systems: it prevents an attacker from generating digests of commonly used passwords or dictionary words that can be compared to the digest of a stolen password. By adding a salt to the beginning or end of a password prior to hashing it, the password is strengthened from being broken by a specific type of attack. Although a salt is not required to be random, a randomized salt—a different value input for each user—will give added protection.

A **nonce** (*number used once*) is an input value that must be unique within some specified scope, such as for a given period or for an entire session. An **initialization vector (IV)** is the most widely used algorithm input. An IV may be considered as a nonce with an additional requirement: it must be selected in a non-predictable way. Most block cipher modes of operation require an IV that is random and unpredictable, or at least unique for each message encrypted with a given key.

Note

Salts are not required to be randomized and can be repeated (but unique and random salts can improve security). A nonce is not required to be randomized but can never be repeated. An IV should be randomized and never repeated.

Digital Certificates

Certification

6.1 Compare and contrast basic concepts of cryptography.

6.4 Given a scenario, implement public key infrastructure.

One of the common applications of cryptography is digital certificates. Using digital certificates involves understanding their purpose, knowing how they are managed, and determining which type of digital certificate is appropriate for different situations.

Defining Digital Certificates

Suppose that Alice receives an encrypted document that says it came from Bob. Although Alice can be sure that the encrypted message was not viewed or altered by someone else while being transmitted, how can she know for certain that Bob was actually the sender? Because Alice's public key is widely available, an attacker could have created a fictitious document, encrypted it with Alice's public key, and then sent it to Alice while pretending to be Bob. Although Alice's key can verify that no one read or changed the document in transport, it cannot verify the sender.

Proof can be provided with asymmetric cryptography by creating a *digital signature*. However, there is a weakness with digital signatures: they do not confirm the true identity of the sender. Digital signatures only show that the private key of the sender was used to encrypt the digital signature, but they do not definitively prove *who* the sender was. If Alice receives a message with a digital signature claiming to be from Bob, she cannot know for certain that it is the *real* Bob whose public key she is retrieving.

Note

Digital signatures are covered in Chapter 3.

For example, suppose Bob created a message along with a digital signature and sent it to Alice. However, Mallory intercepted the message. He then created his own set of public and private keys using Bob's identity. Mallory could then create a new message and digital signature (with the imposter private key) and send them to Alice. Upon receiving the message and digital signature, Alice would unknowingly retrieve the imposter public key (thinking it belonged to Bob) and decrypt it. Alice would be tricked into thinking Bob had sent it when in reality, it came from Mallory. This interception and imposter public key are illustrated in Figure 4-2.

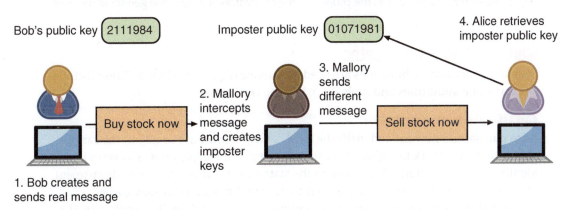

Figure 4-2   Imposter public key

Suppose that Bob wanted to ensure that Alice receives his real public key and not the imposter public key. He could travel to Alice's city, knock on her front door, and say, "I'm Bob and here's my key."

Yet how would Alice even know *this* was the real Bob and not Mallory in disguise? For verification, she could ask to see Bob's passport. This is a document that is provided by a *trusted third party*. Although Alice may not initially trust Bob because she does not know him, she will trust the government agency that required Bob to provide proof of his identity when he applied for the passport. Using a trusted third party who has verified Bob, and who Alice also trusts, would help to solve the problem.

This is the concept behind a digital certificate. A **digital certificate** is a technology used to associate a user's identity to a public key and that has been *digitally signed* by a trusted third party. This third party verifies the owner and that the public key belongs to that owner. When Bob sends a message to Alice, he does not ask her to retrieve his public key from a central site. Instead, Bob attaches the digital certificate to the message. When Alice receives the message with the digital certificate, she can check the signature of the trusted third party on the certificate. If the signature was signed by a party that she trusts, then Alice can safely assume that the public key—contained in the digital certificate—is actually from Bob. Digital certificates make it possible for Alice to verify Bob's claim that the key belongs to him and prevent an attack that impersonates the owner of the public key.

> **Note** 📎
>
> A digital certificate is basically a container for a public key and can be used to identify objects other than users, such as servers and applications. Typically, it contains information such as the owner's name or alias, the owner's public key, the name of the issuer, the digital signature of the issuer, the serial number of the digital certificate, and the expiration date of the public key. It can contain other user-supplied information, such as an email address, postal address, and basic registration information, such as the country or region, postal code, age, and gender of the user.

Managing Digital Certificates

Several entities and technologies are used to manage digital certificates. These include the certificate authorities and tools for managing certificates.

Certificate Authorities

Alice purchases a new car and visits the local county courthouse to fill out the car title application paperwork to register her car. After signing the application and verifying her identity, the information is forwarded to the state capital, where the state's department of motor vehicles (DMV) issues an official car title that is sent to the new owner.

This scenario illustrates some of the entities involved with digital certificates. If a user wants a digital certificate she must, after generating the public and private keys to be used, complete a request with information such as name, address, email address, etc., known as a **Certificate Signing Request (CSR)**. The user electronically signs the CSR by affixing her public key and then sending it to an **intermediate certificate authority (CA)**. The intermediate CA, of which there are many, processes the CSR and verifies the authenticity of the user. The intermediate CAs perform functions on behalf of a **certificate authority (CA)** that is responsible for digital certificates. A CA may also be called a *root CA*. A comparison between the earlier car title scenario and the elements of a digital certificate are shown in Table 4-2.

Table 4-2 Digital certificate elements

Car title scenario	Digital certificate element	Explanation
Car title application	Certificate Signing Request (CSR)	Formal request for digital certificate
Sign car title application	Create and affix public key to certificate	Added to digital certificate for security
Visit county courthouse	Intermediate certificate authority	Party that can process CSR on behalf of CA
Title sent from state DMV	Certificate authority (CA)	Party responsible for digital certificates

> **Note**
>
> Just as there are many county courthouses across a state, there are many intermediate CAs.

Intermediate CAs are subordinate entities designed to handle specific CA tasks such as processing certificate requests and verifying the identity of the individual. Depending upon the type of digital certificate, the person requesting a digital certificate can be authenticated by:

- *Email*. In the simplest form, the owner might be identified only by an email address. Although this type of digital certificate might be sufficient for basic email communication, it is insufficient for other activities, such as transferring money online.
- *Documents*. An intermediate CA can confirm the authenticity of the person requesting the digital certificate by requiring specific documentation such as a birth certificate or a copy of an employee badge that contains a photograph.
- *In person*. In some instances, the intermediate CA might require the applicant to apply in person to prove his existence and identity by providing a government-issued passport or driver's license.

> **Note**
>
> Although the registration function could be implemented directly with the CA, there are advantages to using separate intermediate CAs. If there are many entities that require a digital certificate, or if these are spread out across geographical areas, using a single centralized CA could create bottlenecks or inconveniences. Using multiple intermediate CAs, who can "off-load" these registration functions, can create an improved workflow. This process functions only because the CAs trust the intermediate CAs.

Just as a breach at a state DMV could result in many fraudulent car titles being distributed, so too the consequences of a compromised root CA are very significant. A compromised root CA would likewise taint all its intermediate CAs along with all the digital certificates that they issued. This makes it essential that all root CAs must be kept safe from unauthorized access. A common method to ensure the security and integrity of a root CA is to keep it in an offline state from the network (**offline CA**). It is only brought online (**online CA**) when needed for specific and infrequent tasks, typically limited to the issuance or re-issuance of certificates authorizing intermediate CAs.

Note

As an added measure of protection, offline root CAs can still issue certificates to removable media devices such as a USB drive or DVD, which are then physically transported to the intermediate CAs that need the certificate to perform their tasks. In this way, the root CA never needs to be online.

Certificate Management

There are multiple entities that make up strong certificate management. These include a certificate repository and a means for certificate revocation.

Certificate Repository (CR)

A *certificate repository (CR)* is a publicly accessible centralized directory of digital certificates that can be used to view the status of a digital certificate. This directory can be managed locally by setting it up as a storage area that is connected to the CA server.

Certificate Revocation

Digital certificates normally have an expiration date, such as one year from the date they were issued. However, there are circumstances that might be cause for the certificate to be revoked before it expires. Some reasons might be benign, such as when the certificate is no longer used or the details of the certificate, such as the user's address, have changed. Other circumstances could be more dangerous. For example, if someone were to steal a user's private key, she could impersonate the victim through using digital certificates without the other users being aware of it. In addition, what would happen if digital certificates were stolen from a CA? The thieves could then issue certificates to themselves that would be trusted by unsuspecting users. It is important that the CA publishes approved certificates as well as revoked certificates in a timely fashion; otherwise, it could lead to a situation in which security may be compromised.

Note

There have been several incidences of digital certificates being stolen from CAs or intermediate CAs. The thieves can then trick unsuspecting users into connecting with an imposter site, thinking it is a legitimate site. There have also been charges that nation state actors have stolen digital certificates to trick their own citizens' nation into connecting with a fraudulent email site to monitor their messages and to locate and crack-down on dissidents.

There are two means by which the status of a certificate can be checked to see if it has been revoked. The first is to use a **Certificate Revocation List (CRL)**, which is a list of certificate serial numbers that have been revoked. Many CAs maintain an online

CRL that can be queried by entering the certificate's serial number. In addition, a local computer receives updates on the status of certificates and maintains a local CRL, as illustrated in Figure 4-3.

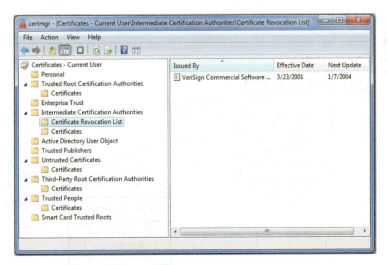

Figure 4-3   Certificate Revocation List (CRL)

The second method is an **Online Certificate Status Protocol (OCSP)**, which performs a real-time lookup of a certificate's status. OCSP is called a request-response protocol. The browser sends the certificate's information to a trusted entity like the CA, known as an *OCSP Responder*. The OCSP Responder then provides immediate revocation information on that one specific certificate.

Note

Initially all modern web browsers (Internet Explorer, Edge, Firefox, Safari on macOS, some versions of Opera, and Google Chrome) used OCSP. However, if the web browser cannot reach the OCSP Responder server, such as when the server is down, then the browser receives back the message that there is a network error (called a *soft-fail*) and the revocation check is simply ignored. Because of this weakness, Google Chrome decided that it would no longer support OCSP but instead would rely entirely on CRLs that are downloaded to Chrome.

A variation of OCSP is called OCSP **stapling**. OCSP requires the OCSP Responder to provide responses to every web client of a certificate in real time, which may create a high volume of traffic. With OCSP stapling, web servers send queries to the Responder OCSP server at regular intervals to receive a signed time-stamped OCSP response. When a client's web browser attempts to connect to the web server, the server can include (*staple*) in the handshake with the web browser the previously received OCSP response. The browser then can evaluate the OCSP response to determine if it is trustworthy. OCSP stapling is illustrated in Figure 4-4.

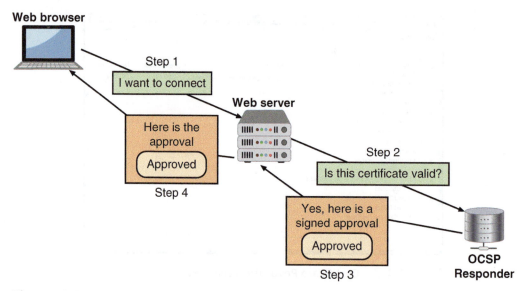

Figure 4-4 OCSP stapling

Types of Digital Certificates

There are several different types of digital certificates. These can be grouped into the broad categories of root certificates, domain certificates, and hardware and software certificates. In addition, there are several certificate formats.

Root Digital Certificates

Suppose that Alice is shopping online and wants to make a purchase. The online retailer asks her to enter her credit card number to complete the transaction. However, how can Alice be certain that she is at the authentic website and not an imposter's look-alike site that only wants to steal her credit card number? The answer is for the online retailer's web server to issue to Alice's web browser a digital certificate that has been signed by a trusted third-party. In this way, Alice can rest assured that her connection is to the authentic online retailer's site.

The process of verifying that a digital certificate is genuine depends upon **certificate chaining**. As its name implies, certificate chaining links several certificates together to establish trust between all the certificates involved. The endpoint of the chain is the **user digital certificate** itself. The beginning point of the chain is a specific type of digital certificate known as a **root digital certificate**. A root digital certificate is created and verified by a CA. And because there is no higher-level authority than a CA, root digital certificates are **self-signed** and do not depend upon any higher-level authority for authentication. Between the root digital certificate and the user certificate can be one or more *intermediate certificates* that have been issued by intermediate CAs. The root digital certificate (verified by a CA) trusts the intermediate certificate (verified by an intermediate CA), which may validate another lower-level intermediate CA, etc., until it reaches the user digital certificate. Certificate chaining is illustrated in Figure 4-5.

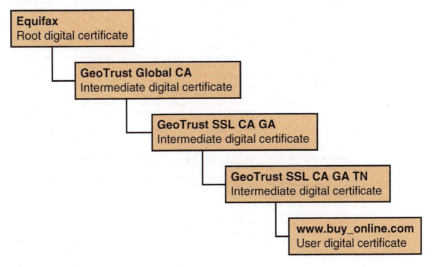

Figure 4-5   Certificate chaining

Note

Why not issue all certificates off the root digital certificate and eliminate the need for certificate chaining? This would require an online CA that could compromise its security.

Root digital certificates and intermediate certificates are packaged as part of modern operating systems. The trusted root digital certificates for a Windows 10 operating system are seen in Figure 4-6. In addition, web browser software also contains root and intermediate digital certificates. Another option is **pinning**, in which a digital certificate is hard-coded (*pinned*) within the app (program) that is using the certificate. Pinning is common for securing mobile messaging apps and for certain web-based services and browsers.

Note

Some browsers use the operating system's list of root digital certificates to determine which CAs are trusted, while other browsers use their own facilities.

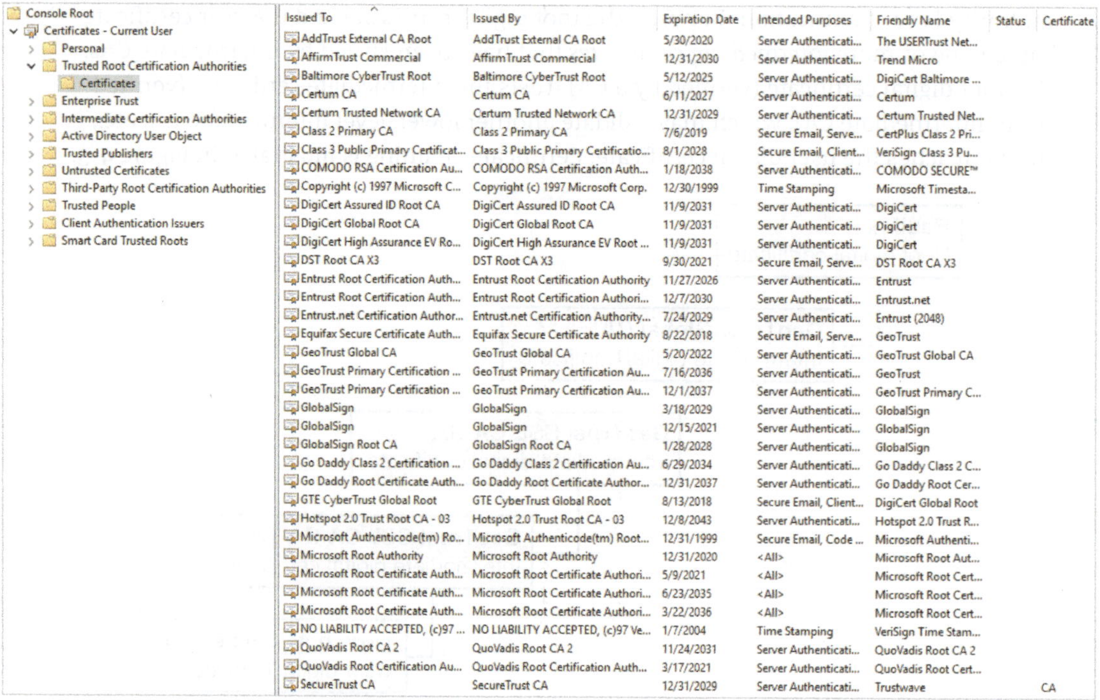

	Issued To	Issued By	Expiration Date	Intended Purposes	Friendly Name	Status	Certificate
Console Root							
⌄ Certificates - Current User	AddTrust External CA Root	AddTrust External CA Root	5/30/2020	Server Authenticati...	The USERTrust Net...		
> Personal	AffirmTrust Commercial	AffirmTrust Commercial	12/31/2030	Server Authenticati...	Trend Micro		
⌄ Trusted Root Certification Authorities	Baltimore CyberTrust Root	Baltimore CyberTrust Root	5/12/2025	Server Authenticati...	DigiCert Baltimore ...		
Certificates	Certum CA	Certum CA	6/11/2027	Server Authenticati...	Certum		
> Enterprise Trust	Certum Trusted Network CA	Certum Trusted Network CA	12/31/2029	Server Authenticati...	Certum Trusted Net...		
> Intermediate Certification Authorities	Class 2 Primary CA	Class 2 Primary CA	7/6/2019	Secure Email, Serve...	CertPlus Class 2 Pri...		
> Active Directory User Object	Class 3 Public Primary Certificat...	Class 3 Public Primary Certificatio...	8/1/2028	Secure Email, Client...	VeriSign Class 3 Pu...		
> Trusted Publishers	COMODO RSA Certification Au...	COMODO RSA Certification Auth...	1/18/2038	Server Authenticati...	COMODO SECURE™		
> Untrusted Certificates	Copyright (c) 1997 Microsoft C...	Copyright (c) 1997 Microsoft Corp.	12/30/1999	Time Stamping	Microsoft Timesta...		
> Third-Party Root Certification Authorities	DigiCert Assured ID Root CA	DigiCert Assured ID Root CA	11/9/2031	Server Authenticati...	DigiCert		
> Trusted People	DigiCert Global Root CA	DigiCert Global Root CA	11/9/2031	Server Authenticati...	DigiCert		
> Client Authentication Issuers	DigiCert High Assurance EV Ro...	DigiCert High Assurance EV Root ...	11/9/2031	Server Authenticati...	DigiCert		
> Smart Card Trusted Roots	DST Root CA X3	DST Root CA X3	9/30/2021	Secure Email, Serve...	DST Root CA X3		
	Entrust Root Certification Auth...	Entrust Root Certification Authority	11/27/2026	Server Authenticati...	Entrust		
	Entrust Root Certification Auth...	Entrust Root Certification Authori...	12/7/2030	Server Authenticati...	Entrust.net		
	Entrust.net Certification Author...	Entrust.net Certification Authority...	7/24/2029	Server Authenticati...	Entrust (2048)		
	Equifax Secure Certificate Auth...	Equifax Secure Certificate Authority	8/22/2018	Secure Email, Serve...	GeoTrust		
	GeoTrust Global CA	GeoTrust Global CA	5/20/2022	Server Authenticati...	GeoTrust Global CA		
	GeoTrust Primary Certification ...	GeoTrust Primary Certification Au...	7/16/2036	Server Authenticati...	GeoTrust		
	GeoTrust Primary Certification ...	GeoTrust Primary Certification Au...	12/1/2037	Server Authenticati...	GeoTrust Primary C...		
	GlobalSign	GlobalSign	3/18/2029	Server Authenticati...	GlobalSign		
	GlobalSign	GlobalSign	12/15/2021	Server Authenticati...	GlobalSign		
	GlobalSign Root CA	GlobalSign Root CA	1/28/2028	Server Authenticati...	GlobalSign		
	Go Daddy Class 2 Certification ...	Go Daddy Class 2 Certification Au...	6/29/2034	Server Authenticati...	Go Daddy Class 2 C...		
	Go Daddy Root Certificate Auth...	Go Daddy Root Certificate Author...	12/31/2037	Server Authenticati...	Go Daddy Root Cer...		
	GTE CyberTrust Global Root	GTE CyberTrust Global Root	8/13/2018	Secure Email, Client...	DigiCert Global Root		
	Hotspot 2.0 Trust Root CA - 03	Hotspot 2.0 Trust Root CA - 03	12/8/2043	Server Authenticati...	Hotspot 2.0 Trust R...		
	Microsoft Authenticode(tm) Ro...	Microsoft Authenticode(tm) Root...	12/31/1999	Secure Email, Code ...	Microsoft Authenti...		
	Microsoft Root Authority	Microsoft Root Authority	12/31/2020	<All>	Microsoft Root Aut...		
	Microsoft Root Certificate Auth...	Microsoft Root Certificate Authori...	5/9/2021	<All>	Microsoft Root Cert...		
	Microsoft Root Certificate Auth...	Microsoft Root Certificate Authori...	6/23/2035	<All>	Microsoft Root Cert...		
	Microsoft Root Certificate Auth...	Microsoft Root Certificate Authori...	3/22/2036	<All>	Microsoft Root Cert...		
	NO LIABILITY ACCEPTED, (c)97 ...	NO LIABILITY ACCEPTED, (c)97 Ve...	1/7/2004	Time Stamping	VeriSign Time Stam...		
	QuoVadis Root CA 2	QuoVadis Root CA 2	11/24/2031	Server Authenticati...	QuoVadis Root CA 2		
	QuoVadis Root Certification Au...	QuoVadis Root Certification Auth...	3/17/2021	Server Authenticati...	QuoVadis Root Cert...		
	SecureTrust CA	SecureTrust CA	12/31/2029	Server Authenticati...	Trustwave		CA

Figure 4-6 Microsoft Windows 10 trusted root digital certificates

Certificate chaining and root digital certificates can be seen by using a web browser to access the Cengage website. The root digital certificate (*DigiCert*) verifies the intermediate certificate (*DigiCert SHA2 High Assurance Server CA*) which in turn authenticates the digital certificate for the Cengage site (**.cengage.com*). This certificate chaining is seen in Figure 4-7. The details of the certificate can be seen in Figure 4-8 with the public key detail information displayed.

Domain Digital Certificates

Most digital certificates are web server digital certificates that are issued from a web server to a client (as illustrated in the previous example). Web server digital certificates perform two primary functions. First, they ensure the authenticity of the web server to the client. Second, web server digital certificates can ensure the authenticity of the cryptographic connection to the web server. Web servers can set up secure cryptographic connections so that all transmitted data is encrypted by providing the server's public key with a digital certificate to the client. This handshake setup between web browser and web server, also called a **key exchange**, is illustrated in Figure 4-9:

1. The web browser sends a message ("ClientHello") to the server that contains information including the list of cryptographic algorithms that the client supports.

Figure 4-7   Certificate chaining for cengage.com

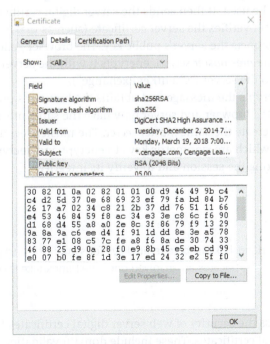

Figure 4-8   Certificate details

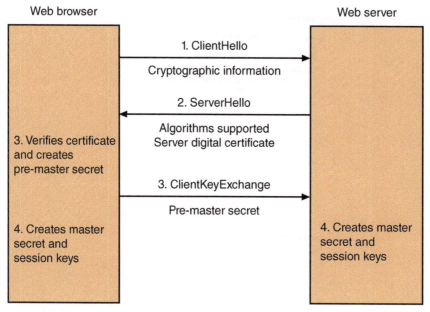

Figure 4-9 Key exchange

2. The web server responds ("ServerHello") by indicating which cryptographic algorithm will be used. It then sends the server digital certificate to the browser.
3. The web browser verifies the server certificate (such as making sure it has not expired) and extracts the server's public key. The browser generates a random value (called the *pre-master secret*), encrypts it with the server's public key, and sends it back to the server ("ClientKeyExchange").
4. The server decrypts the message and obtains the browser's pre-master secret. Because both the browser and server now have the same pre-master secret, they can each create the same *master secret*. The master secret is used to create **session keys**, which are symmetric keys to encrypt and decrypt information exchanged during the session and to verify its integrity.

Note

One of the goals of the handshake is to generate keys for symmetric encryption using 3DES or AES. No public keys or certificates are involved once the handshake is completed.

In order to address the security of web server digital certificates there are several types of domain digital certificates. These include domain validation digital certificates, extended validation digital certificates, wildcard digital certificates, and subject alternative names digital certificates.

Domain Validation

Some CAs issue only entry-level certificates that provide domain-only validation. These digital certificates only authenticate that a specific organization has the right to use a particular domain name. A **domain validation digital certificate** verifies the identity of the entity that has control over the domain name. These certificates indicate nothing regarding the trustworthiness of the individuals behind the site; they simply verify who has control of that domain.

Note

Because domain validation digital certificates are not verifying the identity of a person but only the control over a site, they often can be generated automatically and are very inexpensive or even free.

A domain validation digital certificate displays a green padlock icon in the web browser. This is shown in Figure 4-10 for a Google Chrome browser.

Figure 4-10   Domain validation padlock

Source: Google Chrome web browser

Extended Validation (EV)

An enhanced type of domain digital certificate is the **Extended Validation (EV) certificate**. This type of certificate requires more extensive verification of the legitimacy of the business. Requirements include:

- The CA must pass an independent audit verifying that it follows the EV standards.
- The existence and identity of the website owner, including its legal existence, physical address, and operational presence, must be verified by the CA.
- The CA must verify that the website is the registered holder and has exclusive control of the domain name.
- The authorization of the individual(s) applying for the certificate must be verified by the CA, and a valid signature from an officer of the company must accompany the application.

When a web browser indicates to users that they are connected to a website that uses the higher-level EV, a green padlock along with the site's name is displayed, as seen in Figure 4-11.

Figure 4-11   EV validation padlock

Source: Google Chrome web browser

Wildcard

A **wildcard digital certificate** is used to validate a main domain along with all subdomains. For example, a domain validation digital certificate for *www.example.com* would only cover that specific site. A wildcard digital certificate for **.example.com* would cover *www.example.com, mail.example.com, ftp.example.com*, and any other subdomains.

Subject Alternative Name (SAN)

A **Subject Alternative Name (SAN)** digital certificate, also known as a *Unified Communications Certificate (UCC)*, is primarily used for Microsoft Exchange servers or unified communications (the integration of different types of electronic communication like email, SMS text messaging, fax, etc.). This certificate allows multiple server or domain names to use the same secure certificate by allowing different values to be associated with the certificate.

Hardware and Software Digital Certificates

In addition to root digital certificates and domain digital certificates, there are more specific digital certificates that relate to hardware and software. These include:

- *Machine digital certificate.* A **machine digital certificate** is used to verify the identity of a device in a network transaction. For example, a laser printer may use a machine digital certificate to verify to the client that it is an authentic and authorized device on the network.

> **Note** 📎
>
> Many network devices can create their own self-signed machine digital certificates.

- *Code signing digital certificate.* Digital certificates are used by software developers to digitally sign a program to prove that the software comes from the entity that signed it and no unauthorized third party has altered or compromised it. This is known as a **code signing digital certificate**. When the installation program is launched that contains a code digital certificate, a popup window appears that says *Verified publisher* while an installation program that lacks a code digital certificate says *Publisher: Unknown*.
- *Email digital certificate.* An **email digital certificate** allows a user to digitally sign and encrypt mail messages. Typically, only the user's name and email address are required to receive this certificate.

> **Note** 📎
>
> In addition to email messages, digital certificates also can be used to authenticate the authors of documents. For example, a user can create a Microsoft Word or Adobe Portable Document Format (PDF) document and then use a digital certificate to create a digital signature.

Digital Certificate Formats

The most widely accepted digital certificates are defined by a division of the International Telecommunication Union (ITU) known as the Telecommunication Standardization Sector (ITU-T). These digital certificates adhere to the *X.509* standard. Digital certificates following this standard can be read or written by any application that follows X.509.

Note

X.509 systems also include a method for creating a Certificate Revocation List (CRL).

All X.509 certificates follow the standard ITU-T X.690, which specifies one of three different encoding formats: *Basic Encoding Rules (BER)*, **Canonical Encoding Rules (CER)**, and **Distinguished Encoding Rules (DER)**. The X.509 certificates themselves can be contained within different file formats. Table 4-3 shows several of the different formats.

Table 4-3   X.509 file formats

Name	File extension	Comments
Privacy Enhancement Mail (PEM)	.pem	Designed to provide confidentiality and integrity to emails, it uses DER encoding and can have multiple certificates.
Personal Information Exchange (PFX)	.pfx	The preferred file format for creating certificates to authenticate applications or websites, PFX is password protected because it contains both private and public keys.
PKCS#12	.p12	One of a numbered set of 15 standards defined by RSA Corporation, it is based on the RSA public key algorithm and like PFX contains both private and public keys.

Public Key Infrastructure (PKI)

Certification

1.6 Explain the impact associated with types of vulnerabilities.

6.4 Given a scenario, implement public key infrastructure.

One of the important management tools for the use of digital certificates and asymmetric cryptography is public key infrastructure. It is important to understand public key infrastructure, how it is managed and how key management is performed, as well as knowing PKI trust models.

What Is Public Key Infrastructure (PKI)?

One single digital certificate between Alice and Bob involves multiple entities and technologies. Asymmetric cryptography must be used to create the public and private keys, an intermediate CA must verify Bob's identity, the CA must issue the certificate, the digital certificate must be placed in a CR and moved to a CRL when it expires, and so on. In an organization where multiple users have multiple digital certificates, it can quickly become overwhelming to individually manage all of these entities. In short, there needs to be a consistent means to manage digital certificates.

Public key infrastructure (PKI) is what you might expect from its name: it is the underlying infrastructure for the management of public keys used in digital certificates. PKI is a framework for all the entities involved in digital certificates for digital certificate management—including hardware, software, people, policies, and procedures—to create, store, distribute, and revoke digital certificates. In short, PKI is digital certificate management.

> **Note** 📎
>
> PKI is sometimes erroneously applied to a broader range of cryptography topics beyond managing digital certificates. It is sometimes defined as that which supports other public key-enabled security services or certifies users of a security application. PKI should be understood as the framework for digital certificate management only.

Trust Models

Trust may be defined as confidence in or reliance on another person or entity. One of the principal foundations of PKI is that of trust: Alice must trust that the public key in Bob's digital certificate actually belongs to him.

A **trust model** refers to the type of trust relationship that can exist between individuals or entities. In one type of trust model, *direct trust*, a relationship exists between two individuals because one person knows the other person. Because Alice knows Bob—she has seen him, she can recognize him in a crowd, she has spoken with him—she can trust that the digital certificate that Bob personally gives to her contains his public key. A *third-party trust* refers to a situation in which two individuals trust each other because each trusts a third party. If Alice does not know Bob, this does not mean that she can never trust his digital certificate. Instead, if she trusts a third-party entity who knows Bob, then she can trust that his digital certificate with the public key is Bob's.

> **Note** 📎
>
> An example of a third-party trust is a courtroom. Although the defendant and prosecutor may not trust one another, they both can trust the judge (a third party) to be fair and impartial. In that case, they implicitly trust each other because they share a common relationship with the judge.

Essentially three PKI trust models use a CA. These are the hierarchical trust model, the distributed trust model, and the bridge trust model.

> **Note** 📎
>
> A less secure trust model that uses no CA is called the *web of trust* model and is based on direct trust. Each user signs his digital certificate and then exchanges certificates with all other users. Because all users trust each other, each user can sign the certificate of all other users. Pretty Good Privacy (PGP) uses the web of trust model.

Hierarchical Trust Model

The *hierarchical trust model* assigns a single hierarchy with one master CA called the *root*. This root signs all digital certificate authorities with a single key. A hierarchical trust model is illustrated in Figure 4-12.

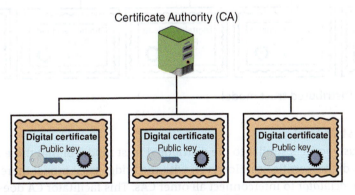

Figure 4-12   Hierarchical trust model

A hierarchical trust model can be used in an organization where one CA is responsible for only the digital certificates for that organization. However, on a larger scale, a hierarchical trust model has several limitations. First, if the CA's single private key were to be compromised, then all digital certificates would be worthless.

Also, having a single CA who must verify and sign all digital certificates may create a significant backlog.

Distributed Trust Model

Instead of having a single CA, as in the hierarchical trust model, the *distributed trust model* has multiple CAs that sign digital certificates. This essentially eliminates the limitations of a hierarchical trust model. The loss of a CA's private key would compromise only those digital certificates for which it had signed, and the workload of verifying and signing digital certificates can be distributed. In addition, these CAs can delegate authority to other intermediate CAs to sign digital certificates. The distributed trust model is the basis for most digital certificates used on the Internet. A distributed trust model is illustrated in Figure 4-13.

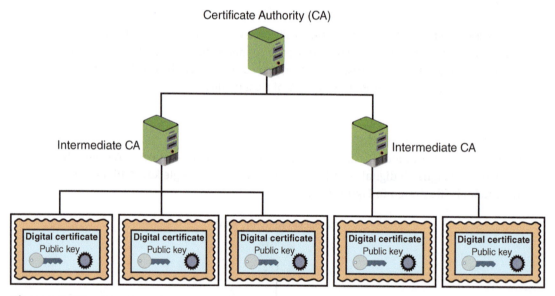

Figure 4-13 Distributed trust model

Bridge Trust Model

The *bridge trust model* is similar to the distributed trust model in that there is no single CA that signs digital certificates. However, with the bridge trust model there is one CA that acts as a *facilitator* to interconnect all other CAs. This facilitator CA does not issue digital certificates; instead, it acts as the hub between hierarchical trust models and distributed trust models. This allows the different models to be linked together. The bridge trust model is shown in Figure 4-14.

Managing PKI

An organization that uses multiple digital certificates on a regular basis needs to properly manage those digital certificates. This includes establishing policies and practices and determining the life cycle of a digital certificate.

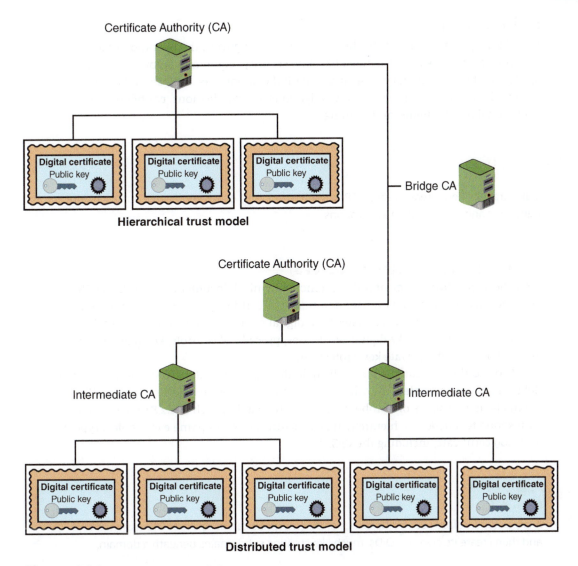

Figure 4-14   Bridge trust model

Certificate Policy (CP)

A *certificate policy (CP)* is a published set of rules that govern the operation of a PKI. The CP provides recommended baseline security requirements for the use and operation of CA, intermediate CA, and other PKI components. A CP should cover such topics as CA or intermediate CA obligations, user obligations, confidentiality, operational requirements, and training.

Note

Many organizations create a single CP to support not only digital certificates but also digital signatures and all encryption applications.

Certificate Practice Statement (CPS)

A *certificate practice statement (CPS)* is a more technical document than a CP. A CPS describes in detail how the CA uses and manages certificates. Additional topics for a CPS include how end users register for a digital certificate, how to issue digital certificates, when to revoke digital certificates, procedural controls, key pair generation and installation, and private key protection.

X.509 certificates contain a specific field that can link to the associated CP. Another field can contain an **object identifier (OID)**, which names an object or entity. OIDs are made up of a series of numbers separated with a dot, such as *1.2.840.113585*, and correspond to a *node* in a hierarchy tree structure. OIDs can name every object type in an X.509 certificate, including the CPS.

Note

A large standardized set of OIDs exists, or an enterprise can have a *root* OID assigned to it and then create its own sub-OIDs, much like creating subdomains beneath a domain.

Certificate Life Cycle

Digital certificates should not last forever. Employees leave, new hardware is installed, applications are updated, and cryptographic standards evolve. Each of these changes affects the usefulness of a digital certificate. The life cycle of a certificate is typically divided into four parts:

1. *Creation*. At this stage the certificate is created and issued to the user. Before the digital certificate is generated, the user must be positively identified. The extent to which the user's identification must be confirmed can vary, depending upon the type of certificate and any existing security policies. Once the user's

identification has been verified, the request is sent to the CA for a digital certificate. The CA can then apply its appropriate signing key to the certificate, effectively signing the public key. The relevant fields can be updated by the CA, and the certificate is then forwarded to the RA (if one is being used). The CA also can keep a local copy of the certificate it generated. A certificate, once issued, can be published to a public directory if necessary.

2. *Suspension*. This stage could occur once or multiple times throughout the life of a digital certificate if the certificate's validity must be temporarily suspended. This may occur, for example, when an employee is on a leave of absence. During this time, it may be important that the user's digital certificate not be used for any reason until she returns. Upon the user's return, the suspension can be withdrawn or the certificate can be revoked.

3. *Revocation*. At this stage the certificate is no longer valid. Under certain situations a certificate may be revoked before its normal expiration date, such as when a user's private key is lost or compromised. When a digital certificate is revoked, the CA updates its internal records and any CRL with the required certificate information and timestamp (a revoked certificate is identified in a CRL by its certificate serial number). The CA signs the CRL and places it in a public repository so that other applications using certificates can access this repository to determine the status of a certificate.

> **Caution** ⚠
>
> Either the user or the CA can initiate a revocation process.

4. *Expiration*. At the expiration stage the certificate can no longer be used. Every certificate issued by a CA must have an expiration date. Once it has expired, the certificate may not be used any longer for any type of authentication and the user will be required to follow a process to be issued a new certificate with a new expiration date.

Key Management

One common vulnerability that allows threat actors to compromise a PKI is improper certificate and key management. Because keys form the foundation of PKI systems, it is important that they be carefully managed. Proper key management includes key storage, key usage, and key handling procedures.

Key Storage

The means of storing keys in a PKI system is important. Public keys can be stored by embedding them within digital certificates, while private keys can be stored on the user's local system. The drawback to software-based storage is that it can leave keys open to attacks: vulnerabilities in the client operating system, for example, can expose keys to attackers.

Storing keys in hardware is an alternative to software-based storage. For storing public keys, special CA root and intermediate CA hardware devices can be used. Private keys can be stored on smart cards or in tokens.

> **Note** 📎
>
> Whether private keys are stored in hardware or software, it is important that they be adequately protected. To ensure basic protection, never share the key in plaintext, always store keys in files or folders that are themselves password protected or encrypted, do not make copies of keys, and destroy expired keys.

Key Usage

If more security is needed than a single set of public and private keys, multiple pairs of dual keys can be created. One pair of keys may be used to encrypt information, and the public key can be backed up to another location. The second pair would be used only for digital signatures, and the public key in that pair would never be backed up.

Key Handling Procedures

Certain procedures can help ensure that keys are properly handled. These procedures include:

- *Escrow.* **Key escrow** refers to a process in which keys are managed by a third party, such as a trusted CA. In key escrow, the private key is split and each half is encrypted. The two halves are registered and sent to the third party, which stores each half in a separate location. A user can then retrieve the two halves, combine them, and use this new copy of the private key for decryption. Key escrow relieves the end user from the worry of losing her private key. The drawback to this system is that after the user has retrieved the two halves of the key and combined them to create a copy of the key, that copy of the key can be vulnerable to attacks.
- *Expiration.* Keys have expiration dates. This prevents an attacker who may have stolen a private key from being able to decrypt messages for an indefinite period. Some systems set keys to expire after a set period by default.
- *Renewal.* Instead of letting a key expire and then creating a new key, an existing key can be renewed. With renewal, the original public and private keys can continue to be used and new keys do not have to be generated. However, continually renewing keys makes them more vulnerable to theft or misuse.
- *Revocation.* Whereas all keys should expire after a set period, a key may need to be revoked prior to its expiration date. For example, the need for revoking a key may be the result of an employee being terminated from his position. Revoked keys cannot be reinstated. The CA should be immediately notified when a key is revoked and then the status of that key should be entered on the CRL.

- *Recovery.* What happens if an employee is hospitalized, yet the organization for which she works needs to transact business using her keys? Different techniques may be used. Some CA systems have an embedded key recovery system in which a *key recovery agent (KRA)* is designated, who is a highly trusted person responsible for recovering lost or damaged digital certificates. Digital certificates can then be archived along with the user's private key. If the user is unavailable or if the certificate is lost, the certificate with the private key can be recovered. Another technique is known as *M-of-N control*. A user's private key is encrypted and divided into a specific number of parts, such as three. The parts are distributed to other individuals, with an overlap so that multiple individuals have the same part. For example, the three parts could be distributed to six people, with two people each having the same part. This is known as the N group. If it is necessary to recover the key, a smaller subset of the N group, known as the M group, must meet and agree that the key should be recovered. If a majority of the M group can agree, they can then piece the key together. M-of-N control is illustrated in Figure 4-15.

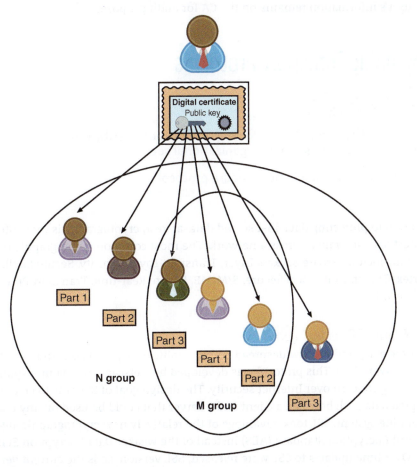

Figure 4-15   M-of-N control

> **Note**
>
> The reason for distributing parts of the key to multiple users is that the absence of one member would not prevent the key from being recovered.

- *Suspension*. The revocation of a key is permanent; key suspension is for a set period. For example, if an employee is on an extended medical leave it may be necessary to suspend the use of her key for security reasons. A suspended key can be later reinstated. As with revocation, the CA should be immediately notified when a key is suspended, and the status of that key should be checked on the CRL to verify that it is no longer valid.
- *Destruction*. Key destruction removes all private and public keys along with the user's identification information in the CA. When a key is revoked or expires, the user's information remains on the CA for audit purposes.

Cryptographic Transport Protocols

 Certification

2.1 Install and configure network components, both hardware- and software-based, to support organizational security.

2.6 Given a scenario, implement secure protocols.

In addition to protecting data-in-use and data-at-rest, cryptography is most often used to protect data-in-transit across a network. The most common cryptographic transport algorithms include Secure Sockets Layer, Transport Layer Security, Secure Shell, Hypertext Transport Protocol Secure, S/MIME, Secure Real-time Transport Protocol, and IP security.

Secure Sockets Layer (SSL)

One of the early and most widespread cryptographic transport algorithms is **Secure Sockets Layer (SSL)**. This protocol was developed by Netscape in 1994 in response to the growing concern over Internet security. The design goal of SSL was to create an encrypted data path between a client and a server that could be used on any platform or operating system. SSL took advantage of the relatively new cryptographic algorithm Advanced Encryption Standard (AES) instead of the weaker Data Encryption Standard (DES). Over time updates to SSL were released; SSL version 3.0 is the current version.

Transport Layer Security (TLS)

Transport Layer Security (TLS) is another widespread cryptographic transport algorithm. SSL v3.0 served as the basis for TLS v1.0. Although the algorithms SSL and TLS are often used interchangeably or even in conjunction with each other (*TLS/SSL*), this is not correct. Although TLS v1.0 was considered marginally more secure than SSL v3.0, subsequent versions of TLS (v1.1 and v1.2) are significantly more secure and address several vulnerabilities present in SSL v3.0 and TLS v1.0.

Even though TLS v1.2 is the current version of the protocol, many websites continue to support older and weaker versions of TLS and SSL in order to provide the broadest range of compatibility for older web browsers. However, most websites are migrating away from older versions and protocols to support TLS v1.2. Table 4-4 lists a survey of web servers that used SSL and TLS in 2014 compared to current usage (servers may support multiple protocols).[2]

Note 🔗

As noted in steps 1 and 2 in Figure 4-9, the web browser provides a list of all the cryptographic algorithms that it supports, but the web server makes the ultimate decision of which will be used.

Table 4-4   Website support of SSL and TLS

Protocol supported	Percentage of websites 2014	Percentage of current websites	Protocol security strength
SSL v2.0	24.2	5.3	Should not be used
SSL v3.0	99.4	17.4	Considered obsolete
TLS v1.0	99.3	95.0	Must be carefully configured
TLS v1.1	25.7	81.9	No known vulnerabilities
TLS v1.2	28.2	84.6	No known vulnerabilities

A *cipher suite* is a named combination of the encryption, authentication, and message authentication code (MAC) algorithms that are used with SSL and TLS. These are negotiated between the web browser and web server during the initial connection handshake. Depending on the different algorithms that are selected, the overall security of the transmission may be either strong or weak. For example, using RC4 instead of AES would significantly weaken the cipher suite. Another factor is the length of the keys. Keys of less than 2048 bits are considered weak, keys of 2048 bits are considered good, while keys of 4096 bits are strong.

> **Note** 📎
>
> Cipher suites typically use descriptive names to indicate their components. For example, CipherSuite *SSL_RSA_WITH_RC4_128_MD5* specifies that RSA will be used for key exchange and authentication algorithm, RC4 encryption algorithm using a 128–bit key will be used, and MD5 will be the MAC algorithm.

Secure Shell (SSH)

Secure Shell (SSH) is an encrypted alternative to the Telnet protocol that is used to access remote computers. SSH is a Linux/UNIX-based command interface and protocol for securely accessing a remote computer. SSH is actually a suite of three utilities— slogin, ssh, and scp—that are secure versions of the unsecure UNIX counterpart utilities. These commands are summarized in Table 4-5. Both the client and server ends of the connection are authenticated using a digital certificate, and passwords are protected by being encrypted. SSH can even be used as a tool for secure network backups.

Table 4-5   SSH commands

UNIX command name	Description	Syntax	Secure command replacement
rlogin	Log on to remote computer	rlogin *remotecomputer*	slogin
Rcp	Copy files between remote computers	rcp [*options*] *localfile remotecomputer:filename*	scp
Rsh	Executing commands on a remote host without logging on	rsh *remotecomputer command*	Ssh

> **Note** 📎
>
> The first version of SSH was released in 1995 by a researcher at the Helsinki University of Technology after his university was the victim of a password-sniffing attack.

Hypertext Transport Protocol Secure (HTTPS)

One common use of TLS and SSL is to secure Hypertext Transport Protocol (HTTP) communications between a browser and a web server. This secure version is actually *plain* HTTP sent over SSL or TLS and is called **Hypertext Transport Protocol Secure (HTTPS)**. HTTPS uses port 443 instead of HTTP's port 80. Users must enter URLs with *https://* instead of *http://*.

Note

Another cryptographic transport protocol for HTTP was Secure Hypertext Transport Protocol (SHTTP). However, it was not as secure as HTTPS and is now considered obsolete.

Secure/Multipurpose Internet Mail Extensions (S/MIME)

Secure/Multipurpose Internet Mail Extensions (S/MIME) is a protocol for securing email messages. It allows users to send encrypted messages that are also digitally signed.

Note

MIME is a standard for how an electronic message will be organized, so S/MIME describes how encryption information and a digital certificate can be included as part of the message body.

Secure Real-time Transport Protocol (SRTP)

The **Secure Real-time Transport Protocol (SRTP)** has several similarities to S/MIME. Just as S/MIME is intended to protect MIME communications, SRTP is a secure extension protecting transmissions using the *Real-Time Transport Protocol (RTP)*. Also, as S/MIME is designed to protect only email communications, SRTP provides protection for Voice over IP (VoIP) communications. SRTP adds security features, such as message authentication and confidentiality, for VoIP communications.

Note

The SRTP protocol was first published in 2004.

IP Security (IPsec)

Internet Protocol Security (IPsec) is a protocol suite for securing Internet Protocol (IP) communications. IPsec encrypts and authenticates each IP packet of a session between hosts or networks. IPsec can provide protection to a much wider range of applications than SSL or TLS.

IPsec is considered to be a *transparent* security protocol. It is *transparent* to the following entities:

- *Applications*. Programs do not have to be modified to run under IPsec.
- *Users*. Unlike some security tools, users do not need to be trained on specific security procedures (such as encrypting with PGP).
- *Software*. Because IPsec is implemented in a device such as a firewall or router, no software changes must be made on the local client.

Unlike SSL, which is implemented as a part of the user application, IPsec is in the operating system or the communication hardware. IPsec is more likely to operate at a faster speed because it can cooperate closely with other system programs and the hardware.

IPsec provides three areas of protection that correspond to three IPsec protocols:

- *Authentication*. IPsec authenticates that packets received were sent from the source. This is identified in the header of the packet to ensure that no specific attacks took place to alter the contents of the packet. This is accomplished by the **Authentication Header (AH)** protocol.
- *Confidentiality*. By encrypting the packets, IPsec ensures that no other parties could view the contents. Confidentiality is achieved through the **Encapsulating Security Payload (ESP)** protocol. ESP supports authentication of the sender and encryption of data.
- *Key management*. IPsec manages the keys to ensure that they are not intercepted or used by unauthorized parties. For IPsec to work, the sending and receiving devices must share a key. This is accomplished through a protocol known as *Internet Security Association and Key Management Protocol/Oakley* (ISAKMP/Oakley), which generates the key and authenticates the user using techniques such as digital certificates.

IPsec supports two encryption modes: transport and tunnel. **Transport mode** encrypts only the data portion (payload) of each packet yet leaves the header unencrypted. The more secure **tunnel mode** encrypts both the header and the data portion. IPsec accomplishes transport and tunnel modes by adding new headers to the IP packet. The entire original packet (header and payload) is then treated as the data portion of the new packet.

> **Note** 📎
>
> Because tunnel mode protects the entire packet, it is generally used in a network-to-network communication, while transport mode is used when a device must see the source and destination addresses to route the packet.

Chapter Summary

- Cryptography that is improperly applied can lead to vulnerabilities that will be exploited. It is necessary to understand the different options that relate to cryptography so that it can be implemented correctly. A key must be strong to resist attacks. A strong key must be random with no predictable pattern. Keys should also be long and the length of time for which a key is authorized for use should be limited. Any attempt to keep an algorithm secret will not result in strong security. A block cipher mode of operation specifies how block ciphers should handle blocks of plaintext. Some of the most common are Electronic Code Book (ECB), Cipher Block Chaining (CBC), Counter (CTR), and the Galois/Counter (GCM) mode. A crypto service provider allows an application to implement an encryption algorithm for execution. Typically, crypto service providers implement cryptographic algorithms by calling crypto modules to perform the specific tasks. Some cryptographic algorithms require that in addition to a key another value can or must be input. A salt is a value that can be used to ensure that plaintext, when hashed, will not consistently result in the same digest. A nonce is a value that must be unique within some specified scope, such as for a given period or for an entire session. An initialization vector (IV) is a nonce that must be selected in a non-predictable way.

- A digital certificate is the user's public key that has been digitally signed by a trusted third party who verifies the owner and that the public key belongs to that owner. It also binds the public key to the certificate. A user who wants a digital certificate generate the public and private keys to be used and then complete a request known as a Certificate Signing Request (CSR). The user electronically signs the CSR by affixing her public key and then sending it to an intermediate certificate authority (CA), who processes the CSR and verifies the authenticity of the user. The intermediate CAs perform functions on behalf of a certificate authority (CA) that is responsible for digital certificates. A common method to ensure the security and integrity of a root CA is to keep it in an offline state from the network (offline CA) rather than having it directly connected to a network (online CA).

- A certificate repository (CR) is a list of approved digital certificates. Revoked digital certificates are listed in a Certificate Revocation List (CRL), which can be accessed to check the certificate status of other users. The status also can be checked through the Online Certificate Status Protocol (OCSP). Because digital certificates are used extensively on the Internet, all modern web browsers are preconfigured with a default list of CAs and the ability to automatically update certificate information. When using OCSP stapling web servers send queries to the Responder OCSP server at regular intervals to receive a signed time-stamped OCSP response.

- There are several different types of digital certificates. The process of verifying that a digital certificate is genuine depends upon certificate chaining, or linking several certificates together to establish trust between all the certificates involved. The endpoint of the chain is the user digital certificate itself. The beginning point of the chain is a specific type of digital certificate known as a root digital certificate, which is created and verified by a CA and also self-signed. Between the root digital certificate and the user certificate can be one or more intermediate certificates that have been issued by intermediate CAs. Root digital certificates and intermediate certificates are packaged as part of modern operating systems, can be part of web browser software, or hard-coded within the app (program) that is using the certificate.

- Domain validation digital certificates verify the identity of the entity that has control over the domain name but indicate nothing regarding the trustworthiness of the individuals behind the site. Extended Validation (EV) certificates requires more extensive verification of the legitimacy of the business. A wildcard digital certificate is used to validate a main domain along with all subdomains. A Subject Alternative Name (SAN) digital certificate, also known as a Unified Communications Certificate (UCC), is primarily used for Microsoft Exchange servers or unified communications. A machine digital certificate is used to verify the identity of a device in a network transaction. Digital certificates are used by software developers to digitally sign a program to prove that the software comes from the entity that signed it and no unauthorized third party has altered or compromised it are called code signing digital certificates. An email digital certificate allows a user to digitally sign and encrypt mail messages. The most widely accepted format for digital certificates is the X.509 international standard.

- A public key infrastructure (PKI) is a framework for all the entities involved in digital certificates—including hardware, software, people, policies, and procedures—to create, store, distribute, and revoke digital certificates. One of the principal foundations of PKI is that of trust. Three basic PKI trust models use a CA. The hierarchical trust model assigns a single hierarchy with one master CA called the root, who signs all digital certificate authorities with a single key. The bridge trust model is similar to the distributed trust model. No single CA signs digital certificates, and yet the CA acts as a facilitator to interconnect all other CAs. The distributed trust model has multiple CAs that sign digital certificates.

- An organization that uses multiple digital certificates on a regular basis needs to properly manage those digital certificates. Such management includes establishing policies and practices and determining the life cycle of a digital certificate. Because keys form the very foundation of PKI systems, it is important that they be carefully managed.

- Cryptography is commonly used to protect data-in-transit. Secure Sockets Layer (SSL) was an early cryptographic transport protocol but is being replaced with the more secure Transport Layer Security (TLS). Secure Shell (SSH) is a Linux/UNIX-based command interface and protocol for securely accessing a remote computer communicating over the Internet. Hypertext Transport Protocol Secure (HTTPS), a secure version for web communications, is HTTP sent over SSL or TLS. Secure/Multipurpose Internet Mail Extensions (S/MIME) is a protocol for securing email messages. IP security (IPsec) is a set of protocols developed to support the secure exchange of packets. The Secure Real-time Transport Protocol (SRTP) provides protection for Voice over IP (VoIP) communications.

Key Terms

Authentication Header (AH)

block cipher mode of
operation

Canonical Encoding Rules
(CER)

certificate authority (CA)

certificate chaining

Certificate Revocation List
(CRL)

Certificate Signing Request
(CSR)

Cipher Block Chaining (CBC)

code signing digital
certificate

Counter (CTR)

crypto modules

crypto service provider

digital certificate

Distinguished Encoding
Rules (DER)

domain validation digital
certificate

Electronic Code Book (ECB)

email digital certificate

Encapsulating Security
Payload (ESP)

Extended Validation (EV)
certificate

Galois/Counter (GCM)

Hypertext Transport
Protocol Secure (HTTPS)

initialization vector (IV)

intermediate certificate
authority (CA)

Internet Protocol Security
(IPsec)

key escrow

key exchange

key strength

machine digital certificate

nonce

object identifier (OID)

offline CA

online CA

Online Certificate Status
Protocol (OCSP)

Personal Information
Exchange (PFX)

pinning

PKCS#12

Privacy Enhancement Mail
(PEM)

public key infrastructure
(PKI)

root digital certificate

salt

secret algorithm

Secure Real-time Transport
Protocol (SRTP)

Secure Shell (SSH)

Secure Sockets Layer (SSL)

Secure/Multipurpose
Internet Mail Extensions
(S/MIME)

self-signed

session keys

stapling

Subject Alternative Name
(SAN)

Transport Layer Security
(TLS)

transport mode

trust model

tunnel mode

user digital certificate

wildcard digital certificate

Review Questions

1. Which of the following is NOT a method
   for strengthening a key?
   a. Randomness
   b. Cryptoperiod
   c. Length
   d. Variability

2. Which of the following block ciphers
   XORs each block of plaintext with the
   previous block of ciphertext before being
   encrypted?

   a. Electronic Code Book (ECB)
   b. Galois/Counter (GCM)
   c. Counter (CTR)
   d. Cipher Block Chaining (CBC)

3. What entity calls in crypto modules to
   perform cryptographic tasks?
   a. Certificate Authority (CA)
   b. OCSP Chain
   c. Intermediate CA
   d. Crypto service provider

4. _____ are symmetric keys to encrypt and decrypt information exchanged during the session and to verify its integrity.
   a. Encrypted signatures
   b. Session keys
   c. Digital certificates
   d. Digital digests

5. Which of these is considered the strongest cryptographic transport protocol?
   a. TLS v1.2
   b. TLS v1.0
   c. SSL v2.0
   d. SSL v2.0

6. The strongest technology that would assure Alice that Bob is the sender of a message is a(n) _____.
   a. digital signature
   b. encrypted signature
   c. digest
   d. digital certificate

7. A digital certificate associates _____.
   a. a user's public key with his private key
   b. the user's identity with his public key
   c. a user's private key with the public key
   d. a private key with a digital signature

8. Digital certificates can be used for each of these EXCEPT _____.
   a. to verify the authenticity of the Registration Authorizer
   b. to encrypt channels to provide secure communication between clients and servers
   c. to verify the identity of clients and servers on the Web
   d. to encrypt messages for secure email communications

9. An entity that issues digital certificates is a _____.
   a. certificate signatory (CS)
   b. digital signer (DS)

   c. certificate authority (CA)
   d. signature authority (SA)

10. A centralized directory of digital certificates is called a(n) _____.
    a. Digital Signature Permitted Authorization (DSPA)
    b. Digital Signature Approval List (DSAP)
    c. Certificate Repository (CR)
    d. Authorized Digital Signature (ADS)

11. _____ performs a real-time lookup of a digital certificate's status.
    a. Certificate Revocation List (CRL)
    b. Real-Time CA Verification (RTCAV)
    c. Online Certificate Status Protocol (OCSP)
    d. CA Registry Database (CARD)

12. What is a value that can be used to ensure that hashed plaintext will not consistently result in the same digest?
    a. Algorithm
    b. Initialization vector (IV)
    c. Nonce
    d. Salt

13. Which digital certificate displays the name of the entity behind the website?
    a. Online Certificate Status Certificate
    b. Extended Validation (EV) Certificate
    c. Session Certificate
    d. X.509 Certificate

14. Which trust model has multiple CAs, one of which acts as a facilitator?
    a. Bridge
    b. Hierarchical
    c. Distributed
    d. Web

15. Which statement is NOT true regarding hierarchical trust models?
    a. It is designed for use on a large scale.
    b. The root signs all digital certificate authorities with a single key.
    c. It assigns a single hierarchy with one master CA.
    d. The master CA is called the root.

16. Public key infrastructure (PKI) _____.
    a. generates public/private keys automatically
    b. creates private key cryptography
    c. is the management of digital certificates
    d. requires the use of an RA instead of a CA
17. A(n) _____ is a published set of rules that govern the operation of a PKI.
    a. signature resource guide (SRG)
    b. enforcement certificate (EF)
    c. certificate practice statement (CPS)
    d. certificate policy (CP)
18. Which of these is NOT part of the certificate life cycle?
    a. Expiration
    b. Revocation

    c. Authorization
    d. Creation
19. _____ refers to a situation in which keys are managed by a third party, such as a trusted CA.
    a. Key authorization
    b. Key escrow
    c. Remote key administration
    d. Trusted key authority
20. _____ is a protocol for securely accessing a remote computer.
    a. Transport Layer Security (TLS)
    b. Secure Shell (SSH)
    c. Secure Sockets Layer (SSL)
    d. Secure Hypertext Transport Protocol (SHTTP)

Hands-On Projects

Note
If you are concerned about installing any of the software in these projects on your regular computer, you can instead install the software in the Windows virtual machine created in the Chapter 1 Hands-On Projects 1-3 and 1-4. Software installed within the virtual machine will not impact the host computer.

Project 4-1: Using SSL Server and Client Tests
In this project, you will use online tests to determine the security of web servers and your local web browser.
1. Go to **www.ssllabs.com**.

Note
It is not unusual for websites to change the location of where files are stored. If the URL above no longer functions, open a search engine and search for "Qualys SSL Server Test".

2. Click **Test your server >>**.
3. Click the first website listed under **Recent Best-Rate**.

4. Note the grade given for this site. Under **Summary** note the **Overall Rating** along with the scores for **Certificate, Protocol Support, Key Exchange**, and **Cipher Strength**, which make up the cipher suite.

5. If this site did not receive an Overall Rating of *A* under **Summary**, you will see the reasons listed. Read through these. Would you agree? Why?

6. Scroll down through the document and read through the **Certificate #1** information. Note the information supplied regarding the digital certificates. Under **Certification Paths** click **Click here to expand** if necessary to view the certificate chaining. What can you tell about it?

7. Scroll down to **Configuration**. Note the list of protocols supported and not supported. If this site was to increase its security, which protocols should it no longer support? Why?

8. Under **Cipher Suites** interpret the suites listed. Notice that they are given in server-preferred order. In order to increase its security, which cipher suite should be listed first? Why?

9. Under **Handshake Simulation** select the web browser and operating system that you are using or is similar to what you are using. Read through the capabilities of this client interacting with this web server. Note particularly the order of preference of the cipher suites. Click the browser's back button when finished.

10. Scroll to the top of the page, then click **Scan Another >>.**

11. This time select one of the **Recent Worst-Rated** sites. As with the previous excellent example, now review the **Summary, Authentication, Configuration, Cipher Suites**, and **Handshake Simulation**. Would you agree with this site's score?

12. If necessary, return to the **SSL Report** page and click **Scan Another >>.**

13. Enter the name of your school or work URL and generate a report. What score did it receive?

14. Review the **Summary, Authentication, Configuration, Cipher Suites**, and **Handshake Simulation**. Would you agree with this site's score?

15. Make a list of the top five vulnerabilities that you believe should be addressed in order of priority. If possible, share this with any IT personnel who may be able to take action.

16. Click **Projects**.

17. Now test the capabilities of your web browser. Click **SSL Client Test**. Review the capabilities of your web browser. Print or take a screen capture of this page.

18. Close this web browser.

19. Now open a different web browser on this computer or on another computer.

20. Return to **www.ssllabs.com** and click **Projects** and then **SSL Client Test** to compare the two scores. From a security perspective, which browser is better? Why?

21. Close all windows.

Project 4-2: Viewing Digital Certificates

In this project, you will view digital certificate information using the Google Chrome web browser.

1. Use the Google Chrome web browser to go to **www.google.com.**

2. Note the green padlock in the address bar. Although you did not enter *https://*, nevertheless Google created a secure HTTPS connection. Why would it do that?

3. Click the three vertical buttons at the far edge of the address bar.
4. Click **More tools**.
5. Click **Developer tools**.
6. Click the **Security** tab (if the tab does not appear click the >> button to display more tabs).
7. Read the information under **Security Overview**.
8. Click **View certificate**.
9. Note the general information displayed under the **General** tab.
10. Now click the **Details** tab. The fields are displayed for this X.509 digital certificate.
11. Click **Valid to** to view the expiration date of this certificate.
12. Click **Public key** to view the public key associated with this digital certificate. Why is this site not concerned with distributing this key? How does embedding the public key in a digital certificate protect it from impersonators?
13. Click the **Certification Path** tab. Because web certificates are based on the distributed trust model, there is a *path* to the root certificate. Click the root certificate and click the **View Certificate** button. Click the **Details tab** and then click **Valid to**. Why is the expiration date of this root certificate longer than that of the website certificate? Click **OK** and then click **OK** again to close the Certificate window.
14. Click **Copy to File** . . .
15. Click **Next**.
16. Note the different file formats that are available. What do you know about each of these formats?
17. Click **Cancel** to close this window.
18. Close all windows.

Project 4-3: Viewing Digital Certificate Revocation Lists (CRL) and Untrusted Certificates

Revoked digital certificates are listed in a Certificate Revocation List (CRL), which can be accessed to check the certificate status of other users. In this project, you will view the CRL and any untrusted certificates on your Microsoft Windows computer.

1. Click the **Windows** + **X** keys.
2. Click **Command Prompt** (Admin).
3. Type **certmgr.msc** and then press **Enter**.
4. In the left pane, expand **Trusted Root Certification Authorities**.
5. In the left pane, double click **Certificates**. These are the CAs approved for this computer. Scroll through this list. How many of these have your heard of before?
6. In the left pane, expand **Intermediate Certification Authorities**.
7. Double-click **Certificates** to view the intermediate CAs. Scroll through this list.
8. Click **Certificate Revocation List**.
9. In the right pane, all revoked certificates will display. Select a revoked certificate and double-click it.

10. Read the information about it and click fields for more detail if necessary. Why do you think this certificate has been revoked? Close the Certificate Revocation List by clicking the **OK** button.
11. In the left pane, expand **Untrusted Certificates**.
12. Click **Certificates**. The certificates that are no longer trusted are listed in the right pane.
13. Double-click one of the untrusted certificates. Read the information about it and click fields for more detail if necessary. Why do you think this certificate is no longer trusted?
14. Click **OK** to close the Certificate dialog box.
15. Close all windows.

Project 4-4: Downloading and Installing a Digital Certificate

In this project, you will download and install a free S/MIME email digital certificate. Note that the Google Chrome browser must be used for downloading the certificate.

1. Use the Google Chrome web browser to go to **www.comodo.com/home /email-security/free-email-certificate.php**.

> **Note** 🔗
>
> It is not unusual for websites to change the location of where files are stored. If the URL above no longer functions, open a search engine and search for "Comodo Free Secure Email Certificate".

2. Click **Sign Up Now**.
3. You will be taken to the **Application for Secure Email Certificate**. Read through the information regarding your browser giving the website permission to generate a key. Follow its instructions.
4. Enter the requested information. Based on the information requested, how secure would you rate this certificate? Under which circumstances would you trust it? Why? Click **I ACCEPT** and then click **Next.**
5. Open your email account that you entered in the application and open the email from Comodo.
6. Click **Click & Install Comodo Email Certificate**.
7. Verify that the certificate is installed. Click **Start** and then type **cmd** and press **Enter**.
8. Type **certmgr.msc** and then press **Enter**.
9. In the left pane, expand **Personal**.
10. In the left pane, click **Certificates**. Your personal certificate should display.
11. Go to **www.comodo.com/support/products/email_certs/outlook.php** to view how to assign a personal certificate to a Microsoft Outlook email account.
12. Read through the steps for assigning a certificate, signing an email and encrypting an email. Do you think an average user would be able to follow these steps? Why or why not? What could be done to simplify the process?
13. Close all windows.

Case Projects

Case Project 4-1: Algorithm Input Values

The most common input values for cryptographic algorithms are salts, nonces, and initialization vectors. Search the Internet for information regarding each of these. How are they used? What are their strengths? How can they be compromised? Write a one paragraph description of each of three values.

Case Project 4-2: Recommended Cryptoperiods

How long should a key be used before it is replaced? Search the Internet for information regarding cryptoperiods for hash, symmetric, and asymmetric algorithms. Find at least three sources for each of the algorithms. Draw a table that lists the algorithms and the recommended time, and then calculate the average for each. Do you agree or disagree? What would be your recommendation on cryptoperiods for each? Why?

Case Project 4-3: Certificate Authorities (CAs)

Operating systems come packaged with many digital certificates from certificate authorities (CAs). Use the Internet to determine how to view the CAs for the type and version of operating system that you are using and view the list. How many have you heard of? How many are unknown? Select three of the publishers and research their organizations on the Internet. Write a one-paragraph summary of each CA.

Case Project 4-4: HTTPS

Hypertext Transport Protocol Secure (HTTPS) is becoming increasingly popular as a security protocol for web traffic. Some sites automatically use HTTPS for all transactions (like Google), while others require that users must configure it in their settings. Some argue that HTTPS should be used on all web traffic. What are the advantages of HTTPS? What are its disadvantages? How is it different from HTTP? How must the server be set up for HTTPS transactions? How would it protect you using a public Wi-Fi connection at a local coffee shop? Should all web traffic be required to use HTTPS? Why or why not? Write a one-page paper of your research.

Case Project 4-5: Block Cipher Modes of Operation

Research block cipher modes of operation. Find information regarding how ECB can be compromised and write a detailed description of that. Then research one of the other modes (CBC, CTR, or GCM) in detail. Draw a picture of how this mode functions by turning plaintext into ciphertext. Write a detailed description of your research.

Case Project 4-6: Digital Certificate Costs

Use the Internet to research the costs of the different types of digital certificates: domain validation, EV, wildcard, SAM, machine, code signing, and email. Look up at least three different providers of each, and create a table listing the type of certificate, the costs, and the length of time the certificate is valid.

Case Project 4-7: Lake Point Consulting Services

Lake Point Consulting Services (LPCS) provides security consulting and assurance services to over 500 clients across a wide range of enterprises in more than 20 states. A new initiative at LPCS is for each of its seven regional offices to provide internships to students who are in their final year of the security degree program at the local college.

Guardian Travel provides emergency assistance to travelers who need help with last-minute travel changes, rebooking flights, ground transportation, and emergency medical services. They are now considering expanding into personalized concierge services to aid travelers with restaurant reservations, tickets to shows, and spa reservations. Guardian Travel would like to create a specialized smartphone app to support their concierge services. One of the contract programmers working on the app has told Guardian Travel that a code signing digital certificate is a waste of money, but one of Guardian Travel's IT staff members says that it is essential. After hearing the discussion in a meeting an executive vice president has asked for LCPS for their help in reviewing all the digital certificates that Guardian Travel uses and how they are currently being managed. Guardian Travel has asked you to conduct a training session to the executive staff and IT personnel about digital certificates

1. Create a PowerPoint presentation that provides an overview of cryptography with specific emphasis on digital signatures, digital certificates, and PKI. The presentation should be at least eight slides in length.
2. The security manager of Guardian Travel has now proposed that all email correspondence, both internal between employees and external to all business partners and customers, should use digital certificates. Several IT staff employees are concerned about this proposal. They have asked you for your opinion on using digital certificates for all email messages. Write a one-page memo to Guardian Travel about the pros and cons of this approach.

Case Project 4-8: Community Site Activity

The Information Security Community Site is an online companion to this textbook. It contains a wide variety of tools, information, discussion boards, and other features to assist learners. Go to **community.cengage.com/Infosec2** and click the *Join or Sign* in icon to login, using your login name and password that you created in Chapter 1. Click **Forums (Discussion)** and click on **Security+ Case Projects (6th edition)**. Read the following case study.

Read again *Today's Attacks and Defenses* at the beginning of the chapter. What if your computer was infected with Spora? Some argue that paying a ransom does not guarantee that you will get your data back. It not only emboldens criminals to spread their crypto-malware but it also offers an incentive for other criminals to get involved in this type of illegal activity. By paying a ransom you may be funding other illicit activity associated with the criminals. Do you agree or disagree? Would you pay or not? Take both the *pro* and *con* sides to this argument and present three to five reasons for each side. Then, give your opinion. Record your answer on the Community Site discussion board.

References

1. *No More Ransom*, retrieved Jan. 14, 2017, https://www.nomoreransom.org/.
2. "SSL Pulse," *Trustworthy Internet Movement*, Mar. 3, 2017, retrieved Mar. 21, 2017, www.trustworthyinternet.org/ssl-pulse/.

NETWORK ATTACKS AND DEFENSES

The chapters in Part 3 deal with securing an enterprise computer network. In Chapter 5, you learn about the attacks that target networks and servers. Chapter 6 demonstrates how to protect a network through network devices, architecture, and technologies. In Chapter 7, you learn how to manage network security as a network administrator. Finally, in Chapter 8 you explore the concepts and tools for protecting wireless networks.

The chapters in Part 2 deal with securing an enterprise computer network. In Chapter 5, you learn about the attacks that target networks and servers. Chapter 6 demonstrates how to protect a network through network devices, architecture and technologies. In Chapter 7 you learn how to manage network security as a network administrator. Finally, in Chapter 8 you explore the concepts and tools for protecting wireless networks.

NETWORKING AND SERVER ATTACKS

After completing this chapter, you should be able to do the following:

Describe the different types of networking-based attacks

Explain how servers are attacked

Today's Attacks and Defenses

Normally, an enterprise would leap at the opportunity to protect its customers' information by plugging vulnerabilities that have been exposed. And government prosecutors would equally be anxious to bring charges against threat actors who steal confidential material. But in a strange twist, tech companies and government agencies are sometimes prohibited from protecting users from attacks.

A group of hactivists known as WikiLeaks posted online 8761 documents, called "Vault 7," purportedly to expose how the Central Intelligence Agency (CIA) conducted covert operations on other nations and U.S. citizens. Several security researchers, after analyzing the documents, confirmed the claims that these documents demonstrated that the CIA exploited zero day vulnerabilities, created their own attack software, and even used attackers' malware, all for spying purposes. By using existing attack software, the CIA could trick investigators into thinking that the attacks came from outside attackers instead of the CIA. However, others claimed that these documents did not conclusively show that CIA operatives masqueraded as attackers. Rather, they say the CIA used a library of malware samples and techniques gleaned from attackers that could be modified by the CIA to save time in programing their own spying software. The CIA declined comment.

In addition to security researchers, several vendors also analyzed the Vault 7 WikiLeaks documents to determine if any of their products were at risk from the exposed software exploits. After studying the documents, Cisco Systems, a manufacturer of networking equipment, discovered a vulnerability in 318 models of Cisco switches that allowed remote attackers to execute code that runs with elevated (administrative) privileges. Cisco announced that it planned to release a fix for the vulnerability.

Not so fast, said the U.S. government.

A statement from the White House press secretary two days after the leak warned that any company that accepted classified material from WikiLeaks could be in violation of the law. That's because the companies would be working with stolen government secrets. Although it was unclear if the government would prosecute a company for using leaked classified documents to patch its products to protect users from attack, it served as an ominous warning to Cisco and other technology vendors.[1]

And in another strange twist, the U.S. Securities and Exchange Commission (SEC) and the Department of Justice (DOJ) filed civil and criminal actions in the largest securities fraud scheme of its kind ever prosecuted. The fraud scheme was the result of online attackers stealing information. This information included the secret plans of organizations, such as the merger or acquisition of another company that could make their stock prices skyrocket. However, the attackers got this information not from servers maintained by these organizations, but from third-party newswires. A newswire is a company that is used by an organization to spread its stories across the Internet and to print sources. It is common practice for public companies to upload draft releases of their proposed actions, such as a merger or acquisition, to the newswires. Because these releases often contain material that is not yet known to the public, such as unreleased earnings and revenue, the newswires agree to keep the information confidential until it is publicly released.

According to the government, attackers used phishing attacks and a type of web server attack known as a SQL injection attack, among other schemes, to access the newswires' servers. Attackers stole the confidential but soon-to-be-released information and quickly purchased the company's stock at a lower cost before the information was publicly released (and the stock price rose). In one instance, the attackers stole and then bought stock in a 36-minute window between the time when the newswire received the information and its public release. In five years over 150,000 confidential press releases from three newswire companies were stolen, resulting in 1000 trades that netted $30 million in profits.

Although the SEC would normally be the agency to investigate and prosecute the threat actors, a recent federal court decision said that these threat actors must use "deceptive methods" to break into a computer in order for the SEC to have jurisdiction. That means that if the threat actors sent malware as an email attachment the SEC could step in, but if the attacker just exploited an existing vulnerability in a web server, the SEC would be prohibited from taking any action.[2]

The impact of the Internet on our world has been nothing short of astonishing. Today's Internet has its roots all the way back in the late 1960s, but it was only used by researchers and the military for almost a quarter of a century. With the introduction of web browser software in the early 1990s, along with the spread of telecommunication connections at work and home, the Internet became useable and accessible to almost everyone. This created a seismic shift across society. First, a virtually limitless amount of information was suddenly available at users' fingertips. Second, not only did it give unprecedented access to information, but the Internet also created a collective force of tremendous proportions. For the first time in human history, mass participation and cooperation across space and time is possible, empowering individuals and groups all over the world. The Internet has truly had a revolutionary impact on how we live.

But for all of the benefits that the Internet has provided, it also has become the primary pathway for threat actors to spread their malware. The Internet has opened the door for them to reach around the world invisibly and instantaneously to launch attacks on any device connected to it. And just as users can surf the web without openly identifying themselves, attackers can also use anonymity to cloak their identity and prevent authorities from finding and prosecuting them.

This chapter begins a study of network attacks and defenses. First the chapter explores some of the common attacks that are launched against networks today. Then it looks specifically at attacks that target network-based servers and the applications that run on those devices.

Networking-Based Attacks

 **Certification**

1.2 Compare and contrast types of attacks.

2.6 Given a scenario, implement secure protocols.

Threat actors place a high priority on targeting networks in their attacks. This is because exploiting a single vulnerability could expose hundreds or thousands of devices. There are several types of attacks that target a network or a process that relies on a network. These can be grouped into interception attacks and poisoning attacks.

Interception

Some attacks are designed to intercept network communications. Three of the most common interception attacks are man-in-the-middle, man-in-the-browser, and replay attacks.

Man-in-the-Middle (MITM)

Suppose that Angie, a high school student, is in danger of receiving a poor grade in math. Her teacher, Mr. Ferguson, mails a letter to Angie's parents requesting a conference regarding her performance. However, Angie waits for the mail and retrieves the letter from the mailbox before her parents come home. She forges her parent's signature on the original letter declining a conference and mails it back to her teacher. Angie then replaces the real letter with a counterfeit pretending to be from Mr. Ferguson that compliments Angie on her math work. The parents read the fake letter and tell Angie they are proud of her, while Mr. Ferguson is puzzled why Angie's parents are not concerned about her grades. Angie has conducted a **man-in-the-middle (MITM)** attack by intercepting legitimate communication and forging a fictitious response to the sender.

A network-based MITM attack involves a threat actor who inserts himself into a conversation between two parties. The actor impersonates both parties to gain access to information they are sending to each other. Neither of the legitimate parties is aware of the presence of the threat actor and thus communicate freely, thinking they are talking only to the authentic party. A conceptual MITM attack is illustrated in Figure 5-1.

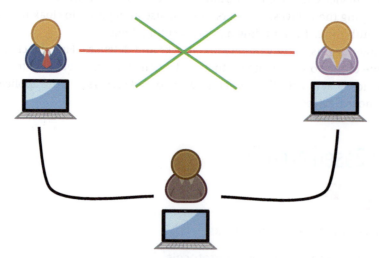

Figure 5-1   Conceptual MITM attack

A MITM could occur between two users. Figure 5-2 illustrates an attack in which a threat actor impersonates both Bob and Alice to intercept a public key. However, many MITM attacks are between a user and a server.

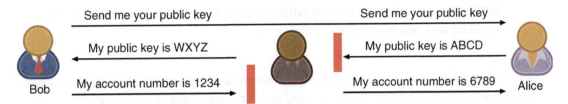

Figure 5-2 MITM attack intercepting public key

Man-in-the-Browser (MITB)

Like a MITM attack, a **man-in-the-browser (MITB)** attack intercepts communication between parties to steal or manipulate the data. But whereas a MITM attack occurs between two *computers*—such as between two user laptops or a user's computer and a web server—a MITB attack occurs between a *browser* and the underlying computer. Specifically, a MITB attack seeks to intercept and then manipulate the communication between the web browser and the security mechanisms of the computer.

> **Note**
>
> Instead of the malicious agent being *external* to the two communicating computers as in a MITM, a MITB is *internal* between web browser and the computer that is running the browser.

A MITB attack usually begins with a Trojan infecting the computer and installing an "extension" into the browser configuration, so that when the browser is launched the extension is activated. When a user enters the URL of a site, the extension checks to determine if this is a site that is targeted for attack. After the user logs in to the site, the extension waits for a specific webpage to be displayed in which a user enters information, such as the account number and password for an online financial institution (a favorite target of MITB attacks). When the user clicks "Submit" the extension captures all the data from the fields on the form and may even modify some of the entered data. The browser then proceeds to send the data to the server, which performs the transaction and generates a receipt that is sent back to the browser. The malicious extension again captures the receipt data and modifies it (with the data the user originally entered) so that it appears that a legitimate transaction has occurred.

There are several advantages to a MITB attack:

- Most MITB attacks are distributed through a Trojan browser extension, which provides a valid function to the user but also installs the MITB malware, making it difficult to recognize that malicious code has been installed.
- Because MITB malware is selective as to which websites are targeted, an infected MITB browser might remain dormant for months until triggered by the user visiting a targeted site.

- MITB software resides exclusively within the web browser, making it difficult for standard anti-malware software to detect it.

Replay

A **replay** attack is a variation of a MITM attack. Whereas a MITM attack alters and then sends the transmission immediately, a replay attack makes a copy of the legitimate transmission before sending it to the recipient. This copy is then used at a later time (the MITM "replays" the transmission). A simple replay would involve the MITM capturing logon credentials between the user's computer and the server. Once that session has ended, the MITM would attempt to log on and replay the captured user credentials.

> **Note** 📎
>
> Although cryptography can be used to thwart a replay attack, there are instances in which cryptographic communications can be manipulated by a replay attack. A threat actor could capture an encrypted administrative message sent from an approved network device to a server. Later, the attacker can send or resend that same message to the server, and the server may respond, thinking it came from the valid device. The response may be such that the threat actor can obtain valuable information about the type of server and the network that can then be used in subsequent attacks.

There are methods to prevent replay attacks. Both sides can negotiate and create a random key that is valid for a limited period or for a specific process. Another option is to use timestamps in all messages and reject any messages that fall outside of a normal window of time.

Poisoning

Poisoning is the act of introducing a substance that harms or destroys a functional living organism. Three types of attacks inject "poison" into a normal network process to facilitate an attack. These are ARP poisoning, DNS poisoning, and privilege escalation.

ARP Poisoning

The TCP/IP protocol suite requires that logical Internet Protocol (IP) addresses be assigned to each host on a network. However, an Ethernet LAN uses the physical media access control (MAC) address to send packets. In order for a host using TCP/IP on an Ethernet network to find the MAC address of another device based on the IP address, it uses the **Address Resolution Protocol (ARP)**. If the IP address for a device is known but the MAC address is not, the sending computer sends an ARP packet to all computers on the network that in effect says, "If this is your IP address, send me back your MAC address." The computer with that IP address sends back a packet with the MAC address so the packet can be correctly addressed. This IP address and the corresponding

MAC address are stored in an ARP cache for future reference. In addition, all other computers that hear the ARP reply also cache that data.

A MAC address is permanently "burned" into a network interface card (NIC) so that there is not a means of altering the MAC address on a NIC. However, because the MAC address is stored in a software ARP cache, it can be changed there, which would then result in the corresponding IP address pointing to a different computer. This attack is known as **ARP poisoning** and relies upon **MAC spoofing** (or imitating another computer by means of changing the MAC address). Table 5-1 illustrates the ARP cache before and after a MITM attack using ARP poisoning.

> **Note**
>
> A variety of different attacks use spoofing. For example, because most network systems keep logs of user activity, attackers may spoof their addresses so that their malicious actions will be attributed to valid users, or spoof their network addresses with addresses of known and trusted hosts so that the target computers will accept their packets and act on them.

Table 5-1   ARP poisoning attack

Device	IP and MAC address	ARP cache before attack	ARP cache after attack
Attacker	192.146.118.2 00-AA-BB-CC-DD-02	192.146.118.3=>00-AA-BB-CC-DD-03	192.146.118.3=>00-AA-BB-CC-DD-03
		192.146.118.4=>00-AA-BB-CC-DD-04	192.146.118.4=>00-AA-BB-CC-DD-04
Victim 1	192.146.118.3 00-AA-BB-CC-DD-03	192.146.118.2=>00-AA-BB-CC-DD-02	192.146.118.2=>00-AA-BB-CC-DD-02
		192.146.118.4=>00-AA-BB-CC-DD-04	192.146.118.4=>00-AA-BB-CC-DD-02
Victim 2	192.146.118.4 00-AA-BB-CC-DD-04	192.146.118.2=>00-AA-BB-CC-DD-02	192.146.118.2=>00-AA-BB-CC-DD-02
		192.146.118.3=>00-AA-BB-CC-DD-03	192.146.118.3=>00-AA-BB-CC-DD-02

> **Note**
>
> ARP poisoning is successful because there are no authentication procedures to verify ARP requests and replies.

Some types of attacks that can be generated using ARP poisoning are listed in Table 5-2.

Table 5-2	Attacks from ARP poisoning
Attack	**Description**
Steal data	An attacker can substitute her own MAC address and steal data intended for another device.
Prevent Internet access	An attacker can substitute an invalid MAC address for the network gateway so that no users can access external networks.
Man-in-the-middle	A man-in-the-middle device can be set to receive all communications by substituting that MAC address.
Denial of Service attack	The valid IP address of the target can be substituted with an invalid MAC address, causing all traffic destined for the target to fail.

DNS Poisoning

The predecessor to today's Internet was the network ARPAnet. This network was completed in 1969 and linked together single computers located at each of four different sites (the University of California at Los Angeles, the Stanford Research Institute, the University of California at Santa Barbara, and the University of Utah) with a 50 Kbps connection. Referencing these computers was originally accomplished by assigning an identification number to each computer (IP addresses were not introduced until later). However, as additional computers were added to the network it became more difficult for humans to accurately recall the identification number of each computer.

Note

On Labor Day in 1969, the first test of the ARPAnet was conducted. A switch was turned on, and to almost everyone's surprise, the network worked. Researchers in Los Angeles then attempted to type the word *login* on the computer in Stanford. A user pressed the letter *L* and it appeared on the screen in Stanford. Next, the letter *O* was pressed, and it too appeared. When the letter *G* was typed, however, the network crashed.

What was needed was a *name system* that would allow computers on a network to be assigned both numeric addresses and more friendly human-readable names composed of letters, numbers, and special symbols (called a *symbolic name*). In the early 1970s, each computer site began to assign simple names to network devices and also manage its own *host table* that mapped names to computer numbers. However, because each site attempted to maintain its own local host table, there were inconsistencies between the sites. A standard master host table was then created that could be downloaded to each site. When TCP/IP was developed, the host table concept was expanded to a hierarchical name system for matching computer names and numbers known as the *Domain Name System (DNS)*, which is the basis for **domain name resolution** of names-to-IP addresses used today.

Because of the important role it plays, DNS can be the focus of attacks. Like ARP poisoning, **DNS poisoning** substitutes a DNS address so that the computer is automatically redirected to another device. Whereas ARP poisoning substitutes a fraudulent MAC address for an IP address, DNS poisoning substitutes a fraudulent IP address for a symbolic name.

DNS poisoning can be done in two different locations: the local host table, or the external DNS server. TCP/IP still uses host tables stored on the local computer. When a user enters a symbolic name, TCP/IP first checks the local host table to determine if there is an entry; if no entry exists, then the external DNS system is used. Attackers can target a local HOSTS file to create new entries that will redirect users to a fraudulent site. A sample local HOSTS file is shown in Figure 5-3.

127.0.0.1	localhost	
161.6.18.20	www.wku.edu	# Western Kentucky University
74.125.47.99	www.google.com	# My favorite search engine
216.77.188.41	www.att.net	# Internet service provider

Figure 5-3   **Sample HOSTS file**

Note

Host tables are found in the */etc/* directory in UNIX, Linux, and macOS, and are located in the *Windows\System32\drivers\etc* directory in Windows.

A second location that can be attacked is the external DNS server. Instead of attempting to break into a DNS server to change its contents, attackers use a more basic approach. Because DNS servers exchange information among themselves (known as *zone transfers*), attackers attempt to exploit a protocol flaw and convince the authentic DNS server to accept fraudulent DNS entries sent from the attacker's DNS server. If the DNS server does not correctly validate DNS responses to ensure that they have come from an authoritative source, it will store the fraudulent entries locally, serve them to users, and spread them to other DNS servers.

Note

The Chinese government uses DNS poisoning to prevent Internet content that it considers unfavorable from reaching its citizenry.

The process of a DNS poisoning attack from an attacker who has a domain name of *www.evil.net* with her own DNS server *ns.evil.net* is shown in Figure 5-4:

1. The attacker sends a request to a valid DNS server asking it to resolve the name *www.evil.net*.
2. Because the valid DNS server does not know the address, it asks the responsible name server, which is the attacker's *ns.evil.net*, for the address.
3. The name server *ns.evil.net* sends the address of not only *www.evil.net* but also all of its records (a zone transfer) to the valid DNS server, which then accepts them.
4. Any requests to the valid DNS server will now respond with the fraudulent addresses entered by the attacker.

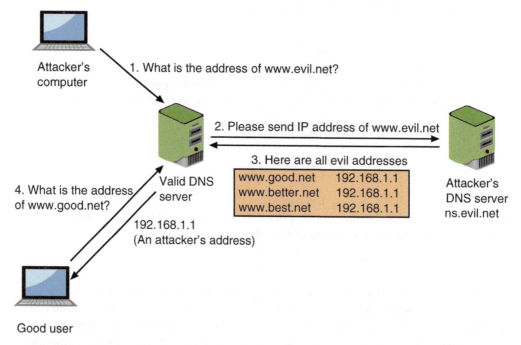

Figure 5-4 DNS server poisoning

Privilege Escalation

Access rights are privileges to access hardware and software resources that are granted to users or devices. For example, Ian may be given access rights to only read a file, while Jaxon has access rights to add content to the file. Operating systems and many applications have the ability to restrict a user's privileges in accessing its specific functions. **Privilege escalation** is exploiting a vulnerability in software to gain access to resources that the user normally would be restricted from accessing.

There are different types of privilege escalation. One type is when a user with a lower privilege uses privilege escalation to grant herself access to functions reserved for higher-privilege users (sometimes called *vertical privilege escalation*). Another type of privilege escalation is when a user with restricted privileges accesses the different restricted functions of a similar user; that is, Mia does not have privileges to access a payroll program but uses privilege escalation to access Li's account that does have these privileges (*horizontal privilege escalation*).

Sometimes privilege escalation is the result of an unintentional relationship between multiple systems. System 1 can access System 2, and because System 2 can access System 3, then System 1 can access System 3. However, the intention may not be for System 1 to access System 3, but instead for System 1 to be restricted to accessing only System 2. This sometimes inadvertent and unauthorized access can result in a privilege escalation, in which threat actors take advantage of access that occurs through succeeding systems. By exploiting the sometimes confusing nature of this access, attackers can often reach restricted resources.

Server Attacks

1.2 Compare and contrast types of attacks.

Whereas some attacks are directed at the network itself, other attacks are directed specifically at network servers. As its name implies, a *server* "serves" or provides resources and services to clients on a network. A compromised server can provide threat actors with its privileged contents or provide an opening for attacking any of the devices that access that server. Typical server attacks include denial of service, web server application attacks, hijacking, overflow attacks, advertising attacks, and exploiting browser vulnerabilities.

Denial of Service (DoS)

A **denial of service (DoS)** attack is a deliberate attempt to prevent authorized users from accessing a system. It does this by overwhelming that system with such a very high number of "bogus" requests that the system cannot respond to legitimate requests. Most DoS attacks today are **distributed denial of service (DDoS)** attacks: instead of only one computer making a bogus request, a DDoS involves hundreds or even tens of thousands of devices flooding the server with requests.

> **Note** 📎
>
> Suppose Gabe is having a conversation with Cora in a coffee shop when a "flash mob" of friends suddenly descends upon them and all start talking to Gabe at the same time. He would be unable to continue his conversation with Cora because he is overwhelmed by the number of voices with which he would have to contend. This is like what happens in a DDoS attack.

There are different types of DoS attacks:

- *Smurf attack.* In a *smurf attack*, an attacker broadcasts a network request to multiple computers but changes the address from which the request came (called **IP spoofing** because it imitates another computer's IP address) to the victim's computer. This makes it appear as if it is asking for a response. Each of the computers then sends a response to the victim's computer so that it is quickly overwhelmed.

- *DNS amplification attack.* Like a smurf attack, a **DNS amplification attack** floods an unsuspecting victim by redirecting valid responses to it. A DNS amplification attack uses publicly accessible and open DNS servers to flood a system with DNS response traffic. A threat actor sends a DNS name lookup request to an open DNS server with the source address spoofed to the victim's address. When the DNS server sends the DNS record response, it is instead sent to the target. As an added step attackers often craft the DNS name lookup request so that it returns all known information about a DNS zone in a single request. This dramatically increases the volume of data sent, which can more quickly overwhelm the victim.

- *SYN flood attack.* An *SYN flood attack* takes advantage of the procedures for initiating a session. Under normal network conditions using TCP/IP, a device contacts a network server with a request that uses a control message, called a synchronize message (SYN), to initialize the connection. The server responds with its own SYN along with an acknowledgment (ACK) that it received the initial request, called a SYN+ACK. The server then waits for a reply ACK from the device indicating that it received the server's SYN. To allow for a slow connection, the server might wait for a period of time for the reply. In an SYN flood attack the attacker sends SYN segments in IP packets to the server but modifies the source address of each packet to computer addresses that do not exist or cannot be reached. The server continues to "hold the line open" and wait for a response (which is never coming) while receiving more false requests and keeping more lines open for responses. After a period of time, the server runs out of resources and can no longer respond to legitimate requests or function properly. Figure 5-5 shows a server waiting for responses during a SYN flood attack.

> **Note** 📎
>
> One report found that almost three out of every four DoS attack victims also saw at least one security incident at the same time as the DoS attack. This may indicate that DoS attacks often serve as decoys to divert attention away from other attacks.[3]

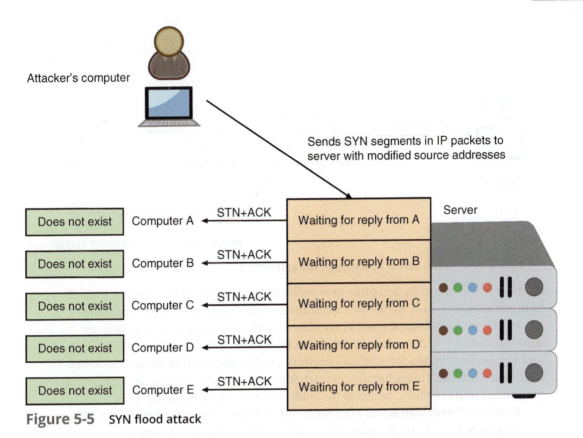

Figure 5-5   SYN flood attack

Web Server Application Attacks

On the international global Internet network, a web server provides services that are implemented as *web applications* through software applications running on the server. Most web applications create dynamic content based on input from the user. For example, a webpage might ask a user to enter a zip code of his vacation destination to receive the latest weather forecast for that region. These dynamic operations of a web application depend heavily upon inputs provided by users.

A typical dynamic web application infrastructure is shown in Figure 5-6. The client's web browser makes a request using the Hypertext Transport Protocol (HTTP) to a web server, which may be connected to one or more web application servers. These application servers run the specific "web apps," which in turn are directly connected to database servers on the internal network. Information from these database servers is retrieved and returned to the web server so that the dynamic information can be sent back to the user's web browser.

Securing web applications is more difficult than protecting other systems. First, by design the dynamic web applications accept user input, such as the zip code of the region for which a weather forecast is needed. Most other systems would categorically reject any user input as being potentially dangerous, not knowing if the

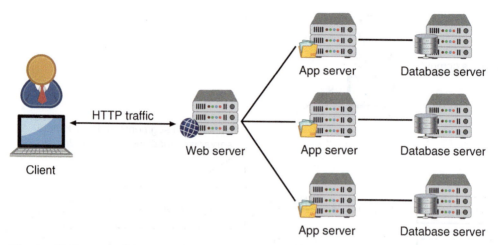

Figure 5-6 Web server application infrastructure

user is a friend or foe. By accepting user input, the web application is exposing itself to threat actors. Second, many web application attacks attempt to exploit previously unknown vulnerabilities. Known as *zero day attacks*, these attacks give victims no time—zero days—to defend against the attacks. Finally, although traditional network security devices can block traditional network attacks, they cannot always block web application attacks. This is because many traditional network security devices ignore the *content* of HTTP traffic, which is the vehicle of web application attacks.

Several different web server application attacks target the input from users. These can be grouped into two categories: cross-site attacks and injection attacks.

Cross-Site Attacks

There are two types of cross-site attacks. These are cross-site scripting attacks and cross-site request forgery attacks.

Cross-Site Scripting (XSS)

Many web applications are designed to customize content for the user by taking what the user enters and then displaying that input back to the user. Typical customized responses are listed in Table 5-3.

Table 5-3 Customized responses

User input	Variable that contains input	Web application response	Coding example
Search term	*search_term*	Search term provided in output	"Search results for *search_term*"
Incorrect input	*user_input*	Error message that contains incorrect input	"*user_input* is not valid"
User's name	*name*	Personalized response	"Welcome back *name*"

Figure 5-7 illustrates a fictitious web application that allows friends to share their favorite bookmarks with each other online. Users can enter their name, a description, and the URL of the bookmark, and then receive a personalized "Thank You" screen. In Figure 5-8 the code that generates the "Thank You" screen is illustrated.

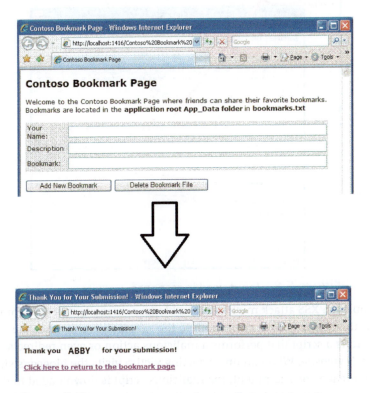

Figure 5-7   Bookmark page that accepts user input

In a **cross-site scripting (XSS)** attack, the threat actor takes advantage of web applications that accept user input *without* validating it before presenting it back to the user. In the previous example, the input that the user enters for *Name* is not verified but instead is automatically added to a code segment that becomes part of an automated response. An attacker can take advantage of this in an XSS attack by tricking a valid website into feeding a malicious script to another user's web browser, which will then execute it.

Note

The term *cross-site scripting* refers to an attack using scripting that originates on one site (the web server) to impact another site (the user's computer).

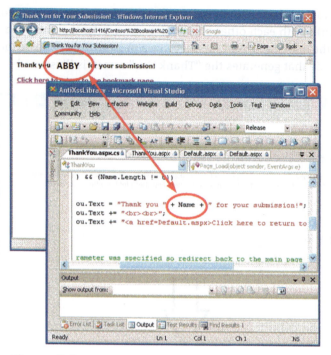

Figure 5-8 Input used in response

For example, an XSS attack might target a blogger's website that asks for user comments. A threat actor posts a comment to the site. However, within the comment the attacker crafts a script that performs a malicious action or even redirects the user to the attacker's website. When an unsuspecting victim visits the blogger's site and clicks on the threat actor's comment, the malicious script is downloaded to the victim's web browser where it is executed. Besides redirecting the victim to a malicious site, other XSS attacks are designed to steal sensitive information that was retained by the browser when visiting specific sites, such as data from an online site where a purchase was made. The XSS attack can steal this information and allow it to be used by an attacker to impersonate the legitimate user.

Note

Some security experts note that XSS is like a phishing attack but without needing to trick the user into visiting a malicious website. Instead, the user starts at a legitimate website and XSS automatically directs her to the malicious site.

An XSS attack requires a website that meets two criteria: it accepts user input without validating it, and it uses that input in a response. Despite the fact that XSS is a widely known type of attack, the number of websites that are vulnerable remains very large. Users can turn off active scripting in their browsers to reduce the risk of XSS, but this limits their ability to use dynamic websites.

> **Note**
>
> The malicious content of an XSS URL is not confined to material posted on a website; it can be embedded into virtually any hyperlink, such as one in an email or text message. That is why users should not blindly click on a URL that they receive.

Cross-Site Request Forgery (XSRF)

A similar attack is a **cross-site request forgery (XSRF)**. This attack uses the user's web browser settings to impersonate that user. If a user is currently authenticated on a website and is then tricked into loading another webpage, the new page inherits the identity and privileges of the victim to perform an undesired function on the attacker's behalf. Figure 5-9 illustrates a cross-site request forgery.

3. Victim unknowingly clicks on email hyperlink

2. Attacker sends email to victim who is logged in to Bank A's website

4. Request is sent to Bank A with victim's verified credentials

1. Attacker forges a fund transfer request from Bank A and embeds it into email hyperlink

5. Bank A validates request with victim's credentials and sends funds to attacker

Figure 5-9   Cross-site request forgery

Injection Attacks

In addition to cross-site attacks on web server applications there are also **injection attacks** that introduce new input to exploit a vulnerability. One of the most common injection attacks, called *SQL injection*, inserts statements to manipulate a database server. SQL stands for *Structured Query Language*, a language used to view and manipulate data that is stored in a relational database. SQL injection targets SQL servers by introducing malicious commands into them.

Most webpages that require users to log on by entering a user name and password typically offer a solution for the user who has forgotten his password by providing an online form, as shown in Figure 5-10. The user enters a valid email address that is already on file. The submitted email address is compared to the stored email address, and if they match, a reset URL is emailed to that address.

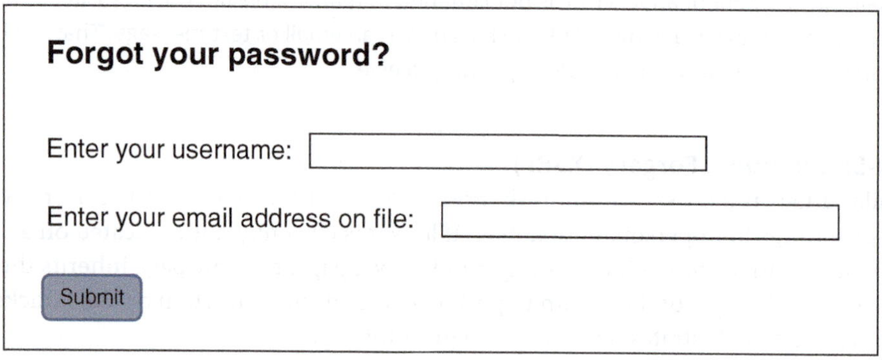

Forgot your password?

Enter your username: ⬚⬚⬚⬚⬚⬚⬚⬚⬚⬚⬚⬚⬚⬚⬚

Enter your email address on file: ⬚⬚⬚⬚⬚⬚⬚⬚⬚⬚⬚⬚⬚⬚⬚

Submit

Figure 5-10   Request form for forgotten password

If the email address entered by the user into the form is stored in the variable $EMAIL, then the underlying SQL statement to retrieve the stored email address from the database would be similar to:

SELECT fieldlist FROM table WHERE field = '$EMAIL'

The *WHERE* clause is meant to limit the database query to only display information when the condition is considered true (that is, when the email address in $EMAIL matches an address in the database).

An attacker using a SQL injection attack would begin by first entering a fictitious email address on this webpage that included a single quotation mark as part of the data, such as *braden.thomas@fakemail.com'*. If the message *E-mail Address Unknown* is displayed, it indicates that user input is being properly filtered and a SQL attack cannot be rendered on the site. However, if the error message *Server Failure* is displayed, it means that the user input is not being filtered and all user input is sent directly to the database. This is because the *Server Failure* message is due to a syntax error created by the additional single quotation mark: the fictitious email address entered would be processed as *braden.thomas@fakemail.com'* (with two single quotation marks) and generate the *Server Failure* error message.

Armed with the knowledge that input is sent unfiltered to the database, the attacker knows that anything he enters into the *Enter your username:* field on the *Forgot your password?* form would be sent to and then processed by the SQL database. Now, instead of entering a user name, the attacker would enter this command, which would let him view all the email addresses in the database: *whatever' or 'a' = 'a*. This command is stored in the variable $EMAIL. The expanded SQL statement would read:

SELECT fieldlist FROM table WHERE field = 'whatever' or 'a' = 'a

These values are:

- *'whatever'*. This can be anything meaningless.
- *or*. The SQL *or* means that as long as either of the conditions are true, the entire statement is true and will be executed.
- *'a' = 'a'*. This is a statement that will always be true.

Because *'a' = 'a'* is always true, the *WHERE* clause is also true. It is not limited as it was when searching for a single email address before it would become true. The result can be that *all* user email addresses will then be displayed.

Note 📎

Whereas this example shows how an attacker could retrieve all email addresses, a more catastrophic attack would be if user passwords were not stored as encrypted and the attacker were able to use SQL injection to extract all these values. This type of attack has been used to steal millions of user passwords. Plaintext passwords should *never* be stored in a database.

By entering crafted SQL statements as user input, information from the database can be extracted or the existing data can be manipulated. SQL injection statements that can be entered and stored in *$EMAIL* and their pending results are shown in Table 5-4.

Table 5-4 **SQL injection statements**

SQL injection statement	Result
whatever' AND email IS NULL; --	Determine the names of different fields in the database
whatever' AND 1=(SELECT COUNT(*) FROM tabname);—	Discover the name of the table
whatever' OR full name LIKE Mia	Find specific users
whatever'; DROP TABLE members; --	Erase the database table
whatever'; UPDATE members SET email = 'attacker-email@evil.net' WHERE email = 'Mia@good.com';	Mail password to attacker's email account

Hijacking

The word *hijacking* means to illegally seize, commandeer, or take control over something to use it for a different purpose. Several server attacks are the result of threat actors "commandeering" a technology and then using it for an attack. Common hijacking attacks include session hijacking, URL hijacking, domain hijacking, and clickjacking.

Session Hijacking

It is important that a user who is accessing a secure web application, such as an online retailer order form, can be verified so as to prevent an imposter from "jumping in" to the interaction and ordering items that are charged to the victim but are sent to another address. This verification is accomplished through a *session token*, which is a random string assigned to that interaction between the user and the web application currently being accessed (a *session*). When the user logs on to the online retailer's web server with her account user name and password, the web application server assigns a unique session token, such as *64da9DACOqgoipxqQDdywg*. Each subsequent request from the user's web browser to the web application contains the session token verifying the identity of the user until she logs out.

> **Note** 📎
>
> A session token is usually a string of letters and numbers of variable length. It can be transmitted in different ways: in the URL, in the header of the HTTP requisition, or in the body of the HTTP requisition.

Session hijacking is an attack in which an attacker attempts to impersonate the user by using her session token. An attacker can attempt to obtain the session token in several different ways. One of the most common methods is to use XSS or other attacks to steal the session token cookie from the victim's computer and then use it to impersonate the victim. Other means include eavesdropping on the transmission or even guessing the session token. Guessing is successful if the generation of the session tokens is not truly random. In such a case, an attacker can accumulate multiple session tokens and then make a guess at the next session token number.

> **Note** 📎
>
> In a highly publicized attack on Yahoo.com, threat actors penetrated Yahoo's network and stole a portion of its User Database (UDB) that contained Yahoo subscriber information. This included user's names, recovery email accounts, and information needed to manually create session tokens for over 500 million Yahoo user accounts. They also accessed Yahoo's Account Management Tool (AMT). Using these tools, the threat actors manufactured session cookies and accessed at least 6500 user accounts.[4]

URL Hijacking

What happens when a user makes a typing error when entering a uniform resource locator (URL) address in a web browser, such as typing *goggle.com* (a misspelling) or *google.net* (incorrect domain) instead of the correct *google.com*? In the past, an error message like *HTTP Error 404 Not Found* would appear. However, today most often the user will be directed to a fake look-alike site filled with ads for which the attacker receives money for traffic generated to the site. These fake sites exist because attackers purchase the domain names of sites that are spelled similarly to actual sites. This is called **URL hijacking** or **typo squatting**. A well-known site like *google.com* may have to deal with more than 1000 typo squatting domains.

> **Note**
>
> The cost of typo squatting is significant because of the large number of misspellings. In one month the typo squatting site *goggle.com* received almost 825,000 unique visitors. It is estimated that typo squatting costs the 250 top websites $285 million annually in lost sales and other expenses.[5]

Enterprises have tried to preempt typo squatting by registering the domain names of close spellings of their website. At one time top-level domains (TLDs) were limited to .com, .org, .net, .int, .edu, .gov and .mil, so it was fairly easy to register close-sounding domain names. However, today there are over 1200 generic TLDs (gTLDs), such as .museum, .office, .global, and .school. Organizations must now attempt to register a very large number of sites that are a variation of their registered domain name.

> **Note**
>
> Some of the most popular new gTLDs are .xyz, .top, .loan, and .win.[6]

In addition to registering names that are similar to the actual names (like *goggle .com* for *google.com*), threat actors are now registering domain names that are *one bit* different (called bitsquatting). This is because the billions of devices that are part of the Internet have multiple instances of a domain name in a DNS server's memory at any time, so the likelihood increases of a RAM memory error of a bit being "flipped." Figure 5-11 illustrates that the change of one bit in the letter *g* (01100111) results in the change of the entire character from *g* to *f*. In this example, a threat actor would register the domain *foo.gl* as a variation of the actual *goo.gl*.

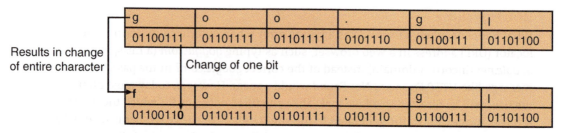

Results in change of entire character

Change of one bit

Figure 5-11 Character change by bit flipping

> **Note** 🖉
>
> An increasing number of registered attacker domains are the result of bitsquatting, such as *aeazon.com* (for *amazon.com*) and *microsmft.com* (for *microsoft.com*). Security researchers found that 20 percent of a sample of 433 registered attacker domains were the result of bitsquatting.[7]

Domain Hijacking

Domain hijacking occurs when a domain pointer that links a domain name to a specific web server is changed by a threat actor. When a domain name is first registered, the owner is given access to a domain control panel. From this panel the owner can point the domain name to the physical web server that contains the website's data, such as the webpages, photos, scripts, etc. When a domain name is hijacked, a threat actor gains access to the domain control panel and redirects the registered domain to a different physical web server.

Clickjacking

Hijacking a mouse click is called **clickjacking**, when the user is tricked into clicking a link that is other than what it appears to be. Suppose a threat actor builds a website with a button labeled *Click here to play music video*. However, the attacker also creates a second page that overlays the first page with a transparent layer that contains a button that purchases an online item sent to the attacker but charged to the victim. When the user clicks the button *Click here to play music video*, that click invokes the purchase button that overlays it. This results in an item bought and charged to the victim's online account.

> **Note** 🖉
>
> For the above scenario to function the victim must be logged into the online retailer and have 1-click ordering turned on.

Clickjacking often relies upon threat actors who craft a zero-pixel IFrame. IFrame (short for *inline frame*) is an HTML element that allows for embedding another HTML document inside the main document. A zero-pixel IFrame is virtually invisible to the naked eye, making it easier to overlay a button in a webpage.

Overflow Attacks

Some attacks are designed to "overflow" areas of memory with instructions from the attacker. This type of attack includes buffer overflow attacks and integer overflow attacks.

Note

Overflow attacks can target either a server or a client.

Buffer Overflow

Consider a teacher working in his office who manually grades a lengthy written examination by marking incorrect answers with a red pen. Because he is frequently interrupted in his grading by students, the teacher places a ruler on the test question he is currently grading to indicate his "return point," or the point at which he should resume the grading. Suppose that two devious students enter his office as he is grading examinations. While one student distracts him, the second student silently slides the ruler down from question 4 to question 20. When the teacher returns to grading, he will resume at the wrong "return point" and not look at the answers for questions 4 through 19.

This scenario is similar to how a buffer overflow attacker attempts to compromise a computer. A storage buffer on a computer typically contains the memory location of the software program that was being executed when another function interrupted the process; that is, the storage buffer contains the "return address" where the computer's processor should resume once the new process has finished. An attacker can substitute her own "return address" in order to point to a different area in the computer's memory that contains his malware code.

A **buffer overflow attack** occurs when a process attempts to store data in RAM beyond the boundaries of a fixed-length storage buffer. This extra data overflows into the adjacent memory locations (a *buffer overflow*). Because the storage buffer typically contains the "return address" memory location of the software program that was being executed when another function interrupted the process, an attacker can overflow the buffer with a new address pointing to the attacker's malware code. A buffer overflow attack is shown in Figure 5-12.

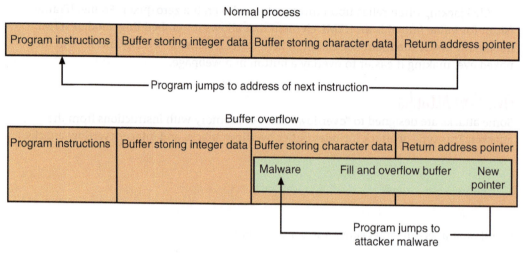

Figure 5-12   Buffer overflow attack

Note

The "return address" is not the only element that can be altered in a buffer overflow attack, but it is one of the most commonly altered elements.

Integer Overflow

Consider a digital clock that can display the hours only as 1 to 12. What happens when the time moves past 12:59? The clock then "wraps around" to the lowest hour value of 1 again.

On a computer, an *integer overflow* is the condition that occurs when the result of an arithmetic operation—like addition or multiplication—exceeds the maximum size of the integer type used to store it. When this integer overflow occurs, the interpreted value then wraps around from the maximum value to the minimum value.

Note

For example, an 8-bit signed integer has a maximum value of 127 and a minimum value of −128. If the value 127 is stored in a variable and 1 is added to it, the sum exceeds the maximum value for this integer type and wraps around to become −128.

In an **integer overflow attack**, an attacker changes the value of a variable to something outside the range that the programmer had intended by using an integer overflow. This type of attack could be used in the following situations:

- An attacker could use an integer overflow attack to create a buffer overflow situation. If an integer overflow could be introduced during the calculations for the length of a buffer when a copy is occurring, it could result in a buffer that is too small to hold the data. An attacker could then use this to create his buffer overflow attack.

- A program that calculates the total cost of items purchased would use the number of units sold times the cost per unit. If an integer overflow were introduced when tallying the number of items sold, it could result in a negative value and a resulting negative total cost, indicating that a refund is due the customer.
- A large positive value in a bank transfer could be wrapped around by an integer overflow attack to become a negative value, which could then reverse the flow of money: instead of adding this amount to the victim's account, it could withdraw that amount and later transfer it to the attacker's account.

Note

An extreme example of an integer overflow attack would be withdrawing $1 from an account that has a balance of 0, which could cause a new balance of $4,294,967,295!

Advertising Attacks

Most websites today rely heavily upon advertising revenue. Ad revenue for Google, which was only $10.4 billion in 2006, had skyrocketed to almost $80 billion just 10 years later.[8] This has not gone unnoticed by threat actors. There are several attacks that attempt to use ads or manipulate the advertising system. Two of the most common are malvertising and ad fraud.

Malvertising

When visiting a typical website it is common for advertisements to be displayed around the pages. For example, visiting a fitness-tracking website often results in ads promoting athletic shoes, sports drinks, weight loss, and other related products being displayed, even when you browse other sites. These ads do not usually come from the main site itself; instead, most mainstream and high-trafficked websites outsource the ad content on their pages to different third-party advertising networks. When a user goes to the site's page, the user's web browser silently connects to dozens of advertising network sites from which ad banners, popup ads, video files, and pictures are sent to the user's computer.

Threat actors have turned to using these third-party advertising networks to distribute their malware to unsuspecting users who visit a well-known website. The threat actors may infect the third-party advertising networks so that their malware is distributed through ads sent to users' web browsers. Or the threat actors might promote themselves as reputable third-party advertisers while in reality they are distributing their malware through the ads. This is known as *malvertising* (for *malicious advertising*) or a *poisoned ad attack*. An ad that contains malware redirects visitors who receive it to the attacker's webpage that then downloads Trojans and ransomware onto the user's computer, often through vulnerabilities in the web browser.

> **Note** 📎
>
> *The New York Times*, Reuters, Yahoo!, Bloomberg, and Google, among many others, have all been infected with malvertising. In one year, 12.4 billion "malvertisements" were distributed, an increase of over 300 percent from the previous year. The growth of malvertising is also credited with a 41 percent increase in ad-blocking software, now used by 198 million users.[9]

Malvertising has a number of advantages for the attacker:

- Malvertising occurs on "big-name" websites, such as news publications that attract many visitors each day. These unsuspecting users, who would avoid or be suspicious of less popular sites, are deceived into thinking that because they are on a reputable site they are free from attacks.
- Usually the website owners have no knowledge of malvertising being distributed through their website. This is because they do not know what type of ad content a third-party ad network is displaying on their site at any given time.
- Ad networks rotate content very quickly, so that not all visitors to a site are infected, making it difficult to determine if malvertising was actually the source of an attack. And even when an ad is pinpointed in an investigation as malicious, it is virtually impossible to prove which ad network was responsible.
- Because advertising networks configure ads to appear according to the user's computer (which browser or operating system they are using) or identifying attributes (their country locations or search keywords they used to find the site) attackers can narrowly target their victims. For example, an attacker who wants to target U.S. federal government employees might distribute ads with malicious content for anyone who entered "Government travel allowance" into a search engine.

> **Note** 📎
>
> Because these attacks can precisely target their victims, often "high value victims" are pinpointed. For example, an attacker might place malicious ads before individuals who are conducting a keyword-search for hotel rates at an upcoming security conference.

Preventing malvertising is a difficult task. Website operators are unaware of the types of ads that are being displayed, users have a false sense of security going to a "mainstream" website, and turning off ads that support plug-ins such as Adobe Flash often disrupts the user's web experience.

Ad Fraud

Suppose that Mario wants to do some online shopping. Using his web browser he goes to his favorite online store, Gear.org. The home page of Gear.org appears, along with a small video window, tempting Mario to click the video to watch it. When he clicks on the video he first sees a short (10–15 second) advertising video called a "pre-roll." The pre-roll ad is a promotional video that plays before the content Mario wants to see.

Note 📎

Pre-roll ads are often "repurposed" TV ads that have been shortened, because the 30-second standard TV ad is too long for pre-rolls, which precede videos that are usually only about two minutes long. Despite the fact that many pre-rolls support a video format called TrueView that allows users to skip the ad after five seconds, almost half of all viewers watch the entire pre-roll ad.

When Mario clicks on the video to view it, an automated advertising auction occurs in the background between the advertiser and the website over what pre-roll video will be displayed. The pre-roll slot is offered by the website and then sold to the advertiser (with the highest bid) within 100 milliseconds. The web browser then directly receives the pre-roll from the advertiser that wins the auction, and the web browser also verifies what site the user is visiting and that the user actually received the pre-roll ad.

Threat actors manipulate this process to earn ad revenue that is directed back to them. Attackers have created essentially a "robo-browser" called Methbot that spoofs all the necessary interactions needed to initiate, carry out, and complete the ad auction. Acting like the website, Methbot contacts an advertiser and says it needs a pre-roll for a video on Gear.org. The super-fast auction occurs and the pre-roll is sent to Methbot. But Methbot also pretends to be the valid web browser and verifies that it received the pre-roll and played it. The advertiser pays the website that the browser claimed to be visiting, but actually the money is sent to the attackers behind Methbot and not to Gear.org. It is estimated that the threat actors sell between 200 million to 300 million false ads each day at 1.3 cents per view, which generates up to $5 million dollars a day in revenue.[10]

Note

Attackers use IP spoofing to mask the fact that Methbot traffic is generated by servers and not by users.

Browser Vulnerabilities

In the early days of the web, users viewed *static* content (information that does not change) such as text and pictures through a web browser. As the Internet increased in popularity, the demand rose for *dynamic* content that can change, such as animated images or customized information. However, basic HTML code could not provide these dynamic functions.

The solution came in several different forms. One solution was to allow scripting code to be downloaded from the web server into the user's web browser. Another solution took the form of different types of additions that could be added to a web browser to support dynamic content. However, these additions have introduced vulnerabilities in browsers that access servers. These web browser additions are extensions, plug-ins, and add-ons.

Scripting Code

One means of adding dynamic content is for the web server to download a "script" or series of instructions in the form of computer code that commands the browser to perform specific actions. *JavaScript* is the most popular scripting code. Because JavaScript cannot create separate "stand-alone" applications, the JavaScript instructions are embedded inside HTML documents. When a website that uses JavaScript is accessed, the HTML document that contains the JavaScript code is downloaded onto the user's computer. The user's web browser then executes that code. Figure 5-13 illustrates how JavaScript works.

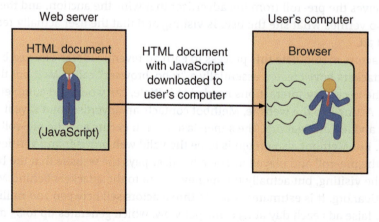

Figure 5-13 JavaScript

Visiting a website that automatically downloads code to run on a local computer can obviously be dangerous: an attacker could write a malicious script and have it downloaded and executed on the user's computer. There are different defense mechanisms intended to prevent JavaScript programs from causing serious harm. These defenses are listed in Table 5-5.

Table 5-5   JavaScript defenses

Defense	Explanation
Limit capabilities	JavaScript does not support certain capabilities. For example, JavaScript running on a local computer cannot read, write, create, delete, or list the files on that computer.
Sandboxing	Only permitting JavaScript to run in a restricted environment ("sandbox") can limit what computer resources it can access or actions it can take.
Same origin	This defense restricts a JavaScript downloaded from Site A from accessing data that came from Site B.

However, there are security concerns with JavaScript. A malicious JavaScript program could capture and remotely transmit user information without the user's knowledge or authorization. For example, an attacker could capture and send the user's email address to a remote source or even send a fraudulent email from the user's email account. Other JavaScript attacks can be even more malicious. An attacker's JavaScript program could scan the user's network and then send specific commands to disable security settings, or redirect a user's browser to an attacker's malicious website.

Extensions

Extensions expand the normal capabilities of a web browser for a specific webpage. Most extensions are written in JavaScript so that the browser can support dynamic actions. Because extensions act as part of the browser itself, they generally have wider access privileges than JavaScript running in a webpage. Extensions are browser-dependent, so that an extension that works in the Google Chrome web browser will not function in the Microsoft Edge browser.

Plug-Ins

A *plug-in* adds new functionality to the web browser so that users can play music, view videos, or display special graphical images within the browser that normally it could not play or display. Technically a plug-in is a *third-party binary library* that lives outside of the "space" that a browser uses on the computer for processing and serves as the link to external programs that are independent of the browser. A single plug-in can be used on different web browsers, such as Google Chrome, Mozilla Firefox, and Microsoft Internet Explorer.

One common plug-in supports Java. Unlike JavaScript, *Java* is a complete programming language that can be used to create stand-alone applications. Whereas JavaScript is embedded in an HTML document, Java can also be used to create a separate program called a *Java applet*. Java applets are stored on the web server and then downloaded onto the user's computer along with the HTML code, as shown in Figure 5-14. Java applets can perform interactive animations, mathematical calculations, or other simple tasks very quickly because the user's request does not have to be sent to the web server for processing and then returned; instead, all of the processing is done on the local computer by the Java applet.

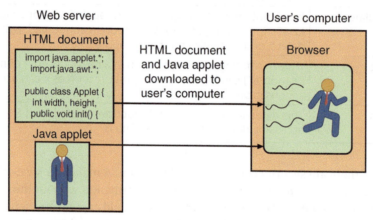

Figure 5-14   Java applet

The most widely used plug-ins for web browsers are Java, Adobe Flash player, Apple QuickTime, and Adobe Acrobat Reader. However, there are tens of thousands of freely available plug-ins, created by not only well-known organizations but also by individual coders.

 Note

One popular blogging tool for users to post their personal blogs supports 39,848 plug-ins.[11]

Add-Ons

Another category of tools that add functionality to the web browser are called *add-ons*. Add-ons add a greater degree of functionality to the entire browser and not just to a single webpage as with a plug-in. In contrast to plug-ins, add-ons can do the following:

- Create additional web browser toolbars
- Change browser menus

- Be aware of other tabs open in the same browser process
- Process the content of every webpage that is loaded

Table 5-6 compares browser extensions, plug-ins, and add-ons.

Table 5-6   Browser additions

Name	Description	Location	Browser support	Examples
Extension	Written in JavaScript and has wider access to privileges	Part of web browser	Only works with a specific browser	Download selective links on webpage, display specific fonts
Plug-in	Links to external programs	Outside of web browser	Compatible with many different browsers	Audio, video, PDF file display
Add-on	Adds functionality to browser itself	Part of web browser	Only works with a specific browser	Dictionary and language packs

It is easy to see how extensions, plug-ins, and add-ons can be security risks. Because of the large number of these browser tools available, created by a large number of programmers, they often have serious security vulnerabilities. Attackers have targeted vulnerable plug-ins as a means to insert malware into a user's computer or in some instances take over complete control of the computer.

Note

Adobe Flash is one of the most popular plug-ins that attackers target. In one five-year span over 324 vulnerabilities in Flash were exploited by attackers.[12]

Due to the risks associated with extensions, plug-ins, and add-ons, efforts are being made to minimize them. Some web browsers now block plug-ins like Adobe Flash, while other browsers use a "Click to Play" feature that enables a plug-in only after the user gives approval. In addition, the most recent version of HTML known as HTML5 standardizes sound and video formats so that plug-ins like Flash are no longer needed. Yet with the large number of these browser tools still available they will likely continue to remain a target of attackers.

Chapter Summary

- Some attacks are designed to intercept network communications. A man-in-the-middle (MITM) attack intercepts legitimate communication and forges a fictitious response to the sender. A man-in-the-browser (MITB) attack occurs between a browser and the underlying computer. A MITB attack seeks to intercept and then manipulate the communication between the web browser and the security mechanisms of the computer. A replay attack makes a copy of the legitimate transmission before sending it to the recipient and then this copy is used at a later time.

- Some types of attacks inject "poison" into a normal network process to facilitate an attack. ARP poisoning changes the ARP cache so the corresponding IP address is pointing to a different computer. DNS poisoning substitutes a DNS address so that the computer is automatically redirected to another device. Privilege escalation is exploiting a vulnerability in software to gain access to resources that the user normally would be restricted from accessing.

- Whereas some attacks are directed at the network itself, other attacks are directed at network servers. A denial of service (DoS) attack is a deliberate attempt to prevent authorized users from accessing a system by overwhelming that system with such a very high number of "bogus" requests so that the system is overwhelmed and cannot respond to legitimate requests. Most DoS attacks today are distributed denial of service (DDoS) attacks using hundreds or even tens of thousands of devices flooding the server with requests. A DNS amplification attack uses publicly accessible and open DNS servers to flood a system with DNS response traffic. An SYN flood attack takes advantage of the procedures for initiating a session.

- A cross-site scripting (XSS) attack is focused not on attacking a web application server to compromise it, but on using the server to launch other attacks on computers that access it. An XSS attack uses websites that accept user input without validating it and uses that input in a response without encoding it. A cross-site request forgery (XSRF) uses the user's web browser settings to impersonate the user. Injection attacks introduce new input to exploit a vulnerability. One of the most common injection attacks, called SQL injection, inserts SQL statements to manipulate a database server.

- Several server attacks are the result of threat actors "commandeering" a technology and then using it for an attack. Session hijacking is an attack in which an attacker attempts to impersonate the user by using the user's session token. Attackers who purchase the domain names of sites that are spelled similarly to actual sites are performing a URL hijacking or typo squatting attack. Domain hijacking occurs when a domain pointer that links a domain name to a specific web server is changed by a threat actor. Hijacking a mouse click is called clickjacking.

- Some attacks can target either a server or a client by "overflowing" areas of memory with instructions from the attacker. A buffer overflow occurs when a process attempts to store data in RAM beyond the boundaries of a fixed-length storage buffer. This extra data overflows into the adjacent memory locations and, under certain conditions, may cause the computer to stop functioning. An integer overflow attack is the result of an attacker changing the value of a variable to something outside the range that the programmer had intended by using an integer overflow.

- Most websites today rely heavily upon advertising revenue. There are several attacks that attempt to use ads or manipulate the advertising system. Malvertising (for malicious advertising) is an attack that uses third-party advertising networks to distribute malware to unsuspecting users who are visiting a well-known website. Threat actors also manipulate the advertising auction process to earn ad revenue that is directed back to them.

- To provide enhanced features, virtually all websites today allow scripting code to be downloaded from the web server into the user's web browser. Another solution to provide these features are different types of additions that are added to a web browser to support dynamic content. However, these have introduced vulnerabilities in browsers that access servers.

Key Terms

Address Resolution
  Protocol (ARP)
ARP poisoning
buffer overflow attack
clickjacking
cross-site request
  forgery (XSRF)
cross-site scripting (XSS)
denial of service (DoS)

distributed denial
  of service (DDoS)
DNS amplification attack
DNS poisoning
domain hijacking
domain name
  resolution
injection attack
integer overflow attack

IP spoofing
MAC spoofing
man-in-the-browser (MITB)
man-in-the-middle (MITM)
privilege escalation
replay
session hijacking
URL hijacking
  (typo squatting)

Review Questions

1. Which attack intercepts communications between a web browser and the underlying computer?
   a. Man-in-the-middle (MITM)
   b. Man-in-the-browser (MITB)
   c. Replay
   d. ARP poisoning

2. Olivia was asked to protect the system from a DNS poisoning attack. What are the locations she would need to protect?
   a. Web server buffer and host DNS server
   b. Reply referrer and domain buffer
   c. Web browser and browser add-on
   d. Host table and external DNS server

3. Newton is concerned that attackers could be exploiting a vulnerability in software to gain access to resources that the user normally would be restricted from accessing. What type of attack is he worried about?
   a. Privilege escalation
   b. Session replay
   c. Scaling exploit
   d. Amplification

4. Which of the following adds new functionality to the web browser so that users can play music, view videos, or display special graphical images within the browser?
   a. Extensions
   b. Scripts
   c. Plug-ins
   d. Add-ons

5. An attacker who manipulates the maximum size of an integer type would be performing what kind of attack?
   a. Integer overflow
   b. Buffer overflow
   c. Number overflow
   d. Heap overflow

6. What kind of attack is performed by an attacker who takes advantage of the inadvertent and unauthorized access built through three succeeding systems that all trust one another?
   a. Privilege escalation
   b. Cross-site attack
   c. Horizontal access attack
   d. Transverse attack

7. Which statement is correct regarding why traditional network security devices cannot be used to block web application attacks?
   a. The complex nature of TCP/IP allows for too many ping sweeps to be blocked.
   b. Web application attacks use web browsers that cannot be controlled on a local computer.
   c. Network security devices cannot prevent attacks from web resources.
   d. Traditional network security devices ignore the content of HTTP traffic, which is the vehicle of web application attacks.

8. What is the difference between a DoS and a DDoS attack?
   a. DoS attacks are faster than DDoS attacks
   b. DoS attacks use fewer computers than DDoS attacks
   c. DoS attacks do not use DNS servers as DDoS attacks do
   d. DoS attacks user more memory than a DDoS attack

9. John was explaining about an attack that accepts user input without validating it and uses that input in a response. What type of attack was he describing?
   a. SQL
   b. XSS
   c. XSRF
   d. DDoS DNS

10. Which attack uses the user's web browser settings to impersonate that user?
    a. XDD
    b. XSRF
    c. Domain hijacking
    d. Session hijacking

11. What is the basis of an SQL injection attack?
    a. To expose SQL code so that it can be examined
    b. To have the SQL server attack client web browsers
    c. To insert SQL statements through unfiltered user input
    d. To link SQL servers into a botnet

12. Which action cannot be performed through a successful SQL injection attack?
    a. Discover the names of different fields in a table
    b. Reformat the web application server's hard drive
    c. Display a list of customer telephone numbers
    d. Erase a database table

13. Attackers who register domain names that are similar to legitimate domain names are performing____.
    a. address resolution
    b. HTTP manipulation
    c. HTML squatting
    d. URL hijacking

14. What type of attack involves manipulating third-party ad networks?
    a. Session advertising
    b. Malvertising
    c. Clickjacking
    d. Directory traversal

15. Why are extensions, plug-ins, and add-ons considered to be security risks?
    a. They are written in Java, which is a weak language.
    b. They have introduced vulnerabilities in browsers.
    c. They use bitcode.
    d. They cannot be uninstalled.

16. What is a session token?
    a. XML code used in an XML injection attack
    b. A random string assigned by a web server

c. Another name for a third-party cookie
    d. A unique identifier that includes the user's email address

17. Which of these is not a DoS attack?
    a. SYN flood
    b. DNS amplification
    c. Smurf attack
    d. Push flood

18. What type of attack intercepts legitimate communication and forges a fictitious response to the sender?
    a. SIDS
    b. interceptor
    c. MITM
    d. SQL intrusion

19. A replay attack____.
    a. can be prevented by patching the web browser
    b. is considered to be a type of DoS attack
    c. makes a copy of the transmission for use at a later time
    d. replays the attack over and over to flood the server

20. DNS poisoning____.
    a. floods a DNS server with requests until it can no longer respond
    b. is rarely found today due to the use of host tables
    c. substitutes DNS addresses so that the computer is automatically redirected to another device
    d. is the same as ARP poisoning

Hands-On Projects

Note

If you are concerned about installing any of the software in these projects on your regular computer, you can install the software in the Windows virtual machine created in the Chapter 1 Hands-On Projects 1-3 and 1-4. Software installed within the virtual machine will not impact the host computer.

Project 5-1: Testing Browser Security

One of the first steps in securing a web browser is to conduct an analysis to determine if any security vulnerabilities exist. These vulnerabilities may be a result of missing patches or out-of-date plug-ins. In this project, you use a plug-in to scan the Firefox or Chrome browser.

1. Open the Firefox or Chrome web browser and enter the URL **browsercheck.qualys .com** (if you are no longer able to access the site through the web address, use a search engine to search for "Qualys Browser Check").
2. Click **FAQ**.
3. Read the information on this page about what the Qualys browser check plug-in will do.
4. Return to the home page.
5. Click **Install Plugin**.
6. Check the box **I have read and accepted the Service User Agreement**.
7. Click **Continue**. An analysis of the browser's security appears.
8. If there are any security issues detected, click the **Fix It** buttons to correct the problem. Follow the instructions on each page to correct the problems.
9. Return to the Qualys scan results page.
10. When the scan is finished click each of the tabs (**Browser/Plugins**, **System Checks**, and **MS Updates**) for each of the browsers listed. Be sure to correct any security problems.
11. Close all windows.

Project 5-2: Configuring Microsoft Windows Data Execution Prevention (DEP)

Data Execution Prevention (DEP) is a Microsoft Windows feature that prevents attackers from using buffer overflow to execute malware. Most modern CPUs support an NX (No eXecute) bit to designate a part of memory for containing only data. An attacker who launches a buffer overflow attack to change the "return address" to point to his malware code stored in the data area of memory would be defeated because DEP will not allow code in the memory area to be executed. If an older computer processor does not support NX, then a weaker software-enforced DEP will be enabled by Windows. Software-enforced DEP protects only limited system binaries and is not the same as NX DEP.

DEP provides an additional degree of protection that reduces the risk of buffer overflows. In this project, you determine if a Microsoft Windows system can run DEP. If it can, you learn how to configure DEP

1. The first step is to determine if the computer supports NX. Use your web browser to go to **www.grc.com/securable**. Click **Download now** and follow the default settings to download the application on your computer.

> **Note** 📎
>
> The location of content on the Internet may change without warning. If you are no longer able to access the program through the above URL, use a search engine to search for "GRC securable".

2. Double-click **Securable.exe** to launch the program. If it reports that **Hardware D.E.P.** is "No," then that computer's processor does not support NX. Close the SecurAble application.
3. The next step is to check the DEP settings in Microsoft Windows. Right-click **Start** and **System** and **Control Panel**.
4. Click **System and Security** and then click **System**.
5. Click **Advanced system settings** in the left pane.
6. Click the **Advanced** tab if necessary.
7. Click **Settings** under **Performance** and then click the **Data Execution Prevention** tab.
8. Windows supports two levels of DEP controls: DEP enabled for only Windows programs and services and DEP enabled for Windows programs and services as well as all other application programs and services. If the configuration is set to *Turn on DEP for essential Windows programs and services only*, click **Turn on DEP for all programs and services except those I select**. This will provide full protection to all programs.
9. If an application does not function properly, it may be necessary to make an exception for that application and not have DEP protect it. If this is necessary, click the **Add** button and then search for the program. Click on the program to add it to the exception list.
10. Close all windows and applications and restart your computer to invoke DEP protection.

Project 5-3: Simulating a Hosts File Attack

Substituting a fraudulent IP address can be done by either attacking the Domain Name System (DNS) server or the local host table. Attackers can target a local hosts file to create new entries that will redirect users to their fraudulent site. In this project, you add a fraudulent entry to the local hosts file.

1. Start your web browser.
2. Go to the Cengage website at **www.cengage.com** and then go to MSN at **www.msn .com** to verify that the names are correctly resolved.
3. Now search based on IP address. Go to **http://69.32.208.74** for Cengage and **http://13.82.28.61** for MSN.

Note 📎

IP addresses are sometimes based on the region in which you live. If you cannot access the above sites by these IP addresses, go to **ipaddress.com/ip_lookup/** and enter the domain name to receive the correct IP address.

4. Click **Start** and then **Windows Accessories**.
5. Right-click **Notepad** and then **More** and select **Run as administrator**. If you receive the message **Do you want to allow this app to make changes to the device?** click **Yes**.
6. Click **File** and then **Open**. Click the **File Type** drop-down arrow to change from **Text Documents (*.txt)** to **All Files (*.*)**.
7. Navigate to the file **C:\Windows\System32\drivers\etc\hosts** and open it.
8. At the end of the file following all hashtags (#) in the first column enter the IP address of **13.82.28.61.** This is the IP address of MSN.
9. Press **Tab** and enter **www.cengage.com**. In this hosts table, www.cengage.com is now resolved to the IP address of MSN, 13.82.28.61.
10. Click **File** and then **Save**.
11. Open your web browser and then enter the URL **www.cengage.com.** What website appears?
12. Return to the hosts file and remove this entry.
13. Click **File** and then **Save**.
14. Close all windows.

Project 5-4: Exploring ARP Poisoning

Attackers frequently modify the Address Resolution Protocol (ARP) table to redirect communications away from a valid device to an attacker's computer. In this project, you view the ARP table on your computer and make modifications to it. You will need to have another "victim's" computer running on your network (and know the IP address), as well as a default gateway that serves as the switch to the network

1. Open a Command Prompt window by right-clicking **Start** and select **Command Prompt (Admin)**.
2. To view your current ARP table, type **arp -a** and then press **Enter**. The Internet Address is the IP address of another device on the network while the physical address is the MAC address of that device.
3. To determine network addresses, type **ipconfig/all** and then press **Enter**.
4. Record the IP address of the default gateway.
5. Delete the ARP table entry of the default gateway by typing **arp -d** followed by the IP address of the gateway, such as **arp -d 192.168.1.1** and then press **Enter**.
6. Create an automatic entry in the ARP table of the victim's computer by typing **ping** followed by that computer's IP address, such as **ping 192.168.1.100**, and then press **Enter**.

7. Verify that this new entry is now listed in the ARP table by typing **arp -a** and then press **Enter**. Record the physical address of that computer.
8. Add that entry to the ARP table by entering **arp -s** followed by the IP address and then the MAC address.
9. Delete all entries from the ARP table by typing **arp -d**.
10. Close all windows.

Case Projects

Case Project 5-1: DoS Attacks

Denial of service (DoS) attacks can cripple an organization that relies heavily on its web application servers, such as online retailers. What are some of the most widely publicized DoS attacks that have occurred recently? Who was the target? How many DoS attacks occur on a regular basis? What are some ways in which DoS attacks can be prevented? Write a one-page paper on your research.

Case Project 5-2: DNS Services

Many organizations offer a free domain name resolution service that resolves DNS requests through a worldwide network of redundant DNS servers. The claim is that this is faster and more reliable than using the DNS servers provided by Internet Service Providers (ISP). They also claim that their DNS servers improve security by maintaining a real-time blacklist of harmful websites and will warn users whenever they attempt to access a site containing potentially threatening content. They also say that using this service can reduce exposure to types of DNS poisoning attacks. Research free DNS services. Identify at least three providers and create a table comparing their features. Are the claims of providing improved security valid? How do they compare with your ISP's DNS service?

Case Project 5-3: Cross-Site Attack Defenses

Use the Internet to research defenses against cross-site attacks (XSS and XSRF). What are the common defenses? How difficult are they to implement? Why are these defenses not used extensively? Write a one-page paper on your research.

Case Project 5-4: SQL Injection Attacks

SQL injection attacks continue to be a significant attack vector for threat actors. Use the Internet to research these attacks. What are some recent attacks that have been initiated by SQL injection? How were they conducted? What defenses are there against them? Write a one-page paper on your research.

Case Project 5-5: Buffer Overflow Attacks

Research the Internet regarding buffer overflow attacks. How do the various types of overflow attacks differ? When did they first start to occur? What can they do and not do? What must a programmer do to prevent a buffer overflow in a program she has written? Write a one-page paper on your research.

Case Project 5-6: Lake Point Consulting Services

Lake Point Consulting Services (LPCS) provides security consulting and assurance services to over 500 clients across a wide range of enterprises in more than 20 states. A new initiative at LPCS is for each of its seven regional offices to provide internships to students who are in their final year of the security degree program at the local college.

Like Magic is a national repair shop that specializes in repairing minor car door "dings," windshield repair, interior fabric repair, and scratch repair. Like Magic allows customers to file a claim through a smartphone app and its website. Recently, however, Like Magic was the victim of an SQL injection attack that resulted in customer account information and credit card numbers being stolen. Several security personnel were fired due to this breach. The vice president of Like Magic is adamant that this will never happen again to them, and has contacted LPSC to help provide training to the technology staff to prevent further attacks.

1. Create a PowerPoint presentation for Like Magic about cross-site attacks, injection attacks, hijacking, and DoS attacks, explaining what they are, how they occur, and what defenses can be set up to prevent them. Your presentation should contain 8 to 10 slides.
2. After the presentation Like Magic asks LPSC to address other weaknesses in their system. You have been placed on the team to examine potential networking-based attacks. One of your tasks is to create a report for a presentation; you are asked to write a one-page narrative providing an overview of the different types of networking-based attacks of interception and poisoning.

Case Project 5-7: Community Site Activity

The Information Security Community Site is an online companion to this textbook. It contains a wide variety of tools, information, discussion boards, and other features to assist learners. Go to **community.cengage.com/Infosec2** and click the *Join or Sign* in icon to log in, using your login name and password that you created in Chapter 1. Click **Forums (Discussion)** and click on **Security+ Case Projects (6th edition)**. Read the following case study.

Read again *Today's Attacks and Defenses* at the beginning of the chapter. Should the government restrict vendors from addressing vulnerabilities in their products, even if the source was from leaked classified material? How would you respond to the charge that this is simply an attempt to keep products vulnerable so that intelligence agencies can manipulate them? To what extent should vendors be pursuing uncovering vulnerabilities in their products? How is this any different from vendors paying security researchers who uncover vulnerabilities? Enter your answers on the InfoSec Community Server discussion board.

References

1. Goodin, Dan, "A simple command allows the CIA to commandeer 318 models of Cisco switches," *Ars Technica*, Mar. 20, 2017, accessed Mar. 20, 2017, arstechnica.com /security/2017/03/a-simple-command-allows-the-cia-to-commandeer-318-models -of-cisco-switches/.

2. Krotoski, Mark and Presley, Susan, "SEC and DOJ hacking prosecutions highlight SEC's increased interest in cybersecurity risks," *Morgan Lewis*, Sep. 15, 2015, accessed Dec. 28, 2015, www.morganlewis.com/pubs/sec-and-doj-hacking-prosecutions-highlight -secs-increased-interest-in-cybersecurity-risks.

3. "Denial of service: How businesses evaluate the threat of DDoS attacks," *Kaspersky*, Sep. 2015, accessed Sep. 9, 2015, press.kaspersky.com/files/2015/09/IT_Risks_Survey _Report_Threat_of_DDoS_Attacks.pdf.

4. "U.S. charges Russian FSB officers and their criminal conspirators for hacking Yahoo and millions of email accounts," *Department of Justice*, Mar. 15, 2017, accessed Apr. 12, 2017, https://www.justice.gov/opa/pr/us-charges-russian-fsb-officers-and-their -criminal-conspirators-hacking-yahoo-and-millions.

5. McNichol, Tom, "Friend me on Facebook," *Bloomberg Businessweek*, Nov. 7, 2011.

6. "New gTLD Overview," *nTLDStats*, retrieved Mar. 28, 2017, ntldstats.com/tld.

7. Domabirg, Artem, "Bitsquatting: DNS hijacking without exploitation," *Diaburg.org*, accessed Mar. 27, 2017, dinaburg.org/bitsquatting.html.

8. "Google's ad revenue from 2001 to 2016," *Statista*, accessed Mar. 28, 2017, www.statista .com/statistics/266249/advertising-revenue-of-google/.

9. Pauli, Darren, "Malware menaces poison ads as Google, Yahoo! look away," *The Register*, accessed Sep. 1, 2015, www.theregister.co.uk/2015/08/27/malvertising_ feature/?page=1.

10. "The Methbot operation," *WhiteOps*, Dec. 20, 2016, accessed Dec. 24, 2016, go.whiteops .com/rs/179-SQE-823/images/WO_Methbot_Operation_WP.pdf.

11. "Plugin Directory," *WordPress*, accessed Aug. 30, 2015, wordpress.org/plugins/

12. "Cisco 2015 Midyear Security Report," *Cisco*, accessed Aug. 30, 2015, www.cisco.com /web/offers/lp/2015-midyear-security-report/index.html.

CHAPTER 6

NETWORK SECURITY DEVICES, DESIGN, AND TECHNOLOGY

After completing this chapter, you should be able to do the following:

List the different types of network security devices and how they can be used

Describe secure network architectures

Explain how network technologies can enhance security

Today's Attacks and Defenses

There has been much debate regarding governments and cryptography. Many governments claim that terrorists are encrypting their electronic correspondence when planning attacks. To protect their citizens, these governments want to eavesdrop on suspected terrorists who use encryption, either by holding the decryption keys themselves so that they can decrypt conversations or by planting a "backdoor" in the encryption algorithm so that it can be compromised. However, a recent event revealed an unintended consequence of such a government-sponsored cryptographic backdoor.

The Computer Security Law of 1987 was passed by the U.S. Congress to improve the security and privacy of sensitive data on federal computer systems. One part of this law tasked the U.S. National Institute of Standards and Technology (NIST) to work with the National Security Agency (NSA) to create standards for federal data security. One of these standards was the pseudo-random number generator Dual_EC_DRBG.

Soon after Dual_EC_DRBG was released in 2006, however, it was demonstrated that this algorithm was not only slow but had a bias in that some numbers appeared more often than other numbers and thus were not truly random. Although some argued that the Dual_EC_DRBG standard should be dropped, it was kept at the NSA's insistence. The agency said that it was worth including because of its theoretical basis and that it should be difficult to predict the numbers the algorithm would generate. (Leaked 2013 documents suggested that the NSA intentionally sabotaged Dual_EC_DRBG to create a cryptographic backdoor but this has never been proved.[1])

Meanwhile, two vulnerabilities were uncovered in networking hardware devices manufactured by Juniper Networks. The first was a hardcoded master password in the Juniper operating system (ScreenOS) that would open a backdoor to allow remote administrative access to the device via Secure Shell (SSH). The second vulnerability would allow an attacker who can monitor traffic through a virtual private network (VPN) to decrypt it. This second vulnerability uses elliptic curve cryptography (ECC) that requires two random numbers, P and Q. The pseudo-random number generator Dual_EC_DRBG was used by ScreenOS to create these values.

In 2007 two Microsoft researchers discovered that if Q was known then someone could examine the random numbers generated by the algorithm and subsequently predict the numbers that would be generated in the future, breaking the encryption. Thus, any algorithm that used random numbers generated by Dual_EC_DRBG could be compromised.

Even though Dual_EC_DRBG was known to have a potential vulnerability, Juniper chose to incorporate Dual_EC_DRBG in its ScreenOS. However, Juniper said that it was using a different point Q, thus preventing anyone from breaking the encryption. Yet, in August 2012 it appears that Juniper changed its Q value back to the original (and vulnerable) value, so that encrypted traffic could have been easily broken. In fact, an attacker would only have to examine 30 bytes of raw output to have the necessary data to initiate the attack. Juniper eventually patched both vulnerabilities.

In a touch of irony, many U.S. government institutions use Juniper devices. This means that government network traffic—much of which was confidential and was protected by ScreenOS's ECC using Dual_EC_DRBG—may also have been compromised for several years. If the U.S. government was behind weakening Dual_EC_DRBG, did it also make its own traffic vulnerable? Many security researchers are wondering if a government-sponsored cryptographic backdoor could come back to haunt them.

At one time the terms *information security* **and** *network security* **were virtually** synonymous. That was because the network was viewed as the protecting wall around which client computers could be kept safe. A secure network would keep attackers away from the devices on the inside.

This approach, however, has proved to be untenable. There are simply too many entry points that circumvent the network and allow malware to enter. For example, users could bring an infected USB flash drive and insert it into their computer, thus introducing malware while bypassing the secure network. Also, malware started taking advantage of common network protocols, such as Hypertext Transfer Protocol (HTTP), and could not always be detected or blocked by network security devices.

This is not to say that network security is unimportant. Having a secure network is essential to a comprehensive information security posture. Not all applications are designed and written with security and reliability in mind, so it falls on the network to provide protection. Also, network-delivered services can scale better for larger environments and can complement server and application functionality. And because an attacker who can successfully penetrate a computer network might have access to hundreds or even thousands of desktop systems, servers, and storage devices, a secure network defense remains a critical element in any enterprise's security plan. Enterprises should make network defenses one of the first priorities in protecting information.

This chapter explores network security, and investigates how to build a secure network through network devices, network architectures, and network technologies.

Security Through Network Devices

 Certification

2.1 Install and configure network components, both hardware- and software-based, to support organizational security.

2.4 Given a scenario, analyze and interpret output from security technologies.

3.2 Given a scenario, implement secure network architecture concepts.

Different network devices can be used to protect a network and its contents. Security can be achieved through using the security features found in standard networking devices as well as hardware designed primarily for security or that provides a significant security function.

> **Note** 🖇
>
> Using both standard networking devices and hardware designed specifically for security can result in a layered security approach, which can significantly improve security. If only one defense mechanism is in place, an attacker has to circumvent only a single defense. A network with layered security makes it more difficult for an attacker because the attacker must have the tools, knowledge, and skills to break through the various layers. A layered approach also can be useful in resisting a variety of types of attacks.

Standard Network Devices

Standard network devices are often classified based on their function in the seven-layer *Open Systems Interconnection (OSI)* reference model: Application (Layer 7), Presentation (Layer 6), Session (Layer 5), Transport (Layer 4), Network (Layer 3), Data Link (Layer 2), and Physical (Layer 1). The security functions of these network devices can be used to provide a degree of network security. However, improperly configured standard network devices can also introduce vulnerabilities. These devices include bridges, switches, routers, load balancers, and proxies.

> **Note** 🖇
>
> Several different data units are represented at the various layers of the OSI model. These data units include bit (Physical), bit/frame (Data Link), packet/datagram (Network), segment (Transport), and data (Session, Presentation, and Application).

Bridges

A network **bridge** is a hardware device or software that is used to join two separate computer networks to enable communication between them. Bridges can connect two local area networks (LANs) or two network segments (like subnets) of a single LAN. A bridge allows a LAN to extend its footprint to cover a larger physical area. Because bridges operate at the Data Link layer (Layer 2) of the OSI model, all networks or segments being connected must use the same Data Link layer protocol, such as Ethernet.

Many laptop computers have both wired and wireless network interface cards. These two adapters allow the laptop to establish simultaneous wired and wireless connections to two different networks. Most operating systems allow for a software network bridge to connect the two networks. Figure 6-1 illustrates the software bridge option for a Microsoft Windows 10 computer.

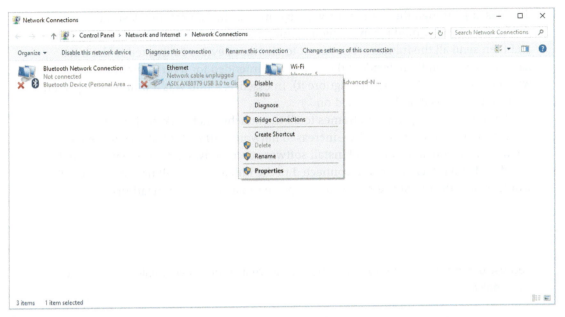

Figure 6-1   Microsoft Windows software network bridge

Note 🔗

A feature of Microsoft Windows known as Internet Connection Sharing (ICS) allows a single Internet connection on a computer to be shared with other computers on the same LAN. However, a software network bridge cannot link ICS connections.

Creating a software network bridge could create a security vulnerability. A bridge that links, for example, a secure wired LAN network with an unsecured wireless network could create an unprotected link between the two, thus permitting access to the secure wired network from the unsecured wireless network.

Note 🔗

Enterprises can configure a wired Ethernet connection to automatically shut off if it detects that the device connecting to it is using software network bridging.

Switches

Early LANs used a *hub*, which is a standard network device for connecting multiple network devices so that they function as a single network segment. Because hubs worked at the Physical layer (Layer 1) of the OSI model, they did not read any of the data passing through them and thus were ignorant of the source and destination of the frames. A hub would receive only incoming frames, regenerate the electrical signal, and then send all the frames received out to all other devices connected to the hub. Each device would then decide if the frame was intended for it (and retain it) or if it was for another device (and then ignore it). In essence, a hub was a multiport repeater: whatever it received, it then passed on.

Because a hub repeated all frames to all the attached network devices, it significantly—and unnecessarily—increased network traffic. But hubs were also a security risk: a threat actor could install software or a hardware device that captured and decoded packets on a client connected to the hub and view all network traffic. This would enable the threat actor to read or capture sensitive communications.

Note 📎

Because of their impact on network traffic and inherent security vulnerability, hubs are rarely used today.

Like a hub, a network **switch** is a device that connects network hosts. However, unlike a hub, a switch has a degree of "intelligence." Operating at the Data Link layer (Layer 2), a switch can learn which device is connected to each of its ports. A switch learns by examining the media access control (MAC) address of frames that it receives and then associates its port with the MAC address of the device connected to that port, storing that information in a *MAC address table*. It can then forward only frames intended for one specific device (*unicast*) or send frames to all devices (*broadcast*). This not only improves network performance but also provides better security. A threat actor who installs software to capture packets on a computer attached to a switch will see only frames that are directed to that device and not those intended for any other network device.

It is important for switches to be properly configured to provide a high degree of security. Proper configuration includes loop prevention and providing a flood guard.

Loop Prevention

In Figure 6-2, computer Alpha, which is connected to Switch A, wants to send frames to computer Beta on Segment 2. Because Switch A does not know where Beta is located, it "floods" the network with the packet (sends it to all destinations). The packet then travels down Segment 1 to Switch B and Segment 2 to Switch C. Switch B then adds Alpha to its lookup table that it maintains for Segment 1, and Switch C also adds it to its lookup table for Segment 3. Yet if Switch B or C has not yet learned the address for Alpha, they will both flood Segment 2 looking for Beta; that is, each switch will take the packet sent by the other switch and flood it back out again because they still do not know where Beta is located. Switch A then will receive the packet from each segment and flood it back out on the other segment. This *switching loop* causes a *broadcast storm* as the frames are broadcast, received, and rebroadcast by each switch. Broadcast storms can cripple a network in a matter of seconds to the point that no legitimate traffic can occur.

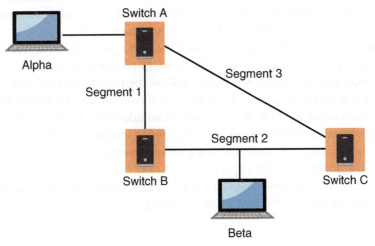

Figure 6-2   **Broadcast storm**

Broadcast storms can be mitigated with **loop prevention**, which uses the IEEE 802.1d standard *spanning-tree algorithm (STA)*. STA can determine that a switch has multiple ways to communicate with a host and then determine the best path of communication while blocking out other paths.

Flood Guard

A MAC address table in a switch contains the MAC-to-port associations that the switch has learned. A threat actor may attempt a *MAC flooding attack* by overflowing the switch with Ethernet frames that have been spoofed so that each frame contains a different source MAC address, each appearing to come from a different computer. This can quickly consume all the memory (called the *content addressable memory or CAM*) for the MAC address table. Once the MAC address table is full and is unable to store any additional MAC address, the switch enters a *fail-open* mode and functions like a network hub, broadcasting frames to all ports. A threat actor could then install software or a hardware device that captures and decodes packets on one client connected to the switch and view all traffic.

The defense against a MAC flooding attack is a **flood guard**. Several vendors of switches have implemented a flood guard technology known as **port security**. Switches that support port security can be configured to limit the number of MAC addresses that can be learned on ports. Restricting the number of incoming MAC addresses for a port prevents overwhelming the MAC address table. If additional MAC addresses are sent to a switch, the port security feature can be configured to ignore the new MAC addresses while allowing normal traffic from the single preapproved MAC address (*restrict mode*), record new MAC addresses up to a specific limit (*sticky mode*), or block the port entirely (*shutdown mode*). MAC address tables can also be converted from a dynamic "learning" mode to a static "permanent" mode when necessary.

> **Note**
>
> Sometimes users who have only a single network connection port in their office might bring their own personal switch to connect to that port so they can then attach more network devices. Port security can usually prevent these personal switches from connecting to the corporate network.

Because a switch can be used for capturing traffic, it is important that the necessary defenses be implemented to prevent unauthorized users from gathering this data. These attacks and defenses are summarized in Table 6-1.

Table 6-1 Protecting a switch

Type of attack	Description	Security defense
MAC flooding	An attacker can overflow the switch's address table with fake MAC addresses, forcing it to act like a hub, sending packets to all devices.	Use a switch that can close ports with too many MAC addresses.
MAC address spoofing	If two devices have the same MAC address, a switch may send frames to each device. An attacker can change the MAC address on her device to match the target device's MAC address.	Configure the switch so that only one port can be assigned per MAC address.
ARP poisoning	The attacker sends a forged ARP packet to the source device, substituting the attacker's computer MAC address.	Use an ARP detection appliance.
Port mirroring	An attacker connects his device to the switch's port.	Secure the switch in a locked room.

Routers

Operating at the Network layer (Layer 3), a **router** is a network device that can forward packets across different computer networks. When a router receives an incoming packet, it reads the destination address and then, using information in its routing table, sends the packet to the next network toward its destination.

Routers can also perform a security function by using an **Access Control List (ACL)**. An ACL is as a set of rules that acts like a "network filter" to permit or restrict data flowing into and out of the router network interfaces. When an ACL is configured on an interface, the router analyzes the data passing through the interface, compares it to the criteria described in the ACL, and either permits the data to continue or prohibits it. Whereas a separate security device can provide more in-depth protection, these separate devices can slow the flow of data as the data must be routed through this device. A router using an ACL, on the other hand, can operate at the higher speed of the router and not delay network traffic.

On external routers that face the Internet, router ACLs can restrict known vulnerable protocols from entering the network. They can also be used to limit traffic entering the network from unapproved networks. When used to protect against IP spoofing that imitates another computer's IP address this defense is called **antispoofing**. Because IP spoofing attacks often utilize known unused and untrusted addresses, an external router ACL can help block these addresses (usually by designating a range of IP addresses) and thus minimize IP spoofing attacks.

Note

Antispoofing ACLs on external routers require frequent monitoring because the address ranges that are denied can frequently change.

Router ACLs can also be used on internal routers that process interior network traffic. These router ACLs usually are less restrictive but more specific than those on external routers because the devices on the internal network are generally considered to be friendly. Internal router ACLs are often configured with explicit *permit* and *deny* statements for specific addresses and protocol services. Internal router ACLs can also limit devices on the network from performing IP spoofing by applying outbound ACLs that limit the traffic to known valid local IP addresses.

Load Balancers

Load balancing is a technology that can help to evenly distribute work across a network. Requests that are received can be allocated across multiple devices such as servers. To the user, this distribution is transparent and appears as if a single server is providing the resources. Load-balancing technology reduces the probability of overloading a single server and ensuring that each networked server benefits from having optimized bandwidth.

Load balancing can be performed either through software running on a computer or as a dedicated hardware device known as a **load balancer**. Load balancers are often grouped into two categories known as *Layer 4 load balancers* and *Layer 7 load balancers*. Layer 4 load balancers act upon data found in Network and Transport layer protocols such as Internet Protocol (IP), Transmission Control Protocol (TCP), File Transfer Protocol (FTP), and User Datagram Protocol (UDP). Layer 7 load balancers distribute requests based on data found in Application layer protocols such as HTTP.

There are different scheduling protocols that are used in load balancers:

- *Round-robin.* In a **round-robin** scheduling protocol, the rotation applies to all devices equally.
- *Affinity.* A scheduling protocol that distributes the load based on which devices can handle the load more efficiently is known as **affinity** scheduling. Affinity scheduling may be based on which load balancers have the least number of connections at a given point in time.
- *Other.* Layer 7 load balancers also can use HTTP headers, cookies, or data within the application message itself to make a decision on distribution.

Note

Load balancing that is used for distributing HTTP requests received is also called *IP spraying*.

When multiple load balancers are used together to achieve *high availability (HA)* they can be placed in different configurations. In an **active-passive** configuration, the primary load balancer distributes the network traffic to the most suitable server while the secondary load balancer operates in a "listening mode." This second load balancer constantly monitors the performance of the primary load balancer and will step in and take over the load balancing duties should the primary load balancer start to experience difficulties or fail. The active-passive configuration allows for uninterrupted service and can also handle planned or unplanned service outages. In an **active-active** configuration, all load balancers are always active. Network traffic is combined and the load balancers then work together as a team.

> **Note** 🔗
>
> Load balancers in an active-active configuration can also remember previous requests from users. In the event the user returns requesting the same information, the user is directed to the load balancer that previously served the request and the information can be immediately provided.

The servers behind load balancers are often given a **virtual IP (VIP)** address. As its name suggests, this is not an actual IP address. Instead, it is an IP address and a specific port number that can be used to reference different physical servers. A VIP with the address and port 172.32.250.1:80 can be configured to accept one type of traffic while the VIP 172.32.250.1:443 can accept another type of traffic. Multiple VIPs can be created using the same IP address as long as a different port number is being used.

The use of a load balancer has security advantages. Because load balancers generally are located between routers and servers, they can detect and stop attacks directed at a server or application. A load balancer can be used to detect and prevent protocol attacks that could cripple a single server. Some load balancers can hide HTTP error pages or remove server identification headers from HTTP responses, denying attackers additional information about the internal network.

Proxies

In the human world, a *proxy* is a person who is authorized to act as the substitute or agent on behalf of another person. For example, an individual who has been granted the power of attorney for a sick relative can make decisions and take actions on behalf of that person as her proxy.

There are also proxies that are used in computer networking. These devices act as substitutes on behalf of the primary device. A **forward proxy** is a computer or an application program that intercepts user requests from the internal secure network and then processes that request on behalf of the user. When an internal client requests a service such as a file or a webpage from an external web server, it normally would connect directly with that remote server. In a network using a forward proxy server, the client first connects to the proxy server, which checks its memory to see if a previous request already has been fulfilled and whether a copy of that file or page is residing on the proxy server in its temporary storage area (*cache*). If it is not, the proxy server connects to the external web server using its own IP address (instead of the internal client's address) and requests the service. When the proxy server receives the requested item from the web server, the item is then forwarded to the client. An **application/multipurpose proxy** is a special proxy server that "knows" the application protocols that it supports. For example, an *FTP proxy server* implements the protocol FTP.

A **reverse proxy** routes requests coming from an external network to the correct internal server. To the outside user, the IP address of the reverse proxy is the final IP address for requesting services, yet only the reverse proxy can access the internal servers. Forward proxy and reverse proxy servers are illustrated in Figure 6-3.

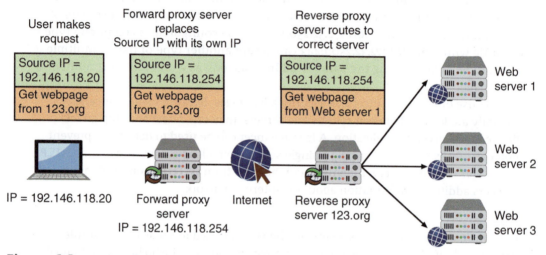

Figure 6-3   Forward and reverse proxy servers

> **Note**
>
> Encrypted traffic entering the network must first be decrypted for a load balancer to direct requests to different servers. A reverse proxy can be the point at which this traffic is decrypted.

Access to forward proxy servers is usually configured in the operating system, as shown in Figure 6-4, or in a user's web browser. However, a **transparent proxy** does not require any configuration on the user's computer. It is often used for content filtering in schools and libraries.

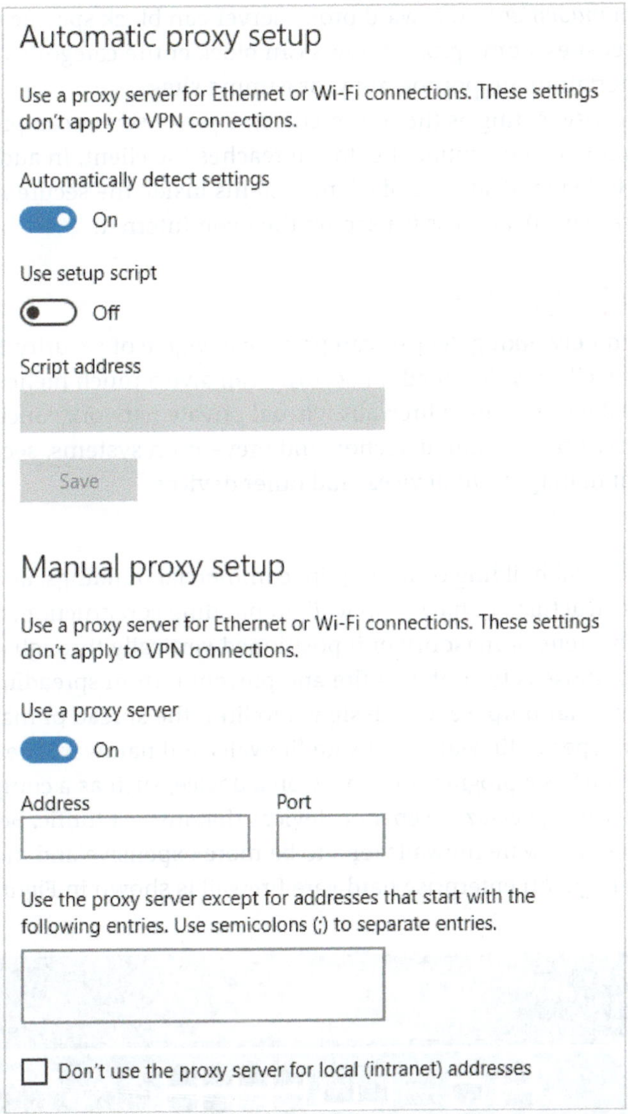

Automatic proxy setup

Use a proxy server for Ethernet or Wi-Fi connections. These settings don't apply to VPN connections.

Automatically detect settings

On

Use setup script

Off

Script address

Save

Manual proxy setup

Use a proxy server for Ethernet or Wi-Fi connections. These settings don't apply to VPN connections.

Use a proxy server

On

Address   Port

Use the proxy server except for addresses that start with the following entries. Use semicolons (;) to separate entries.

☐ Don't use the proxy server for local (intranet) addresses

Figure 6-4   **Configuring access to forward proxy servers**

Although forward proxy servers have some disadvantages, such as the added expense and the fact that caches may not always be current, they have several advantages:

- *Increased speed.* Because forward proxy servers can cache material, a request can be served from the cache instead of retrieving the webpage through the Internet.
- *Reduced costs.* A proxy server can reduce the amount of bandwidth usage because of the cache.

- *Improved management.* A forward proxy server can block specific webpages and/or entire websites. Some proxy servers can block entire categories of websites such as entertainment, pornography, or gaming sites.
- *Stronger security.* Acting as the intermediary, a proxy server can protect clients from malware by intercepting it before it reaches the client. In addition, a proxy server can hide the IP address of client systems inside the secure network. Only the proxy server's IP address is used on the open Internet.

Network Security Hardware

Although standard networking devices can provide a degree of security, hardware devices that are specifically designed for security can give a much higher level of protection. These devices include firewalls, virtual private network concentrators, mail gateways, network intrusion detection and prevention systems, security and information event management devices, and other devices.

Firewalls

Both national and local building codes require commercial buildings, apartments, and other similar structures to have a *firewall*. In building construction, a firewall is usually a brick, concrete, or masonry unit positioned vertically through all stories of the building. Its purpose is to contain a fire and prevent it from spreading. A computer **firewall** serves a similar purpose: it is designed to limit the spread of malware.

There are two types of firewalls: software firewalls and hardware firewalls. A software firewall runs as a program or service on a device, such as a computer or router. Hardware firewalls are specialized separate devices that inspect traffic. Because they are specialized devices, hardware firewalls tend to be more expensive and more difficult to configure and manage. An enterprise hardware firewall is shown in Figure 6-5.

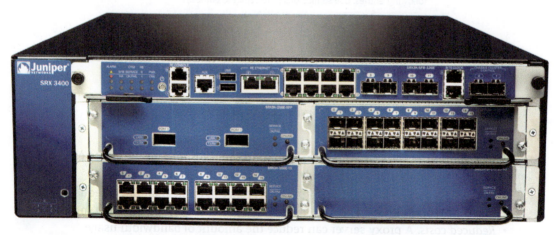

Figure 6-5   Enterprise hardware firewall

Source: https://www.juniper.net/assets/img/products/image-library/srx-series/srx3400/srx3400-frontwtop-high.

Note

A disadvantage of a software firewall is that a malware infection on the device on which it is running, such as a computer, could also compromise the software firewall. Because a hardware firewall does not depend upon an underlying device, this is not an issue with hardware firewalls.

Software firewalls running on a device provide protection to that device only. One common example is a software firewall that runs as a program on the local computer to block or filter traffic coming into and out of the computer. All modern operating systems include a software firewall, usually called a **host-based firewall** or *personal firewall*. The settings for the Windows personal firewall are shown in Figure 6-6. If an application or program running on a computer needs to communicate with another computer on the LAN

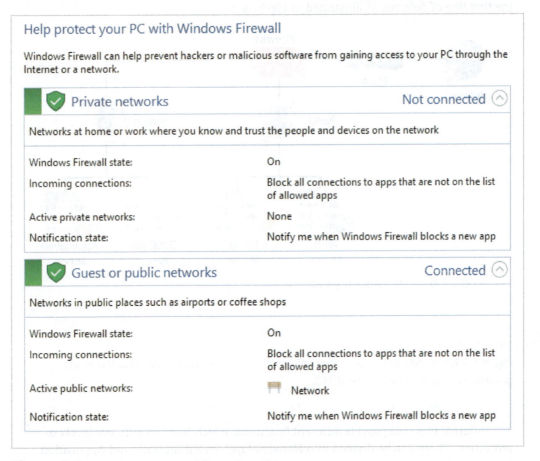

Figure 6-6 Windows personal firewall settings

or an Internet server, the user can create an opening (port) in that personal firewall for that application or program only, approving the application to transmit (called *unblocking*). This is more secure than permanently opening a port in the firewall: when a permanent firewall opening is made it always remains open and is then susceptible to attackers, but when a port is unblocked by a personal firewall it is opened only when an application requires it.

Personal firewalls can limit the spread of malware into the computer as well as preventing a user's infected computer from attacking other computers. For many personal firewalls, inbound connections (data coming in from another source) are always blocked unless there is a specific firewall rule that allows them in. This principle of being always blocked by default is called **implicit deny**. That is, an action is always denied unless it is definitively and explicitly allowed. Outbound connections (data going out to another source) are always allowed unless there is a rule that blocks them and the outbound rules are turned on.

A firewall that protects an entire network is typically a separate hardware device. These hardware firewalls are usually located outside the network security perimeter as the first line of defense, as illustrated in Figure 6-7.

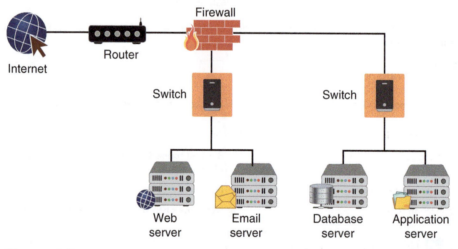

Figure 6-7 Network firewall

Figure 6-7 is not the optimal security configuration. This will be explained below in the discussion of *demilitarized zones (DMZ)*.

Different firewalls provide different functions, which leads to different levels of protection. These can be divided into Network layer-based firewalls and Application layer-based firewalls.

Network-Based Firewalls

A **network-based firewall** functions at the Network layer (Layer 3). Its job is to screen packets based on specific criteria, making it essentially a *packet filter*.

> **Note** 📎
>
> Network-based firewalls are not the same as network firewalls that protect entire networks (discussed in the previous section). A network-based firewall is one that operates at the OSI Network layer (Layer 3).

Packets can be filtered by a firewall in one of two ways. **Stateless packet filtering** looks at the incoming packet and permits or denies it based on the conditions that have been set by the administrator. **Stateful packet filtering** keeps a record of the state of a connection between an internal computer and an external device and then makes decisions based on the connection as well as the conditions. For example, a stateless packet filter firewall might allow a packet to pass through because it is intended for a specific computer on the network. However, a stateful packet filter would not let the packet pass if that internal network computer did not first request the information from the external server.

A firewall can take different actions when it receives a packet: *allow* (let the packet pass through and continue its journey), *drop* (prevent the packet from passing into the network and send no response to the sender), *reject* (prevent the packet from passing into the network but send a message to the sender that the destination cannot be reached), or *ask* (inquire what action to take).

Much like routers, some firewalls use criteria for accepting or rejecting a packet based on an ACL. Sometimes called *rule-based firewalls*, they use a set of individual instructions to control actions. These firewall ACL rules are a single line of textual information containing such information as:

- *Source address.* The source address is the location of the origination of the packet (where the packet is *from*). Addresses generally can be indicated by a specific IP address or range of addresses, an IP mask, the MAC address, or host name.
- *Destination address.* This is the address the connection is attempting to reach (where the packet is going *to*). These addresses can be indicated in the same way as the source address.
- *Source port.* The source port is the TCP/IP port number being used to send packets of data through. Options for setting the source port often include a specific port number, a range of numbers, or *Any* (port).
- *Destination port.* This setting gives the port on the remote computer or device that the packets will use. Options include the same as for the source port.
- *Protocol:* The protocol defines the protocol (such as *TCP, UDP, TCP* or *UDP, ICMP, IP,* etc.) that is being used when sending or receiving packets of data.

- *Direction.* The direction shows the direction of traffic for the data packet (*In, Out,* or *Both*).
- *Action.* The action setting indicates what the firewall should do when the conditions of the rule are met. These options may be the following: *allow, drop, reject,* or *ask*.

Each firewall ACL rule is a separate instruction processed in sequence that tells the firewall precisely what action to take with each packet that comes through it. The rules are stored together in one or more text file(s) that are read when the firewall starts. Rule-based systems are static in nature and cannot do anything other than what they have been expressly configured to do. Although this makes them more straightforward to configure, they are less flexible and cannot adapt to changing circumstances.

Note

Firewall rules are essentially an *IF-THEN* construction. *IF* these rule conditions are met, *THEN* the action occurs.

Application-Based Firewalls

A more "intelligent" firewall is an **application-based firewall**, operating at the Application layer (Layer 7). Application-based firewalls operate at a higher level by identifying the applications that send packets through the firewall and then make decisions about the application instead of filtering packets based on granular rule settings like the destination port or protocol. Applications can be identified by application-based firewalls through predefined application signatures, header inspection, or payload analysis. In addition, application-based firewalls can learn new applications by watching how they behave and even create a baseline of normal behaviors so that an alert can be raised if the application deviates from the baseline.

An example of how an application-based firewall and a network-based ACL firewall compare can be seen in how they filter specific web applications. An organization might frown upon employees using the network during normal business hours to stream online movies, but still need to provide employees with access to an online sales application. Setting an ACL rule in a network-based firewall to prevent streaming video (HTTP on Port 80) would also stop access to the online sales application. An application-based firewall, in contrast, could distinguish between these two applications and allow access to the sales application while blocking streaming video, social networking, and gaming. Or it could allow these applications but limit bandwidth consumption to give priority to business applications.

A special type of application-based firewall is a **web application firewall** that looks at the applications using HTTP. A web application firewall, which can be a separate hardware appliance or a software plugin, can block specific websites or attacks that attempt to exploit known vulnerabilities in specific client software, and can even block cross-site scripting (XSS) and SQL injection attacks.

Note

Cross-site scripting (XSS) and SQL injection attacks are covered in Chapter 5.

Virtual Private Network (VPN) Concentrator

An unsecured public network should never be used for sensitive data transmissions. One solution could be to encrypt documents before transmitting them. However, there are drawbacks. First, the user must consciously perform a separate action (such as encrypt a document) or use specific software (such as PGP) to transmit a secure document. The time and effort required to do so, albeit small, may discourage users from protecting their documents. A second drawback is that these actions protect only documents that are transmitted; all other communications, such as accessing corporate databases, are not secure.

A more secure solution is to use a virtual private network (VPN). A **virtual private network (VPN)** is a technology that enables authorized users to use an unsecured public network, such as the Internet, as if it were a secure private network. It does this by encrypting *all* data that is transmitted between the remote device and the network and not just specific documents or files. This ensures that any transmissions that are intercepted will be indecipherable. There are two common types of VPNs. A **remote access VPN** is a user-to-LAN connection used by remote users. The second type is a **site-to-site VPN**, in which multiple sites can connect to other sites over the Internet. Some VPNs allow the user to always stay connected instead of connecting and disconnecting from it. These are called **always-on VPNs**.

VPN transmissions are achieved through communicating with endpoints. An *endpoint* is the end of the tunnel between VPN devices. An endpoint can be software on a local computer, a dedicated hardware device such as a **VPN concentrator** (which aggregates hundreds or thousands of VPN connections), or integrated into another networking device such as a firewall. Depending upon the type of endpoint that is being used, client software may be required on the devices that are connecting to the VPN. Hardware devices that have a built-in VPN endpoint handle all VPN setup, encapsulation, and encryption in the endpoint. Client devices are not required to run any special software and the entire VPN process is transparent to them.

Note

Software-based VPNs are often used on mobile devices and offer the most flexibility in how network traffic is managed. However, hardware-based VPNs, typically used for site-to-site connections, are more secure, have better performance, and can offer more flexibility.

When using a VPN, there are two options depending upon which traffic is to be protected. When all traffic is sent to the VPN concentrator and protected this is called a **full tunnel**. However, not all traffic—such as web surfing or reading personal email—may need to be protected through a VPN. In this case, **split tunneling**, or routing only some traffic over the secure VPN while other traffic directly accesses the Internet, may be used instead. This can help to preserve bandwidth and reduce the load on the VPN concentrator.

Note

The most common protocols used for VPNs are IPsec and SSL or the weaker TLS.

Mail Gateway

Since developer Ray Tomlinson sent the first email message in 1971, email has become an essential part of everyday life. It is estimated that over 2.3 million emails are sent every second, increasing at a rate of 5 percent each year. By 2019 it is estimated that there will be 246 billion emails sent daily by over 2.9 billion email users.[2]

There are two different electronic email systems that are in use today. An earlier email system uses two TCP/IP protocols to send and receive messages: the **Simple Mail Transfer Protocol (SMTP)** handles outgoing mail, while the **Post Office Protocol (POP)**, (more commonly known as *POP3* for the current version) is responsible for incoming mail. POP3 is a basic protocol that allows users to retrieve messages sent to an email server by using a local program running on their computer called an *email client*. The email client connects to the POP3 server and downloads the messages onto the local computer. After the messages are downloaded, they may be erased from the POP3 server. The SMTP server listens on port 25 while POP3 listens on port 110.

Note

SMTP servers can forward email sent from an email client to a remote domain, known as *SMTP relay*. However, if SMTP relay is not controlled, an attacker can use it to forward spam and disguise his identity to make himself untraceable. An uncontrolled SMTP relay is known as an *SMTP open relay*. The defenses against SMTP open relay are to turn off the mail relay altogether so that all users send and receive email from the local SMTP server only or to limit relays to only local users.

IMAP (Internet Mail Access Protocol) is a more recent and advanced electronic email system for incoming mail. While POP3 is a "store-and-forward" service, IMAP is a "remote" email storage. With IMAP, the email remains on the email server and is not downloaded to the user's computer like POP3 does. Mail can be organized into folders on the mail server and read from any device: desktop computer, tablet, smartphone, etc. IMAP users can even work with email while offline. This is accomplished by downloading a local copy only for display onto the local device without erasing the email on the IMAP server. A user can read and reply to email offline. The next time a connection is established, the new messages are sent and any new email is downloaded. The current version of IMAP is IMAP4.

Note 📎

Older email clients typically used only POP3. Using a web browser to view email messages on an email server, like Google Gmail, generally utilizes IMAP. Most mobile devices are configured to use IMAP.

A **mail gateway** monitors emails for unwanted content and prevents these messages from being delivered. Many mail gateways have monitoring capabilities for both inbound as well as outbound emails. For inbound emails, a mail gateway can search the content in email messages for various types of malware, spam, and phishing attacks. For outbound email, a mail gateway can detect and block the transmission of sensitive data, such as Social Security numbers or healthcare records. In addition, a mail gateway can automatically and transparently encrypt outbound email messages.

Note 📎

One of the primary tasks of a mail gateway is blocking spam. Beyond being annoying and disruptive, spam can pose a serious security risk. Threat actors distribute malware through their email messages as attachments and use spam for social engineering attacks.

There are several different forms of mail gateways. An enterprise may elect to install its own corporate mail gateway on its premises. This filter works with the receiving email server, which is typically based on SMTP for sending email and the IMAP for retrieving email. Another method is for the enterprise to contract with a third-party entity that filters out spam. All email is directed to the third party's remote spam filter where it is cleansed before it is redirected to the organization. This redirection can be accomplished by changing the *MX (mail exchange) record*. The MX record is an entry in the Domain Name System (DNS) that identifies the mail server responsible for handling that domain name. To redirect mail to the third party's remote server, the MX record is changed to show the new recipient. Multiple MX records can be configured in DNS to enable the use of primary and backup mail servers. Each MX record can be prioritized with a preference number that indicates the order in which the mail servers should be used.

> **Note** 📎
>
> Prior to the more comprehensive mail gateways, enterprises often installed basic spam filters with the SMTP server as the simplest and most effective approach. The spam filter and SMTP server could run together on the same computer or on separate computers. The filter (instead of the SMTP server) was configured to listen on port 25 for all incoming email messages and then pass the non-spam email to the SMTP server that is listening on another port (such as port 26). This configuration prevented the SMTP server from notifying the spammer that it was unable to deliver the message.

Network Intrusion Detection and Prevention

An **intrusion detection system (IDS)** can detect an attack as it occurs. An **inline IDS** is connected directly to the network and monitors the flow of data as it occurs. A **passive IDS** is connected to a port on a switch, which receives a copy of network traffic. Table 6-2 lists the differences between inline and passive systems. In addition, IDS systems can be managed **in-band** (through the network itself by using network protocols and tools) or **out-of-band** (using an independent and dedicated channel to reach the device).

Table 6-2   Inline vs. passive IDS

Function	Inline	Passive
Connection	Directly to network	Connected to port on switch
Traffic flow	Routed through the device	Receives copy of traffic
Blocking	Can block attacks	Cannot block attacks
Detection error	May disrupt service	May cause false alarm

IDS systems can use different methodologies for monitoring for attacks. In addition, IDS can be installed on either local hosts or networks.

Monitoring Methodologies

Monitoring involves examining network traffic, activity, transactions, or behavior to detect security-related anomalies. There are four monitoring methodologies: anomaly-based monitoring, signature-based monitoring, behavior-based monitoring, and heuristic monitoring.

Anomaly monitoring is designed for detecting statistical anomalies. First, a baseline of normal activities is compiled over time. (A *baseline* is a reference set of data against which operational data is compared.) Whenever there is a significant deviation from this baseline, an alarm is raised. An advantage of this approach is that it can detect the anomalies quickly without trying to first understand the underlying cause. However, normal behavior can change easily and even quickly, so anomaly-based monitoring is subject to **false positives**, or alarms that are raised when there is no actual abnormal behavior. (A **false negative** is the failure to raise an alarm when there is abnormal behavior.) In addition, anomaly-based monitoring can impose heavy processing loads on the systems where they are being used. Finally, because anomaly-based monitoring takes time to create statistical baselines, it can fail to detect events before the baseline is completed.

A second method for auditing usage is to examine network traffic, activity, transactions, or behavior and look for well-known patterns, much like antivirus scanning. This is known as **signature-based monitoring** because it compares activities against a predefined signature. Signature-based monitoring requires access to an updated database of signatures along with a means to actively compare and match current behavior against a collection of signatures. One of the weaknesses of signature-based monitoring is that the signature databases must be constantly updated, and as the number of signatures grows, the behaviors must be compared against an increasingly large number of signatures. Also, if the signature definitions are too specific, signature-based monitoring can miss variations.

Behavioral monitoring attempts to overcome the limitations of both anomaly-based monitoring and signature-based monitoring by being adaptive and proactive instead of reactive. Rather than using statistics or signatures as the standard by which comparisons are made, behavior-based monitoring uses the "normal" processes and actions as the standard. Behavior-based monitoring continuously analyzes the behavior of processes and programs on a system and alerts the user if it detects any abnormal actions, at which point the user can decide whether to allow or block the activity. One of the advantages of behavior-based monitoring is that it is not necessary to update signature files or compile a baseline of statistical behavior before monitoring can take place. In addition, behavior-based monitoring can more quickly stop new attacks.

The final method takes a completely different approach and does not try to compare actions against previously determined standards (like anomaly-based monitoring and signature-based monitoring) or behavior (like behavior-based monitoring). Instead, it is founded on *experience-based techniques*. Known as **heuristic monitoring**, it attempts to answer the question, *Will this do something harmful if it is allowed to execute?* Heuristic (from the Greek word for *find* or *discover*) monitoring uses an algorithm to determine if a threat exists. Table 6-3 illustrates how heuristic monitoring could trap an application that attempts to scan ports that the other methods might not catch.

Table 6-3	Methodology comparisons to trap port scanning application	
Monitoring methodology	Trap application scanning ports?	Comments
Anomaly-based monitoring	Depends	Only if this application has tried to scan previously and a baseline has been established
Signature-based monitoring	Depends	Only if a signature of scanning by this application has been previously created
Behavior-based monitoring	Depends	Only if this action by the application is different from other applications
Heuristic monitoring	Yes	IDS is triggered if any application tries to scan multiple ports

Types of IDS

Two basic types of IDS exist. A **host-based intrusion detection system (HIDS)** is a software-based application that runs on a local host computer that can detect an attack as it occurs. A HIDS is installed on each system, such as a server or desktop, that needs to be protected. A HIDS relies on agents installed directly on the system being protected. These agents work closely with the operating system, monitoring and intercepting requests in order to prevent attacks. HIDSs typically monitor the following desktop functions:

- *System calls.* Each operation in a computing environment starts with a *system call.* A system call is an instruction that interrupts the program being executed and requests a service from the operating system. HIDS can monitor system calls based on the process, mode, and action being requested.
- *File system access.* System calls usually require specific files to be opened to access data. A HIDS works to ensure that all file openings are based on legitimate needs and are not the result of malicious activity.
- *System Registry settings.* The Windows *Registry* maintains configuration information about programs and the computer. HIDS can recognize unauthorized modification of the Registry.
- *Host input/output.* HIDS monitors all input and output communications to watch for malicious activity. For example, if the system never uses instant messaging and suddenly a threat attempts to open an IM connection from the system, the HIDS would detect this as anomalous activity.

Note

HIDSs are designed to integrate with existing antivirus, antispyware, and firewalls that are installed on the local host computer.

However, there are disadvantages to HIDS. It cannot monitor any network traffic that does not reach the local system. Any data that it accumulates is stored locally and not in a single central repository. And HIDS tend to be resource-intensive and can slow down the system.

Just as a software-based HIDS monitors attacks on a local system, a **network intrusion detection system (NIDS)** watches for attacks on the network. As network traffic moves through the network, NIDS sensors—usually installed on network devices such as firewalls and routers—gather information and report back to a central device. A NIDS may use one or more of the evaluation techniques listed in Table 6-4.

Table 6-4   NIDS evaluation techniques

Technique	Description
Protocol stack verification	Some attacks use invalid IP, TCP, UDP, or ICMP protocols. A protocol stack verification can identify and flag invalid packets, such as several fragmented IP packets.
Application protocol verification	Some attacks attempt to use invalid protocol behavior or have a telltale signature (such as DNS poisoning). The NIDS will re-implement different application protocols to find a pattern.
Creating extended log files	A NIDS can log unusual events and then make these available to other network logging monitoring systems.

Note

A NIDS is not limited to inspecting incoming network traffic. Often, valuable information about an ongoing attack can be gained from observing outgoing traffic as well, such as when a system had been infected and is attacking other devices, producing large amounts of outgoing traffic. A NIDS that examines both incoming and outgoing traffic can detect this.

Once an attack is detected, a NIDS can perform different actions to sound an alarm and log the event. These alarms may include sending email, page, or a cell phone message to the network administrator or even playing an audio file that says "Attack is taking place."

An *application-aware IDS* is a specialized IDS. Instead of applying all IDS rules to all traffic flows, an application-aware IDS can use "contextual knowledge" in real time. It can know the version of the operating system or which application is running as well as what vulnerabilities are present in the systems being protected. This context improves the speed and accuracy of IDS decisions and reduces the risk of false positives.

Intrusion Prevention Systems (IPSs)

As its name implies, an *intrusion prevention system (IPS)* not only monitors to detect malicious activities like an IDS, but also attempts to prevent them by stopping the attack. A **network intrusion prevention system (NIPS)** is like an active NIDS in that it monitors network traffic to immediately react to block a malicious attack by following established rules (a **host-based intrusion prevention system (HIPS)** likewise performs a similar function for hosts). One of the major differences between a NIDS and a NIPS is its location. A NIDS has sensors that monitor the traffic entering and leaving a firewall, and reports back to the central device for analysis. A NIPS, on the other hand, would be located inline on the firewall itself. This allows the NIPS to act more quickly to block an attack.

Like an application-aware IDS, an *application-aware IPS* knows such information as the applications that are running as well as the underlying operating systems so that it can provide more accuracy regarding potential attacks.

Security and Information Event Management (SIEM)

Different network security hardware devices—such as firewalls, NIDS, and NIPS—generate continual security alerts as an enterprise is the target of daily attacks. How can these continual alerts, all from different sources and generated at different points of time, be monitored and managed?

The answer is a **Security and Information Event Management (SIEM)** product. A SIEM consolidates real-time monitoring and management of *security information* with analysis and reporting of *security events*. A SIEM product can be a separate device, software that runs on a computer, or even a service that is provided by a third party. A SIEM "dashboard" is shown in Figure 6-8.

Figure 6-8   SIEM dashboard

https://cdn.alienvault.com/images/uploads/home/screen1

A SIEM typically has the following features:

- *Aggregation.* **SIEM aggregation** combines data from multiple data sources (network security devices, servers, software applications, etc.) to build a comprehensive picture of attacks.
- *Correlation.* The **SIEM correlation** feature searches the data acquired through SIEM aggregation to look for common characteristics, such as multiple attacks coming from a specific source.
- *Automated alerting and triggers.* **SIEM automated alerting and triggers** can inform security personnel of critical issues that need immediate attention. A sample trigger may be *Alert when a firewall, router, or switch indicates 40 or more drop/reject packet events occur from the same IP source address occurring within 60 seconds.*
- *Time synchronization.* Because alerts occur over a wide spectrum of time, **SIEM time synchronization** can show the order of the events.
- *Event duplication.* When the same event occurs that is detected by multiple devices each will generate an alert. The **SIEM event duplication** feature can help filter the multiple alerts into a single alarm.
- *Logs.* **SIEM logs** or records of events can be retained for future analysis and to show that the enterprise has complied with regulations.

Other Network Security Hardware Devices

There are other network security hardware devices that can also be used for security. These are listed in Table 6-5.

Table 6-5   Other network security hardware devices

Name	Description	Comments
Hardware security module	A dedicated cryptographic processor that provides protection for cryptographic keys	A tamper-resistant device that can securely manage, process, and store cryptographic keys
SSL decryptor	A separate device that decrypts SSL traffic	Helps reduce performance degradation and eliminates the need to have multiple decryption licenses spread across multiple devices
SSL/TLS accelerator	A separate hardware card that inserts into a web server that contains one or more co-processors to handle SSL/TLS processing	Used to accelerate the computationally intensive initial SSL connection handshake, during which keys are generated for symmetric encryption using 3DES or AES
Media gateway	A device that converts media data from one format to another	Sometimes called a *softswitch*, converts data in audio or video format

(continues)

Table 6-5 (*continued*)

Name	Description	Comments
Unified Threat Management (UTM)	Integrated device that combines several security functions	Multipurpose security appliance that provides an array of security functions, such as antispam, antiphishing, antispyware, encryption, intrusion protection, and web filtering
Internet content filter	Monitors Internet traffic and block access to preselected websites and files	Restricts unapproved websites based on URL or by searching for and matching keywords such as *sex* or *hate* as well as looking for malware
Web security gateway	Blocks malicious content in real time as it appears without first knowing the URL of a dangerous site	Enables a higher level of defense by examining the content through application-level filtering

Security Through Network Architecture

 **Certification**

3.2 Given a scenario, implement secure network architecture concepts.

The design of a network can provide a secure foundation for resisting attackers. Elements of a secure network architectural design include creating security zones and using network segregation.

Security Zones

A serious security mistake is to create one network that all users can access. A more secure approach is to create *zones* to partition the network so that certain users may enter one zone while access is prohibited to other users. The most common security zones are demilitarized zones, using network address translation to create zones, and other zones.

Demilitarized Zone (DMZ)

Imagine a bank that located its automated teller machine (ATM) in the middle of their vault. This would be an open invitation for disaster by inviting every outside user to enter the secure vault to access the ATM. Instead, the ATM and the vault should be separated so that the ATM is in a public area that anyone can access, while the vault is restricted to trusted individuals. In a similar fashion, locating public-facing servers such as web and email servers inside the secure network is also unwise. An attacker must only break out of the security of the server to access the secure network.

To allow untrusted outside users access to resources such as web and email servers, most networks employ a **demilitarized zone (DMZ)**. The DMZ functions as a separate network that rests outside the secure network perimeter: untrusted outside users can access the DMZ but cannot enter the secure network.

Figure 6-7 (shown earlier) illustrates a DMZ that contains a web server and an email server that are accessed by outside users. In this configuration, a single firewall with three network interfaces is used: the link to the Internet is on the first network interface, the DMZ is formed from the second network interface, and the secure internal LAN is based on the third network interface. However, this makes the firewall device a single point of failure for the network, and it also must take care of all the traffic to both the DMZ and internal network. A more secure approach is to have two firewalls, as seen in Figure 6-9. In this configuration, an attacker would have to breach two separate firewalls to reach the secure internal LAN.

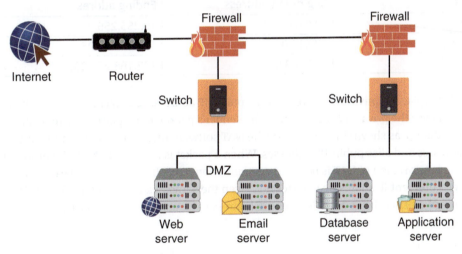

Figure 6-9   DMZ with two firewalls

> **Note**
>
> Some consumer routers advertise support to configure a DMZ. However, this is not a DMZ. Rather, it allows only one local device to be exposed to the Internet for Internet gaming or videoconferencing by forwarding all the ports at the same time to that one device.

Network Address Translation (NAT)

Network address translation (NAT) is a technique that allows private IP addresses to be used on the public Internet. *Private IP addresses*, which are listed in Table 6-6, are IP addresses that are not assigned to any specific user or organization; instead, they can be used by anyone on the private internal network. Private addresses function as regular IP addresses on an internal network; however, if a packet with a private address makes its way to the Internet, the routers drop that packet.

> **Note** 📎
>
> Strictly speaking, NAT is not a specific device, technology, or protocol. It is a technique for substituting IP addresses.

Table 6-6   Private IP addresses

Class	Beginning address	Ending address
Class A	10.0.0.0	10.255.255.255
Class B	172.16.0.0	172.31.255.255
Class C	192.168.0.0	192.168.255.255

NAT replaces a private IP address with a public IP address. As a packet leaves a network, NAT removes the private IP address from the sender's packet and replaces it with an alias IP public address, as shown in Figure 6-10. The NAT software maintains a table of the private IP addresses and alias public IP addresses. When a packet is returned to NAT, the process is reversed. A variation of NAT is *port address translation (PAT)*. Instead of giving each outgoing packet a different IP address, each packet is given the same IP address but a different TCP port number. This allows a single public IP address to be used by several users.

> **Note** 📎
>
> PAT is typically used on home routers that allow multiple users to share one IP address received from an Internet service provider (ISP).

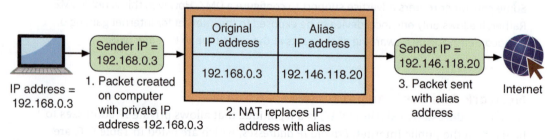

Figure 6-10   Network address translation (NAT)

A device using NAT, such as a NAT router, also can provide a degree of security. Because all outgoing traffic flows through the NAT router, it knows which packets were sent out and what it expects to receive. What happens if a packet arrives at the NAT router for an internal network device but the request for that packet was not first sent out through the router? If the initial request did not come through the NAT router, the router discards all unsolicited packets so that they never enter the internal network. In this way, the NAT router acts like a firewall by discarding unwanted packets. Another element of security that NAT provides is masking the IP addresses of internal devices. An attacker who captures the packet on the Internet cannot determine the actual IP address of the sender. Without that address, it is more difficult to identify and attack a computer. These security advantages enable NAT to create secure zones of a network.

Other Zones

There are other zones that can also be used for security. These are listed in Table 6-7.

Table 6-7   Other network zones

Name	Description	Security benefits
Intranet	A private network that belongs to an organization that can only be accessed by approved internal users	Closed to the outside public, thus data is less vulnerable to external threat actors
Extranet	A private network that can also be accessed by authorized external customers, vendors, and partners	Can provide enhanced security for outside users compared to a publicly accessible website
Guest network	A separate open network that anyone can access without prior authorization	Permits access to general network resources like web surfing without using the secure network

Network Segregation

Another means of providing security is to segregate the network and its resources. **Physical network segregation** simply isolates the network so that it is not accessible by outsiders. A secure government network, for example, might be physically segregated so that it is not connected to any other networks or the Internet. This means that a potential intruder could not access the network remotely. This is sometimes known as an **air gap**, or the absence of any type of connection between devices, in this case the secure network and another network.

Although physically segregating networks provides a high degree of security, it is not usually practical: not being able to access any other networks or the Internet would be an unworkable solution for almost all enterprises. Instead of segregating a network *physically*, a much more practical approach is to segregate the network *logically*. Networks can be segmented by using switches to divide the network into a hierarchy. *Core switches* reside at the top of the hierarchy and carry traffic between switches, while *workgroup switches* are connected directly to the devices on the network. It is often beneficial to group similar users together, such as all the members of the Accounting department. However, grouping by user sometimes can be difficult because all users might not be in the same location and served by the same switch.

> **Note**
>
> Core switches must work faster than workgroup switches because core switches must handle the traffic of several workgroup switches.

It is possible to segment a network by separating devices into logical groups. This is known as creating a **virtual LAN (VLAN)**. A VLAN allows scattered users to be logically grouped together even though they are physically attached to different switches. This can reduce network traffic and provide a degree of security. VLANs can be isolated so that sensitive data is transported only to members of the VLAN.

> **Note**
>
> Although network subnetting and VLANs are often considered to be similar, there are differences between them. Subnets are subdivisions of IP address classes (Class A, B, or C) and allow a single Class A, B, or C network to be used instead of multiple networks. VLANs are devices that are connected logically rather than physically, either through the port they are connected to or by their media access control (MAC) address.

VLAN communication can take place in two ways. If multiple devices in the same VLAN are connected to the same switch, the switch itself can handle the transfer of packets to the members of the VLAN group. However, if VLAN members on one switch need to communicate with members connected to another switch, a special "tagging" protocol must be used, either a proprietary protocol or the vendor-neutral IEEE 802.1Q. These special protocols add a field to the packet that "tags" it as belonging to the VLAN.

> **Note**
>
> Another security advantage of VLANs is that they can be used to prevent direct communication between servers, which can bypass firewall or IDS inspection. Servers that are placed in separate VLANs will require that any traffic headed toward the default gateway for inter-VLAN routing be inspected.

Security Through Network Technologies

2.1 Install and configure network components, both hardware- and software-based, to support organizational security.

Network technologies can also help to secure a network. Two such technologies are network access control and data loss prevention.

Network Access Control (NAC)

The waiting room at a doctor's office is an ideal location for the spread of germs. The patients waiting in this confined space are obviously ill and many have weakened immune systems. During the cold and flu season, doctors routinely post notices that anyone who has flu-like symptoms should not come to the waiting room so that other patients will not be infected. Suppose that a physician decided to post a nurse at the door of the waiting room to screen patients. Anyone who came to the waiting room and exhibited flu-like symptoms would be directed to a separate quarantine room away from other patients. Here the person could receive specialized care without impacting others.

This is the logic behind **network access control (NAC)**. NAC examines the current state of a system or network device before it can connect to the network. Any device that does not meet a specified set of criteria, such as having the most current antivirus signature or the software firewall properly enabled, can connect only to a "quarantine" network where the security deficiencies are corrected. After the problems are solved, the device is connected to the normal network. The goal of NAC is to prevent computers with suboptimal security from potentially infecting other computers through the network.

> **Note** 📎
>
> NAC also can be used to ensure that systems not owned by the organization, such as those owned by customers, visitors, and contractors, can be granted access without compromising security.

NAC uses software "agents" that are installed on devices to gather information and report back (**host agent health checks**). An agent may be a **permanent NAC agent** and reside on end devices until uninstalled or it may be a **dissolvable NAC agent** and disappears after reporting information to the NAC. Instead of installing agents on each device, the NAC technology can be embedded within a Microsoft Windows Active Directory domain controller. When a device joins the domain and a user logs in, NAC uses Active Directory to scan the device to verify that it is in compliance. This is called **agentless NAC**.

An example of the NAC process is illustrated in Figure 6-11:

1. The client performs a self-assessment using a System Health Agent (SHA) to determine its current security posture.

2. The assessment, known as a Statement of Health (SoH), is sent to a server called the Health Registration Authority (HRA). This server enforces the security policies of the network. It also integrates with other external authorities such as antivirus and patch management servers to retrieve current configuration information.

3. If the client is approved by the HRA, it is issued a Health Certificate.

4. The Health Certificate is then presented to the network servers to verify that the client's security condition has been approved.

5. If the client is not approved, it is connected to a quarantine network where the deficiencies are corrected, and then the computer is allowed to connect to the network.

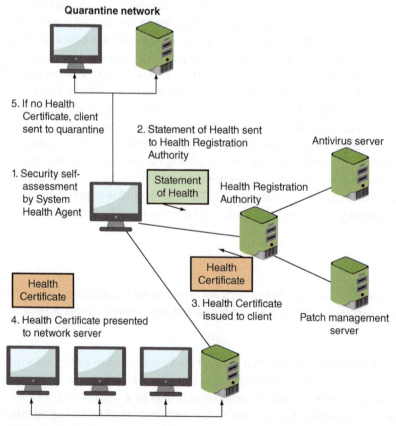

Figure 6-11   Network access control (NAC) framework

NAC typically uses one of two methods for directing the client to a quarantine network and then later to the production network. The first method is the use of a Dynamic Host Configuration Protocol (DHCP) server. The unapproved client is first leased an IP address to the quarantine network and then later leased an IP address to the production network. The second method uses a technique often used by attackers known as Address Resolution Protocol (ARP) poisoning. With this method, the ARP table is manipulated on the client so that it connects to the quarantine network.

Note

ARP poisoning is covered in Chapter 5.

NAC can be an effective tool for identifying and correcting systems that do not have adequate security installed and preventing these devices from infecting others.

Data Loss Prevention (DLP)

In previous generations, most employees drove to the office for a nine-to-five workday to meet with colleagues and create reports at a desk. That has all changed. Work today involves electronic collaboration using mobile technologies—smartphones, tablets, and laptops—over wireless data networks from virtually any location. This means that data, once restricted to papers in the office filing cabinet, now flows freely both in and out of organizations between employees, customers, contractors, and business partners around the world. In addition, the volume of sensitive data has grown exponentially. How can all this data flowing in and out of the organization be protected so that it does not fall into the wrong hands?

One means of securing data is through **data loss prevention (DLP)**. DLP is a system of security tools that is used to recognize and identify data that is critical to the organization and ensure that it is protected. This protection involves monitoring who is using the data and how it is being accessed. DLP's goal is to protect data from unauthorized users. It does this by examining data as it resides in any of three states: data-in-use, data-in-transit, and data-at-rest. Data that is considered critical to the organization or needs to be confidential can be tagged as such. A user who then attempts to access the data to disclose it to another unauthorized user will be prevented from doing so. Two of the most common uses of DLP are monitoring emails through a mail gateway and blocking the copying of files to a USB flash drive (**USB blocking**).

Most DLP systems use *content inspection*. Content inspection is defined as a security analysis of the transaction within its approved context. Content inspection looks at not only the security level of the data, but also who is requesting it, where the data is stored, when it was requested, and where it is going. DLP systems also can use *index matching*. Documents that have been identified as needing protection, such as the program source code for a new software application, are analyzed by the DLP system and complex computations are conducted based on the analysis. Thereafter, if even a small part of that document is leaked, the DLP system can recognize the snippet as being from a protected document.

> **Note**
>
> Index matching is so sensitive that if even a handful of lines of source code from 10,000 lines of protected code are entered in an email message, the DLP system will identify it.

DLP begins with an administrator creating DLP rules based on the data (what is to be examined) and the policy (what to check for). DLPs can be configured to look for specific data (such as Social Security and credit card numbers), lines of computer software source code, words in a sequence (to prevent a report from leaving the network), maximum file sizes, and file types. Because it can be difficult to distinguish a Social Security number from a mistyped telephone number or a nine-digit online order number, DLP can use *fingerprinting* to more closely identify important data. A fingerprint may consist of a Social Security number along with a name to trigger an alarm. In addition, whitelists and blacklists can be created to prevent specific files from being scanned. These rules are then loaded into a DLP server.

Because the data can be leaked by different means, there are three types of DLP sensors:

- *DLP network sensors.* DLP network sensors are installed on the perimeter of the network to protect data-in-transit by monitoring all network traffic. This includes monitoring email, instant messaging, social media interactions, and other web applications. DLP network sensors can even monitor multiple protocols (including HTTP, SMTP, POP, IMAP, FTP, and Telnet).
- *DLP storage sensors.* Sensors on network storage devices are designed to protect data-at-rest. These sensors monitor the devices to ensure that the files on the hard drives that store sensitive data are encrypted. They also scan the drives to determine where specific data is stored.
- *DLP agent sensors.* These sensors are installed on each host device (desktop, laptop, tablet, etc.) and protect data-in-use. The DLP agent sensors watch for actions such as printing or copying to a USB flash drive. They can also read inside compressed (ZIP) files and binary files (such as older Microsoft Office non-XML files).

> **Note**
>
> One of the drawbacks of DLP agent sensors is that the host device must communicate with the DLP server, which can result in performance issues and may not scale well when more devices are added. To limit the performance impact, DLP agent sensors are "event driven" so that the sensor monitors only for specific user actions, such as copying a file to a USB device or printing a document.

When a policy violation is detected by the DLP agent, it is reported back to the DLP server. Different actions can then be taken. This could include blocking the data, redirecting it to an individual who can examine the request, quarantining the data until later, or alerting a supervisor of the request.

Chapter Summary

- Standard network security devices can be used to provide a degree of network security. Hubs should not be used in a network because they repeat all frames to all attached network devices, allowing an attacker to easily capture traffic and analyze its contents. A more secure network device is a switch. A switch forwards frames only to specific devices instead of all devices. A router can forward packets across computer networks. Because packets move through the router, the router can be configured to filter out specific types of network traffic.

- A load balancer can direct requests to different servers based on a variety of factors. Because load balancers are generally located between routers and servers they can detect and stop attacks directed at a server or application. A forward proxy server is a computer or an application program that intercepts user requests from the internal secure network and then processes that request on behalf of the user. Acting as the intermediary, a proxy server can protect clients from malware by intercepting it before it reaches the client. In addition, a proxy server can hide the IP address of client systems inside the secure network. A reverse proxy does not serve clients but instead routes incoming requests to the correct server.

- Hardware devices that are specifically designed for security can give a much higher level of protection. A hardware-based network firewall is designed to inspect packets and either accept or deny entry, and these are generally located outside the network security perimeter as the first line of defense. All modern operating systems include a software firewall usually called a host-based firewall or personal firewall. A network-based firewall functions at the Network layer (Layer 3) of the OSI model. A more "intelligent" firewall is an application-based firewall, operating at the Application layer (Layer 7). Firewalls can either be rule-based or application-aware, and can use stateless packet filtering or stateful packet filtering. A virtual private network (VPN) is a technology that enables authorized users to use an unsecured public network, such as the Internet, as if it were a secure private network.

- A mail gateway monitors emails for unwanted content and prevents these messages from being delivered. Many mail gateways have monitoring capabilities for both inbound as well as outbound emails. An intrusion detection system (IDS) is designed to detect an attack as it occurs. Monitoring involves examining network traffic, activity, transactions, or behavior to detect security-related anomalies. There are four monitoring methodologies: anomaly monitoring, signature-based monitoring, behavior monitoring, and heuristic monitoring. A host intrusion detection system (HIDS) is a software-based application that runs on a local host computer. A network intrusion detection system (NIDS) watches for attacks on the network. As network traffic moves through the network, NIDS sensors (usually installed on network devices such as firewalls and routers) gather information and report back to a central device. A network intrusion prevention system (NIPS) is like a NIDS in that it monitors network traffic to immediately react to block the malicious attack, but it can react more quickly than a NIDS.

- A Security and Information Event Management (SIEM) product consolidates real-time monitoring and management of security information along with an analysis and reporting of security events. Other network security hardware devices include hardware security modules, SSL decryptors, SSL/TLS accelerators, media gateways, Unified Threat Management (UTM) products, Internet content filters, and web security gateways.

- The design of a network can provide a secure foundation for resisting attackers. A secure approach is to create zones to partition the network so that certain users may enter one zone while that access is prohibited to other users. A demilitarized zone (DMZ) functions as a separate network that rests outside the secure network perimeter, so that untrusted outside users can access the DMZ but cannot enter the secure network. Network address translation (NAT) discards packets that were not requested by an internal network device and hides the IP addresses of internal network devices from attackers by substituting a private address with a public address. Other security zones include intranets, extranets, and guest networks.

- Another means of providing security is to segregate the network and its resources. Physical network segregation simply isolates the network so that it is not accessible by outsiders. Logical network segregation segments a network by separating devices into logical groups, known as creating a virtual LAN (VLAN).

- Network technologies can also help to secure a network. Network access control (NAC) examines the current state of a system or network device before it can connect to the network. Any device that does not meet a specified set of criteria can connect only to a "quarantine" network where the security deficiencies are corrected. Data loss prevention (DLP) is a system of security tools that is used to recognize and identify data that is critical to the organization and ensure that it is protected.

Key Terms

Access Control List (ACL)

active-active

active-passive

affinity

agentless NAC

air gap

always-on VPN

anomaly monitoring

antispoofing

application/multipurpose
   proxy

application-based firewall

behavioral monitoring

bridge

data loss prevention (DLP)

demilitarized zone (DMZ)

dissolvable NAC agent

extranet

false negative

false positive

firewall

flood guard

forward proxy

full tunnel

guest network

hardware security
   module

heuristic monitoring

host agent health checks

host-based firewall

host-based intrusion
   detection system (HIDS)

host-based intrusion
   prevention system (HIPS)

IMAP (Internet Mail Access
   Protocol)

implicit deny

in-band IDS

inline IDS

intranet

intrusion detection system
   (IDS)

load balancer

loop prevention

mail gateway

media gateway

network access control
   (NAC)

network address
   translation (NAT)

network intrusion
   detection system (NIDS)

network intrusion
   prevention system (NIPS)

network-based firewall

out-of-band IDS

passive IDS

permanent NAC agent

physical network
   segregation

port security

Post Office Protocol (POP)

remote access VPN

reverse proxy

round-robin

router

Security and Information
   Event Management (SIEM)

SIEM aggregation

SIEM automated alerting
   and triggers

SIEM correlation

SIEM event duplication

SIEM logs

SIEM time synchronization

signature-based monitoring

Simple Mail Transfer
   Protocol (SMTP)

site-to-site VPN

split tunneling

SSL decryptor

SSL/TLS accelerator

stateful packet filtering

stateless packet filtering

switch

transparent proxy

Unified Threat Management
   (UTM)

USB blocking

virtual IP (VIP)

virtual LAN (VLAN)

virtual private network (VPN)

VPN concentrator

web application firewall

Review Questions

1. Isabella is a security support manager for a large enterprise. In a recent meeting, she was asked which of the standard networking devices already present on the network could be configured to supplement the specific network security hardware devices that were recently purchased. Which of these standard networking devices would Isabella recommend?

   a. Router

   b. Hub

   c. Virtual private network

   d. SIEM device

2. Ximena noticed that Sofia had created a network bridge on her new laptop between the unsecured wireless network and the organization's secure intranet. Ximena explained to Sofia the problem associated with setting up the bridge. What did Ximena tell Sofia?
   a. A bridge will block packets between two different types of networks.
   b. A bridge cannot be used on any Internet connection.
   c. A bridge would block packets from reaching the Internet.
   d. A bridge could permit access to the secure wired network from the unsecured wireless network.

3. Which of these would NOT be a filtering mechanism found in a firewall ACL rule?
   a. Source address
   b. Direction
   c. Date
   d. Protocol

4. Which of the following devices can identify the application that send packets and then make decisions about filtering based on it?
   a. Internet content filter
   b. Application-based firewall
   c. Reverse proxy
   d. Web security gateway

5. Which function does an Internet content filter NOT perform?
   a. Intrusion detection
   b. URL filtering
   c. Malware inspection
   d. Content inspection

6. How does network address translation (NAT) improve security?
   a. It filters based on protocol.
   b. It discards unsolicited packets.
   c. It masks the IP address of the NAT device.
   d. NATs do not improve security.

7. Francisco was asked by a student intern to explain the danger of a MAC flooding attack on a switch. What would Francisco say?
   a. Once the MAC address table is full the switch functions like a network hub.
   b. A MAC flooding attack with filter to the local host computer's MAC-to-IP address tables and prevent these hosts from reaching the network.
   c. In a defense of a MAC flooding attack network routers will freeze and not permit any incoming traffic.
   d. A MAC flooding attack will prevent load balances from identifying the correct VIP of the servers.

8. Which device is easiest for an attacker to take advantage of to capture and analyze packets?
   a. Router
   b. Hub
   c. Switch
   d. Load balancer

9. Sebastian was explaining to his supervisor why the enterprise needed to implement port security. His supervisor asked what security action a flood guard could do when a MAC flooding attack occurred. Which of the following was NOT an answer that was given by Sebastian?
   a. Ignore the new MAC addresses while allowing normal traffic from the single pre-approved MAC address
   b. Cause the device to enter a fail-open mode
   c. Record new MAC addresses up to a specific limit
   d. Block the port entirely

10. Which statement regarding a demilitarized zone (DMZ) is NOT true?
    a. It can be configured to have one or two firewalls.
    b. It typically includes an email or web server.

c. It provides an extra degree of security.

d. It contains servers that are used only by internal network users.

11. Which statement about network address translation (NAT) is true?

a. It substitutes MAC addresses for IP addresses.

b. It can be stateful or stateless.

c. It can be found only on core routers.

d. It removes private addresses when the packet leaves the network.

12. Which of these is NOT used in scheduling a load balancer?

a. The IP address of the destination packet

b. Data within the application message itself

c. Round-robin

d. Affinity

13. In which of the following configurations are all the load balancers always active?

a. Active-active

b. Active-passive

c. Passive-active-passive

d. Active-load-passive-load

14. Which device intercepts internal user requests and then processes those requests on behalf of the users?

a. Forward proxy server

b. Reverse proxy server

c. Host detection server

d. Intrusion prevention device

15. Raul was asked to configure the VPN to preserve bandwidth. Which configuration would he choose?

a. Split tunnel

b. Full tunnel

c. Narrow tunnel

d. Wide tunnel

16. Which device watches for attacks and sounds an alert only when one occurs?

a. Firewall

b. Network intrusion detection system (NIDS)

c. Network intrusion prevention system (NIPS)

d. Proxy intrusion device

17. Which of the following is a multipurpose security device?

a. Hardware security module

b. Unified Threat Management (UTM)

c. Media gateway

d. Intrusion Detection/Prevention (ID/P)

18. Which of the following CANNOT be used to hide information about the internal network?

a. Network address translation (NAT)

b. Protocol analyzer

c. Subnetter

d. Proxy server

19. What is the difference between a network intrusion detection system (NIDS) and a network intrusion prevention system (NIPS)?

a. A NIDS provides more valuable information about attacks.

b. There is no difference; a NIDS and a NIPS are equal.

c. A NIPS can take actions more quickly to combat an attack.

d. A NIPS is much slower because it uses protocol analysis.

20. Which is the most secure type of firewall?

a. Stateless packet filtering

b. Stateful packet filtering

c. Network intrusion detection system replay

d. Reverse proxy analysis

Hands-On Projects

> ### Note
>
> If you are concerned about installing any of the software in these projects on your
> regular computer, you can instead install the software in the Windows virtual
> machine created in the Chapter 1 Hands-On Projects 1-3 and 1-4. Software installed
> within the virtual machine will not impact the host computer.

Project 6-1: Using AlienVault SIEM Tools

Security and Information Event Management (SIEM) product consolidates real-time
monitoring and management of security information along with an analysis and reporting of
security events. In this activity, you access online AlienVault, a SIEM product.

1. Use your web browser to go to **www.alienvault.com** (if you are no longer able to
   access the site through the URL, use a search engine to search for "Alienvault").
2. Click **Explore the Online Demo**.
3. Enter the required information and click **Start Online Demo**.
4. The Alienvault online demo appears. Review the information displayed and scroll to the
   bottom of the screen.
5. Under **Sort** click the icon beneath **Intent** on the first line of information that brings up a
   description of this alarm.
6. Click **Recommendations** for suggestions regarding how to mitigate this attack. Is this
   information helpful?
7. Click **Create Rule** to create a SIEM rule.
8. Under **Rule Name** enter **Rule-1**.
9. Under **Suggested From Alarms** scroll down and view the different categories.
10. Click **Destination Countries**. This will allow you to set a rule for an attack coming from
    a specific country.
11. Under **Matching Conditions** change the Destination Countries to **IT** (for Italy).
12. Select several other suggestions and note how the rule is automatically built as you
    proceed. How does a system like this prevent configuration errors?
13. Click **Cancel**.
14. Close the **Suspicious Behavior** window.
15. Under **Dashboards** click **NIDS** to display information from the network intrusion
    detection system. What type of useful information is found here?
16. Click **Environment** and then **Assets**. What does this screen tell you? Where is the
    sensor located? How can this be valuable?
17. Under **Dashboards** click **Overview**.
18. Click the **Export as Report** button.

19. Under **Title** enter **Report-1**.
20. Click **Export**.
21. Click **Print** (you can also select to print to a PDF if your computer has that option).
22. View the report. How could this information be helpful in understanding data from different sensors?
23. How can SIEM data be useful in consolidating real-time attack information?

Project 6-2: Using GlassWire SIEM Tools

Another Security and Information Event Management (SIEM) product is GlassWire. In this activity, you download and install Glasswire.

1. Use your web browser to go to **www.glasswire.com** (if you are no longer able to access the site through the URL, use a search engine to search for "GlassWire").
2. Click **Features** and scroll through the page to read about the different features and configuration options in this product.
3. **Explore the Online Demo**.
4. Click D**ownload GlassWire**
5. Navigate to the location of the downloaded file **GlassWireSetup.ext** and launch this program to install GlassWire by accepting the default settings.
6. Click **Finish** to run GlassWire.
7. Note that the information scrolls horizontally to the left regarding events that are occurring. Open a web browser and surf the Internet for several minutes.
8. Return to GlassWire.
9. Slide the scroller at the bottom of the screen to consolidate the views, as illustrated in Figure 6-12.
10. Click **Apps**. What information is given in the left pane? How can this be useful?
11. Click **Traffic** to view an analysis of the different traffic types.
12. Click the **Resize** button on the GlassWire window and snap this window to the left side of your physical computer screen.
13. Open a web browser, click the **Resize** button, and snap this windows to the right side of your computer screen.
14. Use your web browser to surf the web, and watch the GlassWire screen as well. What can you learn from this?
15. Close the browser window and maximize GlassWire.
16. Click the **Firewall** button. What apps or services have recently gone through your firewall?
17. Click the **Usage** button to see a summary of the local Apps utilized, the Hosts accessed, and the Traffic Type.
18. Click **Alerts**. Scroll through any alerts that have been issued. What can you tell about them?
19. How valuable is this information from GlassWire? How does it compare to AlienVault? Although they are two different products they each may have their own respective place in viewing information about attacks.
20. Close all windows.

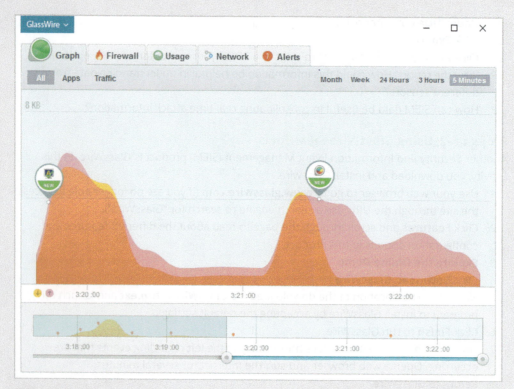

Figure 6-12   **GlassWire**

Source: GlassWire

Project 6-3: Configuring Windows Firewall

In this project, you edit configuration settings on Windows Firewall.

> **Note** 📎
>
> Windows Firewall uses three different profiles: domain (when the computer is connected to a Windows domain), private (when connected to a private network, such as a work or home network), and public (used when connected to a public network, such as a public Wi-Fi). A computer may use multiple profiles, so that a business laptop computer may use the domain profile at work, the private profile when connected to the home network, and the public profile when connected to a public Wi-Fi network. Windows asks whether a network is public or private when you first connect to it.

1. Click **Start**, click the search icon, and enter **Firewall**.
2. Click **Windows Firewall Control panel**.
3. Click **Turn Windows Firewall on or off**. Be sure that the Windows Firewall is turned on for both private and public networks.

4. Under **Public network settings** check **Block all incoming connections, including those in the list of allowed apps**. This provides an extra level of security when using a public network such as a free Wi-Fi network by preventing a malicious incoming connection from another computer on the network. Click **OK**.

5. To allow an inbound connection from an installed application, in the left pane click **Allow an app or feature through Windows Firewall**.

6. Each program or feature of Windows can be chosen to allow an incoming connection on public or private networks. Click **Allow another app**.

7. From here you can select an app that will permit an incoming connection. Because this is a security risk, click **Cancel** and then **OK**.

8. Now check the configuration properties of Windows Firewall. Click **Advanced settings**.

9. Click **Properties** in the right pane.

10. Note the settings on each of the profiles by clicking the **Domain Profile, Private Profile,** and **Public Profile** tabs. Is there any difference in the settings between these profiles? Why?

11. On each tab under Settings, click **Customize**. Be sure that **Display a notification** is set to **Yes**. Why would this be important?

12. Click **OK** to return to the Windows Firewall with Advanced Security page.

13. In addition to being application-aware, Windows Firewall also can be configured for firewall rules. Click **Outbound Rules** in the left pane to block a program from reaching the Internet.

14. In the right pane, click **New Rule**.

15. Click **Port** and then click **Next**.

> **Note** 📎
>
> In addition to ports, the Windows Firewall also can block by program (*Program*) or even by program, port, and IP address (*Custom*).

16. If necessary, click **TCP**.

17. Next to **Specific remote ports:** enter **80**. Click **Next**.

18. If necessary, click **Block the connection**. Click **Next**.

19. Be sure that this new rule applies to all three domains. Click **Next**.

20. Under **Name:** enter **Blocking Port 80**. Click **Finish**.

21. Now open a web browser and try to connect to the Internet. What happens?

22. Click the **Back** button to return to the Windows Firewall screen and click **Action** and **Restore Default Policy** to disable this rule. If a warning dialog box appears, click **Yes**. Click **OK**.

23. Select **Outbound Rules** in the left pane. In the right pane, click **New Rule**.

24. Click **Custom** and **Next**.

25. If necessary, click **All programs** and **Next**.

26. Note that you can configure a firewall rule based on protocol, protocol number, local port, and remote port.
27. Click **Cancel**.
28. Close all windows.

Project 6-4: Using an Internet Content Filter

Internet content filters are used to block inappropriate content. In this project, you download and install the filter K9 Web Protection.

1. Use your web browser to go to **wwwl.k9webprotection.com**.

> **Note** 📎
>
> The location of content on the Internet may change without warning. If you are no longer able to access the program through the above URL, use a search engine to search for "K9 Web Protection".

2. Click **Free Download**.
3. Be sure the radio button **Get K9 Free for your home** is selected. Enter the requested information and then click **Request License**.
4. Go to the email account that you entered and click **Download K9 Web Protection**.
5. Click the operating system that you are using.
6. Click **Save** and save the file to your computer.
7. Click **Run** and follow the instructions to install it to your computer. Accept all default settings.
8. When the installation is complete, reboot the computer.
9. Launch **Blue Coat K9 Web Protection Admin**.
10. Click **SETUP**.
11. Enter your password.
12. Under **Web Categories to Block**, note the different levels of options available.
13. Click **Custom**.
14. Under **Other Categories**, click **Block All**.
15. Click on the other options under **Setup** and note the different configuration settings.
16. Click **Logout**.
17. Open your web browser. Enter the URL **www.google.com**. What happens now that the filter is installed?
18. Close all windows.

Case Projects

Case Project 6-1: Data Loss Prevention Comparison

Research at least four different data loss prevention (DLP) products from four different vendors. Create a table that compares at least six different functions and options. Based on your research which would you choose? What features make this product the optimum? Why? Write a short paragraph that summarizes your research.

Case Project 6-2: UTM Comparison

Create a table of four UTM devices available today. Include the vendor name, pricing, a list of features, the type of protections it provides, etc. Based on your research, assign a value of 1–5 (lowest to highest) that you would give that UTM. Include a short explanation of why you gave it that ranking.

Case Project 6-3: Load-Balancing Algorithms

Different algorithms are used to make decisions on load balancing. These include random allocation, round-robin, weighted round-robin, round-robin DNS load balancing, and others. Use the Internet to research load-balancing algorithms. Create a table that lists at least five algorithms and their advantages and disadvantages. Do any of these algorithms compromise security? Write a one-page paper on your research.

Case Project 6-4: Network Firewall Comparison

Use the Internet to identify three network firewalls, and create a chart that compares their features. Note if they are rule-based or application-aware, perform stateless or stateful packet filtering, what additional features they include (IDS, content filtering, etc.), their costs, etc. Which would you recommend? Why?

Case Project 6-5: Lake Point Consulting Services

Lake Point Consulting Services (LPCS) provides security consulting and assurance services to over 500 clients across a wide range of enterprises in more than 20 states. A new initiative at LPCS is for each of its seven regional offices to provide internships to students who are in their final year of the security degree program at the local college.

Blue Ridge Real Estate is a statewide residential and commercial real estate company. Because the company was the victim of several recent attacks, Blue Ridge wants to completely change its network infrastructure. Currently the company has a small IT staff, so they have contracted with LPSC to make recommendations and install the new equipment. First, however, they have asked LPSC to give a presentation to their executive staff about network security.

1. Create a PowerPoint presentation for the executive staff about network security. Include what it is, why it is important, and how it can be achieved using network devices, technologies, and design elements. Because the staff does not have an IT background,

the presentation cannot be too technical in nature. Your presentation should contain at least 10 slides.

2. Blue Ridge has been working with LPSC and is debating if they should use UTM network security appliances or separate devices (firewall, Internet content filters, NIDS, etc.). Because they appreciated your first presentation, they want your opinion on this subject. Create a memo that outlines the advantages and disadvantages of each approach, and give your recommendation.

Case Project 6-6: Community Site Activity

The Information Security Community Site is an online companion to this textbook. It contains a wide variety of tools, information, discussion boards, and other features to assist learners. Go to **community.cengage.com/Infosec2** and click the *Join or Sign in* icon to log in, using your login name and password that you created in Chapter 1. Click **Forums (Discussion)** and click on **Security+ Case Projects (6th edition)**. Read the following case study.

Some schools and libraries use Internet content filters to prohibit users from accessing undesirable websites. These filters are designed to protect individuals, but some claim it is a violation of their freedom. What are your opinions about Internet content filters? Do they provide protection for users or are they a hindrance? Who should be responsible for determining which sites are appropriate and which are inappropriate? And what punishments should be enacted against individuals who circumvent these filters? Visit the Community Site discussion board and post how you feel about Internet content filters.

References

1. Zetter, Kim, "How a crypto 'backdoor' pitted the tech world against the NSA," *Wired*, Aug. 24, 2013, accessed Apr. 5, 2017, www.wired.com/2013/09/nsa-backdoor/.
2. "Email Market, 2015-2019," *The Radicati Group*, accessed Aug. 30, 2015. http://www.radicati.com/wp/wp-content/uploads/2015/07/Email-Market-2015-2019-Executive-Summary.pdf.

CHAPTER 7

ADMINISTERING A SECURE NETWORK

After completing this chapter, you should be able to do the following:

List and describe the functions of secure network protocols

Explain the placement of security devices and technologies

Tell how security data can be analyzed

Explain how to manage and secure network platforms

Today's Attacks and Defenses

Who hasn't seen a Western movie that involves robbing a bank? The criminals enter the bank, flashing their guns and crying "This is a holdup!" as the robbers leap over the counter and scoop bills and coins into a burlap sack. They then dart out the door and leap onto their horses, only to have a posse hot on their tail with guns blazing. Modern bank robberies—except for the horses and posse—are very much the same. But recently a group of threat actors robbed a major bank in a new way: they changed the bank's web address so all the bank's customers came to them.

The Domain Name System (DNS) is a critical service for web users. It translates domain names in alphanumeric characters (like *www.cengage.com*) to its corresponding IP addresses (like 69.32.208.74), which represent the actual locations of the computers' hosting websites or other services. Imagine what would happen if threat actors could somehow alter the translation so that a name points not to the correct IP address but one that was owned by the threat actors. Anyone entering the domain name in a web browser would be directed to the attacker's site instead. This is just what has happened in some cases. In 2013, for instance, the Syrian Electronic Army group altered the DNS registration of *The New York Times* to redirect visitors to a page that contained the Army's logo.

And this DNS poisoning attack is evidently what occurred at a major Brazilian financial company that has 5 million customers with hundreds of branches, overseas operations in the United States and the Cayman Islands, and over $27 billion in total assets. One afternoon in the Fall of 2016, attackers compromised the bank's DNS account at Registro.br, which is the domain registration service of NIC.br. NIC.br is the registrar for sites ending in the top-level domain (TLD) ".br" (Brazil). The threat actors changed the DNS registration of 36 of the bank's online properties to redirect to their own sites (a later blog post from NIC.br admitted to a vulnerability in its website that would have in some circumstances allowed changes to clients' settings).

The attackers went to great lengths to make their sites appear authentic. These sites even had valid digital certificates, which are intended to verify the identity of the owner by displaying a green padlock along with the bank's name in the web browser, just as they would on the authentic sites. These certificates had been issued six months earlier by a nonprofit certificate authority who had made obtaining a domain validation digital certificate easier in the hopes of increasing HTTPS adoption.

Bank customers using a desktop computer or mobile device to visit the bank's websites were redirected to the attacker's look-alike websites that had been set up on Google's Cloud Platform. Once there, the unknowing victims would enter their user names and passwords— right into the hands of the waiting attackers, who could then use the information to log into the user's accounts and clean out their accounts by transferring money to an account set up by the attackers.

Aside from capturing the customer's login information through this phishing attack, the spoofed websites also infected the victim's devices by downloading malware that disguised itself as an update to a browser security plug-in that the Brazilian bank offered its customers for enhanced security. This malware Trojan gathered login information not only from this Brazilian bank but also from eight other banks. It also captured email and FTP login credentials, as well as contact lists from Microsoft Outlook and Exchange accounts, which were sent to a command and control server hosted in Canada. And just for good measure, the Trojan also included a function to disable the user's antivirus software.

Five hours after the onset of the attack, the Brazilian bank regained control of its domains, likely by calling NIC.br and convincing it to correct the DNS registrations. How many of the bank's millions of customers were caught up in the DNS attack remains unknown; the bank has not shared that information with any external security firms, nor has it publicly disclosed the attack. It's possible that the attackers could have harvested hundreds of thousands—or even millions—of customers' account details from their phishing scheme and malware.

Some evidence indicates that the threat actors may have even simultaneously redirected all transactions at automated teller machines (ATMs) and retail point-of-sale (PoS) systems to the attacker's servers so that they could easily collect the payment card details of anyone who used their card that Saturday afternoon. And the Trojan malware that was downloaded to the victims' computers continued to live on well past the afternoon nightmare.[1]

This type of attack is a known threat on the web, but has not until now been exploited on a massive scale. But half of the top 20 banks (ranked by total assets) do not manage their own DNS but instead leave it in the hands of a third party that could possibly be compromised. Banks should regularly check the security of their DNS and be sure that they have a "registry lock" that some registrars provide to prevent such an attack.

Bank robbery today no longer requires guns or getaway cars. A simple change to a DNS record is sometimes all that it takes.

As you learned in the previous chapter, building a secure network through network devices, architectures, and technologies is important for keeping information secure. But the job does not end there. Properly administering the network is also critical for security. A network that is not properly maintained through proven administrative procedures is at high risk to be compromised.

This chapter looks at administering a secure network. First, you explore secure network protocols and the proper locations for installing security devices. Next, you study the steps for analyzing security data. Finally, you look at how to secure three popular types of network applications: virtualization, cloud computing, and software defined networks.

Secure Network Protocols

 **Certification**

2.6   Given a scenario, implement secure protocols.

In the world of international politics, *protocols* are the forms of ceremony and etiquette. These rules of conduct and communication are to be observed by foreign diplomats and heads of state while in a different country. If they were to ignore these protocols, they would risk offending the citizens of the host country, which might lead to a diplomatic incident or, even worse, a war.

Computer networks also have protocols, or rules for communication. These protocols are essential for proper communication to take place between network devices. The most common protocol used today for both local area networks (LANs) and the Internet is *Transmission Control Protocol/Internet Protocol (TCP/IP)*. TCP/IP is not one single protocol; instead, it comprises several protocols that all function together (called a *protocol suite*). The two major protocols that make up its name, *TCP* and *IP*, are considered the most important protocols. IP is the protocol that functions primarily at the Open Systems Interconnection (OSI) Network layer (Layer 3) to provide addressing and routing. TCP is the main Transport layer (Layer 4) protocol that is responsible for establishing connections and the reliable data transport between devices.

> **Note** 📎
>
> IP is responsible for addressing packets and sending them on the correct route to the destination, while TCP is responsible for reliable packet transmission.

TCP/IP uses its own four-layer architecture that includes the Network Interface, Internet, Transport, and Application layers. This corresponds generally to the OSI reference model, as illustrated in Figure 7-1. The TCP/IP architecture gives a framework for the dozens of protocols and several high-level applications that comprise the suite.

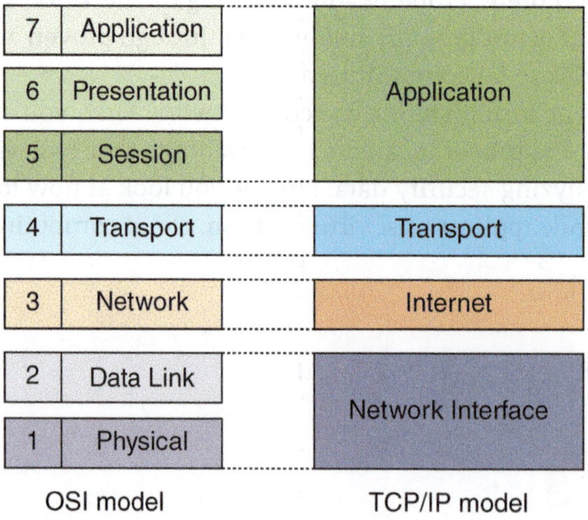

Figure 7-1   OSI model vs. TCP/IP model

> **Note** 📎
>
> The Physical layer is omitted in the TCP/IP model. This is because TCP/IP views the Network Interface layer as the point where the connection between the TCP/IP protocol and the networking hardware occurs.

Some basic TCP/IP protocols that relate to security are Simple Network Management Protocol, Domain Name System, and File Transfer Protocol. There are also email protocols that are not natively secure, but steps can be taken to protect email correspondence. For all these protocols, there are "use cases" regarding when they should be implemented.

> **Note** 📎
>
> There are other TCP/IP security-related protocols such as Secure Sockets Layer (SSL), Transport Layer Security (TLS), Secure Shell (SSH), Hypertext Transfer Protocol Secure (HTTPS), Secure/Multipurpose Internet Mail Extensions (S/MIME), Secure Real-time Transport Protocol (SRTP), and Internet Protocol Security (IPsec). These are covered in Chapter 4.

Simple Network Management Protocol (SNMP)

The **Simple Network Management Protocol (SNMP)** is a popular protocol used to manage network equipment and is supported by most network equipment manufacturers. It allows network administrators to remotely monitor, manage, and configure devices on the network. SNMP functions by exchanging management information between networked devices.

> **Note** 📎
>
> SNMP can be found not only on core network devices such as switches, routers, and wireless access points, but also on some printers, copiers, fax machines, and even uninterruptible power supplies (UPSs).

Each SNMP-managed device must have an agent or a service that listens for commands and then executes them. These agents are protected with a password, called a *community string*, to prevent unauthorized users from taking control of a device. There are two types of community strings: a *read-only* string allows information from the agent to be viewed, and a *read-write* string allows settings on the device to be changed.

There were several security vulnerabilities with the use of community strings in the first two versions of SNMP, known as SNMPv1 and SNMPv2. First, the default SNMP community strings for read-only and read-write were *public* and *private*, respectively. Administrators who did not change these default strings left open the possibility of an attacker taking control of the network device. Also, community strings were transmitted as cleartext with no attempt to encrypt the contents.

Because of the security vulnerabilities of SNMPv1 and SNMPv2, significant security enhancements were made to the next (and now current) version known as **SNMPv3**.

SNMPv3 supports authentication and encryption. Authentication is used to ensure that SNMPv3 information is available only to the intended recipient, while encryption ensures that any messages cannot be read by threat actors.

Note

Because some applications require SNMP messages to be sent through the Internet, the security features of authentication and encryption in SNMPv3 are essential.

Domain Name System (DNS)

The *Domain Name System (DNS)* is a TCP/IP protocol that resolves (maps) a symbolic name (*www.cengage.com*) with its corresponding IP address (*69.32.208.74*). The most popular implementation of DNS is *BIND*, or *Berkeley Internet Name Domain*. BIND software is open source and is the most widely deployed DNS server software. The current version is BIND9.

The DNS database is organized as a hierarchy (tree). Yet to store the entire database of names and IP addresses in one location would present several problems. First, it would cause a bottleneck and slow down the Internet with all users trying to access a single copy of the database. Second, if something happened to this one database, the entire Internet would be affected. Instead of being on a single server, the DNS database is divided and distributed to many different servers on the Internet, each of which is responsible for a different area of the Internet. The steps of a DNS lookup (which uses TCP/IP port 53) are as follows, illustrated in Figure 7-2.

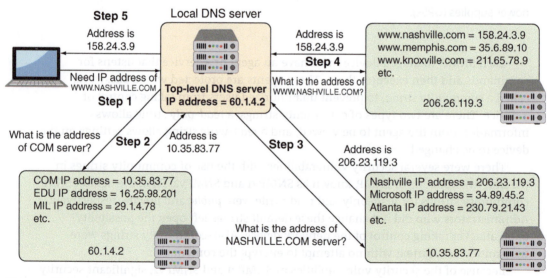

Figure 7-2 DNS lookup

Step 1. The request for the IP address of the site *www.nashville.com* is first compared against the local host table to determine if there is an entry. If no entry exists, the request travels from the user's computer to the local DNS server that is part of the LAN to which it is connected.

Step 2. The local DNS server does not know the IP address of *www.nashville.com*, yet it does know the IP address of a DNS server that contains the top-level domains and their IP numbers. A request is sent to this top-level domain DNS server.

Step 3. This top-level DNS server sends back the IP address of the DNS server that contains information about addresses that end in *.COM*. The local DNS server then sends a request to this second DNS server, which contains the IP address of the DNS server that contains the information about *nashville.com*.

Step 4. After receiving back that information, the local DNS server contacts the third DNS server responsible for *nashville*, which looks up the IP address of *www.nashville.com*.

Step 5. This information is finally returned to the local DNS server, which sends it back to the user's computer.

Because of the important role it plays, DNS is often the focus of attacks. *DNS poisoning* substitutes addresses so that the computer is redirected to another device and is illustrated in this chapter's *Today's Attacks and Defenses* segment. That is, an attacker replaces a valid IP address with a fraudulent IP address for a symbolic name. Substituting a fraudulent IP address can be done in two different locations: the local host table, or the external DNS server.

Note

DNS poisoning is covered in Chapter 5.

DNS poisoning can be thwarted by using **Domain Name System Security Extensions (DNSSEC)**, which is fully supported in BIND9. DNSSEC adds additional *resource records* (these records define the data types being used) and message header information, which can be used to verify that the requested data has not been altered in transmission. Using asymmetric cryptography, a private key that is specific to a zone is used in encrypting a hash of a set of resource records, which is then used to create the digital signature to be stored in the resource record (along with the corresponding public key).

Note

DNSSEC is now widely implemented. About 89 percent of top-level domains (TLDs) zones are signed with digital signatures, and four out of every five requests from a client for a DNS record request DNSSEC digital signature records.[2]

A second attack using DNS is almost the reverse of DNS poisoning; instead of sending a zone transfer to a valid DNS server, an attacker asks the valid DNS server for a zone transfer, known as a *DNS transfer*. With this information, it would be possible for the attacker to map the entire internal network of the organization supporting the DNS server. A zone transfer could also contain hardware and operating system information for each network device, providing the attacker with even more valuable information.

File Transfer Protocol (FTP)

In its early days, prior to the development of the World Wide Web and Hypertext Transfer Protocol (HTTP), the Internet was primarily a medium for transferring files from one device to another. Today transferring files is still an important task. Transferring files can be performed using the **File Transfer Protocol (FTP)**, which is an unsecure TCP/IP protocol. FTP is used to connect to an FTP server, much in the same way that HTTP links to a web server.

> **Note** 🔗
>
> A "light" version of FTP known as *Trivial File Transfer Protocol (TFTP)* uses a small amount of memory, but has limited functionality. It is often used for the automated transfer of configuration files between devices.

There are several different methods for using FTP on a local computer:

- *From a command prompt.* Commands can by typed at an operating system prompt, such as *ls* (list files), *get* (retrieve a file from the server), and *put* (transfer a file to the server).
- *Using a web browser.* Instead of prefacing a URL with the protocol *http://*, the FTP protocol is entered with a preface of *ftp://*.
- *Using an FTP client.* A separate FTP client application can be installed that displays files on the local host as well as the remote server. These files can be dragged and dropped between devices. The FTP client FileZilla is shown in Figure 7-3.

> **Note** 🔗
>
> FTP servers can be configured to allow unauthenticated users to transfer files, known as *anonymous FTP* or *blind FTP*.

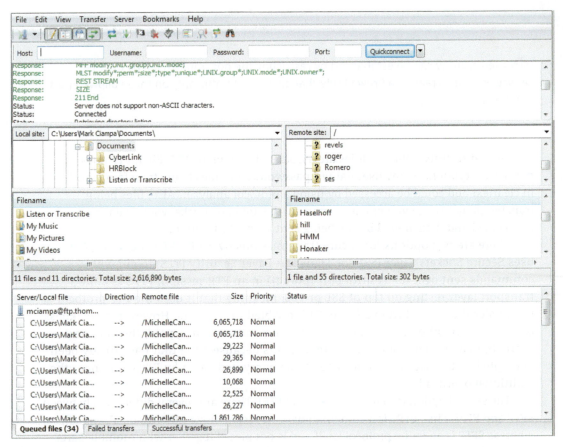

Figure 7-3   FTP client

Source: FileZilla

Using FTP behind a firewall can present a set of challenges. FTP typically uses two ports: TCP port 21 is the FTP control port used for passing FTP commands, and TCP port 20 is the FTP data port through which data is sent and received. Using *FTP active mode*, an FTP client initiates a session to a server by opening a *command channel* connection to the server's TCP port number 21. A file transfer is requested by the client by sending a *PORT* command to the server, which then attempts to initiate a *data channel* connection back to the client on TCP port 20. The client's firewall, however, might see this data channel connection request from the server as unsolicited and drop the packets. This can be avoided by using *FTP passive mode*. In passive mode, the client initiates the data channel connection, yet instead of using the *PORT* command, the client sends a *PASV* command on the command channel. The server responds with the TCP port number to which the client should connect to establish the data channel (typically port 1025 to 5000).

Note

Increased security can be established by restricting the port range used by the FTP service and then creating a firewall rule that allows FTP traffic only on those allowed port numbers.

Several security vulnerabilities are associated with using FTP. First, FTP does not use encryption, so any user names, passwords, and files being transferred are in cleartext and could be accessed by using a protocol analyzer. Also, files being transferred by FTP are vulnerable to man-in-the-middle attacks where data is intercepted and then altered before being sent to the destination.

There are two options for secure transmissions over FTP. **FTP Secure (FTPS)** uses Secure Sockets Layer (SSL) or Transport Layer Security (TLS) to encrypt commands sent over the control port (port 21) in an FTP session. FTPS is a file transport layer resting on top of SSL or TLS, meaning that it uses the FTP protocol to transfer files to and from SSL-, or TLS-enabled FTP servers. However, a weakness of FTPS is that although the control port commands are encrypted, the data port (port 20) may or may not be encrypted. This is because a file that has already been encrypted by the user would not need to be encrypted again by FTPS and incur the additional overhead.

The second option is to use **Secure FTP (SFTP)**. There are several differences between SFTP and FTPS. First, FTPS is a combination of two technologies (FTP and SSL or TLS), whereas SFTP is an entire protocol itself and is not pieced together with multiple parts. Second, SFTP uses only a single TCP port instead of two ports like FTPS. Finally, SFTP encrypts and compresses all data and commands (FTPS might not encrypt data).

Secure Email Protocols

Proof that the email protocols POP and IMAP are not secure can be seen by the large number of high-profile celebrities and politicians whose careers have been damaged or destroyed by the theft of cleartext email messages. And this also highlights the fact that due to the inconvenience of encrypting email messages, few users encrypt their messages.

Securing email messages involves the transmission of the messages as well as the storage of those messages. Whereas Secure/Multipurpose Internet Mail Extensions (S/MIME) is a protocol for securing email messages, it has limitations. S/MIME cannot be used when mail is accessed through a web browser instead of through a dedicated email application. Also, because S/MIME encrypts the entire message, this makes it difficult for any third-party tools that inspect email for malware because it also would be encrypted.

> **Note**
>
> POP, IMAP, and S/MIME are covered in Chapter 6.

Because email protocols are not secure and most users find encrypting and decrypting email cumbersome, some enterprises and government agencies automate the process. All emails are routed through a gateway appliance that automatically encrypts and decrypts messages (but only those messages to and from users within the enterprise).

> **Note**
>
> Some automatic encryption services encrypt any emails that have the word *Secure* in the subject line. Users can also register a personal email address so that forwarded encrypted emails can be read.

Using Secure Network Protocols

Different applications require different secure network protocols. Several of the recommended protocols for specific applications or technologies are summarized in Table 7-1.

Table 7-1   Secure network protocol recommendations

Application or technology	Recommended secure protocol
Voice and video	Secure Real-time Transport Protocol (SRTP)
Time synchronization	Network Time Protocol (NTP)
Email	Secure/Multipurpose Internet Mail Extensions (S/MIME)
Web browsing	Hypertext Transport Protocol Secure (HTTPS)
File transfer	Secure FTP (SFTP)
Remote access	Virtual Private Network (VPN)
Domain name resolution	DNS Security Extensions (DNSSEC)
Routing and switching	IP Security (IPsec)
Network address translation	IP Security (IPsec)
Subscription services	IP Security (IPsec)

Placement of Security Devices and Technologies

3.2 Given a scenario, implement secure network architecture concepts.

The use of network devices—whether it be using the security features found in standard networking devices like bridges, switches, routers, load balancers, and proxies, or using hardware designed primarily for security such as firewalls, virtual private network concentrators, mail gateways, network intrusion detection and prevention systems, and security and information event management (SIEM) devices—is absolutely essential in protecting a network. Whereas improperly configured devices can introduce vulnerabilities, so too can the incorrect placement of these devices within the network. The protection that a firewall provides, for example, can easily be negated if that device is not in the proper location in the network architecture.

The recommended placement for security devices and technologies includes:

- *SSL/TLS accelerator*. In many instances an SSL/TLS accelerator is a separate hardware card that inserts into a web server that contains one or more co-processors to handle SSL/TLS processing. In settings such as a large online retailer selling millions of items daily, a separate SSL/TLS hardware module can be installed as a "virtual SSL/TLS server" alongside the forward proxy server between the user's device and the web servers.

> **Note** 🖉
>
> On peak days, the online retailer Amazon sells over 600 items *each second*, or over 54 million items daily.[3]

- *Taps and port mirrors*. Although a switch limits the frames that are sent to devices, it is still important for a network administrator to be able to monitor network traffic. Monitoring traffic on switches generally can be done in two ways. First, a managed switch on an Ethernet network that supports **port mirroring** allows the administrator to configure the switch to copy traffic that occurs on some or all ports to a designated monitoring port on the switch. Port mirroring is illustrated in Figure 7-4, where the monitoring computer is connected to the mirror port and can view all network traffic moving through the switch (the monitoring computer can be a standalone device or a computer that runs protocol analyzer software). A second method for monitoring traffic is to install a **network tap (test access point)**. A network tap is a separate device that can be installed on the network. A network tap is illustrated in Figure 7-5.

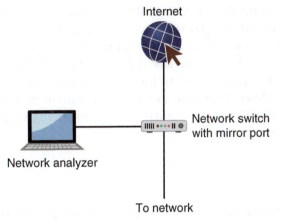

Figure 7-4   Port mirroring

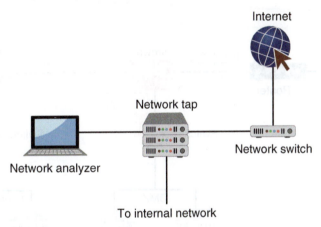

Figure 7-5   Network tap

- *Sensors, collectors, and filters.* The location of *sensors* to monitor traffic (for network intrusion detection and prevention devices), *collectors* to gather traffic (for SIEM devices), and *filters* to block traffic (for Internet content filters) should be placed in the network where the stream of data is largest, allowing them to view, gather, or block traffic. In Figure 7-6 locating a sensor/collector/filter at

Location 1 behind the first firewall would allow monitoring traffic between the internal network and the Internet but would miss traffic between the Internet and DMZ, so that an attack on a web server would be missed. If devices were placed in Location 2 between the first firewall and the DMZ they would miss traffic between the Internet and the internal network. However, placing the sensor/collector/filter at Location 3 would allow them to view all traffic from the Internet and DMZ and the internal network, providing a higher degree of visibility and protection.

> **Note** 📎
>
> Having a sensor/collector/filter at Location 3 still leaves a blind spot: the traffic between the DMZ and internal network could not be monitored. Therefore, multiple sensor/collector/filter devices are needed.

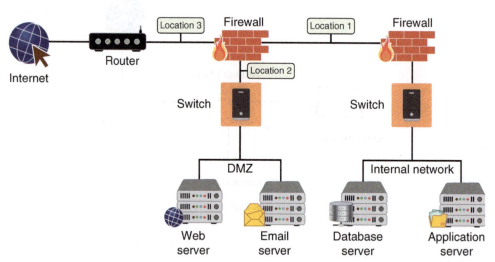

Figure 7-6   Sensor/collector/filter locations

- *Aggregation switch.* As its name implies, an **aggregation switch** is used to combine multiple network connections into a single link. An example of a device that forms a function like an aggregation switch is a load balancer. Aggregation switches, like load balancers, should be located between routers and servers, where they can detect and stop attacks directed at a server or application.
- *Correlation engine.* Like a SIEM, a **correlation engine** aggregates and correlates content from different sources to uncover an attack. Correlation engines should be in the protected internal network using data collected from the logs of different hardware devices.

- *DDoS mitigator.* A **DDoS mitigator** is a hardware device that identifies and blocks real-time distributed denial of service (DDoS) attacks. These devices should be in the network where they can monitor the largest stream of data.

The placement of proxies, firewalls, load balancers, and VPN concentrators is covered in Chapter 6.

Analyzing Security Data

2.4 Given a scenario, analyze and interpret output from security technologies.

Data accumulated by a network or computer can be extremely valuable. Much of the data is accumulated into a **log**, which is a record of events that occur. *Security logs* are particularly important because they can reveal the types of attacks that are being directed at the network and if any of the attacks were successful. A security *access log* can provide details regarding requests for specific files on a system while an *audit log* is used to record which user performed what actions. System *event logs* document any unsuccessful events and the most significant successful events (some system event logs can be tailored to specify the types of events that are recorded). The types of information that can be recorded might include the date and time of the event, a description of the event, its status, error codes, service name, and the user or system responsible for launching the event.

This security data can be analyzed to sound an alert of an attack as well as to later determine how the attack occurred and what can be done to prevent similar future attacks. Other ways in which logs can benefit enterprises include:

- A routine review and analysis of logs helps to identify security incidents, policy violations, fraudulent activity, and operational problems shortly after they have occurred.
- Logs can be useful for performing auditing analysis, supporting the organization's internal investigations, and identifying operational trends and long-term problems.
- Logs can provide documentation that the organization is complying with laws and regulatory requirements.

Data can be accumulated by security devices, security software, and security tools, but there are also some issues involved in the analysis of security data.

Data from Security Devices

Virtually every hardware device designed primarily for security can generate logs, including host-based intrusion detection systems (HIDS), host-based intrusion prevention systems (HIPS), Unified Threat Management (UTM) systems, web application firewalls, host-based firewalls, and to a lesser degree standard networking devices such as bridges, switches, routers, load balancers, and proxies. For example, the types of items that could be examined in a firewall log include:

- *IP addresses that are being rejected and dropped.* It is not uncommon for the owner of a firewall to track down the owner of the site from which the packets are originating and ask why someone at his site is probing these ports. The owner may be able to pinpoint the perpetrator of the probe, even if the owner is an Internet Service Provider (ISP).
- *Probes to ports that have no application services running on them.* Attackers often try to determine if specific ports are already in use to target them for attack. If several probes appear directed at an obscure port number, it may be necessary to investigate if malware is associated with it.
- *Source-routed packets.* Packets with a source address internal to the network but that originates from outside the network could indicate that an attacker is attempting to spoof an internal address to gain access to the internal network.
- *Suspicious outbound connections.* Outbound connections from a public web server could be an indication that an attacker is launching attacks against others from the web server.
- *Unsuccessful logins.* If several unsuccessful logins come from the same domain, it may be necessary to create a new rule to drop all connections from that domain or IP address.

Network device logs that provide the most beneficial security data, in order of importance, are listed in Table 7-2.

Table 7-2 Device logs with beneficial security data

Device	Explanation
Firewalls	Firewall logs can be used to determine whether new IP addresses are attempting to probe the network and if stronger firewall rules are necessary to block them. Outgoing connections, incoming connections, denied traffic, and permitted traffic should all be recorded.
Host-based intrusion detection systems (HIDS) and host-based intrusion prevention systems (HIPS)	Intrusion detection and intrusion prevention systems record detailed security log information on suspicious behavior as well as any attacks that are detected. In addition, these logs also record any actions used to stop the attacks.

(continues)

Table 7-2 (*continued*)

Web servers	Web servers are usually the primary target of attackers. Web server logs can provide valuable information about the type of attack that can help in configuring good security on the server.
DHCP servers	DHCP server logs can identify new systems that mysteriously appear and then disappear as part of the network. They can also show what hardware device had which IP address at a specific time.
VPN concentrators	VPN logs can be monitored for attempted unauthorized access to the network.
Proxies	As intermediate hosts through which websites are accessed, these devices keep a log of all URLs that are accessed through them. This information can be useful when determining if a zombie is "calling home."
Domain Name System (DNS)	A DNS log can show all queries that are received. Some DNS servers also can create logs for error and alert messages.
Email servers	Email servers can show the latest malware attacks that are being launched using attachments.
Routers and switches	Router and switch logs provide general information about network traffic.

Data from Security Software

In addition to hardware devices generating data, security software can also produce important data that can be analyzed. At the very heart of a data loss prevention (DLP) system is logging and monitoring who is using the data and how it is being accessed. A user who repeatedly attempts to send sensitive data by emails through a mail gateway or copy the files to a USB flash drive can be flagged. **Data Execution Prevention (DEP)** is a Microsoft Windows feature that prevents attackers from using buffer overflow to execute malware. DEP events and those from similar software can be logged along with the level of severity, such as *information* (logging the software is starting), *warning* (when configuration changes are made), and *alert* (an active attack has been blocked). **File integrity check (FIC)** is a service that can monitor any changes made to computer files, such as operating system files. These changes can compromise security and indicate a security breach has occurred, and are routinely included in FIC log files.

Note 🖇

Because in modern operating systems, system files are routinely modified in the normal course of the computer's operation, an FIC system must be highly customizable, allowing the user to choose which folders and files to monitor and manage the type of alerts that are generated.

Data from Security Tools

There are other security tools that can produce output to be analyzed. Several of these tools are listed in Table 7-3.

Table 7-3	Security tools	
Tool	**Description**	**Explanation**
Application whitelisting	An application whitelist is an inventory of applications and associated components (libraries, configuration files, etc.) that have been pre-approved and authorized to be active and present on the device.	Unlike most security technologies such as a firewall that attempts to block known malicious activity while permitting all others, application whitelisting technologies are designed to permit only known good activity and block everything else.
Removable media control	Removable media control is a tool that can be used to restrict which removable media, such as USB flash drives, can be attached to a system.	Because removable media can not only introduce malware into a system but also can be used to steal valuable information, removable media control can help prevent these vulnerabilities.
Advanced malware management	Often a third-party service, advanced malware management tools monitor a network for any unusual activity.	Advanced malware management tools often use experience-based techniques such as heuristic monitoring to determine if a threat exists.

Issues in Analyzing Security Data

There are issues associated with *log management*, or generating, transmitting, storing, analyzing, and disposing of computer security log data. This is due to:

- *Multiple devices generating logs.* As noted, virtually every network device, both standard network devices and network security devices, can create logs. And each device might interpret an event in a different context, so that a router looks at a single event differently than a firewall does. This can create a confusing mix of log data.
- *Very large volume of data.* Because each device generates its own data, a very large amount of log data can accumulate in a very short period. In addition, many devices record all events, even those that are not security-related, which increases even more the amount of data that is generated. Filtering through this large volume of data can be overwhelming.
- *Different log formats.* Perhaps the biggest obstacle to log management is that different devices record log information in different formats and even with different data captured. Combining multiple logs, each with a different format, can be a major challenge.

One solution to log management is to use a centralized device log analyzer. These systems are designed to collect and consolidate logs from multiple sources for easy analysis. An example of a centralized device log manager is illustrated in Figure 7-7.

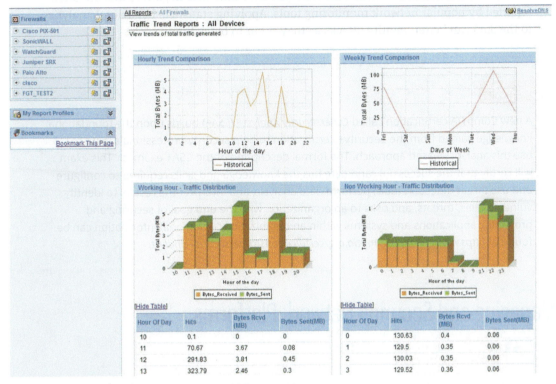

Figure 7-7   Centralized device log analyzer

Source: ManageEngine.com

A greater issue is that too often this data is used only "after the fact": that is, data is analyzed to determine how an attack occurred but not to prevent an attack. As threat actors continue to modify their attacks so that no two attacks appear the same, it is increasingly difficult for enterprises, relying upon traditional static signature-based solutions, to identify a modified attack that has not appeared before. Many enterprises are victims of attacks but are not even aware of it, because their signature-based security tools did not detect it.

Note

Per one study, it takes an enterprise an average of 229 days before it knows that it has been compromised.[4]

However, that is now beginning to change. An *analytics-based* approach is becoming increasingly important. Using data gathered from multiple hardware devices, software security applications, and security tools, an analytics-based approach attempts to differentiate between the false positives and false negatives that are often reported by popular network monitoring tools. Applying statistical behavioral analytics to the data can better identify attacks as they occur to block them.

> **Note** 📎
>
> A new CompTIA certification called *Cybersecurity Analyst+ (CSA+)* builds upon the foundational knowledge gained from the Security+ certification to help security professionals learn to use this analytics-based approach. The formal description of the CSA+ exam is, "This exam will certify that the successful candidate has the knowledge and skills required to configure and use threat detection tools, perform data analysis, and interpret the results to identify vulnerabilities, threats, and risks to an organization with the end goal of securing and protecting applications and systems within an organization." Additional information can be found at *https://certification.comptia.org/certifications/cybersecurity-analyst.*

Managing and Securing Network Platforms

 **Certification**

2.1 Install and configure network components, both hardware- and software-based, to support organizational security.

3.2 Given a scenario, implement secure network architecture concepts.

3.7 Summarize cloud and virtualization concepts.

Some applications and platforms require special security considerations. These include virtualization, cloud computing, and software defined networking.

Virtualization

Virtualization is a means of managing and presenting computer resources by function without regard to their physical layout or location. One type of virtualization in which an entire operating system environment is simulated is known as *host virtualization*. Instead of using a physical computer, a *virtual machine*, which is a simulated software-based emulation of a computer, is created instead. The *host system* (the operating system installed on the computer's hardware) runs a virtual machine monitor program that supports one or more *guest systems* (a foreign virtual operating system) that run applications. For example, a computer that boots to Windows 10 (host) could support a virtual machine of Linux (guest) as well as Windows 8 (guest) or another Windows 10 (guest) system.

> **Note** 📎
>
> Virtualization is used extensively to consolidate network and web servers so that multiple virtual servers can run on a single physical computer. Because a typical server utilizes only about 10 percent of its capacity, there is excess capacity for running virtual machines on a physical server.

The virtual machine monitor program is called a **hypervisor**, which manages the virtual machine operating systems. Hypervisors use a small "layer" of computer code in software or firmware to allocate resources in real time as needed, such as input/output functions and memory allocations. There are two types of hypervisors:

- *Type I*. **Type I hypervisors** run directly on the computer's hardware instead of the underlying operating system. Type I hypervisors are sometimes called "native" or "bare metal" hypervisors.
- *Type II*. Instead of running directly on the computer hardware, **Type II hypervisors** run on the host operating system, much like a regular application. Type I and Type II hypervisors are illustrated in Figure 7-8.

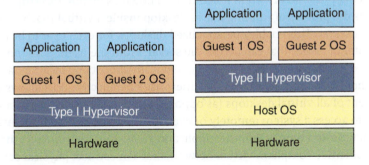

Figure 7-8   Type I and Type II hypervisors

> **Note** 📎
>
> Initially, Type II hypervisors, which run on a host operating system, were popular because network administrators could purchase a Type II hypervisor and install it on an existing file server. However, Type I hypervisors are now more widely used because they provide better performance, as they do not have to rely on the underlying host operating system.

An even more reduced instance of virtualization is a **container** or **application cell**. With both Type I and Type II hypervisors, the entire guest operating system must be started and fully functioning before an application can be launched. A container, on the other hand, holds only the necessary operating system components (such as binary files and libraries) that are needed for that specific application to run. And in some instances, containers can even share binary files and libraries. This not only reduces the necessary hard drive storage space and Random Access Memory (RAM) needed but also allows for containers to start more quickly because the entire operating system does not have to be started. Containers can be easily moved from one computer to another. These are illustrated in Figure 7-9.

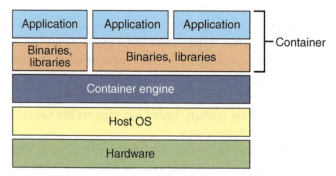

Figure 7-9   Containers

Another application of virtual machines is known as **Virtual Desktop Infrastructure (VDI)**. VDI is the process of running a user desktop inside a virtual machine that resides on a server. This enables personalized desktops for each user to be available on any computer or device that can access the server. From the users' standpoint, their personalized desktop and files can be accessed from almost any location, as if they were sitting at their own computer. From the enterprise's perspective, VDI allows centralized management of all virtual desktops (as opposed to the need for technical support personnel to access a system remotely or even visit a user's desk to troubleshoot), saving substantial time and money. Another application is **Virtual Distributed Ethernet (VDE)**. VDE is an Ethernet-compliant virtual network that can connect physical computers and/or virtual machines together. For example, a VDE can be used to connect computers in a virtual Ethernet environment over the Internet to create and use a VPN.

Virtualization has several advantages. First, new virtual server machines can be quickly made available (*host availability*), and resources such as the amount of RAM or hard drive space can easily be expanded or contracted as needed (*host elasticity*). Also, virtualization can reduce costs. Instead of purchasing one physical server to run one network operating system and its applications, a single physical server can run multiple virtual machines and host multiple operating systems. This results in a significant cost savings in that fewer physical computers must be purchased and maintained. In addition, the cost of electricity to run these servers as well as keep data center server rooms cool is also reduced.

Another advantage of server virtualization is that it can be beneficial in providing uninterrupted server access to users. Data centers must schedule planned "downtime" for servers to perform maintenance on the hardware or software. Often it is difficult, however, to find a time when users will not be inconvenienced by the downtime. This can be addressed by virtualization that supports *live migration*; this technology enables a virtual machine to be moved to a different physical computer with no impact to the users. The virtual machine stores its current state onto a shared storage device immediately before the migration occurs. The virtual machine is then reinstalled on another physical computer and accesses its storage with no noticeable interruption to users. Live migration also can be used for *load balancing*; if the demand for a service or application increases, network managers can quickly move this high-demand virtual machine to another physical server with more RAM or CPU resources.

Host virtualization also has several security-related advantages:

- The latest security updates can be downloaded and run in a virtual machine to determine compatibility, or the impact on other software or even hardware. This is used instead of installing the update on a production computer and then being forced to "roll back" to the previous configuration if it does not work properly.
- A *snapshot* of a state of a virtual machine can be saved for later use. A user can make a snapshot before performing extensive modifications or alterations to the virtual machine, and then the snapshot can be reloaded so that the virtual machine is at the beginning state before the changes were made. Multiple snapshots can be made, all at different states, and loaded as needed.
- Testing the existing security configuration, known as *security control testing*, can be performed using a simulated network environment on a computer using multiple virtual machines. For example, one virtual machine can virtually attack another virtual machine on the same host system to determine vulnerabilities and security settings. This is possible because all the virtual machines can be connected through a virtual network.
- Virtual machines can promote security segregation and isolation. Separating virtual machines from other machines can reduce the risk of infections transferring from one device to another.
- A virtual machine can be used to test for potential malware. A suspicious program can be loaded into an isolated virtual machine and executed (*sandboxing*). If the program is malware, it will impact only the virtual machine, and it can easily be erased and a snapshot reinstalled. This is how antivirus software using heuristic detection can spot the characteristics of a virus.

Note 🖇

Heuristic detection is covered in Chapter 6.

However, there are security concerns for virtualized environments:

- Not all hypervisors have the necessary security controls to keep out determined attackers. If a single hypervisor is compromised, multiple virtual servers are at risk.

- Existing security tools, such as antivirus, antispam, and IDS, were designed for single physical servers and do not always adapt well to multiple virtual machines.

- Virtual machines must be protected from both outside networks and other virtual machines on the same physical computer. In a network without virtual machines, external devices such as firewalls and IDS that reside between physical servers can help prevent one physical server from infecting another physical server, but no such physical devices exist between virtual machines.

- Virtual machines may be able to "escape" from the contained environment and directly interact with the host operating system. It is important to have **virtual machine escape protection** so that a virtual machine cannot directly interact with the host operating system and potentially infect it, which could then be transmitted to all other virtual machines running on the host operating system.

- Because virtual machines can easily and quickly be created and launched, this has led to **virtual machine sprawl**, or the widespread proliferation of virtual machines without proper oversight or management. It is often easy for a virtual machine to be created and then forgotten. A guest operating system that has remained dormant for a period may not contain the latest security updates, even though the underlying host operating system has been updated. When the guest is launched, it will be vulnerable until properly updated.

Cloud Computing

Forty years ago, as computing technology become widespread, enterprises employed an **on-premises** model, in which they purchased all the hardware and software necessary to run the organization. As more resources were needed more purchases were made and more personnel were hired to manage the technology. Because this resulted in spiraling costs, some enterprises turned to **hosted services**. In a hosted services environment, servers, storage, and the supporting networking infrastructure are shared by multiple enterprises over a remote network connection that had been contracted for a specific period. As more resources are needed (such as additional storage space or computing power), the enterprise contacted the hosted service and negotiated an additional fee as well as sign a new contract for those new services.

Today a new model is gaining widespread use. Known as **cloud computing**, this is a pay-per-use computing model in which customers pay only for the online computing resources they need. As computing needs increase or decrease, cloud computing resources can be quickly scaled up or scaled back. Although various definitions of cloud computing have been proposed, the definition from the National Institute of Standards and Technology (NIST) may be the most comprehensive: *Cloud computing* *is a model for enabling convenient, on-demand network access to a shared pool of configurable computing resources (e.g., networks, servers, storage, applications, and services) that can be rapidly provisioned and released with minimal management effort or service provider interaction.*[5]

Table 7-4 lists different characteristics of cloud computing.

Table 7-4   Cloud computing characteristics

Characteristic	Explanation
On-demand self-service	The consumer can make changes, such as increasing or decreasing computing resources, without requiring any human interaction from the service provider.
Universal client support	Virtually any networked device (desktop, laptop, smartphone, tablet, etc.) can access the cloud computing resources.
Invisible resource pooling	The physical and virtual computing resources are pooled together to serve multiple, simultaneous consumers that are dynamically assigned or reassigned based on the consumers' needs; the customer has little or no control or knowledge of the physical location of the resources.
Immediate elasticity	Computing resources can be increased or decreased quickly to meet demands.
Metered services	Fees are based on the computing resources used.

There are different types of clouds. A **public cloud** is one in which the services and infrastructure are offered to all users with access provided remotely through the Internet. Unlike a public cloud that is open to anyone, a **community cloud** is a cloud that is open only to specific organizations that have common concerns. For example, because of the strict data requirements of the Health Insurance Portability and Accountability Act of 1996 (HIPAA), a community cloud open only to hospitals may be used. A **private cloud** is created and maintained on a private network. Although this type offers the highest level of security and control (because the company must purchase and maintain all the software and hardware), it also reduces any cost savings. A **hybrid cloud** is a combination of public and private clouds. **Cloud storage** has no computational capabilities but only provides remote file storage.

There are at least four service models in cloud computing:

- *Software as a Service (SaaS)*. In the **Software as a Service (SaaS)** model the cloud computing vendor provides access to the vendor's software applications running on a cloud infrastructure. These applications, which can be accessed through a web browser, do not require any installation, configuration, upgrading, or management from the user.
- *Platform as a Service (PaaS)*. Unlike SaaS in which the application software belonging to the cloud computing vendor is used, in the **Platform as a Service (PaaS)** model

consumers can install and run their own specialized applications on the cloud computing network. Although customers have control over the deployed applications, they do not manage or configure any of the underlying cloud infrastructure (network, servers, operating systems, storage, etc.).

- *Infrastructure as a Service (IaaS)*. In the **Infrastructure as a Service (IaaS)** model, the customer has the highest level of control. The cloud computing vendor allows customers to deploy and run their own software, including operating systems and applications. Consumers have some control over the operating systems, storage, and their installed applications, but do not manage or control the underlying cloud infrastructure.
- *Security as a Service (SECaaS)*. With the **Security as a Service (SECaaS)** model all security services—such as intrusion detection and SIEM—are delivered from the cloud to the enterprise. This relieves the enterprise from purchasing and managing security hardware and software.

Cloud computing has several potential security issues. It is important that the cloud provider guarantee that the means are in place by which authorized users are given access while imposters are denied. Also, all transmissions to and from "the cloud" must be adequately protected. Finally, the customer's data must be isolated from that of other customers, and the highest level of application availability and security must be maintained.

> **Note** 📎
>
> Another security concern with cloud computing is that often employees, frustrated by the delays in securing computing resources for a project, will privately purchase cloud resources without the knowledge or consent of the enterprise. This can introduce significant security issues if the enterprise's data in the cloud is not properly managed and secured.

One security protection for cloud computing is for an organization to use a **cloud access security broker (CASB)**. A CASB is a set of software tools or services that resides between the enterprises' on-premises infrastructure and the cloud provider's infrastructure. Acting as the "gatekeeper," a CASB ensures that the security policies of the enterprise extend to its data in the cloud. For example, if the enterprise has a policy regarding encrypting data, a CASB can enforce that control so that data copied from the cloud to a local device is encrypted. Another security protection is to utilize cloud-based DLP to extend the enterprise's policies to data stored in the cloud.

Software Defined Network (SDN)

Virtualization has been an essential technology in changing the face of computing over the last decade. Racks of individual physical servers running a single application have been replaced by only a few hardware devices running multiple virtual machines, simulated software-based emulations of computers. Virtual machines have made cloud computing possible; as computing needs increase or decrease, cloud computing resources on virtual machines can be quickly scaled up or back. Networks can also be configured into logical groups to create a *virtual LAN (VLAN)*. A VLAN allows scattered users to be logically grouped together even though they are physically attached to different switches. The computing landscape today would simply not be possible without virtualization.

Yet virtual machines and virtual LANs run into a bottleneck: the physical network. Dating back over forty years, networks comprised of physical hardware like bridges, switches, and routers has collided with the world of virtual machines and VLANs.

Consider this problem. A network manager needs to make sure the VLAN used by a virtual machine is assigned to the same port on a switch as the physical server that is running the virtual machine. But if the virtual machine needs to be migrated, the manager must reconfigure the VLAN every time that a virtual server is moved. In a large enterprise, whenever a new virtual machine is installed it can take hours for managers to perform the necessary reconfiguration. In addition, these managers must configure each vendor's equipment separately, tweaking performance and security configurations for each session and application. This process is difficult to do with conventional network switches because the *control logic* for each switch is bundled together with the *switching logic*.

What is needed is for the flexibility of the virtual world to be applied to the network. This would allow the network manager to quickly and dynamically add, drop, and change network resources on the fly.

The solution is a **software defined network (SDN)**. An SDN virtualizes parts of the physical network so that it can be more quickly and easily reconfigured. This is accomplished by separating the *control plane* from the *data plane*, as illustrated in Figure 7-10. The control plane consists of one or more SDN servers and performs the complex functions such as routing and security checks. It also defines the data flows through the data plane.

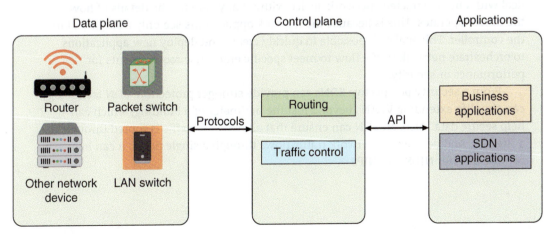

Figure 7-10   Software defined network

> **Note** 📎
>
> In an SDN, the control plane is essentially an application running on a computer that can manage the physical plane.

If traffic needs to flow through the network, it first receives permission from the SDN controller, which verifies that the communication is permitted by the network policy of the enterprise. Once approved, the SDN controller computes a route for the flow to take, and adds an entry for that flow in each of the switches along the path. Because all the complex networking functions are handled by the SDN controller, the switches simply manage "flow tables" whose entries are created by the controller. The communication between the SDN controller and the SDN switches uses a standardized protocol and application program interface (API).

> **Note** 📎
>
> The architecture of SDN is very flexible, using different types of switches from different vendors at different protocol layers. SDN controllers and switches can be implemented for Ethernet switches (Layer 2), Internet routers (Layer 3), Transport (Layer 4) switching, or Application layer switching and routing.

With the decoupling of the control and data planes, SDN enables applications to deal with one "abstracted" network device without any care for the details of how the device operates. This is because the network applications see only a single API to the controller. This makes it possible to quickly create and deploy new applications to orchestrate network traffic flow to meet specific enterprise requirements for performance or security.

From a security perspective SDNs can provide stronger protection. SDN technology can simplify extending VLANs beyond just the perimeter of a building, which can help secure data. Also, an SDN can ensure that all network traffic is routed through a firewall. And because all network traffic flows through a single point, it can help capture data for NIDS and NIPS.

Chapter Summary

- The most common protocol used today for local area networks (LANs) and the Internet is Transmission Control Protocol/Internet Protocol (TCP/IP). TCP/IP is not a single protocol; it is a suite of protocols that all function together. The Simple Network Management Protocol (SNMP) allows network administrators to remotely monitor, manage, and configure devices on the network. SNMP functions by exchanging management information between networked devices. There were several security vulnerabilities with the use of community strings in early versions of SNMP that have been addressed in the most recent version. The Domain Name System (DNS) is a TCP/IP protocol that resolves an IP address with its equivalent symbolic name. The DNS is a database, organized as a hierarchy or tree, of the name of each site on the Internet and its corresponding IP number. Because of the important role it plays, DNS can be the focus of attacks, several of which can be thwarted by using Domain Name System Security Extensions (DNSSEC).

- Transferring files is most commonly performed using the File Transfer Protocol (FTP), which is part of the TCP/IP suite. FTP is used to connect to an FTP server, much in the same way that HTTP links to a web server. Several vulnerabilities are associated with using FTP. There are two options for secure transmissions over FTP. FTPS (FTP using Secure Sockets Layer) is a file transport layer resting "on top" of SSL/TLS. SFTP (Secure FTP) is an entire secure file transfer protocol and not separate elements added together. Securing email messages involves both the transmission of the messages and the storage of those messages. The S/MIME protocol can be used for securing email messages, but it has limitations. Different applications require different secure network protocols.

- The correct placement of security devices is essential for protection. An SSL/TLS accelerator can be a separate hardware card or a separate SSL/TLS hardware module installed as a "virtual SSL server" alongside the forward proxy server between the user's device and the web. Monitoring traffic on switches generally can be done in two ways. First, a managed switch on an Ethernet network that supports port mirroring allows the administrator to configure the switch to copy traffic that occurs on some or all ports to a designated monitoring port on the switch. A second method is to install a network tap (test access point). Sensors to monitor traffic, collectors to gather traffic, and filters to block traffic should be placed in the network where the largest stream of data will allow them to perform their functions. An aggregation switch is used to combine multiple network connections into a single link and should be located between routers and servers. A correlation engine aggregates and correlates content from different sources to uncover an attack and should be in the protected internal network. A DDoS mitigator is a hardware device that identifies and blocks real-time DDoS attacks. These devices should be located in the network where they can monitor the largest stream of traffic.

- A log is a record of events that occur. Security logs are particularly important because they can reveal the types of attacks that are being directed at the network and if any of the attacks were successful. Data can be accumulated by security devices, security software, and security tools. There are issues associated with log management, or generating, transmitting, storing, analyzing, and disposing of computer security log data. One solution to log management is to use a centralized device log analyzer. A greater issue is that too often this data is only used to determine how an attack occurred but it is not used in preventing an attack. An analytics-based approach is becoming increasingly important. Using data gathered from multiple hardware devices, software security applications, and security tools, an analytics-based approach attempts to differentiate between the false positives and false

negatives that are often reported by popular network monitoring tools.

- Some applications and platforms require special security considerations. Virtualization is a means of managing and presenting computer resources by function without regard to their physical layout or location. One type of virtualization in which an entire operating system environment is simulated is known as host virtualization. A reduced instance of virtualization is a container or application cell. Security for virtualized environments can be a concern. A growing number of virtualization security tools are available. Cloud computing is a revolutionary concept. Cloud computing is a "pay-per-use" model in which customers pay only for the online computing resources that they need at any time. Despite its dramatic impact on IT, cloud computing also has security concerns. A software defined network (SDN) virtualizes parts of the physical network so that it can be more quickly and easily reconfigured. This is accomplished by separating the control plane from the data plane.

Key Terms

advanced malware management
aggregation switch
application cell
application whitelisting
cloud access security broker (CASB)
cloud computing
cloud storage
community cloud
container
correlation engine

Data Execution Prevention (DEP)
DDoS mitigator
Domain Name System Security Extensions (DNSSEC)
file integrity check (FIC)
File Transfer Protocol (FTP)
FTP Secure (FTPS)
hosted services
hybrid cloud
hypervisor

Infrastructure as a Service (IaaS)
log
network tap (test access point)
on-premises
Platform as a Service (PaaS)
port mirroring
private cloud
public cloud
removable media control
Secure FTP (SFTP)

Security as a Service (SECaaS)
Simple Network Management
   Protocol (SNMP)
SNMPv3
Software as a Service
   (SaaS)

software defined network
   (SDN)
Type I hypervisor
Type II hypervisor
Virtual Desktop
   Infrastructure (VDI)

Virtual Distributed Ethernet
   (VDE)
virtual machine escape
   protection
virtual machine sprawl
virtualization

Review Questions

1. Which of the following TCP/IP protocols do not relate to security?
   a. IP
   b. SNMP
   c. HTTPS
   d. FTP

2. Aideen sent an email to her supervisor explaining the Domain Name System Security Extensions (DNSSEC). Which of the following statements would Aideen have NOT included in her email?
   a. It is fully supported in BIND9.
   b. It adds additional resource records.
   c. It adds message header information.
   d. It can prevent a DNS transfer attack.

3. What is the recommended secure protocol for voice and video applications?
   a. Secure Real-time Transport Protocol (SRTP)
   b. Hypertext Transport Protocol Secure (HTTPS)
   c. Network Time Protocol (NTP)
   d. Secure/Multipurpose Internet Mail Extensions (S/MIME)

4. Which type of log can provide details regarding requests for specific files on a system?
   a. Audit log
   b. Access log
   c. Event log
   d. SysFile log

5. Which type of device log contains the most beneficial security data?
   a. Firewall log
   b. Email log
   c. Switch log
   d. Router log

6. Which type of cloud is offered to specific organizations that have common concerns?
   a. Public cloud
   b. Hybrid cloud
   c. Private cloud
   d. Community cloud

7. Which of these is NOT correct about an SSL accelerator?
   a. It is a separate hardware card that inserts into a web server.
   b. It contains one or more co-processors to handle SSL/TLS processing.
   c. It can be installed as a "virtual SSL/TLS server" alongside a forward proxy server.
   d. It replaces FTP using Secure Sockets Layer (FTPS) as a file transport layer resting "on top" of SSL/TLS.

8. Catriona needed to monitor network traffic. She did not have the resources to install an additional device on the network. Which of the following solutions would meet her needs?
   a. Network tap
   b. Port mirroring
   c. Aggregation switch
   d. Correlation engine

9. Which version of Simple Network Management Protocol (SNMP) is considered the most secure?
   a. SNMPv2
   b. SNMPv3
   c. SNMPv4
   d. SNMPv5

10. Which Domain Name System (DNS) attack replaces a fraudulent IP address for a symbolic name?
    a. DNS replay
    b. DNS masking
    c. DNS poisoning
    d. DNS forwarding

11. Which of these is the most secure protocol for transferring files?
    a. FTPS c. TCP
    b. SFTP d. FTP

12. Which of the following can be used to prevent a buffer overflow attack?
    a. DEP
    b. FIM
    c. VPN
    d. DNS

13. Which of the following is NOT a service model in cloud computing?
    a. Software as a Service (SaaS)
    b. Hardware as a Service (HaaS)
    c. Platform as a Service (PaaS)
    d. Infrastructure as a Service (IaaS)

14. Eachna is showing a new security intern the log file from a firewall. Which of the following entries would she tell him do not need to be investigated?
    a. Suspicious outbound connections
    b. IP addresses that are being rejected and dropped
    c. Successful logins
    d. IP addresses that are being rejected and dropped

15. Which type of hypervisor does not run on an underlying operating system?
    a. Type I
    b. Type II
    c. Type III
    d. Type IV

16. Which application stores the user's desktop inside a virtual machine that resides on a server and is accessible from multiple locations?
    a. Application cell
    b. Container
    c. VDE
    d. VDI

17. Kyle asked his supervisor which type of computing model was used when the enterprise first started. She explained that the organization purchased all the hardware and software necessary to run the company. What type of model was she describing to Kyle?
    a. Virtual services
    b. Off-premises
    c. On-premises
    d. Hosted services

18. DNSSEC adds additional ____ and message header information, which can be used to verify that the requested data has not been altered in transmission.
    a. resource records
    b. field flags
    c. hash sequences
    d. zone transfers

19. What functions of a switch does a software defined network separate?
    a. Host and virtual
    b. Control plane and physical plane
    c. RAM and hard drive
    d. Network level and resource level

20. Which of the following is NOT a security concern of virtualized environments?
    a. Virtual machines must be protected from both the outside world and from other virtual machines on the same physical computer.
    b. Physical security appliances are not always designed to protect virtual systems.
    c. Virtual servers are less expensive than their physical counterparts.
    d. Live migration can immediately move one virtualized server to another hypervisor.

Hands-On Projects

> **Note**
>
> If you are concerned about installing any of the software in these projects on your regular computer, you can instead install the software in the Windows virtual machine created in the Chapter 1 Hands-On Projects 1-3 and 1-4. Software installed within the virtual machine will not impact the host computer.

Project 7-1: Creating a Virtual Machine from a Physical Computer

The VMware vCenter Converter creates a virtual machine from an existing physical computer. In this project, you download and install vCenter to create a virtual machine.

1. Use your web browser to go to **www.vmware.com**. (The location of content on the Internet may change without warning. If you are no longer able to access the program through this URL, use a search engine to search for "VMware".)
2. Click **Downloads**.
3. Click **vCenter Converter**.
4. If necessary, click **Create an account**, enter the requested information, and log into VMware.
5. If necessary, accept the terms of use and click **I agree**.
6. Click **Manually Download**.
7. When the download completes, run the installation program to install vCenter by accepting the default settings.
8. Launch vCenter to display the VMware vCenter Converter Standalone menu.
9. Click **Convert machine**.
10. Under **Select source type**, choose **This local machine**. Click **Next**.
11. Next to **Select destination type:**, choose **VMware Workstation or other VMware virtual machine**.
12. Under **Select a location for the virtual machine:**, click **Browse**.
13. Navigate to a location to store the new virtual machine. Click **Next** and then click **Next** again.
14. Click **Finish** to create the virtual machine from the physical machine.

> **Note**
>
> Note that depending upon the computer configuration it could take up to 60 minutes to create the virtual machine.

15. When the vCenter has finished, note the location of the image, which will be one or more *.vmx and *.vmdk files in the destination folder. It will be used in the next project.
16. Close all windows.

Project 7-2: Loading the Virtual Machine

In this project, you download a program to load the virtual machine created in Project 7-1.

1. Use your web browser to go to **my.vmware.com**. (The location of content on the Internet may change without warning. If you are no longer able to access the program through this URL, use a search engine to search for "VMware Workstation".)
2. Click **All Downloads**.
3. Click **View Download Components**.
4. Select the Workstation Player for your computer's operating system. Click **Download**.
5. When the download completes, launch the installation program to install VMware Workstation Player.
6. Start VMware Workstation Player after the installation completes.
7. Click **Open a Virtual Machine**.
8. Navigate to the location of the virtual machine that you created in Project 7-1. Click **Open**.
9. Click **Edit virtual machine settings**. Note the different options for configuring the hardware of the virtual machine. Click through these options and if desired change any of the settings. Click **Close**.

> **Note** 📎
>
> Note that to run this virtual machine, a previously unlicensed version of the operating system must first be installed.

10. How easy was it to create a virtual machine from a physical machine?
11. Close all windows.

Project 7-3: Viewing SNMP Management Information Base (MIB) Elements

SNMP information is stored in a management information base (MIB), which is a database for different objects. In this project, you view MIBs.

1. Use your web browser to go to **www.mibdepot.com**. (The location of content on the Internet may change without warning. If you are no longer able to access the program through this URL, use a search engine to search for "MIB Depot".)
2. In the left pane, click **Single MIB View**.
3. Scroll down and click **Linksys** in the right pane. This will display the Linksys MIBs summary information.
4. In the left pane, click **v1 & 2 MIBs** to select the SNMP Version 1 and Version 2 MIBs.
5. In the right pane, click **LINKSYS-MIB** under **MIB Name (File Name)**. This will display a list of the Linksys MIBs.

6. Click **Tree** under **Viewing Mode** in the left pane. The MIBs are now categorized by Object Identifier (OID). Each object in a MIB file has an OID associated with it, which is a series of numbers separated by dots that represent where on the MIB "tree" the object is located.

7. Click **Text** in the left pane to display textual information about the Linksys MIBs. Scroll through the Linksys MIBs and read several of the descriptions. How could this information be useful in troubleshooting?

8. Now look at the Cisco MIBs. Click **Vendors** in the left pane to return to a vendor list.

9. Scroll down and click **Cisco Systems** in the right pane. How many total Cisco MIB objects are listed? Why is there a difference?

10. In the right pane, click the link **Traps**.

11. Scroll down to **Trap 74**, which begins the list of Cisco wireless traps. Notice the descriptive names assigned to the wireless traps.

12. Now scroll down to **Traps 142-143** and click the name **bsnAPIfDown**. Read the description for this SNMP trap. When would it be invoked? Click the browser's **Back** arrow to return to the listing.

13. Close all windows.

Project 7-4: Viewing Logs Using the Microsoft Windows Event Viewer

In this project, you view logs on a Microsoft Windows computer.

1. Launch Event Viewer by clicking **Start** and then type **Administrative Tools** in the Search programs and files box.

2. Click the **Administrative Tools** folder and then double-click **Event Viewer**.

3. The Event Viewer opens to the Overview and Summary page that displays all events from all Windows logs on the system. The total number of events for each type that have occurred is displayed along with the number of events of each type that have occurred over the last seven days, the last 24 hours, or the last hour. Click the > sign under each type of event in the Summary of Administrative Events to view events that have occurred on this system.

4. Select a specific event and then double-click it to display detailed information on the event. Is this information in a format that a custodian could use when examining a system? Is it in a format that an enduser would find helpful?

5. When finished, click the **Back** arrow to return to the Overview and Summary page.

6. In the left pane under **Event Viewer (Local)**, double-click **Windows Logs** to display the default generated logs, if necessary.

7. Double-click **Security**.

8. Select a specific event and then double-click it to display detailed information on the event. When finished, click **Close** and the **Back** arrow to return to the Overview and Summary page.

9. In the left pane under **Event Viewer (Local)**, double-click **Applications and Services Logs** to display the default generated logs, if necessary.

10. Select a specific event and double-click it to display detailed information on the event. When finished, click **Close** and then double-click **Event Viewer (Local)** in the left pane. Leave this window open for the next project.

Project 7-5: Creating a Custom View in Microsoft Windows Event Viewer

Microsoft Windows Event Viewer also can be used to create custom logs and collect copies of events from different systems. In this project, you use the Event Viewer to create a custom log.

1. If necessary, launch Event Viewer by clicking **Start** and then typing **Administrative Tools** in the Search programs and files box. Click the **Administrative Tools** folder and then double-click **Event Viewer**.

2. In the right pane entitled Actions, click **Create Custom View**.

3. Under **Logged** click the **drop-down arrow** next to **Any time**. Several options appear of times to log the events. Click **Custom range** and note that you can create a specific period to log these events. Click **Cancel** and be sure the **Logged** setting is **Any time** to capture all events.

4. Under **Event level**, check each box (**Critical, Error, Warning, Information, Verbose**) to capture all levels of events.

5. Under **By source**, click the radio button if necessary and then click the **drop-down arrow** next to **Event sources**. Scroll through the list of sources that can be used to create a log entry.

6. For this custom view, instead of selecting specific sources, you will use log entries collected from default logs. Under **By log**, click the radio button if necessary and then click the **drop-down arrow** next to **Event logs**.

7. Click the > sign by **Windows Logs** and **Applications and Services Logs**. Any of these logs can be used as input into your custom logs. Click the box next to **Windows Logs** to select all the available Windows logs.

8. You also can include or exclude specific events. Be sure that <**All Event IDs**> is selected.

9. Next to **Keywords** select **Classic**.

10. Next to **User** be sure that <**All Users**> is selected so that any user who logs in to this system will have log entries created.

11. Your completed dialog box will look like that shown in Figure 7-11. Click **OK**. If an Event Viewer dialog box appears, click **Yes**.

12. In the **Save Filter to Custom View** dialog box, next to **Name**, enter **All Events**.

13. Next to **Description**, enter **All Events**. Click **OK**.

14. In the left pane under **Event Viewer (Local)**, double-click **Custom Views** if necessary to display the custom view. Display your view by clicking on it.

15. Close Event Viewer and all windows.

16. Reboot the system.

17. If necessary, launch Event Viewer by clicking **Start** and then typing **Administrative Tools** in the Search programs and files box. Click the **Administrative Tools** folder and then double-click **Event Viewer**.

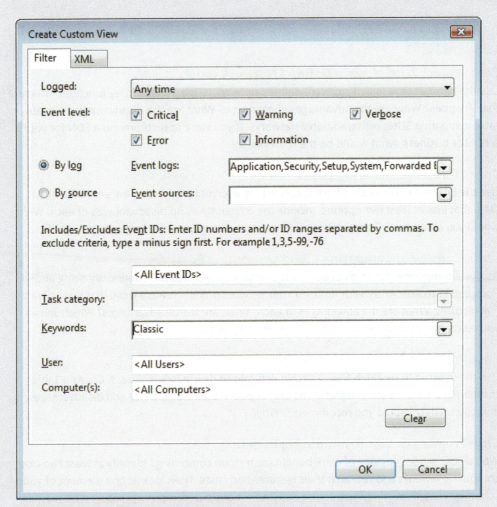

Figure 7-11   Create Custom View dialog box

18. In the left pane under **Event Viewer (Local)**, double-click **Custom Views** if necessary to display the custom views. Display your view by clicking it. What new events have occurred?

19. Close all windows.

Case Projects

Case Project 7-1: Software Defined Network (SDN)

Use the Internet to research software defined network (SDN). How do they function? What are their features? What are the advantages of each type? What are the disadvantages? Create a table comparing SDNs with traditional networks. If you were to recommend a SDN for your school or business, what would be the reason(s)?

Case Project 7-2: Securing Email

Use the Internet to research different options for encrypting and securing email. Create a table that lists at least five options. Include the advantages and disadvantages of each. Which would you recommend? Why? Write a one-paragraph explanation along with your table.

Case Project 7-3: Comparing Cloud Computing Features

As cloud computing increases in popularity, enhanced features are continually being added. Compare Microsoft Azure with Amazon Web Services (AWS). Create a table that lists at least five features. What are the advantages of each? What are the disadvantages? Which would you recommend? Why? Write a one-page summary of your research.

Case Project 7-4: Centralized Device Log Analyzers

Use the Internet to research four different centralized device log analyzers. Create a table comparing their benefits, the platforms they support, their advantages and disadvantages, and costs. Which would you recommend? Why?

Case Project 7-5: Cloud Computing Benefits

Would your school or place of work benefit from cloud computing? Identify at least two cloud computing vendors and research their features and costs. Then look at one element of your school or work network infrastructure and apply it to cloud computing. Would it be feasible? Why or why not? Write a one-page paper on your research and opinions.

Case Project 7-6: Lake Point Security Consulting

Lake Point Consulting Services (LPCS) provides security consulting and assurance services to over 500 clients across a wide range of enterprises in more than 20 states. A new initiative at LPCS is for each of its seven regional offices to provide internships to students who are in their final year of the security degree program at the local college.

Performance Engineered Lubricants (PEL) is a regional petroleum manufacturing and distribution company. PEL is interested in moving to cloud computing, and they have contracted with BPSC to make recommendations.

1. Create a PowerPoint presentation for PEL regarding cloud computing. Include a definition of cloud computing, how it can be used, and why it is important. Your presentation should contain at least 10 slides.

2. PEL is enthusiastic about cloud computing, but is unsure about whether SaaS, PaaS, or IaaS would be best for them. They have multiple customized software applications for the blending of different petroleum products. Create a memo that outlines the advantages and disadvantages of each approach, and give your recommendation.

Case Project 7-7: Information Security Community Site Activity

The Information Security Community Site is an online companion to this textbook. It contains a wide variety of tools, information, discussion boards, and other features to assist learners. Go to **community.cengage.com/Infosec2** and click the *Join or Sign in* icon to log in, using your login name and password that you created in Chapter 1. Click **Forums (Discussion)** and click on **Security+ Case Projects (6th edition)**. Read the following case study.

A hospital decided to use cloud computing for processing and storage to save costs. After several months, it was discovered that the cloud provider's storage facilities were compromised and patient information was stolen. The hospital maintained that the cloud provider should be punished and fined for the breach, while the provider responded that it was still the hospital's responsibility under HIPAA to secure patient information and the hospital was ultimately responsible.

Who do you think should be responsible? The cloud provider or the hospital? If the cloud provider is responsible, then should software companies like Microsoft be held liable for a vulnerability in their software that results in a data breach on a Microsoft server in a LAN? Where does the responsibility for the user end and the vendor begin?

References

1. Greenberg, Andy, "How hackers hijacked a bank's entire online operation," *Wired*, Apr. 4, 2017, accessed Apr. 22, 2017, https://www.wired.com/2017/04/hackers-hijacked-banks-entire-online-operation/.

2. "State of DNSSEC Deployment 2016," *Internet Society*, Dec. 2016, accessed Apr. 21, 2017, https://www.internetsociety.org/sites/default/files/ISOC-State-of-DNSSEC-Deployment-2016-v1.pdf.

3. Popomaronis, Tom, "Prime day gives Amazon over 600 reasons per second to celebrate," *Inc.*, Jul. 13, 2016, accessed Apr. 22, 2017, https://www.inc.com/tom-popomaronis/amazon-just-eclipsed-records-selling-over-600-items-per-second.html.

4. Kahn, Jeremy, "A sentinel that cuts through clutter," *BusinessWeek*, Mar. 14, 2016, accessed Mar. 21, 2016.

5. Mell, Peter, and Grance, Tim, "The NIST definition of cloud computing," NIST Computer Security Division Computer Security Resource Center. Oct. 7, 2009, accessed Apr. 2, 2011, http://csrc.nist.gov/groups/SNS/cloud-computing/.

CHAPTER 8

WIRELESS NETWORK SECURITY

After completing this chapter, you should be able to do the following:

Describe the different types of wireless network attacks

List the vulnerabilities in IEEE 802.11 security

Explain the solutions for securing a wireless network

Today's Attacks and Defenses

Attacks on wireless systems are certainly not uncommon. But it may be surprising to learn that the first recorded attack on a wireless system occurred over 100 years ago, and involved the person credited as the inventor of the radio.

Guglielmo Marconi was an Italian electrical engineer and inventor who pioneered work on long-distance radio transmission. In 1895 Marconi could transmit and receive a signal only less than one mile (1.6 kilometers or km), but through persistence and applying new techniques he was able to increase that distance the following year to 3.7 miles (6 km). Over the next several years the distances gradually became longer, so that by 1900 Marconi was experimenting with transmissions across the Atlantic Ocean, which was achieved the following year. However, skeptics challenged this experiment because it was not independently verified. One of Marconi's skeptics was Nevil Maskelyne, who likewise was an inventor interested in wireless systems. Maskelyne was the manager of a rival wireless company that had been involved in several disputes with Marconi over patents that covered wireless telegraphy systems.

In 1903 Marconi decided to put on a public demonstration of his wireless system. He wanted to show that it could indeed transmit over long distances. But he also wanted to demonstrate that his wireless system was secure. Marconi had often claimed that other signals would not interfere with his wireless transmissions. Maskelyne, on the other hand, was not convinced that Marconi's signal was secure. So, Maskelyne decided to "hack" Marconi's public demonstration.

The demonstration was on June 4, 1903 at the lecture theater of the Royal Institution in London. Marconi was in Cornwall, over 300 miles (482 km) away. The plan was for Marconi's colleague Professor Fleming to be in the theater to receive Marconi's Morse code message sent wirelessly and to be printed on an attached printer. But Maskelyne had his own ideas. He set up a wireless transmitter not far from the lecture theatre. He later claimed that he did not run it at full power because he did not want to block Marconi's signal; instead, he wanted to send his own signal to show that Marconi's signal was not secure.

Toward the end of Fleming's lecture, signals started coming in—but they were not from Marconi. First a brass slide projector arc lamp in the theater, used to display Fleming's presentation, started a rhythmic ticking noise. The audience assumed that the projector was just malfunctioning. But Arthur Blok, Fleming's assistant, quickly recognized it as the "tap-tap" of a human hand keying a message in Morse code. Blok realized that someone was sending powerful wireless pulses into the theatre, strong enough to interfere with the electric arc lamp. Then the wireless receiver came to life, and the Morse code printer started printing—but it was from Maskelyne instead of from Marconi. One word was repeated over and over on the printer: "Rats." Then the printer spelled out an insulting limerick. Marconi's supposedly secure wireless system had been hacked.

Fleming later complained to the *London Times* of "scientific hooliganism." Fleming and Maskelyne exchanged letters, many of which were printed in the *Times*, arguing over the source of the interference (Fleming argued that it was caused by electrical lighting in the theater). It was also discovered that the receiver Fleming was using was not tuned to the specific frequency on which Marconi was transmitting, but was a receiver that could pick up signals across the frequency spectrum. Because this fact was not disclosed to the audience, there was feeling that Marconi had been deceptive in his demonstration. When Maskelyne later wrote about the incident, he ended his account with a Latin legal phrase translated as, "Let him be deceived who wishes to be deceived."

Maskelyne's attack had little impact on Marconi's work or reputation. After sending the first wireless signal across the Atlantic in 1901, Marconi started a commercial transatlantic wireless service 1907. In 1909 he shared the Nobel Prize in Physics in recognition of his contributions to the development of wireless telegraphy. When Marconi died in 1937, the British Broadcasting Company (BBC) observed two minutes of radio silence in respect.

What Maskelyne's attack did do, however, was to make the scientific community realize that Marconi's claim that wireless signals were secure and could not be interfered with was false. Researchers started looking at ways wireless signals could be monitored, jammed, or manipulated. Eventually this led to the development of wireless security measures that were first used in World War I and continue today.[1]

It is difficult to think of a technology over the last decade with a greater impact on our lives than wireless data communications. Because it is no longer necessary to remain connected by cable to a network, users are free to surf the web, check email, download electronic books, or watch videos from virtually anywhere. Free wireless Internet connections are available in coffee shops and libraries across the country. Students use wireless data services on their school campus to access instructional material as well as remain connected to friends. Travelers have wireless access while waiting in airports, traveling on airplanes and trains, and working in their hotel rooms. At work, employees can access remote data during meetings and in conference rooms, thus significantly increasing their productivity. Wireless also has spurred the growth of many other new technologies, such as portable tablet devices. Although wireless voice communication started the revolution in the 1990s, wireless data communications are the driving force in the twenty-first century. It has truly become a wireless world.

Statistics confirm how widespread wireless data technology has become. Over the past five years, mobile data traffic has grown 18-fold, with the amount of global mobile data traffic now exceeding 7.2 exabytes each month (one exabyte is equal to one billion gigabytes). However, not all this traffic is through smartphones on cellular networks. In fact, smartphones represented only 45 percent of the total number of mobile devices and connections; other devices like laptops and tablet computers accounted for a significant percentage of mobile devices. And 60 percent of total mobile data traffic is offloaded onto a fixed network through Wi-Fi, which accounts for 10.7 exabytes of mobile data traffic offloaded each month.[2]

Caution ⚠

Mobile video traffic accounts for about 60 percent of all mobile data traffic. And the top 20 percent of mobile users generate 56 percent of mobile data traffic, and the top 1 percent of mobile users generate 6 percent of total traffic.[3]

Due to the popularity of wireless data, coupled with of the natively unsecure nature of wireless transmissions and the vulnerabilities of early wireless networking standards, wireless networks continue to be targets for attackers. There have been significant changes in wireless network security, however, to the point that today wireless security technology and standards provide users with security comparable to that their wired counterparts enjoy.

This chapter explores wireless network security. You first investigate the attacks on wireless devices that are common today. Next, you explore different wireless security mechanisms that have proven to be vulnerable. Finally, you examine several secure wireless protections.

Wireless Attacks

 Certification

1.2 Compare and contrast types of attacks.

2.1 Install and configure network components, both hardware- and software-based, to support organizational security.

2.5 Given a scenario, deploy mobile devices securely.

3.2 Given a scenario, implement secure network architecture concepts.

> **Note** 📎
>
> Many CompTIA exam objectives include the phrase, "Given a scenario." This indicates that a hands-on simulation related to this objective will likely appear on the Security+ exam. The Hands-On Projects at the end of each chapter serve as training for these scenarios.

There are several attacks that can be directed against wireless data systems. These attacks can be directed against Bluetooth systems, near field communication devices, radio frequency identification systems, and wireless local area networks.

Bluetooth Attacks

Bluetooth is the name given to a wireless technology that uses short-range radio frequency (RF) transmissions and provides rapid device pairings. Named after the tenth-century Danish King Harald "Bluetooth" Gormsson, who was responsible for unifying Scandinavia, it was originally designed in 1994 by the cellular telephone company Ericsson to replace wires with radio-based technology. Bluetooth has moved well beyond its original design. Bluetooth is a *Personal Area Network (PAN)* technology designed for data communication over short distances and enables users to connect wirelessly to a wide range of computing and telecommunications devices. It provides for virtually instantaneous connections between a Bluetooth-enabled device and receiver. Several of these Bluetooth-enabled product pairings are listed in Table 8-1.

Table 8-1   Bluetooth products

Category	Bluetooth pairing	Usage
Automobile	Hands-free car system with cell phone	Drivers can speak commands to browse the cell phone's contact list, make and receive hands-free phone calls, or use its navigation system.
Home entertainment	Stereo headphones with portable music player	Users can create a playlist on a portable music player and listen through a set of wireless headphones or speakers.
Photographs	Digital camera with printer	Digital photos can be sent directly to a photo printer or from pictures taken on one cell phone to another phone.
Computer accessories	Computer with keyboard and mouse	Small travel mouse can be linked to a laptop or a full-size mouse and keyboard that can be connected to a desktop computer.
Gaming	Video game system with controller	Gaming devices and video game systems can support multiple controllers, while Bluetooth headsets allow gamers to chat as they play.
Sports and fitness	Heart-rate monitor with wristwatch	Athletes can track heart rates while exercising by glancing at their watch.
Medical and health	Blood pressure monitors with smartphones	Patient information can be sent to a smartphone, which can then send an emergency phone message if necessary.

Note 📎

Bluetooth is also finding its way into unlikely devices. A Victorinox Swiss Army pocketknife model has Bluetooth technology that can be used to remotely control a computer when projecting a PowerPoint presentation. Bluetooth can be found in items that require tracking in the event they are lost or misplaced, such as luggage and key rings.

The current version is Bluetooth 5 (yet all Bluetooth devices are backward compatible with previous versions). There are two implementations of Bluetooth 5. Bluetooth *Basic Rate/Enhanced Data Rate* (BR/EDR) is designed for devices needing short-range continuous connectivity (such as streaming music to a Bluetooth headset) while Bluetooth *low energy (LE)* is for devices that require short bursts of data over longer distances (such as inventory control devices at a retail store). Compared with the previous version of Bluetooth (4.2) the current Bluetooth 5 has a faster speed of 2 million bits per second (Mbps) vs. 1 Mbps as well as a broader range of coverage of 800 feet (243 meters) vs. 200 feet (60 meters). However, Bluetooth 5 devices can *either* transmit at a faster speed *or* have a broader area of coverage, but not both simultaneously.

The primary type of Bluetooth network topology is a *piconet*. When two Bluetooth devices come within range of each other, after an initial pairing confirmation they automatically connect whenever they meet. One device is the *master*, and controls all the wireless traffic. The other device is known as a *slave*, which takes commands from the master. Slave devices that are connected to the piconet and are sending transmissions are known as *active slaves*; devices that are connected but are not actively participating are called *parked slaves*. Devices can also switch roles so that a slave temporarily becomes a master but then switches back to a slave role or vice versa. An example of a piconet is illustrated in Figure 8-1.

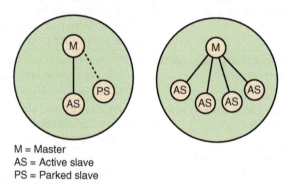

M = Master
AS = Active slave
PS = Parked slave

Figure 8-1   Bluetooth piconet

> **Note** 📎
>
> The Bluetooth specification also allows for a device to a member in two or more overlaying piconets that cover the same area. This group of piconets in which connections exist between different piconets is called a *scatternet*. However, scatternets are rarely used.

The ability for Bluetooth piconets to be established dynamically and automatically "on the fly" as needed (called an **ad hoc topology**) whenever Bluetooth devices enter and leave the coverage area gives Bluetooth its greatest flexibility. However, due to the ad hoc nature of Bluetooth piconets, attacks on wireless Bluetooth technology are not uncommon. Two Bluetooth attacks are bluejacking and bluesnarfing.

Bluejacking

Bluejacking is an attack that sends unsolicited messages to Bluetooth-enabled devices. Usually bluejacking involves sending text messages, but images and sounds also can be transmitted. Bluejacking is usually considered more annoying than harmful because no data is stolen; however, many Bluetooth users resent receiving unsolicited messages.

Note

Bluejacking has been used for advertising purposes by vendors.

Bluesnarfing

Bluesnarfing is an attack that accesses unauthorized information from a wireless device through a Bluetooth connection, often between cell phones and laptop computers. In a bluesnarfing attack, the attacker copies emails, calendars, contact lists, cell phone pictures, or videos by connecting to the Bluetooth device without the owner's knowledge or permission.

Note

To prevent bluesnarfing, a mobile device like a smartphone should have Bluetooth turned off when not being used or set to *undiscoverable*, which keeps Bluetooth turned on, yet it cannot be detected by another device.

Near Field Communication (NFC) Attacks

Near field communication (NFC) is a set of standards used to establish communication between devices in very close proximity. Once the devices are brought within 4 centimeters of each other or tapped together, two-way communication is established. Devices using NFC can be active or passive. A *passive NFC* device, such as an NFC tag, contains information that other devices can read but the tag does not read or receive any information. *Active NFC* devices can read information as well as transmit data.

The NFC communication between a smartphone and an NFC tag functions as follows:

1. The smartphone (*interrogator*) sends out a signal to the tag, which becomes powered by the energy in the interrogator's wireless signal.

Note

The ability of an NFC tag to be powered by the interrogator's signal allows tags to be very small in size. It also does not require a tag to have its own battery or another power source.

2. The interrogator and tag each create a high frequency magnetic field from an internal antenna. Once the fields are created, a connection can be formed between the devices (known as *magnetic induction*). This is illustrated in Figure 8-2 (in this figure the antennas are pictured outside of the interrogator and tag for clarity).

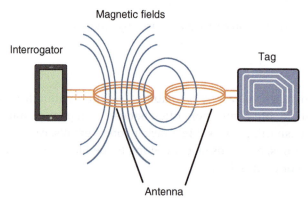

Magnetic fields

Interrogator

Tag

Antenna

Figure 8-2   NFC magnetic induction

3. The interrogator sends a message to the tag to find out what type of communication the tag uses. When the tag responds, the interrogator sends its first commands based on that type.

Note

NFC can use one of three types of communication, known as Type A, Type B, or FeliCa, which is more commonly used in Japan.

4. When the tag receives the instruction, it checks to determine if the instruction is valid. If it is not, the tag ignores the communication. If it is a valid request, the tag responds with the requested information. For sensitive transactions, such as credit card payments, a secure communication channel is established and all transmitted information is encrypted.

Examples of NFC uses include the following:

- *Automobile*. NFC technology can be used to unlock a car door or adjust seats.
- *Entertainment*. NFC devices can be used as a ticket to a stadium or concert, for purchasing food and beverages, and downloading upcoming events by tapping a smart poster.
- *Office*. An NFC-enabled device can be used to enter an office, clock in and out on a factory floor, or purchase snacks from a vending machine.

- *Retail stores*. Coupons or customer reward cards can be provided by tapping the point-of-sale (PoS) terminal.
- *Transportation*. On a bus or train NFC can be used to quickly pass through turnstiles and receive updated schedules by tapping the device on a kiosk.

NFC devices are most often associated with *contactless payment systems*. Users store payment card numbers in a "virtual wallet" on a smartphone to pay for purchases at an NFC-enabled PoS checkout device. Figure 8-3 shows one such contactless payment system.

Figure 8-3   Contactless payment system
REDPIXEL.PL/Shutterstock.com

The use of NFC has risks because of the nature of this technology. The risks and defenses of using NFC are listed in Table 8-2.

Table 8-2 NFC risks and defenses

Vulnerability	Explanation	Defense
Eavesdropping	Unencrypted NFC communication between the device and terminal can be intercepted and viewed.	Because an attacker must be extremely close to pick up the signal, users should remain aware of their surroundings while making a payment.
Data theft	Attackers can "bump" a portable reader to a user's smartphone in a crowd to make an NFC connection and steal payment information stored on the phone.	This can be prevented by turning off NFC while in a large crowd.
Man-in-the-middle attack	An attacker can intercept the NFC communications between devices and forge a fictitious response.	Devices can be configured in pairing so one device can only send while the other can only receive.
Device theft	The theft of a smartphone could allow an attacker to use that phone for purchases.	Smartphones should be protected with passwords or strong PINs.

Note 📎

Even though contactless payment systems using NFC were initially touted as replacing cash and payment cards, acceptance has been slow. Two years after Apple introduced its NFC-based Apple Pay only 13 percent of 680 million iPhone users have used it, and over 60 percent said they are unfamiliar with it. A significant barrier to acceptance is security: over 40 percent of consumers have indicated a concern about the security risks of contactless payment systems.[4]

Radio Frequency Identification (RFID) Attacks

Another wireless technology like NFC is **radio frequency identification (RFID)**. RFID is commonly used to transmit information between employee identification badges, inventory tags, book labels, and other paper-based tags that can be detected by a proximity reader. An RFID tag can easily be affixed to the inside of an ID badge and can be read by an RFID proximity reader as the user walks through the turnstile with the badge in a pocket.

Most RFID tags are passive and do not have their own power supply; instead, the electrical current induced in the antenna by the incoming signal from the transceiver provides enough power for the tag to send a response. Because it does not

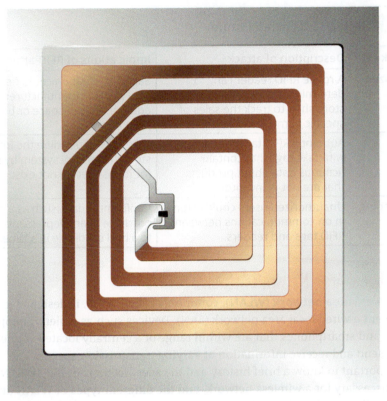

Figure 8-4   RFID tag

Nor Gal/Shutterstock.com

require a power supply, passive RFID tags can be very small, only 0.4 mm × 0.4 mm and thinner than a sheet of paper, as illustrated in Figure 8-4. The amount of data transmitted typically is limited to just an ID number. Passive tags have ranges from about 1/3 inch to 19 feet (10 millimeters to 6 meters). Active RFID tags must have their own power source.

RFID tags are susceptible to different attacks. Table 8-3 lists several attacks that could occur in a retail store that uses RFID inventory tags.

The current version of RFID standards known as *Generation 2* contains some security enhancements over the previous version. These include the ability to permanently render inoperable ("kill") an RFID tag when an item is purchased by a consumer at the PoS terminal and to disguise the tag identifier number. However, Generation 2 does contain significant security vulnerabilities. The disguised tag identifier number is only a pseudo-random number transmitted by the tag, data is not encrypted, and users accessing tag data are not required to prove their identity and authorization to access the data.

Table 8-3	RFID attacks in retail store	
RFID attack type	**Description of attack**	**Implications of RFID attack**
Unauthorized tag access	A rogue RFID reader can determine the inventory on a store shelf to track the sales of specific items.	Sales information could be used by a rival product manufacturer to negotiate additional shelf space or better product placement.
Fake tags	Authentic RFID tags are replaced with fake tags that contain fictitious data about products that are not in inventory.	Fake tags undermine the integrity of the store's inventory system by showing data for items that do not exist.
Eavesdropping	Unauthorized users could listen in on communications between RFID tags and readers.	Confidential data, such as a politician's purchase of antidepressants, could be sold to a rival candidate in a "smear" campaign.

Wireless Local Area Network Attacks

A **wireless local area network (WLAN)**, commonly called *Wi-Fi*, is designed to replace or supplement a wired local area network (LAN). Devices such as tablets, laptop computers, and smartphones that are within range of a centrally located connection device can send and receive information at varying transmission speeds.

It is important to know a brief history and the specifications of IEEE WLANs, the hardware necessary for a wireless network, and the different types of WLAN attacks directed at both the enterprise and home users.

IEEE WLANs

For computer networking and wireless communications, the most widely known and influential organization is the *Institute of Electrical and Electronics Engineers (IEEE)*, which dates to 1884. In the early 1980s, the IEEE began work on developing computer network architecture standards. This work was called Project 802, and quickly expanded into several different categories of network technology.

> **Note** 🖉
>
> One of the most well-known IEEE standards is 802.3, which set specifications for Ethernet local area network technology.

In 1990, the IEEE started work to develop a standard for WLANs operating at 1 and 2 Mbps. Several proposals were recommended before a draft was developed. This draft, which went through seven different revisions, took seven years to complete. In 1997, the IEEE approved the final draft known as *IEEE 802.11*.

Although bandwidth of 2 Mbps was acceptable in 1990 for wireless networks, by 1997 it was no longer sufficient for more recent network applications. The IEEE body revisited the 802.11 standard shortly after it was released to determine what changes could be made to increase the speed. In 1999, a new *IEEE 802.11b* amendment was created, which added two higher speeds (5.5 Mbps and 11 Mbps) to the original 802.11 standard. At the same time the IEEE also issued another standard with even higher speeds, the *IEEE 802.11a* standard with a speed of 54 Mbps.

The success of the IEEE 802.11b standard prompted the IEEE to reexamine the 802.11b and 802.11a standards to determine if a third intermediate standard could be developed. This "best of both worlds" approach would preserve the stable and widely accepted features of 802.11b but increase the data transfer rates to those similar to 802.11a. The *IEEE 802.11g* standard was formally ratified in 2003 and can support devices transmitting at 54 Mbps.

In 2004, the IEEE began work on a new WLAN standard that would significantly increase the speed, range, and reliability of wireless local area networks. This standard, known as *IEEE 802.11n*, was ratified in 2009. The 802.11n standard has four significant improvements over previous standards: speed (600 Mbps), coverage area (doubles the indoor range and triples the outdoor range of coverage), increased resistance to interference, and stronger security.

Work on an updated standard to support the demand for wireless video delivery was started in 2011 called *IEEE 802.11ac*. Building upon many of the enhancements introduced in 802.11n, this standard, ratified in early 2014, has data rates over 7 Gbps. *IEEE 802.11ad* is intended for short-range indoor use. Table 8-4 compares several different IEEE WLAN standards.

Table 8-4   **IEEE WLAN standards**

	802.11	802.11b	802.11a	802.11g	802.11n	802.11ad	802.11ac
Frequency	2.4 GHz	2.4 GHz	5 GHz	2.4 GHz	2.4 & 5 GHz	60 GHz	5 GHz
Maximum data rate	2 Mbps	11 Mbps	54 Mbps	54 Mbps	600 Mbps	7 Gbps	7.2 Gbps
Indoor range (feet/meters)	65/20	125/38	115/35	115/35	230/70	32/10	115/35
Outdoor range (feet/meters)	328/100	460/140	393/120	460/140	820/250	N/A	460/140
Ratification date	1997	1999	1999	2003	2009	2013	2014

WLAN Hardware

Different types of hardware are used in WLANs. A *wireless client network interface card or wireless adapter* performs the same functions as a wired adapter with one major exception: there is no external cable RJ-45 connection. In its place is an antenna (embedded into the adapter or the device) to send and receive signals through the airwaves.

An **access point (AP)** is a centrally located WLAN connection device that can send and receive information. It consists of three major parts:

- An antenna and a radio transmitter/receiver to send and receive wireless signals
- Special bridging software to interface wireless devices to other devices
- A wired network interface that allows it to connect by cable to a standard wired network

An AP has two basic functions. First, it acts as the "base station" for the wireless network. All wireless devices with a wireless NIC transmit to the AP, which in turn redirects the signal if necessary to other wireless devices. The second function of an AP is to act as a bridge between the wireless and wired networks. The AP can be connected to the wired network by a cable, allowing all the wireless devices to access through the AP the wired network (and vice versa), as shown in Figure 8-5.

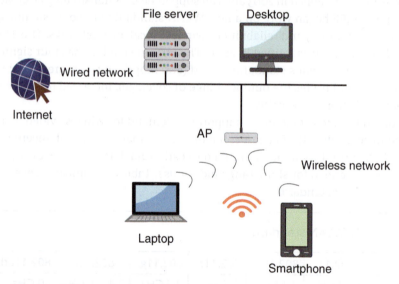

Figure 8-5   Access point (AP) in WLAN

A WLAN using an AP is operating in *infrastructure mode*. The IEEE specifications also define networks that are not using an AP. This is called an *Independent Basic Service Set (IBSS)* or more commonly **ad hoc mode**. In ad hoc mode, devices can only communicate between themselves and cannot connect to another network. The Wi-Fi Alliance has also created a similar technical specification called **Wi-Fi Direct**.

Note 📎

Ad hoc mode is useful for quickly and easily setting up a wireless network anywhere that users need to share data between themselves but do not need a connection to the Internet or an external network. An example might be when a wireless user needs to quickly send a last-minute document to an associate across the table in a meeting room. However, this mode is rarely used.

For a small office or home, instead of using an enterprise-grade AP, another device is commonly used. This device combines multiple features into a single hardware device. These features often include those of an AP, firewall, router, dynamic host configuration protocol (DHCP) server, along with other features. Strictly speaking these devices are *residential WLAN gateways* as they are the entry point from the Internet into the wireless network. However, most vendors instead choose to label their products as simply *wireless routers*.

WLAN Enterprise Attacks

In a traditional wired network, a well-defined boundary or "hard edge" protects data and resources. There are two types of hard edges. The first is a network hard edge. A wired network typically has one point (or a limited number of points) through which data must pass from an external network to the secure internal network. This single data entry point makes it easier to defend against because any attack must likewise pass through this one point. A device like a firewall can be used to block attacks from entering the network. The combination of a single entry point plus security devices that can defend it make up a network's hard edge, which protects important data and resources. This is illustrated in Figure 8-6.

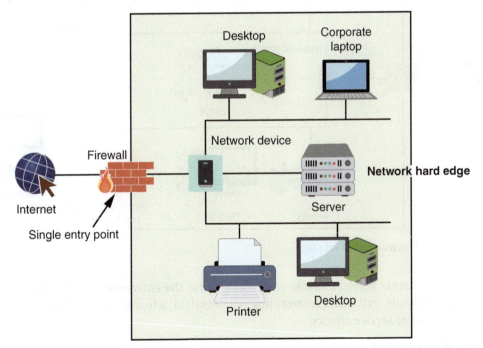

Figure 8-6   Network hard edge

The second hard edge is made up of the walls of the building that houses the enterprise. Because these walls keep out unauthorized personnel, attackers cannot access the network. In other words, the walls serve to physically separate computing resources from attackers.

The introduction of WLANs in enterprises, however, has changed these hard edges to "blurred edges." Instead of a network hard edge with a single data entry point, a WLAN can contain multiple entry points. As shown in Figure 8-7, the RF signals from APs create several data entry points into the network through which attackers can inject attacks or steal data. This makes it difficult to create a hard network edge. In addition, because RF signals extend beyond the boundaries of the building, the walls cannot be considered as a physical hard edge to keep away attackers. A threat actor sitting in a car well outside of the building's security perimeter can still easily pick up a wireless RF signal to eavesdrop on data transmissions or inject malware behind the firewall. An AP whose security settings have not been set or have been improperly configured can allow attackers access to the network.

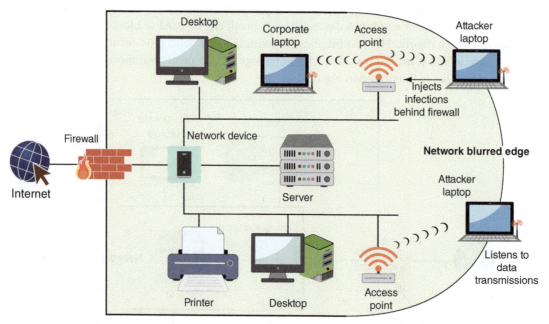

Figure 8-7 Network blurred edge

Several different wireless attacks can be directed at the enterprise. These include rogue access points, evil twins, intercepting wireless data, wireless replay attacks, and wireless denial of service attacks.

Rogue Access Point

Lejla is the manager of a recently opened retail storefront and wants to add wireless access in the employee break room. However, her employer's IT staff turns down her request for a wireless network. Lejla decides to take the matter into her own hands: she purchases an inexpensive wireless router and secretly brings it into the store and connects it to the wired network, thus providing wireless access to her employees.

Unfortunately, Lejla also has provided open access to an attacker sitting in his car in the parking lot who picks up the wireless signal. This attacker can then circumvent the security protections of the company's network.

Lejla has installed a **rogue AP** (*rogue* means someone or something that is deceitful or unreliable). A rogue AP is an unauthorized AP that allows an attacker to bypass many of the network security configurations and opens the network and its users to attacks. For example, although firewalls are typically used to restrict specific attacks from entering a network, an attacker who can access the network through a rogue AP is behind the firewall.

> **Note** 📎
>
> Rogue APs do not even have to be separate network devices. The wireless Hosted Network function in Microsoft Windows makes it possible to virtualize the physical wireless network interface card (NIC) into multiple virtual wireless NICs (Virtual Wi-Fi) that can be accessed by a software-based wireless AP (SoftAP). This means that any computer can easily be turned into a rogue AP. And some smartphone apps allow these devices to also function as APs.

Evil Twin

Whereas a rogue AP is set up by an internal user, an **evil twin** is an AP that is set up by an attacker. This AP is designed to mimic an authorized AP, so a user's mobile device like a laptop or tablet will unknowingly connect to this evil twin instead. Attackers can then capture the transmissions from users to the evil twin AP.

Figure 8-8 illustrates rogue AP and evil twin attacks on an enterprise network, which further create a "blurred edge" to a corporate network.

Intercepting Wireless Data

One of the most common wireless attacks is intercepting and reading data that is being transmitted. An attacker can pick up the RF signal from an open or misconfigured AP and read any confidential wireless transmissions. To make matters worse, if the attacker manages to connect to the enterprise wired network through a rogue AP, she also could read broadcast and multicast wired network traffic that leaks from the wired network to the wireless network. Using a WLAN to read this data could yield significant information to an attacker regarding the wired enterprise network.

Wireless Replay Attack

Another wireless attack is "hijacking" the wireless connection. Using an evil twin, an attacker can trick a corporate mobile device into connecting to the imposter device instead. The attacker could then perform a wireless man-in-the-middle attack. This type of attack makes it appear that the wireless device and the network computers are communicating with each other, when actually they are sending and receiving

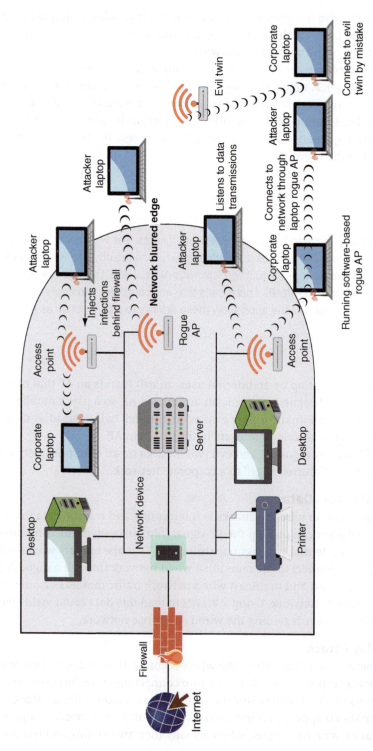

Figure 8-8 Rogue access point and evil twin attacks

data through an evil twin AP (the "man-in-the-middle"). As the man-in-the-middle receives data from the devices, it passes it on to the recipient so that neither computer is aware of the man-in-the-middle's existence.

Man-in-the-middle attacks can be active or passive. In an active attack, the contents are intercepted and altered before they are forwarded to the recipient. In a passive attack, the attacker captures the data that is being transmitted (such as user names and passwords), records it, and then sends it on to the original recipient without the attacker's presence being detected. This is called a **wireless replay attack**.

> **Note** 📎
>
> Wired man-in-the-middle and replay attacks are covered in Chapter 5.

Just as an active man-in-the-middle attack modifies or injects content into a message, another type of wireless attack can inject wireless packets into the enterprise network. For example, an attacker's application could examine incoming wireless packets, and, if the packet data matches a pattern specified in a configuration file, inject custom content into the network to redirect traffic to an attacker's server. In yet another type of attack, a *routing protocol attack*, the attacker injects specific packets into the network to redirect a traffic stream through another router that is controlled by the attacker.

Wireless Denial of Service Attack

Because wireless devices operate using RF signals, there is the potential for two types of signal interference. The wireless device itself may be the source of interference for other devices, and signals from other devices can disrupt wireless transmissions. Several types of devices transmit a radio signal that can cause incidental interference with a WLAN. These devices include microwave ovens, elevator motors, photocopying machines, and certain types of outdoor lighting systems, to name a few. These may cause errors or completely prevent transmission between a wireless device and an AP.

> **Note** 📎
>
> Interference is nothing new for computer networks. Even when using cables to connect network devices, interference from fluorescent light fixtures and electric motors can disrupt data transmission. The solution for wireless devices is the same as that for standard cabled network devices: locate the source of the interference and eliminate the interference. This can be done by moving an AP away from a photocopying machine or microwave oven, for example.

Attackers can likewise use intentional RF interference to flood the RF spectrum with enough interference to prevent a device from effectively communicating with the AP. This wireless DoS attack prevents the transmission of data to or from network devices. In one type of wireless DoS attack, an attacker can intentionally flood the RF spectrum with extraneous RF signal "noise" that creates interference and prevents communications from occurring. This is called **jamming**.

> **Note** 📎
>
> Jamming attacks generally are rare because sophisticated and expensive equipment is necessary to flood the RF spectrum with enough interference to impact the network. In addition, because a very powerful transmitter must be used at a relatively close range to execute the attack, it is possible to identify the location of the transmitter and therefore identify the source of the attack.

Another wireless DoS attack takes advantage of an IEEE 802.11 design weakness. This weakness is the implicit trust of management frames that are transmitted across the wireless network, which includes information such as the sender's source address. Because IEEE 802.11 requires no verification of the source device's identity (and so all management frames are sent in an unencrypted format), an attacker can easily craft a fictitious frame that pretends to come from a trusted client when it is in fact from a malicious attacker. Different types of frames can be "spoofed" by an attacker to prevent a client from being able to remain connected to the WLAN. A client must be both authenticated and associated with an AP before being accepted into the wireless network, and de-authenticated and disassociated when the client leaves the network. An attacker can create false de-authentication or disassociation management frames that appear to come from another client device, causing the client to disconnect from the AP (called a **disassociation attack**). Although the client device can send another authentication request to an AP, an attacker can continue to send spoofed frames to sever any reconnections.

> **Note** 📎
>
> The IEEE 802.11w amendment was designed to protect against wireless DoS attacks. However, it only protects specific management frames instead of all management frames, it requires updates to both the AP and the wireless clients, and it might interfere with other security devices. For these reasons, it has not been widely implemented.

Manipulating duration field values is another wireless DoS attack. The 802.11 standard provides an option using the Request to Send/Clear to Send (RTS/CTS) protocol. A Request to Send (RTS) frame is transmitted by a mobile device to an AP that contains a duration field indicating the length of time needed for both the transmission and the returning acknowledgment frame. The AP, as well as all stations that receive the RTS frame, are alerted that the medium will be reserved for a specific period. Each receiving station stores that information in its net allocation vector (NAV) field, and no station can transmit if the NAV contains a value other than zero. An attacker can send a frame with the duration field set to an arbitrarily high value (the maximum is 32,767), thus preventing other devices from transmitting for lengthy periods of time.

Wireless Home Attacks

Attacks against home WLANs are considered easy because many home users fail to properly configure security on their home wireless networks. Home users face several risks from attacks on their insecure wireless networks. Among other things, attackers can:

- *Steal data*. On a computer in the home WLAN, an attacker could access any folder with file sharing enabled. This essentially provides an attacker full access to steal sensitive data from the computer.
- *Read wireless transmissions*. User names, passwords, credit card numbers, and other information sent over the WLAN could be captured by an attacker.
- *Inject malware*. Because attackers could access the network behind a firewall, they could inject viruses and other malware onto the computer.
- *Download harmful content*. In several instances, attackers have accessed a home computer through an unprotected WLAN and downloaded child pornography to the computer, and then turned that computer into a file server to distribute the content. When authorities have traced the files back to that computer, the unsuspecting owner has been arrested and his equipment confiscated.

Note

Attackers can easily identify unprotected home wireless networks through *war driving*, or searching for wireless signals from an automobile or on foot using a portable computing device.

Vulnerabilities of IEEE Wireless Security

Certification

1.2 Compare and contrast types of attacks.

2.1 Install and configure network components, both hardware- and software-based, to support organizational security.

The original IEEE 802.11 committee recognized that wireless transmissions could be vulnerable. Because of this, they implemented several wireless security protections in the 802.11 standard, while leaving other protections to be applied at the WLAN vendor's discretion. Several of these protections, though well intended, were vulnerable and led to multiple attacks. These vulnerabilities can be divided into Wired Equivalent Privacy (WEP), Wi-Fi Protected Setup (WPS), MAC address filtering, and SSID broadcasting.

Wired Equivalent Privacy

Wired Equivalent Privacy (WEP) is an IEEE 802.11 security protocol designed to ensure that only authorized parties can view transmitted wireless information. WEP accomplishes this confidentiality by encrypting the transmissions. WEP relies on a shared secret key that is known only by the wireless client and the AP. The same secret key must be entered on the AP and on all devices before any transmissions can occur, because it is used to encrypt any packets to be transmitted as well as decrypt packets that are received. IEEE 802.11 WEP shared secret keys must be a minimum of 64 bits in length. Most vendors add an option to use a longer 128-bit shared secret key for higher security.

The shared secret key is combined with an *initialization vector (IV)*, which is a 24-bit value that changes each time a packet is encrypted. The IV and the key are combined and used as a seed for generating a random number necessary in the encryption process. The IV and encrypted ciphertext are both transmitted to the receiving device. Upon arrival, the receiving device first separates the IV from the encrypted text and then combines the IV with its own shared secret key to decrypt the data.

Note

Initialization vectors are covered in Chapter 4.

WEP has several security vulnerabilities. First, to encrypt packets, WEP can use only a 64-bit or 128-bit number, which is made up of a 24-bit IV and either a 40-bit or 104-bit default key. Even if a longer 128-bit number is used, the length of the IV remains at 24 bits. The relatively short length of the IV limits its strength, since shorter keys are easier to break than longer keys.

Second, WEP implementation violates the cardinal rule of cryptography: anything that creates a detectable pattern must be avoided at all costs. This is because patterns provide an attacker with valuable information to break the encryption. The implementation of WEP creates a detectable pattern for attackers. Because IVs are 24-bit numbers, there are only 16,777,216 possible values. An AP transmitting at only 11 Mbps can send and receive 700 packets each second. If a different IV were used for each packet, then the IVs would start repeating in fewer than seven hours (a "busy" AP can produce duplicates in fewer than five hours). An attacker who captures packets for this length of time can see the duplication and use it to crack the code.

Wi-Fi Protected Setup

Wi-Fi Protected Setup (WPS) is an optional means of configuring security on wireless local area networks. Introduced by the Wi-Fi Alliance in early 2007, it is designed to help users who have little or no knowledge of security to quickly and easily implement security on their WLANs.

There are two common WPS methods. The PIN method utilizes a Personal Identification Number (PIN) printed on a sticker of the wireless router or displayed through a software setup wizard. The user types the PIN into the wireless device (like a wireless tablet, laptop computer, or smartphone) and the security configuration automatically occurs. This is the mandatory model, and all devices certified for WPS must support it. The second method is the push-button method: the user pushes a button (usually an actual button on the wireless router and a virtual one displayed through a software setup wizard on the wireless device) and the security configuration takes place. Support for this model is mandatory for wireless routers and optional for connecting devices.

Note

More than 19,677 wireless devices have been certified by the Wi-Fi Alliance to run WPS.

However, there are significant design and implementation flaws in WPS using the PIN method:

- There is no lockout limit for entering PINs, so an attacker can make an unlimited number of PIN attempts.
- The last PIN character is only a checksum.
- The wireless router reports the validity of the first and second halves of the PIN separately, so essentially an attacker must break only two short PIN values (a 4-character PIN and a 3-character PIN).

Due to the PIN being broken down into two shorter values, only 11,000 different PINs must be attempted before determining the correct value. If the attacker's computer can generate 1.3 PIN attempts per second (or 46 attempts per minute), the attacker can crack the PIN in less than four hours and become connected to the WLAN. This effectively defeats security restrictions regarding allowing only authorized users to connect to the wireless network.

Note

Some wireless vendors are implementing additional security measures for WPS, such as limiting the number and frequency of PIN guesses. However, unless it can be verified that WPS supports these higher levels of security, it is recommended that WPS be disabled through the wireless router's configuration settings.

MAC Address Filtering

One means of protecting a WLAN is to control which devices are permitted to join the network. Wireless access control is intended to limit a user's admission to the AP: only those who are authorized can connect to the AP and thus become part of the wireless LAN.

The most common type of wireless access control is **Media Access Control (MAC) address filtering**. The MAC address is a hardware address that uniquely identifies each node of a network. The MAC address is a unique 48-bit number that is "burned" into the network interface card adapter when it is manufactured. This number consists of two parts: a 24-bit organizationally unique identifier (OUI), sometimes called a "company ID," which references the company that produced the adapter, and a 24-bit individual address block (IAB), which uniquely identifies the card itself. A typical MAC address is illustrated in Figure 8-9.

Organizationally Unique
Identifier (OUI)

Individual Address
Block (IAB)

00-50-F2-7C-62-E1

Figure 8-9 MAC address

Note

Other names for the MAC address are vendor address, vendor ID, NIC address, Ethernet address, hardware address, and physical address.

The IEEE 802.11 standard permits controlling but does not specify how it is to be implemented. Since a wireless device can be identified by its MAC address, however, virtually all wireless AP vendors implement MAC address filtering as the means of access control. A wireless client device's MAC address is entered into software running on the AP, which then is used to permit or deny a device from connecting to the network. As shown in Figure 8-10, restrictions can be implemented in one of two ways: a specific device can be permitted access into the network or the device can be blocked.

Filtering by MAC address has several vulnerabilities. First, MAC addresses are initially exchanged between wireless devices and the AP in an unencrypted format. An attacker monitoring the airwaves could easily see the MAC address of an approved device and then substitute it on her own device.

Another weakness of MAC address filtering is that managing several MAC addresses can pose significant challenges. The sheer number of users often makes it difficult to manage all the MAC addresses. As new users are added to the network

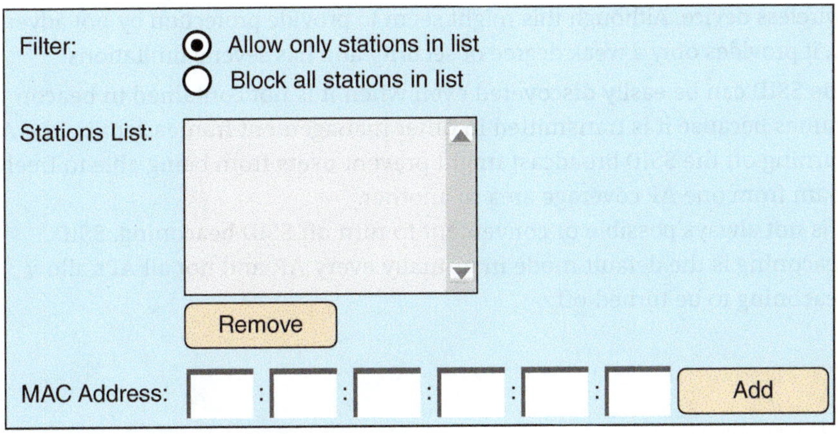

Filter: ⦿ Allow only stations in list
          ◯ Block all stations in list

Stations List:

[▲]
[▼]

[Remove]

MAC Address: [ ] : [ ] : [ ] : [ ] : [ ] : [ ]   [Add]

Figure 8-10   **MAC address filtering**

Note 📎

MAC address filtering is usually implemented by permitting instead of preventing, because it is not possible to know the MAC addresses of all the devices that are to be excluded.

Note 📎

MAC address substitution is possible on Microsoft Windows computers because the MAC address of the wireless NIC is read and then that value is stored in the Windows Registry database, which can easily be changed.

and old users leave, keeping track of MAC address filtering demands almost constant attention. For this reason, MAC address filtering is not always practical in a large and dynamic wireless network.

SSID Broadcasting

Another means of controlling access to the WLAN uses the **Service Set Identifier (SSID)** of the wireless network. The SSID is the user-supplied network name of a wireless network and generally can be any alphanumeric string up to 32 characters. Although normally the SSID is broadcast so that any device can see it, the broadcast can be restricted. Then only those users that know the "secret" SSID in advance would be allowed to access the network.

Some wireless security sources encourage users to configure their APs to prevent the broadcast (beaconing) of the SSID, and instead require the user to enter the SSID manually on the wireless device. Although this might seem to provide protection by not advertising the SSID, it provides only a weak degree of security and has several limitations:

- The SSID can be easily discovered even when it is not contained in beacon frames because it is transmitted in other management frames sent by the AP.
- Turning off the SSID broadcast might prevent users from being able to freely roam from one AP coverage area to another.
- It is not always possible or convenient to turn off SSID beaconing. SSID beaconing is the default mode in virtually every AP, and not all APs allow beaconing to be turned off.

> **Note**
>
> Older versions of Microsoft Windows, when receiving signals from both a wireless network that is broadcasting an SSID and one that is not broadcasting the SSID, will always connect to the AP that is broadcasting its SSID. If such a device is connected to an AP that is not broadcasting its SSID, and another AP is turned on that is broadcasting its SSID, the device will automatically disconnect from the first AP and connect to the AP that is broadcasting.

Wireless Security Solutions

Q Certification

1.5 Given a scenario, troubleshoot security issues related to wireless networking.

2.1 Install and configure network components, both hardware- and software-based, to support organizational security.

2.2 Given a scenario, use appropriate software tools to assess the security posture of an organization.

2.3 Given a scenario, troubleshoot common security issues.

2.5 Given a scenario, deploy mobile devices securely.

3.2 Given a scenario, implement secure network architecture concepts.

3.3 Given a scenario, implement secure systems design.

4.3 Given a scenario, implement identity and access management controls.

6.3 Given a scenario, install and configure wireless security settings.

As a result of wireless security vulnerabilities, both the IEEE and Wi-Fi Alliance organizations worked to create comprehensive security solutions. The results from the IEEE, known as *IEEE 802.11i*, served as the foundation for the Wi-Fi Alliance's Wi-Fi

Protected Access (WPA) and Wi-Fi Protected Access 2 (WPA2). WPA and WPA2 are the primary wireless security solutions today. In addition, there are other security steps that can be taken.

Wi-Fi Protected Access (WPA)

The Wi-Fi Alliance introduced **Wi-Fi Protected Access (WPA)** in October 2003. One of the design goals of WPA was to fit into the existing WEP engine without requiring extensive hardware upgrades or replacements. There were two modes of WPA. *WPA Personal* was designed for individuals or small office/home office (SOHO) settings, which typically have 10 or fewer employees. A more robust *WPA Enterprise* was intended for larger enterprises, schools, and government agencies. WPA addresses both encryption and authentication.

Temporal Key Integrity Protocol (TKIP) Encryption

The heart and soul of WPA is a newer encryption technology called **Temporal Key Integrity Protocol (TKIP)**. TKIP functions as a "wrapper" around WEP by adding an additional layer of security but preserving WEP's basic functionality. TKIP's enhancements are in three basic areas: the required key length is increased from 64 bits to 128 bits (making it harder to break), the IV is increased from 24 bits to 48 bits (effectively eliminating collisions), and a unique "base key" is created for each wireless device using a master key derived in the authentication process along with the sender's unique MAC address (this key is used with the IV to create unique keys for each packet).

With WEP, a small 40-bit encryption key must be manually entered on APs and devices. This key does not change and is the basis for encryption for all transmissions. By contrast, TKIP uses a longer 128-bit *per-packet key*. The per-packet functionality of TKIP means that it dynamically generates a new key for each packet, thus preventing collisions. The result is that TKIP dynamically generates unique keys to encrypt every data packet that is wirelessly communicated during a session.

Note

When using TKIP there are 280 trillion possible keys that can be generated for a given data packet. If a wireless device was transmitting 10,000 packets per second with WEP, collisions could occur in 90 minutes; TKIP ensures that collisions would not occur for more than 900 years.

WPA also includes a *Message Integrity Check (MIC)*, designed to prevent an attacker from conducting active or passive man-in-the-middle attacks by capturing, altering, and resending data packets. MIC provides a strong mathematical function in which the receiver and the transmitter each compute and then compare the MIC. If it does not match, the data is assumed to have been tampered with and the packet is dropped. There is also an optional MIC countermeasure in which all clients are de-authenticated and new associations are prevented for one minute if a MIC error occurs.

Preshared Key (PSK) Authentication

A wireless network in which no authentication is required, such as at a local coffee shop, is using an **open method**. However, most WLANs need to restrict who can access the network through using authentication. Authentication for WPA Personal is accomplished by using a **preshared key (PSK)**; In cryptography, a PSK is a value that has been previously shared using a secure communication channel between two parties. In a WLAN, a PSK is slightly different. It is a secret value that is manually entered on both the AP and each wireless device, making it essentially identical to the "shared secret" used in WEP. Because this secret key is not widely known, it can be assumed that only approved devices have the key value. Devices that have the secret key are then automatically authenticated by the AP.

WPA Vulnerabilities

Although an improvement over WEP, WPA nevertheless has weaknesses. One of the design goals of WPA was to fit into the existing WEP engine without requiring extensive hardware upgrades or replacements. Because most existing WEP devices at the time WPA was released had very limited central processing unit (CPU) capabilities a series of compromises had to be made. This allowed WEP to be modified to run WPA through software-based firmware upgrades on the AP and software upgrades on wireless devices, but these constraints limited the security of WPA, which was designed only as an interim short-term solution to address the critical WEP vulnerabilities and was not seen as a long-term solution.

The vulnerabilities in WPA center around two areas, namely, key management and passphrases. Improper management of the PSK keys can expose a WLAN to attackers. The distribution and sharing of PSK keys is performed manually without any technology security protections. The keys can be distributed by telephone, email, or a text message (none of which are secure). Any user who obtains a key is assumed to be authentic and approved. Yet changing the PSK key on a regular basis requires reconfiguring the key on every wireless device and on all APs. To allow a guest user to have access to a PSK WLAN, the key must be given to that guest. Once the guest departs, this shared secret must be changed on all devices to ensure adequate security for the PSK WLAN. For enterprises, PSK is simply not a viable solution.

A second area of PSK vulnerability is the use of passphrases. A PSK is a passphrase (consisting of letters, digits, punctuation, etc.) that is between 8 and 63 characters in length. PSK passphrases of fewer than 20 characters can be subject to attacks to crack the passphrase. If a user created a PSK passphrase of fewer than 20 characters that was a dictionary word, then a match may be found and the passphrase broken.

Note

The problem with short passphrases was noted even in the IEEE standard, which says, "A key generated from a passphrase of less than about 20 characters is unlikely to deter attacks."[5]

Wi-Fi Protected Access 2 (WPA2)

Shortly after the introduction of IEEE 802.11i, the Wi-Fi Alliance introduced **Wi-Fi Protected Access 2 (WPA2)**, which was the second generation of WPA security. WPA2 is based on the final IEEE 802.11i standard and is almost identical to it. As with WPA, there are two modes of WPA2, *WPA2 Personal* for individuals or SOHOs and *WPA2 Enterprise* for larger enterprises, schools, and government agencies. WPA2 addresses the two major security areas of WLANs, namely, encryption and authentication.

> **Note**
>
> The primary difference between WPA2 and IEEE 802.11i is that WPA2 allows wireless clients using TKIP to operate in the same WLAN, whereas IEEE 802.11i does not permit them to do so.

AES-CCMP Encryption

The WPA2 standard addresses encryption by using the Advanced Encryption Standard (AES) block cipher. AES performs three steps on every block (128 bits) of plaintext. Within the second step, multiple iterations (called rounds) are performed depending upon the key size: a 128-bit key performs 9 rounds, a 192-bit key performs 11 rounds, and a 256-bit key, known as AES-256, uses 13 rounds. Within each round, bytes are substituted and rearranged, and then special multiplication is performed based on the new arrangement. For the WPA2 implementation of AES, a 128-bit key length is used in four stages that make up one round, and each round is then performed 10 times.

The encryption protocol used for WPA2 is the **Counter Mode with Cipher Block Chaining Message Authentication Code Protocol (CCMP)** and specifies the use of CCM (a general-purpose cipher mode algorithm providing data privacy) with AES. The Cipher Block Chaining Message Authentication Code (CBC-MAC) component of CCMP provides data integrity and authentication. CCM itself does not require that a specific block cipher be used, but the most secure cipher AES is mandated by the WPA2 standard. For this reason, CCMP for WLANs is sometimes designated as *AES-CCMP*.

Although CCMP uses a completely different encryption algorithm than TKIP, there are similarities to the process. Both CCMP and TKIP use a 128-bit key for encryption. Also, CCMP includes a 48-bit value that is sent in cleartext, as does TKIP. Although TKIP calls this value a TKIP sequence counter (TSC), CCMP more properly calls it a packet number (PN). Finally, both methods use a 64-bit MIC value. However, CCMP's MIC protects everything in the 802.11 Media Access Control (MAC) header (except for the duration field), while the TKIP MIC protects only the source and destination addresses.

> **Note**
>
> Even though AES is an efficient block cipher, CCMP still requires a separate encryption processor.

IEEE 802.1x Authentication

Authentication for the WPA2 Enterprise model (called the **enterprise method**) uses the **IEEE 802.1x** standard. This standard, originally developed for wired networks, provides a greater degree of security by implementing port-based authentication. IEEE 802.1x blocks all traffic on a port-by-port basis until the client is authenticated using credentials stored on an authentication server. This prevents an unauthenticated device from receiving any network traffic until its identity can be verified. It also strictly limits access to the device that provides the authentication to prevent attackers from reaching it. Figure 8-11 illustrates the steps in an 802.1x authentication procedure.

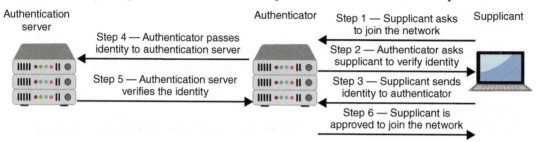

Figure 8-11 IEEE 802.1x process

1. The device (called a *supplicant*) requests from the *authenticator* permission to join the network.
2. The authenticator asks the supplicant to verify its identity.
3. The supplicant sends identity information to the authenticator.
4. The authenticator passes the identity credentials on to an *authentication server*, whose only job is to verify the authentication of devices. The identity information is sent in an encrypted form.
5. The authentication server verifies or rejects the supplicant's identity and returns the information to the authenticator.
6. If approved, the supplicant can now join the network and transmit data.

The most secure form of IEEE 802.1x authentication is **certificate-based authentication** in which each supplicant computer must have a digital certificate as proof of its identity. Certificates can then be automatically deployed to computers without any input of the user. This can be done by the enterprise installing a Public Key Infrastructure (PKI) to deploy certificates.

> **Note** 📎
>
> Although IEEE 802.1x is commonly used on wireless networks, it can be used for wired networks as well. For example, in a public conference room, an RJ-45 network connection may be accessible to both trusted employees and untrusted public users. IEEE 802.1x permits the trusted employees to access both the secure internal corporate network and the Internet, while restricting public users to Internet access only from the same network connection.

It is important that the communication between the supplicant, authenticator, and authentication server in an IEEE 802.1x configuration be secure. A framework for transporting the authentication protocols is known as the **Extensible Authentication Protocol (EAP)**. Despite its name, EAP is a *framework* for transporting authentication protocols instead of the authentication protocol itself. EAP essentially defines the format of the messages and uses four types of packets: *request*, *response*, *success*, and *failure*. Request packets are issued by the authenticator and ask for a response packet from the supplicant. Any number of request-response exchanges may be used to complete the authentication. If the authentication is successful, a success packet is sent to the supplicant; if not, a failure packet is sent.

Note

An EAP packet contains a field that indicates the function of the packet (such as response or request) and an identifier field used to match requests and responses. Response and request packets also have a field that indicates the type of data being transported (such as an authentication protocol) along with the data itself.

A common EAP protocol is **Protected EAP (PEAP)**. PEAP is designed to simplify the deployment of 802.1x by using Microsoft Windows logins and passwords. PEAP is considered a more flexible EAP scheme because it creates an encrypted channel between the client and the authentication server, and the channel then protects the subsequent user authentication exchange. To create this channel, the PEAP client first authenticates the PEAP authentication server using enhanced authentication.

There are several EAP protocols supported in WPA2 Enterprise; the most common are listed in Table 8-5.

Table 8-5   Common EAP protocols supported by WPA2 Enterprise

EAP name	Description
EAP-TLS	This protocol uses digital certificates for authentication.
EAP-TTLS	This protocol securely tunnels client password authentication within Transport Layer Security (TLS) records.
EAP-FAST	This protocol securely tunnels any credential form for authentication (such as a password or a token) using TLS.

Note

WPA2 can support new EAP types as they become available.

Additional Wireless Security Protections

Other security steps can be taken to protect a wireless network. These include rogue AP system detection, using the correct type of AP, AP configuration settings, and wireless peripheral protection.

Rogue AP System Detection

As the cost of consumer wireless routers has fallen, the problem of rogue APs has risen. Identifying these devices in an enterprise is known as **rogue AP system detection**. Several methods can be used to detect a rogue AP by continuously monitoring the RF airspace. This requires a special sensor called a *wireless probe*, a device that can monitor the airwaves for traffic. There are four types of wireless probes:

- *Wireless device probe*. A standard wireless device, such as a portable laptop computer, can be configured to act as a wireless probe. At regular intervals during the normal course of operation, the device can scan and record wireless signals within its range and report this information to a centralized database. This scanning is performed when the device is idle and not receiving any transmissions. When several mobile devices are used as wireless device probes, it can provide a high degree of accuracy in identifying rogue access points.
- *Desktop probe*. Instead of using a mobile wireless device as a probe, a desktop probe utilizes a standard desktop PC. A universal serial bus (USB) wireless adapter is plugged into the desktop computer to monitor the RF frequency in the area for transmissions.
- *Access point probe*. Some AP vendors have included in their APs the functionality of detecting neighboring APs, friendly as well as rogue. However, this approach is not widely used. The range for a single AP to recognize other APs is limited because APs are typically located so that their signals overlap only in such a way as to provide roaming to wireless users.
- *Dedicated probe*. A dedicated probe is designed to exclusively monitor the RF frequency for transmissions. Unlike access point probes that serve as both an AP and a probe, dedicated probes only monitor the airwaves. Dedicated probes look much like standard access points.

Once a suspicious wireless signal is detected by a wireless probe, the information is sent to a centralized database where WLAN management system software compares it to a list of approved APs. Any device not on the list is considered a rogue AP. The WLAN management system can instruct the switch to disable the port to which the rogue AP is connected, thus severing its connection to the wired network.

AP Type

Another means of protection for a wireless network is to choose the best type of AP to match the needs of the network. AP types can be divided into fat vs. thin, controller vs. standalone, and captive portal APs.

Fat vs. Thin APs

Standard APs are *autonomous*, or independent, because they are separate from other network devices and even other autonomous APs. Autonomous APs have the intelligence required to manage wireless authentication, encryption, and other functions for the wireless client devices that they serve. Because everything is self-contained in these single devices they are sometimes called **fat APs**.

Although fat APs are functional for a home or a SOHO setting in which there may be one or two APs, what happens in a large enterprise or college campus where there can be hundreds of APs? In this case fat APs are not a viable option. Because each AP is autonomous, a single wireless network configuration change would require that each AP be reconfigured individually, which could take an extended period and manpower to complete.

When multiple APs are widely deployed, a **thin AP** can be a better solution. These "lightweight" APs do not contain all the management and configuration functions found in fat APs. Much of the configuration is centralized in the wireless switch so that the network administrator can work directly with the switch from the wired network. This can also improve security because managing from a central location instead of visiting and configuring each fat AP reduces the risk of a security setting being overlooked.

Standalone vs. Controller APs

Although thin APs can be managed from a switch, a further improvement can be made by managing from a device that is dedicated for configuring APs. Instead of installing **standalone APs** like fat or thin APs, **controller APs** can be managed through a dedicated *wireless LAN controller (WLC)*. The WLC is the single device that can be configured and then these settings are automatically distributed to all controller APs (a remote office WLAN controller is used to manage multiple WLCs at remote sites from a central location). Controller APs with a WLC are shown in Figure 8-12.

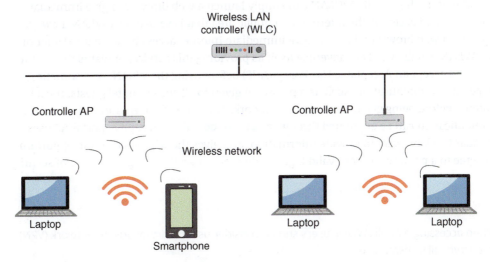

Figure 8-12   Controller APs with WLC

Note

Controller APs handle only the real-time medium access control (MAC) layer functionality within themselves; all other (non-real-time) MAC functionality is processed by the WLC. This type of division is referred to as a *split MAC architecture*.

Besides centralized management, controller APs provide other advantages over standalone APs. As wireless client devices move through a WLAN, a lengthy handoff procedure occurs during which one standalone AP transfers authentication information to another. Slow hand-offs can be unacceptable on WLAN systems using time-dependent communication, such as voice or video. With controller APs, however, this handoff procedure is eliminated because all authentications are performed in the WLC. Another advantage of WLCs are the tools that many provide for monitoring the environment and providing information regarding the best locations for APs, wireless configuration settings, and power settings.

Note

There are disadvantages to controller APs. WLCs still do not provide true convergence (integration) of the wired and wireless networks, but only ease some of the management burdens of WLANs. In addition, these devices are proprietary, which means all the thin APs and WLCs on a network must be from the same vendor to function cohesively.

Captive Portal APs

A home user who installs a WLAN can simply launch a web browser to give immediate and unlimited access to the Internet. In a public area that is served by a WLAN, however, opening a web browser will rarely give immediate Internet access because the owner of the WLAN usually wants to advertise itself as providing this service, or wants the user to read and accept an Acceptable Use Policy (AUP) before using the WLAN. And sometimes a "general" authentication, such as a password given to all current hotel guests, must be entered before being given access to the network. This type of information, approval, or authentication can be supported through a **captive portal AP**. A captive portal AP uses a standard web browser to provide information, and gives the wireless user the opportunity to agree to a policy or present valid login credentials, providing a higher degree of security.

Note

When accessing a public WLAN, users should consider using a virtual private network (VPN) to encrypt all transmissions.

AP Configuration and Device Options

Selecting the proper options for the AP can also enhance security. As noted previously, configuring the APs for MAC address filtering and to prevent the broadcast of the SSID provides little security. However, other AP configuration settings can provide improved security. Some of these settings are designed to limit the spread of the wireless RF signal so that a minimum amount of signal extends past the physical boundaries of the enterprise to be accessible to outsiders. This can be accomplished through a *site survey*, which can also ensure that the signal covers areas that it should. A site survey is an in-depth examination and analysis of a wireless LAN site to determine the best wireless topology.

AP configuration and device options include setting the signal strength and choosing the correct RF spectrum options. One device option is to select the best type of antenna and to correctly locate it.

Signal Strength Settings

A security feature on some APs is the ability to adjust the level of power at which the WLAN transmits. On devices with that feature, the power can be adjusted so that less of the signal leaves the premises and reaches outsiders.

Note

For IEEE WLANs, the maximum transmit power is 200 milliwatts (mW). APs that can adjust the power level usually permit the level to be adjusted in predefined increments, such as 1, 5, 20, 30, 40, 100, or 200 mW.

Spectrum Selection

Some APs provide the ability to adjust frequency spectrum settings. These include:

- *Frequency band*. An increasing number of APs support dual bands of spectrum. If one band is not being used it should be disabled. If both bands are to be used it is recommended that both be set to the same configuration settings.
- *Channel selection*. Some APs have an *Auto* mode in which the AP selects the optimum channel within the frequency band. On those devices in which this mode is not supported, it is important to choose a channel that is different from that of other nearby APs or sources of interference.
- *Channel width*. Channel width controls how much of the spectrum is available to transfer data. However, larger channels are more subject to interference and more likely to interfere with other devices.

Note

A site survey can be helpful in making decisions about bands, channels, and widths.

Antennas

APs use antennas that radiate out a signal in all directions. Because these devices are generally positioned to provide the broadest area of coverage, APs should be located near the middle of the coverage area. Generally, the AP can be secured to the ceiling or high on a wall. It is recommended that APs be mounted as high as possible for two reasons: there may be fewer obstructions for the RF signal, and to prevent thieves from stealing the device. For security purposes, the AP and its antenna should be positioned so that, when possible, a minimal amount of signal reaches beyond the security perimeter of the building or campus. Another option is to use a type of antenna that will focus its signal in a more concentrated direction toward authorized users instead of broadcasting it over a wide area.

Wireless Peripheral Protection

Vulnerabilities in wireless mice and keyboards are not uncommon. One attack could let a threat actor inject mouse movements or keystrokes from a nearby antenna up to 100 yards (91 m) away. This can occur even when the target device is designed to encrypt and authenticate its communications with a paired computer. Protections for wireless peripherals include updating or replacing any vulnerable wireless mice or keyboard devices, switching to more fully tested Bluetooth mice and keyboards, or substituting a wired mouse or keyboard instead of a wireless model.

Chapter Summary

- Bluetooth is a wireless technology that uses short-range RF transmissions. It enables users to connect wirelessly to a wide range of computing and telecommunications devices by providing for rapid "on-the-fly" connections between Bluetooth-enabled devices. The primary type of Bluetooth network topology is a piconet. Two of the common attacks on wireless Bluetooth technology are bluejacking, which is sending unsolicited messages, and bluesnarfing, or accessing unauthorized information from a wireless device through a Bluetooth connection.

- Near field communication (NFC) is a set of standards primarily for smartphones and smart cards that can be used to establish communication between devices in close proximity. Once the devices are either tapped together or brought very close to each other, a two-way communication is established. NFC devices are increasingly used in contactless payment systems so that a consumer can pay for a purchase by simply tapping a store's payment terminal with their smartphone. There are risks with using NFC contactless payment systems because of the nature of this technology.

- A wireless technology similar to NFC is radio frequency identification (RFID). RFID is commonly used to transmit information between paper-based tags that can be detected by a proximity reader. Because RFID tags do not require a power supply they can be very small and thinner than a sheet of paper. RFID tags are susceptible to some types of attacks.

- A wireless local area network (WLAN) is designed to replace or supplement a wired LAN. The IEEE has developed standards for WLANs. An enterprise WLAN requires a wireless client adapter and an AP for communications, whereas a home network uses a wireless router instead of an AP. In a traditional wired network, the security of the network itself along with the walls and doors of the secured building protects the data and resources. Because an RF signal can easily extend past the protective perimeter of a building and because an AP can provide unauthorized entry points into the network, WLANs are frequently the target of attackers.

- A rogue AP is an unauthorized AP that allows an attacker to bypass network security and opens the network and its users to attacks. An evil twin is an AP that is set up by an attacker to mimic an authorized AP and capture the transmissions from users. One of the most common wireless attacks is intercepting and reading data that is being transmitted. In addition, if the attacker manages to connect to the enterprise wired network through a rogue AP, she could also read broadcast and multicast wired network traffic. In wireless replay attacks, attackers capture the data that is being transmitted, record it, and then send it on to the original recipient without their presence being detected. Attackers likewise can use intentional RF interference to flood the RF spectrum with enough interference to prevent a device from effectively

communicating with the AP, performing a wireless DoS attack that prevents the transmission of data to or from network devices. Home wireless networks that are not protected are subject to attackers stealing data, reading transmissions, or injecting malware behind the firewall.

- The original IEEE 802.11 committee recognized that wireless transmissions could be vulnerable and implemented several wireless security protections in the 802.11 standard, while leaving other protections to be applied at the WLAN vendor's discretion. Despite their intended design, several of these protections were vulnerable to attacks. Wired Equivalent Privacy (WEP) was designed to ensure that only authorized parties can view transmitted wireless information by encrypting transmissions. WEP relies on a secret key that is shared between the wireless client device and the AP that is combined with an initialization vector (IV). However, WEP has several security vulnerabilities. Wi-Fi Protected Setup (WPS) is an optional means of configuring security on wireless local area networks and is designed to help users who have little or no knowledge of security to quickly and easily implement security on their WLANs. However, there are significant design and implementation flaws in WPS.

- One method of controlling access to the WLAN so that only approved users can be accepted is to limit a device's access to the AP. Virtually all wireless AP vendors offer Media Access Control (MAC) address filtering. Filtering by MAC address, however, has several vulnerabilities. One weakness is that MAC addresses are initially exchanged between wireless devices and the AP in an unencrypted format. For a degree of protection, some wireless security sources encourage users to configure their APs to prevent the beacon frame from including the Service Set Identifier (SSID) and instead require the user to enter the SSID manually on the wireless device. Although this may seem to provide protection by not advertising the SSID, it provides only a weak degree of security.

- Wi-Fi Protected Access (WPA) was designed to fit into the existing WEP engine without requiring extensive hardware upgrades or replacements. WPA replaces WEP with the Temporal Key Integrity Protocol (TKIP), which uses a longer key and dynamically generates a new key for each packet that is created. WPA authentication for WPA Personal is accomplished by using preshared key (PSK) technology. A key must be created and entered in both the access point and all wireless devices ("shared") prior to ("pre") the devices communicating with the AP. Vulnerabilities still exist in WPA in two areas: key management and passphrases.

- Wi-Fi Protected Access 2 (WPA2) is the second generation of WPA security. Encryption under WPA2 is accomplished by using AES-CCMP. WPA2 authentication is accomplished by the IEEE 802.1x standard. Because it is important that the communication between the supplicant, authenticator, and authentication server in an IEEE 802.1x configuration be secure, a framework for transporting the authentication protocols is known as the Extensible Authentication Protocol (EAP). EAP is a framework for transporting authentication protocols by defining the format of the messages.

- Other steps can be taken to protect a wireless network. The problem of rogue APs is of increasing concern to organizations. Several methods can be used to detect a rogue AP by continuously monitoring the RF airspace. This requires a special sensor called a wireless probe, a device that can monitor the airwaves for traffic. Another means of protection for a wireless network is to choose the best type of AP to match the needs of the network. A thin AP is a "lightweight" AP that does not contain all the management and configuration functions found in fat APs. Much of the configuration is centralized in the wireless switch. Instead of installing standalone APs like fat or thin APs, controller APs can be managed through a dedicated wireless LAN controller (WLC). The WLC is the single device that can be configured and then these settings are automatically distributed to all controller APs. A captive portal AP uses a standard web browser to provide information and give the wireless user the opportunity to agree to a policy or present valid login credentials, providing a higher degree of security.

- Another security feature on some APs is the ability to adjust the level of power at which the WLAN transmits. On devices with that feature, the power can be adjusted so that less of the signal leaves the premises and reaches outsiders. Some APs provide the ability to adjust frequency spectrum settings. For security purposes, the AP and its antenna should be positioned so that, when possible, a minimal amount of signal reaches beyond the security perimeter of the building or campus. Vulnerabilities in wireless mice and keyboards and can be mitigated by replacing vulnerable devices or switching to a wired model instead.

Key Terms

access point (AP)
ad hoc mode
ad hoc topology
bluejacking
bluesnarfing
Bluetooth
captive portal AP
certificate-based
  authentication
controller APs
Counter Mode with Cipher
  Block Chaining Message
  Authentication Code
  Protocol (CCMP)
disassociation attack
EAP-FAST
EAP-TLS

EAP-TTLS
enterprise method
evil twin
Extensible Authentication
  Protocol (EAP)
fat APs
IEEE 802.1x
jamming
Media Access Control (MAC)
  address filtering
near field communication
  (NFC)
open method
preshared key (PSK)
Protected EAP (PEAP)
radio frequency
  identification (RFID)

rogue AP
rogue AP system
  detection
Service Set Identifier (SSID)
standalone APs
Temporal Key Integrity
  Protocol (TKIP)
thin AP
Wi-Fi Direct
Wi-Fi Protected Access
  (WPA)
Wi-Fi Protected Access 2
  (WPA2)
Wi-Fi Protected Setup (WPS)
wireless local area network
  (WLAN)
wireless replay attack

Review Questions

1. Which technology is predominately used for contactless payment systems?
   a. Near field communication (NFC)
   b. Wireless local area network (WLAN)
   c. Bluetooth
   d. Radio Frequency ID (RFID)

2. Which of these Bluetooth attacks involves accessing unauthorized information through a Bluetooth connection?
   a. Bluesnarfing
   b. Bluejacking
   c. Bluecreeping
   d. Bluestealing

3. What is a difference between NFC and RFID?
   a. NFC is based on wireless technology while RFID is not.
   b. RFID is faster than NFC.
   c. RFID is designed for paper-based tags while NFC is not.

   d. NFC devices cannot pair as quickly as RFID devices.

4. Which of these technologies is NOT found in a wireless router?
   a. Access point
   b. Router
   c. Dynamic host configuration protocol (DHCP) server
   d. Firewall

5. Why is a rogue AP a security vulnerability?
   a. It uses the weaker IEEE 80211i protocol.
   b. It conflicts with other network firewalls and can cause them to become disabled.
   c. It allows an attacker to bypass network security configurations.
   d. It requires the use of vulnerable wireless probes on all mobile devices.

6. Which of these is NOT a risk when a home wireless router is not securely configured?
   a. Only a small percentage of the total traffic can be encrypted.
   b. An attacker can steal data from any folder with file sharing enabled.
   c. User names, passwords, credit card numbers, and other information sent over the WLAN could be captured by an attacker.
   d. Malware can be injected into a computer connected to the WLAN.

7. Which of these Wi-Fi Protected Setup (WPS) methods is vulnerable?
   a. Push-button method
   b. PIN method
   c. Piconet method
   d. NFC method

8. Flavio visits a local coffee shop on his way to school and accesses its free Wi-Fi. When he first connects, a screen appears that requires him to first agree to an Acceptable Use Policy (AUP) before continuing. What type of AP has he encountered?
   a. Captive portal
   b. Web-based portal
   c. Rogue portal
   d. Authenticated portal

9. Which of the following is NOT a wireless peripheral protection option?
   a. Update or replacing any vulnerable device
   b. Switch to a more fully tested Bluetooth model
   c. Install a network sensor to detect an attack
   d. Substitute a wired device

10. The primary design of a(n) _____ is to capture the transmissions from legitimate users.
    a. rogue access point
    b. WEP
    c. evil twin
    d. Bluetooth grabber

11. Which of these is a vulnerability of MAC address filtering?
    a. APs use IP addresses instead of MACs.
    b. The user must enter the MAC.
    c. MAC addresses are initially exchanged unencrypted.
    d. Not all operating systems support MACs.

12. Which of these is NOT a limitation of turning off the SSID broadcast from an AP?
    a. Turning off the SSID broadcast may prevent users from being able to freely roam from one AP coverage area to another.
    b. Some versions of operating systems favor a network that broadcasts an SSID over one that does not.
    c. Users can more easily roam from one WLAN to another.
    d. The SSID can easily be discovered, even when it is not contained in beacon frames, because it still is transmitted in other management frames sent by the AP.

13. What is the primary weakness of wired equivalent privacy (WEP)?
    a. It functions only on specific brands of APs.
    b. Its usage creates a detectable pattern.
    c. It slows down a WLAN from 104 Mbps to 16 Mbps.
    d. Initialization vectors (IVs) are difficult for users to manage.

14. WPA replaces WEP with _____.
    a. WPA2
    b. Temporal Key Integrity Protocol (TKIP)
    c. cyclic redundancy check (CRC)
    d. Message Integrity Check (MIC)

15. Adabella was asked by her supervisor to adjust the frequency spectrum settings on a new AP. She brought up the configuration page and looked through the different options. Which of the following frequency spectrum settings would she NOT be able to adjust?
    a. Frequency band
    b. Channel selection
    c. RFID spectrum
    d. Channel width

16. A wireless LAN controller (WLC) was recently installed, and now Kelsey needs to purchase several new APs to be managed by it. Which type of AP should he purchase?
    a. Controller AP
    b. Standalone AP
    c. Fat AP
    d. Any type of AP can be managed by a WLC.

17. AES-CCMP is the encryption protocol standard used in _____ .
    a. WPA
    b. WPA2

    c. IEEE 802.11
    d. NFC

18. Elijah was asked by a student intern to explain the Extensible Authentication Protocol (EAP). What would be the best explanation of EAP?
    a. It is the transport protocol used in TCP/IP for authentication.
    b. It is a framework for transporting authentication protocols.
    c. It is a subset of WPA2.
    d. It is a technology used by IEEE 802.11 for encryption.

19. Minh has been asked to recommend an EAP for a system that uses both passwords and tokens with TLS. Which should she recommend?
    a. EAP-TLS
    b. EAP-TTLS
    c. EAP-SSL
    d. EAP-FAST

20. Which of these is NOT a type of wireless AP probe?
    a. Wireless device probe
    b. WNIC probe
    c. Dedicated probe
    d. AP probe

Hands-On Projects

> ### Note
>
> If you are concerned about installing any of the software in these projects on your regular computer, you can instead install the software in the Windows virtual machine created in the Chapter 1 Hands-On Projects 1-3 and 1-4. Software installed within the virtual machine will not impact the host computer.

Project 8-1: Downloading and Installing a Wireless Monitor

Most Wi-Fi users are surprised to see just how far their wireless signal will reach, and if the network is unprotected this makes it easy for an attacker hiding several hundred feet away to break into the network. There are several tools available that will show the different wireless signals from Wi-Fi networks that can be detected. In this project, you download and install the Xirrus Wi-Fi Inspector program. You will need a computer with a wireless adapter, such as a laptop, to complete this project.

1. Use your web browser to go to **www.xirrus.com/free-tools** (if you are no longer able to access the site through the web address, use a search engine to search for "Xirrus Wi-Fi Inspector").
2. Click **GET WI-FI INSPECTOR**.

> ### Note
>
> Wi-Fi Inspector will run correctly under Windows 10, 8.1, 8.0, 7, and XP.

3. Enter the requested information and download the tool.
4. When finished launch the Wi-Fi Inspector setup program and install the application using the defaults settings.
5. Start Wi-Fi Inspector. It is laid out in 4 tiled windows, each displaying different real-time information about the Wi-Fi networks that can be detected. The windows are Radar, Connection, Networks, and Signal History. This is shown in Figure 8-13.
6. On the **Layout** tab click **Radar** to maximize the radar screen. The Radar screen displays a dynamic view of the Wi-Fi networks in the area. The names of the networks and a corresponding dot are displayed in a circular view, with their relative distance from the center of the radar based on the strength of their Wi-Fi signal (networks from which a strong signal is detected are closer to the center while weaker signals are further away).
7. On **Layout** tab click **Show All** to return to the standard screen layout.
8. In the **Settings** tab click **Settings**.
9. Under **Display Units** change the setting to **Percent**. Click **Ok**.
10. On the **Layout** tab and click **Networks** to maximize the network screen.

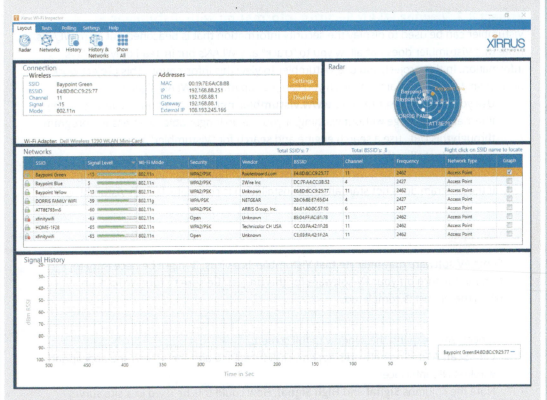

Figure 8-13   Xirrus Wi-Fi Inspector

Source: Xirrus.com

11. Scroll through the list of Wi-Fi networks that are detected. Do you recognize all of them as known networks? Click the **Signal Level** column to show the networks that are the most distant with the weakest signal first. What is the signal strength of the weakest network signal?

12. The Locate Mode can be used to help determine the location of a specific Wi-Fi network. This mode operates like a Geiger counter, using sound and visual information to indicate proximity. When in Locate mode, the selected network is highlighted in yellow on the Networks table, it is displayed on the Radar window, and the selected network is graphed in the History window. In addition, an audible beep sounds, the frequency of which reflects signal strength: the quicker the beep, the closer the network. Select a network that has a weak signal, right-click it, and select the **Locate** option.

13. While carrying the laptop, walk around in your area. How does the radar change? What about the beep sound? Why? How could an attacker use this information?

14. To exit Locate mode right-click the selected network and select **Exit Locate**.

15. Are you surprised by the number of wireless network signals you can detect? Do you think the different owners of these networks are aware that their signals are accessible?

16. Close all windows.

Project 8-2: Viewing WLAN Security Information with Vistumbler

Vistumbler can be used to display the security information that is beaconed out from WLANs. Note that Vistumbler does not allow you to "crack" any WLANs but instead only displays information. In this project, you use Vistumbler to view this information. This project works best when you are in an area in which you can pick up multiple WLAN signals.

1. Use your web browser to go to **www.vistumbler.net**. (The location of content on the Internet may change without warning. If you are no longer able to access the program through this URL, use a search engine and search for "Vistumbler".)
2. Click **EXE Installer (Mirror)**.
3. Follow the prompts to download and install Vistumbler using the default settings.
4. If the program does not start after the installation is complete, launch Vistumbler.

> **Note** 📎
>
> Some AV software may indicate that Vistumbler is a virus. It might be necessary to temporarily turn off your AV software for this project. Be sure to turn AV back on when the project is completed.

5. If necessary, expand the window to full screen.
6. Click **Scan APs**. If no networks appear, click **Interface** and then select the appropriate wireless NIC interface.
7. Note the columns **Signal** and **High Signal**. How could this be used in a site survey?
8. Click **Graph 1**.
9. Click one of the APs displayed at the bottom of the screen. Allow Vistumbler to accumulate data over several minutes. What information is displayed on this graph?
10. Click **Graph 2**.
11. Click another one of the APs displayed at the bottom of the screen. Allow Vistumbler to accumulate data over several minutes. What information is displayed on this graph? How is this different from the previous graph?
12. Click **No Graph** to return to the previous screen.
13. Use the horizontal scroll bar to move to the right. Note the columns **Authentication**, **Encryption**, **Manufacturer**, and **Radio Type**. How would this information be useful to an attacker?
14. Use the horizontal scroll bar to move back to the far left.
15. In the left page, expand the information under **Authentication**. What types are listed?
16. Expand the information under these types and note the information given for the wireless LAN signals. What device does **Mac Address** point to? How could this be useful to an attacker?
17. In the left page, expand the information under **E**ncryption. What types are listed? Which types are most secure? Which types are least secure?
18. Expand the information under these types and note the information given for each WLAN.

19. Record the total number of different WLANs that you can detect, along with the number of encryption types. Which type is most common?

20. Compile all the information from other students regarding the total number of different WLANs and the number of encryption types. Does it surprise you? Why or why not?

21. One of the features of Vistumbler is its ability to use audio and text-to-speech information so that the location and strength of WLANs can be detected without the need to constantly monitor the screen. Be sure that the speakers on the laptop computer are turned on.

22. Click **Options**.

23. Click **Speak Signals**. Now Vistumbler will "speak" the percentage of signal strength.

24. Now carry the laptop away from the AP and note the changes. How would this be helpful to an attacker?

25. Close Vistumbler.

26. Close all windows.

Project 8-3: Configuring Access Points

The ability to properly configure an AP is an important skill for any wireless network professional as well as, to a lesser degree, for endusers. In this project, you use an online emulator from TRENDnet to configure an AP.

1. Use your web browser to go to **http://www.trendnet.com/emulators/TEW-818DRU_v1/login.htm**. (The location of content on the Internet may change without warning; if you are no longer able to access the program through this URL, use a search engine and search for "Trendnet Emulators.")

2. The emulated login screen will appear. Click **Login** without entering a user name or password.

3. An emulated Setup screen displaying what a user would see when configuring an actual TRENDnet is displayed.

4. Be sure that the **BASIC** tab is selected in the left pane. Note the simulated **Network Status** information.

5. Click **Wireless** in the left pane and read the information displayed.

6. Under **Broadcast Network Name (SSID)** click the down arrow next to **Enabled**. What other option is available? Would it be an advantage to change this setting? Why or why not?

7. Under **Frequency (Channel)** note that the default is **Auto**. What does this mean?

8. Click the down arrow on **Auto**. When would you want to change the channel on which the wireless signal is broadcast?

9. Under **Channel BandWidth** click the down arrow on **20 MHz**. What is the other option? Why would you choose this option? What are the advantages and disadvantages of changing the channel bandwidth?

10. Under **Security Policy** there is a single configuration option **Security Mode**. Note the default setting. Is this a good option default option? What does **WPA2-PSK** mean?

11. Click the down arrow on **WPA2-PSK**. What are the other options? What do they mean?

12. Under **WPA** note the option **WPA Encryption**. Click the down arrow on **AES**. What are the other options available and what do they mean?

13. Under **WPA passphrase** how long is the default passphrase? Is that sufficient?

14. In the left pane click **Guest Network**. A guest network allows you to have an additional open network just for occasional guests that does not affect the main wireless network. How could this be an advantage?

15. Note the option under **Internet Access Only**. When would you select this option?

16. Note the option under **Wireless Client Isolation**. Why is this not enabled by default?

17. Under **Security Policy** note that the **Security Mode** is set to **Disable** by default. Why would a guest network's security be turned off by default? (Hint: If it were turned on what would the guests need before they could use the network?)

18. In the left pane click **Advanced**.

19. Click **Security**.

20. Under **Access Control** what is the **LAN Client Filter Function?** Does it provide strong security if it were enabled?

21. How easy is this user interface to navigate? Does it provide enough information for a user to set up the security settings on this system?

22. Close all windows.

Project 8-4: Using Microsoft Windows Netsh Commands

The Windows *netsh* commands for a wireless local area network (WLAN) provide the means to configure wireless connectivity and security settings using the command line instead of a graphical user interface (GUI). Benefits of the wireless *netsh* interface include easier wireless deployment as an alternative to Group Policy, ability to configure clients to support multiple security options, and even the ability to block undesirable networks. In this project, you will explore some of the *netsh* commands.

1. In Microsoft Windows, right-click the **Start** button.

2. Select **Command Prompt (Admin)**. This will open the Windows command window in elevated privilege mode.

> **Note** 📎
>
> For this project, you will need a computer running Microsoft Windows that has a wireless NIC and can access a wireless LAN.

3. Type **netsh** and then press **Enter**. The command prompt will change to *netsh>*.

4. Type **wlan** and then press **Enter**. The command prompt will change to *netsh wlan>*.

5. Type **show drivers** and then press **Enter** to display the wireless NIC driver information. It may be necessary to scroll back toward the top to see all the information.

6. Next view the WLAN interfaces for this computer. Type **show interfaces** and then press **Enter**. Record the SSID value, and the name of the Profile.

7. Now look at the global wireless settings for this computer. Type **show settings** and then press **Enter**.

8. Display all the available networks to this computer. Type **show networks** and then press **Enter**.

9. Windows creates a profile for each network that you connect to. To display those profiles, type **show profiles** and then press **Enter**. If there is a profile of a network that you no longer use, type **delete profile name=***profile-name*.

10. Now disconnect from your current WLAN by typing **disconnect** and then press **Enter**. Note the message you receive, and observe the status in your system tray.

11. Reconnect to your network by typing **connect name=***profile-name* **ssid=***ssid-name* as previously recorded and then press **Enter**.

12. Netsh allows you to block specific networks. Select another network name that you currently are not connected to. Type **show networks**, press **Enter**, and then record the SSID of that network you want to block. Type **add filter permission = block ssid=***ssid-name* **networktype = infrastructure** and then press **Enter**.

13. Type **show networks** and then press **Enter**. Does the network that you previously blocked appear in the list?

14. Now display the blocked network (but do not allow access to it). Type **set blockednetworks display=show** and then press **Enter**.

15. Type **show networks** and then press **Enter**. Does the network that you previously blocked appear in the list?

16. Click the wireless icon in your system tray. Does the network appear in this list?

17. Click the wireless icon in your system tray. What appears next to the name of this blocked network? Click the name of the network. What does it say?

18. Now re-enable access to the blocked network by typing **delete filter permission = block ssid=***ssid-name* **networktype = infrastructure** and then press **Enter**.

19. Type **Exit** and then press **Enter**.

20. Type **Exit** again and then press **Enter** to close the command window.

Case Projects

Case Project 8-1: Comparisons of Virtual Wallets

Using a contactless payment system requires that users store payment card numbers in a "virtual wallet" on a smartphone to pay for purchases at an NFC-enabled PoS checkout device. Each of the major wallets (VISA PayWave, MasterCard PayPass, Google Wallet, Samsung Pay, and Apple Pay) have advantages and disadvantages. Using the Internet research three different virtual wallets. Create a table that lists each of the wallets, their features, strengths and weaknesses, ease of use, security, etc. Which of them would you recommend? In your opinion, what can be done to make these more popular? Write a one-paragraph summary to accompany your table.

Case Project 8-2: Wireless Peripheral Attacks

Attacks on wireless mice and keyboards are not uncommon. Use the Internet to research these attacks. How do the attacks occur? What is the vulnerability that is exploited? How can vendors of these products secure them? Write a one-page paper on your research.

Case Project 8-3: EAP

Use the Internet to research information on the different EAP protocols that are supported in WPA2 Enterprise (see Table 8-5). Write a brief description of each and indicate the relative strength of its security. Write a one-page paper on your research.

Case Project 8-4: Antennas

To many users, antennas are just one of life's great mysteries. They know from experience that any antenna is better than having no antenna, and that the higher the antenna is located, the better the reception will be. Yet the antenna is arguably one of the most important parts of a wireless network. Antennas play a vital role in both sending and receiving signals, and a properly positioned and functioning antenna can make all the difference between a wireless LAN operating at peak efficiency or a network that nobody can use. Use the Internet to research antennas for APs. What different types of antennas are used? What are their strengths? What are their weaknesses? Which types would be used to concentrate a signal to a more confined area? Write a one-page paper on what you find.

Case Project 8-5: Your Wireless Security

Is the wireless network you own as secure as it should be? Examine your wireless network or that of a friend or neighbor and determine which security model it uses. Next, outline the steps it would take to move it to the next highest level. Estimate how much it would cost and how much time it would take to increase the level. Finally, estimate how long it would take you to replace all the data on your computer if it was corrupted by an attacker, and what you might lose. Would this be motivation to increase your current wireless security model? Write a one-page paper on your work.

Case Project 8-6: Lake Point Security Consulting

Lake Point Consulting Services (LPCS) provides security consulting and assurance services to over 500 clients across a wide range of enterprises in more than 20 states. A new initiative at LPCS is for each of its seven regional offices to provide internships to students who are in their final year of the security degree program at the local college.

Pomodoro Fresco is a regional Italian pizza chain that provides free open wireless access to its customers and secure wireless access for its staff. However, Pomodoro Fresco is concerned about the security of the WLAN. They have asked LPCS to make a presentation about wireless attacks and their options for security. LPCS has asked you to help them in the presentation.

1. Create a PowerPoint presentation for the staff about the threats against WLANs and the weaknesses of the IEEE 802.11 security protocols. Also, include information about the more secure WPA2. Your presentation should contain at least 10 slides.
2. After the presentation, Pomodoro Fresco is trying to decide if they should install a captive portal for their customer WLAN. Create a memo to their management outlining the advantages and disadvantages, along with your recommendation.

Case Project 8-7: Information Security Community Site Activity

The Information Security Community Site is an online companion to this textbook. It contains a wide variety of tools, information, discussion boards, and other features to assist learners. Go to **community.cengage.com/Infosec2** and click the *Join or Sign* in icon to log in, using your login name and password that you created in Chapter 1. Click **Forums (Discussion)** and click on **Security+ Case Projects (6th edition)**. Read the following case study.

Unprotected home WLANs carry significant risks for the owners. Threat actors can steal data, read wireless transmissions, inject malware or download harmful content. Many users are uninformed or unsure how to protect their wireless networks. Increasingly wireless routers are preconfigured with random SSIDs and PSK passphrases. But is this the solution? Will users simply change the passphrase to something that is easy to remember? Based on your experiences with users, what recommendations would you have for helping users secure home wireless networks? Post your ideas on the discussion board.

References

1. Baguley, Richard, "Origin of wireless security: the Marconi radio hack of 1903," *Hackaday*, Mar. 2, 2017, accessed Mar. 5, 2017, https://hackaday.com/2017/03/02 /great-hacks-of-history-the-marconi-radio-hack-1903/#more-245251.
2. "Cisco visual networking index: Global mobile data traffic forecast update, 2016-2021 white paper," *Cisco*, Mar. 28, 2017, accessed Apr. 26, 2017, http://www.cisco.com/c/en/us /solutions/collateral/service-provider/visual-networking-index-vni/mobile -white-paper-c11-520862.html.
3. "Cisco visual networking index: Global mobile data traffic forecast update, 2016-2021 white paper," *Cisco*, Mar. 28, 2017, accessed Apr. 26, 2017, http://www.cisco.com/c/en/us /solutions/collateral/service-provider/visual-networking-index-vni/mobile -white-paper-c11-520862.html.
4. Mickle, Tripp, "Apple Pay struggles to gain traction," *Wall Street Journal*, Apr. 6, 2017, accessed Apr. 18, 2017.
5. Nelson, David, et al., "Response to PSK Security Issues," *IEEE P802.11 Wireless LANs*, Nov. 11, 2003, accessed Apr. 28, 2017, https://mentor.ieee.org/802.11/dcn/03/11-03-0932 -01-000i-response-to-pmk-security-issues.doc.

PART IV

DEVICE SECURITY

Chapter 9 Client and Application Security
Chapter 10 Mobile and Embedded Device Security

The chapters in Part 4 explore protecting devices. In Chapter 9, you learn about protecting client devices and the applications that run on those devices. Chapter 10 examines how to secure mobile and embedded devices.

CLIENT AND APPLICATION SECURITY

After completing this chapter, you should be able to do the following:

List the steps for securing a client device

Define application security

Explain how physical security can be used for protection

Today's Attacks and Defenses

Verbal attacks between candidates running for political office have long been a staple of politics. Opponents trade barbs and hurl accusations, trying to discredit one another to win over voters. Now a new type of attack is becoming commonplace in elections: computer attacks.

Recent elections in France, the United States, and other nations have been marred by candidates' information being stolen and published on the Internet. This information ranges from private emails to sensitive campaign tactics. Often "fake news" that pretends to come from the candidates is mixed in with actual stolen information, making it difficult to distinguish fact from fiction. Some claim that these unknown attackers are hactivists who are motivated by ideology. Others claim that nation state actors are behind the malicious actions because foreign governments wish to sway the election in a particular direction, or at least disrupt the election process.

But besides stealing and releasing candidates' personal emails and other sensitive information, these threat actors may also be responsible for other attacks. In August 2016, the FBI issued a "Flash Memorandum" alerting state governments that "foreign hackers" had penetrated the Illinois Board of Election site the previous month. Although the Illinois Board said via a Facebook posting that there was "no evidence that [attackers] added, changed, or deleted any information in the (Illinois Voter Registration System) database" and "their efforts to obtain voter signature images and voter history were unsuccessful," nevertheless they did steal personal data on 200,000 Illinois voters, and resulted in the Illinois voter registration system being shut down for 10 days. The attackers used a SQL injection attack to gain access to the server containing the personal information. Later that same month unknown threat actors injected malware into the Arizona state voter registration system, although Arizona claims that no voter information was stolen.

Attackers are successful in their attacks on candidates and election systems because of weak security. The voting machines used by citizens to cast their votes have been shown to be woefully unsecure. The AVS WINVote voting machine, which was made by Advanced Voting Solutions, passed state voting systems standards and has been used in Virginia and (until recently) Pennsylvania and Mississippi. The security on these machines is shockingly lax. The devices used passwords of "admin," "abcde," and "shoup" to lock down its Windows administrator account, Wi-Fi network, and voting results database respectively (and because these passwords are hard-coded they cannot be changed). These voting machines also used the weak Wired Equivalent Privacy (WEP) to transmit results. Because WEP can easily be broken in a matter of minutes, attackers could easily view confidential ballots. And WINVote runs on a version of the Windows XP Embedded operating system that has not received any security updates since 2004. In addition, these tabulating machines had no firewalls and exposed several Internet ports to attackers.[1]

A growing fear is that as many states and nations move toward online voting, they may be sacrificing a time-honored right for citizens to cast a secret ballot. Thirty-two states and the District of Columbia now offer to all or some voters a form of Internet voting via email or an online portal, or the ability to submit a ballot via fax. Of these, 28 states require a voter casting a ballot over the Internet to waive his or her right to a secret ballot, while four of the states offering Internet voting do not give voters any warning regarding ballot secrecy. Interestingly, only one state has a statutory requirement that votes cast over the Internet remain secret as required by the state constitution. It is unclear if this level of privacy is being accomplished.[2]

As studied in Part 3 of this text, having a secure network is essential to a comprehensive information security posture. Yet attacks invariably make their way past network defenses. This means that protecting individual devices is also essential.

A *client* is a computing device that has software to enable it to send requests to servers. (A *host*, on the other hand, is any end device in a network.) In this chapter, you explore types of client devices and how to secure them. First, you look at basic client hardware and software security. You also explore using physical security to protect client devices. Finally, you learn how secure software applications are developed and deployed.

Client Security

 **Certification**

2.4 Given a scenario, analyze and interpret output from security technologies.

3.3 Given a scenario, implement secure systems design.

Securing the client involves using hardware system security, securing the operating system software running on the client, and protecting peripheral devices connected to the client.

Hardware System Security

Protecting client hardware involves using different tools. These include secure booting tools, a hardware root of trust, and preventing electromagnetic spying. It also includes securing the supply chain through which the hardware is manufactured and delivered.

Secure Booting

Computers are designed to be able to start when powered on without any external assistance from other devices. This process of a computer starting up by itself is called *booting up* or just *booting*.

> **Note** 📎
>
> Early cowboys and workhands were known for wearing tall boots that were tight-fitting. These boots had a tab or loop at the top of the boot through which a tool called a boot hook could be inserted to assist in pulling on the boot. In the mid-1800s the expression *pull yourself up by your own bootstraps* was used to describe an impossible task of lifting oneself off the ground by pulling on the bootstrap. The phrase later came to mean to improve your situation by your own efforts without any external help. It was eventually adopted to describe the computer startup process because these devices do not rely on external assistance on startup.

The booting process on early personal computers used firmware called the **BIOS (Basic Input/Output System)**. The BIOS was a chip that was integrated into the computer's motherboard. Upon startup, the BIOS software would awaken and test the various components of the computer to ensure that they were functioning properly (called the *POST* or *Power On Self Test*). It then referenced the *Master Boot Record* (*MBR*) that specified the computer's *partition table*, which instructed the BIOS where the computer's operating system could be located. Finally, the BIOS passed control over to the installed boot loader that launched the operating system. Booting using a BIOS is illustrated in Figure 9-1

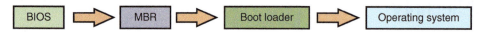

Figure 9-1   Booting using a BIOS

> **Note**
>
> Early Apple computers used what was called OpenFirmware instead of a BIOS but it performed a similar function.

Originally, BIOS firmware was stored in a *ROM (read-only memory)* chip on the motherboard, supplemented by a *CMOS (Complementary Metal-Oxide-Semiconductor)* chip that stored any changes to the BIOS. Later computer systems stored the BIOS contents in *flash memory* so it could be easily updated. This provided the ability to update to the BIOS firmware so new features could be added.

> **Note**
>
> Although BIOS chips were nonvolatile (they retained the information even when the computer was turned off), CMOS needed its own dedicated power source, which was a Lithium-ion battery about the size of a coin that could hold a charge for up to 10 years before needing to be replaced. If the CMOS battery died, the BIOS settings were not lost but instead were reset to their default settings.

However, the ability to update the BIOS with a firmware update also opened the door for a threat actor to create malware to infect the BIOS. Sometimes called a *BIOS attack*, this malware infects the BIOS with malicious code that persistently reinfects the computer whenever it boots.

> **Note**
>
> A BIOS attack does not take advantage of a vulnerability on the computer but exploits only the update feature of the BIOS.

To combat BIOS attacks and add functionality, a new mechanism was developed that replaces the BIOS with **UEFI (Unified Extensible Firmware Interface)**. In conjunction with UEFI, the **Secure Boot** security standard was also created. Secure Boot is designed to ensure that a computer boots using only software that is trusted by the computer manufacturer. When using UEFI and Secure Boot, as computer boots it checks the digital signature of each piece of boot software, including firmware drivers and the operating system. If the signatures are deemed valid the computer boots; otherwise, the computer does not boot.

Note 📎

Manufacturers can update the list of trusted hardware, drivers, and operating systems for a computer, which are stored in the Secure Boot database on the computer. Although it is possible for the user to disable Secure Book to install hardware or run software or operating systems that have not been trusted by the manufacturer, this makes it difficult or impossible to reactivate Secure Boot without restoring the computer back to its original factory state.

Hardware Root of Trust

As previously described, UEFI and Secure Boot ensure the integrity and security of the computer boot process by validating that each digitally signed element has not been modified. This process begins with the validation of the first element (boot software). Once the first element has been validated, it can then validate the next item (like software drivers) and so on until control has been handed over to the operating system. This is called a *chain of trust*: each element relies on the confirmation of the previous element to know that the entire process is secure.

But how does the chain begin? What if a threat actor were to inject malware prior to the start of the chain of trust? If the starting point is software, it can be replaced or modified. That would then compromise each element of the chain. To prevent this, a chain of trust requires a strong starting point.

The strongest starting point is hardware, which cannot be modified. This is known as the **hardware root of trust**. As with UEFI and Secure Boot, security checks are "rooted" in (begin with) hardware checks. Because this chain of trust begins with a hardware verification, each subsequent check can rely upon it.

Electromagnetic Spying

Computer systems, printers, and similar digital devices all emit electromagnetic fields. Security researchers have demonstrated that it is possible to pick up these electromagnetic fields and read the data that is producing them. This *electromagnetic spying*, once thought to be found only in fictional novels and movies, is a reality.

> **Note** 📎
>
> In one case, researchers placed a smartphone next to a computer and could extract the full 4096-bit RSA decryption keys from the computer. This was possible because of the variations in power consumption while the computer was working, electromagnetic noise, timing variations, and even contention for central processing unit (CPU) resources such as caches. The vibration of electronic components in the computer, sometimes heard as a faint high-pitched tone or hiss, is caused by voltage regulation circuits and can be correlated with what the CPU is doing and then captured by the phone. Because the processor changes its power draw according to the type of operation it performs, such as the decryption of ciphertexts, these changes were picked up and used to reveal 4096-bit RSA keys.[3]

The U.S. government has developed a classified standard intended to prevent attackers from picking up electromagnetic fields from government buildings. Known as *Telecommunications Electronics Material Protected from Emanating Spurious Transmissions*, or *TEMPEST*, the exact details are a secret. What is known is that TEMPEST technologies are intended to "reduce the conducted and radiated emissions from within the sensitive environment to an undetectable level outside the shielded enclosure in uncontrolled areas."[4] TEMPEST uses special protective coatings on network cables and additional shielding in buildings.

Supply Chain Infections

A **supply chain** is a network that moves a product from the supplier to the customer. It is made up of vendors that supply raw material, manufacturers who convert the material into products, warehouses that store products, distribution centers that deliver them to the retailers, and retailers who bring the product to the consumer. Today, supply chains are global in scope: manufacturers are usually thousands of miles away overseas and not under the direct supervision of the enterprise that is selling the product.

The fact that products move through many different steps in the supply chain—and that many of these steps are not closely supervised—has opened the door for malware to be injected into products during their manufacturing or storage (called *supply chain infections*). Although personal computers have not seen widespread supply chain infections, other technology devices have been infected. One of the first widespread instances of supply chain infections occurred in 2008 when it was discovered that digital photo frames were infected with a computer virus, which could be spread to the user's computer through a USB flash drive that was inserted into the photo frame to transfer photos. This resulted in a major electronics retailer removing all such frames from their stores. More recently, smartphones using the Android operating system have been the victims of supply chain infections.

Supply chain infections are considered especially dangerous. First, if the malware is planted in the ROM firmware of the device, it can be difficult or sometimes impossible to clean an infected device. Second, users are receiving infected devices at the point of purchase and are completely unaware that a brand new device may be infected. Finally, because it is virtually impossible to closely monitor every step in the supply chain, these infections cannot be easily prevented.

Securing the Operating System Software

There are several different types and uses of operating systems (OSs). Several of the major types are listed in Table 9-1.

Table 9-1 Types of OSs

OS type	Uses	Examples
Network OS	Software that runs on a network device like a firewall, router, or switch	Cisco Internetwork Operating System (IOS), Juniper JUNOS, MikroTik RouterOS
Server OS	Operating system software that runs on a network server to provide resources to network users	Microsoft Windows Server, Apple macOS Server, Red Hat Linux
Workstation OS	Software that manages hardware and software on a client computer	Microsoft Windows, Apple macOS, Ubuntu Linux
Appliance OS	OS in firmware that is designed to manage a specific device like a digital video recorder or video game console	Linpus Linux

(continues)

Table 9-1 (*continued*)

OS type	Uses	Examples
Kiosk OS	System and user interface software for an interactive kiosk	Microsoft Windows, Google Chrome OS, Apple iOS, Instant WebKiosk, KioWare (Android)
Mobile OS	Operating system for mobile phones, smartphones, tablets, and other handheld devices	Google Android, Apple iOS, Microsoft Windows Mobile

Although protections within the OS are designed to provide security, the OS itself must be protected. Securing an OS involves proper configuration, implementing patch management, and using antimalware software. In addition, a secure OS known as a trusted OS can be used in specific settings.

OS Security Configuration

The security of an OS depends upon the proper configuration of its built-in security features. Modern operating systems have hundreds of different security settings that can be configured. A typical OS security configuration should include:

- *Disabling unnecessary ports and services.* One of the primary OS security configurations involves **disabling unnecessary ports and services**, or "turning off" any service that is not being used, such as Microsoft Windows ASP.NET State Service, Portable Device Enumerator Service, and Apple macOS Spotlight Indexing. In addition, closing any unnecessary TCP ports can also enhance security.

- *Disabling default accounts/passwords.* Another important disabling function is **disabling default accounts/passwords**. Some OSs include unnecessary accounts. For example, Microsoft Windows 10 includes a *built-in Administrator account* that can be used for those building new computers to run programs and applications before a user account is created. In addition, some accounts may come with default passwords that should be changed.

- *Employing least functionality.* The concept of **least functionality** states a user should only be given the minimum set of permissions required to perform necessary tasks; all other permissions should be configured as not available to the user. For example, a user should not have the ability to modify system security features such as turning off the host firewall.

- *Application whitelisting/blacklisting.* An increasingly popular approach to client OS security is to employ **application whitelisting/blacklisting**. *Whitelisting* is approving in advance only specific applications to run on the OS so that any item not approved is either restricted or denied ("default-deny"). The inverse of whitelisting is *blacklisting*, creating a list of unapproved software so that any item not on the list of blacklisted applications can run ("default-allow").

Note 📎

The elite Tailored Access Operations (TAO) section of the National Security Agency (NSA) is responsible for compromising networks owned by hostile nations to spy on them. Recently, the head of the TAO spoke at a security conference about the best practices of security from the NSA's perspective (in his own words, "what can you do to defend yourself to make my life hard?"). One of the most important steps was to employ whitelisting for the software that runs on servers. A similar step is to whitelist a predefined set of websites to which users can connect to prevent malware from accessing a command and control structure or to send off stolen information.[6]

Instead of recreating the same security configuration on each computer, tools can be used to automate the process. In Microsoft Windows, a *security template* is a collection of security configuration settings. These settings typically include account policies, user rights, event log settings, restricted groups, system services, file permissions, and registry permissions. Once a single host has been configured properly, a security template from that host can be developed and used for deploying to other systems. Predefined security templates are also available to be imported, and these settings then can be modified to create a unique security configuration for all clients.

Note 📎

Although a Microsoft Windows security template can be deployed manually, this requires an administrator to access each computer and apply the security template either through using the command line or through using a *snap-in*, which is a software module that provides administrative capabilities. A preferred method is to use *Group Policy*, which is a feature that provides centralized management and configuration of computers and remote users who are using specific Microsoft directory services known as *Active Directory (AD)*. Group Policy allows a single configuration to be set and then deployed to many or all users. Group Policy is discussed in Chapter 12.

Patch Management

Early operating systems were simply program loaders whose job was to launch applications. As more features and graphical user interfaces (GUIs) were added, OSs became more complex. And as they became more complex, unintentional vulnerabilities were introduced that could be exploited by attackers. In addition, new attack tools made what were once considered secure functions and services on operating systems now vulnerable.

> **Note**
>
> Microsoft's first operating system, MS-DOS v1.0, had 4000 lines of code, while Windows 10 is estimated to have up to 50 million lines.

To address the vulnerabilities in operating systems that are uncovered after the software has been released, software vendors usually deploy a software "fix." A fix can come in a variety of formats. A security **patch** is a publicly released software security update intended to repair a vulnerability. A *feature update* includes enhancements to the software to provide new or expanded functionality, but do not address security vulnerability. A *service pack* is software that is a cumulative package of all patches and feature updates.

> **Note**
>
> For over 20 years Microsoft released service bulletins that described the patches distributed for a group of software products, such as all the supported versions of Windows. These bulletins included a severity rating system that rated the impact of the vulnerability that the patch is fixing (Critical, Important, Moderate, or Low) and an Exploitability Index, which is the likelihood of an attack based on the vulnerability. In early 2017, Microsoft stopped distributing these service bulletins and instead made the information available in a searchable online database.

Effective patch management involves two types of **patch management tools** to manage patches. The first type includes tools for patch distribution, while the second type involves patch reception.

Patch Distribution

Modern operating systems, such as Red Hat Linux, Apple macOS, Ubuntu Linux, and Microsoft Windows, frequently distribute patches. These patches, however, can sometimes create new problems, such as preventing a custom application from running correctly. Organizations that have these types of applications usually test patches when they are released to ensure that they do not adversely affect any customized applications. In these instances, the organization delays the installation of a patch from the vendor's online update service until the patch is thoroughly tested. But how can an organization prevent its employees from installing the latest patch until it has passed testing, and still ensure that all users download and install necessary patches?

The answer is an *automated patch update service*. This service is used to manage patches within the enterprise instead of relying upon the vendor's online update service. An automated patch update service typically consists of a component installed on one or more servers inside the corporate network. Because these servers can replicate information among themselves, usually only one of the servers must be connected to the vendor's online update service, as seen in Figure 9-2.

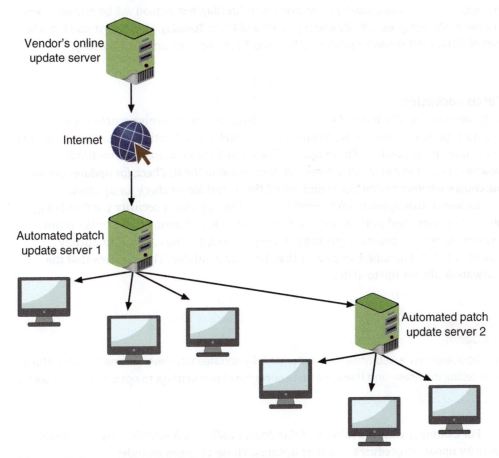

Figure 9-2   Automated patch update service

There are several advantages to an automated patch update service, including:

- Downloading patches from a local server instead of using the vendor's online update service can save bandwidth and time because each computer does not have to connect to an external server.
- Administrators can approve or decline updates for client systems, force updates to install by a specific date, and obtain reports on what updates each computer needs.
- Administrators can approve updates for "detection" only; this allows them to see which computers require the update without installing it.

Note 📎

For several years, Microsoft delivered security patches only on the second Tuesday of the month, known as *Patch Tuesday*. Beginning with Windows 10, Microsoft announced that it will no longer be distributing patches solely on Patch Tuesday, but instead will be pushing them out more frequently, essentially ending the idea of Patch Tuesday. However, through the first part of 2017, most security updates to Windows 10 still occured on Patch Tuesday.

Patch Reception

Early versions of OSs allowed users, to configure how they receive patches. For example, prior to Windows 10, Microsoft users had several options regarding accepting or even rejecting patches. These options included *Install updates automatically*, *Download updates but let me choose whether to install them*, *Check for updates but let me choose whether to download and install them*, and *Never check for updates*.

However, this approach frequently resulted in important security patches being ignored by users and putting their computers at risk. A growing trend today is not to offer users *any* options regarding patches; instead, patches are automatically downloaded and installed whenever they become available. This ensures that the software is always up-to-date.

Note 📎

The Google Chrome web browser is automatically updated whenever it is necessary without even telling the user—and there are no user configuration settings to opt out of the updates.

For example, with the release of Windows 10 Microsoft significantly changed its security update procedures and user options. These changes include:

- *Forced updates*. Users cannot refuse or delay security updates. All updates are downloaded and installed automatically. Windows 10 Home edition users also automatically receive feature updates, although Windows 10 Professional edition users can postpone feature updates for several months.
- *No selective updates*. Unlike in previous versions of Windows, users cannot select individual Windows updates to download and install. However, users can select if they wish to receive updates for other installed Microsoft products (such as Office).
- *More efficient distribution*. If there are multiple Windows 10 devices connected to a network, then each device does not have to download the updates over the Internet individually. Instead, once one device has downloaded the updates these can then be distributed to the other devices across the local network.

In addition, Windows will not download updates on mobile devices unless that device is connected to an unrestricted Wi-Fi network (so that it does not use the cellular data connections that users pay for).

- *Up-to-date resets.* With previous versions of Microsoft Windows, if a computer needed to be reset to its original configuration then all the subsequent patches had to be reinstalled, a process that often would take hours of time and require the user to be at the computer to manage multiple reboots. With Windows 10, a "PC Reset" will install the current up-to-date Windows software.

The patch update options for Microsoft Windows 10 are seen in Figure 9-3.

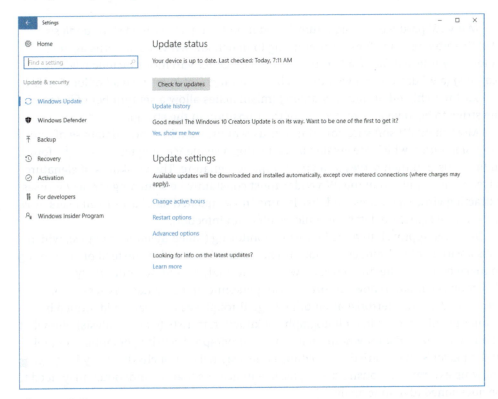

Figure 9-3   Windows 10 update options

Antimalware

Malware can infect both user files as well as OS files. Antimalware software can help protect against these infections. Antimalware includes antivirus, antispam, and antispyware.

Antivirus

One of the first antimalware software security applications was **antivirus (AV)** software. This software can examine a computer for any infections as well as monitor computer activity and scan new documents that might contain a virus (this scanning is typically performed when files are opened, created, or closed). If a virus is detected, options generally include cleaning the file of the virus, quarantining the infected file, or deleting the file. Log files created by AV products can also provide beneficial information regarding attacks.

Note

Viruses are covered in Chapter 2.

Many AV products use signature-based monitoring, also called *static analysis*. The AV software scans files by attempting to match known virus patterns against potentially infected files (called *string scanning*). Other variations include *wildcard scanning* (a wildcard is allowed to skip bytes or ranges of bytes instead of looking for an exact match) and *mismatch scanning* (mismatches allow a set number of bytes in the string to be any value regardless of their position in the string).

Most client AV software contains a virus scanning engine and a database of known virus *signatures*, which are created by extracting a sequence of bytes—a string—found in the virus that then serves as a virus's unique signature. The weakness of signature-based monitoring is that the AV vendor must constantly be searching for new viruses, extracting virus signatures, and distributing those updated databases to all users. Any out-of-date signature database could result in an infection.

A newer approach to AV is heuristic monitoring (called *dynamic analysis*), which uses a variety of techniques to spot the characteristics of a virus instead of attempting to make matches. The difference between static analysis and dynamic analysis detection is similar to how airport security personnel in some nations screen for terrorists. A known terrorist attempting to go through security can be identified by comparing his face against photographs of known terrorists (static analysis). But what about a new terrorist for whom there is no photograph? Security personnel can look at the person's characteristics—holding a one-way ticket, not checking any luggage, showing extreme nervousness—as possible indicators that the individual may need to be questioned (dynamic analysis).

One AV heuristic monitoring technique used is *code emulation* in which a virtual environment is created that simulates the CPU and memory of the computer. Any questionable program code is executed in the virtual environment (no actual virus code is executed by the real CPU) to determine if it is a virus.

Note

Signature-based monitoring and heuristic monitoring are covered in Chapter 6.

Antispam

A *mail gateway* monitors emails for spam and other unwanted content to prevent these messages from being delivered. However, some spam can still slip through. Users can install antispam filtering software on their client computers or configure their local email client (*Microsoft Outlook*) or webmail client (*Gmail.com*) to trap spam.

> **Note**
>
> Spam is covered in Chapter 2 and mail gateways are covered in Chapter 6.

There are different methods for filtering spam on the local email client or web browser client. Many email and webmail clients automatically block potentially dangerous types of file attachments, such as *.exe*, *.bat*, *.vbs*, and *.com*. Users can also create blacklists or whitelists of approved or nonapproved senders, and email can be filtered by region or country.

Another technique is *Bayesian filtering*. The software divides email messages that have been received into two piles, spam and nonspam. The filter then analyzes every word in each email and determines how frequently a word occurs in the spam pile compared to the not-spam pile. A word such as "the" would occur equally in both piles and be given a neutral 50 percent ranking. A word such as "report" may occur frequently in nonspam messages and would receive a 99 percent probability of being a nonspam word, while a word like "sex" may receive a 99 percent probability of being a spam word. Whenever email arrives, the filter looks for the 15 words with the highest probabilities to calculate the message's overall spam probability rating.

> **Note**
>
> Bayesian filters generally trap a much higher percentage of spam than other techniques.

Antispyware

A package known as *antispyware* helps prevent computers from becoming infected by different types of spyware. One common type of antispyware is a *popup blocker*. A *popup* is a small web browser window that appears over a webpage, and most popup windows are created by advertisers and launch as soon as a new website is visited. Using a popup blocker, users can often select the level of blocking, ranging from blocking all popups to allowing specific popups. A popup blocker can be part of an antispyware package, a separate program, or a feature incorporated within a browser that stops popup advertisements from appearing.

Trusted OS

Instead of managing the different security options on an operating system that has been deployed, in some cases it is necessary to tighten security during the design and coding of the OS. This is called *OS hardening*. An operating system that has been designed in this way to be secure is a **trusted OS**. Some of the changes performed through OS hardening to create a trusted OS are listed in Table 9-2.

Table 9-2 Trusted OS hardening techniques

Trusted OS hardening technique	Explanation
Least privilege	Remove all *supervisor* or *administrator* accounts that can bypass security settings and instead split privileges into smaller units to provide the least-privileged unit to a user or process.
Reduce capabilities	Significantly restrict what resources can be accessed and by whom.
Read-only file system	Important operating system files cannot be changed.
Kernel pruning	Remove all unnecessary features that may compromise an operating system.

Peripheral Device Security

Peripheral devices that attached to a client computer must likewise be protected. This includes protection *from* the computer (so that an infected computer does not then infect a peripheral) as well as protection *to* the computer (so that an infected peripheral does not infect the computer). The types of peripheral devices to be secured include devices using Secure Digital Input Output Cards, digital cameras, external storage devices, multifunctional devices, and displays.

Secure Digital Input Output (SDIO) Cards

One type of peripheral that needs to be secured is removable storage for mobile devices. Mobile devices use *flash memory* for storage, which is nonvolatile solid state electronic storage that can be electrically erased and reused. All mobile devices have local nonremovable storage capabilities, and most devices also support removable data storage.

> **Note** 🔗
>
> Some larger laptop computers can accommodate credit card–sized peripheral storage devices that slide into a slot. The original cards were called PC Cards, and later an enhanced type of PC Card was introduced called the CardBus. Today PC Card and CardBus devices are being replaced by ExpressCard technology designed to deliver higher-performance modular expansion in a smaller size. There are two standard ExpressCard form factors: the ExpressCard/34 module (34 mm × 75 mm) and the ExpressCard/54 module (54 mm × 75 mm). Both formats are 5 mm thick.

One popular type of removable data storage is a **Secure Digital (SD)** card. The SD format includes three different form factors of four card "families" available in three different categories of speed ratings. Currently there are three form factors of SD cards: *full SD, miniSD*, and **microSD**. Full SD memory cards are typically used in large consumer electronics devices. The microSD and miniSD cards are commonly used in smaller electronic devices like smartphones, digital cameras, and tablets. A microSD card is illustrated in Figure 9-4.

Figure 9-4   microSD card

ExaMedia Photography/Shutterstock.com

The four families of SD cards are Standard-Capacity (SDSC), High-Capacity (SDHC), eXtended-Capacity (SDXC), and *Secure Digital Input Output* (*SDIO*). SDIO is an SD storage card with integrated wireless transmission capabilities, using Bluetooth or Wi-Fi technology. One popular SDIO device is a **Wi-Fi enabled microSD card** for devices like digital cameras. Once inserted into a digital camera, the SDIO card can wirelessly transmit pictures across the network to a mobile device, laptop, or wireless printer. The security for an SDIO card is the same as for securing a standard Wi-Fi network.

> **Note** 📎
>
> A variation of the SDIO card is an *iSDIO* card that uses TransferJet wireless technology, which is similar to the near field communication (NFC) standard.

Digital Cameras

A **digital camera** uses internal storage and external SD cards to record photographs and capture video. SD speed classes were designed to support video recording. There are three types of speed classes: standard speed class, ultra-high speed (UHS) class, and video speed class.

Note

Video speed class V90 has a minimum sequential write speed of 90 megabits per second (Mbps) and can record 8K video at a frame rate of 120 frames per second.

Protecting data on SD cards can be accomplished by password-protecting the card, using encryption, or write-protecting the card by moving a small external switch to the *Open* position.

External Storage Devices

External storage devices need to be protected, and are increasingly at risk for infection by crypto-malware. Instead of encrypting files on the local hard drive only, crypto-malware encrypts all files on any network or attached device that is connected to that computer. This includes secondary hard disk drives, USB hard drives, network-attached storage devices, network servers, and even cloud-based data repositories like Dropbox, Apple iCloud, and Microsoft OneDrive. Because many users have their computers configured so that files that are dropped into a folder are automatically "synchronized" (copied) to their online data repository, crypto-malware could potentially encrypt and hold hostage all files on the cloud-based data repository.

Note

There are two tests that can be applied to determine if other files (not those stored on the local hard drive) are at risk from crypto-malware. First, if a remote storage device is "mounted" on the local computer and displays a drive letter (like "D:") then those files are at risk. Second, if a cloud storage repository is configured so that files that are automatically placed in a folder are then synced to cloud storage, they too are at risk.

Table 9-3 describes protections for external storage peripherals.

Table 9-3 Protections for external storage peripherals

Device	Recommended protection
External USB or e-SATA storage device	Unplug the device from the computer when not in use and attach it when needed.
Secondary hard disk drive	Unmount the drive when it is not needed by using the *mountvol D: /p* command (where *D* is the drive letter of the mounted drive) or Windows Disk Management utility, and then mount the drive when necessary.

(continues)

Table 9-3 (*continued*)

Device	Recommended protection
Network-attached storage device	Create a new folder and then create a new user account with a strong password that is the only account that has access to it, and log in and out of that, share as needed.
Cloud storage	Turn off automatic synchronization so that files placed in a folder are not immediately synced to the cloud storage; instead, log into the cloud storage provider through a web browser that requires a user name and password to sync files.

Note

If turning off automatic synchronization for cloud storage is not feasible, another option is to take advantage of the short-term "versioning" that many cloud storage providers offer. Older versions of files are retained online for a limited period, such as seven days but sometimes up to a month. If cloud storage files become encrypted they can be rolled back to a previous version of unencrypted files.

Multifunctional Devices

A **multifunctional device (MFD)** combines the functions of a printer, copier, scanner, and fax machine. Although MFDs are often overlooked as requiring protection, these peripheral devices are essentially special-purpose computers with a CPU, a hard drive that stores all received print jobs, faxes, and scanned images, a LAN or wireless LAN connection, a telephone connection for faxes, and a USB port to allow users to print documents stored on that device. *Smart MFDs* even have an OS that allows additional applications to be installed that extend the abilities of the MFD. Not only can an unprotected MFD expose sensitive stored documents on the hard drive to theft, it can also be used to spread malware through the network to all connected client devices.

Note

MFD attacks can also be more "creative" then regular attacks. For example, a threat actor can dial in to the MFD fax and then bridge across to the hard drive to upload malware that can capture all stored images.

Recommended protections for MFDs include:

- Locate the MFD in a secure area, particularly when using a shared office space.
- Configure the MFD with security in mind by changing any default passwords, turning on hard drive encryption, requiring that all stored images be purged

after a short period of time, and setting the device to receive the latest security patches.

- Separate the MFD print server from the network server to protect traffic from interception and to limit and control what traffic is going over that part of the network.
- Link the print management software to existing data loss prevention (DLP) protection.
- Minimize the risk of paper-based thefts by using Secure Job Release, a function that locks print jobs in a queue on the device until the user enters a valid code on the device to initiate printing.
- Make use of semi-visible watermark technology to help classify sensitive documents and highlight what is vulnerable.
- When the MFD is traded, transferred, or retired, the internal hard drive should be wiped, removed, or destroyed.

Displays

Computer displays are often considered "passive" peripherals: a computer sends data to the display that is then projected as words and pictures. However, security researchers have demonstrated that a threat actor can target a display's firmware, which controls the menu to change brightness and other display settings. This could enable an attacker to view what is being projected on the display or even display her own message on the monitor.

Note

In one scenario, an attacker could infect a monitor displaying controls for a nuclear power plant and then display a fictitious emergency message on the screen.

Physical Security

Certification

3.9 Explain the importance of physical security controls.

An often overlooked consideration when protecting a client device is physical security. Preventing a threat actor from physically accessing the device is as important as preventing the attacker from accessing it remotely through a network. Physical security includes external perimeter defenses, internal physical access security, and security for protecting the hardware device itself.

External Perimeter Defenses

External perimeter defenses are designed to restrict access to the areas in which equipment is located. This type of defense includes barriers, security guards, and motion detection devices.

Barriers

Different types of passive barriers can be used to restrict unwanted individuals or vehicles from entering a secure area. **Fencing** is usually a tall, permanent structure to keep out individuals for maintaining security. Most fencing is accompanied with a **sign** that explains the area is restricted and proper **lighting** so the area can be viewed after dark. A **cage** is a fenced secure waiting station area, such as an area that can contain visitors to a facility until they can be approved for entry.

Standard chain link fencing offers limited security because it can easily be circumvented by climbing over it or cutting the links. Most modern perimeter security consists of a fence equipped with other deterrents such as those listed in Table 9-4.

Table 9-4   Fencing deterrents

Technology	Description	Comments
Anticlimb paint	A nontoxic petroleum gel-based paint that is thickly applied and does not harden, making any coated surface very difficult to climb	Typically used on poles, downpipes, wall tops, and railings above head height (8 feet or 2.4 meters)
Anticlimb collar	Spiked collar that extends horizontally for up to 3 feet (1 meter) from the pole to prevent anyone from climbing it; serves as both a practical and visual deterrent	Used for protecting equipment mounted on poles like cameras or in areas where climbing a pole can be an easy point of access over a security fence
Roller barrier	Independently rotating large cups (diameter of 5 inches or 115 millimeters) affixed to the top of a fence prevents the hands of intruders from gripping the top of a fence to climb over it	Often found around public grounds and schools where a nonaggressive barrier is important
Rotating spikes	Installed at the top of walls, gates or fences; the tri-wing spike collars rotate around a central spindle	Designed for high-security areas; can be painted to blend into fencing

Like fencing, a **barricade** is generally designed to block the passage of traffic. However, barricades are most often used for directing large crowds and are generally not designed to keep out individuals. This is because barricades are usually not as tall as fences and can more easily be circumvented by climbing over them. A **bollard** is a short but sturdy vertical post that is used to as a vehicular traffic barricade to prevent a car from "ramming" into a secured area. A pair of bollards is pictured in Figure 9-5.

Figure 9-5 Bollards

MartineDF/Shutterstock.com

Security Guards

Whereas barriers act as passive devices to restrict access, human **security guards** are considered active security elements. Unlike passive devices, a guard can differentiate between an intruder and someone looking for a lost pet. Guards can also make split-second decisions about when it is necessary to take appropriate action.

Some guards are responsible for monitoring activity that is captured by a video camera. **Video surveillance cameras** transmit a signal to a specific and limited set of receivers called *closed circuit television (CCTV)*. CCTV is frequently used for surveillance in areas that require security monitoring such as banks, casinos, airports, and military installations. Some CCTV cameras are fixed in a single position pointed at a door or a hallway. Other cameras resemble a small dome and allow guards to move the camera 360 degrees for a full panoramic view. High-end video surveillance cameras are motion-tracking and automatically follow any movement.

Note 📎

When guards actively monitor a CCTV, it is a preventive measure: any unauthorized activity seen on video surveillance results in the guard taking immediate action by either going to the scene or calling for assistance. When a guard does not actively monitor a CCTV, the video is recorded and, if a security event occurs, the recording is examined later to identify the culprit.

Motion Detection

Motion detection is determining an object's change in position in relation to its surroundings. That is, someone or something has moved in an area in which other objects are still. This movement usually generates an audible **alarm** to warn a guard of an intruder. Motion detection can be performed using the different methods listed in Table 9-5.

Table 9-5	Motion detection methods
Method	**Example**
Visual	CCTV
Radio frequency	Radar, microwave
Vibration	Seismic sensors
Sound	Microphones
Magnetism	Magnetic sensors
Infrared	Passive and active infrared light sensors

Internal Physical Access Security

External perimeter defenses are designed to keep an intruder from entering a campus, building, or other area. In the event that unauthorized personnel defeat external perimeter defenses, they will then face internal physical access security, which is focused on the interior of the area. These protections might be as simple as a **screen filter** that "blacks out" viewers outside the normal direct viewing angle or sophisticated waiting areas for unauthorized visitors. Internal physical access security includes door locks, access logs, mantraps, and protected distribution systems for cabling.

Door Locks

Door locks that require a key or other device to open doors in residences generally fall into four categories. These categories are keyed entry locks (use a key to open the lock from the outside), privacy locks (lock the door but have access to unlock it from the outside via a small hole; typically used on bedroom and bathroom doors), patio locks (lock the door from the inside, but it cannot be unlocked from the outside), and passage locks (latch a door closed yet do not lock; typically used on hall and closet doors).

The standard keyed entry lock, shown in Figure 9-6, is the most common type of door lock for keeping out intruders, but its security is minimal. Because it does not automatically lock when the door is closed, a user may mistakenly think she is locking a door by closing it when she is not. Also, a thin piece of plastic such as a credit card can sometimes be wedged between the lock and the door casing to open it; or the knob itself can be broken off with a sharp blow, such as by a hammer, and then the door can be opened.

Note

Growing in popularity are locks that use Bluetooth or NFC on a smartphone to open the door.

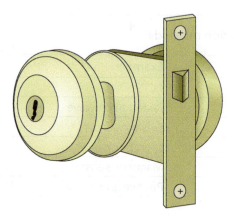

Figure 9-6   Residential keyed entry lock

Door locks in commercial buildings are typically different from residential door locks. For rooms that require enhanced security, a lever coupled with a **deadbolt lock** is common. This lock extends a solid metal bar into the door frame for extra security as shown in Figure 9-7. Deadbolt locks are much more difficult to defeat than keyed entry locks. The lock cannot be broken from the outside like a preset lock, and the extension of the bar prevents a credit card from being inserted to "jimmy" it open. Deadbolt locks also require that a key be used to both open and lock the door.

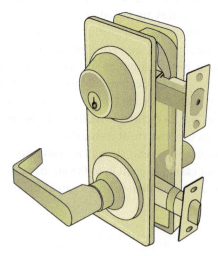

Figure 9-7   Deadbolt lock

> **Note** 📎
>
> The categories of commercial door locks include storeroom (the outside is always locked, entry is by key only, and the inside lever is always unlocked), classroom (the outside can be locked or unlocked, and the inside lever is always unlocked), store entry double cylinder (includes a keyed cylinder in both the outside and inside knobs so that a key in either knob locks or unlocks both at the same time), and communicating double cylinder lock (includes a keyed cylinder in both outside and inside knobs, and the key unlocks its own knob independently).

Any residential or commercial door locks that use keys can be compromised if the keys are lost, stolen, or duplicated. To achieve the best security when using keyed door locks, the following **key management** procedures to regulate the distribution of keys are recommended:

- Keep track of keys issued, to whom, and the date; and require users to sign their name when receiving keys.
- Receive the proper approvals of supervisors or other appropriate persons before issuing keys.
- When making duplicates of master keys, mark them "Do Not Duplicate," and wipe out the manufacturer's serial numbers to keep duplicates from being ordered.
- Secure unused keys in a locked safe.
- Change locks immediately upon loss or theft of keys.

Because of the difficulties in managing keys for large numbers of users, an alternative to a key lock is a more sophisticated door access system using a *cipher lock* as shown in Figure 9-8. Cipher locks are combination locks that use buttons that must be pushed in the proper sequence to open the door.

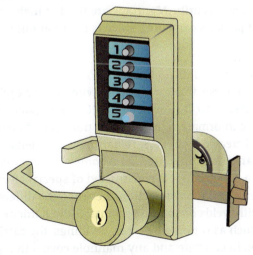

Figure 9-8   Cipher lock

Access Logs

An **access log** is a record or list of individuals who have permission to enter a secure area, along with the time they entered and the time they left the area. Having a record of individuals who were near a suspicious activity can be valuable. In addition, an access list can also identify whether unauthorized personnel have attempted to access a secure area. Access logs were originally paper documents that users had to sign when entering and leaving a secure area. Today cipher locks and other technology can create electronic access logs.

Mantraps

Before electronic security was available, vestibules with two locked doors were used to control access to sensitive areas. Individuals would give their credentials to a security officer, who would then open the first door to a small room (a vestibule) and ask the individuals to enter and wait while their credentials were being checked. If the credentials were approved, the second door would be unlocked; if the credentials were fraudulent, the person would be trapped in the vestibule (a *mantrap*).

A modern **mantrap** is designed to separate a nonsecured area from a secured area. A mantrap device monitors and controls two interlocking doors to a vestibule, as shown in Figure 9-9. When in operation, only one door can be open at any time. By creating a physical *air gap*, or the absence of any type of connection between the areas, this can improve security. Mantraps are used at high-security areas where only authorized persons can enter, such as cash handling areas and research laboratories.

Protected Distribution Systems (PDS)

Cable conduits are hollow tubes that carry copper wire or fiber-optic cables, as shown in Figure 9-10. A **protected distribution system (PDS)** is a system of cable conduits used to protect classified information that is being transmitted between two secure areas. PDS is a standard created by the U.S. Department of Defense (DOD).

Two types of PDS are commonly used. In a *hardened carrier PDS*, the data cables are installed in a conduit that is constructed of special electrical metallic tubing or similar material. All the connections between the different segments are permanently sealed with welds or special sealants. If the hardened carrier PDS is buried underground, such as running between buildings, the carrier containing the cables must be encased in concrete and any manhole covers that give access to the PDS must be locked down. A hardened carrier PDS must be visually inspected on a regular basis.

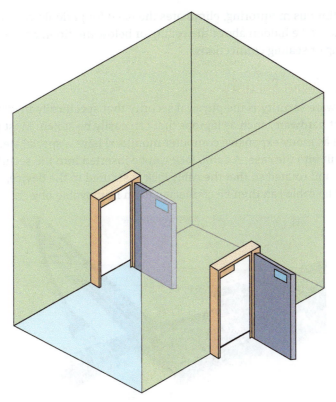

Figure 9-9   Mantrap

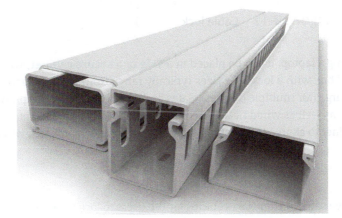

Figure 9-10   Cable conduits
Peter Sobolev/Shutterstock.com

An alternative to a hardened carrier PDS is an *alarmed carrier PDS*. In this type of PDS, the carrier system is deployed with specialized optical fibers in the conduit that can sense acoustic vibrations that occur when an intruder attempts to gain access to the cables, which triggers an alarm. The advantages of an alarmed carrier PDS are that it provides continuous monitoring, eliminates the need for periodic visual inspections, allows the carrier to be hidden above the ceiling or below the floor, and eliminates the need for welding or sealing connections.

Computer Hardware Security

Computer hardware security is the physical security that specifically involves protecting client hardware, such as laptops that can easily be stolen. Most portable devices (as well as many expensive computer monitors) have a special steel bracket security slot built into the case. A **cable lock** can be inserted into the security slot of a portable device and rotated so that the cable lock is secured to the device, as illustrated in Figure 9-11. The cable can then be connected to an immovable object.

Figure 9-11   Cable lock

O.Bellini/Shutterstock.com

When storing a laptop, it can be placed in a **safe** or a **secure cabinet**, which is a ruggedized steel box with a lock. The sizes typically range from small (to accommodate one laptop) to large (for multiple devices). Safes and cabinets also can be prewired for electrical power as well as wired network connections. This allows the laptops stored in the locking cabinet to charge their batteries and receive software updates while not in use.

 Note

Some offices have safes in employee cubicles for the users to lock up important papers when away from their desks, even for a short period of time.

Application Security

Certification

1.6 Explain the impact associated with types of vulnerabilities.

3.4 Explain the importance of secure staging deployment concepts.

3.6 Summarize secure application development and deployment concepts.

Along with securing the client through hardware system security, operating system security, and peripheral device security, as well as protecting it through physical security, it is also important that the applications that run on the client devices are secure. An unsecure application can open the door for attackers to exploit the application, the data that it uses, and even the underlying OS. Table 9-6 lists different attacks that can be launched using vulnerabilities in applications.

Table 9-6   **Attacks based on application vulnerabilities**

Attack	Description	Defense
Executable files attack	Trick the vulnerable application into modifying or creating executable files on the system.	Prevent the application from creating or modifying executable files for its proper function.
System tampering	Use the vulnerable application to modify special sensitive areas of the operating system (Microsoft Windows registry keys, system startup files, etc.) and take advantage of those modifications.	Do not allow applications to modify special areas of the OS.
Process spawning control	Trick the vulnerable application into spawning executable files on the system.	Take away the process spawning ability from the application.

The cause of unsecure applications is usually the result of how the application was designed and written. Some of the most dangerous weaknesses in an application due to poor coding can create vulnerabilities in computer memory or buffer areas that can be easily exploited. These vulnerabilities are summarized in Table 9-7.

Table 9-7 Memory vulnerabilities

Vulnerability	Description	How exploited
Buffer overflow	A process attempts to store data in RAM beyond the boundaries of a fixed-length storage buffer.	Attacker can overflow the buffer with a new address pointing to the attacker's malware code.
Integer overflow	The result of an arithmetic operation like addition or multiplication exceeds the maximum size of the integer type used to store it.	When tallying the number of items sold, it could result in a negative value and a resulting negative total cost, indicating that a refund is due the customer.
Memory leak	An application dynamically allocates memory but does not free that memory when finished using it.	Attacker can take advantage of unexpected program behavior resulting from a low memory condition.
Pointer deference	A pointer with a value of NULL is used as if it pointed to a valid memory area.	Launching the program by an attacker can cause the process to crash, resulting in loss of data.
DLL injection	Inserting code into a running process through a Dynamic Link Library (DLL).	Attacker can use DLL injection vulnerability to cause a program to function in a different way than intended.

Note *Buffer overflow and integer overflow attacks are covered in Chapter 5.*

Poor coding techniques can create vulnerabilities in applications that threat actors can then exploit. Application security includes understanding application vulnerabilities, application development concepts, secure coding techniques, and code testing.

Application Development Concepts

Developing an application requires several different stages. These stages include:

- *Development*. At the **development stage** the requirements for the application are established and it is confirmed that the application meets the intended business needs before the actual coding begins.
- *Testing*. The **testing stage** thoroughly tests the application for any errors that could result in a security vulnerability.
- *Staging*. The **staging stage** is a "quality assurance" test to verify that the code functions as intended.
- *Production*. In the **production stage** the application is released to be used in its actual setting.

An **application development lifecycle model** is a conceptual model that describes the different stages involved in creating an application. There are two major application development lifecycle models. The **waterfall model** uses a sequential design process: as each stage is fully completed the developers then move on to the next stage. This means that once a stage is finished, developers cannot go back to a previous stage without starting all over again. This demands extensive planning in the very beginning and requires that it be followed carefully.

The **agile model** was designed to overcome the disadvantages of the waterfall model. Instead of following a rigid sequential design process, the agile model follows an incremental approach. Developers might start with a simplistic project design and begin to work on small modules. The work on these modules is done in short (weekly or monthly) "sprints," and at the end of each sprint, the project's priorities are again evaluated as tests are being run. This approach allows for software issues to be incrementally discovered so that feedback and changes can be incorporated into the design before the next sprint is started.

One specific type of software methodology that follows the agile model and heavily incorporates security concepts is called **Secure DevOps**. The DevOps methodology includes **security automation** (tools that test for vulnerabilities), **continuous integration** (ensuring that security features are incorporated at each stage), **immutable systems** (once a value or configuration is employed as part of an application, it is not modified; if changes are necessary, a new system must be created), **infrastructure as code** (managing a hardware and software infrastructure using the same principles as developing computer code), and **baselining** (creating a starting point for comparison purposes in order to apply targets and goals to measure success).

Another concept regarding application development involves how the completed application will be used in the context of the larger IT footprint of the enterprise. **Provisioning** is the enterprise-wide configuration, deployment, and management of multiple types of IT system resources, of which the new application would be viewed as a new resource. **Deprovisioning** in application development is removing a resource that is no longer needed.

Because DevOps is based on the agile method there will be continuous modifications throughout the process. With these continual changes, it is important to use tools that support **change management**, or creating a plan for documenting changes to the application. One tool for change management is **version control** software that allow changes to be automatically recorded and if necessary "rolled back" to a previous version of the software.

Note

Despite the clear advantages of DevOps, not all programmers take advantage of it or support it. A recent survey revealed that more than half (52 percent) of programmers said that application security testing often delays development and threatens deadlines. Only 40 percent of developers are incorporating security testing during the programming stage, and 21 percent identify the design stage as the point at which security testing is completed. Only 25 percent of developers said they have authority over decisions regarding security.[7]

Secure Coding Techniques

There are several coding techniques that should be used to create secure applications and limit **data exposure,** or disclosing sensitive data to attackers. These techniques include determining how encryption will be implemented and ensuring that memory management is handled correctly so as not to introduce memory vulnerabilities. Other techniques are summarized in Table 9-8.

Table 9-8 Secure coding techniques

Coding technique	Description	Security advantage
Proper error handling	Taking the correct steps when an error occurs so that the application does not abort unexpectedly.	An application that aborts can expose an OS to attackers.
Proper input validation	Accounting for errors such as incorrect user input (entering a file name for a file that does not exist)	Can prevent Cross-site scripting (XSS) and Cross-site request forgery (XSRF) attacks
Normalization	Organizing data within a database to minimize redundancy	Reduces footprint of data exposed to attackers.
Stored procedure	A subroutine available to applications that access a relational database	Eliminates the need to write a subroutine that could have vulnerabilities
Code signing	Digitally signing applications	Confirms the software author and guarantees the code has not been altered or corrupted
Obfuscation/ camouflaged code	Writing an application in such a way that its inner functionality is difficult for an outsider to understand.	Helps prevent an attacker from understanding a program's function
Dead code	A section of an application that executes but performs no meaningful function.	Provides an unnecessary attack vector for attackers
Server-side execution and validation or Client-side execution and validation	Input validation generally uses the server to perform validation but can also have the client perform validation by the user's web browser.	Adds another validation to the process
Code reuse of third-party libraries and SDKs	Code reuse is using existing software in a new application; a software development kit (SDK) is a set of tools used to write applications.	Existing libraries that have already been vetted as secure eliminate the need to write new code.

Code Testing

There are different tools and processes that can be used to test the quality of application code. At the beginning of the process (and at each sprint for the agile model) a **model verification** test is used to ensure that the projected application meets all specifications at that point. This contrasts with *model validation*, which determines if the product fulfills its intended use when placed in its environment.

Compiled code testing is different from that of **runtime code testing**. Testing of compiled code is searching for errors that could prevent the application from properly compiling from source code to application code, such as programming language syntax errors or type checking errors. Testing of runtime code looks for errors after the program has compiled correctly and is running, such as a pointer deference or memory leak. Most runtime code testing is done in a **sandbox**, which is a testing environment that isolates the untested code from the live production environment. This helps to protect data and even other parts of the code from corruption resulting from a test of an incomplete or "buggy" application.

Static program analyzers are tools that examine the software without actually executing the program; instead, the source code is reviewed and analyzed. **Dynamic analysis (fuzzing)** is a software testing technique that deliberately provides invalid, unexpected, or random data as inputs to a computer program. The program is then monitored to ensure that all errors are trapped. Fuzzing, which is usually done through automated programs, is commonly used to test for security problems in software or computer systems. **Stress testing** puts the application under a heavier than normal load to determine if the program is robust and can perform all error handling correctly.

Integrity measurement is an "attestation mechanism" designed to be able to convince a remote party (external to the coding team) that an application is running only a set of known and approved executables. Whenever a file is called in an executable mode, such as when a program is invoked or a sharable library is mapped, the integrity measurement tool generates a hash digest of that file. On request, the tool can produce a list of all programs run and their corresponding digest values. This list can then be examined to ensure that no unknown or known-vulnerable applications have been run.

Chapter Summary

- The booting process on early personal computers used firmware called the BIOS (Basic Input/Output System). Although the ability to update the BIOS firmware enabled new features to be added, it also opened the door for threat actors to create malware to infect the BIOS. To combat this vulnerability and add additional functionality, UEFI (Unified Extensible Firmware Interface) was developed, in conjunction with the Secure Boot security standard. Secure Boot is designed to ensure that a computer boots using only software that is trusted by the computer manufacturer.

- In a chain of trust each element relies on the confirmation of the previous element to know that the entire process is secure. The strongest starting point is hardware, which cannot be modified. This is known as the hardware root of trust. Computer systems, printers, and similar technology devices all emit electromagnetic fields. It is possible to pick up these electromagnetic fields and read the data that is producing them, possibly compromising that data. A supply chain is a network that moves a product from the supplier to the customer. Because products move unsupervised through many different steps in the supply chain, there is an opportunity for malware to be injected into products during their manufacturing or storage, called supply chain infection.

- Although protections within the operating system (OS) are designed to provide security, the OS itself must be protected.

The security of an OS depends upon the proper configuration of its built-in security features. To address the vulnerabilities in operating systems that are uncovered after the software has been released, software vendors usually deploy a software "fix," generally known as a security patch. Effective patch management involves two patch management tools to manage patches: tools dealing with the distribution of the patch, and tools involving the reception of the patch.

- Antimalware software can help protect against these infections. Antivirus (AV) software can examine a computer for any infections as well as monitor computer activity and scan new documents that might contain a virus. Users can install antispam filtering software on their client computers or configure their local email client or webmail client to trap spam. Antispyware helps prevent computers from becoming infected by different types of spyware. One common type of antispyware is a popup blocker. Instead of managing the different security options on an operating system that has been deployed, in some cases it is necessary to tighten security during the design and coding of the OS. This is called OS hardening. An operating system that has been designed in this way to be secure is a trusted OS.

- Peripheral devices attached to a client computer must likewise be protected. This includes protection from the computer to which it is connected, so that an infected computer does not infect a peripheral, as well as protecting the computer from being infected from malware on a peripheral. One popular type of removable data storage is a Secure Digital (SD) card. SDIO is an SD storage card with integrated wireless transmission capabilities, using Bluetooth or Wi-Fi technology. A popular SDIO device is a Wi-Fi-enabled microSD card for devices like digital cameras. The security for an SDIO card is the same as that for securing a standard Wi-Fi network. Digital cameras use internal storage and external SD cards to record photographs and capture video. Protecting data on SD cards can be accomplished by password-protecting the card, using encryption, or write-protecting the card by moving a small external switch to the *Open* position. External storage devices need to be protected, and are increasingly at risk for infection by crypto-malware.

- A multifunctional device (MFD) is a combination printer, copier, scanner, and fax machine. Although MFDs are often overlooked as requiring protection, these peripheral devices are essentially special-purpose computers that also need to be protected. Computer displays are often considered "passive" peripherals: a computer sends data to the display that is then projected as words and pictures. However, security researchers have demonstrated that a threat actor can target a display's firmware.

- Physical security is an often overlooked consideration when protecting a client device. Preventing a threat actor from physically accessing the device is as important as preventing the attacker from accessing it through a network. Fencing is usually a tall, permanent structure to keep out individuals and secure a restricted area. Like fencing, a barricade is generally designed to block the passage of traffic; however, barricades are most often used for directing large crowds or restricting vehicular traffic and generally are not designed to keep out individuals. A bollard is a short but sturdy vertical post that is used to bar vehicular traffic and to prevent a vehicle from "ramming" into a secured area. Whereas barriers act as passive devices to restrict access, human guards are considered active security elements. Some guards are responsible for monitoring activity that is captured by a video camera. Motion detection is determining an object's change in position in relation to its surroundings. This movement usually generates an audible alarm to warn a guard of an intruder.

- Door locks are important to protect equipment. The standard keyed entry lock is the most common type of door lock for keeping out intruders, but it provides minimal security. For rooms that require enhanced security, a lever coupled with a deadbolt lock, which extends a solid metal bar into the door frame for extra security, is often used. Because of the difficulties in managing keys for hundreds or thousands of users, an alternative to a key lock is a more sophisticated door access system using a cipher lock. An access log is a record or list of individuals who have permission to enter a secure area, along with the time they entered and the time they left the area. A mantrap is designed to separate a nonsecured area from a secured area by controlling two interlocking doors to a small room. A protected distribution system (PDS) is a system of cable conduits used to protect classified information that is being transmitted between two highly sensitive areas.

- Hardware security is physical security that involves protecting the hardware of the host system, particularly portable laptops and tablet computers that can easily be stolen. A cable lock can be inserted into a slot in the device and rotated so that the cable lock is secured to the device, while a cable connected to the lock can then be secured to a desk or chair. Laptops and other portable devices can be placed in a safe or a locking cabinet, which is a ruggedized steel box with a lock.

- Applications that run on client devices need to be secure. An unsecure application can open the door for attackers to exploit the application, the data that it uses, and even the underlying OS. Some of the most dangerous weaknesses in an application are due to poor coding that can create vulnerabilities in computer memory or buffer areas that can be easily exploited. An application development lifecycle model is a conceptual model that describes the different stages involved in creating an application. There are two major application development lifecycle models. The waterfall model uses a sequential design process. The agile model follows an incremental approach. One specific type of software methodology

that follows the agile model and heavily incorporates security concepts is called Secure DevOps. Because DevOps is based on the agile method there will be continuous modifications throughout the process. With these continual changes, it is important to use change management, or creating a plan for documenting changes to the application. There are several coding techniques that should be used to create secure applications.

- There are different tools and processes that can be used to test the quality of the application code. At the beginning of the process (and at each sprint for the agile model) a model verification test ensures that the projected application meets all specifications at that point. Testing of compiled code is different from that of runtime code. Testing of compiled code is searching for errors that could prevent the application from properly compiling from source code to application code, such as programming language syntax errors or type checking errors. Testing of runtime code looks for errors after the program has compiled correctly and is running, such as a pointer deference or memory leak. Static program analyzers examine the software without actually executing the program; instead, the source code is reviewed and analyzed. Dynamic analysis (fuzzing) is a software testing technique that deliberately provides invalid, unexpected, or random data as inputs to a computer program.

Key Terms

access log

agile model

alarm

antivirus (AV)

appliance OS

application development
  lifecycle model

application whitelisting/
  blacklisting

barricade

baselining

BIOS (Basic Input/Output
  System)

bollard

cable lock

cage

change management

client-side execution and
  validation

code reuse of third-party
  libraries and SDKs

code signing

compiled code testing

continuous integration

data exposure

dead code

deadbolt lock

deprovisioning

development stage

digital camera

disabling default accounts/
  passwords

disabling unnecessary ports
  and services

DLL injection

door lock

dynamic analysis (fuzzing)

fencing

hardware root of trust

immutable systems

infrastructure as code

integrity measurement

key management

kiosk OS

least functionality

lighting

mantrap

memory leak

microSD

mobile OS

model verification

motion detection

multifunctional device
  (MFD)

network OS

normalization

obfuscation/camouflaged
  code

patch

patch management tools

pointer deference

production stage

proper error handling

proper input validation

protected distribution
  system (PDS)

provisioning

runtime code testing

safe

sandbox

screen filter

Secure Boot

secure cabinet

secure DevOps

Secure Digital (SD)

security automation

security guard

server OS

server-side execution and
  validation

sign

staging stage

static program analyzer

stored procedure

stress testing

supply chain

testing stage

trusted OS

UEFI (Unified Extensible
  Firmware Interface)

version control

video surveillance camera

waterfall model

Wi-Fi-enabled microSD card

workstation OS

Review Questions

1. Which of the following is NOT a reason why supply chain infections are considered especially dangerous?
   a. If the malware is planted in the ROM firmware of the device this can make it difficult or sometimes even impossible to clean an infected device.
   b. Users are receiving infected devices at the point of purchase and are completely unaware that a brand new device may be infected.
   c. It is virtually impossible to closely monitor every step in the supply chain.
   d. Supply chains take advantage of the trusted "chain of trust" concept.

2. Which type of operating system runs on a firewall, router, or switch?
   a. Server OS
   b. Network OS
   c. Device OS
   d. Resource OS

3. Which of the following is NOT designed to prevent individuals from entering sensitive areas but instead is intended to direct traffic flow?
   a. Barricade
   b. Fencing
   c. Roller barrier
   d. Type V controls

4. Which of the following is NOT a motion detection method?
   a. Magnetism
   b. Radio frequency
   c. Moisture
   d. Infrared

5. Which type of residential lock is most often used for keeping out intruders?
   a. Encrypted key lock
   b. Keyed entry lock
   c. Privacy lock
   d. Passage lock

6. A lock that extends a solid metal bar into the door frame for extra security is the_____.
   a. triple bar lock
   b. deadman's lock
   c. full bar lock
   d. deadbolt lock

7. Which statement about a mantrap is true?
   a. It is illegal in the United States.
   b. It monitors and controls two interlocking doors to a room.
   c. It is a special keyed lock.
   d. It requires the use of a cipher lock.

8. Which of the following is NOT a typical OS security configuration?
   a. Employing least functionality
   b. Restricting patch management
   c. Disabling default accounts/passwords
   d. Disabling unnecessary ports and services

9. Which of the following can be used to secure a laptop or mobile device?
   a. Mobile connector
   b. Cable lock
   c. Mobile chain
   d. Security tab

10. Which of the following is NOT a characteristic of an alarmed carrier PDS?
    a. Requires periodic visual inspections
    b. Uses continuous monitoring
    c. Carrier can be hidden above the ceiling
    d. Eliminates the need to seal connections

11. Which of the following is NOT a memory vulnerability?
    a. DLL injection
    b. Pointer deference
    c. Buffer overflow
    d. Variable overflow

12. Which stage is a "quality assurance" test that verifies the code functions as intended?
    a. Production stage
    b. Testing stage
    c. Staging stage
    d. Development stage
13. Which model uses a sequential design process?
    a. Waterfall model
    b. Rigid model
    c. Agile model
    d. Secure model
14. What allows for a single configuration to be set and then deployed to many or all users?
    a. Snap-In Replication (SIR)
    b. Active Directory
    c. Group Policy
    d. Command Configuration
15. Which of the following is a cumulative package of all patches?
    a. Rollup
    b. Service pack
    c. Patch
    d. Hotfix
16. Which of the following is NOT an advantage to an automated patch update service?
    a. Administrators can approve or decline updates for client systems, force updates to install by a specific date, and obtain reports on what updates each computer needs.
    b. Downloading patches from a local server instead of using the vendor's online update service can save bandwidth and time because each computer does not have to connect to an external server.
    c. Users can disable or circumvent updates just as they can if their

computer is configured to use the vendor's online update service.
    d. Specific types of updates that the organization does not test, such as hotfixes, can be automatically installed whenever they become available.
17. How can an SDIO card be made secure?
    a. Using the security mechanisms on a standard Wi-Fi network.
    b. Turning on patch updates to the SDIO card.
    c. Requiring a username before accessing the SDIO card.
    d. SDIO cards are natively secure and no security settings are needed.
18. How does heuristic detection detect a virus?
    a. A virtualized environment is created and the code is executed in it.
    b. A string of bytes from the virus is compared against the suspected file.
    c. The bytes of a virus are placed in different "piles" and then used to create a profile.
    d. The virus signature file is placed in a suspended chamber before streaming to the CPU.
19. Which of these is a list of approved email senders?
    a. Blacklist
    b. Whitelist
    c. Bluelist
    d. Yellowlist
20. Which of the following types of testing uses unexpected or invalid inputs?
    a. Stress testing
    b. Dynamic analysis
    c. Static analysis
    d. Runtime testing

Hands-On Projects

> **Note**
>
> If you are concerned about installing any of the software in these projects on your regular computer, you can instead install the software in the Windows virtual machine created in the Chapter 1 Hands-On Projects 1-3 and 1-4. Software installed within the virtual machine will not impact the host computer.

Project 9-1: Using the Microsoft Online Security Bulletins

For over 20 years Microsoft released service bulletins that described the patches distributed for a group of software products, such as all the supported versions of Windows. In early 2017, Microsoft stopped distributing these service bulletins and instead made the information available in a searchable online database. All security professionals need to be familiar with using this database. In this project, you explore the online database.

1. Open your web browser and enter the URL **portal.msrc.microsoft.com/en-us/.** (The location of content on the Internet may change without warning. If you are no longer able to access the program through this URL, use a search engine to search for "Microsoft Security TechCenter".)
2. If necessary click **Security Updates**.
3. Click **Guidance** as seen in Figure 9-12.

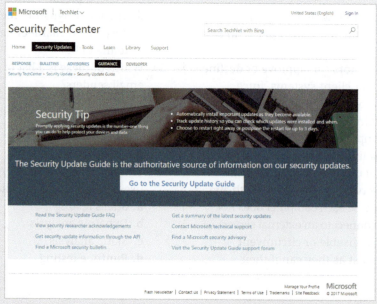

Figure 9-12 **Microsoft Security TechCenter**

4. Click **Read the Security Update Guide FAQ** and read through the information.

5. Click the link **www.icasi.org/cvrf/** (or enter it into another tab in your browser). What is the Common Vulnerability Reporting Framework (CVRF)? How is it used?

6. Return to the Microsoft Security TechCenter.

7. Return to the **Guidance** page.

8. Click **Get a summary of the latest security updates**.

9. If no security updates appear, adjust the **From** date to the first day of the previous month.

10. Scroll through the list of security updates.

11. Click the first link under **KB Article**.

12. Read through this information.

13. Now return to the previous page and select another KB article to read.

14. How useful is this information? Is it presented in a format that is helpful?

15. Now click on the CVE link under **Summary** and read this information. Note the detail of this information.

16. Read the information under **Exploitability Assessment** (if the exploit you selected does not list an Exploitability Assessment then select another that does include the assessment). What does this mean? Open another tab on your web browser and search for **Microsoft Exploitability Index**. Read through the description that you find and keep this tab open.

17. Return to the Microsoft Security TechCenter and view the **Exploitability Assessment**. How serious is this security vulnerability?

18. Scroll down to **Affected Products** (if the exploit you selected does not list Affected Products then select another that does include the information).

19. Select a product that is impacted by this security vulnerability and click the **KB Article**.

20. How important is this information to a security professional? How easy is this online database to use?
    Now compare the Microsoft database with Apple's. Enter the URL **support.apple.com /en-us/HT201222**. (The location of content on the Internet may change without warning. If you are no longer able to access the program through this URL, use a search engine to search for "Apple Security Updates".)

22. Scroll down through the list of Apple security updates. How does this list compare with the updates from Microsoft?

23. Select a recent event under **Name and information link**.

24. Read the information about the update. How does this information compare with Microsoft's information? Why is there such a difference? Which provides better information for security professions?

25. Close all windows.

Project 9-2: Testing Antivirus Software

What happens when antivirus software detects a virus? In this project, you will download a virus test file to determine how your AV software reacts. The file downloaded is not a virus but is designed to appear to an antivirus scanner as if it were a virus.

> **Note** 🔗
>
> You need to have antivirus software installed and running on your computer to perform this project.

1. Open your web browser and enter the URL **www.eicar.org/86-0-Intended-use.html**. (The location of content on the Internet may change without warning. If you are no longer able to access the program through this URL, use a search engine to search for "EICAR AntiVirus Test File".)
2. Read the "INTENDED USE" information.
3. Click **DOWNLOAD**.
4. Click the file **eicar.com**, which contains a fake virus. A dialog box may open that asks if you want to download the file. Wait to see what happens. What does your antivirus software do? Close your antivirus message and if necessary click **Cancel** to stop the download procedure.
5. Now click **eicar_com.zip**. This file contains a fake virus inside a compressed (ZIP) file. What happened? Close your antivirus message and, if necessary, click **Cancel** to stop the download procedure.

> **Note** 🔗
>
> If your antivirus software did not prevent you from accessing the eicar_com.zip file, when the File Download dialog box appeared, click **Save** and download the file to your desktop or another location designated by your instructor. When the download is complete, navigate to the folder that contains the file and right-click it. Then, click **Scan for viruses** on the shortcut menu (your menu command might be slightly different). What happened after the scan?

6. Click **eicarcom2.zip**. This file has a double-compressed ZIP file with a fake virus. What happened? Close your antivirus message and, if necessary, click **Cancel** to stop the download procedure.
7. If necessary, erase any files that were saved to your computer.
8. Close all windows.

Project 9-3: Setting Windows Local Security Policy

The Local Group Policy Editor is a Microsoft Management Console (MMC) snap-in that gives a single user interface through which all the Computer Configuration and User Configuration settings of Local Group Policy objects can be managed. The Local Security Policy settings are among the security settings contained in the Local Group Policy Editor. An administrator can use these to set policies that are applied to the computer. In this project, you view and change local security policy settings.

> **Note** 📎
>
> You will need to be an administrator to open the Local Group Policy Editor.

1. Click **Start**.
2. Type **secpol.msc** into the Search box and then click **secpol**.

> **Note** 📎
>
> If your computer is already joined to a domain then searching for secpol.msc might not launch the application. If this is the case, click **Start** and type **mmc.msc**. On the File menu click **Add/Remove** snap-in and then click **Add**. In **Add Standalone Snap-in**, double-click **Group Policy Object Editor**.

3. First create a policy regarding passwords. Expand **Account Policies** in the left pane and then expand **Password Policy**.
4. Double-click **Enforce password history** in the right pane. This setting defines how many previously used passwords Windows will record. This prevents users from "recycling" old passwords.
5. Change **passwords remembered** to **4**.
6. Click **OK**.
7. Double-click **Maximum password age** in the right pane. The default value is 42, meaning that a user must change his password after 42 days.
8. Change **days** to **30**.
9. Click **OK**.
10. Double-click **Minimum password length** in the right pane. The default value is a length of 8 characters.
11. Change **characters** to **10**.
12. Click **OK**.
13. Double-click **Password must meet complexity requirements** in the right pane. This setting forces a password to include at least two opposite case letters, a number, and a special character (such as a punctuation mark).
14. Click **Enabled**.
15. Click **OK**.
16. Double-click **Store passwords using reversible encryption** in the right pane. Because passwords should be stored in an encrypted format this setting should not be enabled.
17. If necessary, click **Disabled**.
18. Click **OK**.
19. In the left pane, click **Account lockout policy**.

20. Double-click **Account lockout threshold** in the right pane. This is the number of times that a user can enter an incorrect password before Windows will lock the account from being accessed. (This prevents an attacker from attempting to guess the password with unlimited attempts.)
21. Change **invalid login attempts** to **5**.
22. Click **OK**.
23. Note that the Local Security Policy suggests changes to the **Account lockout duration** and the **Reset account lockout counter after** values to 30 minutes.
24. Click **OK**.
25. Expand **Local Policies** in the left pane and then click **Audit Policy**.
26. Double-click **Audit account logon events**.
27. Check both **Success** and **Failure**.
28. Click **OK**.
29. Right-click **Security Settings** in the left pane.
30. Click **Reload** to have these policies applied.
31. Close all windows.

Project 9-4: Configuring Microsoft Windows Security

It is important that security settings be properly configured on a computer in order to protect it. In this project, you examine several security settings on a Microsoft Windows 10 computer.

Note 📎

This project shows how to configure Windows security for a personal computer. If this computer is part of a computer lab or office, these settings should not be changed without the proper permissions.

1. Click **Start** and **Settings**.
2. Click **Update and security**.
3. If necessary click **Windows Update** in the left pane.
4. Click **Advanced options**, then under **Choose how updates are installed** change to **Automatic (recommended)**.

Tip ⓘ

Remember that the safest approach is to restart the device as soon as any updates have been installed.

5. Click **Give me updates for other Microsoft products when I update Windows**. This will allow for updates for Microsoft software such as Office to also be updated.
6. Click **View your update history** to see the updates that have been installed on your computer.

7. Click the **back arrow**.
8. Click the **back arrow** to return to **Update & Security**.
9. Click **Windows Defender**. This is the Microsoft AV product that is part of Windows 10.
10. Be sure that all the settings are set to On.
11. Click **Use Windows Defender**. The Windows Defender dialog box appears.
12. Under **Scan options:** be sure that **Quick** is selected.
13. Now perform a Quick scan of the most essential files. Click **Scan now**. Depending upon your system it may take several minutes to complete. What was the result of the scan?
14. Click the **History** tab. Be sure that **Quarantined items** is selected and click **View details**. Has Defender already identified suspicious files on this computer and placed them in quarantine? When you are finished, close Windows Defender.
15. In the F**ind a setting** search box enter **UAC** and press **Enter**.
16. Click **Change User Account Control Settings**. The **User Account Control Settings** dialog box opens.
17. Move the slider through all the choices and notice the description of each.
18. Position the slider to **Always notify**. Why is this the best security setting? Click **OK** and then **Yes**.
19. Finally, create a recovery drive for this computer. First insert a blank USB flash drive.
20. In the Windows search box enter **recoverydrive.exe** and press **Enter**. Click **Yes** in the UAC.
21. The Recovery Drive dialog box appears. Click **Next**.
22. The system gathers the appropriate files. In the **Select the USB flash drive** dialog box select the appropriate drive. Click **Next**.
23. Click **Create** to complete the process.
24. After the drive has been created close all windows.

Case Projects

Case Project 9-1: Antivirus Comparison

Select four antivirus products, one of which is a free product, and compare their features. Create a table that lists the features. How do they compare with the AV software you currently use? Which would you recommend to others? Why? Create a report on your research.

Case Project 9-2: Analysis of Physical Security

How secure are the host computers at your school or workplace? Perform an analysis of the physical security to protect these devices. Make note of any hardware locks, proximity readers, video surveillance, fencing, etc. Then look at the hardware security around the hosts themselves. What are the strengths? What are the weaknesses? What recommendations would you make for improving host security? Write a one-page paper on your analysis.

Case Project 9-3: Application Patch Management

Select four applications (not OSs) that you frequently use. How does each of them address patch management? Visit their websites to determine what facilities they must alert users to new vulnerabilities. Are the patch management systems adequate? Write a one-page paper on your findings.

Case Project 9-4: UEFI

Use the Internet to research UEFI. What are its advantages? What are its disadvantages? What criticisms have been leveled against it? Do you agree with the criticism? Write a one-page paper on your findings.

Case Project 9-5: Application Whitelisting/Blacklisting

Research the Internet to find three tools that are available for application whitelisting/blacklisting for a client computer and for a network server. Create a table that lists their advantages, disadvantages, ease of use, etc. Would you recommend using these tools? Why or why not? Write a one-page paper on your findings.

Case Project 9-6: Lake Point Security Consulting

Lake Point Consulting Services (LPCS) provides security consulting and assurance services to its clients in a wide range of enterprises. A new initiative at LPCS is for each of its seven regional offices to provide internships to students who are in their final year of the security degree program at the local college.

Each summer LPCS holds a weekly series of workshops for anyone interested who wants to learn more about securing their computer. LPCS has asked you to make the first presentations of the summer series.

1. For the first presentation, create a PowerPoint presentation about the basic steps in securing a client computer, why it is important, what antimalware software should be considered, etc. Because the attendees will not have an IT background, the presentation cannot be too technical in nature. Your presentation should contain at least 10 slides.
2. For the second presentation, create a PowerPoint presentation that covers how to secure a computer from theft. Be sure to cover cable locks, door locks, etc. For this presentation, it should contain 6–10 slides.

Case Project 9-7: Information Security Community Site Activity

The Information Security Community Site is an online companion to this textbook. It contains a wide variety of tools, information, discussion boards, and other features to assist learners. Go to **community.cengage.com/Infosec2** and click the *Join or Sign in* icon to log in, using your login name and password that you created in Chapter 1. Click **Forums (Discussion)** and click on **Security+ Case Projects (6th edition)**. Read the following case study.

Read again *Today's Attacks and Defenses* at the beginning of the chapter. What should be done about protecting the voting process? Should the government set minimum standards for voting machines? With the security risks and privacy risks, what are your thoughts about Internet voting? Do you see a day in which all voting will be done online? Would this help more citizens become involved in the democratic process? Enter your answers on the InfoSec Community Server discussion board.

References

1. "Security assessment of WINVote voting equipment for Department of Elections," *Virginia Information Technologies Agency*, Apr. 14, 2015, May 11, 2017, http://www .elections.virginia.gov/WebDocs/VotingEquipReport/WINVote-final.pdf.

2. "The secret ballot at risk: Recommendations for protecting democracy," *Secret Ballot at Risk*, retrieved May 6, 2017, http://secretballotatrisk.org/.

3. Genkin, Daniel, Shamir, Adi, and Tromer, Eran, "RSA key extraction via low-bandwidth acoustic cryptanalysis," retrieved May 11, 2017, www.tau .ac.il/~tromer /papers/acoustic-20131218.pdf.

4. Arik Hesseldahl, "The tempest surrounding Tempest," *Forbes.com*, Aug. 8, 2000, retrieved May 11, 2017, www.forbes.com/2000/08/10/mu9.html.

5. Koriat, Oren, "Preinstalled malware targeting mobile users," *Check Point Blog*, Mar. 3, 2017, accessed May 5, 2017, http://blog.checkpoint.com/2017/03/10 /preinstalled-malware-targeting-mobile-users/.

6. Horowitz, Michael, "The head of NSA TAO advises on defensive computing for networks," *Computerworld*, Feb. 1, 2016, accessed May 11, 2017, http://www .computerworld.com/article/3028025/security/defending-a-network-from-the-nsa. html.

7. Correa, Danielle, "Sensitive data exposure is top concern for 52% of developers," *SC Magazine*, Dec. 21, 2016, retrieved May 6, 2017, https://www.scmagazineuk.com /sensitive-data-exposure-is-top-concern-for-52-of-developers/article/627593/.

CHAPTER 10

MOBILE AND EMBEDDED DEVICE SECURITY

*After completing this chapter, you should be able
to do the following:*

List and compare the different types of mobile devices and how they are deployed

Explain the risks associated with mobile devices

List ways to secure a mobile device

Describe different types of embedded systems and IoT devices and how to secure them

---

Today's Attacks and Defenses

A relatively new class of mobile technology consists of devices that can be worn by the user instead of being carried. Known as wearable technology, these devices can provide even greater flexibility and mobility. As the cost of wearable technology has decreased while the network speed of the devices has increased, sales of this technology have dramatically risen. Wearable device shipments worldwide totaled 102 million units in 2016, which was an increase of 29 percent over the previous year. It is estimated that wearable device shipments worldwide will increase by 20 percent annually and will reach 213 million units by 2020.[1]

The most common type of wearable technology is a fitness tracker. These devices typically monitor movements by counting steps and distance traveled, record heart rates, provide location data, give alerts of incoming email, calls, or text messages, and even monitor sleep patterns. Another type of wearable technology is a smartwatch, which can perform many of the functions of a fitness tracker as well as show smartphone messages without the need to remove the smartphone from a bag or pocket. The device can also have its own set of sensors and software features to function independently.

As technology continues to advance, fitness trackers are becoming more sophisticated. A project by the National Institutes of Health and the Berkeley Sensor and Actuator Center has recently designed a tracker that measures multiple chemicals in the user's perspiration and then calibrates the data according to the wearer's body temperature. These "sweat trackers" check for lactate and glucose (the chemicals that are produced when bodies burn fuel) as well as the electrolytes sodium and potassium (the chemicals that are needed to retain water). Too much lactate during a workout may indicate muscle fatigue, while low levels of potassium may mean dehydration is starting to occur.

With all this user fitness and health data being collected and transmitted, how secure is it? Security researchers looked at fitness tracking devices and their companion mobile apps from eight different fitness device manufacturers. All the devices, except for one, transmitted a persistent and unique Bluetooth identifier, meaning that the user could be tracked by the beacons, even when the device is not paired with or connected to a smartphone. In addition, the companion smartphone apps for the wearables either exposed login user names and password credentials, transmitted the tracking information that allowed for man-in-the-middle interceptions, or allowed users to submit fake activity tracking information. And some security steps that were taken were only half-hearted. One fitness app used the secure hypertext transport protocol (HTTPS) for transmissions—but only when the user was logging in with her password. All other data was sent without any encryption, so that a snooper could easily read or alter the data. The study also found that often the user's fitness tracking data was being sold or made available to third parties without the user's consent (or consent was buried in legal language). And even the information accessible by users who request their personal information varies from the data actually collected by the companies.

But does it matter that this data could be read or manipulated by someone else? Isn't it just useful to the wearer who wants to track his latest workout? The answer is that fitness tracker data is becoming increasingly important. Some health insurers are now using fitness tracker data to offer lower health insurance premiums. A user's fitness data that was intercepted and altered could result in higher (or lower) insurance premiums. In addition, some courts have admitted fitness app data as evidence in several cases. And police are warning users that a stalker could use stolen fitness tracking data to prey on victims if the stalker knows the route that a person takes every afternoon while running.

As the researchers of the study note, this calls into question the very nature of "self-empowerment," which is often part of the marketing of fitness trackers: encouraging individuals to take personal control of their health and lives. The question could be raised: Can individuals really be empowered when their data is not secure or is sold to nameless third parties without their consent?[2]

If a time traveler living just 15 years ago could be transported to today's world, it is likely that he would be shocked at how mobile devices have dramatically changed the way we live in just a short period of time. Watching cars pass on the road, he would observe that a high percentage of drivers are talking or sending text messages on their mobile phones, often in violation of laws that prohibit it. Sitting in a classroom he would see that almost all students are using their mobile devices to read e-textbooks, access online files, and take notes. Strolling through the mall he would be amazed to see shoppers scan bar codes on their smartphones to determine if the same item is offered at another store in the mall at a lower price or if it would be cheaper to just immediately order it online. All these dramatic changes might even discourage our time traveler from jumping ahead another 15 years to see what a world filled with even more mobile devices would be like.

The statistics confirm that mobile devices have changed—and are continuing to change—our everyday lives. About 92 percent of 18- to 29-year-olds own a smartphone, and almost 80 percent of all Americans own a smartphone, compared with only 35 percent in 2011. And half of the public now owns a tablet computer (tablet ownership in 2010 was a mere 3 percent).[3] Mobile devices have crowded the once-hallowed desktop computer into the shadows. The total time spent browsing the web per month is now higher on smartphones (34 hours per month) than on desktops (29 hours).[4]

Just as users have flocked to mobile devices, so too have attackers. Because mobile devices have become the primary, if not exclusive, computing device for a growing number of users, there has been a dramatic increase in attacks directed at these devices. And unlike desktop computers that can be protected by walls and locked doors, the mobile devices themselves—which can be used virtually anywhere in the world—also must be constantly protected from loss or theft.

In this chapter, you explore mobile device security. You begin by looking at the different types of mobile devices. Next, you look at the risks associated with these devices. Then, you explore how to secure these devices and the applications running on them. Finally, you study embedded systems and the Internet of Things and the increasing risks that they pose to users.

Mobile Device Types and Deployment

 **Certification**

2.5 Given a scenario, deploy mobile devices securely.

There are a variety of different types of mobile devices, which in turn may be connected through different technologies. There are also different ways by which mobile devices are deployed in the enterprise.

Types of Mobile Devices

Most mobile devices have a common set of core features, which serve to differentiate them from other computing devices. There are also additional features that are often found on many (but not all) mobile devices. These features are listed in Table 10-1.

Table 10-1 Mobile device core and additional features

Core features	Additional features
Small form factor	Global Positioning System (GPS)
Mobile operating system	Microphone and/or digital camera
Wireless data network interface for accessing the Internet, such as Wi-Fi or cellular telephony	Wireless cellular connection for voice communications
Applications (apps) that can be acquired through different means	Wireless personal area network interfaces like Bluetooth or near field communication (NFC)
Local non removable data storage	Removable storage media
Data synchronization capabilities with a separate computer or remote servers	Support for using the device itself as removable storage for another computing device

There are several types of mobile devices. These include tablets, smartphones, wearable technology, and portable computers.

Tablets

Tablets are portable computing devices first introduced in 2010. Designed for user convenience, tablets are thinner, lighter, easier to carry, and more intuitive to use than other types of computers. Tablets are often classified by their screen size. The two most common categories of tablet screen sizes are 5–8.5 inches (12.7–21.5 cm) and 8.5–10 inches (12.7–25.4 cm). The weight of tablets is generally less than 1.5 pounds (0.68 kg), and they are less than 1/2 inch (1.2 cm) thick. Figure 10-1 shows a typical tablet computer.

Figure 10-1 Tablet computer

Maximino/Shutterstock.com

Note

Tablets have a sensor called an accelerometer that senses vibrations and movements. It can determine the orientation of the device so that the screen image is always displayed upright.

Tablets generally lack a built-in keyboard or mouse. Instead, they rely on a touchscreen for user input that is manipulated with touch gestures. Table 10-2 lists the touch gestures for an Apple tablet.

Table 10-2 Apple touch gestures

Gesture name	Action	Usage
Tap	Lightly striking the screen.	Make a selection.
Double tap	Two quick taps in succession.	Zoom in or out of content or an image.
Flick	Place finger on the screen and quickly "swipe" in the desired direction.	Scroll or pan quickly.
Drag	Place finger on the screen and move it in the desired direction.	Scroll or move the viewing area.
Pinch open	Place thumb and finger close together on the screen and move them apart.	Zoom in.
Pinch close	Place thumb and finger a short distance apart on the screen and move them toward each other.	Zoom out.
Touch and hold	Touch the screen until the action occurs.	Display an information bubble or magnify content.
Two-finger scroll	Move two fingers together in the same direction.	Scroll content in an element with overflow capability.

Although tablets are primarily display devices with limited computing power, they have proven to be very popular. Besides their portability, a primary reason for their popularity is that tablet computers have an operating system (OS) that allows them to run third-party apps. The most popular OSs for tablets are Apple iOS, Google Android, and Microsoft Windows.

Smartphones

Early cellular telephones were called *feature phones* because they included a limited number of features, such as a camera, an MP3 music player, and ability to send and receive text messages. Many feature phones were designed to highlight a single feature, such as the ability to take high-quality photos or provide a large amount of memory for music storage.

The feature phone has given way to today's *smartphone* that has all the tools of a feature phone but also includes an OS that allows it to run apps and access the Internet. Because it has an OS, a smartphone offers a broader range of functionality. Users can install apps that perform a wide variety of functions for productivity, social networking, music, and so forth, much like a standard computer.

Note

Because of the ability to run apps, smartphones are essentially handheld personal computers.

Wearable Technology

A new class of mobile technology consists of devices that can be worn by the user instead of carried. Known as *wearable technology*, these devices can provide even greater flexibility and mobility.

Fitness trackers are a popular type of wearable technology. Originally designed to monitor and record physical activity, such as counting steps, they have evolved into sophisticated health monitoring devices. Modern fitness trackers can provide continual heart rate monitoring, GPS tracking, oxygen consumption, repetition counting (for weight training), and sleep monitoring. A fitness tracker is displayed in Figure 10-2.

Figure 10-2   Fitness tracker

Stephen VanHorn/Shutterstock.com

> **Note** 🖇
>
> Most fitness trackers use accelerometers to track movement during sleep, with the assumption that movement indicates the user is not sleeping soundly. However, not all movement during sleep is bad and a certain level is entirely natural. And a naturally restless sleeper or someone who moves around while in bed may produce inaccurate sleeping data. Fitness trackers are now becoming more sophisticated in measuring sleep. One tracker also monitors nighttime heart rate data, while another includes a mattress cover that also captures humidity and temperature information.

Another wearable technology is a *smart watch*. This device can serve as an accessory to a smartphone, enabling users to see messages and other information from their smartphones. The device also may have its own set of sensors and software features to function independently. For example, it could serve as a control device for home automation systems.

> **Note** 🖇
>
> A once-promising wearable technology was an optical head-mounted display, the most common being Google Glass. Google Glass could be activated in response to the user's voice commands by saying *OK Glass* or tilting the head 30 degrees upward. Then a specific voice command can be given, such as requesting directions, issuing a command to make a web search, or an action to use one of the device's features. However, due in part to privacy and safety concerns raised about Google Glass, in early 2015 Google discontinued it.

Portable Computers

As a class, *portable computers* are devices that closely resemble standard desktop computers. These portable computers have similar hardware (keyboard, hard disk drive, RAM, etc.) and run the same OS (Windows, Apple macOS, or Linux) and application software (Microsoft Office, web browsers, etc.) that are found on a general-purpose desktop computer. The primary difference is that portable computers are smaller self-contained devices that can easily be transported from one location to another while operating on battery power.

A *laptop* computer is regarded as the earliest portable computer. A laptop is designed to replicate the abilities of a desktop computer with only slightly less processing power yet is small enough to be used on a lap or small table. A *notebook* computer is a smaller version of a laptop computer and is considered a lightweight personal computer. Notebook computers typically weigh less than laptops and are small enough to fit easily inside a briefcase. A *subnotebook* computer is even smaller than standard notebooks and use low-power processors and solid state drives (SSDs). A *2-in-1* computer (also called a *hybrid* or *convertible*) can be used as either a subnotebook or a tablet. These devices have both a touch screen and a physical keyboard; they can be transformed from a subnotebook to a tablet through either a folding design or as a "slate" with a detachable keyboard, as seen in Figure 10-3.

Figure 10-3 2-in-1 computer with slate design

Chesky/Shutterstock.com

A new type of computing device that resembles a laptop computer is a *web-based computer*. It contains a limited version of an OS and a web browser with an integrated media player. Web-based computers are designed to be used while connected to the Internet. No traditional software applications can be installed, and no user files are stored locally on the device. Instead, the device accesses online web apps and saves user files on the Internet. The most common OSs for web-based computers are the Google Chrome OS and Microsoft Windows.

> **Note** 📎
>
> There are several legacy mobile devices that are no longer in use. One of the first mobile devices was a *personal digital assistant (PDA)* that was a handheld mobile device intended to replace paper systems. Most PDAs had a touchscreen for entering data while others had a rudimentary keyboard that contained only a numeric keypad or thumb keyboard. Popular in the 1990s and early 2000s, PDAs fell out of favor as smartphones gained in popularity. A *netbook* computer was a small, inexpensive, and lightweight portable computer that used low-powered processors, featured small screens and keyboards, omitted optical storage, and could not be upgraded. The popularity of netbooks declined once tablet computers were introduced.

Mobile Device Connectivity Methods

Many mobile devices use Wi-Fi as the standard connectivity method to connect to remote networks, with some support for Bluetooth and NFC as personal area network connections. Many devices also support other types of connectivity methods, such as:

- *Cellular.* When not using Wi-Fi, many mobile devices rely on **cellular telephony**. The coverage area for a cellular telephony network is divided into cells; in a typical city the cells, which are hexagon-shaped, measure 10 square miles (26 square kilometers). At the center of each cell is a cell transmitter to which the mobile devices in that cell send and receive the signals. These transmitters are connected a mobile telecommunications switching office (MTSO) that controls all of the transmitters in the cellular network and serves as the link between the cellular network and the wired telephone world. This is illustrated in Figure 10-4.

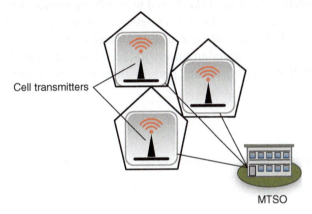

Cell transmitters

MTSO

Figure 10-4   Cellular telephony network

- *Satellite.* Man-made satellites are launched into space and provide communications capabilities around the world. Satellites can transmit television signals, telephone calls, computer communications, and weather information. In **satellite communications (SATCOM)** a repeater is located in a satellite. As an earth station transmits to the satellite at one frequency band, the satellite regenerates and transmits ("repeats") the signal back to earth at another frequency. The transmission time needed to repeat a signal from one earth station to another is approximately 250 milliseconds.

> **Note** 🖉
>
> Sir Isaac Newton in the 1720s was probably the first person to conceive of a man-made satellite. In 1945, Arthur C. Clarke, a science fiction author, wrote an article that envisioned a network of communications satellites placed into space at 22,000 miles (35,400 kilometers) to orbit the planet every 24 hours. At the time of his writing the idea was not well received. In October 1957, the Soviet Union launched the first satellite, Sputnik 1, which circled the globe every 90 minutes. After 18 days, its battery was exhausted and the transmitting ceased.

- *Infrared.* Instead of using radio frequency (RF) for the communication media, light can be used. All the different types of light that travel from the sun to the earth make up the light spectrum, and visible light is a small part of that entire spectrum (all other types of lights, such as x-rays, ultraviolet rays, and microwaves, are invisible to the human eye). **Infrared** light is next to visible light on the light spectrum, and, although invisible, has many of the same characteristics of visible light. At one time, infrared data ports were installed on laptop computers, printers, cameras, watches, and other devices so that data could be exchanged using infrared light. However, due to its slow speed and other limitations, infrared capabilities in mobile devices are rarely found today.
- *ANT.* Similar in function to Bluetooth low energy (LE), **ANT** is a proprietary wireless network technology that is used primarily by sensors for communicating data. Nodes in an ANT network can act as either a slave or master. Each node decides when to transmit based on the activity of other nodes in its area. ANT is often found in fitness trackers, heart rate monitors, watches, power meters that measure cycling performance, and similar devices.

> **Note** 📎
>
> Although not an acronym, the official technology name is in all uppercase (ANT).

- *USB connections.* There are different types and sizes of **USB connections** on mobile devices that are used for data transfer. These include standard size Universal Serial Bus (USB) connectors, mini connectors, and micro connectors, all of which are available as either type A (flat) or type B (square).

> **Note** 📎
>
> Unlike other types of USB connectors, a type C connector is reversible and can be inserted either upside down or right side up.

Enterprise Deployment Models

Due to the widespread use of mobile devices, it is not always feasible to require an employee to carry a company-owned smartphone along with his own personal cell phone. Many organizations have adopted an enterprise deployment model as it relates to mobile devices. These are listed in Table 10-3.

Table 10-3	Enterprise deployment models		
Model name	**Description**	**Employee actions**	**Business actions**
Bring your own device (BYOD)	Allows users to use their own personal mobile devices for business purposes.	Employees have full responsibility for choosing and supporting the device.	This model is popular with smaller companies or those with a temporary staff.
Corporate owned, personally enabled (COPE)	Employees choose from a selection of company approved devices.	Employees are supplied the device chosen and paid for by the company, but they can also use it for personal activities.	Company decides level of choice and freedom for employees.
Choose your own device (CYOD)	Employees choose from a limited selection of approved devices but the employee pays the upfront cost of the device while the business owns the contract.	Employees are offered a suite of choices that the company has approved for security, reliability, and durability.	Company often provides a stipend to pay monthly fees to wireless carrier.
Virtual desktop infrastructure (VDI)	Stores sensitive applications and data on a remote server that is accessed through a smartphone.	Users can customize the display of data as if the data were residing on their own mobile device.	Enterprise can centrally protect and manage apps and data on server instead of distributing to smartphones.
Corporate-owned	The device is purchased and owned by the enterprise.	Employees use the phone only for company-related business.	Enterprise is responsible for all aspects of the device.

There are several benefits of the BYOD, COPE, and CYOD models for the enterprise:

- *Management flexibility*. BYOD and CYOD ease the management burden by eliminating the need to select a wireless data carrier and manage plans for employees.
- *Less oversight*. Businesses do not need to monitor employee telecommunications usage for overages or extra charges.
- *Cost savings*. Because employees are responsible for their own mobile device purchases and wireless data plans (BYOD) or receive a small monthly stipend (CYOD), the company can save money.
- *Increased employee performance*. Employees are more likely to be productive while traveling or working away from the office if they are comfortable with their device.

- *Simplified IT infrastructure.* By using the existing cellular telephony network, companies do not have to support a remote data network for employees.
- *Reduced internal service.* BYOD, COPE, and CYOD reduce the strain on IT help desks because users will be primarily contacting their wireless data carrier for support.

In addition, users are eager to accept this flexibility. The user benefits include:

- *Choice of device.* Users like the freedom of choosing the type of mobile device with BYOD, COPE, and CYOD instead of being forced to accept a corporate device that may not meet their individual needs (corporate-owned).
- *Choice of carrier.* Most users have identified a specific wireless data carrier they want to use and often resist being forced to use a carrier with whom they have experienced a poor past relationship.
- *Convenience.* Because almost all users already have their own device, the BYOD, COPE, and CYOD models provide the convenience of carrying only a single device.

Mobile Device Risks

- 2.5 Given a scenario, deploy mobile devices securely.

There are several security risks associated with using mobile devices. These include mobile device vulnerabilities, connection vulnerabilities, accessing untrusted content, and deployment model risks.

Mobile Device Vulnerabilities

There are several vulnerabilities inherent to mobile devices. The mobile device vulnerabilities include physical security, limited firmware updates, location tracking, and unauthorized recording.

Physical Security

The greatest asset of a mobile device—its portability—is also one of its greatest vulnerabilities. Mobile devices are used in a wide variety of locations both public and private (coffee shops, hotels, conferences, employee homes, while traveling) that are outside of the enterprise's normal physical perimeter. Devices can easily be lost or stolen, and any unprotected data on the device could be retrieved by a thief. About 68 percent of all healthcare security breaches were the result of the loss or theft of a mobile device.[5] One-quarter of all laptop thefts occurred from unattended cars or while traveling on airplanes and trains, 15 percent occurred in airports and hotels, and 12 percent were stolen from restaurants.[6]

Note

It is predicted that the number of mobile devices stolen in airports will dramatically increase due to a new regulation enacted by the U.S. government in 2017. This regulation bans travelers from carrying onboard their laptop computers, tablets, and digital cameras from flights originating from major Middle Eastern airports. However, packing these devices in checked baggage may pose a tempting target for those who have access to checked bags.

In addition to loss or theft, merely using a mobile device in a public area can be considered a risk. Users must constantly guard against shoulder surfing by strangers who want to view sensitive information being displayed or entered on a mobile device.

Note

Shoulder surfing is covered in Chapter 2.

Limited Firmware Updates

Currently there are two dominant OSs for mobile devices. The Apple iOS OS, developed by Apple for its mobile devices, is a closed and proprietary architecture. iOS uses its App Store, which is part of Apple iTunes, as the source for distributing apps. When an operating system update is required, Apple users can either update through iTunes or through the *over-the-air (OTA)* update (called **firmware OTA updates**) that is distributed by Apple through the wireless carriers. This is like the way in which patches are routinely distributed through Apple macOS and Microsoft Windows.

However, the other dominant mobile OS, Google Android, is completely different. Unlike iOS, Android is not proprietary but is open for anyone to use or even modify (however, modifications must adhere to Google's criteria to be able to access Google services). Many original equipment manufacturers (OEMs) worldwide who make mobile devices have flocked to Android because it is freely available. These phones were then sold to consumers through different wireless carriers.

Note

A primary distinction between iOS and Android is that Apple creates both hardware and the OS, while Google only creates the OS.

However, because Google does not create the hardware (like Apple) or control the wireless infrastructure, it is very difficult to distribute security updates to the devices through the wireless carriers for these reasons:

- Many OEMs had modified Android, and were reluctant to distribute updates that could potentially conflict with their changes.
- Wireless carriers needed to perform extensive testing to ensure that the updates did not pose any network issues, which can take considerable time and expense.
- Both OEMs and wireless carriers are hesitant to distribute Google updates because it limits their ability to differentiate themselves from competitors if all versions of Android start to look the same through updates.
- Because OEMs and wireless carriers want to sell as many devices as possible, they have no financial incentive to update mobile devices that users would then continue to use indefinitely.

Note ☍

These issues have resulted in no uniformity as to how Android updates are distributed because Google is not in control. Some devices receive security and feature updates as soon as they are available, some OEMs and wireless carriers only regularly update their major "flagship" models but ignore other devices, while others only promise updates each month or each quarter. And devices that are over two years old or are manufactured by small overseas suppliers may never receive updates

Google has been making efforts to make Android security updates more easily available. These initiatives are summarized in Table 10-4.

Table 10-4 Google security update initiatives

Date	Initiative	Description
2013	Separate Android apps, features, and services from OS	Uncoupling the OS from what runs on the OS (apps) makes it easier to update the OS without "breaking" apps or services.
2015	Monthly security patches	Google began releasing monthly security patches for Android that were separate from normal OS updates; this makes the OS more secure without requiring a OS major update.
2017	Project Treble	This project separates the Android OS from hardware-specific drivers and firmware on Android phones, also making it easier for OEMs to update older devices.

Location Tracking

Mobile devices with *global positioning system (GPS)* capabilities typically support **geolocation**, or the process of identifying the geographical location of the device. Geolocation is provided through the device's *location services*. These services can identify the location of a person carrying a mobile device or a specific store or restaurant. This enables the location of a friend to be identified or the address of the nearest coffee shop to be displayed. Location services are used extensively by social media, navigation systems, weather systems, and other mobile-aware applications. One increasing use of location services is to enable a smartphone to immediately display a coupon whenever a user comes near a store or restaurant.

> **Note** 📎
>
> Banks are expanding the use of geolocation to help reduce bank card fraud. When a user makes a purchase at a specific store the bank can immediately check the location of the cell phone. If the cell phone and the bank card are in the same place, then the purchase may be considered legitimate. But if the cell phone is in Nashville and someone is trying to make a purchase in a store in Tampa, then the payment may be rejected. Geolocation can also help prevent rejecting valid purchases. One credit card issuer says that this can reduce these unnecessary declines by as much as 30 percent.[7]

Mobile devices using location services are at increased risk of targeted physical attacks. An attacker can determine where the user and the mobile device are currently located, and use that information to follow the user to steal the mobile device or inflict harm upon the person. In addition, attackers can compile over time a list of people with whom the user associates and the types of activities they perform in particular locations in order to craft attacks.

A related risk is **GPS tagging** (also called *geo-tagging*), which is adding geographical identification data to media such as digital photos taken on a mobile device. A user who, for example, posts a photo on a social networking site may inadvertently be identifying a specific private location to anyone who can access the photo.

Unauthorized Recording

Video cameras ("webcams") and microphones on mobile devices have been a frequent target of attackers. By infecting a device with malware, a threat actor can secretly "spy" on an unsuspecting victim and record conversations or videos. Some basic precautions against unauthorized recording include:

- Do not use a webcam in any room where private activities take place.
- Place a piece of electrical tape over the lens of a webcam when not in use.

- Only allow permission to access the camera or microphone for apps that require that use.
- Periodically review app permissions on the device and turn off those permissions that are not necessary.

> **Note**
>
> Some webcams have a sliding cover that can be moved over the lens of the camera when not in use.

Connection Vulnerabilities

Vulnerabilities in mobile device connections can also be exploited by threat actors. These vulnerabilities are summarized in Table 10-5.

Table 10-5 Connection vulnerabilities

Name	Description	Vulnerability
Tethering	A mobile device with an active Internet connection can be used to share that connection with other mobile devices through Bluetooth or Wi-Fi.	An unsecured mobile device may infect other tethered mobile devices or the corporate network.
USB On-the-Go (OTG)	A mobile device with a USB connection can act as either a host or a peripheral used for external media access.	Connecting a mobile device as a peripheral to an infected computer could allow malware to be sent to the device.
Connecting to public networks	Mobile devices must at times use public external networks for Internet access.	Because these networks are beyond the control of the organization, attackers can eavesdrop on the data transmissions and view sensitive information.

Accessing Untrusted Content

Mobile devices have the ability to access untrusted content that other types of computing devices generally do not have. One example is *Quick Response (QR)* codes. These codes are a matrix or two-dimensional barcode first designed for the automotive industry in Japan. QR codes consist of black modules (square dots) arranged in a square grid on a white background, which can be read by an imaging device such as a mobile device's camera. A QR code for the Cengage website is illustrated in Figure 10-5.

Figure 10-5   QR code

Source: qrstuff.com

> **Note** 📎
>
> QR codes have become popular outside the automotive industry because of their fast readability and greater storage capacity compared to standard barcodes. QR codes can store website URLs, plain text, phone numbers, email addresses, or virtually any alphanumeric data up to 4296 characters.

An attacker can create an advertisement listing a reputable website, such as a bank, but include a QR code that contains a malicious URL. Once the user snaps a picture of the QR code using his mobile device's camera, the code directs the web browser on his mobile device to the attacker's imposter website or to a site that immediately downloads malware.

Normally users cannot download and install unapproved apps on their iOS or Android device. This is because users must access the Apple App Store or Google Play Store (or other Android store) to download an app to install on a mobile device; in fact, Apple devices can only download from the App store. However, users can circumvent the installed built-in limitations on their smartphone (called **jailbreaking** on Apple iOS devices or **rooting** on Android devices) to download from an unofficial **third-party app store** (called **sideloading**) or even write their own **custom firmware** to run on their device. Because these apps have not been vetted they may contain security vulnerabilities or even malicious code.

> **Note** 📎
>
> Jailbreaking and rooting give access to the file system of the mobile device with full permissions, essentially allowing the user to do anything on the device.

Jailbreaking and rooting is not the same as **carrier unlocking**. Originally almost all cell phones were connected ("locked") to a specific wireless carrier so that neither the phone nor the phone number could be transferred to another carrier. This restriction was enforced by a 2012 decision from the Library of Congress that cell phone unlocking was a violation of the Digital Millennium Copyright Act. However, in 2015, the Unlocking Consumer Choice and Wireless Competition Act was passed that approved carrier unlocking.

> **Note** 📎
>
> All major wireless carriers follow the same industry cell phone unlocking standard to make carrier unlocking easier. However, users who are in a contract with an existing carrier or who owe money on a cell phone purchase must first complete all payments before the device can be unlocked. A user who has a phone that is fully paid and an expired contract or who has been using a prepaid phone that has been in service for at least one year can request carrier unlocking.

Another means by which untrusted content can invade mobile devices is through **short message service (SMS)**, which are text messages of a maximum of 160 characters, or **multimedia messaging service (MMS)**, which provides for pictures, video, or audio to be included in text messages. Threat actors can send SMS messages that contain links to untrusted content, or send a specially crafted MMS video that can introduce malware into the device.

> **Note** 📎
>
> One recent MMS attack took advantage of a multimedia player component in Android named Stagefright. This component is not used just for media playback but also to automatically generate thumbnails and to extract information from video and audio files such as length, height, width, and frame rate. Because Stagefright had high-level system permissions, users did not even have to execute a malicious multimedia file; but simply receiving the file could start the infection.

Deployment Model Risks

Due to the widespread use of mobile devices in the enterprise, there are several risks associated with the different enterprise deployment models:

- Users may erase the installed built-in limitations on their mobile device by jailbreaking or rooting to provide additional functionality. However, this also disables the built-in security features.
- Personal mobile devices are often shared among family members and friends, subjecting sensitive corporate data installed on a user's device to outsiders.

- Different mobile devices have different hardware and different versions of OSs, all of which contain different levels and types of security features. Technical support staff might be called upon to support hundreds of different mobile devices, creating a nightmare for establishing a security baseline.
- Mobile devices might be connected to a user's personal desktop computer that is infected, thus infecting the mobile device and increasing the risk of the organization's network becoming infected when the mobile device connects to it.
- It might be difficult to securing the personal smartphone from an employee who left the company so that any corporate data on it can be erased.

Securing Mobile Devices

 **Certification**

2.5 Given a scenario, deploy mobile devices securely.

Securing mobile devices requires several steps. These include configuring the device, using mobile management tools, and configuring device app security.

Device Configuration

Several things should be considered when setting up a mobile device for use. These include disabling unused features, using strong authentication, managing encryption, segmenting storage, and enabling loss or theft services.

Disable Unused Features

Mobile devices include a wide variety of features for the user's convenience. However, each of these can also serve as a threat vector. It is important to disable unused or rarely used features and turn them back on only when needed. For example, one of the features that should be disabled if it is not being regularly used is Bluetooth wireless data communication to prevent bluejacking and bluesnarfing.

 Note

Bluetooth is covered in Chapter 8.

Use Strong Authentication

Verifying that the authentic user of a mobile device has access to it involves two separate configurations. The first is to restrict unauthorized users with a screen lock. The second is to require a strong passcode.

Screen Lock

A **screen lock** prevents the mobile device from being accessed until the user enters the correct passcode (see the next section), permitting access. Lock screens should be configured so that whenever the device is turned on or is inactive for a period, the user must enter the passcode. Most mobile devices can be set to have the screen automatically lock after anywhere from 5 seconds to 50 minutes of inactivity.

Note

A lock screen is a different setting from the *screen timeout* setting that regulates when the screen goes blank to save battery life.

Some mobile devices can be configured so that after a specific number of failed attempts to enter the correct passcode, such as when a thief is trying to guess the code, additional security protections will occur, including:

- *Extend lockout period*. If an incorrect passcode is entered a specific number of times, the lockout period will be extended. For example, if the incorrect passcode is entered five consecutive times, the mobile device will remain completely locked for one minute. If the incorrect code is entered again after one minute, the device will stay locked for double that time, or two minutes. For each successive incorrect entry, the lockout period will double.
- *Reset to factory settings*. If an incorrect passcode is entered a set number of times, the user will be prompted to enter a special phrase to continue. If the phrase is correctly entered, then the user will have only one more opportunity to enter the correct passcode. If an incorrect passcode is entered again, the device will automatically reset to its factory settings and erase any data stored on it.

Some mobile devices can be configured so that the device automatically unlocks and stays unlocked (ignoring the inactivity setting) until a specific action occurs. This is called **context-aware authentication**, or using a contextual setting to validate the user. An example of context-aware authentication can be seen in the Google Android OS that has a feature called Smart Lock that can be configured in different ways based on different contexts. These are listed in Table 10-6.

Table 10-6 Android Smart Lock configuration options

Configuration name	Explanation	Comments
On-body detection	Device turns on and remains on when it is on the user's body in a pocket or purse.	On-body detection learns the pattern of how the user walks, and if it detects a different walk style it locks the device.
Trusted places detection	Can set a specific location where the phone will turn on and then off when the user leaves the location.	Device will remain unlocked in an 80-meter radius around a building; users can also designate a specific building at a single address.
Trusted devices detection	Device will unlock whenever it is connected to another specific device.	Common trusted devices are Bluetooth watches, fitness trackers, or car systems; users should avoid trusted devices that are always with the device like a Bluetooth mouse.
Trusted face	Whenever the device is turned on it will search for the designated face and unlock if it recognizes the user.	This is the least secure configuration option because the device could be tricked by someone who looks similar.
Trusted voice	If a user says, "OK Google," voice commands can be issued without unlocking the device.	Trusted voice does not completely unlock the device as with other options but only gives the ability to issue some voice commands.

Passcode

Most mobile devices have different options for the type of passcode that can be entered. Although passwords are the most secure option, most users unfortunately opt not to configure their device with a password. This is primarily due to the time needed to enter the password and the difficulty of entering a complex password on the device's small on-screen virtual keyboard.

Another option is to use a **personal identification number (PIN)**. Unlike a password that can be comprised of letters, numbers, and characters, a PIN is made up of numbers only. Although the length of the PIN can usually range from 4–16 numbers, many users choose to set a short four-digit PIN, like those used with a bank's automated teller machine (ATM). However, short PIN codes provide only a limited amount of security. An analysis of 3.4 million users' four-digit (0000–9999) PINs that were compromised revealed that users create predictable PIN patterns. The PIN 1234 was used in more than one out of every 10 PINs. Table 10-7 lists the five most common PINs and their frequency of use. Of the 10,000 potential PIN combinations, 26.83 percent of all PINs could be guessed by attempting just the top 20 most frequent PINs.[8]

Table 10-7 Most common PINs

Pin	Frequency of use
1234	10.71%
1111	6.01%
0000	1.88%
1212	1.19%
7777	0.74%

Note

The research also revealed that the least common PIN was *8068*, which appeared in only 25 of the 3.4 million PINs.

A third option is to use a fingerprint "swipe" on a sensor to unlock the mobile device. Several smartphone devices have the fingerprint sensor on the back of the phone. This allows the user to access the fingerprint reader without the need to move their index finger from the back of the phone (where the index finger is normally located while holding the phone).

Note

Accessing a device through fingerprint, face, or voice, is called *biometrics* and is covered in Chapter 12.

A final option is to draw or swipe a specific pattern connecting dots to unlock the device. This is illustrated in Figure 10-6. Swipe patterns can be detected by threat actors who watch a user draw the pattern or observe any lingering "smear" on the screen.

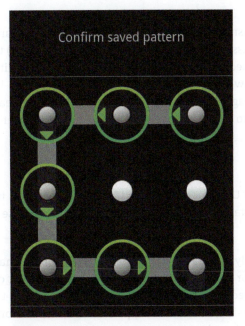

Figure 10-6   Swipe pattern
Source: OnlineAndroidTips.com

Manage Encryption

With previous generations of mobile devices neither Apple iOS nor Google Android provided native encryption, so third-party apps had to be installed to encrypt data. However, later versions of both iOS (iOS version 8 in 2014) and Android (Android 6.0 Marshmallow in 2015) encrypted all data on their mobile devices (*full disk encryption*) by default.

> **Note** 📎
>
> Beginning with Android 7.0, Google provided an encryption option called *file-based encryption*, which is considered more secure than full disk encryption. File-based encryption encrypts different files with different keys so that files can be unlocked independently without requiring an entire partition to be decrypted at once. This allows the device to decrypt and use files needed to boot the system and process critical notifications while not decrypting personal apps and data.

Although data on a mobile device—*local* data-at-rest—is encrypted so that unauthorized users cannot access it, there are significant loopholes in which mobile device data *can* be accessed through data-in-transit and *remote* data-at-rest.

Data-in-Transit

Mobile devices that transmit information using cellular telephony are subject to the 1994 Communications Assistance for Law Enforcement Act (CALEA) that requires telecommunications (telecom) carriers to build surveillance capabilities into their networks. This allows law enforcement agencies to can collect data-in-transit—like phone calls and SMS text messages—crossing through their networks in real time. This Act was later expanded in 2006 to cover "web traffic" and Internet Voice over IP (VoIP) traffic.

> **Note** 📎
>
> In 2015, one of the major U.S. telecoms received 287,980 court orders for user information from all courts (federal, state, and local) covering criminal and civil cases.[9]

However, a relatively new category of mobile apps deliver what is called *over-the-top (OTT)* content, or the delivery of audio, video, and similar content over the Internet without the telecoms being directly involved (other than their networks are being used for transmission). When OTT apps are used, the telecoms can see that the communications are taking place but cannot see the contents of the communication. Even though the courts can ask the app providers to surrender data that they may have stored on their servers from users, there is no requirement about how long they must store the data. One popular OTT app does not store user's messages after they have been delivered so that nothing can be handed over.

> **Note** 📎
>
> Some governments do not like OTT. In 2016, the Brazilian federal police arrested the vice president of Facebook's Latin American operations for not complying with police requests to access WhatsApp (an OTT app owned by Facebook) messages that have been linked to drug trafficking and organized crime cases. In late 2015, another Brazilian judge ordered the complete shutdown of WhatsApp across the entire country for 48 hours after Facebook did not comply with another court order, and in another case, Facebook was fined $250,000 for not complying with three other court requests for OTT data.[10]

Remote Data-at-Rest

Data from mobile devices is routinely backed up to Apple's iCloud or to a Google server. Despite the fact that the data on these servers is encrypted, Apple and Google possess the decryption keys necessary to unlock the data on their servers. Because the data is encrypted on the user's device and is inaccessible to outside parties, courts routinely serve orders to Apple and Google to provide data stored on their servers.

> **Note** 📎
>
> In the first six months of 2016, Apple received 2,564 court orders for data stored on its iCloud servers. While some of the court orders requested only information about an account holder's iTunes or iCloud account, such as a name and an address, other court orders demanded that Apple provide customers' iCloud content, including stored photos, email, iOS device backups, documents, contacts, calendars, and bookmarks.[11]

Because Apple and Google hold the decryption keys to users' data stored on their servers, they can provide the decryption keys to unlock the data to authorities. Those users who are concerned about maintaining the highest level of security on their data often turn off backups to iCloud or Google servers.

Segment Storage

With the exception of corporate-owned devices, each of the other enterprise deployment models (BYOD, COPE, and CYOD) permit the user of a mobile device to use it for both business and personal needs. However, this may result in "co mingling" critical business data with personal photos, downloads, and SMS text messages, something that is not desirable to either the enterprise or the user.

An option on mobile devices that contain both personal and corporate data is **storage segmentation**, or separating business data from personal data. This can be done by using **containerization**, or separating storage into separate business and personal "containers" and managing each appropriately.

There are several advantages to segmenting storage on a mobile device used for both business and personal needs. It helps companies avoid data ownership privacy issues and legal concerns regarding a user's personal data stored on the device. In addition, it allows companies to delete only business data when necessary without touching personal data.

> **Note** 📎
>
> Third-party software is available to create containers on a mobile device's internal memory, or the data can be separately stored on the device's removable storage microSD card.

Enable Loss or Theft Services

One of the greatest risks of a mobile device is the loss or theft of the device. Unprotected devices can be used to access corporate networks or view sensitive data stored on them. To reduce the risk of theft or loss:

- Keep the mobile device out of sight when traveling in a high-risk area.
- Avoid becoming distracted by what is on the device. Always maintain an awareness of your surroundings.

- When holding a device, use both hands to make it more difficult for a thief to snatch.
- Do not use the device on escalators or near transit train doors.
- White or red headphone cords may indicate they are connected to an expensive device. Consider changing the cord to a less conspicuous color.
- If a theft does occur, do not resist or chase the thief. Instead, take note of the suspect's description, including any identifying characteristics and clothing, and then call the authorities. Also contact the organization or wireless carrier and change all passwords for accounts accessed on the device.

If a mobile device is lost or stolen, several security features can be enabled to locate the device or limit the damage. Many of these can be configured through a feature in the operating system or an installed third-party app. These features are listed in Table 10-8.

Table 10-8 Security features for locating lost or stolen mobile devices

Security feature	Explanation
Alarm	The device can generate an alarm even if it is on mute.
Last known location	If the battery is charged to less than a specific percentage, the device's last known location can be indicated on an online map.
Locate	The current location of the device can be pinpointed on a map through the device's GPS.
Remote lockout	The mobile device can be remotely locked and a custom message sent that is displayed on the login screen.
Thief picture	A thief who enters an incorrect passcode three times will have her picture taken through the device's on-board camera and emailed to the owner.

If a lost or stolen device cannot be located, it may be necessary to perform a **remote wipe**, which will erase sensitive data stored on the mobile device. This ensures that even if a thief accesses the device, no sensitive data will be compromised.

Mobile Management Tools

When using mobile devices in the enterprise there are several support tools that can facilitate the management of the devices. These include mobile device management, mobile application management, and mobile content management.

Mobile Device Management (MDM)

Mobile device management (MDM) tools allow a device to be managed remotely by an organization. MDM typically involves a server component, which sends out management commands to the mobile devices, and a client component, which runs on the mobile device to receive and implement the management commands. An administrator can then perform OTA updates or configuration changes to one device, groups of devices, or all devices.

Some of the features that MDM tools provide include the ability to:

- Rapidly enroll new mobile devices (*on-boarding*) and quickly remove devices (*off-boarding*) from the organization's network
- Apply or modify default device settings
- Enforce encryption settings, antivirus updates, and patch management
- Display an acceptable use policy that requires consent before allowing access
- Configure email, calendar, contacts, Wi-Fi, and virtual private network (VPN) profiles OTA
- Discover devices accessing enterprise systems
- Approve or quarantine new mobile devices
- Distribute and manage public and corporate apps
- Securely share and update documents and corporate policies
- Detect and restrict jailbroken and rooted devices
- Selectively erase corporate data while leaving personal data intact
- Send SMS text messages to selected users or groups of users (called **push notification services**)

> **Note** 📎
>
> MDM also can facilitate *asset tracking*, or maintaining an accurate record of company-owned mobile devices.

Mobile Application Management (MAM)

Whereas MDM focuses on the device, *mobile application management (MAM)* covers **application management**, which comprises the tools and services responsible for distributing and controlling access to apps. These apps can be internally developed or commercially available apps.

> **Note** 📎
>
> MDM provides a high degree of control over the device but a lower level of control on the apps, whereas MAM gives a higher level of control over apps but less control over the device.

MAM initially controlled apps through *app wrapping*, which sets up a "dynamic" library of software routines and adds to an existing program (binary) to restrict parts of an app. For example, an app could be wrapped so that when it was launched, a passcode had to be entered before it could be used. Another example is that a wrapped app could require a VPN for specific communications. Using an MAM originally required the use of an MDM as well, although newer versions of some mobile device operating systems have MAM incorporated into the software itself.

Mobile Content Management (MCM)

Content management is used to support the creation and subsequent editing and modification of digital content by multiple employees. It can include tracking editing history, version control (recording changes and "rolling back" to a previous version if necessary), indexing, and searching. A *mobile content management (MCM)* system is tuned to provide content management to hundreds or even thousands of mobile devices used by employees in an enterprise.

Mobile Device App Security

In addition to securing the mobile device, the apps on the device should be secured. Just as the data can be encrypted, so too can the app itself if it is an application created in-house that could provide insight to an attacker about the corporate network or is an app that a competitor might want to steal. Also, apps can require that the user provide authentication such as a passcode before access is granted.

Note

There are also many security apps that can be downloaded to protect mobile devices.

MDMs can also provide app security support. These tools can force *application whitelisting*, which ensures that only preapproved apps can run on the device. MDMs also can enforce **geofencing**. Geofencing uses the device's GPS to define geographical boundaries where the app can be used. For example, a tablet containing patient information that leaves the hospital grounds or an employee who attempts to enter a restricted area with a device can result in an alert sent to an administrator.

Note

Geofencing is commonly used in law enforcement. An individual under house arrest is fitted with an ankle bracelet that alerts authorities if the individual leaves the house.

Embedded Systems and the Internet of Things

Not all computer systems are stand-alone devices with a screen, mouse, and keyboard. Computing capabilities can be integrated into a variety of devices. A growing trend is to add these capabilities to devices that have never had computing power before. These devices include embedded systems and the Internet of Things, and these devices have significant security implications.

Embedded Systems

An **embedded system** is computer hardware and software contained within a larger system that is designed for a specific function. Examples of embedded systems include medical devices, aircraft, vehicles, industrial machines, and **heating, ventilation, and air conditioning (HVAC)** environmental systems that provide and regulate heating and cooling. Industrial enterprises were early adopters of embedded systems. **Industrial control systems (ICS)** control locally or at remote locations by collecting, monitoring, and processing real-time data so that machines can directly control devices such as valves, pumps, and motors without the need for human intervention. Multiple ICS are managed by a larger **supervisory control and data acquisition (SCADA)** system.

Note 📎

SCADA systems are crucial today for industrial organizations. They help to maintain efficiency and provide information on issues to help reduce downtime.

The progression of embedded systems in automobiles is an example of how these systems have dramatically changed human-to-machine interaction. The first automobile embedded systems appeared in mass-production vehicles in the mid-1970s in response to regulations calling for higher fuel economy and emission standards, and handled basic functions such as engine ignition timing and transmission shifting. By the 1980s, more sophisticated computerized engine-management systems enabled the use of reliable electronic fuel-injection systems, and later active safety systems such as anti-lock braking and traction and stability control features were added, all controlled by embedded systems. Today embedded systems in cars use sonar, radar, and laser emitters to control brakes, steering, and the throttle to perform functions such as blind-spot and pedestrian collision warnings, automated braking, safe distance-keeping, and fully automated parking. Some of the embedded systems in cars are shown in Figure 10-7.

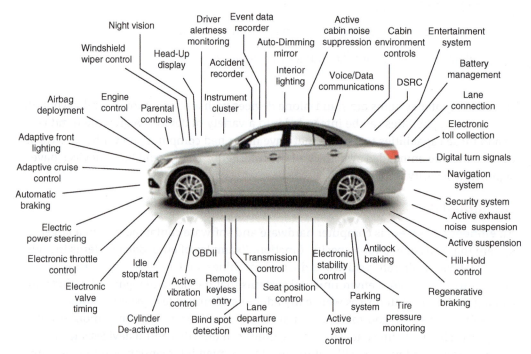

Figure 10-7 **Embedded systems in cars**

© 2016 ChipsEtc.com

> **Note** 📎
>
> There are over 50 embedded systems in today's average car. With the introduction of self-driving autonomous cars, the number of embedded systems in a car will skyrocket into the hundreds.

Although all embedded systems are different based on the requirements and capabilities of the underlying system, they still all have hardware that is operated by software, just as with a standard computer system. The hardware is typically a **system on a chip (SoC)**, which is all the necessary hardware components contained on a single microprocessor chip. The software is often a **real-time operating system (RTOS)** that is specifically designed for an SoC in an embedded system. Standard computer systems, such as a laptop with a mouse and a keyboard or a tablet with a touchscreen, typically receive irregular "bursts" of input data from a user or a network connection. Embedded systems, on the other hand, receive very large amounts of data very quickly, such as an aircraft preparing to land on a runway at night during a storm. RTOS is tuned to accommodate very high volumes of data that must be immediately processed for critical decision making.

Internet of Things

The Telecommunication Standardization Sector of the International Telecommunication Union (ITU-T) defines the **Internet of Things (IoT)** as *A global infrastructure for the information society, enabling advanced services by interconnecting (physical and virtual) things based on existing and evolving interoperable information and communication technologies.*[12] More simply put, the IoT is connecting any device to the Internet for the purpose of sending and receiving data to be acted upon. Although this definition could encompass laptop computers and tablets, more often IoT refers to devices that heretofore were not considered as computing devices connected to a data network. IoT devices include wearable technology and multifunctional devices as well as many everyday home automation items such as thermostats, coffee makers, tire sensors, slow cookers, keyless entry systems, washing machines, electric toothbrushes, headphones, and light bulbs, to name just a few. It is estimated that by 2020 there will be over 26 billion IoT devices.[13]

An example of IoT and the great promise it holds can be seen in devices that can be used for *body area networks (BAN)*, which is a network system of IoT devices in close proximity to a person's body that cooperate for the benefit of the user. Sensors are placed on the human body to monitor electrocardiogram (EKG) impulses, blood pressure, glucose, and other human biological functions. These are then transmitted via computer or smartphone to a third-party physician who can make a decision regarding any medications to prescribe or lifestyle changes to recommend. This *managed body sensor network (MBSN)* is illustrated in Figure 10-8.

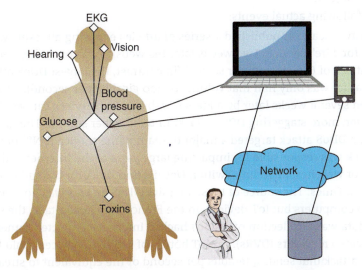

Figure 10-8   Managed body sensor network (MBSN)

A more robust approach is the *autonomous body sensor network (ABSN)*. Instead of only reading and transmitting information, an ABSN introduces actuators in addition to the sensors so that immediate effects can be made on the human body. Dozens of IoT micro-stimulator implant devices can be used to treat paralysis and other conditions. These devices take in signals from the human nervous system and then stimulate nerves through electrical charges that cause muscles to contract and limbs to move, bypassing areas of the nervous system that have been impaired by strokes or spinal cord or brain injuries. The ABSN can expand the use of functional electric stimulation to restore sensation, mobility, and function to those persons with paralyzed limbs and organs. Another ABSN being tested installs "stretchy" microprocessors on the tips of cardiac catheters, which are threaded through arteries into the heart. These catheters will be used to monitor the heart's electrical activity to pinpoint the location of irregular heartbeats, and if necessary can treat the heart by "zapping" the tissue that is malfunctioning.

> **Note** 📎
>
> One type of ABSN has already been approved for use. In late 2011, the Federal Communications Commission (FCC) gave approval for the use of medical micropower networks (MMN). Four blocks of the 400 MHz spectrum (two of the four channels are 426-432 and 438-444 MHz while the other two are above and below the 420-450 MHz band) are allocated for low-power wide-band networks.

Security Implications

Consider the following actual events:

- A security researcher published a series of articles exposing attackers who ran a "DDoS-for-hire" service. Two weeks later his website was overwhelmed with a DDoS attack of 620 gigabits per second (in contrast, the largest DDoS attack three years earlier was only half that volume or 300 gigabits per second). This was followed several weeks later by a French web hosting service that was the victim of an even more staggering DDoS attack: 1.1 terabits per second. The following month, a DDoS attack targeted a major domain name service (DNS) provider and the attack was responsible for impacting large parts of the Internet and disabling dozens of websites, including Twitter, Netflix, Spotify, Airbnb, Reddit, and The New York Times. The source of these massive DDoS attacks was not traditional desktop computers but IoT devices. In the French web host attack, the source of the data was a collection of 145,607 hacked Internet-connected cameras and digital video recorders (DVRs). An IoT botnet of 1 million devices could launch a DDoS attack that sends 4 terabits per second or the equivalent to streaming 800,000 high-definition movies simultaneously.[14]

- A worm was discovered that was actively targeting Windows computers that managed large-scale SCADA systems, which are often found in military installations, oil pipeline control systems, manufacturing environments, and even nuclear power plants. Named Stuxnet, this malware attempted to gain administrative access to other computers through the network to control the SCADA system. It appears that Stuxnet's primary target was nuclear reactors at the Bushehr nuclear power plant. Located in southwestern Iran near the Persian Gulf, Bushehr was a source of tension between Iran and the West (including the United States) because of fear that spent fuel from the reactor could be reprocessed elsewhere in the country to produce weapons-grade plutonium for use in nuclear warheads. Stuxnet was ultimately not successful in its attack.[15]
- Marc G. was in the kitchen when he began to hear strange sounds coming from the nursery of his two-year-old daughter Allyson. Marc and his wife entered the nursery and heard a stranger's voice calling out Allyson's name, cursing at her and calling her vile names. The parents discovered that the voice was coming from the electronic baby monitor in Allyson's room that contained a camera, microphone, and speaker connected to their home Wi-Fi network. Because they did not have any security set on their wireless network, the attacker had been able to take control of the baby monitor from an unknown remote location. When Marc and his wife stepped in front of the camera, the attacker turned his verbal attack toward them. They quickly unplugged the device. The parents surmised that the attacker knew their daughter's name because he saw "Allyson" spelled out on the wall in her room. This situation is not unique: it is estimated that there are more than 100,000 wireless IoT cameras that can easily be exploited because they have virtually no security.[16]

These three events illustrate the fact that security in embedded systems and particularly IoT devices is lacking and can result in a wide range of attacks.

There are several reasons why IoT and embedded system devices are so vulnerable:

- Most IoT vendors are concerned primarily with making products as inexpensive as possible, which means leaving out all security protections.
- Those devices that do have any security capabilities implemented have notoriously weak security. For example, several attacks using compromised IoT devices used firmware that was traced back to a single Chinese electronics supplier. The firmware had a hard-coded backdoor so that the default user name and password could not be changed. The user names ("root," "admin," "support," etc.) and passwords ("admin," "888888," "default," "123456," "54321," and even "password") were simple and well-known.
- Few, if any, IoT devices have been designed with the capacity for being updated to address exposed security vulnerabilities.
- IoT and embedded systems that can receive patches often see long gaps between the discovery of the vulnerability and a patch being applied. Many IoT and embedded devices run the Linux OS. The average lifetime of a critical

security bug in the Linux kernel, from the time the Linux code is finalized to a vulnerability being uncovered and then a patch issued, is over three years.

There are several initiatives underway to address security vulnerabilities in IoT and embedded devices. Some of these initiatives are listed in Table 10-9. However, these initiatives are scattered and do not represent a comprehensive solution to the problem. It is predicted that as use of embedded systems and IoT devices continues to grow, so too will attacks on them.

Table 10-9 Embedded system and IoT security initiatives

Organization	Initiative	Explanation
U.S. Federal Trade Commission (FTC)	Prize competition	A contest for developers to create a system for automatic software updates to be distributed to IoT devices; top prize is $25,000.
Z-Wave Alliance	Security 2 (S2) framework	A framework that requires a QR code or PIN on each IoT device for authenticating it to the network, uses an Elliptic Curve Diffie–Hellman secure key exchange and a Transport Layer Security (TLS) tunnel.
Industrial Internet Consortium	Industrial Internet Security Framework (IISF)	A set of best practices to help developers and users assess risks and defend against them; has created a systematic way to implement security in IoT and a common language communication.
European Commission	European Union Telecomm Law and Regulations	Update laws and regulations by creating rules that force companies to meet tough security standards and go through a multi-pronged certification processes to guarantee privacy.
IEEE	P2413 Standard for an Architectural Framework for the Internet of Things (IoT)	An architectural framework for IoT that defines relationships among various IoT verticals (e.g., transportation, healthcare, etc.) and common architecture elements, and provides a blueprint for data abstraction and protection, security, privacy, and safety.

Note @

Visa has announced that it is partnering with IBM to add payment capabilities to many IoT devices. Their objective is to create additional "points of sale" where they did not already exist. This would allow a wearable fitness band to tell its owner when it is time to replace athletic shoes and even allow them to be ordered through the band itself. Many security researchers question if adding payment capabilities to already vulnerable IoT devices is a wise step.

Chapter Summary

- There are several types of mobile devices. Tablet computers are portable computing devices smaller than portable computers, larger than smartphones, and focused on ease of use. Tablets generally lack a built-in keyboard and rely on a touch screen. A smartphone includes an operating system that allows it to run apps and access the Internet, and it offers a broader range of functionality. A new class of mobile technology is wearable technology, devices that can be worn by the user instead of being carried.

- Portable computers are devices that closely resemble standard desktop computers. A laptop is designed to replicate the abilities of a desktop computer with only slightly less processing power yet is small enough to be used on a lap or small table. A notebook computer is a smaller version of a laptop computer that is designed to include only the most basic frequently used features of a standard computer in a smaller size that is easy to carry. A subnotebook computer is even smaller than the standard notebook. A 2-in-1 computer can be used as either a subnotebook or a tablet. Web-based computers are designed to be used primarily while connected to the Internet.

- Many mobile devices use Wi-Fi as the standard connectivity method to connect to remote networks, with some support for Bluetooth and NFC as personal area network connections. Many devices also support other types of connectivity methods. Cellular telephony divides the coverage area into cells. Satellite communications (SATCOM) uses a repeater located in a satellite to "bounce" signals to and from earth. At one time, infrared data ports were installed on devices so that data could be exchanged using infrared light. However, due to its slow speed and other limitations, infrared capabilities in mobile devices are rarely found. ANT is a proprietary wireless network technology that is used primarily for sensors communicating data. There are different types and sizes of USB connections on mobile devices that are used for data transfer.

- It is not always feasible to require an employee to carry a company-owned smartphone along with a personal cell phone. Many organizations have adopted an enterprise deployment model as it relates to mobile devices. Bring your own device (BYOD) allows users to use their own personal mobile devices for business purposes. Corporate owned, personally enabled (COPE) gives employees a choice from a selection of company approved devices. Choose your own device (CYOD) gives employees a limited selection of approved devices but the employee pays the upfront cost of the device while the business owns the contract. Corporate-owned devices are purchased and owned by the enterprise.

- Several risks are associated with using mobile devices. Mobile devices are used in a wide variety of locations that are outside of the organization's normal physical perimeter. Devices can easily be lost or stolen, and any unprotected data on the device can be retrieved by a thief. The Google Android OS, unlike Apple iOS, has weaknesses in patching and updating the OS. Geolocation, or the process of identifying the geographical location of a device, can be helpful but also is a security risk because it can identify the location of a person carrying a mobile device. Video cameras and microphones on mobile devices have been used by attackers to secretly "spy" on an unsuspecting victim. Vulnerabilities in mobile device connections can also be exploited by threat actors.

- Mobile devices have the ability to access untrusted content that other types of computing devices generally do not have. One example is Quick Response (QR) codes that can be created to direct a victim to a malicious website. Users can circumvent the installed built-in limitations on their smartphone (jailbreaking on Apple iOS devices or rooting on Android devices) to download from an unofficial third-party app store (called sideloading) or even write their own custom firmware to run on their device. Because these apps have not been vetted, they may contain security vulnerabilities or even malicious code. Other means by which untrusted content can invade mobile devices include short message service (SMS), text messages of a maximum of 160 characters, or multimedia messaging service (MMS), which provides for pictures, video, or audio to be included in text messages. There are several risks associated with the different enterprise deployment models.

- There are several security considerations when initially setting up a mobile device. It is important to disable unused features and turn off those that do not support the business use of the device or that are rarely used. A lock screen prevents the mobile device from being used until the user enters the correct passcode. Some mobile devices can be configured so that after a specific number of failed attempts to enter the correct passcode, such as when a thief is trying to guess the code, additional

security protections will occur. Most mobile devices have different options for the type of passcode that can be entered. Although passwords are the most secure option, many users instead opt for a weaker personal identification number (PIN), fingerprint reader, or draw or swipe a specific pattern connecting dots to unlock the device. Although later versions of both iOS and Android encrypt all data on mobile devices, there are significant loopholes through which mobile device data can be accessed.

- There are several support tools that can facilitate the management of mobile devices in the enterprise. Mobile device management (MDM) tools allow a device to be managed remotely by an organization. Mobile application management (MAM) covers application management, which comprises the tools and services responsible for distributing and controlling access to apps. A mobile content management (MCM) system provides content management to mobile devices used by employees in an enterprise. In addition to securing the mobile device itself, the apps on the device also should be secured.

- An embedded system is computer hardware and software contained within a larger system that is designed for a specific function. Although embedded systems differ based on the requirements and capabilities of the underlying system, they all have hardware that is operated by software, just as with a standard computer system. The Internet of Things (IoT) is connecting any device to the Internet for the purpose of sending and receiving data to be acted upon. Security in embedded systems and particularly in IoT devices is lacking and can result in a wide range of attacks. There are several initiatives underway to address security vulnerabilities.

Key Terms

ANT
application management
bring your own device (BYOD)
carrier unlocking
cellular telephony
choose your own device
   (CYOD)
containerization
content management
context-aware
   authentication
corporate-owned
corporate owned,
   personally enabled (COPE)
custom firmware
embedded system
firmware OTA updates

geofencing
geolocation
GPS tagging
heating, ventilation, and air
   conditioning (HVAC)
industrial control systems
   (ICS)
infrared
Internet of Things (IoT)
jailbreaking
multimedia messaging
   service (MMS)
personal identification
   number (PIN)
push notification services
real-time operating system
   (RTOS)

remote wipe
rooting
satellite communications
   (SATCOM)
screen lock
short message service (SMS)
sideloading
storage segmentation
supervisory control and
   data acquisition (SCADA)
system on a chip (SoC)
tethering
third-party app store
USB connections
USB On-the-Go (OTG)

Review Questions

1. Which technology is NOT a core feature of a mobile device?
   a. Physical keyboard
   b. Small form factor
   c. Local non-removable data storage
   d. Data synchronization capabilities

2. Agape was asked to make a recommendation regarding short-range wireless technologies to be supported in a new conference room that was being renovated. Which of the following would she NOT consider due to its slow speed and its low deployment levels today?
   a. ANT
   b. Bluetooth
   c. Infrared
   d. NFC

3. Calista is designing the specifications for new laptop computers to be purchased by her company. She is comparing the different types and sizes of USB

connections found on the devices. Which type USB connection would she NOT find on a laptop?
   a. Type D
   b. Mini
   c. Micro
   d. Standard

4. In her job interview, Xiu asks about the company policy regarding smartphones. She is told that employees may choose from a limited list of approved devices but that she must pay for the device herself; however, the company will provide her with a monthly stipend. Which type of enterprise deployment model does this company support?
   a. BYOD
   b. COPE
   c. CYOD
   d. Corporate-owned

5. Pakpao has been asked to provide research regarding a new company initiative to add Android smartphones to a list of approved devices. One of the considerations is how frequently the smartphones receive firmware OTA updates. Which of the following reasons would Pakpao NOT list in his report as a factor in the frequency of Android firmware OTA updates?

   a. Both OEMs and wireless carriers are hesitant to distribute Google updates because it limits their ability to differentiate themselves from competitors if all versions of Android start to look the same through updates.

   b. Because many of the OEMs had modified Android, they are reluctant to distribute updates that could potentially conflict with their changes.

   c. Wireless carriers are reluctant to provide firmware OTA updates because of the bandwidth it consumes on their wireless networks.

   d. Because OEMs and wireless carriers want to sell as many devices as possible, they have no financial incentive to update mobile devices that users would then continue to use indefinitely.

6. What is the process of identifying the geographical location of a mobile device?

   a. Geotracking

   b. Geolocation

   c. geoID

   d. Geomonitoring

7. Which of these is NOT a risk of connecting a mobile device to a public network?

   a. Public networks are beyond the control of the employee's organization.

   b. Replay attacks can occur on public networks.

   c. Public networks may be susceptible to man-in-the-middle attacks.

   d. Public networks are faster than local networks and can spread malware more quickly to mobile devices.

8. Paavo was reviewing a request by an executive for a new subnotebook computer. The executive said that he wanted USB OTG support and asked Paavo's opinion regarding its security. What would Paavo tell him about USB OTG security?

   a. USB OTG uses strong security and the executive should have no concerns.

   b. Subnotebooks do not support USB OTG.

   c. An unsecured mobile device could infect other tethered mobile devices or the corporate network.

   d. Connecting a mobile device as a peripheral to an infected computer could allow malware to be sent to that device.

9. A friend of Ukrit told him that he has just downloaded and installed an app that allows him to circumvent the built-in limitations on his Apple iOS smartphone. What is this called?

   a. Rooting

   b. Sideloading

   c. Jailbreaking

   d. Ducking

10. Which of the following technologies provides for pictures, video, or audio to be included in text messages?

    a. MMS

    b. QS

    c. SMS

    d. ANT

11. What prevents a mobile device from being used until the user enters the correct passcode?
    a. Swipe identifier (SW-ID)
    b. Screen lock
    c. Screen timeout
    d. Touch swipe

12. Gaetan has attempted to enter the passcode for his mobile device but keeps entering the wrong code. Now he is asked to enter a special phrase to continue. Which configuration setting is enabled on Gaetan's mobile device?
    a. Reset to factory settings
    b. Extend lockout period
    c. Enable high security
    d. Lock device

13. What does containerization do?
    a. It splits operating system functions only on specific brands of mobile devices.
    b. It places all keys in a special vault.
    c. It slows down a mobile device to half speed.
    d. It separates personal data from corporate data.

14. What allows a device to be managed remotely?
    a. Mobile device management (MDM)
    b. Mobile application management (MAM)
    c. Mobile resource management (MRM)
    d. Mobile wrapper management (MWM)

15. Which of these is NOT a security feature for locating a lost or stolen mobile device?
    a. Remote lockout
    b. Last known good configuration
    c. Alarm
    d. Thief picture

16. What enforces the location in which an app can function by tracking the location of the mobile device?
    a. Location resource management
    b. Geofencing
    c. GPS tagging
    d. Graphical Management Tracking (GMT)

17. Which of these is considered the strongest type of passcode to use on a mobile device?
    a. Password
    b. PIN
    c. Fingerprint swipe
    d. Draw connecting dots pattern

18. Jabez needs to alert through an SMS text message those corporate users who have a specific brand and type of mobile device regarding a serious malware incident. What technology will she use?
    a. MCM
    b. COPE
    c. MAM
    d. Push notification services

19. Which tool manages the distribution and control of apps?
    a. MAM
    b. MDM
    c. MCM
    d. MFM

20. Which type of OS is typically found on an embedded system?
    a. SoC
    b. RTOS
    c. OTG
    d. COPE

Hands-On Projects

If you are concerned about installing any of the software in these projects on your regular computer, you can instead install the software in the Windows virtual machine created in the Chapter 1 Hands-On Projects 1-3 and 1-4. Software installed within the virtual machine will not impact the host computer.

Project 10-1: Creating and Using QR Codes

Quick Response (QR) codes can be read by an imaging device such as a mobile device's camera or online. In this project, you create and use QR codes.

1. Use your web browser to go to **www.qrstuff.com**. (The location of content on the Internet may change without warning. If you are no longer able to access the program through this URL, use a search engine to search for "Qrstuff".)

2. First create a QR code. Under **DATA TYPE** be sure that **Website URL** is selected.

3. Under **CONTENT** enter the URL **http://www.cengagebrain.com** as illustrated in Figure 10-9. Note how the **QR CODE PREVIEW** changes.

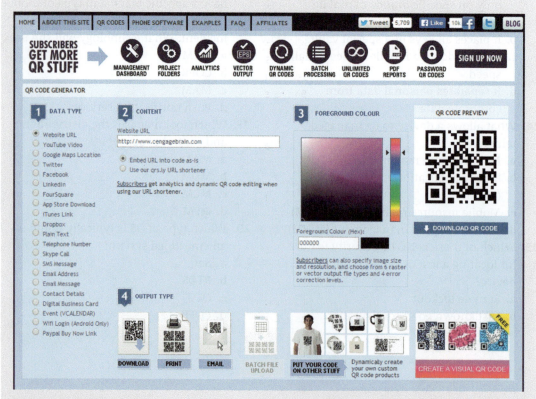

FIGURE 10-9 QR code

Source: http://www.qrstuff.com/

4. Under **OUTPUT TYPE**, click **DOWNLOAD** to download an image of the QR code.

5. Navigate to the location of the download and open the image. Is there anything you can tell by looking at this code?

6. Now use an online reader to interpret the QR code. Use your web browser to go to **blog .qr4.nl/Online-QR-Code_decoder.aspx** (The location of content on the Internet may change without warning. If you are no longer able to access the program through this URL, use a search engine and search for "Free Online QR Code Reader").

7. Click **Choose File**.

8. Navigate to the location of the QR code that you downloaded on your computer and click **Open**.

9. Click **Upload**.

10. In the textbox, what does it display? How could an attacker use a QR code to direct a victim to a malicious website?

11. Return to **www.qrstuff.com**.

12. Click **Google Maps Location** under **DATA TYPE**.

13. Under **Or use the field below to geo-locate an address** to enter an address with which you are familiar. Click **go**.

14. The latitude and longitude will be automatically entered under **CONTENT**.

15. Under **OUTPUT TYPE**, click **DOWNLOAD** to download an image of this QR code.

16. Navigate to the location of the download and open the image. How does it look different from the previous QR code? Is there anything you can tell by looking at this code?

17. Use your web browser to return to **blog.qr4.nl/Online-QR-Code_decoder.aspx**.

18. Click **Choose File**.

19. Navigate to the location of the Google Maps Location QR code that you downloaded on your computer and click **Open**.

20. Click **Upload**.

21. In the textbox, a URL will be displayed. Paste this URL into a web browser.

22. What does the browser display? How could an attacker use this for a malicious attack?

23. Return to **www.qrstuff.com**.

24. Click each option under **DATA TYPE** to view the different items that can be created by a QR code. Select three and indicate how they could be used by an attacker.

25. Close all windows.

Project 10-2: Using Software to Locate a Missing Laptop

If a mobile device is lost or stolen, there are several different security features that can be used to locate the device or limit the damage. Many of these can be used through an installed third-party app. In this project, you download and install software that can locate a missing laptop computer. Note that for this project a portable computer or desktop computer can be used.

1. Open your web browser and enter the URL **preyproject.com**. (The location of content on the Internet may change without warning. If you are no longer able to access the program through this URL, use a search engine and search for "Prey Project".)

2. Click **Features**.
3. Read through the information so you will understand what Prey does.
4. Return to the home page.
5. Click **Download**.
6. Select the latest version for your computer.
7. When the file finishes downloading, run the program and follow the default installation procedures.
8. Click **Finish** to configure the Prey settings.
9. Be sure that **New user** is selected. Click **Next**.
10. Enter your information to create an account and click **Create**.
11. Go to **panel.preyproject.com**.
12. Enter your login information, and on the **All your devices** page, click the name of your recently added device.
13. You will then receive in your email information about this added device.
14. Notice that your device is shown on a map regarding its current location. How accurate is this?
15. Click **Hardware information**. How accurate is this information?
16. Click **Map and actions**.
17. Under **Actions** in the right pane, click **Sound alarm**. Read the popup window about this function. How would it be useful? Depending upon your setting either click **Close** (to cancel this) or **Confirm** (to sounds the alarm).
18. Under **Actions** in the right pane, click **Send message**. Click **Confirm**. Notice that the message appears on the screen. Is this wording strong enough to compel the person to return a missing laptop? Should a reward be offered? How would you frame this message?
19. Close the message.
20. Under **Actions** in the right pane, click **Lock device**. Read about the function this will perform. How useful would this be? Depending upon your setting either click **Close** (to cancel this) or **Confirm** (to lock the device).
21. Click **Activity log**. Read through the list of events that have occurred.
22. Click **Set device to missing** and read through what occurs when this is selected. Click **Advanced Options**. How helpful would it be to have a photo of the person who is using the device and a screen capture of what they are doing on the device?
23. Click **Yes, my device is missing**. It may take up to 10 minutes for the alarm to sound depending on how frequently the device checks into Prey.
24. When a report is generated, click **Reports** and read the information about the location of the device. Would this be sufficient information to find the missing device?
25. Change the settings so that your device is no longer registered as missing.
26. Close all windows.

Project 10-3: Installing Bluestacks Android Emulator

In this project, you install an Android emulator on a personal computer to test different tools. Note that you will need a Google account to access these tools.

1. Use your web browser to go to **www.bluestacks.com**. (The location of content on the Internet may change without warning. If you are no longer able to access the program through this URL, use a search engine and search for "Bluestacks".)
2. Click **Download BlueStacks**.
3. When the download is complete, launch the installation file and accept the defaults to install Bluestacks.
4. Click **Sign in with Google**.
5. Enter your Google account information.
6. Click **Done**.
7. Click the right arrow in the window.
8. Click **Continue**.
9. If necessary sign in with your Google account.
10. Click **OK**.
11. Click the right arrow in the window.
12. If necessary personalize the information and click the right arrow in the window.
13. Click **Finish**.
14. Click **Got it**.
15. Remain in Bluestacks for the next project.

Project 10-4: Installing Security Apps Using Bluestacks

In this project, you download and install Android apps to test different antimalware tools.

1. Click **Search apps**.
2. In the search bar enter **Antivirus**.
3. Select **Norton Security**.
4. Click **Install**.
5. Click **Accept**.
6. After the app has installed, click **OPEN**.
7. If the button **Agree and launch** appears, click it to start the app.
8. After the app has loaded and scanned, click through the various options for this app. Would you use this antivirus app on your Android device?
9. Click **Play Store**.
10. Click the magnifying glass to start another search.
11. In the search bar enter **Antivirus**.
12. This time select a different antivirus product. Install it and then view the different options.
13. Click **Play Store**.
14. Click the magnifying class to start another search.
15. Enter **Security** and press **Enter**.
16. Scroll down through the different apps available.
17. Select a different security app and install it.
18. How easy were these apps to install and configure? How do they compare with comparable desktop antimalware apps?
19. Close all windows.

Project 10-5: Installing the Andy Android Emulator

In this project, you install an Android emulator on a personal computer that can be used to test different tools or sideloading apps.

1. Use your web browser to go to **www.andyroid.net** (The location of content on the Internet may change without warning. If you are no longer able to access the program through this URL, use a search engine and search for "Andy Android emulator".)
2. Click **FAQS**.
3. Read the file **Andy FAQ**.
4. Read the system requirements to be sure that your device can support Andy.
5. Read through the other FAQ information.
6. Click **Download**.
7. When the download is complete, launch the installation file and accept the defaults to install Andy. Note that additional unnecessary software is offered during the installation process; these offers may be declined.
8. Once the application starts, press F11 if necessary to go from full screen mode to a smaller window.
9. If the **One time setup** screen appears, click **Continue**. You will need a Google account to access apps from the Google Play Store. In the **Add a Google Account** screen, answer the question **Do you want to add an existing account or create a new one?** by clicking either **Existing** if you already have an account or **New** to create an account. Follow the prompts to sign in or create your new account.
10. If you are asked **Join Google+**, click **Not now**.
11. Uncheck **Keep this phone backed up with my Google Account**. Click **Next**.
12. When the **One time setup** screen appears again, click **Continue**.
13. Under **Enable App Sync**, enter your Google account password.
14. When asked **Do you want the browser to remember this password?** click **Not now**.
15. When the **One time setup** screen appears again, click **Let's go!**
16. Remain in Bluestacks for the next project.

Project 10-6: Installing Security Apps Using Bluestacks Android Emulator

In this project, you download and install Android apps to test different antimalware tools.

1. Click **Accept**.
2. In the Google Play Store, click **APPS**.
3. Click the magnifying glass to open the online search tool. If you were not asked to complete the "One Time Setup" in the previous project, you may be asked to perform that function now.
4. Enter **Lookout Security & Antivirus**.
5. If necessary, click on the Lookout Security & Antivirus icon.
6. Click **INSTALL**.
7. Click **ACCEPT**.
8. After Lookout has installed, click **OPEN**.

9. The **Welcome to Lookout!** screen appears. Click **Next**.

10. After reading the explanations about Lookout, click **Next** on each successive screen. Click **Done** on the final screen.

11. Create a password and enter it under **Password** and **Confirm password**.

12. Click **Start Protecting**.

13. If you are asked to upgrade, click **No Thanks**.

14. Click **Continue to Lookout Free**.

15. Click **Done**.

16. Click **Change Settings**.

17. Read through these configuration settings. Would you consider them adequate for a mobile device? Why or why not?

18. Click the **Home** button.

19. Under **RECENTLY PLAYED**, click Lookout.

20. Click **Scan Now** to scan the apps contained in Bluestacks. Would this be easy to use on a mobile device?

21. Explore the different options of Lookout.

22. Click the **Home** button.

23. Under **RECENTLY PLAYED**, click **Search**.

24. Enter **Security** and press **Enter**.

25. Scroll down through the different apps available.

26. Select a different mobile antivirus app and install it. Compare its features to Lookout. Which do you prefer? Why?

27. Click the **Home** button.

28. Under **RECENTLY PLAYED**, click **Search**.

29. Enter **Security** and press **Enter**.

30. Select a different security app and install it. How easy were these apps to install and configure? How do they compare with comparable desktop antimalware apps?

31. Close all windows.

Case Projects

Case Project 10-1: Mobile Device Management Tools

Use the Internet to identify and compare three different mobile device management (MDM) tools. Create a table that lists their various features for on-boarding, off-boarding, configuration, quarantine, modification of device settings, etc. Which of the tools would you recommend for a small business with 10 employees who use smartphones but has a single person managing IT services? Why?

Case Project 10-2: Enterprise Deployment Model Comparison

Research the different enterprise deployment models listed in Table 10-3. Create a detailed chart listing their typical features, how they are used, and their advantages and disadvantages to both the enterprise as well as to the employee. Which of them is the most secure option? Which is the least secure option? Which of them is most advantageous for the enterprise? Which would you prefer to use? Which would you recommend for your school or place of employment? Why? Create a one-paragraph summary along with your chart.

Case Project 10-3: Rooting and Jailbreaking

Research rooting and jailbreaking. What are the advantages? What are the disadvantages? How frequently is this technology used? Can a device that has been broken return to its default state? If so, how? Finally create a list of at least seven reasons why rooting and jailbreaking is considered harmful in a corporate environment.

Case Project 10-4: Security for Missing Mobile Devices

If a mobile device is lost or stolen, several security features can be used to locate the device or limit the damage. Many of these can be used through an installed third-party app. Use the Internet to identify four apps, two each for iOS and Android, and create a table that compares their features. Use the information in Table 10-8 as a starting point. Create your own table comparing their different features. Include a paragraph that outlines which app you would prefer for iOS and Android.

Case Project 10-5: Internet of Things

Use the Internet to research the Internet of Things (IoT). In your own words, what is IoT? How is it being used today? How will it be used in the near future? What impact will IoT have on technology, society, and the economy over the next five years? What are its advantages and disadvantages? Finally, visit the IoT List site (**iotlist.co**) and identify five of the most unusual IoT devices. Write a one-page paper on the information that you find.

Case Project 10-6: Lake Point Security Consulting

Lake Point Consulting Services (LPCS) provides security consulting and assurance services to over 500 clients across a wide range of enterprises in more than 20 states. A new initiative at LPCS is for each of its seven regional offices to provide internships to students who are in their final year of the security degree program at the local college.

The Carlyle-Stedman Museum provides patrons with mobile devices that contain prerecorded information that can be listened to while viewing the museum's artifacts. Recently an incident occurred in which a patron circumvented the security on the device and, because it was not examined after it was turned in, the next patron who tried to use it was exposed to inappropriate content. The executive board of Carlyle-Stedman decided that something must be done to prevent this from reoccurring, and wants to ensure that all employee mobile devices are also secure. They have asked LPSC to make a presentation about mobile device security, and you have been given this assignment.

1. Create a PowerPoint presentation for the staff about the security risks of mobile technology and steps to be taken to secure mobile devices. Be sure to cover these from the perspective of the organization, the IT department, and the end user. Your presentation should contain at least 8 slides.

2. After the presentation, the IT director at Peabody has asked LPCS for recommendations on using MDM, MAM, and MCM for the museum. Write a one-page memo listing the features of these tools and how they could be used to help Peabody.

Case Project 10-7: Information Security Community Site Activity

The Information Security Community Site is an online companion to this textbook. It contains a wide variety of tools, information, discussion boards, and other features to assist learners. Go to *community.cengage.com/Infosec2* and click the *Join or Sign in* icon to log in, using your login name and password that you created in Chapter 1. Click **Forums (Discussion)** and click on **Security+ Case Projects (6th edition)**. Read the following case study.

Read again the information in the chapter regarding the security risks of data-in-transit and remote data-at-rest. What are your feelings regarding CALEA and the ability of the government to access data on iCloud and Google servers? Do you believe this is a safeguard for the nation, or is it a serious violation of personal privacy? What are the advantages and the risks of a government that has these powers? How could they be abused? Post your thoughts about app data sharing on the discussion board.

References

1. "IDC forecasts wearables shipments to reach 213.6 million units worldwide in 2020 with watches and wristbands driving volume while clothing and eyewear gain traction," *IDC*, Jun. 15, 2016, accessed May 26, 2017, http://www.idc.com/getdoc.jsp?containerId=prUS41530816.

2. Hilts, Andrew, Parsons, Christopher, and Knockel, Jeffrey, "Every Step You Fake: A Comparative Analysis of Fitness Tracker Privacy and Security," Open Effect Report, Apr. 19, 2016, accessed May 11, 2017, https://openeffect.ca/reports/Every_Step_You_Fake.pdf.

3. Smith, Aaron, "Record shares of Americans now own smartphones, have home broadband," *Pew Research Center*, Jan. 12, 2017, accessed May 11, 2017, http://www.pewresearch.org/fact-tank/2017/01/12/evolution-of-technology/.

4. Chaffey, Dave, "Mobile marketing statistics compilation", *Smart Insights*, Mar. 1, 2017, accessed May 11, 2017, http://www.smartinsights.com/mobile-marketing/mobile-marketing-analytics/mobile-marketing-statistics/.

5. "Lost and stolen mobile devices are leading cause of healthcare data breaches," *Accellion*, Feb. 23, 2015, accessed May 15, 2017, http://www.accellion.com/blog/lost-and-stolen-mobile-devices-are-leading-cause-healthcare-data-breaches.

6. "Survey: IT Security and Laptop Theft," *Kensington*, Aug. 2016, accessed May 15, 2017, https://www.kensington.com/a/283005.

7. "Visa Tech Matters," *Visa*, Feb. 12, 2015, accessed May 26, 2017, http://visacorporate.tumblr.com/post/110835709353/visatechmatters-visa-launches-mobile-location.

8. "Pin analysis," *DataGenetics*, accessed Mar. 10, 2014, http://datagenetics.com/blog/september32012/index.html.

9. "AT&T Transparency Report," accessed May 19, 2017, https://images.apple.com/legal/privacy/transparency/requests-2016-H1-en.pdfhttps://about.att.com/content/dam/csr/Transparency%20Reports/ATT_Transparency%20Report_Jan%202016.pdf.

10. Thubron, Rob, "Facebook's Latin America VP arrested in Brazil after failing to provide WhatsApp user data," *Techspot*, Mar. 2, 2016, retrieved May 26, 2017, http://www.techspot.com/news/63970-facebook-latin-america-vp-arrested-brazil-after-failing.html.

11. "Report on Government Information Requests: January 1–June 30, 2016," accessed May 19, 2017.

12. Overview of the Internet of things, Series Y: Global information infrastructure, internet protocol aspects and next-generation networks - Next Generation Networks –Frameworks and functional architecture models, Jun. 2012, Retrieved May 18, 2017, https://www.itu.int/rec/T-REC-Y.2060-201206-I.

13. Morgan, Jacob, "A simple explanation of 'The Internet of Things,'" *Forbes*, May 13, 2014, retrieved May 18, 2017, https://www.forbes.com/sites/jacobmorgan/2014/05/13/simple-explanation-internet-things-that-anyone-can-understand/#5c3dcca81d09.

14. Hinden, Bob, "The Internet of insecure things," *The Internet Protocol Journal*, Mar. 2017, retrieved Mar. 15, 2017, http://ipj.dreamhosters.com/internet-protocol-journal/issues/current-issue/.

15. Kushner, David, "The real story of Stuxnet," *IEEE Spectrum*, Feb. 26, 2013, retrieved May 26, 2017, http://spectrum.ieee.org/telecom/security/the-real-story-of-stuxnet.

16. Abramson, Alana, "Baby monitoring hacking alarms Houston parents," *ABC News*, Aug. 13, 2013, retrieved May 26, 2017, http://abcnews.go.com/blogs/headlines/2013/08/baby-monitor-hacking-alarms-houston-parents/.

IDENTITY AND ACCESS MANAGEMENT

The chapters in this part explore managing identities and access to services and devices. Chapter 11 examines how to manage authentication credentials and accounts. In Chapter 12, you learn about managing and implementing access control.

AUTHENTICATION AND ACCOUNT MANAGEMENT

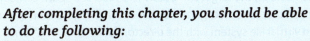

After completing this chapter, you should be able to do the following:

Describe the different types of authentication credentials

Explain what single sign-on can do

List the account management procedures for securing passwords

Today's Attacks and Defenses

What would you call malware that is so sophisticated it has gone undetected for over five years, can completely bypass data loss prevention (DLP), and uses zero-day vulnerabilities that we still do not even know about today? What if, in addition, it can change itself for each attack, is likely the work of nation state actors with the intent of harming other nations, and is estimated to cost millions of dollars to create? Whatever you call it, it undoubtedly belongs in the malware hall of fame.

Security researchers have recently reported on "ProjectSauron" (so named because the word "Sauron" is found in parts of the code). Here are some of its characteristics: it is a modular platform that is designed to enable long-term cyberespionage campaigns against targeted governments; it uses a modified scripting engine to implement its core platform and has 50 different plugins, so that no attack ever looks the same; it steals documents, records keystrokes, and hijacks encryption keys from both infected computers and attached USB flash drives; and virtually all of the files are unique and have different file names and sizes, meaning that they are individually built for each target.

ProjectSauron is so sophisticated that it can steal data from ultra-secure computers that are "air-gapped" (not connected to the Internet because the data that they contain is highly sensitive). Although that sounds virtually impossible, ProjectSauron contains a special module designed to move data from air-gapped networks to Internet-connected systems using removable USB flash drives. Once ProjectSauron infects computers that are not air-gapped but are connected to the local network, it waits for a user to insert a USB drive into an infected computer. These USB devices then secretly create several hundred megabytes of reserved space to store hidden data on the target computer. This reserved space contains a customized and encrypted partition that is not recognized by the operating system on the computer. The partition has its own virtual file system with the directories "In" and "Out." Once an infected USB flash drive is inserted into an air-gapped computer, data can be secretly downloaded and later transported to the attackers when the USB device is inserted back into a networked computer.

But perhaps the most amazing feature of ProjectSauron is how it steals user passwords. Managing passwords for multiple users in a Microsoft Windows environment requires Password Policy settings that are configured by using Group Policy at the domain level. However, prior to Group Policy, Microsoft had another means of enforcing password policies, which still exists on Windows systems for backward compatibility but is rarely used. Password enforcement was done through using password filters.

Password filters contain the restrictions regarding user passwords for that system, such as the minimum length of a password or if letters, numbers, and symbols are all required. The password filter function is itself implemented by a password filter dynamic link library (DLL). By default, Windows has its own password filter file PASSFILT.DLL, and users can edit this file or write their own password filter DLLs that enforce password policies. Password filters can be used to manage domain or local account passwords (to use the password filter for domain accounts the DLL must be installed and registered on each domain controller). Password filters provided a way to implement password policy and change notification to large numbers of users without using Group Policy.

When a user attempts to change her password, the Local Security Authority (LSA) reviews the password filters that have been registered on the system, first to validate the new password and then, after all filters have validated the new password, to notify the filters that the change has been made. When the user enters a new password, while it is still as plaintext, the password is run through the password filter process to ensure that it meets the necessary criteria.

And that's where the writers behind ProjectSauron were very creative. This malware registered itself on domain controllers as a password filter. Whenever anyone signed in to the computer this malicious password filter was given the plaintext password to examine. Only ProjectSauron did not examine the password; it simply stole it. This allowed ProjectSauron to steal passwords undetected.[1]

Authentication **in information security is the process of ensuring that the person or** system desiring access to resources is *authentic*, and not an imposter. Authentication is an essential element of IT security, and can never be taken lightly.

In this chapter, you study authentication and the secure management of user accounts that enforces authentication. First, you look at the different types of authentication credentials that can be used to verify a user's identity. Next you see how a single sign-on might be used. Finally, you look into the techniques and technology used to manage user accounts in a secure fashion.

Authentication Credentials

 Certification

1.2 Compare and contrast types of attacks.

2.5 Given a scenario, deploy mobile devices securely.

3.9 Explain the importance of physical security controls.

4.1 Compare and contrast identity and access management concepts.

4.2 Given a scenario, install and configure identity and access services.

4.3 Given a scenario, implement identity and access management controls.

6.1 Compare and contrast basic concepts of cryptography.

6.2 Explain cryptography algorithms and their basic characteristics.

Consider this scenario: Ermanno works on a local military base. One afternoon he stops at the gym on the base to exercise. After Ermanno locks his car, he walks into the club and is recognized by Li, the clerk at the desk. Li congratulates Ermanno for winning the base's recent competition for doing the most pushups in one minute. She then allows him to enter the locker room. Once inside the locker room, Ermanno opens his locker's combination lock with a series of numbers that he has memorized. When he starts exercising, Kristen walks over to Ermanno and says, "I was standing across the room and saw someone doing pushups, and I knew it had to be you. Nobody can do them as fast as you can."

In this scenario, Ermanno has been demonstrated to be *genuine* or *authentic*, and not an imposter, by five separate elements. These are illustrated in Figure 11-1 and explained here:

- *Somewhere he is.* Because the military base is surrounded by fencing and guards, an imposter of Ermanno would not be approved to enter the base. This means that the *location* of Ermanno can help prove his authenticity.
- *Something he has.* By locking the doors of his car with his car's wireless key fob, an item that only the real Ermanno would possess, what he *has* helps to prove his genuineness.
- *Something he is.* Access to the locker room is protected by what Ermanno *is*. Li must recognize his unique characteristics (his hair color, face, body type, voice, etc.) before he will be allowed to enter the locker room, so these characteristics serve to confirm his authenticity.
- *Something he knows.* The contents of Ermanno's locker are protected by what only the real Ermanno *knows*, namely, the lock combination. The lock will not open for an imposter, but only for the real Ermanno who knows the combination.
- *Something he does.* Because only Ermanno can do the record number of pushups, what he *does* helps to uniquely prove his authenticity.

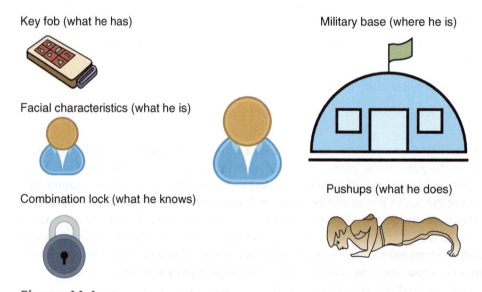

Key fob (what he has)

Military base (where he is)

Facial characteristics (what he is)

Pushups (what he does)

Combination lock (what he knows)

Figure 11-1   Ermanno's authenticity

Because only the real or "authentic" Ermanno possesses these elements— where he is, what he has, what he is, what he knows, and what he does—they can be considered as types of **authentication** or proof of his genuineness. These types of authentication confirm his identity and can be used to protect his belongings by preventing access by an imposter.

In information technology (IT), these five elements are known as *authentication credentials*. Although there are many different authentication credentials that can be presented to an IT system to verify the genuineness of the user, all credentials can be classified into one of these five categories.

What You Know: Passwords

In most computer systems, a user logging in would be asked to identify herself. This is done by entering an identifier known as the *user name*, such as *MDenton*. Yet because anyone could enter this user name, the next step is for the user to *authenticate* herself by proving that she actually is *MDenton*. This is often done by providing information that only she would know, namely, a password. A **password** is a secret combination of letters, numbers, and/or characters that only the user should have knowledge of. Passwords are by far the most common type of authentication used today based on **something you know** that no one else knows.

Despite their widespread use, passwords provide only weak protection. Although there are several different attacks that can be launched against passwords, there are steps that can be taken to strengthen passwords.

> **Note** 📎
>
> Password security has been exploited since the early days of computers. In 1961, MIT developed the Compatible Time-Sharing System (CTSS) in which passwords were first used to authenticate computer users. In the spring of 1962, a Ph.D. researcher, who had been allotted only four hours per week of computing resources, submitted a request to the CTSS computer to print the list of all password files. Because there were no safeguards, the computer produced the list, which the researcher then used to log in with other users' passwords and gain more computing time.

Password Weaknesses

The weakness of passwords centers on human memory. Human beings can memorize only a limited number of items. Passwords place heavy loads on human memory in multiple ways:

- The most effective passwords are long and complex. However, these are difficult for users to memorize and then accurately recall when needed.
- Users must remember multiple passwords for many different accounts. Most users have accounts for different computers and mobile devices at work, school, and home; multiple email accounts; online banking accounts; Internet site accounts;

and so on. According to one study, in the United States, the average number of online accounts registered to a single email address was 130. At the current rate of growth, the average number of accounts per Internet user will reach 207 by 2020.[2]

- For the highest level of security, each account password should be unique, which further strains human memory.
- Many security policies mandate that passwords expire after a set period of time, such as every 45–60 days, when a new one must be created. Some security policies even prevent a previously used password from being recycled and used again, forcing users to repeatedly memorize new passwords.

Because of the burdens that passwords place on human memory, users take shortcuts to help them memorize and recall their passwords. One shortcut is to create and use a *weak password*. Weak passwords use a common word as a password (*princess*), a short password (*desk*), a predictable sequence of characters (*abc123*), or personal information (*Hannah*) in a password. Even when users attempt to create stronger passwords, they generally follow predictable patterns of *appending* and *replacing*:

- *Appending*. When users combine letters, numbers, and punctuation (*character sets*), they do it in a pattern. Most often they only add a number after letters (*caitlin1 or cheer99*). If they add all three character sets, it is in the sequence *letters+punctuation+number (braden.8 or chris#6)*.
- *Replacing*. Users also use replacements in predictable patterns. Generally, a zero is used instead of the letter *o* (*passw0rd*), the digit 1 for the letter *i* (*dennis*), or a dollar sign for an *s* (*be$tfriend*).

> **Note** 🔗
>
> Attackers are aware of these patterns in passwords and can search for them, making it faster and easier to crack the password.

The widespread use of weak passwords can be easily illustrated. Several recent attacks have stolen hundreds of millions of passwords, which are often posted on the Internet. An analysis of over 562 million stolen user names and passwords revealed that the most common length of a password was only 9 characters, while fewer than 1 percent of the passwords were over 14 characters. The number of passwords that used uppercase characters (6 percent), special symbols (4 percent), or a space (0.03 percent) were very low. Only 1 million of the accounts were from domains of large companies, which means that over 98 percent of the stolen passwords were from user personal accounts. The ten most common passwords in the 562 million stolen passwords are very weak and are listed in Table 11-1.[3]

Another common shortcut that dramatically weakens passwords is to reuse the same password (or a slight derivation of it) for multiple accounts. Although this makes it easier for the user, it also makes it easier for an attacker who compromises one account to access all other accounts.

Table 11-1 Ten most common passwords

Rank	Password
1	123456
2	123456789
3	abc123
4	password
5	password1
6	12345678
7	111111
8	1234567
9	12345
10	1234567890

Note 📎

An analysis of stolen passwords from five countries—United States, Russia, China, Pakistan, and India—revealed that users in Russia have the strongest passwords. Russians have a lower percentage of passwords that are fewer than 10 characters and a higher percentage that are 14 characters in length; U.S. users on average have passwords only eight characters long. The percentage of users having a password that were in the top 100 password patterns revealed that Russia also had the fewest number of users (30 percent) while over half of the U.S. users had passwords based on these patterns. And only 4 percent of Russian users had their name or email address in their password, while 14 percent of users in China had their name or email address as a password.[4]

A noted security expert summarized the password problem well by stating:

The problem is that the average user can't and won't even try to remember complex enough passwords to prevent attacks. As bad as passwords are, users will go out of the way to make it worse. If you ask them to choose a password, they'll choose a lousy one. If you force them to choose a good one, they'll write it [down] and change it back to the password they changed it from the last month. And they'll choose the same password for multiple applications.[5]

Attacks on Passwords

Many users think that passwords are compromised by password guessing: a threat actor enters different passwords at the login prompt until he guesses the right password and is admitted access (called an **online attack**). However, this is not used because it is impractical. Even at two or three tries per second, it could take thousands of years to guess the right password. In addition, most accounts can be set to disable all logins after a limited number of incorrect attempts (such as five), thus locking out the attacker.

Instead of randomly guessing a password, attackers use far more sophisticated methods. Attacks that can be used to discover a password include social engineering (phishing, shoulder surfing, or dumpster diving) or capturing (installing a keylogger or using man-in-the-middle attacks). But these attacks have their limitations, such as the need to physically access a user's computer or watch the user enter a password.

Most password attacks today instead are an **offline attack**. When a password is first created, a one-way hash algorithm creates a message digest (or hash) of the password. This digest is then stored instead of the original plaintext password. When a user later attempts to log in, she enters her password and another digest is created from it. This is then compared against the stored digest, and if they match, the user is authenticated.

> **Note** 📎
>
> Hash algorithms are covered in Chapter 3.

In an offline attack, threat actors steal the file of password digests and load that file onto their own computers. They can then attempt to discover the passwords by comparing the stolen digests with their own digests that they have created, called *candidates*. Several offline password attack techniques attempt to match an attacker's known password digest with stolen digests. These password attacks are brute force, mask, rule, dictionary, rainbow tables, and password collections.

Brute Force Attack

In an automated **brute force attack**, every possible combination of letters, numbers, and characters is used to create candidate digests that are then matched against those in the stolen digest file. This is the slowest yet most thorough method.

> **Note** 📎
>
> When cracking passwords using a brute force attack, attackers often use computers with multiple graphics processing units (GPUs). Whereas the central processing unit (CPU) of a computer can do a wide variety of tasks, a GPU, which is separate from the CPU, is used to render screen displays on computers. GPUs are very good at performing video processing, which involves the very repetitive work of performing the same function over and over to large groups of pixels on the screen. This makes GPUs superior to CPUs at repetitive tasks like breaking passwords.

Although offline attacks require that the digest be broken through a brute force or similar attack, one attack does not even require breaking the digest. Microsoft Windows operating systems hash passwords in two ways. The first is known as the *LM (LAN Manager) hash*. The LM hash is not actually a hash, because a hash is a mathematical function used to fingerprint the data. The LM hash uses a *cryptographic one-way function (OWF)*: instead of encrypting the password with another key, the password itself is the key. The LM hash is considered to be a very weak function for storing passwords. To address the security issues in the LM hash, Microsoft later introduced the stronger **NTLM (New Technology LAN Manager) hash**. However, NTLM has a serious security vulnerability: an attacker who could steal the digest of an NTLM password would not need to try to break it. Instead, he could simply pretend to be the user and send that hash to the remote system to then be authenticated. This is known as a **pass the hash** attack.

Mask Attack

Brute force attacks can be very slow because every character combination must be generated. A variation of a brute force attack is a *mask attack*. A mask attack is a more targeted brute force attack that uses placeholders for characters in certain positions of the password. The goal of a mask attack is to reduce the number of potential candidates that must be created to speed up the cracking process.

Consider attempting to break the stolen hash of the nine-character password *Fabio1998*. A brute force attack using the character set of all 26 uppercase letters (*A, B, C*, etc.), all 26 lowercase letters (*a, b, c*, etc.), and 10 digits (*0-9*) means that for each of the nine characters in *Fabio1998* a total of 62 (26+26+10) different characters would have to be substituted (*aaaaaaaaA, aaaaaaaaB, aaaaaaaaC*, etc.). Such a process would take an extensive amount of time.

Note

The number of different potential passwords of a nine-character password like *Fabio1998* that used a character set of uppercase letters, lowercase letters, and digits only would be 1.3537087e+16.

However, what if assumptions were made based on how most users create passwords? Because most users create passwords based on a name followed by a year, a mask *string* could be created that anticipates this. A mask of *?u ?l ?l ?l ?l ?d ?d ?d ?d* (*u* = uppercase, *l* = lowercase, and *d* = digit) would tell the password cracking program, *Use an uppercase letter for the first position, a lowercase letter for the next four positions, and digits for the remaining four positions*. Using a mask would significantly reduce the time needed to crack a password. The parameters that typically can be entered in a mask attack include:

- *Password length*. The minimum and maximum lengths of the passwords to be generated (such as a range from *1–45*) can be entered.

- *Character set.* This is the set of letters, symbols, and characters that make up the password. Because not all systems accept the same character set for passwords, if characters can be eliminated from the character set, this will dramatically increase the speed of the attack.
- *Language.* Many programs allow different languages to be chosen, such as Arabic, Dutch, English, French, German, Italian, Portuguese, Russian, or Spanish.
- *Pattern.* If any part of the password is known, a pattern can be entered to reduce the number of passwords generated. A question mark (?) can replace one symbol and an asterisk (*) can replace multiple symbols. For example, if the first two letters of a six-character password were known to be *sk*, the pattern could be *sk????*.
- *Skips.* Because most passwords are word-like combinations of letters, some brute force attack programs can be set to skip nonsensical combinations of characters (*wqrghea*) so that only passwords such as *elmosworld* and *carkeys* are created.

Rule Attack

Whereas a mask attack is sometimes using an "educated guess" on what the format of the underlying password could be, a *rule attack* is more focused. A rule attack conducts a statistical analysis on the stolen passwords that is then used to create a mask to break the largest number of passwords. There are three basic steps in a rule attack:

1. A small sample of the stolen password plaintext file is obtained.
2. Statistical analysis is performed on the sample to determine the length and character sets of the passwords, as seen in Figure 11-2.
3. A series of masks are generated that will be most successful in cracking the highest percentage of passwords. This is illustrated in Figure 11-3.

```
[*] Length Statistics...
[+]                               8: 62% (612522)
[+]                               6: 18% (183307)
[+]                               7: 14% (146152)
[+]                               5: 02% (26438)
[+]                               4: 01% (15088)
[+]                               3: 00% (2497)
[+]                               2: 00% (308)
[+]                               1: 00% (113)

[*] Charset statistics...
[+]                  loweralphanum: 47% (470580)
[+]                     loweralpha: 46% (459208)
[+]                        numeric: 05% (56637)
```

Figure 11-2 Rule attack statistical analysis

```
[*] Advanced Mask statistics...
[+]          ?1?1?1?1?1?1?1?1: 04%  (688053)
[+]            ?1?1?1?1?1?1?1: 04%  (601257)
[+]          ?1?1?1?1?1?1?1?1: 04%  (585093)
[+]      ?1?1?1?1?1?1?1?1?1?1: 03%  (516862)
[+]            ?d?d?d?d?d?d?d: 03%  (487437)
[+]    ?d?d?d?d?d?d?d?d?d?d?d: 03%  (478224)
[+]        ?d?d?d?d?d?d?d?d?d: 02%  (428306)
[+]          ?1?1?1?1?1?1?d?d: 02%  (420326)
[+]      ?1?1?1?1?1?1?1?1?1?1: 02%  (416961)
[+]                ?d?d?d?d?d: 02%  (390546)
[+]      ?d?d?d?d?d?d?d?d?d?d: 02%  (307540)
[+]            ?1?1?1?1?1?d?d: 02%  (292318)
[+]          ?1?1?1?1?1?1?d?d: 01%  (273640)
```

Figure 11-3   Rule attack generated masks

Note

A rule attack is not intended to crack every password, but instead gives the highest probability of the largest number of passwords that can be broken.

Dictionary Attack

Another common password attack is a **dictionary attack**. A dictionary attack begins with the attacker creating digests of common dictionary words as candidates and then comparing them against those in a stolen digest file. A dictionary attack is shown in Figure 11-4. Dictionary attacks can be successful because users often create passwords that are simple dictionary words.

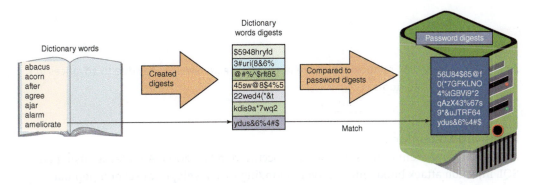

Figure 11-4   Dictionary attack

A dictionary attack that uses a set of dictionary words and compares it with the stolen digests is known as a *pre-image attack*, in that one known digest (dictionary word) is compared to an unknown digest (stolen digest). A *birthday attack* is slightly different, in that the search is for *any* two digests that are the same. A password attack that is a combination of a dictionary attack and a mask attack is called a *hybrid attack*.

> **Note**
>
> Birthday attacks are covered in Chapter 3.

Rainbow Tables

Rainbow tables make password attacks easier by creating a large pregenerated data set of candidate digests. There are two steps in using a rainbow table. First is creating the table itself. Next, that table is used to crack a password. A rainbow table is a compressed representation of cleartext passwords that are related and organized in a sequence (called a *chain*). To create a rainbow table, each chain begins with an initial password that is hashed and then fed into a function that produces a different cleartext password. This process is repeated for a set number of rounds. The initial password and the last digest value of the chain comprise a rainbow table entry.

Using a rainbow table to crack a password also requires two steps. First, the password to be broken is hashed and run through the same procedure used to create the initial table. This results in the initial password of the chain. Then the process is repeated, starting with this initial password until the original digest is found. The password used at the last iteration is the cracked password.

Although generating a rainbow table requires a significant amount of time, once it is created it has three significant advantages over other password attack methods: a rainbow table can be used repeatedly for attacks on other passwords; rainbow tables are much faster than dictionary attacks; and the amount of memory needed on the attacking machine is greatly reduced.

> **Note**
>
> Although once popular, rainbow tables are not used as extensively today due to advances in other password attack tools.

Password Collections

A watershed moment in password attacks occurred in late 2009. An attacker using an SQL injection attack broke into a server belonging to a developer of several popular social media applications. This server contained more than 32 million user passwords, all in cleartext. These passwords were later posted on the Internet.

Attackers seized this opportunity to examine actual user passwords. These passwords provided two key elements for password attacks. First, this "treasure-trove" collection of passwords gave attackers, for the first time, a large corpus of real-world passwords. Because users repeat their passwords on multiple accounts, attackers could now use these passwords as candidate passwords in their attacks with a high probability of success. Most password cracking software tools accept these stolen "wordlists" as input.

Second, these password collections have provided attackers advanced insight into the strategic thinking of how users create passwords. For example, on those occasions when users mix uppercase and lowercase in passwords, users tend to capitalize at the beginning of the password, much like writing a sentence. Likewise, punctuation and numbers are more likely to appear at the end of the password, again mimicking standard sentence writing. And a high percentage of passwords were comprised of a name and date, such as *Braden2008*. Such insights are valuable in rule attacks, significantly reducing the amount of time needed to break a password when compared to a raw brute force attack.

Note @

Websites host lists of these leaked passwords that attackers can download along with important statistics and masks for a rule attack. These sites also attempt to crack submitted password collections. One website cracked 1.07 *billion* submitted passwords in a single year.[6]

Most threat actors do not use a single password attack tool but use several in combination. Table 11-2 lists a common sequence of attack tools on passwords.

Table 11-2 Common sequence of password attack tools

Order	Password attack	Explanation
1	Custom wordlist	Download a stolen password collection
2	Custom wordlist using rule attack	Generate password statistics using a rule attack to create specialized masks
3	Dictionary attack	Perform a dictionary attack on passwords
4	Dictionary attack using rules	Conduct a refined dictionary attack using results from a rule attack
5	Updated custom wordlist using rules	Input any cracked passwords from previous steps to create more refined rules
6	Hybrid attack	Perform a focused dictionary attack with a mask attack
7	Mask attack	Conduct a mask attack on harder passwords that have not already been cracked
8	Brute force attack	Last resort effort on any remaining passwords

> **Note**
>
> Table 11-2 assumes that a sample of the passwords in plaintext can be examined; if this is not available, then most attacks will skip to Step 3 that results in enough cracked passwords so that rules can be developed for the next step.

Password Security

Securing passwords from attacks depends upon the user as well as the enterprise. For the user, this involves properly managing passwords, while for the enterprise it involves protecting password digests.

Managing Passwords

Due to the advanced nature of password attack tools, it is critical that users create and manage secure passwords. The most critical factor in a strong password is not complexity but length: a longer password is always more secure than a shorter password. This is because the longer a password is, the more attempts an attacker must make to break it. The formula for determining the number of possible passwords requires knowing only two items: the character set being used and the password length. Since the character set of most passwords is equal to the number of keys on a keyboard that can be used, the formula is *Number-of-Keyboard-Keys ^ Password-Length = Total-Number-of-Possible-Passwords.* Table 11-3 illustrates the number of possible passwords for different password lengths using a standard 95-key keyboard, along with the average attempts needed to break a password.

Table 11-3 Number of possible passwords

Keyboard keys	Password length	Number of possible passwords	Average attempts to break password
95	2	9025	4513
95	3	857,375	428,688
95	4	81,450,625	40,725,313
95	5	7,737,809,375	3,868,904,688
95	6	735,091,890,625	367,545,945,313

> **Note**
>
> The average attempts to break a password is calculated as one-half of the total number of possible passwords. That is because an attack could break the password on the first attempt or on the very last attempt.

Obviously, a longer password takes significantly more time to attempt to break than a short password.

In addition to having long passwords (a strong password should be a minimum of 20 characters in length) there are other general recommendations regarding creating passwords:

- Do not use passwords that consist of dictionary words or phonetic words.
- Do not repeat characters (*xxx*) or use sequences (*abc, 123, qwerty*).
- Do not use birthdays, family member names, pet names, addresses, or any personal information.

Another recommendation is to use non-keyboard characters, or special characters that do not appear on the keyboard, thus extending the number of possible keys beyond 95. These characters are created by holding down the *ALT* key while simultaneously typing a number on the numeric keypad (but not the numbers across the top of the keyboard). For example, *ALT + 0163* produces the £ symbol. A list of all the available non-keyboard characters based on the Unicode character set can be seen by clicking *Start* and entering *charmap.exe*, and then clicking on a character. The code *ALT + 0xxx* will appear in the lower-right corner of the screen (if that character can be reproduced in Windows). Figure 11-5 shows a Windows character map.

Figure 11-5   Windows character map

However, due to the limitations of human memory, it is virtually impossible for users to apply all these recommendations and then memorize long, complex, and unique passwords for all accounts. Instead of relying on human memory for passwords, security experts universally recommend that technology be used instead to store and manage passwords. The technology used for securing passwords are called *password managers*. There are three basic types of password managers:

- *Password generators*. These are web browser extensions that generate passwords. The user enters a master password and the password generator creates a password based on the master password and the website's URL "on the fly." The disadvantage of password generators is that the browser extension must be installed on each computer and web browser.
- *Online vaults*. An online vault also uses a web browser extension but instead of creating the user's password each time it retrieves the password from a central repository that is online. The disadvantage is that these online sites that store the passwords are vulnerable to attackers.
- *Password management applications*. A password management application is a program installed on a computer through which the user can create and store multiple strong passwords in a single user "vault" file that is protected by one strong master password. Users can retrieve individual passwords as needed by opening the user file, thus freeing the user from need to memorize multiple passwords. The disadvantage is that the program must be carried with the user or installed on multiple computers.

Note 🔗

A password management application is recognized as having the highest level of security. These applications are more than a password-protected list of passwords. They typically include drag-and-drop capabilities, enhanced encryption, in-memory protection that prevents the OS cache from being exposed to reveal retrieved passwords, and timed clipboard clearing. Some password management applications can even require that a secret key file be present when entering the master password to open the vault: if the vault file was stolen, it still could not be opened without the secret key file being present, even if the correct master password was entered. The value of using a password management application is that unique strong passwords such as *WUuAôxB$2aWøBnd&Tf7MfEtm* can be easily created and used for all accounts.

Protecting Password Digests

Just as users must protect their passwords, enterprises likewise must protect the stored password digests. One means of protecting digests is to use salts while another is choosing to use the most secure hash algorithm for creating the password digests.

Salts

One means for an enterprise to protect stored digests is to add *a salt* that consists of a random string that is used in hash algorithms. Passwords can be protected by adding this random string to the user's plaintext password before it is hashed. Salts make dictionary attacks and brute force attacks for cracking large number of passwords much more difficult and limits the impact of rainbow tables.

Note

Salts are covered in Chapter 3.

Another benefit of a salt is that if two users choose the same password, this will not help the attacker. Without salts, an attacker who can crack User #1's password would also immediately know User #2's password without performing any computations. By adding salts, however, each password digest will be different.

Note

Salts should be random (never sequential like *0001, 0002*, etc.) and unique for each user.

Key Stretching

Using general-purpose hash algorithms like MD5 and SHA is not considered secure for creating digests because these hashing algorithms are designed to create a digest as quickly as possible. The fast speed of general-purpose hash algorithms works in an attacker's favor. When an attacker is creating candidate digests, a general-purpose hashing algorithm can rapidly create a very large number of passwords for matching purposes.

A more secure approach for creating password digests is to use a specialized password hash algorithm that is intentionally designed to be slower. This would then limit the ability of an attacker to crack passwords because it requires significantly more time to create each candidate digest, thus slowing down the entire cracking process. This is called **key stretching**.

Two popular key stretching password hash algorithms are **bcrypt** and **PBKDF2**. These can be configured to require more time to create a digest. A network administrator can specify the number of iterations (*rounds*), which sets how "expensive" (in terms of computer time and/or resources) the password hash function will be. Whereas the increased time is a minor inconvenience when one user logs in and waits for the password digest to be generated, it can significantly reduce attackers' speed of generating candidates.

Note

Using a general password algorithm, an attacker could generate about 95^8 candidate passwords in 5.5 hours. However, using bcrypt, in that same time only 71,000 candidate passwords could be generated.

However, the problem with key stretching is that CPUs continue to process faster and faster, so that yesterday's key stretching algorithms may become too fast with tomorrow's processors. The original standards written in 2000 for key stretching recommended at least 1,000 iterations. Today iterations of 100,000 are not uncommon. Recently an open competition was initiated to develop an even stronger key stretching algorithm. After working through 24 proposals, a winner was announced: *Argon2*. Argon2 can be configured based on several different parameters: adding a salt (which must be between 8–16 characters), the number of iterations (default of 3), and the memory usage (default parameter of 12).

One recommendation for enterprises using salts and key stretching is to use a process such as the following:

1. Use a strong random number generator to create a salt of at least 128 bits.
2. Input the salt and the user's plaintext password into the PBKDF2 algorithm that is using HMAC-SHA-256 as the core hash.
3. Perform at least 30,000 iterations on PBKDF2.
4. Capture the first 256 bits of output from PBKDF2 as the password digest.
5. Store the iteration count, the salt, and the password digest in a secure password database.

Note

It is also recommended that periodically the number of iterations be increased by at least 10,000 rounds.

What You Have: Tokens, Cards, and Cell Phones

Another type of authentication credential is based on the approved user having a specific item in his possession (**something you have**). Such items are often used in conjunction with passwords. Because the user is using more than one type of authentication credential—both what a user knows (the password) and what the user has—this type of authentication credential is called **multifactor authentication**. Using just one type of authentication is called *single-factor authentication*.

The most common items that are used for authentication are tokens, cards, and cell phones.

Tokens

A **security token** is a means of authentication based on what the user has. Tokens can be used to create a *one-time password* (OTP), an authentication code that can be used only once for a limited period. A **hardware security token** is typically a small device (usually one that can be affixed to a keychain) with a window display, as shown in Figure 11-6. A **software security token** is stored on a general-purpose device like a laptop computer or smartphone instead of being a separate hardware device.

Figure 11-6 Hardware security token

There are two types of OTPs. A **time-based one-time password (TOTP)** changes after a set period. As illustrated in Figure 11-7, the token and a corresponding authentication server share an algorithm (each user's token has a different algorithm), and the token generates a code from the algorithm once every 30 to 60 seconds. This code is valid for only the brief period that it is displayed on the token. When the user logs in, she enters her user name along with the code currently being displayed on the token. When the authentication server receives it, the server looks up the algorithm associated with that specific user, generates its own code, and then compares it with what the user entered. If they are identical, the user is authenticated. An attacker who steals the code would have to use it within the token's time limit.

Instead of changing after a set number of seconds, an **HMAC-based one-time password (HOTP)** password is "event-driven" and changes when a specific event

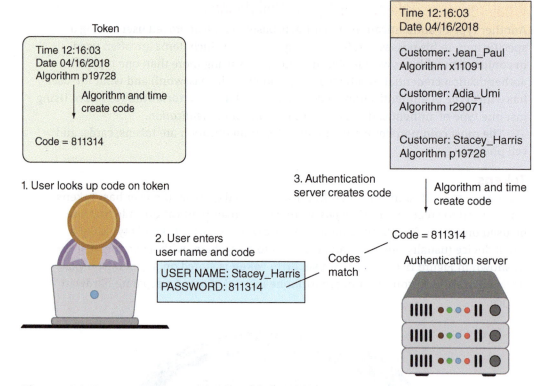

Figure 11-7   **Time-based one-time password (TOTP)**

Note 📎

The code is not transmitted to the token; instead, both the token and authentication server have the same algorithm and time setting.

occurs, such as when a user enters a personal identification number (PIN) on the token's keypad, which triggers the token to create a random code. For example, after entering the PIN *1694*, the code *190411* is displayed.

Tokens have several advantages over passwords. First, standard passwords are static: they do not change unless the user is forced to create a new password. Because passwords do not change frequently, this can give an attacker a lengthy period in which to crack and then use the password. In contrast, tokens produce dynamic passwords that change frequently. Second, a user might not know if an attacker has stolen her password, and confidential information could be accessed without the user knowing it was taking place. If a token is stolen, it would become obvious and steps could be taken immediately to disable that account.

Cards

Several types of cards can be used as authentication credentials. A **smart card**, as illustrated in Figure 11-8, contains an *integrated circuit* chip that can hold information, which then can be used as part of the authentication process. Smart cards can be either contact cards, which contain a tell-tale "pad" allowing electronic access to the contents of the chip, or contactless cards that do not require physical contact with the card itself (called a **proximity card**).

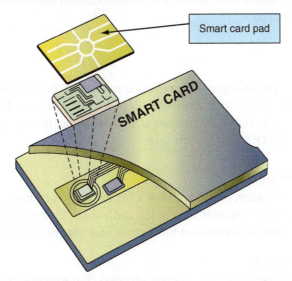

Smart card pad

Figure 11-8 Smart card

 Note

Smart cards and proximity cards are often used as a means of controlling physical access to a secure room or building.

One type of smart card is currently being distributed by the U.S. government. A **common access card (CAC)** is a U.S. Department of Defense (DoD) smart card that is used for identification of active-duty and reserve military personnel along with civilian employees and special contractors. A CAC resembles a credit card. In addition to an integrated circuit chip, it has a bar code and magnetic stripe along with the bearer's picture and printed information. This card can be used to authenticate the owner as well as for encryption. The smart card standard covering all U.S. government employees is the **Personal Identity Verification (PIV)** standard.

Smart cards, CAC, and PIV can all take advantage of *certificate-based authentication*, which is using digital certificates to identify a user, computer, or device before granting access. An advantage of using certificate-based authentication is that there is no additional hardware needed, because certificates are stored locally on the computer or device. This saves on both hardware costs and the costs of managing the distribution, replacement, and revocation of standard tokens.

Note

Digital certificates are covered in Chapter 4 and certificate-based authentication in IEEE 802.1x is covered in Chapter 8.

Cell Phones

Tokens and cards are increasingly being replaced today with cell phones. A code can be sent to a user's cell phone through a software security token app on the device or as a text message when using TOTP. Cell phones also allow a user to send a request via the phone to receive an HOTP authorization code.

What You Are: Biometrics

In addition to authentication based on what a person knows or has, another category rests on the features and characteristics of the individual. This type of authentication, **something you are**, involves standard biometrics and cognitive biometrics.

Standard Biometrics

Standard biometrics uses a person's unique physical characteristics for authentication (what he *is*). Standard biometrics can use several unique characteristics of a person's face, hands, or eyes to authenticate a user. Authentication using standard biometrics can be done divided into those that use specialized biometric scanners and those that use standard technology input devices for recognition. However, there are several issues regarding using biometrics.

Note

Standard biometrics is commonly used in physical security to restrict access to a secure area.

Specialized Biometric Scanners

Some types of biometric authentication require specialized and dedicated biometric scanners that are used to inspect the person's features. A **retinal scanner** uses the human retina as a biometric identifier. The retina is a layer at the back (posterior) portion of the eyeball that contains cells sensitive to light, which trigger nerve impulses that pass these through the optic nerve to the brain, where a visual image is formed. Due to the complex structure of the capillaries that supply the retina with blood, each person's retina is unique.

> **Note** 📎
>
> The network of blood vessels in the retina is so complex that even identical twins do not share a similar pattern. Even though retinal patterns may be altered in cases of diabetes, glaucoma, or retinal degenerative disorders, the retina generally remains unchanged through a person's lifetime.

A retinal scanner maps the unique patterns of a retina by directing a beam of low-energy infrared light (IR) into a person's eye as they look in the scanner's eyepiece (the beam cannot be detected by the user). Because retinal blood vessels are more absorbent of IR than the rest of the eye, the amount of reflection varies during the scan. This pattern of variations is recorded and used for comparison when the user attempts to authenticate.

A **fingerprint scanner**, which uses a fingerprint as a biometric identifier, has become the most common type of standard biometrics. Every user's fingerprint consists of several ridges and valleys, with ridges being the upper skin layer segments of the finger and valleys the lower segments. In one method of fingerprint scanning, the scanner locates the point where these ridges end and split, converts them into a unique series of numbers, and then stores the information as a template. A second method creates a template from selected locations on the finger.

There are two basic types of fingerprint scanners. A *static fingerprint scanner* requires the user to place the entire thumb or finger on a small oval window on the scanner. The scanner takes an optical "picture" of the fingerprint and compares it with the fingerprint image on file. The other type of scanner is known as a dynamic fingerprint scanner. A *dynamic fingerprint scanner* has a small slit or opening, as shown in Figure 11-9.

Figure 11-9   Dynamic fingerprint scanner

Note

Dynamic fingerprint scanners work on the same principle as stud finders that carpenters use to locate wood studs behind drywall. This is known as capacitive technology.

Standard Input Devices

Unlike fingerprints and retinas that require specialized scanners, other types of biometrics can use standard computer input devices for recognition, such as a microphone or camera.

Because all users' voices are different, **voice recognition**, using a standard computer microphone, can be used to authenticate users based on the unique characteristics of a person's voice. Several characteristics make each person's voice unique, from the size of the head to age. These differences can be quantified and a user voice template can be created.

Note

Voice recognition is not to be confused with speech recognition, which accepts spoken words for input as if they had been typed on the keyboard.

One of the concerns regarding voice recognition is that an attacker could record the user's voice and then create a recording to use for authentication. However, this would be extremely difficult to do. Humans speak in phrases and sentences instead of isolated words. The *phonetic cadence*, or speaking two words together in a way that one word "bleeds" into the next word, becomes part of each user's speech pattern. It would be extremely difficult to capture several hours of someone's voice, parse it into separate words, and then combine the words in real time to defeat voice recognition security.

Note

To protect against even the remote possibility of an attacker attempting to mimic a user's voice, identification phrases can be selected that would rarely (if ever) come up in normal speech.

An **iris scanner**, which can use a standard computer webcam, uses the unique characteristic of the iris, which is a thin, circular structure in the eye. A human iris is seen in Figure 11-10. The iris is responsible for controlling the diameter and size of the pupils to regulate the amount of light reaching the retina. Iris recognition identifies the unique random patterns in an iris for authentication.

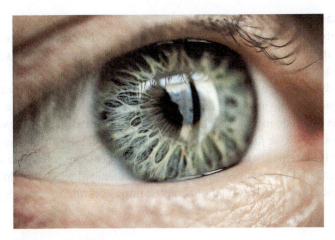

Figure 11-10   Iris

creativemarc/Shutterstock.com

Note 📎

A person's eye color is actually the color of the iris, which is most often brown, blue, or green. In some cases, it can be hazel, grey, violet, or even pink.

A biometric authentication that is becoming increasingly popular on smartphones is **facial recognition**. Every person's face has several distinguishable "landmarks" that make up their facial features. These landmarks are called *nodal points* and each human face has approximately 80 nodal points, such as the width of the nose, the depth of the eye sockets, the shape of the cheekbones, and the length of the jaw line. Using a standard computer webcam, facial recognition software can measure the nodal points and create a numerical code (*faceprint*) that represents the face.

Note 📎

Facial recognition is frequently used by law enforcement agencies to scan crowds for missing children, fugitive criminals, or even terrorists. This type of recognition is much less precise than personal facial recognition using a smartphone or computer for authentication. This is because variations in the lighting in a large crowd make recognition difficult, a cap or hat can obscure the subject's face, or the subject might not look directly into the camera. These limitations can partially be overcome by using a 3-D camera to compare against 3-D images.

Biometric Disadvantages

Standard biometrics has three disadvantages. The first is the cost for fingerprint and retinal identification that requires specialized biometric scanners. These scanners must be installed at each location where authentication is required.

The second disadvantage is that biometric authentication is not foolproof: genuine users may be rejected while imposters are accepted. The **false acceptance rate (FAR)** or *false positive* is the frequency at which imposters are accepted as genuine while the **false rejection rate (FRR)** or *false negative* is the frequency that legitimate users are rejected. Biometric systems are tuned so that the FAR and FRR are equal over the size of the population (called the **crossover error rate (CER)**). Ideally the CER should be as low as possible to produce the lowest number of accepted imposters and rejected legitimate users.

> **Note**
>
> False positives and false negatives are covered in Chapter 6.

A third disadvantage is that with increasing frequency, biometric systems can be "tricked." Security researchers have demonstrated that pictures of an iris can fool an iris recognition system while fingerprints can be collected from water glasses and used to trick fingerprint readers on smartphones. Many security researchers advocate that biometrics should only be used in multifactor authentication systems and not as a single-factor authentication system, and should not be used for the most sensitive authentication apps, such as mobile payments.

> **Note**
>
> Tricking an iris recognition system requires a picture of the authentic user's eye to be made with a digital camera in "night" mode or with the infrared filter removed. The iris picture is then printed on a color laser printer. To emulate the curvature of the eye, a normal contact lens is placed on top of the print. This can successfully trick the iris recognition system into thinking the user's real eye is in front of the camera.

Cognitive Biometrics

Whereas standard biometrics considers a person's physical characteristics, the field of *cognitive biometrics* is related to the perception, thought process, and understanding of the user. Cognitive biometrics is considered to be much easier for the user to remember because it is based on the user's life experiences. This also makes it more difficult for an attacker to imitate.

One type of cognitive biometrics introduced by Microsoft is called picture password for Windows 10 touch-enabled devices. Users select a picture to use for which there should be at least 10 "points of interest" on the photograph that could serve as "landmarks" or places to touch, connect with a line, or draw a circle around. Specific gestures—tap, line, or circle—are then used to highlight any parts of the picture and these gestures are recorded. When logging in, a user reproduces those same gestures on the photograph, as illustrated in Figure 11-11. For an attacker to replicate these actions, she would need to know the parts of the image that were highlighted, the order of the gestures, as well as the direction, and the starting and ending points, of the circles and lines.

Figure 11-11   Picture password authentication

Pressmaster/Shutterstock.com

A similar example of cognitive biometrics requires the user to identify specific faces. Users are provided a random set of photographs of different faces, typically three to seven, to serve as their password. They are taken through a "familiarization process" that is intended to imprint the faces in the user's mind. When the user logs in, he must select his assigned faces from three to five different groups, with each group containing nine faces. These groups are presented one at a time until all the faces have been correctly identified.

Another example of cognitive biometrics based on a life experience that the user remembers is the process that begins with the user selecting one of several "memorable events" in her lifetime, such as taking a special vacation, celebrating a personal achievement, or attending a specific family dinner. Then the user is asked specific questions about that memorable event, such as what type of food was served, how old the person was when the event occurred, where the event was located, who was in attendance, and the reason for the event. The user authenticates by answering the same series of questions when logging in.

Cognitive biometrics is considered much easier for the end user and may provide a higher degree of protection. It is predicted that cognitive biometrics could become a key element in authentication in the future.

What You Do: Behavioral Biometrics

Another type of authentication is based on actions that the user is uniquely qualified to perform, or **something you do**. This is sometimes called *behavioral biometrics*. One type of behavioral biometrics is *keystroke dynamics*, which attempts to recognize a user's unique typing rhythm. All users type at a different pace. During World War II, the U.S. military could distinguish enemy coders who tapped out Morse code from Allied coders by their unique rhythms. A study funded by the U.S. National Bureau of Standards concluded that the keystroke dynamics of entering a user name and password could provide up to 98 percent accuracy.[8]

Keystroke dynamics uses two unique typing variables. The first is known as *dwell time*, which is the time it takes for a key to be pressed and then released. The second characteristic is *flight time*, or the time between keystrokes (both "down" when the key is pressed and "up" when the key is released are measured). Multiple samples are collected to form a user typing template, as shown in Figure 11-12. When the user enters his user name and password, they are sent, along with the user's individual typing sample obtained by entering the user name and password, to the authentication server. If both the password and the typing sample match, those stored on the authentication server, and the user is approved; if the typing template does not match even though the password does, the user is not authenticated. This is shown in Figure 11-13.

Keystroke dynamics holds a great deal of potential. Because it requires no specialized hardware and because the user does not have to take any additional steps beyond entering a user name and password, some security experts predict that keystroke dynamics will become widespread in the near future.

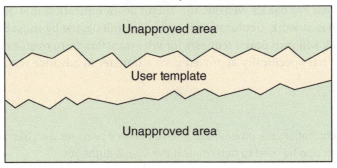

Figure 11-12   Typing template

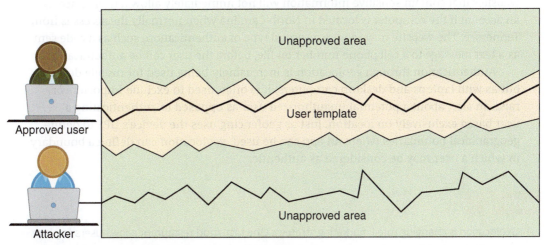

Figure 11-13   Authentication by keystroke dynamics

Where You Are: Geolocation

A final type of authentication can be based where the user is located, or **somewhere you are**. Also known as *geolocation*, it is the identification of the location of a person or object using technology. However, unless the location is within a restricted area that is already secured with a security perimeter, such as a military base or a secured building, this type of authentication is most often used to *reject* imposters instead of *accepting* authorized users. In other words, although geolocation may not uniquely identify the user, it can indicate if an impersonator is trying to perform an action from a location different from the normal location of the user.

Geolocation has been used for laptop and desktop computers for several years, particularly financial institutions. For example, where does Alice normally access her bank's website? If it is typically from her home computer on nights and weekends, then this information can be used to establish a geolocation pattern based the Internet

Protocol (IP) address of Alice's computer. If a computer located in China suddenly attempts to access her bank's website, this might be an indication that an attacker instead of Alice is at work. Geolocation is done to some degree by most banks, so that generally a bank will turn down requests for wire transfers from overseas locations unless the user has specifically approved such a transfer in advance with the bank.

> **Note** 📎
>
> In addition to geolocation, the time of day, Internet service provider, and basic device configuration can also be used to determine if the user is authentic.

Geolocation is not restricted to financial institutions. Some online retailers or other websites that contain sensitive information will not immediately allow a user to access an account if the computer is located in North Carolina when normally the access is from Tennessee. The website may require a second type of authentication, such as a code sent as a text message to a cell phone number on file, before the user can be authenticated.

Authentication through geolocation is increasingly being used for mobile devices, but as with laptops and desktop computers, it is often used to exclude imposters or raise an alert about a potential unauthorized user as opposed to authenticating a user based exclusively on location. Just as geofencing uses the device's GPS to define geographical boundaries where an app can be used, geolocation can define a boundary in which a user may be considered as authentic.

> **Note** 📎
>
> Geolocation is changing retail marketing strategy. One fast–food restaurant allows users to place an order via a mobile app. The app can then monitor the location of the customer and determine when the food should be prepared so it is ready when the customer arrives to pick it up.

Single Sign-on

 **Certification**

4.1 Compare and contrast identity and access management concepts.

4.2 Given a scenario, install and configure identity and access services.

One of the problems facing users today is the fact that they have multiple accounts across multiple platforms that all should use a unique user name and password. The difficulty in managing all of these different authentication credentials frequently causes users to compromise and select the least burdensome password and then use it for all accounts.

A solution to this problem is to have one user name and password to gain access to all accounts so that the user has only one user name and password to remember.

This is the idea behind *identity management*, which is using a single authentication credential that is shared across multiple networks. When those networks are owned by different organizations, it is called **federation** (sometimes called *federated identity management* or *FIM*). One application of federation is **single sign-on (SSO)**, or using one authentication credential to access multiple accounts or applications. SSO holds the promise of reducing the number of user names and passwords that users must memorize (potentially, to just one).

Note 📎

Several large Internet providers support SSO, but only for their own suite of services and applications. For example, a Google user can access all of Google's features, such as Gmail, Google Docs and Spreadsheets, Calendar, and Photos, by entering a single Google account user name and password. Microsoft offers a similar service through its Microsoft Account. An advantage besides only using a single user name and password is that settings made on one device are automatically synced with all other devices. However, these SSOs are proprietary and restricted to Google or Microsoft applications and are not "federated" with other organizations.

There are several current technologies for federation systems. These are listed in Table 11-4.

Table 11-4 Federation systems technologies

Name	Description	Explanation
OAuth	Open source federation framework	OAuth 2.0 is a framework to support the development of authorization protocols.
Open ID Connect	Provides user authentication information	Authentication protocol that can be used in OAuth 2.0 as a standard means to obtain user identity.
Shibboleth	Open source software package for designing SSO	Uses federation standards to provide SSO and exchanging attributes.

Note 📎

OAuth relies upon token credentials. A user sends her authentication credentials to a server (such as a web application server) and also authorizes the server to issue token credentials to a third-party server. These token credentials are used in place of transferring the user's user name and password. The tokens are not generic, but are for specific resources on a site for a limited period.

Account Management

4.1 Compare and contrast identity and access management concepts.

4.2 Given a scenario, differentiate common account management practices.

Managing the login credentials such as passwords in user accounts (**credential management**) can be accomplished by setting restrictions regarding the creation and use of passwords. Although these restrictions can be performed on a user-by-user basis, this quickly becomes cumbersome and is a security risk: it is too easy to overlook one setting in one user account and create a security vulnerability.

A preferred approach is to assign privileges by group (**group policy**). In a Microsoft Windows environment, there are two categories of group password settings. The first category is called *Password Policy Settings* and is configured by using Group Policy at the domain level. There are six common domain password policy settings called Microsoft setting objects. These are detailed in Table 11-5.

Table 11-5 Password policy settings (Windows Group Policy)

Password setting name	Microsoft setting object	Description	Recommended setting
Password reuse	Enforce password history	Determines the number of unique new passwords a user must use before an old password can be reused (from 0 to 24).	24 new passwords
Password expiration	Maximum password age	Determines how many days a password can be used before the user is required to change it. The value of this setting can be between 0 (password never expires) and 999.	90 days
Password history	Minimum password age	Determines how many days a new password must be kept before the user can change it (from 0 to 999). This setting is designed to work with the Enforce password history setting so that users cannot quickly reset their passwords the required number of times, and then change back to their old passwords.	1 day

(continues)

Table 11-5 (*continued*)

Password setting name	Microsoft setting object	Description	Recommended setting
Password length	Minimum password length	Determines the minimum number of characters a password can have (0–28).	12 characters
Password complexity	Passwords must meet complexity requirements	Determines whether the following are used in creating a password: Passwords cannot contain the user's account name or parts of the user's full name that exceed two consecutive characters; must contain characters from three of the following four categories—English uppercase characters (A through Z), English lowercase characters (a through z), digits (0 through 9), and non-alphabetic characters (!, $, #, %).	Enabled
Password encryption	Store passwords using reversible encryption	Provides support for applications that use protocols which require knowledge of the user's password for authentication purposes. An attacker who can circumvent the encryption will be able to log on to the network with these passwords.	Disabled

The second category is the *Account Lockout Policy*, which is an Active Directory Domain Services (AD DS) security feature. The **password lockout** prevents a logon after a set number of failed logon attempts within a specified period and can also specify the length of time that the lockout is in force. This helps prevent attackers from online guessing of user passwords. These settings are listed in Table 11-6.

In addition to account policy enforcement, other steps should be taken regarding user accounts. For example, a **shared account** (an account used by more than one user), a **generic account** (an account not tied to a specific person, such as *HelpDesk_1*), and a **guest account** (given to temporary users) should be prohibited. A **service account** is a user account that is created explicitly to provide a security context for services running on a server. These accounts should be carefully configured so as not to provide more privileges than are absolutely necessary. A **privileged account** is an account to which powerful rights, privileges, and permissions are granted so that a user could perform nearly any action; these should also be closely monitored.

Table 11-6 Account lockout policy settings (Windows Active Directory)

Microsoft setting object	Description	Recommended setting	Comments
Account lockout duration	Determines the length of time a locked account remains unavailable before a user can try to log on again (a value of 0 sets account to remain locked out until an administrator manually unlocks it).	15 minutes	Setting this attribute too high may increase help desk calls from users who unintentionally lock themselves out.
Account lockout threshold	Determines the number of failed log in attempts before a lockout occurs.	30 invalid attempts	Setting this attribute too low may result in attackers using the lockout state as a denial of service (DoS) attack by triggering a lockout on a large number of accounts.
Reset account lockout counter after	Determines the length of time before the account lockout threshold setting resets to zero.	15 minutes	This reset time must be less than or equal to the value for the account lockout duration setting.

Account passwords should be **disabled** (made inactive) instead of the account being immediately deleted. This serves to create an audit trail to conform with compliance issues, and also makes the reestablishment of an account easier if it becomes necessary. Finally, attention should be given regarding policies for **password recovery** in the event a user forgets a password. Simply providing a password over the telephone is discouraged; rather, a process needs to be in place in which the user can authenticate himself or herself prior to being provided a new password.

Also, care must be taken with **transitive trust**. Transitive trust is a two-way relationship that is automatically created between parent and child domains in a Microsoft Active Directory forest. When a new domain is created, it shares resources with its parent domain by default, which can enable an authenticated user to access resources in both the child and the parent.

Chapter Summary

- Different authentication credentials can be presented to an information technology system to verify the genuineness of the user. These can be classified into five categories: what you know, what you have, what you are, what you do, and where you are.

- The most common "what you know" type of authentication is a password. A password is a secret combination of letters, numbers, and/or characters that only the user should have knowledge of and is the most common type of authentication in use today. Passwords provide a weak degree of protection because they rely on human memory. Human beings have a finite limit to the number of items that they can memorize. Because of the burdens that passwords place on human memory, users often take shortcuts to help them recall their passwords.

- Many users erroneously think passwords are compromised by password guessing: a threat actor enters different passwords at the login prompt until he guesses the right password and is admitted access, called an online attack. Although there are several different types of password attacks, the most common password attacks today use offline attacks. Attackers steal the file of password digests and then load that file onto their own computers so they can attempt to discover the passwords by comparing the stolen digest passwords with candidate digests that they have created. An automated brute force attack uses every possible combination of letters, numbers, and characters to create candidates that are matched with those in the stolen file. A mask attack is a more targeted brute force attack that uses placeholders for characters in certain positions of the password. A rule attack conducts a statistical analysis on the stolen passwords that is then used to create a mask to break the largest number of passwords.

- A dictionary attack begins with the attacker creating digests of common dictionary words, which are then compared with those in a stolen password file. Attackers often use rainbow tables, which make password attacks easier by creating a large pregenerated data set of encrypted passwords. Large collections of stolen password files have allowed attackers to create a larger number of accurate candidates and to understand how users create passwords.

- Securing passwords from attacks depends upon the user as well as the enterprise. However, due to the limitations of human memory it is virtually impossible for users to apply all these recommendations and then memorize long, complex, and unique passwords for all accounts. Instead of relying on human memory for passwords, security experts universally recommend that technology be used instead to store and manage passwords called password managers. Enterprises likewise must protect the stored password digests. One means for an enterprise to protect stored digests is to add a salt that consists of a random string that is used in hash algorithms. Another means is to use specialized password hash algorithms that are intentionally designed to be slower, called key stretching.

- Another type of authentication credential is based on the approved user having a specific item in her possession ("what you have"). A hardware token is typically a small device (usually one that can be affixed to a keychain) with a window display that generates a code from the algorithm once every 30 to 60 seconds. Several different types of cards can be used as authentication credentials. A smart card contains an integrated circuit chip that can hold information, which can then be used as part of the authentication process. Tokens and cards are being replaced with cell phones.

- The features and characteristics of the individual ("what you are") can serve as authentication. Standard biometrics uses a person's unique physical characteristics for authentication. This includes fingerprints, retinas, voice, iris, and facial recognition. There are also disadvantages to biometrics. Cognitive biometrics is related to the perception, thought process, and understanding of the user. Cognitive biometrics is considered to be much easier for the user because it is based on the user's life experiences, which also makes it very difficult for an attacker to imitate.

- Behavioral biometrics, or "what you do," authenticates by normal actions that the user performs. Behavioral biometric technologies include keystroke dynamics. A final type of authentication, geolocation, is the identification of the location ("where you are") of a person or object using technology. Although geolocation may not uniquely identify the user, it can indicate if an attacker is trying to perform a malicious action from a location different from the normal location of the user.

- One of the problems facing users today is that they have multiple accounts across multiple platforms that all ideally use a unique user name and password. The difficulty in managing all these different authentication credentials frequently causes users to compromise and select the least burdensome password and then use it for all accounts. A solution to this problem is to have one user name and password to gain access to all accounts so that the user has only one user name and password to remember. This is called single sign-on (SSO). Examples of popular SSOs include Shibboleth, OpenID Connect, and OAuth.

- Managing the passwords in user accounts can be accomplished by setting restrictions regarding the creation and use of passwords. Although these restrictions can be performed on a user-by-user basis, this quickly becomes cumbersome and is a security risk: it is too easy to overlook one setting in one user account and create a security vulnerability. It may be more secure for an administrator to set these restrictions in a group policy.

Key Terms

authentication	dictionary attack	generic account
bcrypt	disabled	group policy
brute force attack	facial recognition	guest account
common access card (CAC)	false acceptance rate (FAR)	hardware security token
credential management	false rejection rate (FRR)	HMAC-based one-time
crossover error	federation	password (HOTP)
rate (CER)	fingerprint scanner	iris scanner

key stretching

multifactor authentication

NTLM (New Technology LAN
  Manager) hash

OAuth

offline attack

online attack

Open ID Connect

pass the hash

password

password complexity

password expiration

password history

password length

password lockout

password recovery

password reuse

PBKDF2

Personal Identity
  Verification (PIV)

privileged account

proximity card

rainbow tables

retinal scanner

security token

service account

shared account

Shibboleth

single sign-on (SSO)

smart card

software security token

something you are

something you do

something you have

something you know

somewhere you are

standard biometrics

time-based one-time
  password (TOTP)

transitive trust

voice recognition

Review Questions

1. Which authentication factor is based on a unique talent that a user possesses?
   a. What you have
   b. What you are
   c. What you do
   d. What you know

2. Which of these is NOT a characteristic of a weak password?
   a. A common dictionary word
   b. A long password
   c. Using personal information
   d. Using a predictable sequence of characters

3. Each of the following accounts should be prohibited EXCEPT:
   a. Shared accounts
   b. Generic accounts
   c. Privileged accounts
   d. Guest accounts

4. Ilya has been asked to recommend a federation system technology that is an open-source federation framework that can support the development of authorization protocols. Which of these technologies would he recommend?
   a. OAuth
   b. Open ID Connect
   c. Shibboleth
   d. NTLM

5. How is key stretching effective in resisting password attacks?
   a. It takes more time to generate candidate password digests.
   b. It requires the use of GPUs.
   c. It does not require the use of salts.
   d. The license fees are very expensive to purchase and use it.

6. Which of these is NOT a reason why users create weak passwords?
   a. A lengthy and complex password can be difficult to memorize.
   b. A security policy requires a password to be changed regularly.
   c. Having multiple passwords makes it hard to remember all of them.
   d. Most sites force users to create weak passwords even though they do not want to.

7. What is a hybrid attack?
   a. An attack that uses both automated and user input
   b. An attack that combines a dictionary attack with a mask attack
   c. A brute force attack that uses special tables
   d. An attack that slightly alters dictionary words

8. A TOTP token code is generally valid for what period of time?
   a. Only while the user presses SEND
   b. For as long as it appears on the device
   c. For up to 24 hours
   d. Until an event occurs

9. What is a token system that requires the user to enter the code along with a PIN called?
   a. Single-factor authentication system
   b. Token-passing authentication system
   c. Dual-prong verification system
   d. Multifactor authentication system

10. Which of these is a U.S. Department of Defense (DoD) smart card that is used for identification of active-duty and reserve military personnel?
    a. Personal Identity Verification (PIV) card
    b. Secure ID Card (SIDC)
    c. Common Access Card (CAC)
    d. Government Smart Card (GSC)

11. Which of the following should NOT be stored in a secure password database?
    a. Iterations
    b. Password digest
    c. Salt
    d. Plaintext password

12. Creating a pattern of where a user accesses a remote web account is an example of which of the following?
    a. Keystroke dynamics
    b. Geolocation

   c. Time-Location Resource Monitoring (TLRM)
   d. Cognitive biometrics

13. Timur was making a presentation regarding how attackers break passwords. His presentation demonstrated the attack technique that is the slowest yet most thorough attack that is used against passwords. Which of these password attacks did he demonstrate?
    a. Dictionary attack
    b. Hybrid attack
    c. Custom attack
    d. Brute force attack

14. Which human characteristic is NOT used for biometric identification?
    a. Retina
    b. Iris
    c. Height
    d. Fingerprint

15. _____ biometrics is related to the perception, thought processes, and understanding of the user.
    a. Cognitive
    b. Standard
    c. Intelligent
    d. Behavioral

16. Using one authentication credential to access multiple accounts or applications is known as _____.
    a. single sign-on
    b. credentialization
    c. identification authentication
    d. federal login

17. What is a disadvantage of biometric readers?
    a. Speed
    b. Cost
    c. Weight
    d. Standards

18. Which type of password attack is a more targeted brute force attack that uses placeholders for characters in certain positions of the password?
    a. Rainbow attack
    b. Mask attack
    c. Rule attack
    d. Pass the hash attack
19. Why should the account lockout threshold not be set too low?
    a. It could decrease calls to the help desk.
    b. The network administrator would have to reset the account manually.
    c. The user would not have to wait too long to have her password reset.
    d. It could result in denial of service (DoS) attacks.
20. Which one-time password is event-driven?
    a. HOTP
    b. TOTP
    c. ROTP
    d. POTP

Hands-On Projects

> **Note** 📎
>
> If you are concerned about installing any of the software in these projects on your regular computer, you can instead install the software in the Windows virtual machine created in the Chapter 1 Hands-On Projects 1–3 and 1–4. Software installed within the virtual machine will not impact the host computer.

Project 11-1: Using an Online Password Cracker

In this project, you create a hash on a password and then crack it through an online dictionary attack to demonstrate the speed of cracking passwords that use dictionary words.

1. The first step is to use a general-purpose hash algorithm to create a password hash. Use your web browser to go to **www.fileformat.info/tool/hash.htm** (if you are no longer able to access the program through this URL, use a search engine and search for "Fileformat.info").
2. Under **String hash**, enter the simple password **apple123** in the **Text:** line.
3. Click **Hash**.
4. Scroll down the page and copy the MD5 hash of this password to your Clipboard by selecting the text, right-clicking, and choosing **Copy**.
5. Open a new tab on your web browser.
6. Go to **https://crackstation.net/**.
7. Paste the MD5 hash of *apple123* into the text box beneath **Enter up to 10 non-salted hashes:**.
8. In the RECAPTCHA box, enter the current value being displayed in the box that says **Type the text**.
9. Click **Crack Hashes**.
10. How long did it take to crack this hash?
11. Click the browser tab to return to FileFormat.Info.
12. Under **String hash**, enter the longer password **12applesauce** in the **Text:** line.

13. Click **Hash**.
14. Scroll down the page and copy the MD5 hash of this password to your Clipboard.
15. Click to browser tab to return to the CrackStation site.
16. Paste the MD5 hash of *12applesauce* into the text box beneath **Enter up to 10 non-salted hashes:**.
17. In the RECAPTCHA box, enter the current value being displayed in the box that says **Type the text**.
18. Click **Crack Hashes**.
19. How long did it take this online rainbow table to crack this stronger password hash?
20. Click the browser tab to return to FileFormat.Info and experiment by entering new passwords, computing their hash, and testing them in the CrackStation site. If you are bold, enter a string hash that is similar to a real password that you use.
21. What does this tell you about the speed of password cracking tools? What does it tell you about how easy it is for attackers to crack weak passwords?
22. Close all windows.

Project 11-2: Cracking Passwords Using Hashcat GUI

In this project, you create a hash on a password and then crack it through an advanced password cracking tool called Hashcat. This tool demonstrates the strength of very powerful password cracking tools.

1. Open your web browser and enter the URL **www.hashcat.net** (if you are no longer able to access the site through this URL, use a search engine to search for "Hashcat").
2. Under **Download** click the latest version of **hashcat binaries**.
3. Download Hashcat.
4. Enter the URL **www.7-zip.org** to download the 7-Zip program to unpack Hashcat.
5. Click **Download** to download either the 32-bit or 64-bit version.
6. Launch 7-Zip and install the program.
7. Navigate to the location of the Hashcat download.
8. Right-click on the Hashcat file and select **7-Zip**.
9. Select **Extract files** and choose the location to extract the Hashcat files.
10. For computers with an Intel CPU, install the latest Intel OpenCL Runtime version. Enter the URL **software.intel.com/en-us/articles/opencl-drivers** (if you are no longer able to access the site through the web address, use a search engine to search for "Intel OpenCL drivers"). Under **OpenCL Runtime for Intel Core and Intel Xeon Processor** click **OpenCL Runtime XX.X for Intel Core and Intel Xeon Processors for Windows (64-bit & 32-bit)**. Download and install these drivers.

Note

Note that not all Intel processors fully support OpenCL Runtime.

11. For computers with an AMD CPU, install the latest AMD drivers. Enter the URL **support.amd.com/en-us/download**. Click **Download Now** and follow the instructions to install these drivers.

12. For computers with NVidia video cards, install the latest NVidia drivers. Enter the URL **www.nvidia.com/Download/index.aspx?lang=en-us** and follow the instructions to download and install the NVidia drivers.

13. Download a graphical user interface (GUI) for Hashcat. Enter the URL **hashkiller.co.uk /hashcat-gui.aspx**.

14. Download the latest version of HashcatGUI into the same directory as the Hashcat files unpacked in Step 9.

15. If necessary install the Microsoft .NET framework. Enter the URL **www.microsoft.com /en-us/download/details.aspx?id=21** and follow the instructions to download and install .NET Framework 3.5.

16. Download a sample wordlist file. Enter the URL **hashkiller.co.uk/downloads.aspx**.

17. Click **HashKiller Output Wordlist** and download this file into the same directory as the Hashcat files unpacked in Step 9.

18. Right-click on the Wordlist file and select **7-Zip**.

19. Select **Extract files** and extract the Wordlist file to this directory.

20. Create a text file that contains a password in MD5 format. Open Notepad and enter **c24a542f884e144451f9063b79e7994e** (the hash for "password12").

21. Save this file as **Hashes1.txt**.

22. Navigate to the Hashcat directory.

23. Launch the Hashcat GUI by clicking **App.HashcatGUI.exe**.

24. Click the tab **Wordlists & Markov**.

25. Click **Add Wordlists**.

26. Navigate to the file **hashkiller-dict.txt** and select this file.

27. Click the tab **Hashcat**.

28. Click the file location finder (...) after **Hash File:**.

29. Navigate to the file **Hashes1.txt** and select this file. This will be the input file for Hashcat to crack.

30. Under **Rules:** check the first box.

31. Click the file location finder (...) after **Rules:**.

32. Open the folder **Rules** and select **best64.rule**. This will be the file that contains the "rules" that Hashcat will follow to crack the password.

33. Click the file location finder (...) after **Output:**.

34. Enter the filename **Hashes1-Output.txt**.

35. Click the down arrow next to **Format:**.

36. Select **hash[:salt]:plain**. This will be the format of the output file, which will contain both the hash and the resulting plaintext password.

37. Click the file location finder (...) after **Binary**.

38. Navigate to the file **hashcat64.exe** and select this file if necessary.

39. If an error message occurs under **OpenCL Platform #1: NVIDIA Corporation** then close the message box.

40. Return to the **Hashcat** tab and under **Output:** check the box **CPU Only**.

41. Click the button at the bottom of the main Hashcat page (could be labeled "**Power of the Atom**" or "**I'm a HashKiller**") to start the cracking process again, without using the GPU.

42. While the process is working, you can press **S** to view the status.

43. When the cracking process is complete, navigate to the **Hashes1-Output.txt** and open it. The broken hashes will follow the original hash with a colon, such as "c24a542f884e14 4451f9063b79e7994e:password12."

44. Close all windows.

Project 11-3: Using Facial Recognition Software with Federation Technology

Facial recognition is a biometric authentication that is becoming increasingly popular on smartphones. In this project, you download and use a facial recognition app that uses the federation technologies OAuth running on OpenID Connect and utilizes multifactor authentication as well. You need either an Apple iOS or Android device for this project.

1. On your mobile device launch either the Apple iTunes or Android Play Store app.

2. Search for **BioID Facial Recognition Authenticator**.

3. Download and install this app on your mobile device.

4. Click **Open**.

5. Use your web browser to go to **mobile.bioid.com** (if you are no longer able to access the program through this URL, use a search engine and search for "BioID Facial Recognition").

6. Click **Sign up for free**.

7. Enter the requested information and click **Register**.

8. Go to your email account and confirm your account by clicking the link.

9. Return to your mobile device and sign in to BioID and click **Register**.

10. Click **Yes**.

11. Click **Allow**.

12. Follow the instructions to take four sets of pictures.

13. Click **Verify**. You are now logged in using BioID. Close this app and log in again using different positions of your face in different locations. How easy is this to use? How accurate is it?

14. Open a web browser and enter the URL **BioID.com**.

15. Click **Log in**.

16. Click on your name to view your account information.

17. Under **Biometric template**, click **Examine**. Read through the information and delete any photos that you consider would not be helpful in recognizing your face. Be sure to keep at least five photos.

18. Return to the **Manage your BioID account** page.

19. Under **Challenge-response** click **Enable** and read through the information. What additional degree of protection would this give you? Close the pop-up window.

20. Under **Time-based one-time password (TOTP)** click **Synchronize**. Read this information. What additional degree of protection would this give you? Click the browser back button.

21. Under **Multi-factor authentication** click **Configure**. Read this information. What additional degree of protection would this give you? Click the browser back button.
22. How much would you trust this application for your authentication? Would you use it to replace your passwords? Why or why not?
23. Close all windows.

Project 11-4: Practicing Keystroke Dynamics

One type of behavioral biometrics is keystroke dynamics, which attempts to recognize a user's unique typing rhythm. In this project, you download an application that illustrates keystroke dynamics.

1. Use your web browser to go to **www.epaymentbiometrics.ensicaen.fr/index.php /app/resources/65** (if you are no longer able to access the program through this URL, use a search engine and search for "GreyC-Keystroke Software").
2. Click **Softwares**.
3. Click **GREYC-KeyStroke Application**.
4. Click **Download**.
5. After the file downloads, uncompress the files.
6. Navigate to the directory of the files and double-click **GreycKeystroke.exe**.
7. Click **OK** to launch the application.
8. Click **Parameters**.
9. Point to **Password**.
10. This is the text that will be entered to determine your keystroke dynamics. Replace the current text with **Cengage** and press **Enter**.
11. Now register yourself. Click **Execution Mode**.
12. Point to **Enroll User**.
13. In the text field, enter your name and press **Enter**.
14. Now you will determine your keystroke dynamics.
15. Under **Password:** type **Cengage** and press **Enter**.
16. Notice that the graphs illustrate your keystroke dynamics for the time between two keys pressure, time between two keys release, time between one release and one pressure, and time between one pressure and one release.
17. Now change the color of the next attempt and run the test again. Click **View**.
18. Click **Graph color**.
19. Click **green**.
20. Under **Password:** type **Cengage** and press **Enter**.
21. Your graph should look similar to the first attempt.
22. Now run the test with a partner. Click **Execution Mode**.
23. Click **Enroll User**.
24. Ask your partner to enter his or her name, and press **Enter**.
25. Click **View**, then click **Graph color**.
26. Click **blue**.
27. Ask your partner under **Password:** to type **Cengage** and press **Enter**.

28. Click **View**, then click **Graph color**.
29. Click **black**.
30. Ask your partner under **Password:** to type **Cengage** and press **Enter**.
31. The results may look similar to Figure 11-14. How different are the dynamics between you and your partner?

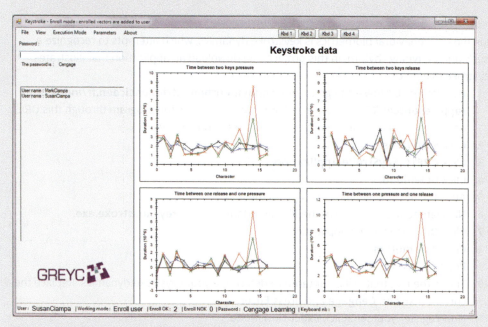

Figure 11-14   GreyC Keystroke dynamics
Source: GREYC-KeyStroke Software

32. Now determine the mean (average) of the keystroke dynamics for your partner. Click **View**.
33. Point to **Show mean vector**.
34. Select your partner's name.
35. Notice that another line appears with the average of your partner.
36. Now show your average. Click **View**, then click **Show mean vector**.
37. Select your name.
38. Can you determine that your keyboard dynamics are different from your partner's through these graphs?
39. To run the test again, click **View** and **Clear graph**.
40. Close GreyC Keystroke when finished and close all windows.

Project 11-5: Installing a Password Management Program

The drawback to using strong passwords is that they can be very difficult to remember, particularly when a unique password is used for each account that a user has. As another option, password management programs allow users to store account information such as a user name and password. These programs are themselves protected by a single strong password. One example of a password storage program is KeePass Password Safe, which is an open-source product. In this project, you download and install KeePass.

1. Use your web browser to go to **keepass.info** and then click **Downloads** (if you are no longer able to access the program through this URL, use a search engine and search for "KeePass").

2. Under **Professional Edition**, locate the most recent portable version of KeePass and click it to download the application. Save this file in a location such as your desktop, a folder designated by your instructor, or your portable USB flash drive. When the file finishes downloading, install the program. Accept the installation defaults.

> **Note** 🔗
>
> Because this is the portable version of KeePass it does not install under Windows. To use it, you must double-click the file name KeePass.exe.

3. Launch KeePass to display the opening screen.

4. Click **File** and **New** to start a password database. Enter a strong master password for the database to protect all the passwords in it. When prompted, enter the password again to confirm it.

5. Click **Edit** and **Add Entry**. You will enter information about an online account that has a password that you already use.

6. Create a group by clicking **Edit** and then **Add Group** and then enter **Web Sites**.

7. Select the **Web Sites** group and click **Edit** and then **Add Entry**.

8. Enter a title for your website (such as *Google Gmail*) under **Title**.

9. Under **User name**, enter the user name that you use to log in to this account.

10. Erase the entries under **Password** and **Repeat** and enter the password that you use for this account and confirm it.

11. Enter the URL for this account under **URL**.

12. Click **OK**.

13. Click **File** and **Save**. Enter your last name as the file name and then click Save.

14. Exit KeePass.

15. If necessary, navigate to the location of KeePass and double-click the file **KeePass.exe** to launch the application.

16. Enter your master password to open your password file.

17. If necessary, click the group to locate the account you just entered; it will be displayed in the right pane.

18. Click under **URL** to go to that website.

19. Click KeePass in the taskbar so that the window is now on top of your browser window.

20. Drag and drop your user name from KeePass into the login user name box for this account in your web browser.

21. Drag and drop your password from KeePass for this account.

22. Click the button on your browser to log in to this account.

23. Because you can drag and drop your account information from KeePass, you do not have to memorize any account passwords and can instead create strong passwords for each account. Is this an application that would help users create and use strong passwords? What are the strengths of such password programs? What are the weaknesses? Would you use KeePass?

24. Close all windows.

Project 11-6: Using Cognitive Biometrics

Cognitive biometrics holds great promise for adding two-factor authentication without placing a tremendous burden on the user. In this project, you participate in a demonstration of Passfaces.

1. Use your web browser to go to **www.passfaces.com/demo** (if you are no longer able to access the program through this URL, use a search engine and search for "Passfaces demo").

2. Under **First Time Users**, enter the requested information and then click **START THE DEMO**.

3. Click **Start the Demo**.

4. If you are prompted, accept **demo** as the name and then click **OK**.

5. When asked, click **NEXT** to enroll now.

6. When the **Enroll in Passfaces** dialog box displays, click **NEXT**.

7. Look closely at the three faces you are presented with. After you feel familiar with the faces, click **NEXT**.

8. You will then be asked to think of associations with the first face (who it looks like or who it reminds you of). Follow each step with the faces and then click **NEXT** after each face.

9. When the **STEP 2 Practice Using Passfaces** dialog box displays, click **NEXT**.

10. You will then select your faces from three separate screens, each of which has nine total faces. Click on the face (which is also moving as a hint).

11. You can practice one more time. Click **NEXT**.

12. When the **STEP 3 Try Logging On with Passfaces** dialog box displays, click **NEXT**. Identify your faces, and click **NEXT**.

13. Click **DONE** and click **OK**.

14. Click **Try Passfaces** and then click **Logon**.

15. Click **OK** under the user name and identify your faces.

16. Is this type of cognitive biometrics effective? If you came back to this site tomorrow, would you remember the three faces?

17. Close all windows.

Project 11-7: Using Windows Picture Password

In this project, you use another cognitive biometrics tool, Windows Picture Password.

1. Select a photo or image that you want to use as a picture password. Be sure the image is clear enough so that you can create lines, dots, or circles easily and distinctively.

2. Click **Start** and then **Settings** and then **Accounts** and finally **Sign-in options**.

3. On the right pane scroll down to **Picture Password**.

4. Click **Add**.
5. Enter your password when requested and click **OK**.
6. Windows displays a generic image along with details. Click **Choose Picture**.
7. Navigate to the location of the picture that you want to use.
8. Double-click that picture.
9. Click **Use this picture**.
10. You will now create three gestures for this photo. They can be any combinations of circles, lines, and taps. On the initial screen use your mouse, stylus, or finger to draw a circle, line, or dot on the screen.
11. Windows will then prompt you to add two more gestures.
12. Windows displays an outline of the gestures for your review. You can either click **Start** over or accept these gestures.
13. Be sure to remember each gesture in sequence and where they occur on the photo. When requested, draw them again for confirmation.
14. Close all windows.
15. Now try your picture password. Click **Start** and **Sign out**.
16. Press any key when the lock screen appears to see the different sign-in options along with your picture.
17. Draw the gestures to sign in. If you are unable to recreate them click **Sign-in options** to enter your password.
18. How easy is picture password to use? How difficult? Would you consider it more or less secure than a password? Why?

Case Projects

Case Project 11-1: Testing Password Strength

How strong are your passwords? Various online tools can provide information on password strength, but not all feedback is the same. First, assign the numbers 1 through 3 to three of the passwords you are currently using, and write down the number (not the password) on a piece of paper. Then, enter those passwords into these three online password testing services:

- How Secure Is My Password (*howsecureismypassword.net/*)
- Password Checker Online (*password-checker.online-domain-tools.com*)
- The Password Meter (*www.passwordmeter.com/*)

Record next to each number the strength of that password as indicated by these three online tools. Then use each online password tester to modify the password by adding more random numbers or letters to increase its strength. How secure are your passwords? Would any of these tools encourage someone to create a stronger password? Which provided the best information? Create a one-paragraph summary of your findings.

Case Project 11-2: Password Management Applications

Research at least four password management applications, one of which is a stand-alone application and another of which is a browser-based application. Create a table that lists and compares their features. Which would you recommend? Why? Create a report on your findings.

Case Project 11-3: Create Your Own Cognitive Biometric Memorable Event

What type of cognitive biometric "memorable event" do you think would be effective? Design your own example that is different from those given in the chapter. There should be five steps, and each step should have at least seven options. The final step should be a fill-in-the-blank user response. Compare your steps with those of other learners. Which do you think would be the easiest for users?

Case Project 11-4: Standard Biometric Analysis

Use the Internet and other sources to research the two disadvantages of standard biometrics: cost and error rates. Select one standard biometric technique (fingerprint, palm print, iris, facial features, etc.) and research the costs for having biometric readers for that technique located at two separate entrances into a building. Next, research ways in which attackers attempt to defeat this particular standard biometric technique. Finally, how often will this technique reject authorized users while accepting unauthorized users compared to other standard biometric techniques? Based on your research, would you recommend this technique? Why or why not? Write a one-page paper on your findings.

Case Project 11-5: Password Requirements

Visit the website Passwords Requirements Shaming (*password-shaming.tumblr.com*), which is a list of password requirements for different websites that are considered weak. Read through several of the submissions. Select three that you consider the most egregious. Why are they the worst? Next, indicate what you would suggest to make the requirement stronger, but a requirement that most users could meet. Write a one-paragraph summary.

Case Project 11-6: Lake Point Security Consulting

Lake Point Consulting Services (LPCS) provides security consulting and assurance services to over 500 clients across a wide range of enterprises in more than 20 states. A new initiative at LPCS is for each of its seven regional offices to provide internships to students who are in their final year of the security degree program at the local college.

"It's Late" is a regional coffee shop that serves "quick, casual food" such as sandwiches, soups, and salads. Each location also provides free wireless LAN access to its customers. Recently, one of the location's networks was successfully attacked and personal customer information was stolen, such as names, email addresses, birthdates, and similar information. The attack was traced to a manager's account that used the name of his spouse as the password. The new director of IT has asked LPSC to assist them by conducting a workshop regarding the risks of weak passwords and how to create and manage strong passwords.

1. Create a PowerPoint presentation for the executive management about the weaknesses and risks of using passwords, and how employees should create strong passwords. Your presentation should contain at least 10 slides.

2. After the presentation, the It's Late director of IT has contacted you. She recently read an article in a trade magazine about SSO and believes that this could be a solution to their problem. Create a memo to this director about SSO and how it could or could not address the password issue.

Case Project 11-7: Community Site Activity

The Information Security Community Site is an online companion to this textbook. It contains a wide variety of tools, information, discussion boards, and other features to assist learners. Go to *community.cengage.com/Infosec2* and click the *Join or Sign in* icon to log in, using your login name and password that you created in Chapter 1. **Click Forums (Discussion)** and click on **Security+ Case Projects (6th edition)**. Read the following case study.

Take the challenge to convince three of your friends that they must strengthen their passwords. Create a script of what you will say to them in an attempt to convince them of the dangers of weak passwords and the seriousness of the problem, and to inform them about what practical solutions are available. Then approach each friend individually and see whether you can be successful. Make a record of their responses and reactions to stronger passwords.

Record what occurred on the Community Site discussion board. What did you learn from this? How hard or easy is it to challenge users to create strong passwords? What arguments did you hear against it? What helped convince them to create stronger passwords?

References

1. "The ProjectSauron Apt," *Kaspersky Global research and Analysis Team*, Aug. 9, 2016, accessed May 21, 2017, https://securelist.com/files/2016/07/The-ProjectSauron-APT_research_KL.pdf.

2. Le Bras, Tom, "Online overload – it's worse than you think," *Dashlane Blog,* accessed May 22, 2017, https://blog.dashlane.com/infographic-online-overload-its-worse-than-you-thought/.

3. Lady, Kyle, "A security analysis of over 500 million usernames and passwords," *Duo Labs*, May 11, 2017, retrieved May 22, 2017, https://duo.com/blog/a-security-analysis-of-over-500-million-usernames-and-passwords.

4. Ahmad, Faizan, "Password strength analysis based on countries," *FSecurity*, Nov. 7, 2016, retrieved Jun. 3, 2017, http://fsecurify.com/password-analysis-based-on-countries/.

5. Schneier, Bruce, *Secrets and lies: Digital security in a networked world* (New York: Wiley Computer Publishing), 2004.

6. "Statistics," *Hashes.org*, retrieved May 22, 2017, https://hashes.org/stats.php.

7. Zhao, Ziming, Ahn, Gail-Joon, Seo, Jeong-Jun, and Hu, Hongxin, "On the security of Picture Gesture Authentication," *USENIX Security Symposium, 2013*, retrieved Mar. 22, 2014, www.public.asu.edu/~zzhao30/publication/ZimingUSENIX2013.pdf.

8. "Products," *BioPassword*, 2007, retrieved May 1, 2011, http://stage1.biopassword.com/keystroke-dynamics-history.php.

CHAPTER 12

ACCESS MANAGEMENT

After completing this chapter, you should be able to do the following:

Define access management and list the access control models

Describe how to manage access through account management

List the best practices for access control

Describe how to implement access control

Explain the different types of identity and access services

Elma Magkamit was considered to be a model employee for the city of West Linn, Oregon. In 1994, she applied for a position as an accountant in the city's finance department. On her job application, she stated that she was a certified public accountant (CPA) who had graduated from the university (had the city checked more closely they would have found she neither had a college degree nor a CPA). After being hired as an accountant, she was appointed as finance director seven years later. Ms. Magkamit was well respected in her field and was a member of the Oregon Municipal Finance Officers Association and the Government Finance Officers Association (GFOA).

Because she was so highly respected inside City Hall as well as among her peers in government accounting, Ms. Magkamit took control of West Linn's accounting—complete control. She sidestepped the important principle of separation of duties, in which responsibilities are distributed among several employees. Ms. Magkamit was the only employee who wrote checks, reconciled the bank statements, and made adjusting entries to the general ledger. No one else had oversight over her work.

For five years Ms. Magkamit stole voided checks from the accounts payable printer, took them home, and typed in her name or a fake consulting business as the payee. She never entered the checks into the general ledger; instead, she altered the bank statements and reconciled around them. She used correcting fluid to "white out" entries, cut and pasted strips of paper over portions of the statement, and folded over other parts of the statements before making her own photocopies for the city records. No one could tell funds were missing because the financial reporting adjustments and reports were purposefully made to look confusing and were poorly formatted.

Each month Ms. Magkamit wrote a check to herself averaging about $30,000. However, she did not write checks for the months of June and July, which were the months in which any new external auditors would be closely looking over the accounts—if the city hired new auditors. The City Council had a disagreement with the former external auditors, who were later fired. But the city never got around to replacing them, evidently because they thought Ms. Magkamit was doing such a good job and auditors were not needed.

The West Linn local charter required Ms. Magkamit to perform financial audits. Due to her power and prestige, she simply ignored the rules. Oregon state law also required audits and when the Oregon secretary of state's office asked West Linn for the audits, she ignored these requests as well.

Ms. Magkamit resigned her position after about five years—perhaps because she no longer needed any more income. She had forged and deposited 57 city checks into her personal account. The money supported her gambling habit and was used to purchase expensive clothing, $17,000 in jewelry, a luxury car, and a nice home on a golf course. In total, Ms. Magkamit had embezzled over $1.42 million from West Linn.

The following year, after a new finance director and new city manager were hired, an internal accountant was trying to straighten out the city's financial records when he discovered that a check was missing from the city's copy of the bank statement. The check was for $36,884.70 and made payable to "Larry Magkamit, Magkamit Consulting." This led to more intense scrutiny with more discrepancies being uncovered, with everything pointing to Ms. Magkamit. She was later arrested and indicted on 114 felony counts of theft and forgery. She was found guilty and sentenced to eight years in prison and ordered to repay the city for the embezzled funds.

The fallout from Ms. Magkamit's embezzlement was far-reaching. As the largest-ever Oregon city government embezzlement, employees were terminated, taxpayers lost money, the city's bond rating was suspended, and residents voted down a five-year levy to finance the police department, which was attributed to the public's lack of trust in the city's management. Eventually new internal controls were implemented with clear separation of duties over the bank reconciliation process, access to cash, and printing and control over the check stock. Other new controls included documenting procedures, double reviewing, mandatory "sign offs" on purchases, and rotating job functions.[1]

Consider this scenario: Braden has been assigned to help complete a project for his company at its office in a different city. Braden enters the building and explains to the security guard who he is and why he is there. He shows his company ID badge to the guard, who takes time to examine the photo on the ID badge and compare it to Braden's face, and then make several telephone calls to confirm Braden's presence. Once Braden's identity is confirmed, the guard hands a package to Braden that was left at the desk for him that contains a temporary passcode to the office that Braden will be using.

This scenario reflects actions that are like those used in information security. In Chapter 11, you learned that a user first must be identified as an authorized user, such as by logging in with a user name and password to a laptop computer. Because that laptop connects to the corporate network that contains critical data, it is likewise important to restrict user access to only the software, hardware, and other resources for which the user has been pre-approved (much like Braden is only approved for access to a single office and not to every office in the building). Managing access to resources is an important function in information security.

This chapter introduces you to the principles and practices of access management. You first examine what access management is and how to manage access through account management. Then the chapter surveys best practices for access control and ways to implement it. Finally, you explore identity and access services.

What Is Access Control?

Certification

4.1 Compare and contrast identity and access management concepts.

4.3 Given a scenario, implement identity and access management controls.

5.8 Given a scenario, carry out data security and privacy practices.

Note 🔗

Many CompTIA exam objectives include the phrase, "Given a scenario." This indicates that a hands-on simulation related to this objective will likely appear on the Security+ exam. The Hands-On Projects at the end of each chapter serve as training for these scenarios.

As its name implies, **access control** is granting or denying approval to use specific resources; it is controlling access. *Physical access control* consists of fencing, hardware door locks, and mantraps to limit contact with *devices*. In a similar way, *technical* *access control* consists of technology restrictions that limit users on digital devices from accessing *data*. Access control has a set of associated terminology used to describe its actions. There are also standard access control models that are used to help enforce access control.

> **Note** 📎
>
> Most home users have full privileges on their personal computers so they can install programs, access files, or delete folders at will and give no thought to access control. In the enterprise, however, where multiple individuals could potentially have access to sensitive information, access control is essential.

Access Control Terminology

Suppose that Gabe is babysitting his sister Mia one afternoon. Before leaving the house, his mother tells Gabe that a package delivery service is coming to pick up a box, which is inside the front door. Soon there is a knock at the door, and as Gabe looks out he sees the delivery person standing on the porch. Gabe asks her to display her employee credentials, which the delivery person is pleased to do. Gabe then opens the door and allows her inside, but only to the area by the front door, to pick up the box. Gabe then signs the delivery person's tablet device so there is a confirmation record that the package was picked up.

This scenario illustrates the basic steps in limiting access. The package delivery person first presents her ID to Gabe to be reviewed. A user accessing a computer system would likewise present credentials or **identification**, such as a user name, when logging on to the system. Identification is the process of recognizing and distinguishing the user from any other user. Checking the delivery person's credentials to be sure that they are authentic and not fabricated is *authentication*. Computer users, likewise, must have their credentials authenticated to ensure that they are who they claim to be, often by entering a password, fingerprint scan, or other means of authentication. **Authorization**, granting permission to take an action, is the next step. Gabe allowed the package delivery person to enter the house because she had been preapproved by Gabe's mother and her credentials were authentic. Likewise, once users have presented their identification and been authenticated, they can be authorized to log in to the system and access resources.

Gabe only allowed the package delivery person access to the area by the front door to retrieve the box; he did not allow her to go upstairs or into the kitchen. Likewise, computer users are granted *access* only to the specific services, devices, applications, and files needed to perform their job duties. Gabe signing on the tablet is akin to **accounting**, which is a record that is preserved of who accessed the network, what resources they accessed, and when they disconnected from the network. Accounting data can be used to provide an audit trail, for billing, determining trends, identifying resource utilization, and future capacity planning.

Note

Authentication, authorization, and accounting are sometimes called AAA ("triple-A"), providing a framework for controlling access to computer resources.

The basic steps in this access control process are summarized in Table 12-1.

Table 12-1 Basic steps in access control

Action	Description	Scenario example	Computer process
Identification	Review of credentials	Delivery person shows employee badge	User enters user name
Authentication	Validate credentials as genuine	Gabe reads badge to determine it is real	User provides password
Authorization	Permission granted for admittance	Gabe opens door to allow delivery person in	User authorized to log in
Access	Right given to access specific resources	Delivery person can only retrieve box by door	User allowed to access only specific data
Accounting	Record of user actions	Gabe signs to confirm the package was picked up	Information recorded in log file

Other terminology is used to describe how computer systems impose technical access control:

- *Object*. An object is a specific resource, such as a file or a hardware device.
- *Subject*. A subject is a user or a process functioning on behalf of the user that attempts to access an object.
- *Operation*. The action that is taken by the subject over the object is called an operation. For example, a user (subject) may attempt to delete (operation) a file (object).

Individuals are given different roles in relationship to access control objects or resources. These roles are summarized in Table 12-2.

Table 12-2 Roles in access control

Role	Description	Duties	Example
Privacy officer	Manager who oversees data privacy compliance and manages data risk	Ensures the enterprise complies with data privacy laws and its own privacy policies	Decides that users can have permission to access SALARY.XLSX
Custodian or **steward**	Individual to whom day-to-day actions have been assigned by the owner	Periodically reviews security settings and maintains records of access by end users	Sets and reviews security settings on SALARY.XLSX
Owner	Person responsible for the information	Determines the level of security needed for the data and delegates security duties as required	Determines that the file SALARY.XLSX can be read only by department managers
End user	User who accesses information in the course of routine job responsibilities	Follows organization's security guidelines and does not attempt to circumvent security	Opens SALARY.XLSX

Note 📎

Instead of the formal terms *custodian* or *steward*, the more generic term *administrator* is commonly used to describe this role.

Figure 12-1 illustrates the technical access control process and terminology.

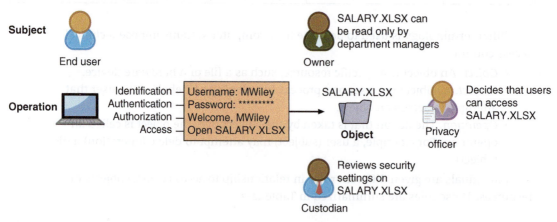

Figure 12-1 Technical access control process and terminology

> **Note**
>
> A common attack that exploits vulnerabilities in access control to gain access to restricted resources is called privilege escalation. Privilege escalation is covered in Chapter 5.

Access Control Models

Consider a network system administrator who needs to act as an access control custodian. One afternoon she must give a new employee access to specific servers and files. With tens of thousands of files scattered across a multitude of different servers, and with the new employee being given different access privileges to each file (for example, he can view one file but not edit it, but for a different file he can edit but not delete), controlling access could prove to be a daunting task. However, this job is made easier by the fact that the hardware and software have a predefined *framework* that the custodian can use for controlling access. This framework, called an **access control model**, is embedded in the software and hardware. The custodian can use the appropriate model to configure the necessary level of control.

> **Note**
>
> Access control models are variously referred to as access control models, methods, modes, techniques, or types. They are used by custodians for access control but are neither created nor installed by custodians or users. Instead, these models are already part of the software and hardware.

There are five major access control models: Discretionary Access Control, Mandatory Access Control, Role-Based Access Control, Rule-Based Access Control, and Attribute-Based Access Control.

Discretionary Access Control (DAC)

The **Discretionary Access Control (DAC)** model is the least restrictive. With the DAC model, every object has an owner, who has total control over that object. Most importantly, the owner has discretion (the choice) as to who can access their objects, and can grant permissions to other subjects over these objects. For example, with DAC, the owner Jose can access the files EMPLOYEES.XLSX and SALARIES.XLSX as well as paste the contents of EMPLOYEES.XLSX into a newly created document MY_DATA.XLSX. He also could give Juan access to all these files but allow Ricardo to only read EMPLOYEES.XLSX. As owner, Jose has the choice of which other subjects can have access to his objects.

DAC is used on several operating systems (OSs). Figure 12-2 illustrates the DAC that a Microsoft Windows owner has over an object. These controls can be configured so that another user can have full or limited access over a file, printer, or other object.

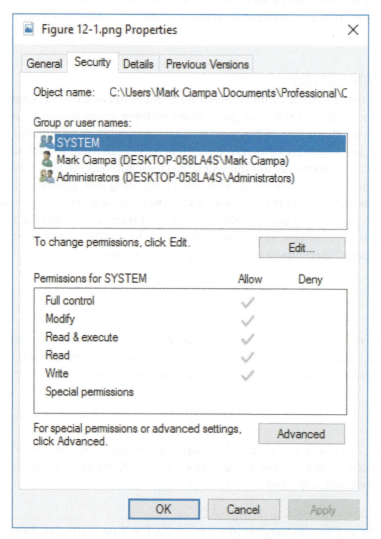

Figure 12-2 Windows Discretionary Access Control (DAC)

DAC has two significant weaknesses. First, although it gives a degree of freedom to the subject, DAC poses risks in that it relies on decisions by the end user to set the proper level of security. As a result, incorrect permissions might be granted to a subject or permissions might be given to an unauthorized subject. A second weakness is that a subject's permissions will be "inherited" by any programs that the subject executes. Threat actors often take advantage of this inheritance because end users frequently have a high level of privileges. Malware that is downloaded onto a user's computer that uses the DAC model would then run at the same high level as the user's privileges.

Mandatory Access Control (MAC)

The opposite of DAC is the most restrictive access control model, **Mandatory Access Control (MAC)**. MAC assigns users' access controls strictly according to the custodian's desires. This is considered the most restrictive access control model because the user has no freedom to set any controls or distribute access to other subjects. This model is typically found in military settings in which security is of supreme importance.

There are two key elements to MAC:

- *Labels*. In a system using MAC, every entity is an object (laptops, files, projects, and so on) and is assigned a classification label. These labels represent the relative importance of the object, such as *confidential*, *secret*, and *top secret*. Subjects (users, processes, and so on) are assigned a privilege label (sometimes called a *clearance*).
- *Levels*. A hierarchy based on the labels is also used, both for objects and subjects. *Top secret* has a higher level than *secret*, which has a higher level than *confidential*.

MAC grants permissions by matching object labels with subject labels based on their respective levels. To determine if a file can be opened by a user, the object and subject labels are compared. The subject must have an equal or greater level than the object in order to be granted access. For example, if the object label is *top secret*, yet the subject has only a lower *secret* clearance, access is denied. Subjects cannot change the labels of objects or other subjects to modify the security settings.

> **Note**
>
> In the original MAC model, all objects and subjects were assigned a numeric access level and the access level of the subject had to be higher than that of the object for access to be granted. For example, if EMPLOYEES.XLSX was assigned Level 500 while SALARIES.XLSX was assigned Level 700, then a user with an assigned level of 600 could access EMPLOYEES.XLSX (Level 500) but not SALARIES.XLSX (Level 700). This model was later modified to use labels instead of numbers.

There are two major implementations of MAC. The first is called the *lattice model*. A *lattice* is a type of screen or fencing that is used as a support for climbing garden plants. Different "rungs" on the MAC lattice model have different security levels, and subjects are assigned a "rung" on the lattice just as objects are. There can even be multiple lattices placed beside each other to allow for different groups of labels. For example, one subject label lattice could use the clearances *confidential*, *secret*, and *top secret* while a corresponding subject label lattice could use *public, restricted*, and *top clearance*. The rungs of each subject lattice would still align with the rungs on the object security lattice.

Another implementation of MAC is the *Bell-LaPadula (BLP) model*. Although this model is very similar to the lattice model, it contains an additional restriction not found in the original lattice model. This protection prevents subjects from creating a new object or performing specific functions on objects that are at a lower level than their own. For example, a user with clearance *secret* should not have the ability to open a document at the *secret* level and then paste its contents to a newly created document at the *confidential* level. A variation of the BLP model is the *Biba Integrity model*, which goes beyond the BLP model and adds protecting data integrity in addition to confidentiality.

Microsoft Windows uses a MAC implementation called *Mandatory Integrity Control (MIC)*. Based on the Biba model, MIC ensures data integrity by controlling access to securable objects. A *security identifier (SID)* is a unique number issued to the user, group, or session. Each time a user logs in, the system retrieves the SID for that user from the database, and then uses that SID to identify the user in all subsequent interactions with Windows security. Windows links the SID to an *integrity level*. Objects such as files, processes, services, and devices are assigned integrity levels—*low, medium, high,* and *system*—that determine their levels of protection or access. To write to or delete an object, the integrity level of the subject must be equal to or greater than the object's level. This ensures that processes running with a low integrity level cannot write to an object with a medium integrity level.

> **Note** 📎
>
> MIC works in addition to Windows DAC. Windows first checks any requests against MIC, and if they pass, then it checks DAC.

This can be seen in practice through a Window's feature known as *User Account Control (UAC)*. The standard user (lower level) who attempts to install software (higher level) is first required by UAC to enter the higher-level administrative password before being allowed to proceed (which elevates the action to the higher level). As an additional check, an administrative user also must confirm the action (yet he does not need to enter the administrative password, as shown in Figure 12-3). In this way, UAC attempts to match the subject's privilege level with that of the object.

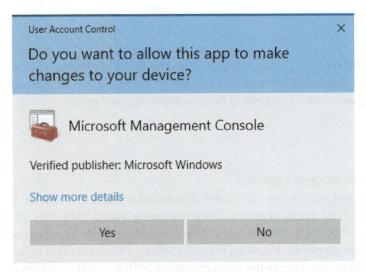

Figure 12-3   Windows User Account Control (UAC) prompt

By default, Windows switches to "Secure Desktop mode" when the UAC prompt appears. Secure Desktop mode allows only trusted processes with the integrity level *System* to run, which prevents malware from "spoofing" what appears on the screen to trick users. Secure Desktop mode is similar to what appears when a Windows login screen appears or the keystroke combination Ctrl-Alt-Delete is pressed. In Secure Desktop mode, users cannot click on any icon other than the Windows prompt.

Role-Based Access Control

The third access control model is **Role-Based Access Control (RBAC)** sometimes called *Non-Discretionary Access Control*. RBAC is considered a more "real-world" access control than the other models because the access under RBAC is based on a user's job function within an organization. Instead of setting permissions for each user or group, the RBAC model assigns permissions to particular roles in the organization, and then assigns users to those roles. Objects are set to be a certain type, to which subjects with that particular role have access. For example, instead of creating a user account for Ahmed and assigning specific privileges to that account, the role *Business_Manager* can be created based on the privileges an individual in that job function should have. Then Ahmed and all other business managers in the organization can be assigned to that role. The users and objects inherit all the permissions for the role.

> **Note**
>
> Roles are different from groups. Although users may belong to multiple groups, a user under RBAC can be assigned only one role. In addition, under Role-Based Access Control, users cannot be given permissions beyond those available for their role.

Rule-Based Access Control

The **Rule-Based Access Control** model, also called the *Rule-Based Role-Based Access Control (RB-RBAC)* model or *automated provisioning*, can dynamically assign roles to subjects based on a set of rules defined by a custodian. Each resource object contains a set of access properties based on the rules. When a user attempts to access that resource, the system checks the rules contained in that object to determine if the access is permissible.

Rule-Based Access Control is often used for managing user access to one or more systems, where business changes may trigger the application of the rules that specify access changes. For example, a subject on Network A wants to access objects on Network B, which is located on the other side of a router. This router contains the set of access control rules and can assign a certain role to the user, based on her network address or protocol, which will then determine whether she will be granted access. Similar to MAC, Rule-Based Access Control cannot be changed by users. All access permissions are controlled based on rules established by the custodian or system administrator.

Attribute-Based Access Control

While the Rule-Based Access Control model uses predefined rules, **Attribute-Based Access Control (ABAC)** uses more flexible policies that can combine attributes. These policies can take advantage of many different types of attributes, such as object attributes, subject attributes, and environment attributes. ABAC rules can be formatted using an *If-Then-Else* structure, so that a policy can be created such as *If this subject has the role of manager then grant access else deny access*.

> **Note**
>
> ABAC systems can also enforce both DAC and MAC models.

Table 12-3 summarizes the features of the five access control models.

Table 12-3 Access control models

Name	Explanation	Description
Mandatory Access Control (MAC)	End user cannot set controls	Most restrictive model
Discretionary Access Control (DAC)	Subject has total control over objects	Least restrictive model
Role-Based Access Control (RBAC)	Assigns permissions to particular roles in the organization and then users are assigned to roles	Considered a more "real-world" approach
Rule-Based Access Control	Dynamically assigns roles to subjects based on a set of rules defined by a custodian	Used for managing user access to one or more systems
Attribute-Based Access Control (ABAC)	Uses policies that can combine attributes	Most flexible model

Managing Access Through Account Management

 **Certification**

4.3 Given a scenario, implement identity and access management controls.

Because access management is closely linked to the permissions on accounts, properly configuring those accounts is a first step in providing strong security. These accounts include not only user accounts but also service accounts and privileged accounts. Account management includes account setup as well as account auditing.

Account Setup

When initially setting up accounts, there are several items that need to be taken into consideration. These include employee accounts, creating location-based policies, establishing standard naming conventions, creating time-of-day restrictions, and enforcing least privilege.

Employee Accounts

Employee accounts are often the source of entry points by threat actors, so securing these accounts is of high priority. Securing employee accounts involves configurations in the context of employee onboarding and offboarding.

Employee Onboarding

Employee onboarding refers to the tasks associated with hiring a new employee (*onboarding*). Whereas at one time there was little advanced preparation for "new hires," today that is generally not the case. There are several steps that should be taken to not only make the new employee feel part of the team but also so that the employee can become productive as soon as possible. Several recommended employee onboarding steps are listed in Table 12-4.

Table 12-4 General employee onboarding procedures

Category	Recommendations
Scheduling	Contact employee to confirm start date, time, place, parking, dress code, etc.; identify computer needs and requirements; provide name of their onboarding buddy
Job duties	Prepare employee's calendar for the first two weeks; add regularly scheduled staff and department meetings to employee's calendar; plan employee's first assignment
Socializing	Email department of new hire, including start date, employee's role, and biography; set up meetings with important contacts for the employee's first week; arrange for lunch with the appropriate persons; set up campus tour
Work space	Create welcome packet with job description, welcome letter, contact names and phone lists, campus map, parking, mission, and values of the enterprise; set up cubicle or office space with supplies; order office or work area keys; add employee to email lists
Training	Remind employee to sign up for new employee orientation session; arrange pertinent trainings required for the job; provide information on setting up voicemail and computer

In addition to these general onboarding procedures there are several steps to be taken regarding the setup and account configuration of new employees. In a common Microsoft Windows environment using Active Directory (AD) the steps may include:

- *Provision the new computer.* The new computer can be added to the AD domain and then moved into a specific organizational unit (OU), or the computer account can be set up inside the correct OU before it is joined. In addition, the appropriate applications should be installed.
- *Create email mailboxes and AD users.* New email mailboxes and corresponding new AD user accounts should be set up.
- *Add user accounts to groups.* Once an AD account is created, it is necessary to add that account to one or more AD security groups.
- *Create home folder.* Home folders are typically folders on a file server that contain a storage repository for the files the employee will be creating and using.
- *Review security settings.* It is important to review the security settings of the different accounts to ensure that they fit within the policy guidelines of the enterprise.

Employee Offboarding

Employee offboarding entails actions to be taken when an employee leaves an enterprise. The necessary steps should include backing up all employee files from the local computer and file server, archiving email, forwarding email to a manager or coworker, hiding the name from the email address book, etc.

In addition, when an employee leaves an organization, that employee's accounts should be immediately disabled. *Orphaned accounts* are user accounts that remain active after an employee has left an organization, while a *dormant account* is one that has not been accessed for a lengthy period. Both these types of accounts can be a security risk. For example, an employee who left under unfavorable circumstances might be tempted to "get even" with the organization by stealing or erasing sensitive information through her account. Dormant accounts can also provide an avenue for an attacker to exploit without the fear of the actual user or a system administrator noticing.

Several recommendations for dealing with orphaned or dormant accounts include:

- *Establish a formal process*. It is important that a formal procedure be in place for disabling accounts for employees who are dismissed, resign, or retire from the organization.
- *Terminate access immediately*. It is critical that access be ended as soon as the employee is no longer part of the organization.
- *Monitor logs*. Current employees are sometimes tempted to use an older dormant account instead of their own account. Monitoring logs can help prevent use of other accounts.

Locating and terminating orphaned and dormant accounts, however, remains a problem for many organizations. To assist with controlling orphaned and dormant accounts, *account expiration* can be used. Account expiration is the process of setting a user's account to expire. Account expiration can be explicit, in that the account expires on a set date, or it can be based on a specific number of days of inactivity.

> **Note** 📎
>
> Some OSs have an option to set a maximum number of days that an account will remain active after a password has expired and has not been reset. Once that maximum is reached, the account will automatically be disabled.

It is generally recommended not to immediately delete an AD account after an employee leaves the enterprise (although it should be disabled). This is to protect any data for evidence if necessary and because automated tasks such as creating reports may be tied to user accounts. Many organizations disable accounts for a minimum of 30 days and then purge disabled accounts twice per year.

Note

If an AD account is deleted as part of an automated task, it is not possible to simply recreate the account with the same user name. This is because the SID, which is what the automated task looks at and not the visible name of the account, will be different.

Location-Based Policies

Mobile devices with global positioning system (GPS) capabilities typically support geolocation, or the process of identifying the geographical location of the device. This can be used to support geofencing, or defining geographical boundaries where the app can be used. For example, a tablet containing patient information that leaves the hospital grounds or an employee who attempts to enter a restricted area with a device can result in an alert sent to an administrator.

Note

Geolocation and geofencing are covered in Chapter 10.

Geofencing relies upon **location-based policies**, or establishing the geographical boundaries of where a mobile device can and cannot be used. These policies are often first prescribed by generating an IP location data file, which is a text file containing comma separated fields in the format *IP_From, IP_To, Country_Code, Country_Name, Region, City* (for example, *10.0.0.255, 10.0.5.0, US, United States, Tennessee, Nashville*). This policy then becomes the basis for how authorization requests from mobile devices are evaluated. When setting up accounts with mobile devices, location-based policies can be helpful in controlling access.

Note

Location-based policies can support multiple geographical zones using mobile device management (MDM) systems. These policies are enforced automatically as the device moves into and out of a specific network zone. Policies can include such actions as disabling the camera to prevent users from taking unauthorized pictures in specific geographic locations, disabling automatic screen lock so that users do not have to unlock their device repeatedly while at work, or disabling apps and browsers entirely.

Standard Naming Conventions

Suppose a student was asked to name a Word document containing an assignment with her name, course, and assignment number. Would she use *Roma_CIS100_Assignment1,* or *Assign1-Roma-CIS,* or *100RRomanelli1*—or one of several other options? Just as there is no set standard for naming user data files, the same is true of naming accounts: there are no **standard naming conventions**, or "rules" that have been established for creating account names. Because this can lead to confusion, it is important that each enterprise create a standard naming convention for account names. Options typically include first initial of first name followed by last name (*RRomanelli*), first name with a punctuation mark followed by last name (*Roma.Romanelli*), last name followed by department code (*Romanelli1912*), or similar variations. In the event two names appear to be the same, a standard policy should also be established for resolving such conflicts, such as adding a middle initial (*RARomanelli*).

Note 📎

If a standard naming convention includes appending different data together to form a user name, the potential exists that the result might be offensive or humorous. It is recommended that even with an automated user name creation system, account names should still be manually reviewed.

Time-of-Day Restrictions

A **Time-of-day restriction** can be used to limit when a user can log into their account to access resources. When setting these restrictions, a custodian would typically indicate the times a user is restricted from accessing the system or resources. Figure 12-4 illustrates time of day restrictions implemented by indicating the specific days and times, while Figure 12-5 shows setting the restrictions with a graphical interface.

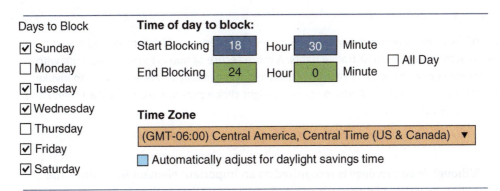

Figure 12-4   Time-of-day restrictions setting specific times and days

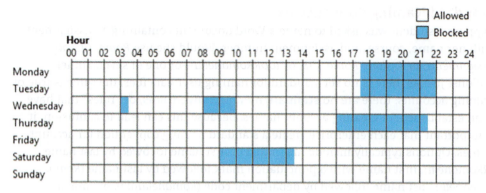

Figure 12-5   Time-of-day restrictions using GUI

Least Privilege

Consider the rooms in a large office building, each of which has a door with a lock. Different classifications of employees can be provided different keys to open doors based on their jobs. For example, a typical office worker would not be given a key that opens every door in the building; there simply is no need for this classification of worker to have access to the contents of every room. A member of the building's security staff, on the other hand, would have a key that could open any office because her job function would require it.

Limiting access to rooms in a building is a model of the information technology security principle of **least privilege**. Least privilege in access control means that only the minimum amount of privileges necessary to perform a job or function should be allocated. This helps reduce the attack surface by eliminating unnecessary privileges that could provide an avenue for an attacker. Least privilege should apply both to user accounts and to processes running on the system.

> **Note** 📎
>
> One of the reasons home computers are so frequently and easily compromised is that they use an account with administrative rights. A more secure option is to use an account with lower privileges and then invoke administrative privileges only when necessary. To invoke administrative privileges, Windows users can right-click a program from the Start menu and select *Run as administrator*.

Although least privilege is recognized as an important element in security, the temptation to assign higher levels of privileges is great due to the challenges of assigning users lower security levels. Several of those challenges are listed in Table 12-5.

| Table 12-5 | Challenges of least privilege |

Challenge	Explanation
Legacy applications	Many older software applications were designed to run only with a high level of privilege. Many of these applications were internally developed and are no longer maintained or are third-party applications that are no longer supported. Redeveloping the application may be seen as too costly. An alternative is to run the application in a virtualized environment.
Common administrative tasks	In some organizations, basic system administration tasks are performed by the user, such as connecting printers or defragmenting a disk. Without a higher level of privilege, users must contact the help desk so that a technician with administrative privileges can help with the tasks.
Software installation/ upgrade	A software update that is not centrally deployed can require a higher privilege level, which can mean support from the local help desk. This usually results in decreased productivity and increased support costs.

Account Auditing

Once accounts have been created, it is important that they be periodically maintained and audited to ensure they follow all enterprise policies. These audits include:

- *Recertification.* **Recertification** is the process of periodically revalidating a user's account, access control, and membership role or inclusion in a specific group. The recertification process validates whether the permissions are still required for a valid business purpose. The process is not done in secret; rather, it starts by sending a recertification notification and approval to the participants being examined. A recertification policy includes activities to ensure that users provide confirmation that they have a valid and ongoing need for a specified resource or membership.
- *Permission auditing and review.* **Permission auditing and review** is intended to examine the permissions that a user has been given to determine if each is still necessary. Whereas individual user account permissions may not change regularly, groups to which a user is assigned may be given increased privileges, yet the user herself does not require these permissions. In that case, a new group account should be created with limited permissions and the appropriate users added to that group.
- *Usage auditing and review.* **Usage auditing and review** is an audit process that looks at the applications that the user is provided, how frequently they are used, and how they are being used. As with permission auditing and review, if a user does not access an application, this could indicate that the user no longer needs access to that application and it should be removed.

Best Practices for Access Control

 **Certification**

5.1 Explain the importance of policies, plans, and procedures related to organizational security.

Enforcing technical access control using the various access control models is only one means of providing security. In addition, establishing a set of "best practices" for limiting access also can help secure systems and their data. These practices include separation of duties, job rotation, mandatory vacations, and a clean desk policy.

Separation of Duties

News headlines such as "County Official Charged with Embezzlement" appear all too frequently. Often this fraud results from a single user being trusted with a set of responsibilities that place the person in complete control of the process. For example, one person may be given total control over the collection, distribution, and reconciliation of money. If no other person is involved, it might be too tempting for that person to steal, knowing that nobody else is watching and that there is a good chance the fraud will go undetected. To counteract this possibility, most organizations require that more than one person be involved with functions that relate to handling money, because it would require a conspiracy of all the individuals for fraud to occur.

Likewise, a foundational principle of computer access control is not to give one person total control. Known as **separation of duties**, this practice requires that if the fraudulent application of a process could potentially result in a breach of security, the process should be divided between two or more individuals. For example, if the duties of the owner and the custodian are performed by a single individual, it could provide that person with total control over all security configurations. It is recommended that these responsibilities be divided so that the system is not vulnerable to the actions performed by a single person.

Job Rotation

Another way to prevent one individual from having too much control is to use **job rotation**. Instead of one person having sole responsibility for a function, individuals are periodically moved from one job responsibility to another. Employees can rotate either within their home department or across positions in other departments. The best rotation procedure involves multiple employees rotating across many positions for different lengths of time to gain exposure to different roles and functions.

Job rotation has several advantages:

- It limits the amount of time that individuals are in a position to manipulate security configurations.
- It helps to expose any potential avenues for fraud by having multiple individuals with different perspectives learn about the job and uncover vulnerabilities that someone else may have overlooked.

- Besides enhancing security, it can reduce "burnout," increase employee satisfaction, provide a higher level of employee motivation, enhance and improve skills and competencies leading to promotional advancement, and provide an increased appreciation for peers and decreased animosity between departments.

> **Note**
>
> Job rotation also has disadvantages. In some cases, employees may not be in a specific job long enough to develop proficiency, and productivity may be lost in the time it takes to train employees in new tasks. Also, job rotation is often limited to less specialized positions. For these reasons, job rotation might not always be practical.

Mandatory Vacations

In many fraud schemes, the perpetrator must be present every day to continue the fraud or keep it from being exposed. Many organizations require **mandatory vacations** for all employees to counteract this. For sensitive positions within an organization, an audit of the employees' activities is usually scheduled while they are away on vacation.

Clean Desk Policy

A **clean desk** policy is designed to ensure that all confidential or sensitive materials, either in paper form or electronic, are removed from a user's workspace and secured when the items not in use or an employee leaves her workspace. This not only reduces the risk of theft or "prying eyes" reading confidential information, but it can also increase the employee's awareness about the need to protect sensitive information.

A clean desk policy may include such statements as:

- Computer workstations must be locked when the workspace is unoccupied and turned off at the end of the business day.
- Confidential or sensitive information must be removed from the desk and locked in a drawer or safe when the desk is unoccupied and at the end of the work day.
- File cabinets must be kept closed and locked when not in use or not attended, and keys may not be left at an unattended desk.
- Laptops must be either locked with a locking cable or locked in a drawer or filing cabinet.
- Mass storage devices such as USB flash drives or portable external hard drives must be locked in a drawer or filing cabinet.
- Paper documents no longer needed must be shredded using the official shredder bins.
- Printouts should be immediately removed from the printer.
- Whiteboards containing confidential or sensitive information should be erased.

Implementing Access Control

 **Certification**

4.3 Given a scenario, implement identity and access management controls.

4.4 Given a scenario, differentiate common account management practices.

Several technologies can be used to implement access control. These include access control lists and group-based access control.

Access Control Lists (ACLs)

Similar to an Access Control List (ACL) used in a router that acts like a "network filter" to permit or restrict data flowing into and out of the router network interfaces, an access management ACL is a set of permissions that is attached to an object. This list specifies which subjects are allowed to access the object and what operations they can perform on it. When a subject requests to perform an operation on an object, the system checks the ACL for an approved entry in order to decide if the operation is allowed.

 Note

Router ACLs are covered in Chapter 6.

Although ACLs can be associated with any type of object, these lists are most often viewed in relation to files maintained by the OS. All OSs use a *file system*, which is a method for storing and organizing computer files to facilitating access. ACLs provide **file system security** for protecting files managed by the OS. ACL have also been ported to SQL and relational database systems so that ACLs can provide **database security** as well.

Note

ACLs are the oldest and most basic form of access control. These became popular in the 1970s with the growth of multiuser systems, particularly UNIX systems, when it became necessary to limit access to files and data on shared systems. Later, as multiuser operating systems for personal use became popular, the concept of ACLs was added to them. Today all major operating systems—UNIX/Linux, Apple macOS, and Windows—make use of ACLs at some level.

The structure behind ACL tables can be complex. In the Microsoft Windows, Linux, and macOS operating systems, each entry in the ACL table is known as an *access control entry (ACE)*. In Windows, the ACE includes four items of information:

- *An SID for the user account, group account, or logon session.* An SID is a unique number issued to the user, group, or session that is used to identify the user in all subsequent interactions with Windows security.
- *An access mask that specifies the access rights controlled by the ACE.* An *access mask* is a value that specifies the rights that are allowed or denied, and is also used to request access rights when an object is opened.
- *A flag that indicates the type of ACE.* This flag corresponds to a particular set of operations that can be performed on an object.
- *A set of flags that determines whether objects can inherit permissions.*

Note

When an SID has been used as the unique identifier for a user or group, it cannot ever be used again to identify another user or group.

Although widely used, ACLs have limitations. First, using ACLs is not efficient. The ACL for each file, process, or resource must be checked every time the resource is accessed. ACLs control not only user access to system resources but also application and system access. This means that in a typical computing session, ACLs are checked whenever a user accesses files, when applications are opened (along with the files and applications those applications open and modify), when the operating system performs certain functions, and so on. A second limitation to ACLs is that they can be difficult to manage in an enterprise setting where many users need to have different levels of access to many different resources. Selectively adding, deleting, and changing ACLs on individual files, or even groups of files, can be time-consuming and open to errors, particularly if changes must be made frequently.

Group-Based Access Control

In an organization with hundreds of computers, how can access control be implemented? One solution for organizations is to use **group-based access control** that permits the configuration of multiple computers by setting a single policy for enforcement. One example of group-based access control is Microsoft Windows *Group Policy*, which is a feature that provides centralized management and configuration of computers and remote users using Microsoft Active Directory (AD) directory services. Group Policy is usually used in enterprise environments to enforce access control by restricting user actions that may pose a security risk, such as changing access to certain folders or downloading executable files. Group Policy can control an object's script for logging on and off the system, folder redirection, selected browser settings, and Windows Registry settings (the *registry* is a database that stores settings and options for the operating system).

Group Policy settings are stored in *Group Policy Objects (GPOs)*. These objects may, in turn, be linked to multiple domains or websites, which allows for multiple systems and users to be updated by a change to a single GPO. Group Policies are analyzed and applied for computers when they start up and for users when they log in. Every one to two hours, the system looks for changes in the GPO and reapplies them as necessary.

Note

The time period to look for changes in the GPO can be adjusted.

A *Local Group Policy (LGP)* has fewer options than a Group Policy. Generally, a LGP is used to configure settings for systems that are not part of Active Directory. Although older versions of Windows using LGP could not be used to apply policies to individual users or groups of users, recent Windows versions support multiple Local Group Policy objects, which allows setting Local Group Policy for individual users.

Note

Although group policies can assist custodians in managing multiple systems, some security settings configured by Group Policy can be circumvented by a determined user. For this reason, Group Policy is often viewed as a way to establish a security configuration baseline for users, but not as an "ironclad" security solution.

Identity and Access Services

 **Certification**

2.6 Given a scenario, implement secure protocols.

6.3 Given a scenario, install and configure wireless security settings.

A user accessing a computer system must present credentials or identification when logging in to the system. Different services can be used to provide identity and access services. These include RADIUS, Kerberos, Terminal Access Control Access Control

Systems, generic servers built on the Lightweight Directory Access Protocol, Security Assertion Markup Language, and authentication framework protocols.

RADIUS

RADIUS, or **Remote Authentication Dial In User Service**, was developed in 1992 and quickly became the industry standard with widespread support across nearly all vendors of networking equipment. RADIUS was originally designed for remote dial-in access to a corporate network. However, the word *Remote* in the name RADIUS is now almost a misnomer because RADIUS authentication is used for more than connecting to remote networks. With the development of IEEE 802.1x port security for both wired and wireless LANs, RADIUS has seen even greater usage.

Note

IEEE 802.1x is covered in Chapter 8.

A RADIUS client is not the device requesting authentication, such as a desktop system or wireless laptop computer. Instead, a RADIUS client is typically a device such as a wireless access point (AP) or dial-up server that is responsible for sending user credentials and connection parameters in the form of a RADIUS message to a RADIUS server. The RADIUS server authenticates and authorizes the RADIUS client request, and sends back a RADIUS message response. RADIUS clients also send RADIUS accounting messages to RADIUS servers. The strength of RADIUS is that messages are never sent directly between the wireless device and the RADIUS server. This prevents an attacker from penetrating the RADIUS server and compromising security.

Note

RADIUS standards also support the use of what are called RADIUS proxies. A RADIUS proxy is a computer that forwards RADIUS messages between RADIUS clients, RADIUS servers, and other RADIUS proxies.

The detailed steps for RADIUS authentication with a wireless device in an IEEE 802.1x network, which are illustrated in Figure 12-6, are:

1. A wireless device, called the *supplicant* (it makes an "appeal" for access), sends a request to an access point (AP) requesting permission to join the wireless LAN (WLAN). The AP prompts the user for the user ID and password.

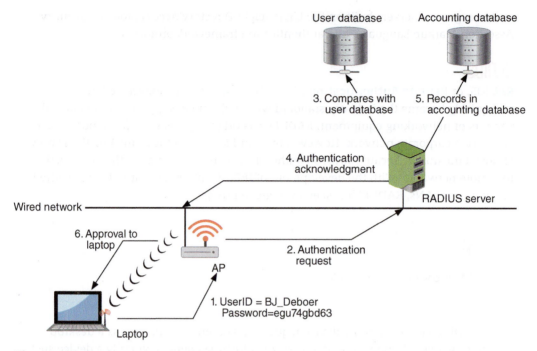

User database   Accounting database

3. Compares with   5. Records in
   user database   accounting database

4. Authentication
   acknowledgment

RADIUS server

Wired network

6. Approval to
   laptop

AP

2. Authentication
   request

1. UserID = BJ_Deboer
   Password=egu74gbd63

Laptop

Figure 12-6 RADIUS authentication

2. The AP, serving as the *authenticator* that will accept or reject the wireless device, creates a data packet from this information called the *authentication request*. This packet includes information such as identification of the specific AP that is sending the authentication request and the user name and password. For protection from eavesdropping, the AP (acting as a RADIUS client) encrypts the password before it is sent to the RADIUS server. The authentication request is sent over the network from the AP to the RADIUS server. This communication can be done over either a local area network or a wide area network. This allows the RADIUS clients to be remotely located from the RADIUS server. If the RADIUS server cannot be reached, the AP can usually route the request to an alternate server.

3. When an authentication request is received, the RADIUS server validates that the request is from an approved AP and then decrypts the data packet to access the user name and password information. This information is passed on to the appropriate security user database. This could be a text file, UNIX password file, a commercially available security system, or a custom database.

4. If the user name and password are correct, the RADIUS server sends an authentication acknowledgment that includes information on the user's network system and service requirements. For example, the RADIUS server may tell the AP that the user needs TCP/IP. The acknowledgment can even contain

filtering information to limit a user's access to specific resources on the network. If the user name and password are not correct, the RADIUS server sends an authentication reject message to the AP and the user is denied access to the network. To ensure that requests are not responded to by unauthorized persons or devices on the network, the RADIUS server sends an authentication key, or signature, identifying itself to the RADIUS client.

5.   If accounting is also supported by the RADIUS server, an entry is started in the accounting database.

6.   Once the server information is received and verified by the AP, it enables the necessary configuration to deliver the wireless services to the user.

RADIUS allows an organization to maintain user profiles in a central database that all remote servers can share. Doing so increases security, allowing a company to set up a policy that can be applied at a single administered network point. Having a central service also means that it is easier to track usage for billing and for keeping network statistics.

Kerberos

Kerberos is an authentication system developed by the Massachusetts Institute of Technology (MIT) in the 1980s and used to verify the identity of networked users. Named after a three-headed dog in Greek mythology that guarded the gates of Hades, Kerberos uses encryption and authentication for security. Kerberos will function under Windows, Apple macOS, and Linux.

Note

Kerberos is used most often by universities and government agencies.

Kerberos has often been compared to using a driver's license to cash a check. A state agency, such as the Department of Motor Vehicles (DMV), issues a driver's license that has these characteristics:

- It is difficult to copy.
- It contains specific information (name, address, weight, height, etc.).
- It lists restrictions (must wear corrective lenses, etc.).
- It will expire at some future date.

Kerberos, which works in a similar fashion, is typically used when a user attempts to access a network service and that service requires authentication. The user is provided a ticket that is issued by the Kerberos authentication server, much as a driver's license is issued by the DMV. This ticket contains information linking it to the user. The user presents this ticket to the network for a service. The service then examines the ticket to verify the identity of the user. If the user is verified, he is then accepted. Kerberos tickets share some of the same characteristics as a driver's license: tickets are difficult to copy (because they are encrypted), they contain specific user information, they restrict what a user can do, and they expire after a few hours or a day. Issuing and submitting tickets in a Kerberos system is handled internally and is transparent to the user.

Note

Kerberos is available as a free download.

Terminal Access Control Access Control System+ (TACACS+)

Similar to RADIUS, *Terminal Access Control Access Control System (TACACS)* is an authentication service commonly used on UNIX devices that communicates by forwarding user authentication information to a centralized server. The centralized server can be either a TACACS database or a database such as a Linux or UNIX password file with TACACS protocol support. The first version was simply called TACACS, while a later version introduced in 1990 was known as *Extended TACACS (XTACACS)*. The current version is **TACACS+**.

Note

TACACS is a proprietary system developed by Cisco Systems.

There are several differences between TACACS+ and RADIUS. These are summarized in Table 12-6.

Table 12-6 Comparison of RADIUS and TACACS+

Feature	RADIUS	TACACS+
Transport protocol	User Datagram Protocol (UDP)	Transmission Control Protocol (TCP)
Authentication and authorization	Combined	Separate
Communication	Unencrypted	Encrypted
Interacts with Kerberos	No	Yes
Can authenticate network devices	No	Yes

Lightweight Directory Access Protocol (LDAP)

A **directory service** is a database stored on the network itself that contains information about users and network devices. It contains information such as the user's name, telephone extension, email address, login name, and other facts. The directory service also keeps track of all the resources on the network and a user's privileges to those resources, and grants or denies access based on the directory service information. Directory services make it much easier to grant privileges or permissions to network users.

The International Organization for Standardization (ISO) created a standard for directory services known as *X.500*. The purpose of the X.500 standard was to standardize how the data was stored so that any computer system could access these directories. It provides the capability to look up information by name (a *white-pages service*) and to browse and search for information by category (a *yellow-pages service*). The information is held in a *directory information base (DIB)*. Entries in the DIB are arranged in a tree structure called the *directory information tree (DIT)*. Each entry is a named object and consists of a set of attributes. Each attribute has a defined attribute type and one or more values. The directory defines the mandatory and optional attributes for each class of object. Each named object may have one or more object classes associated with it.

> ### Note
>
> The X.500 standard itself does not define any representation for the data stored like user names. What is defined is the structural form of names. Systems that are based on X.500, such as Microsoft Active Directory, define their own representation.

The X.500 standard defines a protocol for a client application to access an X.500 directory called the *Directory Access Protocol (DAP)*. However, the DAP is too large to run on a personal computer. The **Lightweight Directory Access Protocol (LDAP)**, sometimes called X.500 Lite, is a simpler subset of DAP. The primary differences between DAP and LDAP are:

- Unlike X.500 DAP, LDAP was designed to run over TCP/IP, making it ideal for Internet and intranet applications. X.500 DAP requires special software to access the network.
- LDAP has simpler functions, making it easier and less expensive to implement.
- LDAP encodes its protocol elements in a less complex way than X.500 that enables it to streamline requests.

If the information requested is not contained in the directory, DAP only returns an error to the client requesting the information, which must then issue a new search request. By contrast, LDAP servers return only results, making the distributed X.500 servers appear as a single logical directory.

By default, LDAP traffic is transmitted in cleartext. LDAP traffic can be made secure by using Secure Sockets Layer (SSL) or Transport Layer Security (TLS). This is known as **LDAP over SSL (LDAPS)**.

LDAP makes it possible for almost any application running on virtually any computer platform to obtain directory information. Because LDAP is an open protocol, applications need not worry about the type of server hosting the directory. Today many LDAP servers are implemented using standard relational database management systems as the engine, and communicate via Extensible Markup Language (XML) documents served over the Hypertext Transport Protocol (HTTP).

However, a weakness of LDAP is that it can be subject to LDAP injection attacks. These attacks, similar to SQL injection attacks, can occur when user input is not properly filtered. This may allow an attacker to construct LDAP statements based on user input statements. The attacker could then retrieve information from the LDAP database or modify its content. The defense against LDAP injection attacks is to examine all user input before processing.

Note

SQL injection attacks are covered in Chapter 5.

Security Assertion Markup Language (SAML)

Security Assertion Markup Language (SAML) is an XML standard that allows secure web domains to exchange user authentication and authorization data. This allows a user's login credentials to be stored with a single identity provider instead of being stored on each web service provider's server. SAML is used extensively for online ecommerce business-to-business (B2B) and business-to-consumer (B2C) transactions.

The steps of a SAML transaction, which are illustrated in Figure 12-7, are:

1. The user attempts to reach a website of a service provider that requires a username and password.
2. The service provider generates a SAML authentication request that is then encoded and embedded into a URL.
3. The service provider sends a redirect URL to the user's browser that includes the encoded SAML authentication request, which is then sent to the identity provider.
4. The identity provider decodes the SAML request and extracts the embedded URL. The identity provider then attempts to authenticate the user either by asking for login credentials or by checking for valid session cookies.
5. The identity provider generates a SAML response that contains the authenticated user's username, which is then digitally signed using asymmetric cryptography.

6. The identity partner encodes the SAML response and returns that information to the user's browser.

7. Within the SAML response, there is a mechanism so that the user's browser can forward that information back to the service provider, either by displaying a form that requires the user to click on a *Submit* button or by automatically sending to the service provider.

8. The service provider verifies the SAML response by using the identity provider's public key. If the response is successfully verified, the user is logged in.

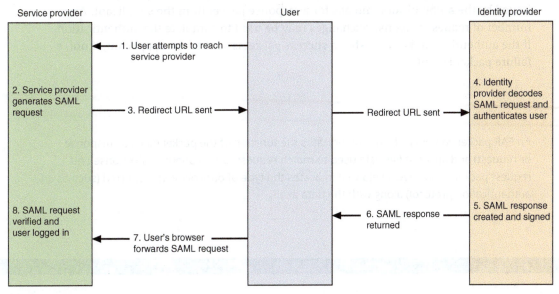

Figure 12-7   SAML transaction

 Note

SAML works with multiple protocols including Hypertext Transfer Protocol (HTTP), Simple Mail Transfer Protocol (SMTP), and File Transfer Protocol (FTP).

Authentication Framework Protocols

Authentication using the *IEEE 802.1x* standard provides a greater degree of security by implementing port-based authentication. IEEE 802.1x blocks all traffic on a port-by-port basis until the client is authenticated using credentials stored on an authentication server. This prevents an unauthenticated device from receiving any network traffic until its identity can be verified. It also strictly limits access to the device that provides the authentication to prevent attackers from reaching it.

It is important that the communication between the supplicant, authenticator, and authentication server in an IEEE 802.1x configuration be secure. A framework for transporting the authentication protocols is known as the *Extensible Authentication Protocol (EAP)*. EAP was created as a more secure alternative than the weak **Challenge-Handshake Authentication Protocol (CHAP)**, the Microsoft version of CHAP **(MS-CHAP)**, and **Password Authentication Protocol (PAP)**. Despite its name, EAP is a *framework* for transporting authentication protocols instead of the authentication protocol itself. EAP essentially defines the format of the messages and uses four types of packets: *request, response, success,* and *failure*. Request packets are issued by the authenticator and ask for a response packet from the supplicant. Any number of request-response exchanges may be used to complete the authentication. If the authentication is successful, a success packet is sent to the supplicant; if not, a failure packet is sent.

> **Note** 📎
>
> An EAP packet contains a field that indicates the function of the packet (such as response or request) and an identifier field used to match requests and responses. Response and request packets also have a field that indicates the type of data being transported (such as an authentication protocol) along with the data itself.

Chapter Summary

- Access control is the process by which access to resources or services is denied or granted. *Physical access control* consists of protections to limit contact with devices, while technical access control is the technology restrictions that limit users on digital devices from accessing data. Access control has its own set of terminologies. Individuals are given different roles in relationship to access control objects or resources. These include privacy officers, custodian or stewards, owners, and end users.

- Hardware and software have a predefined framework that the custodian can use for controlling access; this is called an access control model. There are five major access control models. The Discretionary Access Control model gives the user full control over any objects that he owns. In the Mandatory Access Control model, the end user cannot change any security settings. Role-Based Access Control maps the user's job function with security settings. Rule-Based Access Control dynamically assigns roles based on a set of rules. Attribute-Based Access Control uses more flexible policies that can combine attributes. These policies can take advantage of many different types of attributes.

- Because access management is closely linked to the permissions on accounts, properly configuring those accounts is a first step in providing strong security. Employee onboarding refers to the tasks associated when hiring a new employee, while employee offboarding refers to the tasks associated when an employee is released from an enterprise. There are specific recommendations regarding setting up and disabling user accounts.

- Location-based policies establish the geographical boundaries of where a mobile device can and cannot be used. When setting up accounts with mobile devices, location-based policies can be helpful in controlling access. There are no standard naming conventions that have been established for creating account names. This may lead to confusion, so it is important that each enterprise create a standard naming convention for account names. Time-of-day restrictions can be used to limit when users can log in to their account and access resources. Least privilege in access control means that only the minimum amount of privileges necessary to perform a job or function should be allocated.

- Once accounts have been created, it is important that they be periodically maintained and audited to ensure they still follow all enterprise policies. This includes recertification, permission auditing and review, and usage auditing and review.

- Best practices for implementing access control include separation of duties (dividing a process between two or more individuals), job rotation (periodically moving employees from one job responsibility to another), mandatory vacations (requiring that employees take periodic vacations), and following a clean desk policy (ensuring that all confidential or sensitive materials, either in paper form or electronic, are removed from a user's workspace and secured).

- Implementing access control methods includes using access control lists (ACLs), which are provisions attached to an object. ACLs define which subjects are allowed to access which objects and specify which operations they can perform. Group-based access control permits the configuration of multiple computers by setting a single policy for enforcement. Group Policy is a Microsoft Windows feature that provides centralized management and configuration of computers that use Active Directory.

- Different services can be used to provide identity and access services. RADIUS has become the industry standard with widespread support across nearly all vendors of networking equipment. The strength of RADIUS is that messages are never directly sent between the wireless device and the RADIUS server. This prevents an attacker from penetrating the RADIUS server and compromising security. Kerberos is an authentication system used to verify the identity of networked users. Similar to RADIUS, TACACS+ is a protocol specifications that forwards user name and password information to a centralized server.

- A directory service is a database stored on the network itself that contains information about users and network devices, including all the resources on the network and a user's privileges to those resources, and can grant or deny access based on the directory service information. One implementation of a directory service as an authentication is the Lightweight Directory Access Protocol (LDAP); a secure version is LDAP over SSL (LDAPS). Security Assertion Markup Language (SAML) is an XML standard that allows secure web domains to exchange user authentication and authorization data with one another.

A framework for transporting the authentication protocols is known as the Extensible Authentication Protocol (EAP). EAP was created as a more secure alternative than the weak Challenge-Handshake Authentication Protocol (CHAP), the Microsoft version of CHAP (MS-CHAP), and Password Authentication Protocol (PAP).

Key Terms

access control

access control model

accounting

Attribute-Based Access
  Control (ABAC)

authorization

Challenge-Handshake
  Authentication Protocol
  (CHAP)

clean desk

custodian (steward)

database security

directory service

Discretionary Access
  Control (DAC)

employee offboarding

employee onboarding

file system security

group-based access control

identification

job rotation

Kerberos

LDAP over SSL (LDAPS)

least privilege

Lightweight Directory
  Access Protocol (LDAP)

location-based policies

Mandatory Access Control
  (MAC)

mandatory vacations

MS-CHAP

owner

Password Authentication
  Protocol (PAP)

permission auditing and
  review

privacy officer

RADIUS (Remote
  Authentication Dial In
  User Service)

recertification

Role-Based Access Control
  (RBAC)

Rule-Based Access Control

Security Assertion Markup
  Language (SAML)

separation of duties

standard naming
  conventions

TACACS+

time-of-day restriction

usage auditing and review

Review Questions

1. What is the current version of TACACS?
   a. XTACACS
   b. TACACS+
   c. TACACS v9
   d. TRACACS
2. How is the Security Assertion Markup Language (SAML) used?

   a. It allows secure web domains to exchange user authentication and authorization data.
   b. It is a backup to a RADIUS server.
   c. It is an authenticator in IEEE 802.1x.
   d. It is no longer used because it has been replaced by LDAP.

3. A RADIUS authentication server requires the _____ to be authenticated first.
   a. authenticator
   b. user
   c. authentication server
   d. supplicant

4. Which of the following is NOT true regarding how an enterprise should handle an orphaned or dormant account?
   a. A formal procedure should be in place for disabling accounts for employees who are dismissed, resign, or retire from the organization.
   b. Access should be ended as soon as the employee is no longer part of the organization.
   c. Logs should be monitored because current employees are sometimes tempted to use an older dormant account instead of their own account.
   d. All orphaned and dormant accounts should be deleted immediately whenever they are discovered.

5. With the development of IEEE 802.1x port security, what type of authentication server has seen even greater usage?
   a. RADIUS
   b. Lite RDAP
   c. DAP
   d. RDAP

6. Which of the following is NOT part of the AAA framework?
   a. Authentication
   b. Access
   c. Authorization
   d. Accounting

7. What is the version of the X.500 standard that runs on a personal computer over TCP/IP?

8. Raul has been asked to serve as the individual to whom day-to-day actions have been assigned by the owner. What role is Raul taking?
   a. Privacy officer
   b. End user
   c. Custodian
   d. Operator

9. Which access control model is the most restrictive?
   a. DAC
   b. MAC
   c. Role-Based Access Control
   d. Rule-Based Access Control

10. Which type of access control model uses predefined rules that makes it flexible?
    a. ABAC
    b. DAC
    c. MAC
    d. Rule-Based Access Control

11. Which can be used to establish geographical boundaries where a mobile device can and cannot be used?
    a. Location-based policies
    b. Restricted access control policies
    c. Geolocation policies
    d. Mobile device policies

12. Which statement about Rule-Based Access Control is true?
    a. It requires that a custodian set all rules.
    b. It is considered obsolete today.
    c. It dynamically assigns roles to subjects based on rules.
    d. It is considered a real-world approach by linking a user's job function with security.

Column two, question 7 answers:
   a. Lite RDAP
   b. DAP
   c. LDAP
   d. IEEE X.501

13. Which of the following would NOT be considered as part of a clean desk policy?
    a. Do not share passwords with other employees.
    b. Lock computer workstations when leaving the office.
    c. Place laptops in a locked filing cabinet.
    d. Keep mass storage devices locked in a drawer when not in use.

14. Which of these is a set of permissions that is attached to an object?
    a. Access control list (ACL)
    b. Subject Access Entity (SAE)
    c. Object modifier
    d. Security entry designator

15. Which Microsoft Windows feature provides group-based access control for centralized management and configuration of computers and remote users who are using Active Directory?
    a. Windows Registry Settings
    b. AD Management Services (ADMS)
    c. Group Policy
    d. Resource Allocation Entities

16. What can be used to provide both file system security and database security?
    a. RBASEs
    b. LDAPs
    c. CHAPs
    d. ACLs

17. What is the least restrictive access control model?
    a. DAC
    b. ABAC
    c. MAC
    d. Rule-Based Access Control

18. What is the secure version of LDAP?
    a. LDAPS
    b. Secure DAP
    c. X.500
    d. 802.1x

19. Which of the following is the Microsoft version of EAP?
    a. EAP-MS
    b. MS-CHAP
    c. PAP-MICROSOFT
    d. AD-EAP

20. Which of the following involves rights given to access specific resources?
    a. Identification
    b. Access
    c. Authorization
    d. Accounting

Hands-On Projects

> ### Note 📎
>
> If you are concerned about installing any of the software in these projects on your regular computer, you can instead install the software in the Windows virtual machine created in the Chapter 1 Hands-On Projects 1-3 and 1-4. Software installed within the virtual machine will not impact the host computer.

Project 12-1: Using Windows Local Group Policy Editor

The Windows Local Group Policy (LGP) has fewer options than a domain-based Group Policy, and generally an LGP is used to configure settings for systems that are not part of Active Directory. In this project, you explore different options of using the Windows LGP. Note that Windows 10 Home edition does not contain the LGP; this activity requires Windows 10 Professional.

1. Click **Start** and type **mmc** in the search bar.
2. If you are prompted by UAC, enter the password or click **Yes**.
3. Click **File** and **Add/Remove Snap-in**.
4. In **Add or Remove Snap-ins** dialog box, click **Group Policy Object Editor** and click **Add**.
5. In the **Select Group Policy Object** dialog box, click **Browse**.
6. Click **This computer** and then **OK**.
7. Click **Finish**.
8. Click **OK** to display the Console Root screen as shown in Figure 12-8.

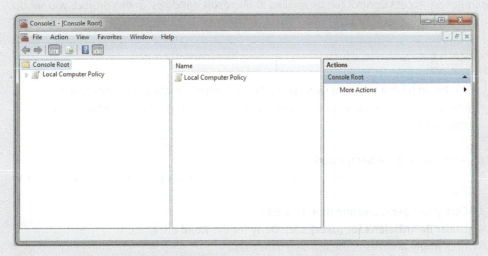

Figure 12-8   Console Root screen

9. Administrative Templates are registry-based policy settings that appear in the Local Group Policy Editor. In the left pane under **Console Root**, click **Local Computer Policy**.
10. Double-click **Computer Configuration**.
11. Double-click **Administrative Templates**.
12. Click **All Settings**. In the middle pane, scroll down through the different LPGs that can be set on the local computer. Which settings can you identify that directly relate to security?
13. Now change the LGP so that only strong TLS cryptography will be used. In the left pane, double-click **Network**.
14. Click **SSL Configuration Settings**.
15. In the center pane, double-click **SSL Cipher Suite Order**. This identifies which SSL suites will be supported.
16. Click **Enabled** if necessary.
17. Open a blank Notepad document.
18. Now copy and paste all suites listed in the left pane under **SSL Cipher Suites** into the Notepad document. Note that this is one continuous line with no line breaks and no additional space.
19. Locate **SSL_CK_RC4_128_WITH_MD5** in the Notepad document. This is one of the weakest SSL cipher suites.
20. Erase this listing. Make sure that there are no additional spaces or commas.
21. Copy this line onto the clipboard and paste it under **SSL Cipher Suites**.
22. Click **Apply**.
23. Click **OK**.
24. Close all windows.

Project 12-2: Using Discretionary Access Control to Share Files in Windows

Discretionary Access Control can be applied in Microsoft Windows. In this project, you set up file sharing with other users.

> **Note** 📎
>
> You should have a standard user named "Abby Lomax" created in Windows and a Notepad document Sample.txt created by an administrative user to complete this assignment.

1. Right-click the file **Sample.txt**.
2. To see the current permissions on this file, click **Properties**, and then click the **Security** tab.
3. Click your user name and then click **Edit**.
4. Under **Permissions for [user]**, click **Deny** for the **Read** attribute.
5. Click **Apply** and **Yes** at the warning dialog box.
6. Click **OK** in the Properties dialog box and then click **OK** in the Sample.txt dialog box.
7. Double-click the file **Sample.txt** to open it. What happens?

8. Now give permissions to Abby Lomax to open the file. Right-click the file **Sample.txt**.
9. Click **Share with** and then click **Specific people**.
10. Click the drop-down arrow and select **Abby Lomax**. Click **Add**.
11. Click **Share**.
12. Click **Done** when the sharing process is completed.
13. Now log in as Abby Lomax. Click **Start** and the **right arrow** and then **Switch User**.
14. Log in as Abby Lomax.
15. Right-click **Start** and then click **Explore**.
16. Navigate to your account name and locate the file Sample.txt.
17. Double-click **Sample.txt** to open the file. Using DAC, permissions have been granted to another user.
18. Close all windows.

Project 12-3: Enabling IEEE 802.1x

In this project, you enable support for 802.1x on a Microsoft Windows computer with a wired connection (there are different steps for wireless devices).

> **Note**
>
> You must be logged in as an Administrator for this project.

1. First you must enable the Wired AutoConfig service, which by default is turned off. Click the **Start** button and in the **Search** box, type services.msc and then press **Enter**.
2. If you are prompted by UAC, enter the password or click **Yes**.
3. In the **Services** dialog box, click the **Standard** tab at the bottom of the screen.
4. Scroll down to **Wired AutoConfig** and then right-click it and click **Start**. The service is now enabled.
5. Open the Network Connections by clicking the **Start** button and then clicking **Control Panel**.
6. Click **Network and Internet**.
7. Click **Network and Sharing Center**.
8. In the left pane, click **Change adapter settings**.
9. Double-click the network interface card being used.
10. Click **Properties**.
11. If you are prompted by UAC, enter the password or click **Yes**.
12. Click **Authentication**.
13. Click **Enable IEEE 802.1X authentication** if necessary.
14. If necessary, under Choose a network authentication method, select **Microsoft Protected EAP (PEAP)**.
15. Click **Additional Settings** and view the different IEEE 802.1X options.
16. Click **Cancel**.
17. Click **OK**.
18. Close all windows.

Project 12-4: Exploring User Account Control (UAC)—Part 1

Microsoft Windows provides several options with user account control (UAC). In this project, you configure and test UAC settings. Note that during this project the UAC dialog box may appear after specific steps. Be sure to always confirm the selection by clicking **OK** or **Yes**.

1. First ensure that UAC is set at its highest level. Click the **Start** button and then enter **UAC** in the search bar.
2. The User Account Control Settings dialog box displays. If necessary, move the slider up to the higher level of **Always notify**.
3. Click **OK**.
4. Click **Start** and type **mmc** in the search bar.
5. The UAC confirmation box displays. Click **No**.
6. Click the **Start** button and then enter **UAC** in the search bar.
7. The User Account Control settings dialog box displays. Move the slider down to the lowest level of **Never notify me when:**.
8. Click **OK**.
9. Click **Start** and type **mmc** in the search bar. What happens?
10. Click the **Start** button and then enter **UAC** in the search bar.
11. Change the account settings to **Notify me only when apps try to make changes to my computer (default)** and click **OK**.
12. Now click **Start** and type **mmc** in the search bar. What happens? Close the Console1 dialog box.
13. Click the **Start** button and then enter **UAC** in the search bar.
14. Change the account settings to **Notify me only when apps try to make changes to my computer (do not dim my desktop)** and click **OK**.
15. Click **Start** and type **mmc** in the search bar. What happens?
16. Click the **Start** button and then enter **UAC** in the search bar.
17. The User Account Control Settings dialog box displays. Move the slider up to the higher level of **Always notify**.
18. Click **OK**.

Project 12-5: Exploring User Account Control (UAC)—Part 2

In this project, you configure and test additional UAC settings. Note that Windows 10 Home edition does not contain the Local Group Policy Editor needed for this project; this activity requires Windows 10 Professional.

1. Change the settings to disable secure desktop mode in UAC.
2. Click **Start** and enter **gpedit.msc** in the search bar.
3. If necessary click **Computer Configuration**.
4. Expand **Windows Settings.**
5. Expand **Security Settings.**
6. Expand **Local Policies.**
7. Expand **Security Options.**
8. Navigate to **User Account Control: Switch to the secure desktop when prompting for elevation** and double-click.

9. Change **Enabled** to **Disabled**.
10. Click **Apply** and then **OK**.
11. Click the **Start** button and then enter **UAC** in the search bar.
12. What is different about your desktop now?
13. Return to the Security Options in gpedit.msc.
14. Review the other UAC options available.
15. Navigate to **User Account Control: Switch to the secure desktop when prompting for elevation** and double-click.
16. Change **Disabled** to **Enabled**.
17. Click **Apply** and then **OK**.
18. Close all windows.

Case Projects

Case Project 12-1: Security Assertion Markup Language (SAML)

Use the Internet to research SAML. What are its features? How is it being used? What are its advantages and disadvantages? Write a one-page paper on your research.

Case Project 12-2: User Account Control (UAC)

Microsoft Windows User Account Control (UAC) provides a higher level of security for users. Research UAC using the Internet. What were its design goals? Were they achieved? How secure is UAC? What are its strengths? What are its weaknesses? Write a one-page paper on your findings.

Case Project 12-3: Best Practices for Access Control

Search the Internet for one instance of a security breach that occurred for each of the four best practices of access control (separation of duties, job rotation, mandatory vacations, and clean desk). Write a short summary of that breach. Then rank these four best practices from most effective to least effective. Give an explanation of your rankings.

Case Project 12-4: Group Policies

Write a one-page paper on Microsoft's Group Policies. Explain what they are, how they can be used, and what their strengths and weaknesses are.

Case Project 12-5: TACACS+

How does TACACS+ work? In what settings is it most likely to be found? How widespread is its usage? What are its advantages? What are its disadvantages? When would you recommend using it over RADIUS or Kerberos? Use the Internet to answer these questions about TACACS+ and write a one-page paper on your findings.

Case Project 12-6: LDAP

Use the Internet to research LDAP. Describe the settings in which it would be used and what its different database options are. Write a one-page paper on your research.

Case Project 12-7: Lake Point Security Consulting

Lake Point Consulting Services (LPCS) provides security consulting and assurance services to over 500 clients across a wide range of enterprises in more than 20 states. A new initiative at LPCS is for each of its seven regional offices to provide internships to students who are in their final year of the security degree program at the local college.

Built-Right Construction is a successful developer of commercial real estate projects. Built-Right has caught the attention of Premiere Construction, a national builder, who wants to purchase Built-Right to make them a subsidiary. Premiere Construction has contracted with LPSC to help them provide training to the Built-Right office staff regarding best practices of access control. LPSC has asked you for assistance on this project.

1. Create a PowerPoint presentation for the staff about the best practices of access control (separation of duties, job rotation, mandatory vacations, and clean desk). Explain what each is and how it can be used to create a secure environment. Because the staff does not have an IT background, the presentation cannot be too technical in nature. Your presentation should contain at least 10 slides.

2. After the presentation, Premiere Construction has asked you how best to handle the staff's objections regarding these practices, because some of the staff members see them as restrictive. Create a memo to Premiere Construction on how you would address those objections in the next round of training.

Case Project 12-8: Information Security Community Site Activity

The Information Security Community Site is an online companion to this textbook. It contains a wide variety of tools, information, discussion boards, and other features to assist learners. Go to **community.cengage.com/Infosec2** and click the *Join or Sign in* icon to log in, using your login name and password that you created in Chapter 1. Click **Forums (Discussion)** and click on **Security+ Case Projects (6th edition)**. Read the following case study.

It is your first week in technical support at a local college. An instructor has called the help desk saying that she cannot install a new software application on her desktop computer, and you have been asked to visit her office to make the installation. (The policy at the college is that all systems have least privilege and, for security reasons, users cannot install applications.) When you arrive at her office, you are immediately confronted with an angry instructor who complains that she cannot do her job because of all the restrictions. She demands that you provide her with the ability to install her own applications. Two other instructors hear the commotion and come to her office with the same complaints. What is the best way to handle the situation? Should you try to explain the reasoning behind the restrictions? Or should you simply say, "That's the way it is" and walk away? Or is there a better approach? Enter your answers on the Community Site discussion board.

References

1. Seals, Richard, "From worst to first," *Fraud*, Mar. 2013, accessed May 27, 2017, http://www.fraud-magazine.com/article.aspx?id=4294977156.

PART VI

RISK MANAGEMENT

The chapters in this part explore topics as they relate to risk management. Chapter 13 examines how to assess the vulnerability of an enterprise and how to practice data privacy security. In Chapter 14, you learn about business continuity. Chapter 15 concludes with a detailed look at controlling risk.

CHAPTER 13

VULNERABILITY ASSESSMENT AND DATA SECURITY

After completing this chapter, you should be able to do the following:

Explain how to assess the security posture of an enterprise

Define vulnerability assessment and explain why it is important

Explain the differences between vulnerability scanning and penetration testing

Describe the techniques for practicing data privacy and security

Today's Attacks and Defenses

How do threat actors carry out their attacks? A single attack can be analyzed for clues, but this only reveals the tactics of those behind this specific attack. A more comprehensive look at attacker behavior is to set up a *honeypot*, which is a computer with limited security and loaded with fake software and data files that entice attackers to launch attacks, thereby revealing multiple attack techniques. Honeypots can even reveal the attackers' way of thinking.

Recently, a security research group set up a series of honeypots that were deployed worldwide. These honeypots were configured with unpublished IP addresses so that the only "hits" would come from services that were scanning a wide range of IP addresses, presumably searching for something to attack. When an unsolicited connection attempt was made, the honeypot captured the attacker's attempts to break in as well as background information on the attacker.

The research group later published information about the attackers' attempts to break in to the honeypots via Microsoft Remote Desktop Protocol (RDP) by guessing passwords. RDP allows a client to connect to a remote computer and access its resources. The research group also ran a test to determine how many possible targets are on the Internet running RDP. They discovered 10,822,679 different IP addresses of devices listening for this type of traffic, spread out worldwide.

After 334 days, the honeypots recorded 221,203 different login attempts, an average of 662 attempts each day. These attempts came from 5,076 distinct IP addresses from 119 different countries. The attackers used 1,806 different user names and 3,969 different passwords.

The analysis revealed some interesting facts. Almost 40 percent of the attacks originated from China, with the United States as the second most common source of attacks (24 percent). Because RDP was the protocol being analyzed, it is no real surprise that the most commonly attempted user names were those that would typically be used by a network administrator (who would set up the RDP account). The user names "administrator" (34 percent), "Administrator" (24 percent), "user1" (3 percent), and "admin" (2 percent) were the most common. Evidently, the attackers think that there is a large group of administrators with the first name "alex," because that user name was attempted 4,051 times, or about 1 percent of the total.

But what may be most interesting is the passwords that were guessed. Shockingly, the most common password attempted was just "x," attempted 11,865 times (5.36 percent). Equally surprising, the second most common password attempted was "Zz" (10,591 or 4.79 percent). And fourth on the list was "1," tried 5,679 times (2.57 percent). Keeping with the trend of names, "alex" was attempted as a password 4,032 times (1.82 percent).

Why were these weak passwords attempted by the attackers? Were they completely ignorant about the types of passwords that administrators would set up? Who would use "x" or "Zz" or "1" as a password? Or do the attackers know something that we do not know? Are they attempting these passwords because they were successful using them in the past? Here's what the researchers said: "We guess that these passwords are selected because whomever is conducting these scans believes that there is a chance they will work. Maybe the scanners have inside knowledge about actual usernames and passwords in use, or maybe they're just using passwords that have been made available from previous security breaches in which account credentials were leaked."[1]

"How vulnerable are we?" is a question that too few enterprises ask themselves in regard to their IT security. Too often, enterprises create a false sense of security and invulnerability by purchasing expensive security devices, installing the latest antimalware software, conducting employee training sessions, and hiring a staff of security technicians. Although each of these defenses is important, they should not be considered the final solution to protecting against attacks. Simply having the right security tools does not guarantee a secure system. In other words, these defenses should never create the mindset, *"We're safe now."*

It is a fact that *all* computer systems, and the information contained on those systems, are vulnerable to attack; all security experts say that it's not a matter of *if* an attack will penetrate defenses, but only a matter of *when*. Because successful attacks are inevitable, enterprises must protect themselves by realistically evaluating their vulnerabilities, assessing how an attacker could penetrate their defenses, and then taking proactive steps to defend against those attacks.

In this chapter, you learn what a vulnerability assessment is and examine the tools and techniques associated with it. Next, you explore the differences between vulnerability scanning and penetration testing. Finally, you look at the steps for practicing data security.

Assessing the Security Posture

 Certification

2.2 Given a scenario, use appropriate software tools to assess the security posture of an organization.

3.2 Given a scenario, implement secure network architecture concepts.

The first step in any security protection plan begins with an assessment of the security posture of the enterprise. This will reveal existing vulnerabilities that must be addressed. A variety of techniques and tools can be used in evaluating the levels of vulnerability.

What Is Vulnerability Assessment?

Vulnerability assessment is a systematic and methodical evaluation of the security posture of the enterprise. It examines the exposure of assets to attackers, forces of nature, and any other entity that could cause potential harm. Its goal is to identify and prioritize the vulnerabilities in a system.

Note 📎

Although closely related, risk management is not identical to vulnerability assessment. Risk management looks at the dangers that an asset faces. Vulnerability assessment examines the consequences for the asset if it is successfully compromised, and it does this by testing its security. A vulnerability assessment drives the risk management process.

Vulnerability assessment attempts to identify what needs to be protected (asset identification), what the pressures are against those assets (threat evaluation), how susceptible the current protection is (vulnerability appraisal), and what damages could result from the threats (risk assessment). Once this is completed, an analysis of what to do about it (risk mitigation) can take place.

Note

Risk management is covered in Chapter 15.

Asset Identification

The first step in a vulnerability assessment is to determine the assets that need to be protected. An asset is defined as any item that has a positive economic value, and *asset identification* is the process of inventorying these items. An organization has many different types of assets, including people (employees, customers, business partners, contractors, and vendors) and physical assets (buildings, automobiles, and plant equipment). In addition, the elements of IT are also key assets. This includes data (all information used and transmitted by the organization, such as employee databases and inventory records), hardware (computers, servers, networking equipment, and telecommunications connections), and software (application programs, operating systems, and security software).

Note

Asset identification can be a lengthy and complicated process. However, it is one of the most critical steps in vulnerability assessment. If an organization does not know *what* needs to be protected, then how can the organization protect it?

After an inventory of the assets has been taken, it is important to determine each item's relative value. Some assets are of critical value while other assets are of lesser importance. Factors that should be considered in determining the relative value include how critical the asset is to the goals of the organization, how much revenue it generates, how difficult it would be to replace, and the impact to the organization if the asset were unavailable. Some organizations assign a numeric value (such as 5 being extremely valuable and 1 being the least valuable) to each asset. For example, a web application server that receives and processes online orders could be considered a critical asset because without it no orders would be received. For this reason, it might be assigned a value of 5. A desktop computer used by an employee might have a lesser value because its loss would not negatively impact the daily workflow of the organization nor prove to be a serious security risk. It might be assigned only a value of 2.

Threat Evaluation

After assets have been inventoried, the next step is to determine the potential threats against the assets that come from threat actors. Threats are not limited to attackers, but also include natural disasters, such as fire or severe weather. Common threat agents are listed in Table 13-1.

Table 13-1 Common threats

Category of threat	Example
Natural disasters	Fire, flood, or earthquake destroys data
Compromise of intellectual property	Software is pirated or copyright infringed
Espionage	Spy steals production schedule
Extortion	Mail clerk is blackmailed into intercepting letters
Hardware failure or errors	Firewall blocks all network traffic
Human error	Employee drops laptop computer in parking lot
Sabotage or vandalism	Attacker implants worm that erases files
Software attacks	Virus, worm, or denial of service compromises hardware or software
Software failure or errors	Bug prevents program from properly loading
Technical obsolescence	Program does not function under new version of operating system
Theft	Desktop system is stolen from unlocked room
Utility interruption	Electrical power is cut off

Determining threats that could pose a risk to assets can be a complicated process. One way to approach this task is a process known as threat modeling. The goal of *threat modeling* is to better understand who the attackers are, why they attack, and what types of attacks might occur. Threat modeling often constructs scenarios of the types of threats that assets can face. A valuable tool used in threat modeling is the construction of an attack tree. An *attack tree* provides a visual image of the attacks that could occur against an asset. Drawn as an inverted tree structure, an attack tree displays the goal of the attack, the types of attacks that could occur, and the techniques used in the attacks.

A partial attack tree for stealing a car stereo system is shown in Figure 13-1. At the top of the tree (Level 1) is the goal of the attack, which is to steal a car stereo. The next level, Level 2, lists the ways an attack could occur: someone could break the glass out of a car window and steal the stereo, someone could steal the keys to the car to get to the stereo, or someone could "carjack" the car and drive away. To steal the keys (Level 3), a purse snatcher might grab the purse containing the keys, or someone, such as a parking lot attendant, might make a copy of them. The attendant might copy the keys because of pressure in the form of threats, blackmail, or bribes (Level 4). The attack tree presents a picture of the threats against an asset.

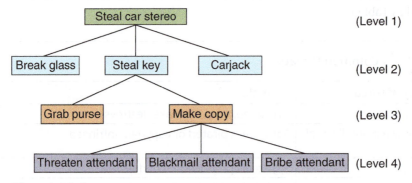

Figure 13-1 Attack tree for stealing a car stereo

Figure 13-2 shows a partial attack tree for an attacker who is attempting to log in to a restricted account. The attacker might attempt to learn the password (Level 2) by looking for one that is written down and stored under a mouse pad in an office (Level 3). He could also try to get the password from the user (Level 3) by installing a keylogger on the computer or by shoulder surfing (Level 4). An alternative approach might be to steal the password digest file to use offline cracking (Level 2). Attack trees help list the types of attacks that can occur and trace how and from where the attacks might originate.

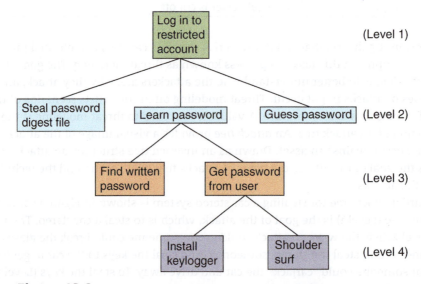

Figure 13-2 Attack tree for logging into restricted account

Note

These abbreviated examples of attack trees are not intended to show every possible threat, as an actual attack tree would.

Vulnerability Appraisal

After the assets have been inventoried and the threats have been determined, the next natural question is, "What are our current weaknesses that might expose the assets to these threats?" Known as *vulnerability appraisal*, this process in effect takes a snapshot of the current security of the organization.

Note

Hardware and software assessment tools may be used to assist with determining the vulnerabilities of hardware and software assets. These tools are discussed later in this chapter.

Revealing the vulnerabilities of an asset is not always as easy as it might seem. Every asset must be viewed in light of each threat; it is not sufficient to limit the assessment to only a few of the obvious threats against an asset. Each threat can reveal multiple vulnerabilities, and it is important that each vulnerability be cataloged.

Note

Determining vulnerabilities often depends on the background and experience of the assessor. It is recommended that teams composed of diverse members be responsible for listing vulnerabilities instead of only one person.

Risk Assessment

The next step is to perform a risk assessment. A *risk assessment* involves determining the damage that would result from an attack and the likelihood that the vulnerability is a risk to the organization.

Determining the damage from an attack first requires a realistic look at several different types of attacks that might occur. Based upon the vulnerabilities recognized in the vulnerability appraisal, a risk assessment of the impact can then be undertaken. Not all vulnerabilities pose the same risk. One way to determine the severity of a risk is to gauge the impact the vulnerability would have on the organization if it were exploited. A sample scale for ranking vulnerabilities is shown in Table 13-2.

Table 13-2 Vulnerability impact scale

Impact	Description	Example
No impact	This vulnerability would not affect the organization.	The theft of a mouse attached to a desktop computer would not affect the operations of the organization.
Small impact	Small impact vulnerabilities would produce limited periods of inconvenience and possibly result in changes to a procedure.	A specific brand and type of hard disk drive that fails might require that spare drives be made available and that devices with those drives be periodically tested.
Significant	A vulnerability that results in a loss of employee productivity due to downtime or causes a capital outlay to alleviate it could be considered significant.	Malware that is injected into the network could be classified as a significant vulnerability.
Major	Major vulnerabilities are those that have a considerable negative impact on revenue.	The theft of the latest product research and development data through a backdoor could be considered a major vulnerability.
Catastrophic	Vulnerabilities that are ranked as catastrophic are events that would cause the organization to cease functioning or be seriously crippled in its capacity to perform.	A tornado that destroys an office building and all the company's data could be a catastrophic vulnerability.

Note

Risk assessment can be done using qualitative or quantitative risk calculation tools to help determine the risk likelihood and risk impact. These tools are covered in Chapter 15.

Risk Mitigation

Once the risks are determined and ranked, the final step is to determine what to do about the risks, or *risk mitigation*. Realistically, risk can never be entirely eliminated; it would cost too much or take too long. Some risks must simply be accepted by default (war is an example of such a risk that cannot be protected against, and thus most assets cannot be insured against war), that is, some degree of risk must always be assumed. An organization should not ask, "How can we eliminate all risk?" but rather, "How much acceptable risk can we tolerate?" Once the "toleration" level is known, steps can be taken to mitigate the risk.

Note

Chapter 15 covers different ways to mitigate and control risk.

Table 13-3 summarizes the steps in performing vulnerability assessment.

Table 13-3 Vulnerability assessment actions and steps

Vulnerability assessment action	Steps
1. Asset identification	a. Inventory the assets
	b. Determine the assets' relative value
2. Threat identification	a. Classify threats by category
	b. Design attack tree
3. Vulnerability appraisal	a. Determine current weaknesses in protecting assets
	b. Use vulnerability assessment tools
4. Risk assessment	a. Estimate impact of vulnerability on organization
	b. Calculate risk likelihood and impact of the risk
5. Risk mitigation	a. Decide what to do with the risk

Vulnerability Assessment Tools

Many tools are available to perform vulnerability assessments. These include port scanners, protocol analyzers, vulnerability scanners, honeypots and honeynets, banner grabbing tools, crackers, command line tools, and other tools.

Note

Although the primary purpose of assessment tools is to help security personnel identify security weaknesses, these tools can likewise be used by attackers to uncover vulnerabilities to be exploited in an attack.

Port Scanners

Most communication in TCP/IP networks involves the exchange of information between a program running on one system (known as a *process*) and the same, or a corresponding process, running on a remote system. TCP/IP uses a numeric value as an identifier to the applications and services on these systems. This value is known as the *port number*. Each packet/datagram contains the source port and destination port, which identifies both the originating application/service on the local system and the corresponding application/service on the remote system.

Note

The term *port* is also used to refer to a physical outlet on the computer, such as a Universal Serial Bus (USB) port.

Because port numbers are 16 bits in length, they can have a decimal value from 0 to 65,535. TCP/IP divides port numbers into three categories:

- *Well-known port numbers (0–1023).* Reserved for the most universal applications
- *Registered port numbers (1024–49151).* Other applications that are not as widely used
- *Dynamic and private port numbers (49152–65535).* Available for use by any application

Note

Although previous versions of the Security+ exam objectives required test-takers to know specific ports and associated protocols, such as File Transfer Protocol (FTP)—Data (TCP and UDP, Port 20), DNS (TCP and UDP, Port 53), and Hypertext Transfer Protocol (HTTP) (TCP Port 80)—these are no longer required. However, having a knowledge of common ports is important for a security professional. A list of all well-known and registered TCP/IP port numbers can be found at *www.iana.org/assignments/port-numbers*.

Because port numbers are associated with applications and services, if an attacker knows that a specific port is accessible, this could indicate what services are being used. For example, if port 20 is available, an attacker could assume that FTP is being used. With that knowledge, he can target his attacks to that service. It is important to implement port security by disabling unused application/service ports to reduce the number of threat vectors.

When performing a vulnerability assessment, *port scanner* software can be used to search a system for port vulnerabilities. Port scanners, such as the one shown

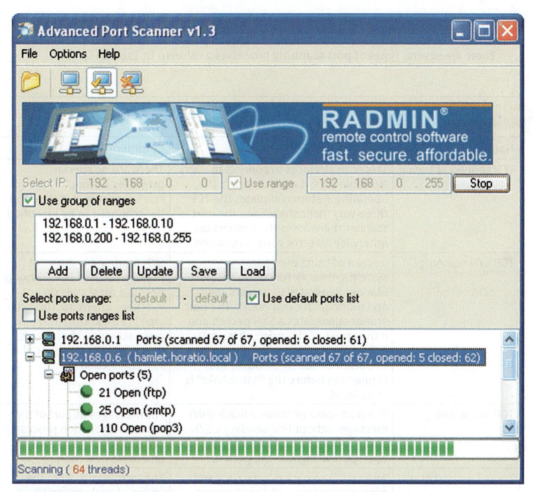

Figure 13-3   Port scanner

Source: RADMIN Advanced Port Scanner. Copyright © 1999-2014 Famatech. All rights reserved

in Figure 13-3, are typically used to determine the state of a port to know what applications/services are running. There are three port states:

- *Open*. An *open port* means that the application or service assigned to that port is listening for any instructions. The host system will send back a reply to the scanner that the service is available and listening; if the operating system receives packets destined for this port, it will give them over to that service process.
- *Closed*. A *closed port* indicates that no process is listening at this port. The host system will send back a reply that this service is unavailable and any connection attempts will be denied.

- *Blocked*. A *blocked port* means that the host system does not reply to any inquiries to this port number.

There are several types of port scanning processes as shown in Table 13-4.

Table 13-4 Port scanning

Name	Scanning process	Comments
TCP connect scanning	This scan attempts to connect to every available port. If a port is open, the operating system completes the TCP three-way "handshake" and the port scanner then closes the connection; otherwise an error code is returned.	There are no special privileges needed to run this scan. However, it is slow and the scanner can be identified.
TCP SYN scanning	Instead of using the operating system's network functions, the port scanner generates IP packets itself and monitors for responses. The port scanner generates a SYN packet, and if the target port is open, that port will respond with a SYN+ACK packet. The scanner host then closes the connection before the "handshake" is completed.	SYN scanning is the most popular form of TCP scanning because most sites do not log these attempts. This scan type is also known as "half-open scanning," because it never actually opens a full TCP connection.
TCP FIN scanning	The port scanner sends a finish (FIN) message without first sending a SYN packet. A closed port will reply, but an open port will ignore the packet.	FIN messages as part of the normal negotiation process can pass through firewalls and avoid detection.
Xmas Tree port scan	An Xmas Tree packet is a packet with every option set to *on* for whatever protocol is in use. When used for scanning, the TCP header of an Xmas Tree packet has the flags finish (FIN), urgent (URG), and push (PSH) all set to *on*. By observing how a host responds to this "odd" packet, assumptions can be made about its operating system.	The term comes from the image of each option bit in a header packet being represented by a different-colored "light bulb." When all are turned on, it can be said that the packet "was lit up like a Christmas tree."

Protocol Analyzers

A **protocol analyzer** is hardware or software that captures packets to decode and analyze their contents. Network traffic can be viewed by a stand-alone protocol analyzer device or a computer that runs protocol analyzer software such as the Wireshark software shown in Figure 13-4. Protocol analyzers can fully decode application-layer network protocols such as HTTP or FTP.

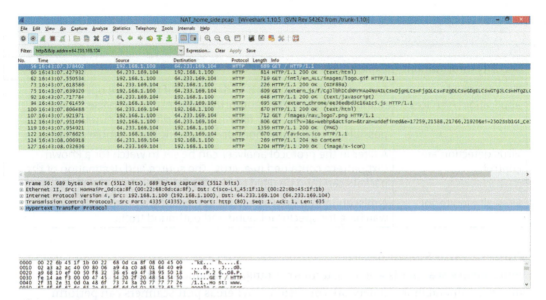

Figure 13-4   Protocol analyzer

Source: Wireshark Software

Protocol analyzers are widely used by network administrators for network monitoring. They can assist in network troubleshooting by detecting and diagnosing network problems such as addressing errors and protocol configuration mistakes. They also are used for network traffic characterization. Protocol analyzers can be used to paint a picture of the types and makeup of network traffic. This representation can be used to fine-tune the network and manage bandwidth to provide the highest level of service to users.

In addition, protocol analyzers can be helpful in a security analysis of the network. The types of security-related information available from a protocol analyzer are summarized in Table 13-5.

Table 13-5   Protocol analyzer security information

Security information	Explanation
Unanticipated network traffic	Most network managers know the types of applications that they expect to see utilizing the network. Protocol analyzers can help reveal unexpected traffic and even pinpoint the computers that are involved.
Unnecessary network traffic	Network devices might by default run network protocols that are not required and could pose a security risk. As a precaution, a protocol analyzer can be set to filter traffic so it can help identify unnecessary network traffic and the source of it.

(continues)

Table 13-5 (*continued*)

Security information	Explanation
Unauthorized applications/services	Servers can be monitored to determine if they have open port numbers to support unauthorized applications/services. Many protocol analyzers allow filtering on specified port numbers, so it is possible to constantly monitor for specific port number requests.
Virus detection and control	A filter in the protocol analyzer can be set to watch for a known text pattern contained in a virus. The source and destination of the packets can then be used to identify the location of the virus.
Firewall monitoring	A misconfigured firewall can be detected by a protocol analyzer watching for specific inbound and outbound traffic.

Vulnerability Scanners

Vulnerability scanner is a generic term for a range of products that look for different vulnerabilities in networks or systems. Whereas port scanners can perform only one task, vulnerability scanners for enterprises are intended to identify several vulnerabilities and alert network administrators to these problems.

There are two types of vulnerability scanners. An **active scanner** sends "probes" to network devices and examines the responses received back to evaluate whether a specific device needs remediation. Active scanners can also be used to simulate a network attack to uncover a vulnerability or to examine a device following an attack to determine how security was breached. Some active scanners can even take action to automatically resolve specific security issues, such as blocking a potentially dangerous IP address. A **passive scanner** can identify the current software operating systems and applications being used on the network, and indicate which devices might have a vulnerability (an example would be an OS that has not been patched). Although passive scanners can provide information about weaknesses, they cannot take action to resolve security problems.

Note

Passive scanners can run continuously or at specified intervals.

A vulnerability scanner can:

- Alert when new systems are added to the network
- Detect when an application is compromised or subverted
- Detect when an internal system begins to port scan other systems

- Detect which ports are served and which ports are browsed for each individual system
- Identify which applications and servers host or transmit sensitive data
- Maintain a log of all interactive network sessions
- Track all client and server application vulnerabilities
- Track which systems communicate with other internal systems

Some of the specific types of vulnerability scanners are listed in Table 13-6.

Table 13-6 Types of vulnerability scanners

Type	Description	Uses
Network mapping scanner	Combines network device discovery tools and network scanners to find open ports or discover shared folders.	Can be used to create visual maps of the network that also identify vulnerabilities that need correction.
Wireless scanner	Can discover malicious wireless network activity such as failed login attempts, record these to an event log, and alert an administrator.	Detects security weaknesses inside the local wireless network with internal vulnerability scanning.
Configuration compliance scanner	Used to evaluate and report any compliance issues related to specific industry guidelines.	A compliance audit is a comprehensive review of how an enterprise follows regulatory guidelines, as seen in Figure 13-5.

Note

Another type of vulnerability scanner, a rogue AP system detection scanner, is covered in Chapter 8.

Honeypots and Honeynets

A **honeypot** is a computer typically located in an area with limited security and loaded with software and data files that appear to be authentic, but are actually imitations of real data files. The honeypot is intentionally configured with security vulnerabilities so that it is open to attacks. It is intended to trick attackers into revealing their attack techniques. It can then be determined if actual production systems could thwart such an attack. Figure 13-6 shows the results from a honeypot dashboard, listing the attacker probes by IP address, targeted port, and even originating continent.

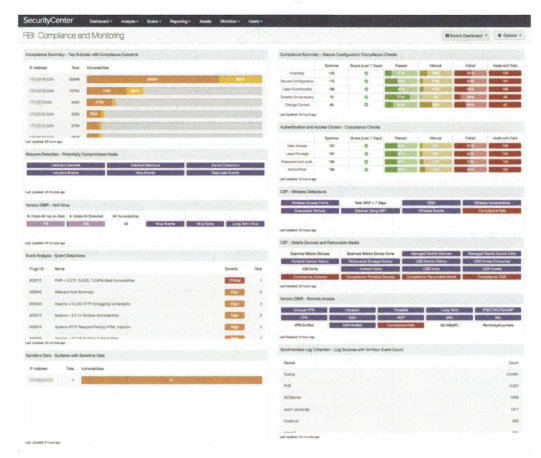

Figure 13-5   Configuration compliance scanner

Source: Tenable

> **Note** 📎
>
> A honeypot also can direct an attacker's attention away from legitimate servers by encouraging attackers to spend their time and energy on the decoy server, distracting their attention from the data on the real server.

Similar to a honeypot, a **honeynet** is a network set up with intentional vulnerabilities. Its purpose is also to invite attacks so that the attacker's methods can be studied and that information can be used to increase network security. A honeynet typically contains one or more honeypots.

Figure 13-6 Honeypot dashboard

Source: Elasticsearch BV

Banner Grabbing Tools

A *banner* is a message that a service transmits when another program connects to it. For example, the banner for a Hypertext Transfer Protocol (HTTP) service typically shows the type of server software, its version number, when it was last modified, and other similar information. When a program is used to intentionally gather this information, the process is called **banner grabbing**.

Banner grabbing can be used as an assessment tool to perform an inventory on the services and systems operating on a server. This can be done by using a tool to create a connection with the device and then querying each port.

Note

Attackers can also make use of banner grabbing when performing reconnaissance on a system.

Crackers

Although often considered the tool of threat actors, *crackers* can also be used in a vulnerability assessment. Crackers are intended to break ("crack") the security of a system. Using a cracker in a vulnerability assessment can help determine how secure that system is. A **wireless cracker** is designed to test the security of a wireless LAN system by attempting to break its protections of Wi-Fi Protected Access (WPA) or Wi-Fi

Protected Access 2 (WPA2). A **password cracker** is intended to break the digest of a password to determine its strength.

> **Note**
>
> Examples of password crackers are covered in the Hands-On Projects in Chapter 11.

Command-Line Tools

There are several command-line tools that can be used to assess the vulnerability of a network. The command-line tools that are native to common operating systems are listed in Table 13-7.

Table 13-7 Operating system command-line tools

Name	Description	How used
Ping	Tests the connection between two network devices	Can flood the network to determine how it responds to a Denial of Service attack
Netstat	Displays detailed information about how a device is communicating with other network devices	Used to determine the source of malware that is sending out stolen information or communicating with a command and control server
Tracert	Shows the path that a packet takes	Can detect faulty or malicious routing paths
Nslookup	Queries the Domain Name System (DNS) to obtain a specific domain name or IP address mapping	Used to verify correct DNS configurations
Dig	Linux command-line alternative to Nslookup	More robust tool that can also verify DNS configurations
Arp	View and modify Address Resolution Protocol (ARP) cache	Can view ARP cache to uncover ARP poisoning attack
Ipconfig	Displays all current TCP/IP network configuration values and refreshes Dynamic Host Configuration Protocol (DHCP) and DNS settings	Used to alter current settings such as IP address, subnet mask, and default gateway to test if configurations are secure
IP and Ifconfig	Linux implementations of Ipconfig	Like Ipconfig, it can test to determine if configurations are secure.
Tcpdump	Linux command-line protocol analyzer	Can monitor network traffic for unauthorized traffic

In addition to operating system tools there are a variety of third-party tools that can be used for vulnerability assessment. **Nmap** (*network mapper*) is a security vulnerability scanner that can determine which devices are connected to the network and the services they are running. It does this by sending special packets to the targeted host and analyzing the responses. Nmap can build an extensive mapping of the network and devices, as seen in Figure 13-7.

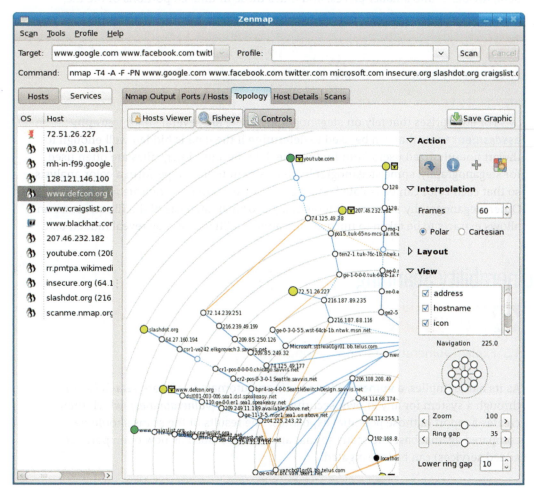

Figure 13-7   Nmap

Source: Insecure.org

Whereas Nmap is a GUI utility, **Netcat** is a command-line alternative to Nmap with additional features scanning for vulnerabilities. Netcat can be used by itself or driven by other programs and scripts.

Other Tools

There are several other tools that can be used in a vulnerability assessment. An **exploitation framework** is used to replicate attacks during a vulnerability assessment by providing a structure of exploits and monitoring tools. These are used to validate security defenses and reveal what data would be at risk.

Steganography is a technology that hides the existence of data in a seemingly harmless data file, image file, audio file, or video file. Steganography typically takes the data, divides it into smaller pieces, and hides these in unused portions of the file.

Note

Steganography is covered in Chapter 3.

For enterprises that rely on steganography, there are several **steganography assessment tools** that can be used to determine if the data is hidden well enough to thwart unauthorized users from finding the data. Because image files are often used for steganography, some steganography assessment tools can perform a color analysis so that each color can be isolated and viewed; a variation may indicate a hidden bit. Other steganography assessment tools can perform an analysis of the file structure and allows extracts to be taken to uncover any abnormalities that may reveal hidden text.

Vulnerability Scanning

 Certification

1.5 Explain vulnerability scanning concepts.

As its name implies, a **vulnerability scan** is an automated software search (*scan*) through a system for any known security weaknesses (*vulnerabilities*), which then creates a report of those potential exposures. The results of the scans should be compared against baseline scans so that any changes (such as new open ports or added services) can be investigated.

Note

Vulnerability scanning should be conducted on existing systems and particularly as new technology equipment is deployed; the new equipment should be scanned immediately and then added to the regular schedule of scans for all equipment.

A vulnerability scan examines the current security by **passively testing security controls**: it does not attempt to exploit any weaknesses that it finds; rather, it is intended to only report back what it uncovers. The heart of a vulnerability scan is to *identify*. Specifically, a scan looks to **identify vulnerabilities** or security weaknesses found in the system, to **identify a lack of security controls** that are missing to establish a secure framework, and to **identify common misconfigurations**, which are settings in hardware and software.

There are two methods for performing a vulnerability scan. An **intrusive vulnerability scan** attempts to actually penetrate the system in order to perform a simulated attack, while a **non-intrusive vulnerability scan** uses only available information to hypothesize the status of the vulnerability. These two methods are compared in Table 13-8.

Table 13-8 Intrusive and non-intrusive vulnerability scans

Type of scan	Description	Advantages	Disadvantages
Intrusive vulnerability scanning	Vulnerability assessment tools use intrusive scripts to penetrate and attack.	By attacking a system in the same manner as an attacker would, more accurate results are achieved.	The system may be unavailable for normal use while the scan is being conducted. Also, it may disable security services for the duration of the attack.
Non-intrusive vulnerability scanning	Through social engineering and general reconnaissance efforts, information is gathered regarding the known vulnerabilities and weaknesses of the system.	Organizations can avoid any disruption of service or setting off alerts from IPS, IDS, and firewalls. These scans also mimic the same reconnaissance efforts used by attackers.	Time is needed for all the information to be analyzed so that the security status of the system based on the data can be determined.

Some intrusive vulnerability scanners permit the user name and password (*credentials*) of an active account to be stored and used by the scanner, which allows the scanner to test for additional internal vulnerabilities if an attacker could successfully penetrate the system. This is called a **credentialed vulnerability scan**, while scans that do not use credentials are called **non-credentialed vulnerability scans**.

 Note

Vulnerability scans can generate a high number of *false positives*. A vulnerability scan report should be examined by trained security personnel to identify and correct any problems.

Penetration Testing

1.4 Explain penetration testing concepts.

Unlike a vulnerability scan, **penetration testing** (*pentest*) is designed to exploit any weaknesses in systems that are vulnerable. Instead of using automated software, penetration testing relies upon the skill, knowledge, and cunning of the tester. The tester herself is usually an independent contractor not associated with the organization. Such testers have the organization's permission to exploit vulnerabilities in a system and then privately provide information back to that organization. It is not unusual for only a limited number of personnel to even be aware that a pentest is being performed. Testers are typically outside (instead of inside) the security perimeter.

> **Note** 📎
>
> The end product of a penetration test is the penetration test report. The report focuses on what data was compromised, how and why it was compromised, and includes details of the actual attack method and the value of the data exploited. If requested, potential solutions can be provided, but often it is the role of the organization to determine how best to solve the problems.

Three different techniques can be used by a penetration tester, based upon the requirements established by the enterprise. Each technique varies in the amount of knowledge the tester has regarding the details of the systems that are being evaluated:

- *Black box*. In a **black box** test, the tester has no prior knowledge of the network infrastructure that is being tested. The tester must determine the location and types of systems and devices before starting the actual tests. This technique most closely mimics an attack from outside the organization.
- *White box*. The opposite of a black box test is a **white box** test, in which the tester has an in-depth knowledge of the network and systems being tested, including network diagrams, IP addresses, and even the source code of custom applications.
- *Gray box*. Between a black box test and a white box test is a **gray box** test, in which some limited information has been provided to the tester.

Note 📎

The Computer Fraud and Abuse Act (18 U.S.C. 1030) states that it is a federal crime if a party "intentionally accesses a computer without authorization or exceeds authorized access."[2] This means that penetration testers should always receive prior approval by the organization before conducting a test.

In black box and gray box testing, the first task of the tester is to perform preliminary information gathering on her own from outside the organization, sometimes called *open source intelligence* (OSINT). There are two methods by which this information is gathered. **Active reconnaissance** involves actively probing the system, much like an attacker would do, to find information. The disadvantage of active reconnaissance is that the probes are likely to alert the uninformed security professionals of the enterprise of some action being taken against it, which may cause the network to become more restrictive and difficult to probe. Instead of probing the system for information, **passive reconnaissance** takes an entirely different approach: the tester uses tools that do not raise any alarms. This may include searches online for publicly accessible information that can reveal valuable insight about the system. Other non-intrusive tools for reconnaissance, such as banner grabbing, can also be used. In short, active reconnaissance relies on traffic being sent to the targeted system while passive reconnaissance calls for the tester to quietly "make do" with whatever information she can accumulate from public sources.

Note 📎

The amount of information gathered through a passive reconnaissance can be surprising. Not only can technical information such as IP addresses, subdomains, and open ports be identified through technology tools, but a wide variety of information that can then be used in a social engineering attack can also be accumulated. This includes company contact names, phone numbers, and email addresses from a corporate web site directory, news about other companies with which the target company is a partner, company privacy policies that can help identify the types of security mechanisms in place, job boards, and even disgruntled employee blogs or websites.

Once the tester has gathered the information, the next step is to perform an **initial exploitation** by using that information to determine if it provides entry to the secure network. Once inside the network, the tester attempts to perform a **pivot**, or moving around inside the network to other resources. The pentester's goal is that of *privilege escalation*, or exploiting a vulnerability to access an ever-higher level of resources. To achieve this goal, testers must rely on **persistence**, or endurance and "doggedness" to continue to probe for weaknesses and exploit them.

Vulnerability scanning and penetration testing are important tools in a vulnerability assessment. Table 13-9 compares their features.

Table 13-9 Vulnerability scan and penetration test features

Feature	Vulnerability scan	Penetration test
Frequency	When new equipment is installed and at least once per month thereafter	Once per year
Goals	Reveal known vulnerabilities that have not yet been addressed	Discover unknown exposures to the normal business processes
Tester	In-house technician	Independent external consultant
Location	Performed from inside	Performed from outside
Disruption	Passive evaluation with no disruption	Active attack with potential disruption
Tools	Automated software	Knowledge and skills of tester
Cost	Low (approximately $1500 plus staff time)	High (approximately $12,500)
Report	Comprehensive comparison of current vulnerabilities compared to baseline	Short analysis of how the attack was successful and the damage to data
Value	Detects weaknesses in hardware or software	Preventive; reduces the organization's exposure

Note

It is not uncommon for some self-appointed "security experts" to claim they have performed in-depth penetration testing while in reality, they have conducted only less-intensive vulnerability scanning.

Practicing Data Privacy and Security

 **Certification**

2.2 Given a scenario, use appropriate software tools to assess the security posture of an organization.

5.8 Given a scenario, carry out data security and privacy practices.

It is universally understood that a fundamental goal of security is to keep sensitive data away from the hands of threat actors. In fact, security is most often associated with theft prevention; preventing data from being stolen is often cited by enterprises as a primary objective of their information security. Enterprise data theft may involve stealing proprietary business information, such as research for a new product or a list of customers that competitors would be eager to acquire.

Personal data theft involves user personal data such as credit card numbers that can then be used to purchase thousands of dollars of merchandise online before the victim is even aware the number has been stolen. Personal data theft can also lead to *identity theft*, or stealing another person's personal information, such as a Social Security number, and then using the information to impersonate the victim, generally for financial gain.

Whereas *security* is often viewed as keeping sensitive data away from attackers, it is also important to keep private data from leaking into the hands of *any* unauthorized persons, whether they are seeking the data or not. Inadvertent data leaks can be as deadly as an overt theft by an attacker. From 2005 through early 2017, over 907 million electronic data records in the United States had been breached, exposing to attackers a range of personal electronic data, such as addresses, Social Security numbers, health records, and credit card numbers, with the overwhelming number of breaches as the result of inadvertent actions.[3]

Practicing data privacy and security involves understanding what privacy is and its risks, as well as practical steps in keeping data safe.

What Is Privacy?

Privacy is defined as the state or condition of being free from public attention to the degree that you determine. That is, privacy is freedom from attention, observation, or interference, based on your decision. Privacy is the right to be left alone to the level that you choose.

Prior to the current age of technology, almost all individuals (with the exception of media celebrities and politicians) generally were able to choose the level of privacy that they desired. Those who wanted to have very open and public lives could freely provide information about themselves to others. Those who wanted to live a very quiet or even unknown life could limit what information was disseminated. In short, both those wanting a public life and those wanting a private life could choose to do so by controlling information about themselves.

However, today that is no longer possible. Data is collected on almost all actions and transactions that individuals perform. This includes data collected through web surfing, purchases (online and in stores), user surveys and questionnaires, and through a wide array of other sources. It also is collected on benign activities such as the choice of movies streamed through the Internet, the location signals emitted by a cell phone, and even the path of walking as recorded by a surveillance camera. This data is then aggregated by *data brokers*. One data broker holds an average of 1,500 pieces of information per person on more than 200 million consumers around the world.[4] These brokers then sell the data to interested third parties such as marketers or even governments.

Note

Unlike consumer reporting agencies, which are required by federal law to give consumers free copies of their credit reports and allow them to correct errors, data brokers are not required to show consumers information that has been collected about them or provide a means of correcting it.

Risks Associated with Private Data

The risks associated with the use of private data fall into three categories:

- *Individual inconveniences and identity theft*. Data that has been collected on individuals is frequently used to direct ad marketing campaigns toward the person. These campaigns, which include email, direct mail marketing promotions, and telephone calls, generally are considered annoying and unwanted. In addition, personal data can be used as the basis for identity theft.

Note

Identity theft is covered in Chapter 1.

- *Associations with groups*. Another use of personal data is to place what appear to be similar individuals together into groups. One data broker has 70 distinct segments (*clusters*) within 21 consumer and demographic characteristic groups (*life stages*). These groups range from *Boomer Barons* (baby boomer-aged households with high education and income), *Hard Changers* (well-educated and professionally successful singles), and *True Blues* (working parents who hold blue-collar jobs with teenage children about to leave home). Once a person is placed in a group, the characteristics of that group are applied, such as whether a person is a "potential inheritor," an "adult with senior parent," or whether a household has a "diabetic focus" or "senior needs." However, these assumptions may not always be accurate for the individual that has been placed within that group. Individuals might be offered fewer or the wrong types of services based on their association with a group.
- *Statistical inferences*. Statistical inferences are often made that go beyond groupings. For example, researchers have demonstrated that by examining only four data points of credit card purchases (such as the dates and times of purchases) by 1.1 million people, they were able to correctly identify 90 percent of them.[5] In another study, the *Likes* indicated by Facebook users can statistically reveal their sexual orientation, drug use, and political beliefs.[6]

The issues raised regarding how private data is gathered and used are listed in Table 13-10.

Table 13-10 Issues regarding how private data is gathered and used

Issue	Explanation
The data is gathered and kept in secret.	Users have no formal rights to find out what private information is being gathered, who gathers it, or how it is being used.
The accuracy of the data cannot be verified.	Because users do not have the right to correct or control what personal information is gathered, its accuracy may be suspect. In some cases, inaccurate or incomplete data may lead to erroneous decisions made about individuals without any verification.
Identity theft can impact the accuracy of data.	Victims of identity theft often have information added to their profile that was the result of actions by the identity thieves, and even the victims have no right to see or correct the information.
Unknown factors can impact overall ratings.	Ratings are often created from combining thousands of individual factors or data streams, including race, religion, age, gender, household income, zip code, presence of medical conditions, transactional purchase information from retailers, and hundreds more data points about individual consumers. How these different factors impact a person's overall rating is unknown.
Informed consent is usually missing or is misunderstood.	Statements in a privacy policy such as "We may share your information for marketing purposes with third parties" is not clearly informed consent to freely allow the use of personal data. Often users are not even asked for permission to gather their information.
Data is being used for increasingly important decisions.	Private data is being used on an ever-increasing basis to determine eligibility in significant life opportunities, such as jobs, consumer credit, insurance, and identity verification.

Note 🔗

The inaccuracy of data is of particular concern. A study of financial data used by consumer reporting agencies found that 20 percent of consumers discovered an error on at least one of their three credit reports that had impacted their credit score. After the information was corrected, over 10 percent of consumers saw their credit score increase, while one in 20 consumers had a score change of over 25 points. And one in 250 consumers who corrected their data had a maximum score change of over 100 points.[7]

The risks associated with private data have led to concern by individuals regarding how their private data is being used. According to one survey, 91 percent "agree" or "strongly agree" that consumers have lost control over how personal information is collected and used by companies, 80 percent of those who use social networking sites say they are concerned about third parties like advertisers or businesses accessing the data they share on these sites, 70 percent of social networking site users say that they are at least somewhat concerned about the government accessing some of the information they share on social networking sites without their knowledge.[8]

Maintaining Data Privacy and Security

In addition to the need to keep data secure to prevent theft, there is likewise a need to keep data private and secure for **legal and compliance issues**, which is following the requirements of legislation, prescribed rules and regulations, specified standards, or the terms of a contract. Several federal and state laws have been enacted to protect the privacy of electronic data, and businesses that fail to protect data they possess may face serious financial penalties. Some of these laws include the Health Insurance Portability and Accountability Act of 1996 (HIPAA), the Sarbanes-Oxley Act of 2002 (Sarbox), the Gramm-Leach-Bliley Act (GLBA), the Payment Card Industry Data Security Standard (PCI DSS), and various state notification and security laws. Some of the legal and compliance issues relate to **data retention**, or how long data must be kept and how it is to be secured.

Note

Laws related to privacy are covered in Chapter 1.

There are several important steps in maintaining data privacy and security. These include creating and following an overall security methodology, properly labeling and handling sensitive data, and ensuring that data is destroyed when no longer needed.

Security Methodology

A *methodology* is a body of methods or rules employed by a discipline. Although there are a wide variety of ways by which sensitive data can be compromised, a standard methodology should be used in mitigating and deterring attacks. These techniques include creating a security posture, selecting and configuring controls, hardening, and reporting.

Creating a Security Posture

A *security posture* may be considered as an approach, philosophy, or strategy regarding data privacy and security. A healthy security posture results from a sound and workable strategy toward managing risks associated with handling this data.

Several elements make up a security posture, including:

- *Initial baseline configuration.* A baseline is the standard security checklist against which systems are evaluated for a security posture. A baseline outlines the major security considerations for a system and becomes the starting point for solid security. It is critical that a strong baseline be created when developing a security posture.

- *Continuous security monitoring.* Continual observation of systems and networks through vulnerability scanning and penetration testing can provide valuable information regarding the current state of preparedness. In particular, system logs—including event logs, audit logs, security logs, and access logs—should be closely monitored.
- *Remediation.* As vulnerabilities are exposed through monitoring, a plan must be in place to address the vulnerabilities before they are exploited by attackers.

Selecting Appropriate Controls

Selecting the appropriate controls to use is another key to mitigating and deterring attacks. Although many different controls can be used, there are common controls that are important to meet specific security goals. Table 13-11 summarizes some of these.

Table 13-11 Appropriate controls for different security goals

Security goal	Common controls
Confidentiality	Encryption, steganography, access controls
Integrity	Hashing, digital signatures, certificates, nonrepudiation tools
Availability	Redundancy, fault tolerance, patching
Safety	Fencing and lighting, locks, CCTV, escape plans and routes, safety drills

Configuring Controls

Another key to mitigating and deterring attacks is the proper configuration and testing of the controls that are already in place. One category of controls is those that can either *detect* or *prevent* attacks. For example, a closed-circuit television (CCTV) camera's primary purpose in a remote hallway may be to detect if a criminal is attempting to break into an office to steal confidential data. The camera itself, however, cannot prevent the attack; it can only be used to record it for future prosecution or to alert a person monitoring the camera. Other controls can be configured to include prevention as their primary purpose. A security guard whose desk is positioned at the entrance of the hallway has the primary purpose of preventing the criminal from entering the hallway. In the same way, different information security controls can be configured to detect attacks and sound alarms, or to prevent attacks from occurring.

One example of configuring controls regards what occurs when a normal function is interrupted by a failure: does safety take priority or does security? For example, consider a school door that is controlled by a special electromagnetic lock requiring the electrical current to be on for the door to function properly. If the electricity goes off (fails), should the door automatically be unlocked to allow any occupants to leave the building (safety) or should the door automatically lock to prevent any intruders from entering the building (security)? Which takes precedence, safety or security? In this scenario, a door that automatically unlocks is called a *fail-open* lock, which errs on the side of permissiveness, while one that automatically locks is called a *fail-safe* (or *fail-secure*) lock, which is a control that puts the system on the highest level of security.

The same question should be asked about what occurs when a security hardware device fails or a program aborts: which state should it enter? A firewall device that goes into a fail-safe control state could prevent all traffic from entering or exiting, resulting in no traffic coming into the network. That also means that internal nodes cannot send traffic out, thereby restricting their access to the Internet. If the firewall goes into a fail-open state, then all traffic would be allowed, opening the door for unfiltered attacks to enter the system. If a software program abnormally terminates, a fail-open state could allow an attacker to launch an insecure activity, whereas the fail-safe state would close the program or even stop the entire operating system to prevent any malicious activity.

Hardening

The purpose of hardening is to eliminate as many security risks as possible and make the system more secure. A variety of techniques can be used to harden systems. Types of hardening techniques include:

- Protecting accounts with passwords
- Disabling any unnecessary accounts
- Disabling all unnecessary services
- Protecting management interfaces and applications

Reporting

It is important to provide information regarding the events that occur so that action can be taken. This reporting can take the form of *alarms* or *alerts* that sound a warning message of a specific situation that is occurring. For example, an alert could signal that someone is trying to guess a user's password by entering several different password attempts. The reporting also can involve providing information on *trends* that may indicate an even more serious impending situation. A trend report may indicate that multiple user accounts are experiencing multiple password attempts.

Data Labeling and Handling

It is not uncommon for sensitive data to be exposed simply because it was mislabeled. Data that should have been private was inadvertently or mistakenly labeled as that which could be publicly distributed. By applying the correct **data sensitivity labeling** (applying it to the correct category of data) can help ensure proper data handling. Table 13-12 lists different categories of data labeling and handling.

Data Destruction

Because data itself is intangible, destroying data that is no longer needed involves destroying the media on which the data is stored. If any data other than data labeled public is on paper, that media should never be thrown away in a dumpster, recycle bin, or trash receptacle. Paper media can be destroyed by **burning** (lighting it on fire), **shredding** (cutting

Table 13-12	Data sensitivity labeling and handling	
Data label	**Description**	**Handling**
Confidential	Highest level of sensitivity	Should only be made available to users with highest level of preapproved authentication
Private	Restricted data with a medium level of confidentiality	For users who have a need-to-know basis of the contents
Proprietary	Belongs to the enterprise	Can be available to any current employees or contractors
Public	No risk of release	For all public consumption; data is assumed to be public if no other data label is attached
Personally Identifiable Information (PII)	Data that could potentially identify a specific individual	Should be kept secure so that an individual cannot be singled out for identification
Protected Health Information (PHI)	Data about a person's health status, provision of health care, or payment for health care	Must be kept secure as mandated by HIPAA

Note

In addition to labels, a color coding scheme can also be used to help identify the least confidential through the most confidential data labels. A spectrum of colors from green, blue, yellow, orange, to red can help clearly indicate the sensitivity of the document. Some organizations color the label or insert a colored cover sheet in the sensitive document.

it into small strips or particles), **pulping** (breaking the paper back into wood cellulose fibers after the ink is removed), or **pulverizing** ("hammering" the paper into dust).

If data is on an electronic media, the data should never be erased using the operating system "delete" command (**purging**). This is because the data still could be retrieved by using third-party tools. Instead, **data sanitation tools** can be employed to securely remove data. One technique is called **wiping** (overwriting the disk space with zeros or random data). For a magnetic-based hard disk drive, **degaussing** will permanently destroy the entire drive by reducing or eliminating the magnetic field.

Note

There is no universal agreement on the differences between purging and wiping.

Chapter Summary

- Vulnerability assessment is a systematic and methodical evaluation of the exposure of assets to attackers, forces of nature, and any other entity that could cause potential harm. Generally, five steps are involved in vulnerability assessment. The first step is to determine the assets that need to be protected. An asset is defined as any item that has a positive economic value, and asset identification is the process of inventorying these items. After an account of the assets has been made, it is important to determine each item's relative value. Once the assets have been inventoried, the next step is to determine the potential threats against the assets that come from threat agents. One tool used to assist in determining potential threats is a process known as threat modeling. The third step is a vulnerability appraisal, which takes a snapshot of the security of the organization as it currently stands. The next step is to perform a risk assessment, which involves determining the damage that would result from an attack and the likelihood that the vulnerability is a risk to the organization. The last step is to determine what to do about the risks. Because risk cannot ever be entirely eliminated, an organization must decide how much acceptable risk can be tolerated.

- Many assessment tools can be used to perform vulnerability assessments. Port scanner software searches a system to determine the state of ports to show what applications are running and to point out port vulnerabilities that could be exploited.

A protocol analyzer captures each packet to decode and analyze its contents. A vulnerability scanner is a generic term that refers to a range of products that look for vulnerabilities in networks or systems. A honeypot is a computer typically located in an area with limited security and loaded with software and data files that appear to be authentic but are not. The honeypot is intentionally configured with security vulnerabilities to trick attackers into revealing their attack techniques. Similar to a honeypot, a honeynet is a network set up with intentional vulnerabilities.

- Banner grabbing can be used to perform an inventory on the services and systems operating on a server. Although often considered as the tool of threat actors, crackers can also be used in a vulnerability assessment as well. There are several command-line tools that can be used to assess the vulnerability of a network as well as third-party tools. An exploitation framework is used to replicate attacks during a vulnerability assessment by providing a structure of exploits and monitoring tools. Steganography assessment tools can be used to determine if the data is hidden well enough in an image, audio, or video file to thwart unauthorized users from finding the data.

- A vulnerability scan searches a system for any known security weaknesses and creates a report of those potential exposures. An intrusive vulnerability scan attempts to actually penetrate the system in order to perform a simulated attack, while a non-intrusive vulnerability scan uses only available information to hypothesize the status of the vulnerability. These scans are conducted using an automated software package that examines the system for known weaknesses by testing the security controls.

- Penetration testing is designed to exploit any weaknesses discovered in systems. Penetration testers do not use automated software as with vulnerability scanning. Testers are typically outside the security perimeter and may even disrupt the operation of the network or devices instead of passively probing for a known vulnerability. Penetration testers can use black box (no knowledge of network or systems), white box (full knowledge of systems), or gray box (limited knowledge) techniques in their testing. Active reconnaissance involves actively probing the system, much like an attacker would do, to find information. Passive reconnaissance includes searches online for publicly accessible information that can reveal valuable insight about the system.

- Privacy is defined as the state or condition of being free from public attention to the degree that you determine, or the right to be left alone to the level that you choose. Prior to the current age of technology, individuals were generally able to choose the level of privacy that they desired. Today, that is no longer possible, for data is collected on almost all actions and transactions that individuals perform. There are several risks associated with the use of private data. In addition to the need to keep data secure to prevent theft, there is a need to keep data private and secure for legal and compliance issues.

- There are several important steps in maintaining data privacy and security. Several standard techniques can be used in mitigating and deterring attacks. A security posture is a philosophy regarding security. A healthy security posture results from a sound and workable strategy toward managing risks. Another key to mitigating and deterring attacks is the selection of appropriate controls and the proper configuration of those controls. One category of controls is those that can either detect attacks or prevent attacks. The purpose of hardening is to eliminate as many security risks as possible and make the system more secure. Reporting can provide information regarding the events that occur so that action can be taken. Reporting also can involve providing information on trends that may indicate an even more serious impending situation. By applying the correct data sensitivity labeling (applying it to the correct category of data) can help ensure proper data handling. Because data itself is intangible, destroying data that is no longer needed involves destroying the media on which the data is stored.

Key Terms

active reconnaissance

active scanner

banner grabbing

black box

burning

confidential

configuration compliance
  scanner

credentialed vulnerability
  scan

data retention

data sanitation tools

data sensitivity labeling

degaussing

Dig

exploitation framework

gray box

honeynet

honeypot

identify a lack of security
  controls

identify common
  misconfigurations

identify vulnerabilities

initial exploitation

intrusive vulnerability scan

IP and Ifconfig

Ipconfig

legal and compliance issues

Netcat

Netstat

network mapping scanner

Nmap

non-credentialed
  vulnerability scan

non-intrusive vulnerability
  scan

Nslookup

passive reconnaissance

passive scanner

passively testing security
  controls

password cracker

penetration testing

persistence

Personally Identifiable
  Information (PII)

Ping

pivot

privacy

private

proprietary

Protected Health
  Information (PHI)

protocol analyzer

public

pulping

pulverizing

purging

shredding

steganography assessment
  tools

Tcpdump

Tracert

vulnerability scan

vulnerability scanner

white box

wiping

wireless cracker

wireless scanner

Review Questions

1. At what point in a vulnerability assessment would an attack tree be utilized?
   a. Vulnerability appraisal
   b. Risk assessment
   c. Risk mitigation
   d. Threat evaluation
2. Which of the following is NOT true about privacy?
   a. Today, individuals can achieve any level of privacy that is desired.
   b. Privacy is difficult due to the volume of data silently accumulated by technology.

   c. Privacy is freedom from attention, observation, or interference based on your decision.
   d. Privacy is the right to be left alone to the degree that you choose.
3. Which of the following is NOT a risk associated with the use of private data?
   a. Individual inconveniences and identity theft
   b. Associations with groups
   c. Statistical inferences
   d. Devices being infected with malware

4. Which of the following is NOT an issue raised regarding how private data is gathered and used?
   a. The data is gathered and kept in secret.
   b. By law, all encrypted data must contain a "backdoor" entry point.
   c. Informed consent is usually missing or is misunderstood.
   d. The accuracy of the data cannot be verified.

5. Which of the following is a systematic and methodical evaluation of the exposure of assets to attackers, forces of nature, and any other entity that could cause potential harm?
   a. Vulnerability assessment
   b. Penetration test
   c. Vulnerability scan
   d. Risk appraisal

6. Which of these should NOT be classified as an asset?
   a. Business partners
   b. Buildings
   c. Employee databases
   d. Accounts payable

7. Which of the following command-line tools tests a connection between two network devices?
   a. Netstat
   b. Ping
   c. Nslookup
   d. Ifconfig

8. Which statement regarding vulnerability appraisal is NOT true?
   a. Vulnerability appraisal is always the easiest and quickest step.
   b. Every asset must be viewed in light of each threat.

   c. Each threat could reveal multiple vulnerabilities.
   d. Each vulnerability should be cataloged.

9. Which of the following constructs scenarios of the types of threats that assets can face to learn who the attackers are, why they attack, and what types of attacks may occur?
   a. Vulnerability prototyping
   b. Risk assessment
   c. Attack assessment
   d. Threat modeling

10. Which of the following tools is a Linux command-line protocol analyzer?
    a. Wireshark
    b. Tcpdump
    c. IP
    d. Arp

11. Which of the following is a command-line alternative to Nmap?
    a. Netcat
    b. Statnet
    c. Mapper
    d. Netstat

12. Which of these is NOT a state of a port that can be returned by a port scanner?
    a. Open
    b. Busy
    c. Blocked
    d. Closed

13. Which of the following data sensitivity labels is the highest level of data sensitivity?
    a. Ultra
    b. Confidential
    c. Private
    d. Secret

14. Which of the following data sensitivity labels has the lowest level of data sensitivity?
    a. Unrestricted
    b. Public
    c. Free
    d. Open

15. Which of the following is NOT a function of a vulnerability scanner?
    a. Detects which ports are served and which ports are browsed for each individual system
    b. Alerts users when a new patch cannot be found
    c. Maintains a log of all interactive network sessions
    d. Detects when an application is compromised

16. Which of the following must be kept secure as mandated by HIPAA?
    a. PII
    b. PHI
    c. PHIL
    d. PLILP

17. Which statement regarding a honeypot is NOT true?
    a. It is typically located in an area with limited security.
    b. It is intentionally configured with security vulnerabilities.
    c. It cannot be part of a honeynet.
    d. It can direct an attacker's attention away from legitimate servers.

18. Which of the following sends "probes" to network devices and examines the responses to evaluate whether a specific device needs remediation?
    a. Active scanner
    b. Probe scanner
    c. Passive scanner
    d. Remote scanner

19. If a tester is given the IP addresses, network diagrams, and source code of customer applications, the tester is using which technique?
    a. Black box
    b. White box
    c. Gray box
    d. Blue box

20. If a software application aborts and leaves the program open, which control structure is it using?
    a. Fail-safe
    b. Fail-secure
    c. Fail-open
    d. Fail-right

Hands-On Projects

> **Note**
>
> If you are concerned about installing any of the software in these projects on your regular computer, you can instead install the software in the Windows virtual machine created in the Chapter 1 Hands-On Projects 1-3 and 1-4. Software installed within the virtual machine will not impact the host computer.

Project 13-1: Using an Online Vulnerability Scanner

Online software vulnerability scanners can compare all applications on a computer with a list of known patches from the different software vendors and then alert the user to any applications that are not properly patched or automatically install the patches when one is detected as missing. In this project, you use the Secunia Personal Software Inspector (PSI) to determine if your computer is missing any security updates.

> **Note**
>
> The current version of PSI contains several advanced features. It supports applications from more than 3000 different software vendors and encapsulates all the vendor patches for your computer into one proprietary installer. This installer suppresses any required dialogs so everything can be patched silently without any user intervention. You can even create rules, such as telling PSI to ignore patching a specific application.

1. Open your web browser and enter the URL **www.flexerasoftware.com** (if you are no longer able to access the program through this URL, use a search engine and search for "Flexera Personal Software Inspector").
2. Under **Solutions for Enterprises** click **Visit Site**.
3. Under **Free Trials** click **Free Personal Software Inspector**.
4. Click **Get free download**.
5. Enter the requested information and click **Download Now**.
6. Click **Download Now**.
7. When the download completes, install PSI.
8. Select the appropriate language and click **OK**.
9. Click **Next** on the Welcome screen, then click **I accept the terms of the License Agreement**. Click **Next**.
10. Check the box **Update programs automatically (recommended)** if necessary. Click **Next**.
11. Click **Finish** when the installation is complete.

12. When asked **Would you like to launch Secunia PSI now?**, click **Yes**. Depending upon the computer, it may take several minutes to load the program and its modules.
13. If necessary, click **Scan now**.
14. When the scan is finished, the results appear.
15. Applications that can be automatically updated start the download and installation automatically. On any applications that need manual updates, you can go to the application and then update it.
16. How hard or easy is this vulnerability assessment program to use? Would you recommend it to others?
17. Close all windows.

> **Note**
>
> The Secunia PSI application will continually run in the background checking for updates. If you do not want this functionality, you can click Settings and uncheck Start on boot.

Project 13-2: Using an Online Port Scanner

Internet port scanners are available that will probe the ports on a system to determine which ports are open, closed, or blocked. In this project, you perform a scan using an online Internet-based scanner.

1. Use your web browser to go to **www.t1shopper.com/tools/port-scan/** (if you are no longer able to access the program through this URL, use a search engine to search for "Online Port Scan").
2. Note that your IP address is automatically entered in the field **Host name or IPv4 address:**.
3. You can scan a specific port number, a range of numbers, or specific recommended numbers. Select each of the 14 recommended ports to scan by clicking **Check All**.
4. Click **Scan Ports**.
5. Each port is scanned. This may take several minutes. If that port is blocked, which is the most secure setting, it will respond that the IP address "isn't responding on port ##."
6. When the scan finishes, note any ports that are open, closed, or blocked.
7. Click the browser's back button.
8. Click **Uncheck All**.
9. Now enter a range of ports. Under **Beginning port number** enter **1**.
10. Under **Ending port number** enter **200**.
11. Click **Scan Ports**.
12. When the scan finishes, note any ports that are open, closed, or blocked.
13. Click the browser's back button.
14. Erase the beginning and ending port numbers.

15. Now scan a web server, such as your school's or www.cengage.com to view its ports. Enter the address under **Host name or IPv4 address:**.

16. Select each of the 14 recommended ports to scan by clicking **Check All**.

17. Click **Scan Ports**. Each port is scanned.

18. Did you discover any open or closed ports? If so, which ones? Why were they open or closed instead of blocked?

19. Close all windows.

Project 13-3: Using a Local Port Scanner

In this project, you download and install the port scanner Nmap on a local computer.

1. Use your web browser to go to **nmap.org/download.html** (if you are no longer able to access the program through this URL, use a search engine to search for "Nmap").

2. Under **Microsoft Windows binaries**, click the link next to **Latest stable release self-installer:**.

3. When the download completes, launch the installation program by accepting the default configuration settings.

4. Launch Nmap.

5. Next to **Target:** enter the IP address of a computer on the network to which the computer is connected. Then, click the **Scan** button.

> **Note** 📎
>
> If you do not know the address of any of the devices on the network, click **Start** and enter **cmd** and press **Enter**. At the prompt, enter **arp -a** to view the arp cache of IP addresses and MAC addresses of devices on the network of which the computer is aware. Select one of the IP addresses of the devices on the network to scan.

6. Nmap scans the ports of that computer and displays the results. Scroll down through the results of the port scan. How could this information be valuable to an attacker?

7. For a summary of open ports, click **Topology**.

8. Click **Hosts Viewer**.

9. Click the **Services** tab.

10. Expand each of the entries listed.

11. Close the Hosts Viewer window.

12. Click **Controls**. What information is being provided? How would this be useful to an attacker?

13. Close all windows.

Case Projects

Case Project 13-1: Microsoft Windows 10 Privacy

Starting with Microsoft Windows 10, Microsoft by default gathers information about user preferences. For example, Windows 10 assigns an advertising ID to users, and then uses it to deliver customized ads and information. This has caused alarm among some users regarding intrusion into their privacy. Using the Internet, research the information gathered through Windows 10. What are the advantages of this data collection? What are the disadvantages? Is this any different from how other operating systems and websites gather information? Should Microsoft be more upfront about the collection of this data? Is there a way to turn the data collection off? If so, how is it done? Should it be easier to turn it off for users who do not want their data collected? Write a one-page paper on your research and opinions.

Case Project 13-2: Risk Management Study

Perform an abbreviated risk management study on your personal computer. Conduct an asset identification, threat identification, vulnerability appraisal, risk assessment, and risk mitigation. Under each category, list the elements that pertain to your system. What major vulnerabilities did you uncover? How can you mitigate the risks? Write a one-page paper on your analysis.

Case Project 13-3: Compare Port Scanners

Use the Internet to locate three port scanner applications that you can download to your computer. Install and run each application and examine the results. Based on your study, what are the strengths and weaknesses of each scanner? Which scanner would you recommend? Why?

Case Project 13-4: Compare Protocol Analyzers

Several very good protocol analyzers are available. Three of the most popular are Wireshark (*www.wireshark.org*), which is an open source product, Microsoft Message Analyzer (*www.microsoft.com/en-us/download/details.aspx?id=44226*), and Colasoft Capsa (*www.colasoft.com/capsa*), which has a free version along with an Enterprise and Professional edition. Research these three protocol analyzers and compare their features. Next download and install each product, and perform a basic protocol analysis (there are several free tutorials available regarding how to use these tools). Create a document that lists the features and strengths of each product. Which would you prefer? Why?

Case Project 13-5: Attack Tree

Select an attack, such as "Break into Instructor's Lab Computer" or "Steal Credit Card Number from Online User," and then develop an attack tree for it. The tree should have at least four levels with three boxes on each level. Share your tree with at least two other learners and ask if they can think of other attacks that they would add.

Case Project 13-6: Command-Line Tools

Use the Internet to research each of the command-line tools found in Table 13-7. Select five of the tools and design a command line with the appropriate options that could be used to investigate the security configuration or settings of a network or computer. Then run those command lines with the options, and capture the screen of results. Create a table that lists the tool, a description of the options that you used, and embed the screen capture into the document as an appendix.

Case Project 13-7: Lake Point Security Consulting

Lake Point Consulting Services (LPCS) provides security consulting and assurance services to over 500 clients across a wide range of enterprises in more than 20 states. A new initiative at LPCS is for each of its seven regional offices to provide internships to students who are in their final year of the security degree program at the local college.

Predish Real Estate and Auction (PREA) buys and sells high-end residential and commercial real estate across a multistate region. One of the tools that PREA offers is a sophisticated online website that allows potential buyers to take virtual tours of properties. However, PREA's site was recently compromised by attackers who defaced the site with malicious messages, causing several customers to threaten to withdraw their listings. PREA's senior management has demanded a top-to-bottom review of their security by an independent third party. LPCS has been hired to perform the review, and they have contracted with you to work on this project.

1. The first task is to perform a vulnerability assessment of PREA. Create a PowerPoint presentation for the president and his staff about the steps in a vulnerability assessment. List in detail the actions under each step and what PREA should expect in the assessment. Your presentation should contain at least 10 slides.

2. One of the activities recommended by LPCS is to perform a penetration test. However, the IT staff is very resistant to the idea and has tried to convince PREA's senior management that it is too risky and that a vulnerability scan would serve the same purpose. PREA has asked you for your opinion of performing a penetration test or a vulnerability scan. Create a memo that outlines the differences and what your recommendation would be.

Case Project 13-8: Community Site Activity

The Information Security Community Site is an online companion to this textbook. It contains a wide variety of tools, information, discussion boards, and other features to assist learners. Go to **community.cengage.com/Infosec2** and click the *Join or Sign in* icon to log in, using your login name and password that you created in Chapter 1. Click **Forums (Discussion)** and click on **Security+ Case Projects (6th edition)**. Read the following case study.

Bob is invited to attend a weekly meeting of computer enthusiasts on campus. At the meeting, much of the talk centers around the latest attack software and how to bypass weak security settings on the school network. As the meeting starts to break up, Bob is approached by Alice, who strikes up a conversation with him about the latest attack software. Alice soon confides in Bob that she has plans to break into the school's web server that night and deface it (she has a friend who works in the school's IT department and the friend has shared some helpful information with her). Alice goes on to say that she would give Bob the chance to "show he's a man" by helping her break into the server. Bob declines the invitation and leaves.

Later that week, Bob receives an email from Alice who says she wasn't successful in breaking into the server that night, but knows that she has the right information now. She asks Bob to meet her at the library that night to watch her. Bob thinks about it and accepts the invitation. That night Alice shows Bob some of the information she has acquired through her friend in IT and says she's ready to launch her attack. Alice then pauses and gives Bob the chance to make up for being "chicken" earlier in the week. Bob again declines. Alice then tells Bob that she knows he's really stupid because he can't do it and he lacks the nerve. After several minutes of her accusations, Bob finally gives in and uses the information Alice has to break into the web server.

The next day two campus security officers appear at Bob's dorm room. It turns out that Alice is working undercover for campus security and turned Bob in to them. In addition, the web server that Bob thought he was breaking into turned out to be a honeypot the school had set up. Bob was required to go before the school's Office of Judicial Affairs (OJA) to determine if he should be suspended.

When Bob appeared before the OJA he claimed in his defense that he was entrapped in two different ways. First, he was entrapped by Alice to break into the server. Second, he claimed that the honeypot itself was entrapment. He claimed that he should not be suspended from school.

What do you think? Did Alice entrap Bob? Is a honeypot entrapment? (You may want to research *honeypot entrapment* on the Internet.) If you were in Bob's place, what would you say? Enter your answers on the Information Security Community Site discussion board.

References

1. Hodgman, Roy, "The attacker's dictionary," *Rapid7 Community*, Mar. 1, 2016, retrieved Jun. 3, 2017, https://community.rapid7.com/community/infosec/blog/2016/03/01/the-attackers-dictionary.

2. "18 U.S. Code § 1030—Fraud and related activity in connection with computers," *Legal Information Institute*, retrieved Jun. 14, 2017, www.law.cornell.edu/uscode/text/18/1030.

3. "Data Breaches," *Privacy Rights Clearinghouse*, updated Feb. 16, 2017, accessed Feb. 16, 2017, www.privacyrights.org/data-breaches.

4. Tucker, Patrick, "Has big data made anonymity impossible?", *MIT Technical Review*, May 7, 2013, accessed Sep. 12, 2015, http://www.technologyreview.com/news/514351/has-big-data-made-anonymity-impossible.

5. Hardesty, Larry, "Privacy challenges," *MIT News*, Jan. 29, 2015, accessed Sep. 12, 2015, http://news.mit.edu/2015/identify-from-credit-card-metadata-0129.

6. Halliday, Josh, "Facebook users unwittingly revealing intimate secrets, study finds", *The Guardian*, Mar. 11, 2013, accessed Sep. 12, 2015, http://www.theguardian.com/technology/2013/mar/11/facebook-users-reveal-intimate-secrets.

7. Dixon, Pam and Gellman, Robert, *The scoring of America: How secret consumer scores threaten your privacy and your future*, Apr. 2, 2014, accessed Sep. 12, 2015, http://www.worldprivacyforum.org/wp-content/uploads/2014/04/WPF_Scoring_of_America_April2014_fs.pdf.

8. Madden, Mary, "Public perceptions of privacy and security in the post-Snowden era," *Pew Research Center*, Nov. 12, 2014, accessed Sep. 12, 2015, http://www.pewinternet.org/2014/11/12/public-privacy-perceptions/.

CHAPTER 14

BUSINESS CONTINUITY

After completing this chapter, you should be able to do the following:

Define business continuity

Describe how to achieve fault tolerance through redundancy

Explain different environmental controls

Describe forensics and incident response procedures

Today's Attacks and Defenses

One of the most important defenses against attacks is to create data backups on a regular basis. In the event an attack is successful, a current data backup can be used to restore the system to its former state. For a home user, creating a data backup generally means copying files from a computer's hard drive onto other digital media that is then stored in a secure remote location. Today a growing number of home users are turning to online data backup services, which automatically copy data to the "cloud," a remote storage facility via the Internet. Using cloud technology allows data to be easily backed up to a remote location.

But what about for enterprises? Many organizations have massive volumes of data that must be stored in a remote location. A home user might typically have only a few megabytes (MB) or even less of new data per day that must be backed up over the Internet.

But an enterprise measures its data use not in MB or gigabytes (GB) but in terabytes (TB) (1 TB = 1,000 GB; 10 TB can hold the entire printed collection of the Library of Congress), petabytes (PB) (1 PB = 1,000 TBs; the contents of 20 million four-drawer filing cabinets could be stored in 1 PB), and even exabytes (EB) (1 EB = 1,000 PBs; 1 EB is equal to one trillion books of 400 pages each). Using even a high-speed Internet connection, it would require up to 26 years to move 1 EB from the enterprise's data center to an online storage facility.

Amazon Web Services (AWS) recently introduced a new means to move data from a corporate customer's data center to Amazon's cloud computing servers. This solution is not a new and cutting-edge technology to transmit the data, but instead uses something much more common: a truck.

Known as the AWS Snowmobile solution, it all begins with an initial assessment by Amazon of the enterprise's data center. Once the assessment is completed, a 45-foot (13.7 meter) shipping container is driven to the organization's site on a semi-tractor trailer ("18-wheeler"), the same that are commonly used to transport goods around the country. This container, which has networking and storage hardware, can hold up to 100 PB of data. A removable, high-speed network switch directly connects Snowmobile to the enterprise's local network so that the shipping container can be accessed like a regular network storage device. Massive volumes of data, including video libraries, image repositories, or even a complete data center migration, can then be encrypted and copied to the Snowmobile at fast local network speeds. The same 1 EB that would take 26 years to transfer over the Internet would take ten Snowmobiles fewer than six months to complete.

Once the data has been transferred, the shipping container is driven back to an AWS location. To protect the data in transport, dedicated security personnel, GPS tracking, alarm monitoring, and 24/7 video surveillance keeps the data secure while on the road. An optional escort security vehicle can accompany the truck if desired. Once it arrives at the Amazon site, the data is imported into Amazon's cloud repository for safe keeping, where it costs only about half a cent per GB per month to store the data.

Earthquakes, tsunamis, tornados, hurricanes, floods, wildfires—these and other natural disasters can have a major impact on businesses around the world. By some estimates, world economic losses over the last 20 years to such disasters averaged about $175 billion annually (2011 saw a huge spike of $465 billion in disasters).[1] The top three natural disasters are flooding, earthquakes, and severe weather, all of which are virtually impossible to predict to make quick preparations.[2] Not all disasters, however, are acts of nature. Sabotage, acts of terrorism, and even cyberattacks on information technology also can quickly bring a business to its knees—or put it out of operation entirely. The ability of an organization to maintain its operations and services in the face of catastrophe is crucial if it is to survive.

Although preparation for disaster is an essential business element for organizations both large and small, it remains sadly lacking in practice. Many organizations are completely unprepared. It is estimated that one out of every three small businesses impacted by a disaster does not recover.[3] And many organizations that do have plans on paper have never tested those plans to determine whether they would truly bring the business through an unforeseen event.

In this chapter, you learn about the critical importance of keeping an organization operational in the face of disaster. You first learn what business continuity is and why it is important. Next, you investigate how to prevent disruptions through redundancy and how to protect resources with environmental controls. Finally, you see how incident response procedures and forensics are used when an event occurs.

What Is Business Continuity?

 **Certification**

3.8 Explain how resiliency and automation strategies reduce risk.

5.2 Summarize business impact analysis concepts.

5.6 Explain disaster recovery and continuity of operation concepts.

Business continuity can be defined as the ability of an organization to maintain its operations and services in the face of a disruptive event, whether the event is as basic as an electrical outage or as catastrophic as a hurricane. Business continuity preparedness involves business continuity planning, business impact analysis, and disaster recovery planning.

Business Continuity Planning (BCP)

Business continuity planning (BCP) is the development of strategic plans that provide alternative modes of operation for business activities which, if interrupted, could result in a significant loss to the enterprise. BCP is the process of identifying exposure to threats, creating preventive and recovery procedures, and then testing them to determine if they are sufficient. In short, BCP is designed to ensure that an organization can continue to function (*continuity of operations*) in the event of a natural (flood, hurricane, earthquake, etc.) or man-made (plane crash, terrorist attack, denial-of-service attack, etc.) disaster; it is *recovery planning*.

Note 📎
BCP may also include succession planning, or determining in advance who will be authorized to take over in the event of the incapacitation or death of key employees.

BCP consists of three essential elements:

- *Business recovery planning*. This involves the resumption of critical business functions and processes that relate to and support the delivery of the core products or services to a customer.
- *Crisis management and communications*. Crisis management and communications is the process of giving an effective response to an event. It is intended to stabilize the situation through effective leadership communication.
- *Disaster recovery*. This element addresses the recovery of critical information technology (IT) assets, including systems, applications, databases, storage and network assets.

BCP is sometimes confusing due to conflicting terminology. Because BCP is used across a wide range of industries and by different regulatory groups and agencies, many of these use their own unique terminology that is similar to BCP but slightly different. Table 14-1 lists several of the terms that are similar to BCP but have different meanings.

Table 14-1 BCP terminology

Terminology	Definition	How compares to BCP
Resumption planning	Used for the recovery of critical business functions separate from IT, such as resuming a critical manufacturing process	Part of the BCP process
Contingency actions	Tactical solutions addressing a core business resource or process, such as how to handle the loss of a specific vendor	Contingency planning is usually considered an isolated action and not part of an overall BCP
Emergency response	The immediate actions taken to preserve lives and safeguard property and assets, such as an evacuation plan	Emergency response is a subset of a BCP
Disaster recovery	The recovery and resumption of critical technology assets in the event of a disaster	Disaster recovery is a component of an overall BCP program

Business Impact Analysis (BIA)

One important tool in BCP is a *business impact analysis (BIA)*. A BIA identifies business functions and quantifies the impact a loss of these functions may have on business operations. These range from the **impact on property** (tangible assets), **impact on finance** (monetary funding), **impact on safety** (physical protection), **impact on reputation** (status), and even the **impact on life** (wellbeing).

A BIA is designed to identify those processes that are critically important to an enterprise. A BIA will help determine the **mission-essential function**, or the activity that serves as the core purpose of the enterprise. For example, a mission-essential function for a hospital could be to *Deliver health care services to individuals and their families*, while a nonessential function is to *Generate and distribute a monthly online newsletter*. In addition, a BIA can also help in the **identification of critical systems** that in turn support the mission-essential function. In a hospital setting, a critical system could be *Maintain an emergency room facility for the community*. Whereas this is a critical system, is not the core purpose of the hospital.

Identifying the **single point of failure**, which is a component or entity in a system which, if it no longer functions, will disable the entire system, is also a goal of a BIA. A patient information database in a hospital could be considered a single point of failure. Minimizing these single failure points results in **high availability**, or a system that can function for an extended period with little downtime. This availability is often expressed as a percentage of uptime in a year. Table 14-2 lists the percentage availability and the corresponding downtimes.

Table 14-2 Percentage availability and downtimes

Percentage availability	Name	Weekly downtime	Monthly downtime	Yearly downtime
90%	One Nine	16.8 hours	72 hours	36.5 days
99%	Two Nines	1.68 hours	7.20 hours	3.65 days
99.9%	Three Nines	10.1 minutes	43.2 minutes	8.76 hours
99.99%	Four Nines	1.01 minutes	4.32 minutes	52.56 minutes
99.999%	Five Nines	6.05 seconds	25.9 seconds	5.26 minutes
99.9999%	Six Nines	0.605 second	2.59 seconds	31.5 seconds

Note

A service level agreement (SLA) is a service contract between a vendor and a client that specifies what services will be provided, the responsibilities of each party, and any guarantees of service. Most SLAs are based on percentages of guaranteed uptime.

Because privacy of data is of high importance today, many BIAs also contain a **privacy impact assessment**, which is used to identify and mitigate privacy risks. This includes an examination of what personally identifiable information (PII) is being collected, the reasons why it is collected, and the safeguards regarding how the data will be accessed, shared, and stored. A **privacy threshold assessment** can determine if a system contains PII, whether a privacy impact assessment is required, and if any other privacy requirements apply to the IT system. A privacy threshold assessment should be submitted to an organization's privacy officer for review and approval.

> **Note**
>
> Privacy officers are covered in Chapter 12.

Disaster Recovery Plan (DRP)

Whereas BCP looks at the needs of the business as a whole in recovering from a catastrophe, a subset of it focuses on continuity in the context of IT. Closely related is a **disaster recovery plan (DRP)**, which is involved with restoring the IT functions and services to their former state. A DRP is a written document that details the process for restoring IT resources following an event that causes a significant disruption in service. Comprehensive in scope, a DRP is intended to be a detailed document that is updated regularly. Most DRPs have a common set of features, cover specific topics, and require testing for verification.

> **Note**
>
> Many enterprises also participate in *IT contingency planning (ITCP)* (a *contingency* is a future event or circumstance that might possibly occur but cannot be predicted with any certainty), which is developing an outline of procedures that are to be followed in the event of major IT incident such as a denial-of-service attack or an incident that directly impacts IT like a building fire.

Features

All disaster recovery plans are different, but most address the common features included in the following typical outline:

Unit 1: Purpose and Scope—The reason for the plan and what it encompasses are clearly outlined. Those incidences that require the plan to be enacted also should be listed. Topics found under Unit 1 include:

- Introduction
- Objectives and constraints

- Assumptions
- Incidents requiring action
- Contingencies
- Physical safeguards
- Types of computer service disruptions
- Insurance considerations

Unit 2: Recovery Team—The team that is responsible for the direction of the disaster recovery plan is clearly defined. It is important that each member knows her role in the plan and be adequately trained. This part of the plan is continually reviewed as employees leave the organization, home telephone or cell phone numbers change, or new members are added to the team. The Unit 2 DRP addresses the following:

- Organization of the disaster/recovery team
- Disaster/recovery team headquarters
- Disaster recovery coordinator
- Recovery team leaders and their responsibilities

Unit 3: Preparing for a Disaster—A DRP lists the entities that could impact an organization and the procedures and safeguards that should constantly be in force to reduce the risk of the disaster. Topics for Unit 3 include:

- Physical/security risks
- Environmental risks
- Internal risks
- External risks
- Safeguards

Unit 4: Emergency Procedures—The Emergency Procedures unit answers the question, "What should happen when a disaster occurs?" Unit 4 outlines the step-by-step procedures that should occur, including the following:

- Disaster recovery team formation
- Vendor contact list
- Use of alternate sites
- Off-site storage

Unit 5: Restoration Procedures—After the initial response has put in place the procedures that allow the organization to continue functioning, this unit addresses how to fully recover from the disaster and return to normal business operations. This unit should include:

- Central facilities recovery plan
- Systems and operations
- Scope of limited operations at central site
- Network communications
- Client computer recovery plan

Topics

Most DRPs also cover a standard set of topics. One common topic is the sequence in restoring systems. After a disaster has occurred, what should be the sequence in which different systems are reinstated (**order of restoration**) to functioning order? That is, which systems should have priority and be restored before other systems? There are several factors that may be considered. One factor is obvious dependencies: that is, the network must be restored before applications that rely on the network are restored. A second factor is the processes that are of fundamental importance to an enterprise: critical systems that support the mission-essential function and those systems that require high availability need to be restored before other systems. Another factor is the **alternative business practices**, or those "workaround" activities that can temporarily substitute for normal business activities. That is, how long can a manual workaround process meet the temporary needs without causing bigger problems such as unmanageable backlogs?

Another common topic found in a DRP is what should be done if a disaster makes the current location for processing data no longer available. In that case, an **alternative processing site** must be identified. This would also involve how and when to perform **failover**, or moving data input and output processes from the primary location to an alternative processing site. This typically involves temporarily suspending data input and output as well as stopping any data mirroring activities at the primary site so that applications can be started at the alternative site along with data input/output and data mirroring activities. *Failback* is the process of resynchronizing data back to the primary location, halting data input/output and application activity from the alternative site before restoring functions back to the original location.

Testing

Disaster exercises are designed to test the effectiveness of the DRP. Plans that may look solid on paper often make assumptions or omit key elements that can be revealed only with a mock disaster. The objectives of these disaster exercises are to test the efficiency of interdepartmental planning and coordination in managing a disaster, test current procedures of the DRP, and determine the strengths and weaknesses in responses.

One way in which DRPs can be tested is by using **tabletop exercises**. Tabletop exercises simulate an emergency situation but in an informal and stress-free environment. Table 14-3 lists the features of a tabletop exercise. Tabletop exercises should generate an **after-action report**. The purpose of this report is to analyze the exercise results with the purpose of identifying strengths to be maintained and weaknesses to be addressed for improvement.

Table 14-3 Features of tabletop exercises

Feature	Description
Participants	Individuals on a decision-making level
Focus	Training and familiarizing roles, procedures, and responsibilities
Setting	Informal
Format	Discussion guided by a facilitator
Purpose	Identify and solve problems as a group
Commitment	Only moderate amount of time, cost, and resources
Advantage	Can acquaint key personnel with emergency responsibilities, procedures, and other members
Disadvantage	Lack of realism; does not provide a true test

Fault Tolerance Through Redundancy

 **Certification**

2.2 Given a scenario, use appropriate software tools to assess the security posture of an organization.

3.8 Explain how resiliency and automation strategies reduce risk.

5.2 Summarize business impact analysis concepts.

5.6 Explain disaster recovery and continuity of operation concepts.

One of the means to prevent certain issues from crippling an enterprise is to incorporate **fault tolerance** into IT systems. A "fault" is a malfunction or deviation from the systems' normal expected behavior, while "tolerance" is the capacity for enduring. Fault tolerance refers to a system's ability to deal with malfunctions.

Note 🖉

Fault tolerance is a realization that systems will always have faults or the potential for faults, so they must be designed in such a way that the system will be "forgiving" of those faults. The system should compensate for the faults yet continue to function.

Because no IT system can ever be completely free of faults, the solution to fault tolerance is to build in **redundancy**, or the use of duplicated equipment to improve the availability of the system. The goal of redundancy is to reduce a variable known as the **mean time to recovery (MTTR)**. This is the average amount of time that it will take a device to recover from a failure that is not a terminal failure. Some systems are designed to have a MTTR of zero, which means they have redundant components that can take over the instant the primary component fails. Redundancy planning can involve redundancy for servers, storage, networks, power, sites, and data.

Servers

Because servers play such a key role in a network infrastructure, the loss of a single server that supports a critical application can have a significant impact. In the past, some organizations would stockpile spare parts to replace one that has failed (such as a server's power supply) or even entire redundant servers as standbys. However, the time it takes to install a new part or add a new server to the network and then load software and backup data was sometimes more than an organization could tolerate.

Another approach that some organizations took was to design the network infrastructure so that multiple servers are incorporated into the network yet appear to users and applications as a single computing resource. One method to do this is by *clustering*, or combining two or more devices to appear as a single unit. A *server cluster* is the combination of two or more servers that are interconnected to appear as one, as shown in Figure 14-1. These servers are connected through both a *public cluster connection* so that clients see them as a single unit as well as a *private cluster connection* so that the servers can exchange data when necessary. There are two types of server clusters. In an *asymmetric server cluster*, a standby server exists only to take

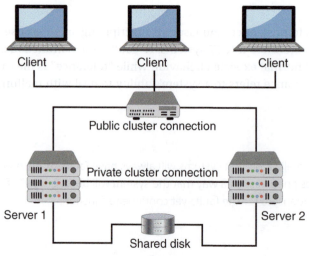

Figure 14-1 Server cluster

over for another server in the event of its failure. The standby server performs no useful work other than to be ready if it is needed. In a *symmetric server cluster*, every server in the cluster performs useful work. If one server fails, the remaining servers continue to perform their normal work as well as that of the failed server.

Today, however, just as virtualization has reduced the number of physical servers that are needed in a data center, so too has virtualization impacted the number of server clusters that are needed for server redundancy in disaster recovery. Because a virtualized image can be quickly moved to another physical server, the need for server clusters supporting large numbers of physical servers for disaster recovery has diminished. Tools are available so that as one virtual machine is shut down, a copy of that virtual machine is automatically launched.

Storage

A trend in data storage technologies for computers today is to use solid state drives (SSDs), which essentially store data on chips instead of magnetic platters. Because SSDs lack spinning platters, actuator arms with read/write heads, and motors, they are more resistant to failure and are considered more reliable than traditional hard disk drives (HDDs). However, due primarily to lower cost, HDDs still serve as the backbone of data storage for servers.

Because HDDs are mechanical devices, they often are the first component of a system to fail. Some organizations maintain a stockpile of hard drives as spare parts to replace those that fail. Yet how many spare hard drives should an organization keep on hand?

A statistical value that is used to answer this question is **mean time between failures (MTBF)**. MTBF refers to the average (*mean*) amount of time until a component fails, cannot be repaired, and must be replaced. Calculating the MTBF involves taking the total time measured divided by the total number of failures observed. For example, if 15,400 hard drive units were run for 1000 hours each and that resulted in 11 failures, the MTBF would be (15,400 × 1000) hours/11, or 1.4 million hours. This MTBF rating can be used to determine the number of spare hard drives that should be available for a quick replacement. If an organization had 1000 hard drives operating continuously with an MTBF rating of 1.4 million hours, it could be expected that one drive would fail every 58 days, or 19 failures over three years. This data can help an organization know how many spare hard drives are needed.

Note 📎

The MTBF certainly does not mean that a single hard drive is expected to last 1.4 million hours (159 years)! MTBF is a statistical measure and, as such, cannot predict anything for a single unit.

Instead of waiting for a hard drive to fail, a more proactive approach can be used. A system of hard drives based on redundancy can be achieved through using a technology known as **RAID (Redundant Array of Independent Drives),** which uses multiple hard disk drives for increased reliability and performance. RAID can be implemented through either software or hardware. Software-based RAID is implemented at the operating system level, while hardware-based RAID requires a specialized hardware controller either on the client computer or on the array that holds the RAID drives.

> **Note**
>
> RAID originally stood for *Redundant Array of Inexpensive Disks*.

Originally, there were five standard RAID configurations (called *levels*), and several additional levels have since evolved. These additional levels include "nested" levels and nonstandard levels that are proprietary to specific vendors. Nested RAIDs are usually described by combining the numbers indicating the RAID levels with a "+" in between, such as *RAID Level 0+1*. With nested RAID, the elements can be either individual disks or entire RAIDs.

The most common levels of RAID are:

- *RAID Level 0 (striped disk array without fault tolerance).* RAID 0 technology is based on *striping*. Striping partitions divide the storage space of each hard drive into smaller sections (*stripes*), which can be as small as 512 bytes or as large as several megabytes. Data written to the stripes is alternated across the drives, as shown in Figure 14-2. Although RAID Level 0 uses multiple drives, it is not fault-tolerant; if one of the drives fails, all the data on that drive is lost.

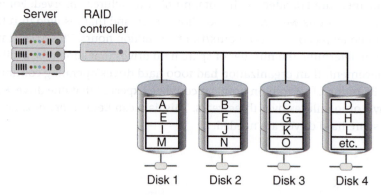

Figure 14-2 RAID Level 0

- *RAID Level 1 (mirroring).* RAID Level 1 uses *disk mirroring*. Disk mirroring involves connecting multiple drives in the server to the same disk controller card. When a request is made to write data to the drive, the controller sends that request to each drive; when a read action is required, the data is read twice, once from each drive. By "mirroring" the action on the primary drive, the other drives become exact duplicates. In case the primary drive fails, the other drives take over with no loss of data. This is shown in Figure 14-3. A variation of RAID Level 1 is to include *disk duplexing*. Instead of having a single disk controller card that is attached to all hard drives, disk duplexing has separate cards for each disk. A single controller card failure affects only one drive. This additional redundancy protects against controller card failures.

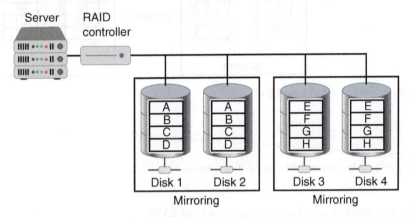

Figure 14-3 RAID Level 1

- *RAID 5 (independent disks with distributed parity).* RAID Level 5 distributes *parity* data (a type of error checking) across all drives instead of using a separate drive to hold the parity error checking information. Data is always stored on one drive while its parity information is stored on another drive, as shown in Figure 14-4. Distributing parity across other disks provides an additional degree of protection.

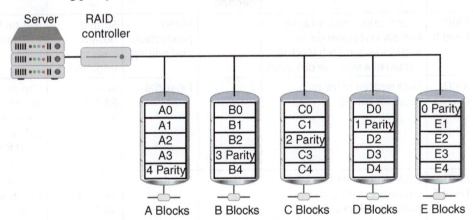

Figure 14-4 RAID Level 5

- *RAID 0+1 (high data transfer).* RAID 0+1 is a nested-level RAID. It acts as a mirrored array whose segments are RAID 0 arrays. RAID 0+1 can achieve high data transfer rates because there are multiple stripe segments. RAID Level 0+1 is shown in Figure 14-5.

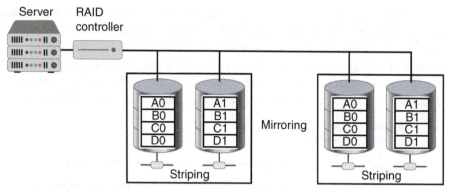

Figure 14-5 RAID Level 0+1

Many operating systems support one or more levels of RAID.

Table 14-4 summarizes the common levels of RAID.

Table 14-4 Common RAID levels

RAID level	Description	Minimum number of drives needed	Typical application	Advantages	Disadvantages
RAID Level 0	Uses a striped disk array so that data is broken down into blocks and each block is written to a separate disk drive	2	Video production and editing	Simple design, easy to implement	Not fault-tolerant
RAID Level 1	Data written twice to separate drives	2	Financial	Simplest RAID to implement	Can slow down system if RAID controlling software is used instead of hardware
RAID Level 5	Each entire data block is written on a data disk and parity for blocks in the same rank is generated and recorded on a separate disk	3	Database	Most versatile RAID	Can be difficult to rebuild if a disk fails
RAID Level 0+1	A mirrored array with segments that are RAID 0 arrays	4	Imaging applications	High input/output rates	Expensive

Note

Apple's macOS also supports a concatenated disk set, sometimes called "Just a Bunch of Disks" (JBOD). This combines several smaller disks into a single large disk. A concatenated disk set can create a mirrored or striped RAID set with disks that are of different sizes.

Networks

Due to the critical nature of connectivity today, redundant networks also may be necessary. A redundant network waits in the background during normal operations and uses a replication scheme to keep its copy of the live network information current. If a disaster occurs, the redundant network automatically launches so that it is transparent to users. A redundant network ensures that network services are always accessible.

Virtually all network hardware components can be duplicated to provide a redundant network. Some manufacturers offer switches and routers that have a primary active port as well as a standby failover network port for physical redundancy. If a special packet is not detected in a specific time frame on the primary port, the failover port automatically takes over. Load balancers can provide a degree of network redundancy by blocking traffic to servers that are not functioning. Also, multiple redundant switches and routers can be integrated into the network infrastructure.

Note

Some enterprises contract with more than one Internet service provider (ISP) for remote site network connectivity. In case the primary ISP is no longer available, the secondary ISP will be used. Enterprises can elect to use redundant fiber-optic lines to the different ISPs, each of which takes a diverse path through an area.

Just as virtualization has an impact on server redundancy, so too have virtual software defined networks (SDNs) impacted the need for network redundancy of physical devices. This is because the functionality that the SDN controller offers can increase network reliability and may lessen the need for redundant equipment. One technique that an SDN controller can use to increase network reliability is to set up multiple paths between the origin and the destination so that the network is not impacted by the outage of a single link.

Note

SDNs are covered in Chapter 7.

Power

Maintaining electrical power is essential when planning for redundancy. An *uninterruptible power supply (UPS)* is a device that maintains power to equipment in case of an interruption in the primary electrical power source.

There are two primary types of UPS. An *off-line UPS* is considered the least expensive and simplest solution. During normal operation, the equipment being protected is served by the standard primary power source. The off-line UPS battery charger is also connected to the primary power source to charge its battery. If power is interrupted, the UPS quickly (usually within a few milliseconds) begins supplying power to the equipment. When the primary power is restored, the UPS automatically switches back into standby mode.

An *on-line UPS* is always running off its battery while the main power runs the battery charger. An advantage of an on-line UPS is that it is not affected by dips or sags in voltage. An on-line UPS can clean the electrical power before it reaches the server to ensure that a correct and constant level of power is delivered to the server. The on-line UPS also can serve as a surge protector, which keeps intense spikes of electrical current, common during thunderstorms, from reaching systems.

A UPS is more than just a big battery, however. UPS systems also can communicate with the network operating system on a server to ensure that an orderly shutdown occurs. Specifically, if the power goes down, a UPS can complete the following tasks:

- Send a message to the network administrator's computer, or page or telephone the network manager, to indicate that the power has failed
- Notify all users that they must finish their work immediately and log off
- Prevent any new users from logging on
- Disconnect users and shut down the server

Because a UPS can supply power for a limited amount of time, some organizations turn to a *backup generator* to create power. Backup generators can be powered by diesel, natural gas, or propane gas to generate electricity. Unlike portable residential backup generators, commercial backup generators are permanently installed as part of the building's power infrastructure. They include automatic transfer switches that can, in less than one second, detect the loss of a building's primary power and switch to the backup generator.

Recovery Sites

Just as redundancy can be planned for servers, storage, networks, and power, it also can be planned for the entire site. A major disaster such as a flood or hurricane can inflict such extensive damage to a building that the organization must temporarily move to another location. Many organizations maintain redundant recovery sites in case this occurs. Three basic types of redundant sites are used: hot sites, cold sites, and warm sites.

- *Hot site.* A **hot site** is generally run by a commercial disaster recovery service that allows a business to continue computer and network operations to maintain business continuity. A hot site is essentially a duplicate of the production site and has all the equipment needed for an organization to continue running, including office space and furniture, telephone jacks, computer equipment, and a live telecommunications link. Data backups of information can be quickly moved to the hot site, and in some instances the production site automatically synchronizes all its data with the hot site so that all data is immediately accessible. If the organization's data processing center becomes inoperable, typically all data processing operations can be moved to a hot site within an hour.

- *Cold site*. A **cold site** provides office space, but the customer must provide and install all the equipment needed to continue operations. In addition, there are no backups of data immediately available at this site. A cold site is less expensive, but requires more time to get an enterprise in full operation after a disaster.
- *Warm site*. A **warm site** has all the equipment installed but does not have active Internet or telecommunications facilities, and does not have current backups of data. This type of site is much less expensive than constantly maintaining those connections as required for a hot site; however, the amount of time needed to turn on the connections and install the backups can be as much as half a day or more.

> ### Note 📎
>
> Businesses usually have an annual contract with a company that offers hot and cold site services with a monthly service charge. Some services also offer data backup services so that all company data is available regardless of whether a hot site or cold site is used.

A growing trend is to use cloud computing in conjunction with sites. Some organizations back up their applications and data to the cloud and then, if a disaster occurs, restore it to hardware in a hot, cold, or warm site. Other organizations also back up to the cloud but, instead of restoring to hardware at a site, they restore to virtual machines in the cloud, which then can be accessed from almost any location. This approach reduces or even eliminates the need for maintaining sites.

Data

An enterprise **data backup** is copying information to a different medium and storing it at an off-site location so that it can be used in the event of a disaster. Backing up data involves data backup calculations, using different types of data backups, and off-site backups.

Data Backup Calculations

Two elements are used in the calculation of when backups should be performed. The first is known as the **recovery point objective (RPO)**, which is defined as the maximum length of time that an organization can tolerate between backups. Simply put, RPO is the "age" of the data that an organization wants the ability to restore in the event of a disaster. For example, if an RPO is six hours, this means that an organization wants to be able to restore systems back to the state they were in no longer than six hours ago. To achieve this, it is necessary to make backups at least every six hours; any data created or modified between backups will be lost.

Related to the RPO is the **recovery time objective (RTO)**. The RTO is the length of time it will take to recover the data that has been backed up. An RTO of two hours means that data can be restored within that timeframe.

Types of Data Backups

One of the keys to backing up files is to know which files need to be backed up. **Backup utilities**, or software that can be used for backups, can internally designate which files have already been backed up by setting an *archive bit* in the properties of the file. A file with the archive bit cleared (set to 0) indicates that the file has been backed up. Any time the contents of that file are changed, the archive bit is set (to 1), meaning that this modified file now needs to be backed up. The archive bit is illustrated in Figure 14-6.

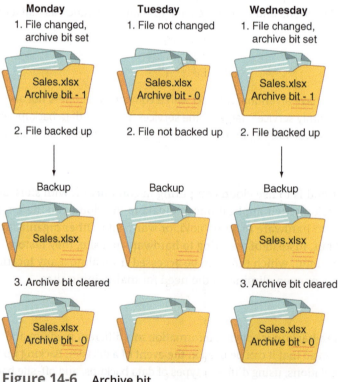

Figure 14-6   Archive bit

There are different types of backups, and three of the most common are summarized in Table 14-5. The archive bit is not always cleared after each type of backup; this provides additional flexibility regarding which files should be backed up.

Table 14-5 Types of data backups

Type of backup	How used	Archive bit after backup	Files needed for recovery
Full backup	Starting point for all backups	Cleared (set to 0)	The full backup is needed
Differential backup	Backs up any data that has changed since last full backup	Not cleared (set to 1)	The full backup and only last differential backup are needed
Incremental backup	Backs up any data that has changed since last full backup or last incremental backup	Cleared (set to 0)	The full backup and all incremental backups are needed

A more comprehensive backup technology than using full, differential and incremental backups is known as *continuous data protection (CDP)*. As its name implies, CDP performs continuous data backups that can be restored immediately, thus providing excellent RPO and RTO times. CDP maintains a historical record of all changes made to data by constantly monitoring all writes to the hard drive. It does this by creating a **snapshot** of the data, which is essentially a series of "reference markers" of the data at a specific point in time.

> **Note** 🖉
>
> Many CDP products even let users restore their own documents. A user who accidentally deletes a file can search the CDP system by entering the name of the document and then view the results through an interface that looks like a web search engine. Clicking the desired file then restores it. For security purposes, users may search only for documents for which they have permissions.

Off-Site Backups

Most security experts recommend that at minimum, a *3-2-1 backup* plan should be used. This plan says that there should always be *three* different copies of backups (that does not count the original data itself) on at least *two* different types of storage media or devices to store these backups (such as separate hard drives or network attached storage devices) and one of the backups should be stored at a different location (an **off-site backup**).

> **Note** 📎
>
> Home users should likewise follow the *3-2-1 backup* plan by always maintaining *three* different copies of your backups (that does not count the original data itself) by using at least *two* different types of media on which to store these backups (a separate hard drive, an external hard drive, a USB device, etc.) and store *one* of the backups off-site.

In the past, off-site backups were stored in a secure location like a local bank vault. Later, services became available in which a courier would routinely visit the enterprise and pick up magnetic tapes or hard drives that contained the most recent backups and transport them to the vendor's secure site. However, the **location selection** of where the media should be stored was often an issue, given that the **distance** may cause security concerns (transporting media over long distances increased the risk of accident or theft) or cause a delay in accessing the media in the event the data backup needed to be quickly restored.

> **Note** 📎
>
> One of the most secure off-site backup facilities is in a former salt mine facility in Kansas. It is 650 feet (198 meters) or about 45 stories beneath the surface. The facility is encased in solid stone and covers the equivalent of 35 football fields with over 1.7 million square feet (.52 million square meters) of storage space. The temperature and humidity levels remain constant year-round and protects against natural disasters (tornado, hurricane, flooding, etc.) as well as man-made disasters (explosion, fire, civil unrest, etc.). It serves as the single largest storage facility. for the movie and television film industry worldwide.

Today most organizations store their off-site backups using an online cloud repository. These online sites often use CDP to continually backup data and provide the highest degree of protection today to users. There are several Internet services available that provide features similar to these:

- *Automatic continuous backup.* Once the initial backup is completed, any new or modified files are also backed up. Usually the backup software "sleeps" while the computer is being used and performs backups only when there is no user activity. This helps to lessen any impact on the computer's performance or Internet speed.
- *Universal access.* Files backed up through online services can be made available to another computer.

- *Delayed deletion.* Files that are copied to the online server will remain accessible for up to 30 days before they are deleted. This allows a user to have a longer window of opportunity to restore a deleted file.
- *Online or media-based restore.* If a file or the entire computer must be restored, then this can be done online. Some services also provide the option of shipping backup files on a new media device such as an SSD or on optical media.

However, there are **legal implications** (consequences as determined by law) of off-site backups. The primary issue involves **data sovereignty**, which is the concept that data stored in a digital format is subject to the laws of the country in which the storage facility resides instead of being subject to the laws of the country in which the data originated or is used. For example, data that has been created in Florida and then uploaded to a cloud provider who stores the data on its server in Dublin would be subject to the laws of Ireland and not the United States.

Note

Data that has been backed up to cloud repositories may be physically stored almost anywhere. Google currently has 15 different locations in the Americas, Asia, and Europe in which user data is stored.

Data sovereignty has caused a patchwork of laws enacted primarily to protect the privacy of user data. Currently, the strictest data sovereignty laws are found in Germany, France, and Russia, which mandate that its citizens' data must be stored on physical servers within that country's physical borders. Certain United States federal agencies require their data be stored exclusively within the United States. In addition, conflicting court rulings have created different legal interpretations on data sovereignty. These relate to the concept of *jurisdiction*, or the power or right of a legal or political agency to exercise its authority over a territory. In 2013, a search warrant was served on Microsoft by the U.S. Department of Justice in a drug-trafficking investigation seeking emails sent by the defendant. Because those files were stored at one of Microsoft's data centers in Ireland, Microsoft refused to turn over the emails, arguing that they fall outside the investigators' jurisdiction. Two federal courts agreed with the Justice Department before a Court of Appeals sided with Microsoft in mid-2016. However, in early 2017, a federal magistrate judge handed down an opinion ordering Google to comply with a search warrant to produce foreign-stored emails.

Despite conflicting laws and court rulings, complying with data sovereignty is considered important. Organizations should identify a cloud services provider whose data center locations ensure that it fully complies with all applicable data sovereignty laws.

Environmental Controls

Q **Certification**

3.3 Given a scenario, implement secure systems design.

3.9 Explain the importance of physical security controls.

"An ounce of prevention is worth a pound of cure" is an adage that emphasizes taking proactive steps to avoid disruptions rather than just trying to recover from them. Just as using fault tolerance to build in redundancy is considered proactive, so too is having proper environmental controls that regulate the surroundings of the data. Preventing disruptions through environmental controls involves fire suppression, electromagnetic disruption protection, and proper configuration of HVAC systems.

Fire Suppression

Damage inflicted as a result of a fire is a constant threat to persons as well as property. **Fire suppression** includes the attempts to reduce the impact of a fire.

For a fire to occur, four entities must be present at the same time:

- A type of *fuel* or combustible material
- Sufficient *oxygen* to sustain the combustion
- Enough *heat* to raise the material to its ignition temperature
- A chemical *reaction* that is the fire itself

The first three factors form a fire triangle, which is illustrated in Figure 14-7. To extinguish a fire, any one of these elements must be removed.

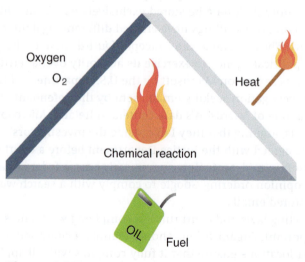

Figure 14-7 Fire triangle

Fires are divided into five categories. Table 14-6 lists the types of fires, their typical fuel source, how they can be extinguished, and the types of handheld fire extinguishers that should be used.

Table 14-6 Fire types

Class of fire	Type of fire	Combustible materials	Methods to extinguish	Type of fire extinguisher needed
Class A	Common combustibles	Wood, paper, textiles, and other ordinary combustibles	Water, water-based chemical, foam, or multipurpose dry chemical	Class A or Class ABC extinguisher
Class B	Combustible liquids	Flammable liquids, oils, solvents, paint, and grease, for example	Foam, dry chemical, or carbon dioxide to put out the fire by smothering it or cutting off the oxygen	Class BC or Class ABC extinguisher
Class C	Electrical	Live or energized electric wires or equipment	Foam, dry chemical, or carbon dioxide to put out the fire by smothering it or cutting off the oxygen	Class BC or Class ABC extinguisher
Class D	Combustible metals	Magnesium, titanium, and potassium, for example	Dry powder or other special sodium extinguishing agents	Class D extinguisher
Class K	Cooking oils	Vegetable oils, animal oils, or fats in cooking appliances	Special extinguisher converts oils to noncombustible soaps	Wet chemical extinguisher

Note

In Europe and Australia, Class K is known as Class F.

In a server closet or room that contains computer equipment, using a handheld fire extinguisher is not recommended because the chemical contents can contaminate electrical equipment. Instead, stationary fire suppression systems are integrated into the building's infrastructure and release fire suppressant in the room. These systems can be classified as *water sprinkler systems* that spray the area with pressurized water; *dry chemical systems* that disperse a fine, dry powder over the fire; and *clean agent systems* that do not harm people, documents, or electrical equipment in the room. Table 14-7 lists the types of stationary fire suppression systems.

Table 14-7 Stationary fire suppression systems

Category	Name	Description	Comments
Water sprinkler system	Wet pipe	Water under pressure used in pipes in the ceiling	Used in buildings with no risk of freezing
	Alternate	Pipes filled with water or compressed air	Can be used when environmental conditions dictate
	Dry pipe	Pipes filled with pressurized water and water is held by control valve	Used when water stored in pipes overhead is a risk
	Pre-action	Like dry pipe but requires a preliminary action such as a smoke detector alarm before water is released into pipes	Used in areas that an accidental activation would be catastrophic, such as in a museum or storage area for rare books
	Deluge	All sprinklers connected to system are opened at once instead of only those in the immediate area of the fire	Used for special hazards where a rapid fire spread may occur
Dry chemical system	Dry chemicals	Dry powder is sprayed onto the fire, inhibiting the chain reaction that causes combustion and putting the fire out	Used frequently in industrial settings and in some kitchens
Clean agent system	Low-pressure carbon dioxide (CO_2) systems	Chilled, liquid CO_2 is stored and becomes a vapor when used that displaces oxygen to suppress the fire	Used in areas of high voltage and electronic areas
	High-pressure carbon dioxide systems	Like the low-pressure CO_2 systems, but used for small and localized applications	Used in areas of high voltage and electronic areas
	FM 200 systems (Heptafluoropropane)	Absorbs the heat energy from the surface of the burning material, which lowers its temperature below the ignition point and extinguishes the fire	One of the least toxic vapor extinguishing agents currently used; can be used in computer rooms, vaults, phone rooms, mechanical rooms, museums, and other areas where people may be present
	Inergen systems	A mix of nitrogen, argon, and carbon dioxide	Used to suppress fires in sensitive areas such as telecommunication rooms, control rooms, and kitchens
	FE-13 systems	Developed initially as a chemical refrigerant, FE-13 works like FM 200 systems	Safer and more desirable if the area being protected has people in it

> **Note** 📎
>
> Clean agents can extinguish a fire through the reduction of heat, the reduction or isolation of oxygen, or inhibiting the chemical reaction.

Electromagnetic Disruption Protection

Computer systems, printers, and similar digital devices all emit electromagnetic fields, and often these can result in interference, called **electromagnetic interference (EMI)**. EMI is caused by a short-duration burst of energy by the source called an **electromagnetic pulse (EMP)**. Reducing or eliminating the unintentional generation, spread, and reception of electromagnetic energy is called *electromagnetic compatibility (EMC)*. The goal of EMC is the correct operation of different types of equipment that function in the same electromagnetic environment.

> **Note** 📎
>
> Electromagnetic spying, or picking up electromagnetic fields and reading the data that is producing them, is covered in Chapter 9.

One means of protecting against EMP is a **Faraday cage**. A Faraday cage is a metallic enclosure that prevents the entry or escape of an electromagnetic field. A Faraday cage, consisting of a grounded, fine-mesh copper screening, as shown in Figure 14-8, is often used for testing in electronic labs. In addition, lightweight and portable *Faraday bags* made of special materials can be used to shield cell phones and portable computing devices like tablets and notebook computers. Faraday bags are often used in crime scene investigations. Phones, tablets, or laptops found on-scene are placed in Faraday bags, thus eliminating inbound and outbound signals and preventing the devices from being remotely wiped of evidence.

HVAC

Data centers or rooms that house computer systems and network equipment typically have special cooling requirements. First, additional cooling is necessary due to the number of systems generating heat in a confined area. Second, data centers need more precise cooling. Electronic equipment radiates a drier heat than the human body, so the cooling requires different settings from those used in an office area. The control and monitoring of *heating, ventilation, and air conditioning (HVAC)* environmental systems that provide and regulate heating and cooling are important

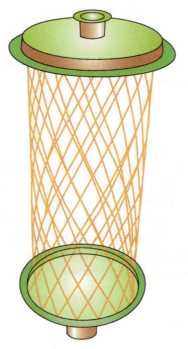

Figure 14-8   Faraday cage

for data centers. Temperatures and relative humidity (RH) levels that are too low or high, or that change abruptly, may result in unreliable components or even system failures. Controlling environmental factors also can reduce *electrostatic discharge (ESD)*, the sudden flow of electric current between two objects, which can destroy electronic equipment.

Note

Embedded systems that include HVAC environmental systems are covered in Chapter 10.

Because network equipment and servers in a data center generate large amounts of heat, a **hot aisle/cold aisle** layout can be used to reduce the heat by managing air flow. In a data center using a hot aisle/cold aisle layout, the server racks are lined up in alternating rows, with cold air intakes facing one direction and hot air exhausts facing the other direction. The rows composed of the rack fronts are the cold aisles and face air conditioner output ducts. The rows that are the backs of the racks where the heated exhausts exit are the hot aisles and generally face the air conditioner return ducts.

Incident Response

5.4 Given a scenario, follow incident response procedures.

5.5 Summarize basic concepts of forensics.

When an unauthorized incident occurs, an immediate response is necessary. This response often involves using forensics. It requires an incident response plan and following basic forensic procedures.

What Is Forensics?

Forensics, also known as **forensic science**, is the application of science to questions that are of interest to the legal profession. Forensics is not limited to analyzing evidence from a murder scene; it also can be applied to technology. As computers are the foundation for communicating and recording information, computer forensics uses technology to search for computer evidence of a crime, can attempt to retrieve information—even if it has been altered or erased—that can be used in the pursuit of the attacker or criminal. Digital evidence can be retrieved from computers, mobile devices, cell phones, digital cameras, and virtually any device that has memory or storage.

The importance of computer forensics is due in part to the following:

- *Amount of digital evidence*. Just as technology is widely used in all areas of life today, so too criminals use technology in the preparation and often the execution of their crimes. This leaves behind large volumes of digital evidence that can be retrieved through computer forensics.
- *Increased scrutiny by the legal profession*. No longer do attorneys and judges freely accept computer evidence. The procedures used in retrieving, transporting, and storing digital evidence are now held to the same standards as those used with physical evidence.
- *Higher level of computer skill by criminals*. As criminals become increasingly sophisticated in their knowledge of computers and techniques such as encryption, a computer forensics expert is often needed to retrieve the evidence.

Incident Response Plan

An **incident response plan (IRP)** is a set of written instructions for reacting to a security incident. Without an IRP, enterprises are at risk of being unable to quickly identify the attack, contain its spread, recover, and learn from the attack to improve defenses.

The six action steps to be taken when an incident occurs, called the **incident response process**, also make up the six elements of an IRP. These are listed in Table 14-8.

Table 14-8 Incident response process

Action step	Description
Preparation	Equipping IT staff, management, and users to handle potential incidents when they arise
Identification	Determining whether an event is actually a security incident
Containment	Limiting the damage of the incident and isolating those systems that are impacted to prevent further damage
Eradication	Finding the cause of the incident and temporarily removing any systems that may be causing damage
Recovery	After ensuring no threat remains, permitting affected systems to return to normal operation
Lessons learned	Completing incident documentation, performing detailed analysis to increase security and improve future response efforts

At a minimum, an IRP should contain the following information:

- *Documented incident definitions.* The IRP should provide clear descriptions of the types and categories of **documented incident definitions**, which outline in detail what is—and is not—an incident that requires a response.
- *Cyber-incident response teams.* A **cyber-incident response team** is responsible for responding to security incidents. In addition to technical specialists who can address specific threats, it should also include members who are public-relations employees and managers who can guide enterprise executives on appropriate communication. Each member should have clearly designated duties (**roles and responsibilities**) in the cyber-incident response team.
- *Reporting requirements/escalation.* The **reporting requirements/escalation** indicates to whom information should be distributed and at what point the security event has escalated to the degree that specific actions should be implemented.
- *Exercises.* It is important to test the IRP by conducting simulated **exercises** to make necessary adjustments. These can be conducted via tabletop exercises that simulate an emergency situation but are in an informal and stress-free environment.

Forensics Procedures

When responding to a criminal event that requires an examination using computer forensics, five basic steps are followed, which are similar to those of standard forensics. The steps are: secure the crime scene, preserve the evidence, establish a chain of custody, examine the evidence, and enable recovery.

Secure the Crime Scene

When an illegal or unauthorized incident occurs that involves a computer or other electronic device that contains digital evidence, action must be taken immediately. A delay of even a few minutes can allow the digital evidence to become contaminated by other users or give a person time to destroy the evidence. When an event occurs, those individuals in the immediate vicinity should perform damage control, which is the effort to minimize any loss of evidence. The steps in *damage control* include:

- Report the incident to security or the police.
- Confront any suspects (if the situation allows).
- Neutralize the suspected perpetrator from harming others (if necessary).
- Secure physical security features.
- Quarantine electronic equipment.
- Contact the cyber-incident response team.

Organizations should instruct their users that the cyber-incident response team must be contacted immediately. This team serves as first responders whenever digital evidence needs to be preserved. If the team is external to the organization, it is important that they accurately monitor their time (**track man hours**) and expenses from the start of the investigation. This information can be entered into evidence in court to prove that the cyber-incident response team was present from the beginning.

After the cyber-incident response team arrives, the first job is to secure the crime scene, which includes:

- The physical surroundings of the computer should be clearly documented (many forensics experts use a video camera to **capture video** of the entire process).
- Photographs of the area should be taken before anything is touched to help document that the computer was working prior to the attack. (Some defense attorneys have argued that a computer was not functioning properly and thus the attacker could not be held responsible for any damages.) The computer should be photographed from several angles, including the images displayed on the screen. Because digital pictures can be altered, some security professionals recommend that photographs be taken with a standard camera using film.
- Cables connected to the computer should be labeled to document the computer's hardware components and how they are connected.
- The team should take custody of the entire computer along with the keyboard and any peripherals. In addition, USB flash drives and any other media must be secured.
- The team must speak with those present (**witness interviews**) and everyone who had access to the system and document their findings, including what those people were doing with the system, what its intended functions were, and how it has been affected by the unauthorized actions.
- The length of time that has passed since the initial incident should be noted.

Preserve the Evidence

The next task is **preservation of the evidence**, or ensuring that important proof is not destroyed. Because digital computer evidence is very fragile, it can easily and unintentionally be altered or destroyed through normal use or even by turning on the computer. Only properly trained computer evidence specialists should process computer evidence so that the integrity of the evidence is maintained and can hold up in a court of law.

One of the first steps is for a **legal hold** to be issued. A legal hold is a notification sent from the legal team to employees instructing them not to delete electronically stored information or paper documents that may be relevant to the incident.

> **Note** 📎
>
> There is a tendency to issue legal holds that are too broad in scope. For example, to place a legal hold on all email correspondence may result in retaining thousands or millions of unneeded messages and associated attachments, while placing a legal hold on all portable devices requiring them to be locked away makes them useless to the organization. Instead, appropriate filters should be used to capture only data that is relevant.

The cyber-incident response team first captures any volatile data that would be lost when the computer is turned off. Any data such as contents of RAM, current network connections, logon sessions, **network traffic and logs** (recorded information about any network activity), and any open files must be captured and saved. Because different data sources have different degrees of preservation, an **order of volatility** must be used to preserve the most fragile data first. Table 14-9 lists the order of volatility.

Table 14-9 Order of volatility

Location of data	Sequence to be retrieved
Register, cache, peripheral memory	First
Random access memory (RAM)	Second
Network state	Third
Running processes	Fourth

Volatile data is the most difficult type of data to capture. Not only does it have a short "shelf life," but accessing information at a lower level also can destroy data at higher levels. For example, executing a command to retrieve from a running process can destroy the current contents of registers and RAM. Securing this volatile information can best be performed by using tools that allow **capturing the system image**, which is a snapshot of the current state of the computer that contains all current settings and data. In addition, capturing the current image on the screen by taking a **screenshot** is also important.

After retrieving the volatile data, the team next focuses on the hard drive. A *mirror image backup*, also called a *bit-stream backup*, is an evidence-grade backup because its accuracy meets evidence standards. A mirror image backup is not the same as a normal copy of the data. Standard file copies or backups include only files. Mirror image backups replicate all sectors of a computer hard drive, including all files and any hidden data storage areas. Using a standard copy procedure can miss significant data and can even taint the evidence. For example, copying a file may change file date information on the source drive, which is information that is often critical in a computer forensic investigation.

To guarantee accuracy, mirror image backup programs rely upon *hashing algorithms* as part of the validation process. The digest of the original source data is compared against the digest of the copied data to help create a snapshot of the current system based on the contents of the drives. This is done to document that any evidence retrieved came from the system and was not "planted" there.

Mirror image backups are considered a primary key to uncovering evidence because they create exact replicas of the crime scene. Defense teams often focus on mirror image backups; if they can prove that the copy of the data was contaminated or altered in any fashion, then any evidence gathered from the data will likely be dismissed. For this reason, mirror image backup software should be used only by trained professionals and done in a controlled manner, using hardware that does not influence the accuracy of the data it captures.

Note 📎

Mirror image backups can be performed using handheld devices that capture through the hard drive, USB, or FireWire connection. The devices are one-way data transfers that can only copy from the external data source to prevent inadvertent corruption. Some devices even use Global Positioning System (GPS) to specify the location of the data capture.

Establish the Chain of Custody

As soon as the team begins its work, it must start and maintain a strict chain of custody. The **chain of custody** documents that the evidence was always under strict control and no unauthorized person was given the opportunity to corrupt the evidence. A chain of custody includes documenting all the serial numbers of the systems involved, who handled and had custody of the systems and for what length of time, how the computer was shipped, and any other steps in the process. In short, a chain of custody is a detailed document describing where the evidence was at all times. Gaps in this chain of custody can result in severe legal consequences. Courts have dismissed cases involving computer forensics because a secure chain of custody could not be verified.

Examine for Evidence

After a computer forensics expert creates a mirror image of a system, the original system is secured and the mirror image examined to reveal evidence. This includes searching word processing documents, email files, spreadsheets, and other documents for evidence. The cache and cookies of the web browser can reveal websites that have been visited. The frequency of emails to particular individuals may be useful. In short, all exposed data is examined for clues. Depending on the volume of data, sometimes a big data analysis may be conducted on the data.

Hidden clues also can be mined and exposed. One source of hidden data is called *slack*. Windows computers use two types of slack. The first is RAM slack. Windows stores files on a hard drive in 512-byte blocks called sectors, and multiple sectors are used to make up a cluster. Clusters are made up of blocks of sectors. When a file that is being saved is not long enough to fill up the last sector on a disk (a common occurrence because a file size only rarely matches the sector size), Windows pads the remaining cluster space with data that is currently stored in RAM. This padding creates *RAM slack*, which can contain any information that has been created, viewed, modified, downloaded, or copied since the computer was last booted. Thus, if the computer has not been shut down for several days, the data stored in RAM slack can come from activity that occurred during that time. RAM slack is illustrated in Figure 14-9.

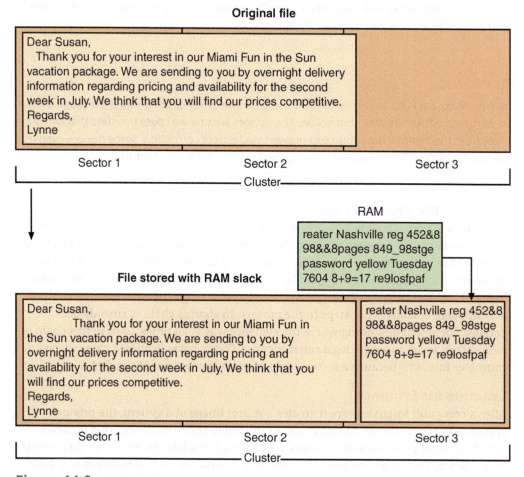

Figure 14-9 RAM slack

RAM slack pertains only to the last sector of a file. If additional sectors are needed to round out the block size for the last cluster assigned to the file, then a different type of slack is created. This is known as *drive file slack* (sometimes called *drive slack*) because the padded data that Windows uses comes from data stored on the hard drive. Such data could contain remnants of previously deleted files or data from the format pattern associated with disk storage space that has yet to be used by the computer. Drive file slack is illustrated in Figure 14-10. Both RAM slack and drive slack can hold valuable evidence.

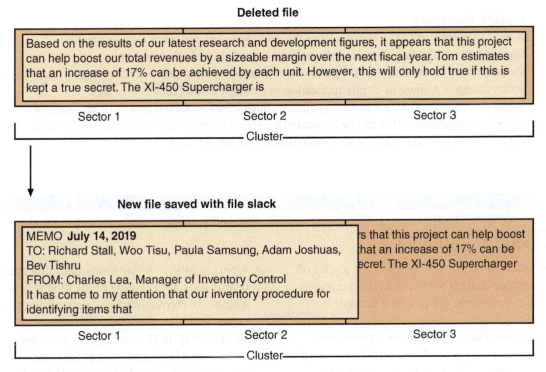

Deleted file

Based on the results of our latest research and development figures, it appears that this project can help boost our total revenues by a sizeable margin over the next fiscal year. Tom estimates that an increase of 17% can be achieved by each unit. However, this will only hold true if this is kept a true secret. The XI-450 Supercharger is

Sector 1   Sector 2   Sector 3
└─────────────────── Cluster ───────────────────┘

New file saved with file slack

MEMO **July 14, 2019**
TO: Richard Stall, Woo Tisu, Paula Samsung, Adam Joshuas, Bev Tishru
FROM: Charles Lea, Manager of Inventory Control
It has come to my attention that our inventory procedure for identifying items that

rs that this project can help boost that an increase of 17% can be ecret. The XI-450 Supercharger

Sector 1   Sector 2   Sector 3
└─────────────────── Cluster ───────────────────┘

Figure 14-10   Drive file slack

An additional source of hidden clues can be gleaned from *metadata*, or data about data. Although some metadata is user-supplied information, most metadata about a file is generated and recorded automatically without the user's knowledge. Examples of metadata include the file type, authorship, and edit history. Some electronic files may contain hundreds of pieces of such information.

Another example of metadata is the date and time that a file was created or accessed. The **time offset** is the amount of time added to or subtracted from Coordinated Universal Time (UTC) to arrive at the current "actual" (called *civil*) time, which may be affected by daylight savings time and different regional time zones. However, different operating systems store time values differently. Microsoft Windows uses a 64-bit time stamp that counts the number of 100 nanosecond intervals that have occurred since January 1, 1601 at 00:00:00 Greenwich Mean Time (GMT). The Linux operating system uses a 32-bit time stamp that recognizes the number of seconds that have occurred since January 1, 1970 at 00:00:00 GMT. It is important when examining evidence to be aware of how the particular operating system stores time and record its time offset.

Upon completion of the examination, a detailed report is required that lists the steps that were taken and any evidence that was uncovered in the forensic investigation.

Enable Recovery

A final analysis looks at recovering from the security event and what lessons can be learned from it. The forensics procedures have gathered **strategic intelligence**, or the collection, processing, analysis, and dissemination of intelligence for forming policy changes. A more in-depth application of strategic intelligence is **strategic counterintelligence**, which involves gaining information about the attacker's intelligence collection capabilities. This can be facilitated by **active logging**, or maintaining active logs regarding the reconnaissance activities conducted by the attacker.

Chapter Summary

- Business continuity, which is the ability of an organization to maintain its operations and services in the face of a disruptive event, involves the process of identifying exposure to threats, creating preventive and recovery procedures, and then testing the procedures to determine if they are sufficient. Business continuity planning (BCP) is the development of strategic plans that provide alternative modes of operation for business activities. One important tool in BCP is a business impact analysis (BIA), which analyzes the most important mission-essential function and identifies critical systems. Because privacy of data is of high importance today, many BIAs will also contain a privacy impact assessment, which is used to identify and mitigate privacy risks.

- Whereas business continuity planning and testing look at the needs of the business as a whole in recovering from a catastrophe, a subset of BCP focuses on continuity in the context of IT. In IT contingency planning, an outline of procedures that are to be followed in the event of a major IT incident or an incident that directly impacts IT is developed. Closely related is the disaster recovery plan (DRP), which is the plan for restoring IT functions and services to their former state. Disaster recovery planning involves creating, implementing, and testing disaster recovery plans. Most DRPs also cover a standard set of topics. One common topic is the sequence in which different systems are reinstated. Another common topic found in a DRP is identifying an alternative processing site to be used if a disaster makes the current location for processing data no longer available. Disaster exercises are designed to test the effectiveness of the DRP.

- One of the means to prevent certain issues from crippling an enterprise is to incorporate fault tolerance into IT systems. Because no IT system can ever be completely free of faults, the solution to fault tolerance is to build in redundancy, or the use of duplicated equipment to improve the availability of the system. Because servers play such a key role in a network infrastructure, the loss of a single server that supports a critical application can have a significant impact. A common approach is for the organization to design the network infrastructure so that multiple servers are incorporated into the network yet appear to users and applications as a single computing resource. One method of doing this is by using a server cluster, which is the combination of two or more servers that are interconnected to appear as one. A system of hard drives based on redundancy can be achieved through using a technology known as RAID (Redundant Array of Independent Drives), which uses multiple hard disk drives for increased reliability and performance.

- Most network hardware components can be duplicated to provide a redundant network. Maintaining electrical power is also essential when planning for redundancy. An uninterruptible power supply (UPS) is a device that maintains power to equipment in the event of an interruption in the primary electrical power source. Just as redundancy can be planned for servers, storage, networks, and power, it also can be planned for the entire site. A major disaster such as a flood or hurricane can inflict such extensive damage to a building that the organization may have to temporarily move to another location. Many organizations maintain redundant sites in case this occurs. Three basic types of redundant sites are used: hot sites, cold sites, and warm sites.

- The most important redundancy is that of the data itself, which is accomplished through data backups. A data backup is copying information to a different medium and storing it so that it can be used in the event of a disaster. The storage location is preferably at an off-site facility. The recovery point objective (RPO) is the maximum length of time that an organization can tolerate between backups. The recovery time objective (RTO) is the length of time it will take to recover data that has been backed up. There are three common types of backups: full backup, differential backup, and incremental backup. Another newer backup technology is continuous data protection (CDP), which performs continuous data backups that can be restored immediately, thus providing excellent RPO and RTO times. Today most organizations store their off-site backups using an online cloud repository. However, there are legal implications of off-site backups.

- Damage inflicted as a result of a fire is a constant threat, to persons as well as property. Fires are divided into five categories. In a server closet or room that contains computer equipment, using a handheld fire extinguisher is not recommended because the chemical contents can contaminate electrical equipment. Instead, stationary fire suppression systems are integrated into the building's infrastructure and release the suppressant in the room. These systems can be classified as water sprinkler systems that spray the area with pressurized water; dry chemical systems that disperse a fine, dry powder over the fire; and clean agent systems that do not harm people, documents, or electrical equipment in the room.

- Computer systems and similar devices emit electromagnetic fields that are produced by signals or the movement of data. A defense for shielding an electromagnetic field is a Faraday cage, which is a metallic enclosure that prevents the entry or escape of an electromagnetic field. Controlling environmental factors also can reduce electrostatic discharge (ESD), the sudden flow of electric current between two objects, which can destroy electronic equipment. The control and maintenance of HVAC systems that provide and regulate heating and cooling are important for data centers. Temperatures and relative humidity levels that are too low or high, or that change abruptly, may result in unreliable components or even system failures.

- Forensic science is the application of science to questions that are of interest to the legal profession. Computer forensics attempts to retrieve information that can be used in the pursuit of a computer crime. An incident response plan (IRP) is a set of written instructions for reacting to a security incident. Forensics procedures are carried out in five major steps. First, the crime scene is secured and documented. Next, the data is preserved by capturing any volatile data and then performing a mirror image backup along with hashing the image. A strict chain of custody, or documentation of evidence, must be established at all times. After a computer forensics expert creates a mirror image of a system, the original system is secured and the mirror image examined to reveal evidence. A final analysis looks at recovering from the security event and what lessons can be learned from it.

Key Terms

active logging
after-action report
alternative business practices
alternative processing site
backup utilities
business continuity
capture video
capturing the system image
chain of custody
cold site
containment
cyber-incident response team

data backup
data sovereignty
differential backup
disaster recovery plan (DRP)
distance
documented incident definitions
electromagnetic interference (EMI)
electromagnetic pulse (EMP)
eradication
exercises
failover

Faraday cage
fault tolerance
fire suppression
forensics (forensic science)
full backup
high availability
hot aisle/cold aisle
hot site
identification
identification of critical systems
impact on finance
impact on life
impact on property

impact on reputation
impact on safety
incident response plan (IRP)
incident response process
incremental backup
legal hold
legal implications
lessons learned
location selection
mean time between failures (MTBF)
mean time to recovery (MTTR)
mission-essential function
network traffic and logs
off-site backup

order of restoration
order of volatility
preparation
preservation of the evidence
privacy impact assessment
privacy threshold assessment
RAID (Redundant Array of Independent Drives)
recovery
recovery point objective (RPO)
recovery time objective (RTO)
redundancy

reporting requirements/escalation
roles and responsibilities
screenshot
single point of failure
snapshot
strategic counterintelligence
strategic intelligence
tabletop exercises
time offset
track man hours
warm site
witness interviews

Review Questions

1. Raul has been asked to help develop an outline of procedures to be followed in the event of a major IT incident or an incident that directly impacts IT. What type of planning is this?
   a. Disaster recovery planning
   b. IT contingency planning
   c. Business impact analysis planning
   d. Risk IT planning

2. Dilma has been tasked with creating a list of potential employees to serve in an upcoming tabletop exercise. Which employees will be on her list?
   a. All employees
   b. Individuals on a decision-making level
   c. Full-time employees
   d. Only IT managers

3. What is the average amount of time that it will take a device to recover from a failure that is not a terminal failure?
   a. MTTR
   b. MTBR

   c. MTBF
   d. MTTI

4. Which of the following is NOT a category of fire suppression systems?
   a. Water sprinkler system
   b. Wet chemical system
   c. Clean agent system
   d. Dry chemical system

5. Which of the following is NOT required for a fire to occur?
   a. A chemical reaction that is the fire itself
   b. A type of fuel or combustible material
   c. A spark to start the process
   d. Sufficient oxygen to sustain the combustion

6. An electrical fire like that which would be found in a computer data center is known as what type of fire?
   a. Class A
   b. Class B
   c. Class C
   d. Class D

7. Which level of RAID uses disk mirroring and is considered fault-tolerant?
   a. Level 1
   b. Level 2
   c. Level 3
   d. Level 4

8. What is the amount of time added to or subtracted from Coordinated Universal Time to determine local time?
   a. Time offset
   b. Civil time
   c. Daylight savings time
   d. Greenwich Mean Time (GMT)

9. What does the abbreviation RAID represent?
   a. Redundant Array of IDE Drives
   b. Resilient Architecture for Interdependent Discs
   c. Redundant Array of Independent Drives
   d. Resistant Architecture of Inter-Related Data Storage

10. Which of these is an example of a nested RAID?
   a. Level 1-0
   b. Level 0-1
   c. Level 0+1
   d. Level 0/1

11. A(n) _____ is always running off its battery while the main power runs the battery charger.
   a. secure UPS
   b. backup UPS
   c. off-line UPS
   d. on-line UPS

12. Which type of site is essentially a duplicate of the production site and has all the equipment needed for an organization to continue running?
   a. Cold site
   b. Warm site
   c. Hot site
   d. Replicated site

13. Which of the following can a UPS NOT perform?
   a. Prevent certain applications from launching that will consume too much power
   b. Disconnect users and shut down the server
   c. Prevent any new users from logging on
   d. Notify all users that they must finish their work immediately and log off

14. Which of these is NOT a characteristic of a disaster recovery plan (DRP)?
   a. It is updated regularly.
   b. It is a private document used only by top-level administrators for planning.
   c. It is written.
   d. It is detailed.

15. What does an incremental backup do?
   a. Copies all files changed since the last full or incremental backup
   b. Copies selected files
   c. Copies all files
   d. Copies all files since the last full backup

16. Which question is NOT a basic question to be asked regarding creating a data backup?
   a. What media should be used?
   b. How long will it take to finish the backup?
   c. Where should the backup be stored?
   d. What information should be backed up?

17. The chain of _____ documents that the evidence was under strict control at all times and no unauthorized person was given the opportunity to corrupt the evidence.
   a. forensics
   b. evidence
   c. custody
   d. control

18. What is the maximum length of time that an organization can tolerate between data backups?
    a. Recovery time objective (RTO)
    b. Recovery service point (RSP)
    c. Recovery point objective (RPO)
    d. Optimal recovery timeframe (ORT)

19. Margaux has been asked to work on the report that will analyze the exercise results with the purpose of identifying strengths to be maintained and weaknesses to be addressed for improvement. What report will she be working on?

    a. Identification of critical systems report
    b. Containment report
    c. Business continuity report
    d. After-action report

20. When an unauthorized event occurs, what is the first duty of the cyber-incident response team?
    a. To log off from the server
    b. To secure the crime scene
    c. To back up the hard drive
    d. To reboot the system

Hands-On Projects

Note

If you are concerned about installing any of the software in these projects on your regular computer, you can instead install the software in the Windows virtual machine created in the Chapter 1 Hands-On Projects 1-3 and 1-4. Software installed within the virtual machine will not impact the host computer.

Project 14-1: Using Windows File History to Perform Data Backups

The software backup utility File History is the Microsoft Windows 10 primary tool for backing up user files. Once configured, File History will automatically back up files to a storage device on a schedule. Note that File History is designed to back up user files and does not create a system image of the drive. In this project, you configure and use File History.

1. Connect an external storage device such as a large capacity USB flash drive or external hard drive to the computer as a repository for the backups (you cannot back up files to the same drive that contains the user files).
2. Click **Start** and then **Settings**.
3. Click **Update and Security**.
4. Click **Backup**.
5. Click **Add a drive**.
6. Select the drive that will be used for your backups.
7. Be sure that **Automatically back up my files** is set to **On**.

8. Click **More options**.

9. Click the down arrow under **Back up my files**. Note the default setting is **Every hour (default)**. Scroll through the other options. Which would you consider the best option for you? Why?

10. Click the down arrow under **Keep my backups**. Note the default setting is **Forever**. Scroll through the other options. What is the advantage to having backups kept indefinitely? What is the disadvantage? Which would you consider the best option for you? Why?

11. Look at the list of items that File History automatically backs up under **Back up these folders**. By default, File History is set to back up important folders in the user account's home folder, such as Desktop, Documents, Downloads, Music, Pictures, Videos, and so on. Do these folders include all your important data? Click **Add a folder** and add an additional folder to be part of the backup.

12. Under **Exclude these folders**, click **Add a folder** and select the folder that does not contain your important data such as **Downloads**.

13. Under **Related settings** click **See advanced settings**.

14. Click **Advanced settings**.

15. Under **Event logs**, click **Open File History event logs to view recent events or errors**. This allows you to see the log of any errors that may have occurred during the backup. Why is this important? How often should this log be viewed?

16. How easy is File History to use? Would you recommend it as a basic file backup software utility? Why or why not?

17. Close all windows.

Project 14-2: Entering and Viewing Metadata

Although most file metadata is not accessible to users, with some types of metadata, users can enter and change it. In this project, you view and enter metadata in a Microsoft Word document.

1. Use Microsoft Word to create a document containing your name. Save the document as **Metadata1.docx**.

2. Click the **File** tab on the Ribbon.

3. Click the drop-down arrow next to **Properties** and click **Advanced Properties**.

4. Enter the following information in the Advanced Properties dialog box:
   - Title—**Project 14-2**
   - Author—**Your name**
   - Category—**Computer Forensics**
   - Comments—**Viewing metadata in Microsoft Word**

5. Click **OK**.

6. Save **Metadata1.docx**.

7. Click the **File** tab on the Ribbon.

8. Click the drop-down arrow next to **Document Properties** and then click **Advanced Properties**.

9. Click the **Statistics** tab on the Properties dialog box and view the information it contains. How could a computer forensics specialist use this metadata when examining this file?

10. Click the **Custom** tab. Notice that there are several predefined fields that can contain metadata.

11. In the Name box, enter **Editor**.

12. Be sure the Type is set to **Text**.

13. Enter your name in the **Value** field, and then press **Enter**.

14. Select three predefined fields and enter values for each field. Click **OK**. Save your document when you are finished.

15. Close the Document Properties Information panel and return to **Metadata1.docx**.

16. Erase your name from **Metadata1.docx** so you have a blank document. However, this file still has the metadata. Enter today's date and save this as **Metadata2.docx**.

17. Close **Metadata2.docx**.

18. Reopen **Metadata2.docx**.

19. Click the **File** tab on the Ribbon.

20. Click the drop-down arrow next to **Properties** and click **Show Document Panel**.

21. What properties carried over to **Metadata2.docx** from **Metadata1.docx**, even though the content of the file was erased? Why did this happen? Could a computer forensics specialist use this technique to examine metadata, even if the contents of the document were erased?

22. Close all windows.

Project 14-3: Viewing Windows Slack and Hidden Data

RAM slack, drive slack, and other hidden data can be helpful to a computer forensics investigator. In this project, you will download and use a program to search for hidden data.

1. Use your web browser to go to **www.briggsoft.com** (if you are no longer able to access the program through this URL, use a search engine and search for "Directory Snoop").

2. Scroll down to the current version of **Directory Snoop** and click **Download Free Trial**.

3. Follow the default installation procedures to install Directory Snoop.

4. Launch Directory Snoop.

5. Depending on the file system on your computer, click **FAT Module** or **NTFS Module**.

6. Under Select Drive, click **C:** or the drive letter of your hard drive. If the **RawDisk Driver** dialog box appears, click **Install Driver** and then **OK** and then click the appropriate drive again.

7. Click to select a file and display its contents, preferably a user-created document (like a Microsoft Word file). Scroll down under **Text data** to view the contents that you can read.

8. Select other files to look for hidden data. Did you discover anything that might be useful to a computer forensics specialist?

9. Create a text document using Notepad. Click the **Start** button, enter **Notepad** in the Search box, and then click the link.
10. Enter the text **Now is the time for all good men to come to the aid of their country**.
11. Save the document on your desktop as **Country.txt**.
12. Exit Notepad.
13. Now delete this file. Right-click **Start**, click **File Explorer**, and then navigate to **Country.txt**.
14. Right-click **Country.txt** and then click **Delete**.
15. Now search for information contained in the file you just deleted. Return to **Directory Snoop**, click the top-level node for the **C:** drive, and then click the **Search** icon.
16. Click **Files**.
17. Enter **country** as the item that you are searching for.
18. Click **Search in slack area also**.
19. Click **Ok**. Was the program able to find this data? Why or why not?
20. Close all windows.

Project 14-4: Viewing and Changing the Backup Archive Bit

One of the keys to backing up files is to know which files need to be backed up. Backup software can internally designate which files have already been backed up by setting an archive bit in the properties of the file. A file with the archive bit cleared (set to 0) indicates that the file has been backed up. However, when the contents of that file are changed, the archive bit is set (to 1), meaning that this modified file now needs to be backed up. In this project, you view and change the backup archive bit.

1. Start Microsoft Word and create a document that contains your name and today's date.
2. Save this document as **Bittest.docx**, and then close Microsoft Word.
3. Click **Start**, enter **cmd**, and then press **Enter**. The Command Prompt window opens.
4. Navigate to the folder that contains **Bittest.docx**.
5. Type **attrib/?** and then press **Enter** to display the options for this command.
6. Type **attrib Bittest.docx** and then press **Enter**. The attributes for this file are displayed. The A indicates that the bit is set and the file should be backed up.
7. You can clear the archive bit like the backup software does after it copies the file. Type **attrib –a Bittest.docx** and then press **Enter**.
8. Now look at the setting of the archive bit. Type **attrib Bittest.docx** and then press **Enter**. Has it been cleared?
9. Close the Command Prompt window.

Case Projects

Case Project 14-1: Business Impact Analysis

Using your school or organization, develop a brief business impact analysis. What are the impacts? What is the mission-essential function? What are the critical systems? What is the single point of failure? Use the steps outlined earlier in the chapter. Share your plan with others if possible. What did you learn? Modify your plan accordingly.

Case Project 14-2: Continuous Data Protection (CDP)

Use the Internet to research continuous data protection (CDP). Identify three different solutions and compare their features. Create a table of the different features to make a side-by-side comparison. Which product would you consider to be the best solution for an enterprise environment? Why?

Case Project 14-3: Personal Disaster Recovery Plan

Create a one-page document of a personal disaster recovery procedure for your home computer. Be sure to include what needs to be protected and why. Also include information about where your data backups are stored and how they can be retrieved. Does your DRP show that what you are doing to protect your assets is sufficient? Should any changes be made?

Case Project 14-4: RAID

Use the Internet to research the hardware and costs of adding two levels of hardware RAID. Compare their features as well. Determine which current operating systems support which RAID levels. Create a chart that lists the features, costs, and operating systems supported.

Case Project 14-5: Forensics Tools

Search the Internet for websites that advertise computer forensic tools. Locate reviews of four tools. Create a chart that lists the tool, the type of data that it searches for, its features, the cost, etc. Which would you recommend if you could purchase only one tool and budget were not a concern?

Case Project 14-6: Online Backup Services

Several good online backup services can help make data backup easy for the user. Use a search engine to search for *online backup service reviews*, and select three different services. Research these services and note their features. Create a table that lists each service and compare their features. Be sure to also include costs. Which would you recommend? Why?

Case Project 14-7: Free Synchronization Storage

Although not as full-featured as online backup services, several free synchronization storage tools allow users to back up data by synchronization: when you place a file in a designated folder, it is automatically stored to the remote site. Several of these sites offer free storage from 5 GB to unlimited space. Use a search engine to search for *free cloud synch storage*, and select three different services. Research these services and note their features. Create a table that lists each product and compare their features. Be sure to include storage space limits. How do they compare to online backup services? Which would you recommend? Why?

Case Project 14-8: Lake Point Security Consulting

Lake Point Consulting Services (LPCS) provides security consulting and assurance services to over 500 clients across a wide range of enterprises in more than 20 states. A new initiative at LPCS is for each of its seven regional offices to provide internships to students who are in their final year of the security degree program at the local college.

Miles Comfort Coaches (MCC) is a regional charter bus service. Recently an IT employee was caught using the MCC network servers to store pirated software, yet because there were no incident response procedures in place, he was able to erase the software and destroy the evidence. MCC has approached LPSC to provide external forensics response services. However, several employees who are aware of the forensic analysis performed on the employee's computer have now raised concern about MCC scanning their computers. MCC has asked LPSC to help educate all employees about computer forensics.

1. Create a PowerPoint presentation that provides an explanation of computer forensics, why it is important, and the basic forensics procedures that should be used. The presentation should be 10 slides in length.
2. Comfort Coaches has asked that you draft a memo to all employees regarding the steps to take when they suspect that an incident has occurred that may require digital evidence to be secured. Write a one-page memo to Comfort Coaches' employees about these steps.

Case Project 14-9: Community Site Activity

The Information Security Community Site is an online companion to this textbook. It contains a wide variety of tools, information, discussion boards, and other features to assist learners. Go to **community.cengage.com/Infosec2** and click the *Join or Sign in* icon to log in, using your login name and password that you created in Chapter 1. Click **Forums (Discussion)** and click on **Security+ Case Projects (6th edition)**. Read the following case study.

The issue of data sovereignty remains contentious around the world. Do you agree that data stored in a digital format is subject to the laws of the country in which the storage facility resides? Or should it instead be subject to the laws of the country in which the data originated or is used? Should cloud service providers give to law enforcement agencies data stored on overseas servers when requested? What if their refusal resulted in a criminal being set free for lack of evidence? Record your answer on the Community Site discussion board.

References

1. "Economic loss from natural disaster events globally from 2000 to 2016 (in billion U.S. dollars)," *Statista*, retrieved Jun. 13, 2017, https://www.statista.com/statistics/510894/natural-disasters-globally-and-economic-losses/.
2. "Economic loss from natural disaster events globally in 2016, by peril (in billion U.S. dollars)," *Statista*, retrieved Jun. 13, 2017, https://www.statista.com/statistics/510922/natural-disasters-globally-and-economic-losses-by-peril/.
3. Hill, Logan, "The workday after tomorrow," *Bloomberg Businessweek*, Nov. 12-18, 2012, pp. 101–103.

CHAPTER 15

RISK MITIGATION

After completing this chapter, you should be able to do the following:

Explain how to manage risk

Describe strategies for reducing risk

List practices for mitigating risk

Describe common security issues

Today's Attacks and Defenses

Of all the technology devices that carry risk in the event of a successful attack, a heart pacemaker would certainly be at the top of the list. If someone could manipulate the configuration settings of a pacemaker, it could certainly result in death. It might be assumed that the manufacturers of these products would take whatever steps were necessary to ensure that their products were sound, stable, and above all secure.

Recently, security researchers examined how today's pacemaker systems work and the quality of their security.[1] The researchers looked at "pacemaker systems," which included pacemakers, Implantable Cardioverter Defibrillators (ICD), Pulse Generators, and Cardiac Rhythm Management (CRM) systems. There are four components to these pacemaker systems: the implanted pacemaker devices themselves, pacemaker programmers (not people but devices used to program or configure the pacemaker), home monitoring systems, and the supporting/update infrastructure. Each of these components is vital to the safe functioning of the pacemaker system.

What the security researchers found was that the architecture and technical implementation of these pacemaker systems across the four largest manufacturers was very similar. They suspected that is most likely due to the technical constraints associated with implanted heart technologies: the devices must be very small and very stable. But the researchers also found that some similarities show a "cross-pollination" between the pacemaker manufacturers. Because systems were so similar, the researchers hoped that the pacemaker manufacturers are working together to share security designs.

First the researchers acquired pacemaker programmers, home monitors, and pacemaker devices made by the four different manufacturers. Despite the fact that these devices are supposed to be controlled so that they are returned to the manufacturer after use by a hospital or physician, the researchers were able to easily purchase these devices online through online auction websites. And many of these devices were purchased at a very low cost: programmers cost $500-$3,000, home monitoring equipment $15-$300, and pacemaker devices $200-$3,000.

The researchers focused on seven different pacemaker programmers from four different manufacturers. They found that six pacemaker programmers store cleartext (not encrypted) data on the hard drives in the programmers, while one pacemaker programmer uses an unencrypted flash drive. The operating systems on the programmers are very old: DOS, Windows XP, and even OS/2, whose last update was 2001. All the programmers boot directly into the programming software without any authentication. And the pacemaker programmers do not authenticate to specific pacemaker devices: any pacemaker programmer can program any pacemaker from that specific vendor.

Older pacemaker programmers used a specialized device called a "telemetry wand" for communication between the programmer and the pacemaker device for transmitting signals. This telemetry wand requires that the programmer and the pacemaker system be within a short range of each other. Today's programmers from all vendors utilize longer range radio frequency (RF) communications in addition to the close proximity telemetry wand. All the pacemaker programmers first require the use of a telemetry wand in order to communicate with the pacemaker. The telemetry wand retrieves a token from the pacemaker device itself, which can be the device serial number or a static AES key. This token value is then used to create a session key before communications is passed from the telemetry wand to the RF communications. These session token generation algorithms are stored within the programmer logic and software. Once a proper session is established, the programmer can perform a variety of functions from a distance on the pacemaker, including altering how it functions.

The results of the study showed that pacemaker programmers can be easily purchased online, and the security of the programmers is essentially non-existent. And the programmers are using out-of-date software riddled with security issues: across the four programmers built by four different vendors, the researchers said that they discovered over 8,000 vulnerabilities associated with outdated libraries and software in the programmers. And programmers now can reach longer distances to manipulate a pacemaker. This all adds up to the technology devices that carry the highest risk in the event of a successful attack—heart pacemakers—being very vulnerable.

It is no surprise that the use of technology in the workplace can increase the overall business risk to an organization. At the very heart of information security, therefore, should be the concept of risk. Many different types of risk are encountered in an organization. Although some risks have a small impact and can be easily managed, other risks can threaten the very existence of the business. Because information security risks can be avenues through which an attacker could cripple an organization, they can never be taken lightly.

In this final chapter, you learn how organizations can establish and maintain security in the face of risk. First, you learn about risk and steps to manage it. Then, you study strategies for reducing risk and practices for mitigating risks. Finally, you explore troubleshooting common security issues that may increase risk.

Managing Risk

 **Certification**

1.2 Compare and contrast types of attacks.

5.3 Explain risk management processes and concepts.

At a basic level, *risk* may be defined as a situation that involves exposure to some type of danger. At a more advanced level, risk can be described as a function of threats, consequences of those threats, and the resulting vulnerabilities. The objective of managing risk is to create a level of protection that mitigates the vulnerabilities to the threats and reduces the potential consequences; that is, to reduce risk to an acceptable level.

Note

Risk is introduced and discussed in Chapter 1.

Managing risk involves knowing what threats are being faced and assessing those risks.

Threat Assessment

One of the first steps in managing risk is determining what threats an enterprise may be facing. This is known as a **threat assessment**. A threat assessment is a formal process of examining the seriousness of a potential threat as well as the likelihood that it will be carried out.

There are a multitude of different types of threats. Three broad categories of threats are:

- *Environmental.* An **environmental threat** is a threat related to the natural surroundings of an enterprise. This would include tornados, floods, and hurricanes.
- *Manmade.* A **manmade threat** is that of human origin, such as the vandalism of a wireless antenna.
- *Internal vs. external.* An **internal threat** comes from within an organization (such as employee theft), while an **external threat** is from the outside (like the actions of a hactivist).

Threats may be further divided into several threat classifications. These are listed in Table 15-1.

Table 15-1 Threat classifications

Threat category	Description	Example
Strategic	Action that affects the long-term goals of the organization	Theft of intellectual property, not pursuing a new opportunity, loss of a major account, competitor entering the market
Compliance	Following (or not following) a regulation or standard	Breach of contract, not responding to the introduction of new laws
Financial	Impact of financial decisions or market factors	Increase in interest rates, global financial crisis
Operational	Events that impact the daily business of the organization	Fire, hazardous chemical spill, power blackout
Technical	Events that affect information technology systems	Denial of service attack, SQL injection attack, virus
Managerial	Actions related to the management of the organization	Long-term illness of company president, key employee resigning

A threat assessment should also be used to determine the **asset value** or relative worth of an asset that is at risk. An *asset* is defined as any item that has a positive economic value. An organization has many different types of assets, including people (employees, customers, business partners, contractors, and vendors) and physical assets (buildings, automobiles, and plant equipment). In addition, the elements of IT are also key assets, such as data (all information used and transmitted by the organization, including employee databases and inventory records), hardware (computers, servers, networking equipment, and telecommunications connections), and software (application programs, operating systems, and security software). Some assets are of critical value while other assets are of lesser importance. The value of an asset is determined by how important the asset is to the goals of the organization, how much revenue it generates, how difficult it would be to replace, and the impact to the organization if the asset were unavailable.

Note

Asset identification is covered in Chapter 13.

In addition to examining assets within the enterprise, a **supply chain assessment** can also be useful. A *supply chain* is a network that moves a product from the supplier to the customer and is comprised of vendors that supply raw material, manufacturers who convert the material into products, warehouses that store products, distribution centers that deliver them to the retailers, and retailers who bring the product to the consumer. Today, supply chains are global in scope: manufacturers are often thousands of miles away and not under the direct supervision of the enterprise that is selling the product. Because these supply chains are so critical in today's environment, they should also be viewed as assets to the enterprise and their threats should also be cataloged.

Note

Supply chain infections are covered in Chapter 9.

Assessing threats should not be considered a straightforward exercise. Consider a threat actor who performs **device driver manipulation**, or altering a device driver for use in an attack. An attacker may use **shimming**, or transparently adding a small coding library that intercepts calls made by the device and changes the parameters passed between the device and the device driver. This **refactoring** (changing the design of existing code) can be very difficult to detect yet is a real threat.

Risk Assessment

Once the threats to assets have been determined, the risks that these assets face must be examined. Risk assessment involves testing, change management, privilege management, incident management, risk calculations, and representing risk information.

Testing

Assessing risk should include testing of technology assets to identity any vulnerabilities. This involves an automated software *vulnerability scan* through a system for any known security weaknesses, which then creates a report of those potential exposures. The results of the scans should be compared against baseline scans so that any changes (such as new open ports or added services) can be investigated. An *intrusive vulnerability scan* that attempts to actually penetrate the system to perform a simulated attack is preferable to a *non-intrusive vulnerability scan* that uses only available information to hypothesize the status of the vulnerability. In addition, a *penetration test* (*pentest*) that is designed to exploit any weaknesses in systems that are vulnerable should be performed. Instead of using automated software, penetration testing relies upon the skill, knowledge, and cunning of the tester, who is usually an independent contractor not associated with the organization.

> **Note**
>
> Vulnerability scans and penetration testing are covered in Chapter 13.

Due to the nature of penetration testing, it is important for **penetration testing authorization**, or permission to perform the test, to be obtained. In a similar fashion, **vulnerability testing authorization** should also be secured. The reasons authorization should be obtained include:

- *Legal authorization.* A penetration or vulnerability test is an attempt to break into a computer network. Because computer crime can carry severe penalties, a tester should have written and signed authority to conduct these tests.
- *Indemnification.* Penetration testing may result in disruption or even damage to data, or a third party may want to file a claim against the tester (such as a tester of a hospital system who corrupts patient information). Having prior authorization can help limit these risks.
- *Limit retaliation.* Although not common, there have been instances of penetration testers who have been successful in entering computer networks only to have technical support personnel "turn the tables" and instigate a retaliation attack against the tester.

Note

Many cloud providers allow customers to perform penetration tests and vulnerability scans on their cloud systems but only after a request has been formally approved.

Change Management

Change management refers to a methodology for making modifications to a system and keeping track of those changes. In some instances, changes to network or system configurations are made haphazardly to alleviate a pressing problem. Without proper documentation, a future change may negate or diminish a previous change or even unknowingly create a security vulnerability. Change management seeks to approach changes systematically and provide the necessary documentation of the changes.

Note

Because change management documentation provides a wealth of information that would be valuable to attackers, it must be secured. Limited copies should be available on a checkout-only basis, with clear markings that they should not be copied, distributed, or removed from the premises.

Although change management involves all types of changes to information systems, two major types of changes regarding security need to be properly documented. The first is any change in system architecture, such as new servers, routers, or other equipment being introduced into the network. These devices might be replacements for existing equipment or new equipment to expand the capability of the network. A detailed list of the attributes of the new equipment should be compiled, including:

- IP and MAC addresses
- Equipment name
- Equipment type
- Function
- Inventory tag number
- Location
- Manufacturer
- Manufacturer serial number
- Model and part number
- Software or firmware version

The second type of change is that of classification, which primarily refers to files or documents. The classification designation of government documents is typically

Top Secret, Secret, Confidential, and *Unclassified*. Many organizations do not have four levels of document classification; they may simply have Standard documents and Confidential documents. Whatever system of classification is used, it is important to clearly label documents that are not intended for public use.

Because the impact of changes can potentially affect all users, and uncoordinated changes can result in security vulnerabilities, many organizations create a *change management team (CMT)* to oversee the changes. Any proposed change (addition, modification, relocation, removal) of the technical infrastructure, or any component, hardware or software, including any interruption of service, must first be approved by the CMT. The team might typically be composed of representatives from all areas of IT, network security, and upper-level management. The duties of the CMT include:

- Review proposed changes
- Ensure that the risk and impact of the planned change is clearly understood
- Recommend approval, disapproval, deferral, or withdrawal of a requested change
- Communicate proposed and approved changes to coworkers

Privilege Management

A *privilege* is a subject's access level over an object, such as a user's ability to open a payroll file. *Privilege management* is the process of assigning and revoking privileges to objects; that is, it covers the procedures of managing object authorizations.

One element of privilege management is a periodic review of a subject's privileges over an object, known as *privilege auditing* (an *audit* is a methodical examination and review that produces a detailed report of its findings). Audits are usually associated with reviewing financial practices, such as an examination of an organization's financial statements and accounting documents to be sure that they follow the generally accepted accounting principles and mandated regulations. Auditing IT functions, particularly security functions, can be equally important. Audits serve to verify that the organization's security protections are being enacted and that corrective actions can be swiftly implemented before an attacker exploits a vulnerability.

Note

The roles of owners, stewards, and custodians are covered in Chapter 12.

It is important to periodically examine a subject's privilege over an object to ensure that the subject has the correct privileges. The correct privileges should follow the principle of least privilege in which users should be given only the minimal amount of privileges necessary to perform their job functions. This helps to ensure that users do not exceed their intended authorization. Most organizations have a written policy that mandates regular reviews. Figure 15-1 shows a sample review.

Review of User Access Rights

- User access rights will be reviewed on a regular basis by the IT Security Manager. External audits of access rights will be carried out at least once per year.

- The organization will institute a review of all network access rights every six months in order to positively confirm all current users. Any lapsed accounts that are identified will be disabled immediately and deleted within three business days unless they can be positively reconfirmed.

- The organization will institute a review of access to applications once per year. This will be done in cooperation with the application owner and will be designed to positively and deleted within three business days unless they can be positively reconfirmed. This review will be conducted as follows:

  1. The IT Security Manager will generate a list of users, by application.

  2. The appropriate list will be sent to each application owner who will be asked to confirm that all users identifier are authorized to have access to the application.

  3. The IT Security Manager will ensure that a response is received within 10 business days.

  4. Any user not confirmed will have his/her access to the system disabled immediately and deleted within three business days.

  5. The IT Security Manager will maintain a permanent record of list that were distributed to application owners, application owner responses, and a record of any action taken.

Figure 15-1   Sample user access rights review

Incident Management

When an unauthorized incident occurs, such as an unauthorized employee copying sensitive material, a response is required. *Incident response* can be defined as the components required to identify, analyze, and contain an incident. *Incident handling* is the planning, coordination, and communications functions that are needed to resolve an incident in an efficient manner. *Incident management* can be defined as the "framework" and functions required to enable incident response and incident handling within an organization. The objective of incident management is to restore normal operations as quickly as possible with the least possible impact on either the business or the users.

Note

One part of incident response procedures may include using forensic science and basic forensics procedures to properly respond to a computer forensics event. Computer forensic procedures are covered in Chapter 14.

Risk Calculation

An organization that can accurately calculate risk is better prepared to address the risk. For example, if a customer database is determined to be of high value and to have a high risk, the necessary resources should be used to strengthen the defenses surrounding that database.

There are two approaches to risk calculation. One is **qualitative risk calculation**. This approach uses an "educated guess" based on observation. For example, if it is observed that the customer database contains important information, it would be assigned a high asset value. Also, if it is observed that this database has been frequently the target of attacks, it would be assigned a high-risk value as well. Qualitative risk typically assigns a numeric value (1–10) or label (*High, Medium,* or *Low*) that represents the risk.

The second approach, **quantitative risk calculation**, is considered more scientific. Instead of arbitrarily assigning a number or label based on observation, the quantitative risk calculation attempts to create "hard" numbers associated with the risk of an element in a system by using historical data. In the example, if the customer database has a higher risk calculation than a product database, more resources would be allocated to protecting it.

Quantitative risk calculations can be divided into the *likelihood* of a risk and the *impact* of a risk being successful.

Risk Likelihood

Historical data is valuable in providing information on how likely it is that a risk will become a reality within a specific period of time. For example, when considering the risk of equipment failure, several quantitative tools can be used to predict the likelihood of the risk, including:

- *Mean time between failures (MTBF)*. MTBF calculates the average (*mean*) amount of time until a component fails, cannot be repaired, and must be replaced. It is a reliability term used to provide the amount of failures. Calculating the MTBF involves taking the total time measured divided by the total number of failures observed.

> **Note** 📎
>
> Although MTBF is sometimes used to advertise the reliability of consumer hardware products like hard disk drives, this value is seldom considered by the purchaser. This is because most consumer purchases are simply price-driven. MTBF is considered more important for industries than for consumers.

- *Mean time to recovery (MTTR)*. MTTR is the average amount of time that it will take a device to recover from a failure that is not a terminal failure. Although MTTR is sometimes called *mean time to repair* because in most systems this means replacing a failed hardware instead of repairing it, mean time to recovery is considered a more accurate term.

Note

MTBF and MTTR were covered in Chapter 14.

- *Mean time to failure (MTTF)*. MTTF is a basic measure of reliability for systems that cannot be repaired. It is the average amount of time expected until the first failure of a piece of equipment.
- *Failure in time (FIT)*. The FIT calculation is another way of reporting MTBF. FIT can report the number of expected failures per 1 billion hours of operation for a device. This term is used particularly by the semiconductor industry. FIT can be stated as *devices for 1 billion hours, 1 billion devices for 1000 hours each*, or in other combinations.

Other historical data for calculating the likelihood of risk can be acquired through a variety of sources. These are summarized in Table 15-2.

Table 15-2 Historical data sources

Source	Explanation
Police departments	Crime statistics on the area of facilities to determine the probability of vandalism, break-ins, or dangers potentially encountered by personnel
Insurance companies	Risks faced by other companies and the amounts paid out when these risks became reality
Computer incident monitoring organizations	Data regarding a variety of technology-related risks, failures, and attacks

Once historical data is compiled, it can be used to determine the likelihood of a risk occurring within a year. This is known as the **Annualized Rate of Occurrence (ARO)**.

Risk Impact

Once historical data is gathered so that the ARO can be calculated, the next step is to determine the impact of that risk. This can be done by comparing it to the monetary loss associated with an asset to determine the cost that represents how much money would be lost if the risk occurred.

> **Note** 📎
>
> When calculating the loss, it is important to consider all costs. For example, if a network firewall failed, the costs would include the amount needed to purchase a replacement, the hourly wage of the person replacing the equipment, and the pay for employees who could not perform their job functions because they could not use the network while the firewall was not functioning.

Two risk calculation formulas are commonly used to calculate expected losses. The **Single Loss Expectancy (SLE)** is the expected monetary loss every time a risk occurs. The SLE is computed by multiplying the Asset Value (AV) by the Exposure Factor (EF), which is the proportion of an asset's value that is likely to be destroyed by a particular risk (expressed as a percentage). The SLE formula is:

$$SLE = AV \times EF$$

For example, consider a building with a value of $10,000,000 (AV) of which 75 percent of it is likely to be destroyed by a tornado (EF). The SLE would be calculated as follows:

$$\$7,500,000 = \$10,000,000 \times 0.75$$

The **Annualized Loss Expectancy (ALE)** is the expected monetary loss that can be expected for an asset due to a risk over a one-year period. It is calculated by multiplying the SLE by the ARO, which is the probability that a risk will occur in a particular year. The ALE formula is:

$$ALE = SLE \times ARO$$

In this example, if flood insurance data suggests that a serious flood is likely to occur once in 100 years, then the ARO is 1/100 or 0.01. The ALE would be calculated as follows:

$$\$75,000 = 0.01 \times \$7,500,000$$

Representing Risks

There are different tools that can be used to represent risks identified through a risk assessment. A **risk register** is a list of potential threats and associated risks. These are sometimes rated both before and after controls have been implemented. Often shown as a table, a risk register can help provide a clear snapshot of vulnerabilities and risks. A sample risk register is shown in Figure 15-2.

Risk Id	Risks	Current risk			Status	Owner	Raised	Mitigation Strategies	Residual risk		
		Likelihood	Impact	Severity					Likelihood	Impact	Severity
Category 1: Projecty selection and project finance											
RP-01	Financial attraction of project to investors	4	4	15	Open		01-march	• Data collection • Information of financial capability of investor • Giving them assurance of tremendous future return.	4	3	12
RP-02	Availability of finance	3	4	12	Open		03-march	• Own resources • Commitment with financial institution • Exclusive management of investor.	3	3	9
RP-03	Level of demand for project	3	3	9	Open		08-march	• Making possibility and identification of low cost and best quality material • Eradication of extra expenses from petty balance.	2	3	6
RP-04	Land acquisition (site availability)	3	3	9	Open		13-march	• Making feasibilites • Analysis and interpretation of feasibilities • Possession and legal obligation of land.	2	2	4
RP-05	_High finance costs	2	2	4	Open		15-march	• Lowering operational expenses and transportation expenses • Proper management of current expenses.	1	2	2

Figure 15-2   Risk register

Another tool is called a *risk matrix*. This is a visual color-coded tool that lists the impact and likelihood of risks. Figure 15-3 illustrates a risk matrix.

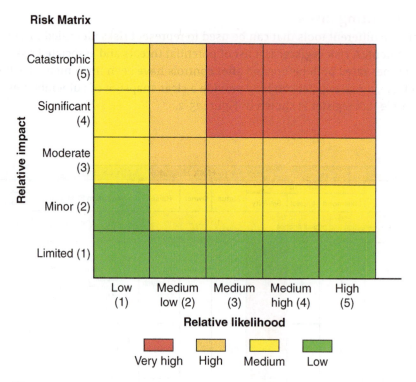

Figure 15-3 Risk matrix

Strategies for Reducing Risk

 **Certification**

3.1 Explain use cases and purpose for frameworks, best practices and secure configuration guides.

3.8 Explain how resiliency and automation strategies reduce risk.

5.7 Compare and contrast various types of controls.

What strategies can help reduce risk for an enterprise? Several approaches are used to reduce risk. These include using control types, distributing allocation, and implementing automation.

Using Control Types

A **security control** is any device or process that is used to reduce risk. That is, it attempts to limit exposure to a danger. There are two levels of security controls. **Administrative controls** are the processes for developing and ensuring that policies and procedures are carried out. In other words, administrative controls are the actions that users *may do, must do,* or *cannot do.* The second class consists of security controls carried out or managed by devices, called **technical controls**.

> **Note** 📎
>
> Remember from Chapter 1 that the goal of security is not to eliminate all risk, simply because that is not possible. Instead, the goal in designing and implementing controls is to reach a balance between achieving an acceptable level of risk, minimizing losses, and an acceptable level of expense. Some assets, however, must be protected irrespective of the perceived risk. For example, controls based upon regulatory requirements may be required regardless of risk.

The subtypes of controls that can be either technical or administrative (sometimes called *activity phase controls*) may be classified as follows:

- *Deterrent controls.* A **deterrent control** attempts to discourage security violations before they occur.
- *Preventive controls.* A **preventive control** works to prevent the threat from coming in contact with the vulnerability.
- *Physical controls.* A **physical control** implements security in a defined structure and location.
- *Detective controls.* A **detective control** is designed to identify any threat that has reached the system.
- *Compensating controls.* A **compensating control** is a control that provides an alternative to normal controls that for some reason cannot be used.
- *Corrective controls.* A control that is intended to mitigate or lessen the damage caused by the incident is called a **corrective control**.

These controls are summarized in Table 15-3.

Table 15-3 Activity phase controls

Control name	Description	When it occurs	Example
Deterrent control	Discourage attack	Before attack	Signs indicating that the area is under video surveillance
Preventive control	Prevent attack	Before attack	Security awareness training for all users
Physical control	Prevent attack	Before attack	Fences that surround the perimeter
Detective control	Identify attack	During attack	Installing motion detection sensors
Compensating control	Alternative to normal control	During attack	An infected computer is isolated on a different network
Corrective control	Lessen damage from attack	After attack	A virus is cleaned from an infected server

> **Note**
>
> Security professionals do not universally agree on the nomenclature and classification of activity phase controls. Some researchers divide controls into administrative, logical, and physical. Other security researchers specify up to18 different activity phase controls.

Distributing Allocation

Another approach is to modify the *response* to the risk instead of merely accepting the risk. **Distributive allocation** refers to "spreading" the risk. Ways to distribute risk include:

- *Transference*. Risk transference makes a third party responsible for the risk.
- *Risk avoidance*. Risk avoidance involves identifying the risk and making the decision to not engage in the activity.
- *Mitigation*. Risk mitigation is the attempt to address the risk by making it less serious.

Implementing Technology

Risk is often introduced through human error. A misconfigured security setting or a door left ajar can result in a risk to be exploited. Using technology as a strategy for reducing risk can minimize these errors. Implementing technology involves using automation, images and templates, and non-persistence tools.

Automation

Change is the driving factor in enterprises today. What was commonplace just a few years ago can be quickly replaced by the latest technology. Enterprises that cannot quickly adapt to this changing environment find themselves left behind and struggling to catch up.

Most enterprise data centers have workflows that are dynamic processes that continuously change based on the current demands of the market and the pressures of stiff competition. Data centers must be able to quickly adapt as new data sources are identified and utilized. This demand for continual change results in existing work environments that require manual effort. However, relying on human effort in a quickly changing environment is an open door for mistakes and adding risk.

The solution is automation. **Automation** can be defined as that which replaces human physical activity. It is self-acting, self-operating, and self-regulating. Using technology to automate IT processes is called **automated courses of action**. IT automation can also provide **scalability**, or the ability to continue to function as the size or volume of the enterprise data center expands to meet the growing demands. It can also provide **elasticity**, which is the ability to revert to its former size after expanding.

In addition, IT automation can provide **continuous monitoring**, or sustained and continual surveillance. Continuous monitoring allows for a continuous stream of near real-time views of the state of risk to clients, security devices, networks, cloud devices, applications and data. Continuous monitoring can provide valuable insight into assessing existing security controls.

> **Note** 📎
>
> Continuous monitoring is also used by regulatory agencies to ensure compliance. The Federal Information Security Management Act (FISMA) originally required annual audits to ensure that organizations are in compliance with federal regulations. Revised guidelines call on agencies and departments to provide FISMA auditors with real-time information about the state of their systems and networks, which can be provided through continuous monitoring.

Secure configuration guides are available to help IT security personnel configure hardware devices and software to repel attacks. **Vendor-specific guides** are useful for configuring web servers, operating systems, applications servers, and network infrastructure devices, and **general-purpose guides** can also be beneficial but are more "generic" in scope. Yet how can an enterprise know that these secure configuration guides have been followed?

The answer is another benefit of automation called **configuration validation**, or reviewing the configuration of systems to determine if security settings are correct. Many configuration validation tools are web-based and can generate reports based on the current configuration settings of products using a common interface. Figure 15-4 shows a report from a configuration validation tool.

▽ Systems

System	ConfigStore Name	Config. Item	Field name (Ref.)	Operator	Value Low	Value High	Comparison Value	Compliance	Compliant (1=Yes, 0=No, ' '=Not valuated)
B4X 0020270862	RFCDES_TYPE_3_CHECK	PMIB4X001	RFCDEST	Contains	*	#	PMIB4X001	Yes	1
			LOGON_CLIENT	Ignore	#	#	001	Not valuated	
			LOGON_USER	Ignore	#	#	PIRWBUSER	Not valuated	
			PASSWORD_STATUS	Ignore	#	#	S	Not valuated	
			HOST_NAME	Ignore	#	#	ldcib4x	Not valuated	
			SYSTEM_IDENTIFIER	Ignore	#	#	B4X	Not valuated	
			SYSTEM_NUMBER	Ignore	#	#	#	Not valuated	
			TRUSTED_SYSTEM	Ignore	#	#	#	Not valuated	
			CV_USER_PROFILE_RESULT	Not equal	CRITICAL_USER_PROFILE	#	CRITICAL_USER_PROFILE	No	0
			CV_CONFIG_DEST_LONG_SID	Ignore	#	#	B4X	Not valuated	
			CV_REMARK	Ignore	#	#	Profile: SAP_ALL	Not valuated	

Figure 15-4   Configuration validation report
Source: SAP

Images and Templates

Risk is introduced when variances to standards are allowed, such as when an IT security technician configures the host-based firewall settings for one user to allow a specialized application to run. Standardization can prevent these variances. A **master image** is a copy of a properly configured and secured computer software system that can be replicated to other computers. This eliminates the need for configuring individualized security settings, which often leads to errors. In general terms, a template is a form, mold, or pattern that is used as a guide to making something, such as a ruler serving as a template to draw a straight line. A computer **template** is a type of document in which the standardized content has already been created so that the user needs only to enter specialized and variable components. Using a template reduces the amount of data to be entered and helps minimize errors that could introduce risk.

Non-Persistence Tools

Persistence is a continued or prolonged state, whereas *non-persistence* is temporary. Often in IT, it is advisable to "start from a clean slate" so that any unwanted data or changes are not continued. For example, a non-persistent desktop is a virtual desktop that does not keep any user data, personalized settings, or any other changes that have been made, so that each time an end user logs on, the user receives a "fresh" or generic virtual desktop image. **Non-persistence tools** are those that are used to ensure that unwanted data is not carried forward, but instead a clean image is used. Table 15-4 lists several common non-persistence tools that can reduce risk.

Table 15-4 Non-persistence tools

Tool name	Description	How used
Live boot media	A "lightweight" bootable image on a USB flash drive or optical media	Temporarily creates a secure, non-persistent client for use on a public computer for accessing a secure remote network
Revert to known state	Restore device to a previous secure condition	Used to reset a device to a stable and secure setting
Rollback to known configuration	Undo recent changes that cause errors or weaken security	Can restore a device to a previous configuration
Snapshot	An instance (image) of a virtual machine	Used to replace a corrupted or infected virtual machine

Note

The option "Start Windows using Last Known Good Configuration" was available through Microsoft Windows 7 on bootup; however, it is no longer available under subsequent versions.

Practices for Reducing Risk

Certification

5.1 Explain the importance of policies, plans, and procedures related to organizational security.

In addition to the overall strategies for reducing risk, there are several practices that can be used. These include using security policies, awareness and training, agreements, and personnel management.

Security Policies

An important means of reducing risks is through a security policy. It is important to know the definition of a policy, what a security policy is, and the different types of policies that are used.

Definition of a Policy

Several terms are used to describe the "rules" that a user follows in an organization. A *standard* is a collection of requirements specific to the system or a procedure that must be met by everyone. For example, a standard might describe how to secure a computer at home that remotely connects to the organization's network. Users must follow this standard if they want to be able to connect. A *guideline* is a collection of suggestions that should be implemented. These are not requirements to be met but are strongly recommended. A *policy* is a document that outlines specific requirements or rules that must be met.

A policy generally has these characteristics:

- Communicates a consensus of judgment
- Defines appropriate behavior for users
- Identifies what tools and procedures are needed
- Provides directives for Human Resources action in response to inappropriate behavior
- May be helpful if it is necessary to prosecute violators

> **Note**
>
> A policy is considered the correct tool for an organization to use when establishing security because a policy applies to a wide range of hardware or software (it is not a standard) and is required (it is not just a guideline).

What Is a Security Policy?

If the question "What is a security policy?" were posed to both a manager and a security technician, the answers would likely be different. A manager might say that a security policy is as a set of management statements that defines an organization's philosophy of how to safeguard its information. A security technician might respond that a security policy is the rules for computer access and specific information on how these will be carried out. These two responses are not conflicting but are actually complementary and reflect the different views of a security policy.

At its core, a **security policy** is a written document that states how an organization plans to protect the company's information technology assets. The policy outlines the protections that should be enacted to ensure that the organization's assets face minimal risks. A security policy, along with the accompanying procedures, standards, and guidelines, is key to implementing information security in an organization. Having a written security policy empowers an organization to take appropriate action to safeguard its data.

An organization's information security policy can serve several functions:

- It can be an overall intention and direction, formally expressed by the organization's management. A security policy is a vehicle for communicating an organization's information security culture and acceptable information security behavior.
- It details specific risks and how to address them, and so provides controls that executives can use to direct employee behavior.
- It can help to create a security-aware organizational culture.
- It can help to ensure that employee behavior is directed and monitored in compliance with security requirements.

An effective security policy must carefully balance two key elements: trust and control. There are three approaches to trust: trust everyone all of the time (the easiest model to enforce because there are no restrictions, but is impractical because it leaves systems vulnerable to attack); trust no one at any time (this model is the most restrictive, but is also impractical, for few individuals would work for an organization that did not trust its employees); and trust some people some of the time (this approach exercises caution in the amount of trust given, for access is provided as needed, with technical controls to ensure the trust is not violated).

A security policy attempts to provide the right amount of trust by balancing *no trust* and *too much trust*. It does this by trusting some of the people some of the time and providing the right level of access to resources for the employees to perform their job functions—but no more than that. Deciding on the level of trust may be a delicate matter; too much trust may lead to security problems, while too little trust may make it difficult to find and keep good employees.

Control is the second element that must be balanced. One of the goals of a security policy is to implement control. Deciding on the level of control for a specific policy is not always straightforward. The security needs and the culture of the organization play a major role when deciding what level of control is appropriate. If policies are too restrictive or too hard to implement and comply with, employees will either ignore them or find a way to circumvent the controls. Management must commit to the proper level of control that a security policy should address.

> **Note** 📎
>
> The purpose of security policies is not to serve as a motivational tool to force users to practice safe security techniques. The results from research have indicated that the specific elements of a security policy do not have an impact on user behavior. Relying on a security policy as the exclusive defense mechanism will not provide adequate security for an organization.

Types of Security Policies

Because a security policy is so comprehensive and is often detailed, most organizations choose to break the security policy down into smaller "subpolicies" that can be more easily referred to. The term *security policy* then becomes an umbrella term for all the subpolicies included within it.

Many types of security policies exist. Some of these types are listed in Table 15-5.

Table 15-5 Types of security policies

Name of security policy	Description
Acceptable encryption policy	Defines requirements for using cryptography
Antivirus policy	Establishes guidelines for effectively reducing the threat of computer viruses on the organization's network and computers
Audit vulnerability scanning policy	Outlines the requirements and provides the authority for an information security team to conduct audits and risk assessments, investigate incidents, ensure conformance to security policies, or monitor user activity
Automatically forwarded email policy	Prescribes that no email will be automatically forwarded to an external destination without prior approval from the appropriate manager or director
Database credentials coding policy	Defines requirements for storing and retrieving database user names and passwords
Demilitarized zone (DMZ) security policy	Defines standards for all networks and equipment located in the DMZ
Email policy	Creates standards for using corporate email
Email retention policy	Helps employees determine what information sent or received by email should be retained and for how long
Extranet policy	Defines the requirements for third-party organizations to access the organization's networks
Information sensitivity policy	Establishes criteria for classifying and securing the organization's information in a manner appropriate to its level of security
Router security policy	Outlines standards for minimal security configuration for routers and switches
Server security policy	Creates standards for minimal security configuration for servers
VPN security policy	Establishes requirements for remote access virtual private network (VPN) connections to the organization's network
Wireless communication policy	Defines standards for wireless systems used to connect to the organization's networks

In addition to the security policies listed in Table 15-5, most organizations have security policies that address acceptable use, personal email, and social media networks and applications.

Acceptable Use Policy (AUP)

An **acceptable use policy (AUP)** is a policy that defines the actions users may perform while accessing systems and networking equipment. The *users* are not limited to employees; the term can also include vendors, contractors, or visitors, each with different privileges. AUPs typically cover all computer use, including mobile devices.

An AUP may have an overview regarding what is covered by the policy, as in the following sample:

> *Internet/intranet/extranet-related systems, including but not limited to computer equipment, software, operating systems, storage media, network accounts providing electronic mail, and web browsing, are the property of the Company. These systems are to be used for business purposes in serving the interests of the company, and of our clients and customers, in the course of normal operations. Personal use is strictly prohibited.*

The AUP usually provides explicit prohibitions regarding security and proprietary information:

> *Keep passwords secure and do not share accounts. Authorized users are responsible for the security of their passwords and accounts. System-level passwords should be changed every 30 days; user-level passwords should be changed every 45 days.*

> *All computers and laptops should be secured with a password-protected screensaver with the automatic activation feature set at 10 minutes or less, or by logging off when the host is unattended.*

> *Postings by employees from a Company device or using a Company email address to personal blogs or personal social media accounts is prohibited.*

Unacceptable use may also be outlined by the AUP, as in the following sample:

> *The following actions are not acceptable ways to use the system:*
>
> - *Introduction of malicious programs into the network or server*
> - *Revealing your account password to others or allowing use of your account by others, including family and other household members when work is being done at home*
> - *Using the Company's computing asset to actively engage in procuring or transmitting material that is in violation of sexual harassment or hostile workplace laws in the user's local jurisdiction*
> - *Any form of harassment via email, telephone, or paging, whether through language, frequency, or size of messages*
> - *Unauthorized use or forging of email header information*

Acceptable use policies are generally considered to be the most important information security policies. It is recommended that all organizations, particularly educational institutions and government agencies, have an AUP in place.

Personal Email Policy

A **personal email policy** generally covers three important elements: using company email to send personal email messages, accessing personal email at a place of employment, and forwarding company emails to a personal email account. Here are some elements of a sample personal email policy:

- *Email accounts are solely for the purpose of conducting Company business. Only users who have been appropriately authorized, for Company purposes, may use Company email accounts.*
- *Email is to be used for Company business only. Company confidential information must not be shared outside of the Company, without authorization, at any time. Employees must not conduct personal business using a Company computer or Company email.*
- *The Company owns any communication sent via email or that is stored on company equipment. Management and other authorized staff have the right to access any material in your email or on your computer at any time. Employees should not consider electronic communication to be private.*
- *Forwarding Company emails to private email accounts is strictly prohibited. Copying Company emails ("CC") to private email accounts is strictly prohibited.*

Note

Many recent high-profile security incidents, particularly relating to the federal government, have occurred because users have forwarded personal emails to private email accounts, in violation of stated personal email policies. Using a personal email account for any type of storage of enterprise emails should be strictly prohibited.

Social Media Policy

Grouping individuals and organizations into clusters or groups based on some sort of affiliation is called a **social media network**. Although physical social networking is achieved in person at schools or work, social networking is increasingly performed online. The websites that facilitate linking individuals with common interests like hobbies, religion, politics, or school contacts are called *social media sites* and function as an online community of users. A user who is granted access to a social media site can read the profile pages of other members and interact with them and can read information posted by others and share documents, photos, and videos. The popularity of online social media sites has skyrocketed.

> **Note** 🖇
>
> As of 2017, there were over 1.9 billion monthly active Facebook users. The highest traffic on Facebook occurs between 1:00 to 3:00 PM, and Thursdays and Fridays are busier than any other days of the week. The average time spent per Facebook visit is 20 minutes per visit. Every 60 seconds on Facebook 510,000 comments are posted, 293,000 statuses are updated, and 136,000 photos are uploaded. It is estimated that there are 83 million fake profiles on Facebook.[2]

For users, social media sites carry risks. These risks include:

- *Personal data can be used maliciously.* Users post personal information on their pages for others to read, such as birthdays, where they live, their plans for the upcoming weekend, and the like. However, attackers can use this information for a variety of malicious purposes. For example, knowing that a person is on vacation could allow a burglar to break into an empty home. Providing too much personal information could be used in identity theft. And even personal information that appears to be harmless can be very valuable. For example, the challenge password question when resetting a password, such as *What high school did you attend?* can easily be gathered from a user's social media page.

- *Users may be too trusting.* Attackers often join a social media site and pretend to be part of the network of users. After several days or weeks, users begin to feel they know the attackers and may start to provide personal information or click on embedded links provided by the attacker that loads malware onto the user's computer.

- *Accepting friends may have unforeseen consequences.* Some social media users readily accept any "friend" request they receive, even if they are not familiar with that person. This can result in problems, because whoever is accepted as a friend may then be able to see not only all that user's personal information, but also the personal information of her friends.

- *Social media security is lax or confusing.* Because social media sites by design are intended to share information, these sites have often made it too easy for unauthorized users to view other people's information. To combat this problem, many sites change their security options on a haphazard basis, making it difficult for users to keep up with the changes.

Likewise, for enterprises, employee use of social media can also pose risks. It is important that a **social media policy** that outlines acceptable employee use of social media be enforced. The reasons for a social media policy and its elements include:

- *Setting standards for employee use.* A social media policy gives the employer the opportunity to establish clear guidelines and expectations for employees. With policy guidelines in place, employees can exercise creativity and show their personalities on social media while representing the enterprise.

- *Defining limitations.* By its very nature, social media is designed for individuals to freely and frequently post personal information and opinions. However, this is the opposite of what most enterprises permit. Often employees may not understand what is and is not appropriate to say online. A policy helps define what actions are permissible.
- *Protecting the enterprise's reputation.* A social media policy lowers the risk of legal issues and helps protect the enterprise by outlining to employees the potential risks and the steps to take in the event of an adverse action.
- *Creating consistency across channels.* A single inappropriate social media post may conflict with the "brand" an enterprise is attempting to convey or put an enterprise's reputation in serious jeopardy. A social media policy can help create consistency across different social media channels.

Awareness and Training

One of the key defenses in information security is to provide security awareness and training to users (sometimes called **continuing education**). All computer users in an organization have a shared responsibility to protect the assets of the organization. It cannot be assumed that all users have the knowledge and skill to protect these assets. Instead, users need training in the importance of securing information, the roles that they play in security, and the steps they need to take to prevent attacks. And because new attacks appear regularly, and new security vulnerabilities are continuously being exposed, user awareness and training must be ongoing. User awareness is an essential element of security.

All users need continuous training in the new security defenses and to be reminded of company security policies and procedures. Opportunities for security education and training can be at any of the following times:

- When a new employee is hired
- After a computer attack has occurred
- When an employee is promoted or given new responsibilities
- During an annual departmental retreat
- When new user software is installed
- When user hardware is upgraded

Note 📎

Education in an enterprise is not limited to the average employee. Human resource personnel also need to keep abreast of security issues because in many organizations, it is their role to train new employees on all aspects of the organization, including security. Even upper management needs to be aware of the security threats and attacks that the organization faces, if only to acknowledge the necessity of security in planning, staffing, and budgeting.

One of the challenges of organizational education and training is to understand the traits of learners. Table 15-6 lists general traits of individuals born in the United States since 1946.

Table 15-6 Traits of learners

Year born	Traits	Number in U.S. population
Prior to 1946	Patriotic, loyal, faith in institutions	75 million
1946–1964	Idealistic, competitive, question authority	80 million
1965–1981	Self-reliant, distrustful of institutions, adaptive to technology	46 million
1982–2000	Pragmatic, globally concerned, computer literate, media savvy	76 million

In addition to traits of learners, training style also impacts how people learn. The way that one person was taught may not be the best way to teach all others. Most people are taught using a *pedagogical* approach (from a Greek word meaning *to lead a child*). For adult learners, however, an *andragogical* approach (the art of helping an adult learn) is often preferred. Some of the differences between pedagogical and andragogical approaches are summarized in Table 15-7.

Table 15-7 Approaches to training

Subject	Pedagogical approach	Andragogical approach
Desire	Motivated by external pressures to get good grades or pass on to next grade	Motivated by higher self-esteem, more recognition, desire for better quality of life
Student	Dependent on teacher for all learning	Self-directed and responsible for own learning
Subject matter	Defined by what the teacher wants to give	Learning is organized around situations in life or at work
Willingness to learn	Students are informed about what they must learn	A change triggers a readiness to learn or students perceive a gap between where they are and where they want to be

In addition to training styles, there are different learning styles. Visual learners learn through taking notes, being at the front of the class, and watching presentations. Auditory learners tend to sit in the middle of the class and learn best through lectures and discussions. The third style is kinesthetic, which many information technology professionals tend to be. These students learn through a lab environment or other hands-on approaches. Most people use a combination of learning styles, with one style being dominant. To aid in knowledge retention, trainers should incorporate all three learning styles and present the same information using different techniques. For example, a course could include a lecture, PowerPoint slides, and an opportunity to work directly with software and replicate what is being taught.

Another common approach is to use **role-based awareness training**. Role-based training involves specialized training that is customized to the specific role that an employee holds in the organization. An office associate, for example, should be provided security training that is different from that provided to an upper-level manager, because the duties and tasks of these two employees are significantly different. Role-based awareness training should be developed for data owners, system administrators, system owners, privileged users, executive users, and general users.

> **Note** 🖉
>
> All training should include a feedback mechanism by which participants can provide input on the training's effectiveness so that any needed modifications can be made for future training. In addition, such feedback can provide data to validate compliance where training is required.

Agreements

In a highly publicized security event, attackers penetrated the network of the Target Corporation and stole the credit and debit card numbers of customers who made purchases during a three-week period. More than 110 million customers were affected. The attack, however, was not the result of a successful penetration by the attackers directly into the Target network. Instead, the attackers entered through a third-party entity. This particular entity was a refrigeration, heating, and air conditioning subcontractor that had worked at a number of Target stores. Evidently, Target provided this third-party subcontractor access to the Target network so that the subcontractor could monitor energy consumption and temperatures in stores that used their equipment. Attackers were able to compromise the subcontractor's computers and steal their login credentials, which then enabled them to access the Target network and craft their attack. Evidence seems to indicate that the third-party subcontractor was using free antivirus software on its computers that did not continually monitor for malware, and this allowed the attackers to successfully compromise its systems.

> **Note** 🖉
>
> As a result of this attack, Target paid over $10 million to individual victims, $39 million to banks, $86 million to credit card companies, and $18 million to 47 states.[3]

As an increasing number of organizations turn to third-party vendors to create partnerships, the risk of *third-party integration*, or combining systems and data with outside entities, continues to grow. The risks of this integration include:

- *On-boarding and off-boarding.* **Partner on-boarding** refers to the start-up relationship between partners, while *partner off-boarding* is the termination of such an agreement. Significant consideration must be given to how the entities will combine their services without compromising their existing security defenses. Also, when the relationship ends, particularly if it has been in effect for a significant length of time, work must be done to ensure that as the parties and their IT systems separate, no gaping holes are left open for attackers to exploit.
- *Application and social media network sharing.* How will different applications be shared between the partners? Who will be responsible for support and vulnerability assessments? And as social media becomes more critical for organizations in their interaction with customers, which partner will be responsible for sharing social media information?
- *Privacy and risk awareness.* What happens if the privacy policy of one of the partners is less restrictive than that of the other partner? And how will risk assessment be performed on the combined systems?
- *Data considerations.* All parties must have a clear understanding of who owns data that is generated through the partnership and how that data will be backed up. Restrictions on unauthorized data sharing also must be reached.

One of the means by which the parties can reach an understanding of their relationships and responsibilities is through interoperability **agreements**, or formal contractual relationships, particularly as they relate to security policy and procedures. This is part of the **standard operating procedures**, or those actions and conduct that are considered normal. These agreements, which should be regularly reviewed to verify compliance and performance standards, include:

- A **Service Level Agreement (SLA)** is a service contract between a vendor and a client that specifies what services will be provided, the responsibilities of each party, and any guarantees of service.
- A **Blanket Purchase Agreement (BPA)** is a prearranged purchase or sale agreement between a government agency and a business. BPAs are often used by federal agencies to satisfy repetitive needs for products and services.
- A **Memorandum of Understanding (MOU)** describes an agreement between two or more parties. It demonstrates a "convergence of will" between the parties so that they can work together. An MOU generally is not a legally enforceable agreement, but is more formal than an unwritten agreement.
- An **Interconnection Security Agreement (ISA)** is an agreement that is intended to minimize security risks for data transmitted across a network. Examples of network interconnections usually include corporate virtual private network (VPN) tunnels that are used to connect to a network. The ISA ensures the adequate security of both entities as they share data across networks.

- A **non-disclosure agreement (NDA)** is a legal contract between parties that specifies how confidential material will be shared between the parties but restricted to others. An NDA creates a confidential relationship between the parties to protect any type of confidential and proprietary information.

Personnel Management

Risk can also be reduced by having in place procedures that affect the hiring and termination of personnel. When hiring, a **background check** should be conducted. Background checking is the process of authenticating the information supplied to a potential employer by a job applicant in the applicant's resume, application, and interviews. In most cases, lying about background and credentials will prevent the applicant from being hired.

When an employee leaves, an **exit interview** is usually conducted. An exit interview is a "wrap-up" meeting between management representatives and the person leaving an organization either voluntarily or through termination. The purpose of the interview is to gather useful feedback that can help guide future practices and improve recruiting and retention.

> **Note**
>
> The specific questions asked in an exit interview vary for terminated employees and those leaving voluntarily. For an employee leaving voluntarily, the most important question regards why they are leaving. If these reasons are repeated by several individuals, it may indicate that company procedures, pay scales, and benefits need to be reviewed.

Troubleshooting Common Security Issues

 **Certification**

2.3 Given a scenario, troubleshoot common security issues.

The security professional should have the knowledge and skills to **troubleshoot common security issues**, or those that regularly appear and provide an entry point to threat actors. A list of some of the most common security issues include:

- Access violations
- Asset management
- Authentication issues
- Baseline deviation
- Certificate issues

- Data exfiltration
- License compliance violation (availability/integrity)
- Logs and events anomalies
- Misconfigured devices (firewalls, content filters, access points, etc.)
- Permission issues
- Personnel issues (policy violations, insider threats, social engineering, social media, personal email)
- Unauthorized software
- Unencrypted credentials
- Weak security configurations

Chapter Summary

- A risk is a situation that involves exposure to some type of danger. One of the first steps in managing risk is determining what threats an enterprise may be facing. A threat assessment is a formal process of examining the seriousness of a potential threat as well as the likelihood that it will be carried out. There are many different types of risks that can be classified into different categories. A threat assessment should also be used to determine the asset value or relative worth of the asset that is at risk.

- Once the threats to assets have been determined, the risks that these assets face must be examined. Assessing risks should include testing of technology assets to identify any vulnerabilities. Change management refers to a methodology for making changes and keeping track of those changes. Without proper documentation in procedures, a change may negate or diminish a previous change or even unknowingly create a security vulnerability. Change management seeks

to approach changes systematically and provide the necessary documentation of them. Privilege management is the process of assigning and revoking privileges to objects; that is, it covers the procedures of managing object authorizations. One element of privilege management involving periodic review of a subject's privileges over an object is known as privilege auditing. Incident management is the framework and functions required to enable incident response and incident handling within an organization. The objective of incident management is to restore normal operations as quickly as possible with the least possible impact on the organization.

- There are two approaches to risk calculation: qualitative risk calculation, which uses an "educated guess" based on observation, and quantitative risk calculation, which is considered more scientific. Quantitative risk calculations can be divided into the likelihood of a risk and the impact of a risk being successful. The tools used for calculating risk likelihood include mean time between failures (MTBF), mean time to recovery (MTTR), mean time to failure (MTTF), failure in time (FIT), and the Annualized Rate of Occurrence (ARO). Risk impact calculation tools include Single Loss Expectancy (SLE) and Annual Loss Expectancy (ALE).

- Several approaches are used to reduce risk. A security control is any device or process that is used to reduce risk. Another approach is to modify the response to the risk instead of merely accepting the risk. Using technology as a strategy for reducing risk can minimize human errors that introduce risk. Using technology to automate IT processes is called automated courses of action. Risk is introduced when variances to standards are allowed, so standardization can prevent these variances. A master image is a copy of a properly configured and secured computer software system that can be replicated to other computers. A computer template is a type of document in which the standardized content has already been created so that the user needs to enter only specialized and variable components. Non-persistence tools are those that are used to ensure that unwanted data is not carried forward but instead a clean image is used.

- A policy is a document that outlines specific requirements or rules that must be met. A security policy is a written document that states how an organization plans to protect the company's information technology assets. An effective security policy must carefully balance two key elements, trust and control. Because a security policy is comprehensive and often detailed, most organizations choose to break the security policy down into smaller subpolicies. The term "security policy" is a general term for all the subpolicies included within it.

- An acceptable use policy (AUP) defines the actions users may perform while accessing systems and networking equipment. A personal email policy generally covers three important elements: using company email to send personal email messages, accessing personal email at a place of employment, and forwarding company emails to a personal email account. A social media policy outlines acceptable employee use of social media. To develop the knowledge and skills necessary to support information security, users need to receive ongoing awareness and training, which involves instruction regarding compliance, secure user practices, and an awareness of threats. There are also techniques that should be considered to make the training informative and useful.

- Different parties can reach an understanding of their relationships and responsibilities is through interoperability agreements, or formal contractual relationships, particularly as they relate to security policy and procedures. This is part of the standard operating procedures, or those actions and conduct that are considered normal. Risk can also be reduced by having in place procedures that affect the hiring and termination of personnel. When hiring, a background check should be conducted. When an employee leaves, an exit interview is usually conducted.

Key Terms

acceptable use policy (AUP)

administrative controls

agreements

Annualized Loss Expectancy
(ALE)

Annualized Rate of
Occurrence (ARO)

asset value

automated courses of
action

automation

background check

Blanket Purchase
Agreement (BPA)

change management

compensating control

configuration validation

continuing education

continuous monitoring

corrective control

detective control

deterrent control

device driver manipulation

distributive allocation

elasticity

environmental threat

exit interview

external threat

general-purpose guides

Interconnection Security
Agreement (ISA)

internal threat

live boot media

manmade threat

master image

Memorandum of
Understanding (MOU)

non-disclosure agreement
(NDA)

non-persistence tools

partner on-boarding

penetration testing
authorization

personal email policy

physical control

preventive control

qualitative risk calculation

quantitative risk
calculation

refactoring

revert to known state

risk register

role-based awareness
training

rollback to known
configuration

scalability

secure configuration guides

security control

security policy

Service Level Agreement
(SLA)

shimming

Single Loss Expectancy (SLE)

snapshot

social media network

social media policy

standard operating
procedures

supply chain assessment

technical controls

template

threat assessment

troubleshoot common
security issues

vendor-specific guides

vulnerability testing
authorization

Review Questions

1. Which of the following threats would be classified as the actions of a hactivist?
   a. External threat
   b. Internal threat
   c. Environmental threat
   d. Compliance threat

2. Which of these is NOT a response to risk?
   a. Mitigation
   b. Transference
   c. Resistance
   d. Avoidance

3. Agnella was asked to create a report that listed the reasons why a contractor should be provided penetration testing authorization. Which of the follow would she NOT list in her report?
   a. Legal authorization
   b. Indemnification
   c. Limit retaliation
   d. Access to resources

4. Which of the following risk control types would use video surveillance systems and barricades to limit access to secure sites?
   a. Operational
   b. Managerial
   c. Technical
   d. Strategic

5. Which of the following approaches to risk calculation typically assigns a numeric value (1–10) or label (*High*, *Medium*, or *Low*) represents a risk?
   a. Quantitative risk calculation
   b. Qualitative risk calculation
   c. Rule-based risk calculation
   d. Policy-based risk calculation

6. Which of the following is the average amount of time that it will take a device to recover from a failure that is not a terminal failure?
   a. MTTF
   b. MTTR
   c. FIT
   d. MTBF

7. Which of the following covers the procedures of managing object authorizations?
   a. Asset management
   b. Task management
   c. Privilege management
   d. Threat management

8. Which statement does NOT describe a characteristic of a policy?
   a. Policies define appropriate user behavior.
   b. Policies identify what tools and procedures are needed.
   c. Policies communicate a unanimous agreement of judgment.
   d. Policies may be helpful if it is necessary to prosecute violators.

9. Tomassa is asked to determine the expected monetary loss every time a risk occurs. Which formula will she use?
   a. AV
   b. ARO
   c. ALE
   d. SLE

10. What is a collection of suggestions that should be implemented?
    a. Policy
    b. Guideline
    c. Standard
    d. Code

11. Simona needs to research a control that attempts to discourage security violations before they occur. Which control will she research?
    a. Deterrent control
    b. Preventive control
    c. Detective control
    d. Corrective control

12. Which statement is NOT something that a security policy must do?
    a. State reasons why the policy is necessary.
    b. Balance protection with productivity.
    c. Be capable of being implemented and enforced.
    d. Be concise and easy to understand.

13. What describes the ability of an enterprise data center to revert to its former size after expanding?
    a. Scalability
    b. Elasticity
    c. Contraction
    d. Reduction

14. Which policy defines the actions users may perform while accessing systems and networking equipment?
    a. End-user policy
    b. Acceptable use policy
    c. Internet use policy
    d. User permission policy

15. While traveling abroad, Giuseppe needs to use public Internet café computers to access the secure network. Which of the following non-persistence tools should he use?
    a. Snapshot
    b. Live boot media
    c. Revert to known state
    d. Secure Configuration

16. Bria is reviewing the company's updated personal email policy. Which of the following will she NOT find in it?
    a. Employees should not use company email to send personal email messages.
    b. Employees should not access personal email at work.
    c. Employees should not forward company emails to a personal email account.
    d. Employees should not give out their company email address unless requested.

17. For adult learners, which approach is often preferred?
    a. Pedagogical
    b. Andragogical
    c. Institutional
    d. Proactive

18. Which of the following is NOT a security risk of social media sites for users?
    a. Personal data can be used maliciously.
    b. Users may be too trusting.
    c. Social media security is lax or confusing.
    d. Social media sites use popup ads.

19. Which of the following is NOT a time employee training should be conducted?
    a. After monthly patch updates.
    b. When a new computer is installed.
    c. During an annual department retreat.
    d. When an employee is promoted.

20. Bob needs to create an agreement between his company and a third-party organization that demonstrates a "convergence of will" between the parties so that they can work together. Which type of agreement will Bob use?
    a. SLA
    b. BPA
    c. ISA
    d. MOU

Hands-On Projects

> **Note** 📎
>
> If you are concerned about installing any of the software in these projects on your regular computer, you can instead install the software in the Windows virtual machine created in the Chapter 1 Hands-On Projects 1-3 and 1-4. Software installed within the virtual machine will not impact the host computer.

Project 15-1: Viewing Your Annual Credit Report

Security experts recommend that one means to reduce personal risk for consumers is to receive a copy of their credit report at least once per year and check its accuracy to protect their identity. In this project, you access your free credit report online.

1. Use your web browser to go to **www.annualcreditreport.com**. Although you could send a request individually to one of the three credit agencies, this website acts as a central source for ordering free credit reports. Figure 15-5 shows the website.

Figure 15-5   Credit report website

Source: AnnualCreditReport.com

2. Click **Request your free credit reports.**
3. Read through the three steps and click **Request your credit reports.**
4. Enter the requested information and click **Continue** and then **Next.**
5. Click **TransUnion.** Click **Next.**
6. After the brief processing completes, click **Continue.**
7. You may then be asked personal information about your transaction history to verify your identity. Answer the requested questions and click **Next.**
8. Follow the instructions to print your report.
9. Review it carefully, particularly the sections of "Potentially negative items" and "Requests for your credit history." If you see anything that might be incorrect, follow the instructions on that website to enter a dispute.
10. Follow the instructions to exit from the website.
11. Close all windows.

Project 15-2: Using a Non-Persistent Web Browser

Non-persistence tools are those that are used to ensure that unwanted data is not carried forward but instead a clean image is used. One common tool is a web browser that retains no information such as cookies, history, passwords, or any other data and requires no installation but runs from a USB flash drive. In this project, you download and install a non-persistent web browser.

1. Use your web browser to go to **www.browzar.com** (if you are no longer able to access the program through this URL, use a search engine and search for "Browzar").
2. Click **Key Features** and read about the features of Browzar.
3. Click **Help & FAQs** and read the questions and answers.
4. Click **Download now – It's FREE!**
5. Choose one of the available themes and click **Download.**
6. Click **Accept.**
7. Click **Download.**
8. Click on the downloaded file to run Browzar. Note that no installation is required and it can be run from a USB flash drive.
9. From Browzar go to **www.google.com**.
10. Enter **Cengage** in the search bar to search for information about Cengage.
11. Now click the red **X** in the upper right corner to close the browser. What information appears in the popup window? What happened when you closed the browser?
12. Launch Browzar again.
13. Click **Tools.**
14. Click **Secure delete.**
15. Click **More** >>. What additional protections does Secure Delete give?
16. Close all windows.

Project 15-3: Creating and Using a Non-Persistent Live Boot Media

Another non-persistence tool is a live boot media, which is an operating system that boots from a USB flash drive or optical disc but retains no information. In this project, you create a Linux live boot media USB flash drive using UNetbootin. Note that you will need a flash drive of at least 32 GB formatted as FAT32.

1. Use your web browser to go to **unetbootin.github.io** (if you are no longer able to access the program through this URL, use a search engine and search for "unetbootin").
2. Read through the features of UNetbootin.
3. Under **Supported Distributions** note that UNetbootin had built-in support for several different Linux distributions.
4. Click **Linux Mint.**
5. On the Linux Mint website click **Read more** to see more information on Linux Mint. It is a graphical user interface distribution that has many similarities to Microsoft Windows and Apple macOS.
6. Click your browser's **Back** button to return to UNetbootin.
7. Select the operating system of your computer and click **Download.**
8. When the download completes, launch the UNetbootin application. Note that no installation is required. The UNetbootin screen is shown in Figure 15-6.

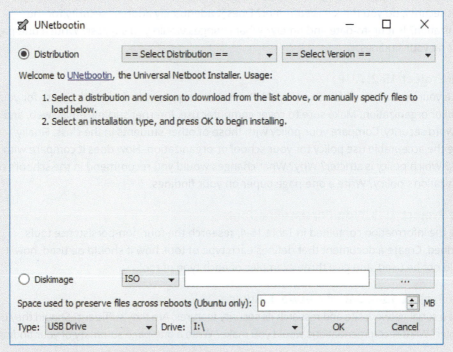

Figure 15-6   UNetbootin screen

Source: UNetbootin

9. Click the down arrow under **Select Distribution.** Scroll through the list of natively supported distributions from which a live boot media can be created.
10. Click **Linux Mint.**
11. Under **Type:** be sure that **USB Drive** is selected and that is the correct flash drive on which to install it is selected under **Drive:.**
12. Click **OK.** UNetbootin will download the Linux Mint files and then create the bootable USB flash drive. Note that this may take several minutes to complete depending upon your network bandwidth.
13. After the installation is complete, reboot the computer to boot from the USB flash drive (many systems require pressing the **F12** key when rebooting to choose an alternative booting device).
14. Boot from the USB flash drive to load the live boot media Linux Mint.
15. Reboot your computer again to access the operating system on the hard drive.

Case Projects

Case Project 15-1: Security Policy Review
Locate the security policy for your school or organization. Based on what you now know about security, do you think it is sufficient? Does it adequately address security for the organization? Is it up-to-date and timely? What changes would you suggest? Write a one-page paper on your findings.

Case Project 15-2: AUP
Create your own acceptable use policy (AUP) for the computers and network access for your school or organization. Make sure to cover computer use, Internet surfing, email, web, and password security. Compare your policy with those of other students in the class. Finally, locate the acceptable use policy for your school or organization. How does it compare with yours? Which policy is stricter? Why? What changes would you recommend in the school's or organization's policy? Write a one-page paper on your findings.

Case Project 15-3: Non-Persistence Tools
Using the information contained in Table 15-4, research the four non-persistence tools described. Create a document that defines each type of tool, how it should be used, how it should not be used, and give three examples of each type of tool.

Case Project 15-4: Social Network Advice
Select a social network site and research its security features. Are they sufficient? Should they be stronger? What recommendations would you make? Write a one-page summary of your findings.

Case Project 15-5: User Awareness and Training
What user security awareness and training is available at your school or place of business? How frequently is it performed? Is it available online or in person? Is it required? Are the

topics up-to-date? On a scale of 1–10, how would you rate the training? Write a one-page summary.

Case Project 15-6: Lake Point Security Consulting

Lake Point Consulting Services (LPCS) provides security consulting and assurance services to over 500 clients across a wide range of enterprises in more than 20 states. A new initiative at LPCS is for each of its seven regional offices to provide internships to students who are in their final year of the security degree program at the local college.

Chef's Market is a regional restaurant chain that was recently purchased by new owners, who want to create new security policies. Because they have no experience in this area, they have hired LPSC to help them.

1. Create a PowerPoint presentation that explains what a security policy is, the security policy cycle, and the steps in developing a security policy. The presentation should be 10 slides in length.
2. Chef's Market is ready to start developing security policies and wants to make the security-related human resource policy its first. Create a one-page draft of a policy for them.

Case Project 15-7: Community Site Activity

The Information Security Community Site is an online companion to this textbook. It contains a wide variety of tools, information, discussion boards, and other features to assist learners. Go to *community.cengage.com/Infosec2* and click the *Join or Sign in* icon to log in, using your login name and password that you created in Chapter 1. Click **Forums (Discussion)** and click on **Security+ Case Projects (6th edition)**. Read the following case study.

What is your reaction to *Today's Attacks and Defenses* regarding the lack of security on heart pacemakers? Should the federal government place security standards on these devices? If that is the case, should security standards be placed on other devices in which individuals could be harmed if they are compromised? Should security standards for cars, wireless cameras, household door locks, and other technology be government regulated? What are the advantages and disadvantages? Record your answers on the Community Site discussion board.

References

1. Rios, Billy, and Butts, Jonathan, "Security evaluation of the implantable cardiac device ecosystem architecture and implementation interdependencies," *WhiteScope*, May 17, 2017, retrieved May 27, 2017, https://drive.google.com/file/d /oB_GspGER4QQTYkJfaVl BeGVCSW8/view
2. "The top 20 valuable Facebook statistics—updated May 2017," *Zephoria*, May 8, 2017, retrieved Jun. 22, 2017, https://zephoria.com/top-15-valuable-facebook-statistics/
3. Fingas, Jon, "Target settles with 47 states over its 2013 data breach," *Engadget*, May 23, 2017, retrieved Jun. 22, 2017, https://www.engadget.com/2017/05/23/target-settles-with -states-over-data-breach/

CompTIA SYO-501 Certification Exam Objectives

This Appendix shows the domains and objectives of the CompTIA Security+ exam (SY0-501), keyed to chapters and sections in this text. Bloom's Taxonomy is an industry-standard classification system used to help identify the level of ability that learners need to demonstrate proficiency. It is often used to classify educational learning objectives into different levels of complexity. The column "Bloom's Taxonomy" reflects the level of coverage in *Security+ Guide to Network Security Fundamentals, 6 th edition* for the respective SY0-501 objective domains. In all instances, the level of coverage for this text meets or exceeds that indicated by CompTIA for that objective. See the Introduction of this text for more information.

Security + Exam Domain/Objectives	Chapter	Section	Bloom's Taxonomy
1.0 Threats, Attacks, and Vulnerabilities			
1.1 Given a scenario, analyze indicators of compromise and determine the type of malware. • Viruses • Crypto-malware • Ransomware • Worm • Trojan • Rootkit • Keylogger • Adware • Spyware • Bots • RAT • Logic bomb • Backdoor	2	Attacks Using Malware	Analyze

(continues)

Security + Exam Domain/Objectives	Chapter	Section	Bloom's Taxonomy
1.2 Compare and contrast types of attacks.	2	Social Engineering Attacks	Understand
• Social engineering			
○ Phishing			
○ Spear phishing	3	Cryptographic Attacks	Analyze
○ Whaling			
○ Vishing			
○ Tailgating	5	Networking-Based Attacks	Understand
○ Impersonation	5	Server Attacks	Understand
○ Dumpster diving			
○ Shoulder surfing			
○ Hoax	8	Wireless Attacks	Apply
○ Watering hole attack	8	Vulnerabilities of IEEE Wireless Security	Understand
○ Principles (reasons for effectiveness)			
▪ Authority			
▪ Intimidation	11	Authentication Credentials	Create
▪ Consensus			
▪ Scarcity			
▪ Familiarity	15	Managing Risk	Apply
▪ Trust			
▪ Urgency			
• Application/service attacks			
○ DoS			
○ DDoS			
○ Man-in-the-middle			
○ Buffer overflow			
○ Injection			
○ Cross-site scripting			
○ Cross-site request forgery			
○ Privilege escalation			
○ ARP poisoning			
○ Amplification			
○ DNS poisoning			
○ Domain hijacking			
○ Man-in-the-browser			
○ Zero day			
○ Replay			
○ Pass the hash			
○ Hijacking and related attacks			
▪ Clickjacking			
▪ Session hijacking			
▪ URL hijacking			
▪ Typo squatting			
○ Driver manipulation			
▪ Shimming			
▪ Refactoring			
○ MAC spoofing			

Security + Exam Domain/Objectives	Chapter	Section	Bloom's Taxonomy
• Wireless attacks			
○ Replay			
○ IV			
○ Evil twin			
○ Rogue AP			
○ Jamming			
○ WPS			
○ Bluejacking			
○ Bluesnarfing			
○ RFID			
○ NFC			
○ Disassociation			
• Cryptographic attacks			
○ Birthday			
○ Known plain text/cipher text			
○ Rainbow tables			
○ Dictionary			
○ Brute force			
▪ Online vs. offline			
○ Collision			
○ Downgrade			
○ Replay			
○ Weak implementations			
1.3 Explain threat actor types and attributes.			
• Types of actors	1	What Is Information Security?	Analyze
○ Script kiddies			
○ Hacktivist	1	Who Are the Threat Actors?	Apply
○ Organized crime			
○ Nation states/APT			
○ Insiders			
○ Competitors			
• Attributes of actors			
○ Internal/external			
○ Level of sophistication			
○ Resources/funding			
○ Intent/motivation			
• Use of open-source intelligence			
1.4 Explain penetration testing concepts.	13	Penetration Testing	Apply
• Active reconnaissance			
• Passive reconnaissance			
• Pivot			
• Initial exploitation			
• Persistence			
• Escalation of privilege			
• Black box			
• White box			
• Gray box			
• Pen testing vs. vulnerability scanning			

(continues)

Security + Exam Domain/Objectives	Chapter	Section	Bloom's Taxonomy
1.5 Explain vulnerability scanning concepts. • Passively test security controls • Identify vulnerability • Identify lack of security controls • Identify common misconfigurations • Intrusive vs. non-intrusive • Credentialed vs. non-credentialed • False positive	13	Vulnerability Scanning	Apply

1.6 Explain the impact associated with types of vulnerabilities.
 	
• Race conditions
• Vulnerabilities due to:
  ○ End-of-life systems
  ○ Embedded systems
  ○ Lack of vendor support
• Improper input handling
• Improper error handling
• Misconfiguration/weak configuration
• Default configuration
• Resource exhaustion
• Untrained users
• Improperly configured accounts
• Vulnerable business processes
• Weak cipher suites and implementations
• Memory/buffer vulnerability
  ○ Memory leak
  ○ Integer overflow
  ○ Buffer overflow
  ○ Pointer dereference
  ○ DLL injection
• System sprawl/undocumented assets
• Architecture/design weaknesses
• New threats/zero day
• Improper certificate and key management
	1
	
	3
	
	4
	
	5
	
	9
	
	10
		Challenges of Securing Information
		
		Cryptographic Attacks
		
		Public Key Infrastructure (PKI)
		
		Server Attacks
		
		Application Security
		
		Embedded Systems and the Internet of Things
			Understand
			
			Understand
			
			Understand
			
			Understand
			
			Understand
			
			Understand

2.0: Technologies and Tools			

2.1 Install and configure network components, both hardware- and software-based, to support organizational security.
• Firewall
  ○ ACL
  ○ Application-based vs. network-based
  ○ Stateful vs. stateless
  ○ Implicit deny
• VPN concentrator
  ○ Remote access vs. site-to-site
  ○ IPSec
	4
	
	6
	
	6
	
	7
		Cryptographic Transport Protocols
		
		Security through Network Devices
		Security through Network Technologies
		
		Managing and Securing Network Platforms
			Apply
			
			Analyze
			
			Analyze
			
			Apply

Security + Exam Domain/Objectives	Chapter	Section	Bloom's Taxonomy
▪ Tunnel mode			
▪ Transport mode			
▪ AH	8	Wireless Attacks	Analyze
▪ ESP	8	Vulnerabilities of IEEE Wireless Security	Analyze
○ Split tunnel vs. full tunnel			
○ TLS	8	Wireless Security Solutions	Evaluate
○ Always-on VPN			
• NIPS/NIDS			
○ Signature-based			
○ Heuristic/behavioral			
○ Anomaly			
○ Inline vs. passive			
○ In-band vs. out-of-band			
○ Rules			
○ Analytics			
▪ False positive			
▪ False negative			
• Router			
○ ACLs			
○ Antispoofing			
• Switch			
○ Port security			
○ Layer 2 vs. Layer 3			
○ Loop prevention			
○ Flood guard			
• Proxy			
○ Forward and reverse proxy			
○ Transparent			
○ Application/multipurpose			
○ Load balancer			
○ Scheduling			
▪ Affinity			
▪ Round-robin			
○ Active-passive			
○ Active-active			
○ Virtual IPs			
• Access point			
○ SSID			
○ MAC filtering			
○ Signal strength			
○ Band selection/width			
○ Antenna types and placement			
○ Fat vs. thin			
○ Controller-based vs. standalone			
• SIEM			
○ Aggregation			
○ Correlation			
○ Automated alerting and triggers			
○ Time synchronization			

(continues)

Security + Exam Domain/Objectives	Chapter	Section	Bloom's Taxonomy
• Event deduplication ○ Logs/WORM • DLP ○ USB blocking ○ Cloud-based ○ Email • NAC ○ Dissolvable vs. permanent ○ Host health checks ○ Agent vs. agentless • Mail gateway ○ Spam filter ○ DLP ○ Encryption • Bridge • SSL/TLS accelerators • SSL decryptors • Media gateway • Hardware security module			
2.2 Given a scenario, use appropriate software tools to assess the security posture of an organization. • Protocol analyzer • Network scanners • Rogue system detection • Network mapping • Wireless scanners/cracker • Password cracker • Vulnerability scanner • Configuration compliance scanner • Exploitation frameworks • Data sanitization tools • Steganography tools • Honeypot • Backup utilities • Banner grabbing • Passive vs. active • Command line tools ○ ping ○ netstat ○ tracert ○ nslookup/dig ○ arp ○ ipconfig/ip/ifconfig ○ tcpdump ○ nmap ○ netcat	8 13 13 14	Wireless Security Solutions Assessing the Security Posture Practicing Data Privacy and Security Fault Tolerance Through Redundancy	Evaluate Analyze Evaluate Evaluate

(Continued)

Security + Exam Domain/Objectives	Chapter	Section	Bloom's Taxonomy

2.3 Given a scenario, troubleshoot common security issues.
• Unencrypted credentials/clear text
• Logs and events anomalies
• Permission issues
• Access violations
• Certificate issues
• Data exfiltration
• Misconfigured devices
  ◦ Firewall
  ◦ Content filter
  ◦ Access points
• Weak security configurations
• Personnel issues
  ◦ Policy violation
  ◦ Insider threat
  ◦ Social engineering
  ◦ Social media
  ◦ Personal email
• Unauthorized software
• Baseline deviation
• License compliance violation (availability/integrity)
• Asset management
• Authentication issues
	15	Troubleshooting Common Security Issues	Analyze

2.4 Given a scenario, analyze and interpret output from security technologies. • HIDS/HIPS • Antivirus • File integrity check • Host-based firewall • Application whitelisting • Removable media control • Advanced malware tools • Patch management tools • UTM • DLP • Data execution prevention • Web application firewall	6 7 9	Security through Network Devices Analyzing Security Data Client Security	Analyze Analyze Analyze

2.5 Given a scenario, deploy mobile devices securely.
• Connection methods
  ◦ Cellular
  ◦ WiFi
  ◦ SATCOM
  ◦ Bluetooth
	8
	8
		Wireless Attacks
		Wireless Security Solutions
			Apply
			Evaluate

(continues)

Security + Exam Domain/Objectives	Chapter	Section	Bloom's Taxonomy
o NFC	10	Mobile Device Types and Deployment	Analyze
o ANT			
o Infrared	10	Mobile Device Risks	Analyze
o USB	10	Securing Mobile Devices	Create
• Mobile device management concepts			
o Application management			
o Content management	11	Authentication Credentials	Analyze
o Remote wipe			
o Geofencing			
o Geolocation			
o Screen locks			
o Push notification services			
o Passwords and pins			
o Biometrics			
o Context-aware authentication			
o Containerization			
o Storage segmentation			
o Full device encryption			
• Enforcement and monitoring for:			
o Third-party app stores			
o Rooting/jailbreaking			
o Sideloading			
o Custom firmware			
o Carrier unlocking			
o Firmware OTA updates			
o Camera use			
o SMS/MMS			
o External media			
o USB OTG			
o Recording microphone			
o GPS tagging			
o WiFi direct/ad hoc			
o Tethering			
o Payment methods			
• Deployment models			
o BYOD			
o COPE			
o CYOD			
o Corporate-owned			
o VDI			
2.6 Given a scenario, implement secure protocols.	4	Cryptographic Transport Protocols	Apply
• Protocols			
o DNSSEC			
o SSH			
o S/MIME	5	Networking-Based Attacks	Analyze

Security + Exam Domain/Objectives	Chapter	Section	Bloom's Taxonomy
○ SRTP ○ LDAPS ○ FTPS ○ SFTP ○ SNMPv3 ○ SSL/TLS ○ HTTPS ○ Secure POP/IMAP • Use cases ○ Voice and video ○ Time synchronization ○ Email and web ○ File transfer ○ Directory services ○ Remote access ○ Domain name resolution ○ Routing and switching ○ Network address allocation ○ Subscription services	7 12	Secure Network Protocols Identity and Access Services	Apply Apply
3.0: Architecture and Design			
3.1 Explain use cases and purpose for frameworks, best practices and secure configuration guides. • Industry-standard frameworks and reference architectures ○ Regulatory ○ Non-regulatory ○ National vs. international ○ Industry-specific frameworks • Benchmarks/secure configuration guides ○ Platform/vendor-specific guides ▪ Web server ▪ Operating system ▪ Application server ▪ Network infrastructure devices ○ General purpose guides • Defense-in-depth/layered security ○ Vendor diversity ○ Control diversity ▪ Administrative ▪ Technical ○ User training	1 15	Defending Against Attacks Strategies for Reducing Risk	Analyze Understand

(continues)

Security + Exam Domain/Objectives	Chapter	Section	Bloom's Taxonomy
3.2 Given a scenario, implement secure network architecture concepts.	6	Security Through Network Devices	Analyze
• Zones/topologies	6	Security Through Network Architecture	Analyze
○ DMZ			
○ Extranet			
○ Intranet			
○ Wireless	7	Placement of Security Devices and Technologies	Apply
○ Guest			
○ Honeynets			
○ NAT	7	Managing and Securing Network Platforms	Apply
○ Ad hoc			
• Segregation/segmentation/isolation			
○ Physical			
○ Logical (VLAN)	8	Wireless Attacks	Apply
○ Virtualization	8	Wireless Security Solutions	Evaluate
○ Air gaps			
• Tunneling/VPN			
○ Site-to-site			
○ Remote access	13	Assessing the Security Posture	Apply
• Security device/technology placement			
○ Sensors			
○ Collectors			
○ Correlation engines			
○ Filters			
○ Proxies			
○ Firewalls			
○ VPN concentrators			
○ SSL accelerators			
○ Load balancers			
○ DDoS mitigator			
○ Aggregation switches			
○ Taps and port mirror			
• SDN			
3.3 Given a scenario, implement secure systems design.	3	Using Cryptography	Analyze
• Hardware/firmware security			
○ FDE/SED			
○ TPM	8	Wireless Security Solutions	Evaluate
○ HSM			
○ UEFI/BIOS			

Security + Exam Domain/Objectives	Chapter	Section	Bloom's Taxonomy
○ Secure boot and attestation ○ Supply chain ○ Hardware root of trust ○ EMI/EMP	9	Client Security	Evaluate

• Operating systems
  ○ Types
    ▪ Network
    ▪ Server
    ▪ Workstation
    ▪ Appliance
    ▪ Kiosk
    ▪ Mobile OS
  ○ Patch management
  ○ Disabling unnecessary ports and services
  ○ Least functionality
  ○ Secure configurations
 	
  ○ Trusted operating system
  ○ Application whitelisting/ blacklisting
  ○ Disable default accounts/ passwords
• Peripherals
  ○ Wireless keyboards
  ○ Wireless mice
  ○ Displays
  ○ WiFi-enabled MicroSD cards
  ○ Printers/MFDs
  ○ External storage devices
  ○ Digital cameras
	14	Environmental Controls	Apply

3.4 Explain the importance of secure staging deployment concepts.
• Sandboxing
• Environment
  ○ Development
  ○ Test
  ○ Staging
  ○ Production
• Secure baseline
• Integrity measurement
	9	Application Security	Understand

(continues)

Security + Exam Domain/Objectives	Chapter	Section	Bloom's Taxonomy

3.5 Explain the security implications of embedded systems.
• SCADA/ICS
• Smart devices/IoT
  ○ Wearable technology
  ○ Home automation
• HVAC
• SoC
• RTOS
• Printers/MFDs
• Camera systems
• Special purpose
  ○ Medical devices
  ○ Vehicles
  ○ Aircraft/UAV
	10	Embedded Systems and the Internet of Things	Understand

3.6 Summarize secure application development and deployment concepts.
• Development life-cycle models
  ○ Waterfall vs. Agile
• Secure DevOps
  ○ Security automation
  ○ Continuous integration
  ○ Baselining
  ○ Immutable systems
  ○ Infrastructure as code
• Version control and change management
• Provisioning and deprovisioning
• Secure coding techniques
  ○ Proper error handling
  ○ Proper input validation
  ○ Normalization
  ○ Stored procedures
  ○ Code signing
  ○ Encryption
  ○ Obfuscation/camouflage
  ○ Code reuse/dead code
  ○ Server-side vs. client-side execution and validation
  ○ Memory management
  ○ Use of third-party libraries and SDKs
  ○ Data exposure
• Code quality and testing
  ○ Static code analyzers
  ○ Dynamic analysis (e.g., fuzzing)
  ○ Stress testing
	9	Application Security	Understand

Security + Exam Domain/Objectives	Chapter	Section	Bloom's Taxonomy
○ Sandboxing ○ Model verification • Compiled vs. runtime code			
3.7 Summarize cloud and virtualization concepts. • Hypervisor ○ Type I ○ Type II ○ Application cells/containers • VM sprawl avoidance • VM escape protection • Cloud storage • Cloud deployment models ○ SaaS ○ PaaS ○ IaaS ○ Private ○ Public ○ Hybrid ○ Community • On-premise vs. hosted vs. cloud • VDI/VDE • Cloud access security broker • Security as a Service	7	Managing and Securing Network Platforms	Apply
3.8 Explain how resiliency and automation strategies reduce risk. • Automation/scripting ○ Automated courses of action ○ Continuous monitoring ○ Configuration validation • Templates • Master image • Non-persistence ○ Snapshots ○ Revert to known state ○ Rollback to known configuration ○ Live boot media • Elasticity • Scalability • Distributive allocation • Redundancy • Fault tolerance • High availability • RAID	14 14 15	What is Business Continuity? Fault Tolerance Through Redundancy Strategies for Reducing Risk	Understand Analyze Understand

(continues)

Security + Exam Domain/Objectives	Chapter	Section	Bloom's Taxonomy

3.9 Explain the importance of physical security controls.
• Lighting
• Signs
• Fencing/gate/cage
• Security guards
• Alarms
• Safe
• Secure cabinets/enclosures
• Protected distribution/ Protected cabling
• Airgap
• Mantrap
• Faraday cage
• Lock types
• Biometrics
• Barricades/bollards
• Tokens/cards
• Environmental controls
  ○ HVAC
  ○ Hot and cold aisles
  ○ Fire suppression
• Cable locks
• Screen filters
• Cameras
• Motion detection
• Logs
• Infrared detection
• Key management
	9
	
	11
	
	14
		Physical Security
		
		Authentication Credentials
		
		Environmental Controls
			Understand
			
			Analyze
			
			Understand

4.0: Identity and Access Management			

4.1 Compare and contrast identity and access management concepts.
• Identification, authentication, authorization, and accounting (AAA)
• Multifactor authentication
  ○ Something you are
  ○ Something you have
  ○ Something you know
  ○ Somewhere you are
  ○ Something you do
• Federation
• Single sign-on
• Transitive trust
	11
	
	11
	11
	
	12
		Authentication and Account Management
		Single Sign-On
		Account Management
		
		What Is Access Control?
			Analyze
			
			Analyze
			Analyze
			
			Analyze

Security + Exam Domain/Objectives	Chapter	Section	Bloom's Taxonomy
4.2 Given a scenario, install and configure identity and access services. • LDAP • Kerberos • TACACS+ • CHAP • PAP • MSCHAP • RADIUS • SAML • OpenID Connect • OAUTH • Shibboleth • Secure token • NTLM	11 11	Authentication Credentials Single Sign-On	Apply Apply

4.3 Given a scenario, implement identity and access management controls.
 • Access control models
   ○ MAC
   ○ DAC
   ○ ABAC
   ○ Role-based access control
   ○ Rule-based access control
 • Physical access control
   ○ Proximity cards
   ○ Smart cards
 • Biometric factors
   ○ Fingerprint scanner
   ○ Retinal scanner
   ○ Iris scanner
   ○ Voice recognition
   ○ Facial recognition
   ○ False acceptance rate
   ○ False rejection rate
   ○ Crossover error rate
 • Tokens
   ○ Hardware
   ○ Software
   ○ HOTP/TOTP
 • Certificate-based authentication
   ○ PIV/CAC/smart card
   ○ IEEE 802.1x
 • File system security
 • Database security
	8
	
	 11
	
	 12
	 12
	
	 12
		Wireless Security Solutions
		
		 Authentication and Account Management
		
		 What Is Access Control?
		 Implementing Access Control
		 Managing Access through Account Management
			Apply
			
			 Apply
			
			 Apply
			 Apply
			
			 Analyze

(continues)

Security + Exam Domain/Objectives	Chapter	Section	Bloom's Taxonomy
4.4 Given a scenario, differentiate common account management practices.	11	Account Management	Analyze
• Account types			
○ User account	12	Managing Access Through Account Management	Analyze
○ Shared and generic accounts/credentials			
○ Guest accounts	12	Implementing Access Control	Analyze
○ Service accounts			
○ Privileged accounts			
• General Concepts			
○ Least privilege			
○ Onboarding/offboarding			
○ Permission auditing and review			
○ Usage auditing and review			
○ Time-of-day restrictions			
○ Recertification			
○ Standard naming convention			
○ Account maintenance			
○ Group-based access control			
○ Location-based policies			
• Account policy enforcement			
○ Credential management			
○ Group policy			
○ Password complexity			
○ Expiration			
○ Recovery			
○ Disablement			
○ Lockout			
○ Password history			
○ Password reuse			
○ Password length			
5.0: Risk Management			
5.1 Explain the importance of policies, plans, and procedures related to organizational security.	12	Best Practices for Access Control	Understand
• Standard operating procedure			
• Agreement types			
○ BPA	15	Practices for Reducing Risk	Apply
○ SLA			
○ ISA			
○ MOU/MOA			
• Personnel management			
○ Mandatory vacations			
○ Job rotation			
○ Separation of duties			
○ Clean desk			
○ Background checks			
○ Exit interviews			
○ Role-based awareness training			

Security + Exam Domain/Objectives	Chapter	Section	Bloom's Taxonomy

• Data owner
  ▪ System administrator
  ▪ System owner
  ▪ User
  ▪ Privileged user
  ▪ Executive user
 ○ NDA
 ○ Onboarding
 ○ Continuing education
 ○ Acceptable use policy/
 rules of behavior
 ○ Adverse actions
• General security policies
 ○ Social media networks/
 applications
 ○ Personal email			

5.2 Summarize business impact analysis concepts.
  • RTO/RPO
  • MTBF
  • MTTR
  • Mission-essential functions
  • Identification of critical systems
  • Single point of failure
  • Impact
   ○ Life
   ○ Property
   ○ Safety
   ○ Finance
   ○ Reputation
  • Privacy impact assessment
  • Privacy threshold assessment
	14
	
	14
		What Is Business Continuity?
		Fault Tolerance Through Redundancy
			Understand
			
			Analyze

5.3 Explain risk management processes and concepts.
  • Threat assessment
   ○ Environmental
   ○ Manmade
   ○ Internal vs. external
  • Risk assessment
   ○ SLE
   ○ ALE
   ○ ARO
   ○ Asset value
   ○ Risk register
   ○ Likelihood of occurrence
   ○ Supply chain assessment
   ○ Impact
	1
	
	15
		What Is Information Security?
		
		Managing Risk
			Apply
			
			Understand

(continues)

Security + Exam Domain/Objectives	Chapter	Section	Bloom's Taxonomy

○ Quantitative
○ Qualitative
○ Testing
  ■ Penetration testing authorization
  ■ Vulnerability testing authorization
○ Risk response techniques
  ■ Accept
  ■ Transfer
  ■ Avoid
  ■ Mitigate
● Change management			

5.4 Given a scenario, follow incident response procedures. ● Incident response plan ○ Documented incident types/category definitions ○ Roles and responsibilities ○ Reporting requirements/ escalation ○ Cyber-incident response teams ○ Exercise ● Incident response process ○ Preparation ○ Identification ○ Containment ○ Eradication ○ Recovery ○ Lessons learned	14	Incident Response	Apply
5.5 Summarize basic concepts of forensics. ● Order of volatility ● Chain of custody ● Legal hold ● Data acquisition ○ Capture system image ○ Network traffic and logs ○ Capture video ○ Record time offset ○ Take hashes ○ Screenshots ○ Witness interviews ● Preservation ● Recovery ● Strategic intelligence/ counterintelligence gathering ● Active logging ● Track man-hours	14 14	Forensics Procedures Incident Reponse	Apply Apply

Security + Exam Domain/Objectives	Chapter	Section	Bloom's Taxonomy

5.6 Explain disaster recovery and continuity of operation concepts.
• Recovery sites
  ○ Hot site
  ○ Warm site
  ○ Cold site
• Order of restoration
• Backup concepts
  ○ Differential
  ○ Incremental
  ○ Snapshots
  ○ Full
• Geographic considerations
  ○ Off-site backups
  ○ Distance
  ○ Location selection
  ○ Legal implications
  ○ Data sovereignty
• Continuity of operation planning
  ○ Exercises/tabletop
  ○ After-action reports
  ○ Failover
  ○ Alternate processing sites
  ○ Alternate business practices
	14
	
	14
		What Is Business Continuity?
		Fault Tolerance Through Redundancy
			Understand
			
			Apply

5.7 Compare and contrast various types of controls. • Deterrent • Preventive • Detective • Corrective • Compensating • Technical • Administrative • Physical	15	Strategies for Reducing Risk	Understand

5.8 Given a scenario, carry out data security and privacy practices.
 	
• Data destruction and media sanitization
  ○ Burning
  ○ Shredding
  ○ Pulping
  ○ Pulverizing
  ○ Degaussing
  ○ Purging
  ○ Wiping
• Data sensitivity labeling and handling
  ○ Confidential
  ○ Private
  ○ Public
	12
	
	13
		What Is Access Control?
		
		Practicing Data Privacy and Security
			Understand
			
			Analyze

Security + Exam Domain/Objectives	Chapter	Section	Bloom's Taxonomy
○ Proprietary			
○ PII			
○ PHI			
• Data roles			
○ Owner			
○ Steward/custodian			
○ Privacy officer			
• Data retention			
• Legal and compliance			
6.0: Cryptography and PKI			
6.1 Compare and contrast basic concepts of	3	Defining Cryptography	Understand
cryptography.	3	Cryptographic Algorithms	Analyze
• Symmetric algorithms	3	Cryptographic Attacks	Analyze
• Modes of operation			
• Asymmetric algorithms			
• Hashing	4	Implementing	Analyze
• Salt, IV, nonce		Cryptography	
• Elliptic curve	4	Types of Digital Certificates	Analyze
• Weak/deprecated algorithms			
• Key exchange			
• Digital signatures	11	Authentication Credentials	Analyze
• Diffusion			
• Confusion			
• Collision			
• Steganography			
• Obfuscation			
• Stream vs. block			
• Key strength			
• Session keys			
• Ephemeral key			
• Secret algorithm			
• Data-in-transit			
• Data-at-rest			
• Data-in-use			
• Random/pseudo-random number generation			
• Key stretching			
• Implementation vs. algorithm selection			
○ Crypto service provider			
○ Crypto modules			
• Perfect forward secrecy			
• Security through obscurity			
• Common use cases			
○ Low power devices			
○ Low latency			
○ High resiliency			

Security + Exam Domain/Objectives	Chapter	Section	Bloom's Taxonomy

○ Supporting confidentiality
   ○ Supporting integrity
   ○ Supporting obfuscation
   ○ Supporting authentication
   ○ Supporting non-repudiation
   ○ Resource vs. security constraint			

6.2 Explain cryptography algorithms and their basic characteristics.	3 3	Defining Cryptography Cryptographic Algorithms	Understand Understand

• Symmetric algorithms
   ○ AES
   ○ DES
   ○ 3DES
   ○ RC4
   ○ Blowfish/ Twofish
   ○ Cipher modes
   ○ CBC
   ○ GCM
   ○ ECB
   ○ CTM
   ○ Stream vs. block
  • Asymmetric algorithms
   ○ RSA
   ○ DSA
   ○ Diffie-Hellman
     ■ Groups
     ■ DHE
     ■ ECDHE
   ○ Elliptic curve
   ○ PGP/GPG
  • Hashing algorithms
   ○ MD5
   ○ SHA
   ○ HMAC
  • RIPEMD
  • Key stretching algorithms
   ○ BCRYPT
   ○ PBKDF2
  • Obfuscation
   ○ XOR
   ○ ROT13
   ○ Substitution ciphers
	4
	
	11
		Implementing
		  Cryptography
		
		Authentication and
		  Account Management
			Apply
			
			Analyze

6.3 Given a scenario, install and configure wireless security settings.
  • Cryptographic protocols
   ○ WPA
   ○ WPA2
   ○ CCMP
   ○ TKIP
	8
	
	12
		Wireless Security
		  Solutions
		
		Identity and Access
		  Services
			Evaluate
			
			Apply

(continues)

Security + Exam Domain/Objectives	Chapter	Section	Bloom's Taxonomy

• Authentication protocols
  ○ EAP
  ○ PEAP
  ○ EAP-FAST
  ○ EAP-TLS
  ○ EAP-TTLS
  ○ IEEE 802.1x
  ○ RADIUS Federation
• Methods
  ○ PSK vs. Enterprise vs. Open
  ○ WPS
  ○ Captive portals			

6.4 Given a scenario, implement public key infrastructure.
• Components
  ○ CA
  ○ Intermediate CA
  ○ CRL
  ○ OCSP
  ○ CSR
  ○ Certificate
  ○ Public key
  ○ Private key
  ○ Object identifiers (OID)
• Concepts
  ○ Online vs. offline CA
  ○ Stapling
  ○ Pinning
  ○ Trust model
  ○ Key escrow
  ○ Certificate chaining
• Types of certificates
  ○ Wildcard
  ○ SAN
  ○ Code signing
  ○ Self-signed
  ○ Machine/computer
  ○ Email
  ○ User
  ○ Root
  ○ Domain validation
  ○ Extended validation
• Certificate formats
  ○ DER
  ○ PEM
  ○ PFX
  ○ CER
  ○ P12
  ○ P7B
	3
	
	4
	4
		Cryptographic Algorithms
		
		Digital Certificates
		Public Key Infrastructure
			Apply
			
			Apply
			Apply

GLOSSARY

A

accept A response to risk that acknowledges the risk but takes no steps to address it.

acceptable use policy (AUP) A policy that defines the actions users may perform while accessing systems and networking equipment.

access control The mechanism used in an information system for granting or denying approval to use specific resources.

Access Control List (ACL) A set of rules to permit or restrict data from flowing into or out of a network.

access control model A predefined framework found in hardware and software that a custodian can use for controlling access.

access log A paper or electronic record of individuals who have permission to enter a secure area, the time that they entered, and the time they left the area.

access point (AP) A centrally located WLAN connection device that can send and receive information.

accounting A record that is preserved of who accessed the network, what resources they accessed, and when they disconnected from the network.

active logging Maintaining active logs regarding the reconnaissance activities conducted by the attacker.

active reconnaissance Actively probing a system like an attacker would do to find information.

active scanner A vulnerability scanner that sends "probes" to network devices and examine

the responses received back to evaluate whether a specific device needs remediation.

active-active A configuration in which all load balancers are always active.

active-passive A configuration in which the primary load balancer distributes the network traffic to the most suitable server while the secondary load balancer operates in a "listening mode."

ad hoc mode A WLAN functioning without an AP.

ad hoc topology A configuration in which networks can be created "on the fly" as needed.

Address Resolution Protocol (ARP) Part of the TCP/IP protocol for determining the MAC address based on the IP address.

administrative controls Security controls for developing and ensuring that policies and procedures are carried out; regulating the human factors of security.

Advanced Encryption Standard (AES) A symmetric cipher that was approved by the NIST in late 2000 as a replacement for DES. To date, AES is the most secure symmetric cipher.

advanced malware management A third-party service that monitors a network for any unusual activity.

Advanced Persistent Threat (APT) A new class of attack that uses innovative attack tools to infect a system and then silently extracts data over an extended period.

adware A software program that delivers advertising content in a manner that is unexpected and unwanted by the user.

affinity A scheduling protocol that distributes the load based on which devices can handle the load more efficiently.

after-action report A report to analyze the exercise results with the purpose of identifying strengths to be maintained and weaknesses to be addressed for improvement.

agentless NAC A network access control (NAC) agent that is not installed on an endpoint device but is embedded within a Microsoft Windows Active Directory domain controller.

aggregation switch A device used to combine multiple network connections into a single link.

agile model An application development life-cycle model that follows an incremental approach.

agreements Formal contractual relationships, particularly as they relate to security policy and procedures.

air gap The absence of any type of connection between devices.

alarm An audible sound to warn a guard of an intruder.

algorithm Procedures based on a mathematical formula used to encrypt and decrypt the data. Also called a cipher.

alternative business practices "Workaround" activities that can temporarily substitute for normal business activities.

alternative processing site A different location to be used for processing data.

always-on VPN A VPN that allows the user to always stay connected instead of connecting and disconnecting from it.

Annualized Loss Expectancy (ALE) The expected monetary loss that can be anticipated for an asset due to a risk over a one-year period.

Annualized Rate of Occurrence (ARO) The likelihood of a risk occurring within a year.

anomaly monitoring A monitoring technique used by an intrusion detection system (IDS) that creates a baseline of normal activities and compares actions against the baseline. Whenever there is a significant deviation from this baseline, an alarm is raised.

ANT A proprietary wireless network technology that is used primarily by sensors for communicating data.

antispoofing A defense used to protect against IP spoofing that imitates another computer's IP address.

antivirus (AV) Software that can examine a computer for any infections as well as monitor computer activity and scan new documents that might contain a virus.

appliance OS OS in firmware that is designed to manage a specific device like a digital video recorder or video game console.

application cell See *container*.

application development lifecycle model A conceptual model that describes the different stages involved in creating an application

application management The tools and services responsible for distributing and controlling access to apps.

application whitelisting An inventory of applications and associated components (libraries, configuration files, etc.) that have been pre-approved and authorized to be active and present on the device.

application whitelisting/blacklisting Creating a list of applications that are permitted (whitelisting) or denied (blacklisting) to run.

application/multipurpose proxy A special proxy server that "knows" the application protocols that it supports.

application-aware IDS A specialized intrusion detection system (IDS) that can use "contextual knowledge" in real time.

application-aware IPS An intrusion prevention system (IPS) that "knows" contextual information such as the applications that are running as well as the underlying operating systems.

application-based firewall A firewall that functions at the OSI Application layer (Layer 7).

architecture/design weaknesses Deficiencies in software due to poor design.

ARP poisoning An attack that corrupts the ARP cache.

asset An item that has value.

asset value The relative worth of an asset that is at risk.

asymmetric cryptographic algorithm Cryptography that uses two mathematically related keys.

Attribute-Based Access Control (ABAC) An access control model that uses more flexible policies that can combine attributes.

attributes Characteristic features of different groups of threat actors.

authentication Proving that a user is genuine, and not an imposter.

Authentication Header (AH) An IPsec protocol that authenticates that packets received were sent from the source.

authority A social engineering effectiveness principle in which an attack is directed by someone impersonating an authority figure or falsely citing their authority.

authorization Granting permission to take an action.

automated courses of action Using technology to automate IT processes.

automation That which replaces human physical activity.

availability Security actions that ensure that data is accessible to authorized users.

avoid A response to risk that identifies the risk and the decision is made to not engage in the risk-provoking activity.

B

backdoor Software code that gives access to a computer, program or a service that circumvents any normal security protections.

background check Authenticating the information supplied to a potential employer by a job applicant in the applicant's resume, application, and interviews.

backup utilities Software that can be used for performing backups.

banner grabbing Gathering information from messages that a service transmits when another program connects to it.

barricade A structure designed to block the passage of traffic.

baselining Creating a starting point for comparison purposes to apply targets and goals to measure success.

bcrypt A popular key stretching password hash algorithm.

behavior monitoring A monitoring technique used by an intrusion detection system (IDS) that uses the normal processes and actions as the standard and compares actions against it.

BIOS (Basic Input/Output System) Firmware that wakens and tests the various components of the computer upon startup.

birthday attack A statistical phenomenon that makes finding collisions easier.

black box A penetration test in which the tester has no prior knowledge of the network infrastructure that is being tested.

Blanket Purchase Agreement (BPA) A prearranged purchase or sale agreement between a government agency and a business.

block cipher A cipher that manipulates an entire block of plaintext at one time.

block cipher mode of operation A process that specifies how block ciphers should handle plaintext.

Blowfish A block cipher that operates on 64-bit blocks and can have a key length from 32 to 448 bits.

bluejacking An attack that sends unsolicited messages to Bluetooth-enabled devices.

bluesnarfing An attack that accesses unauthorized information from a wireless device through a Bluetooth connection.

Bluetooth A wireless technology that uses short-range radio frequency (RF) transmissions and provides rapid ad hoc device pairings.

bollard A short but sturdy vertical post that is used to block vehicular traffic.

bot An infected computer that is under the remote control of an attacker for the purpose of launching attacks, also known as a zombie.

bridge   A hardware device or software that is used to join two separate computer networks to enable communication between them.

bring your own device (BYOD)   Allows users to use their own personal mobile devices for business purposes.

brute force attack   A password attack in which every possible combination of letters, numbers, and characters is used to create encrypted passwords that are matched against those in a stolen password file.

buffer overflow attack   An attack that occurs when a process attempts to store data in RAM beyond the boundaries of a fixed-length storage buffer.

burning   Lighting paper on fire to destroy the data printed on it.

business continuity   The ability of an organization to maintain its operations and services in the face of a disruptive event.

cable lock   A device that can be inserted into the security slot of a portable device and rotated so that the cable lock is secured to the device to prevent it from being stolen.

cage   A fenced secure waiting area that can contain visitors until they are approved for entry.

Canonical Encoding Rules (CER)   An X.509 encoding format.

captive portal AP   An infrastructure that is used on public access WLANs that uses a standard web browser to provide information, and gives the wireless user the opportunity to agree to a policy or present valid login credentials to provide a higher degree of security.

capture video   Using a video camera to clearly document the entire process of a forensics investigation.

capturing the system image   Taking a snapshot of the current state of the computer that contains all current settings and data.

carrier unlocking   Uncoupling a phone from a specific wireless provider.

cellular telephony   A communications network in which the coverage area is divided into hexagon-shaped cells.

certificate authority (CA)   The entity that is responsible for digital certificates.

certificate chaining   Linking several certificates together to establish trust between all the certificates involved.

Certificate Revocation List (CRL)   A list of certificate serial numbers that have been revoked.

Certificate Signing Request (CSR)   A user request for a digital certificate.

certificate-based authentication   An authentication method in which each supplicant computer must have a digital certificate as proof of its identity.

chain of custody   A process of documentation that shows that the evidence was always under strict control and no unauthorized individuals were given the opportunity to corrupt the evidence.

Challenge-Handshake Authentication Protocol (CHAP)   A weak version of Extensible Authentication Protocol (EAP).

change management   A methodology for making modifications to a system and keeping track of those changes.

choose your own device (CYOD)   Employees choose from a limited selection of approved devices but the employee pays the upfront cost of the device while the business owns the contract.

cipher   *See* algorithm.

Cipher Block Chaining (CBC)   A process in which each block of plaintext is XORed with the previous block of ciphertext before being encrypted.

clean desk   A policy designed to ensure that all confidential or sensitive materials are removed from a user's workspace and secured when the items are not in use or an employee leaves her workspace.

clickjacking   Hijacking a mouse click.

client-side execution and validation   Input validation that is performed by the user's web browser.

cloud access security broker (CASB)   A set of software tools or services that resides between the enterprises' on-premises infrastructure and the cloud provider's infrastructure to ensure that the security policies of the enterprise extend to their data in the cloud.

cloud computing   A pay-per-use computing model in which customers pay only for the online computing resources that they need, and the resources can be easily scaled.

cloud storage   A cloud system that has no computational capabilities but provides remote file storage.

code reuse of third-party libraries and SDKs   Using existing software or software development kits (SDKs) in a new application.

code signing   Digitally signing applications.

code signing digital certificate   Certificate used by software developers to digitally sign a program to prove that the software comes from the entity that signed it and that no unauthorized third party has altered it.

cold site   A remote site that provides office space; the customer must provide and install all the equipment needed to continue operations.

collision   When two files have the same hash.

collision attack   An attempt to find two input strings of a hash function that produce the same hash result.

common access card (CAC)   A U.S. Department of Defense (DoD) smart card used for identification of active-duty and reserve military personnel along with civilian employees and special contractors.

community cloud   A cloud that is open only to specific organizations that have common concerns.

compensating control   A control that provides an alternative to normal controls that for some reason cannot be used.

competitors   Threat actors that launch attack against an opponents' system to steal classified information.

compiled code testing   Searching for errors that could prevent an application from properly compiling from source code to application code.

confidential   The highest data label level of sensitivity.

confidentiality   Security actions that ensure that only authorized parties can view the information.

configuration compliance scanner   A device that can evaluate and report any compliance issues related to specific industry guidelines.

configuration validation   Reviewing the configuration of systems to determine if security settings are correct.

confusion   A means to thwart statistical analysis so that the key does not relate in a simple way to the ciphertext.

consensus   A social engineering effectiveness principle in which the victim is influenced by what others do.

container   A virtualized environment that holds only the necessary operating system components (such as binary files and libraries) that are needed for a specific application to run. Also called an *application cell*.

containerization   Separating storage into separate business and personal "containers."

containment   An action step in the incident response process that involves limiting the damage of the incident and isolating those systems that are impacted to prevent further damage.

content management   Tools used to support the creation and subsequent editing and modification of digital content by multiple employees.

context-aware authentication   Using a contextual setting to validate a user.

continuing education   Providing security awareness and training to users.

continuous integration   Ensuring that security features are incorporated at each stage of application development.

continuous monitoring   Sustained and continual surveillance.

control diversity   Having different groups responsible for regulating access to a system.

controller AP   An AP that is managed through a dedicated wireless LAN controller (WLC).

corporate-owned   A mobile device that is purchased and owned by the enterprise.

corporate owned, personally enabled (COPE) Employees choose from a selection of company-approved devices.

corrective controls Controls that are intended to mitigate or lessen the damage caused by an incident.

correlation engine A device that aggregates and correlates content from different sources to uncover an attack.

Counter (CTR) A process in which both the message sender and receiver access a counter, which computes a new value each time a cipher-text block is exchanged.

Counter Mode with Cipher Block Chaining Message Authentication Code Protocol (CCMP) The encryption protocol used for WPA2 that specifies the use of a general-purpose cipher mode algorithm providing data privacy with AES.

credential management Managing the login credentials such as passwords in user accounts.

credentialed vulnerability scan A scan that provides credentials (user name and password) to the scanner so that tests for additional internal vulnerabilities can be performed.

crossover error rate (CER) The biometric error rate in which the FAR and FRR are equal over the size of the population.

cross-site request forgery (XSRF) An attack that uses the user's web browser settings to impersonate that user.

cross-site scripting (XSS) An attack that injects scripts into a web application server to direct attacks at clients.

crypto modules Cryptography modules that are invoked by crypto service providers.

crypto service provider A service used by an application to implement cryptography.

cryptography The practice of transforming information so that it is secure and cannot be accessed by unauthorized persons.

crypto-malware Malware that encrypts all the files on the device so that they cannot be opened.

custodian (steward) Individual to whom day-to-day actions have been assigned by the owner.

custom firmware Firmware that is written by users to own and run on their own mobile devices.

cyber-incident response team A group responsible for responding to security incidents.

data backup The process of copying information to a different medium and storing it at an offsite location so that it can be used in the event of a disaster.

Data Encryption Standard (DES) One of the first widely popular symmetric cryptography algorithms. No longer considered secure.

Data Execution Prevention (DEP) A Microsoft Windows feature that prevents attackers from using buffer overflow to execute malware.

data exposure Disclosing sensitive data to attackers.

data loss prevention (DLP) A system of security tools that is used to recognize and identify data that is critical to the organization and ensure that it is protected.

data retention How long data must be kept and how it is to be secured.

data sanitation tools Tools that can be employed to securely remove data from electronic media.

data sensitivity labeling Applying the correct category to data to ensure proper data handling.

data sovereignty The concept that data stored in a digital format is subject to the laws of the country in which the storage facility resides.

data-at-rest Data that is stored on electronic media.

database security Security functions provided by access control lists (ACLs) for protecting SQL and relational database systems.

data-in-transit Actions that transmit the data across a network.

data-in-use Data actions being performed by "endpoint devices," such as printing a report from a desktop computer.

DDoS mitigator   A hardware device that identifies and blocks real-time distributed denial of service (DDoS) attacks.

dead code   A section of an application that executes but performs no meaningful function.

deadbolt lock   A door lock that extends a solid metal bar into the door frame for extra security.

default configurations   The *out-of-the-box* security configuration settings.

defense-in-depth   Creating multiple layers of security defenses through which an attacker must penetrate; *also called* layered security.

degaussing   Permanently destroying a hard drive by reducing or eliminating the magnetic field.

demilitarized zone (DMZ)   A separate network that rests outside the secure network perimeter: untrusted outside users can access the DMZ but cannot enter the secure network.

denial of service (DoS)   An attack that attempts to prevent a system from performing its normal functions by overwhelming the system with requests.

deprecated algorithm   A cryptographic algorithm that is still available but should not be used because of known vulnerabilities.

deprovisioning   Removing a resource that is no longer needed.

detective control   A control that is designed to identify any threat that has reached the system.

deterrent control   A control that attempts to discourage security violations before they occur.

development stage   A stage of application development in which the requirements for the application are established and it is confirmed that the application meets the intended business needs before the actual coding begins.

device driver manipulation   Altering a device driver for use in an attack.

dictionary attack   A password attack that creates encrypted versions of common dictionary words and compares them against those in a stolen password file.

differential backup   A backup that copies any data that has changed since last full backup.

Diffie-Hellman (DH)   A key exchange that requires all parties to agree upon a large prime number and related integer so that the same key can be separately created.

Diffie-Hellman Ephemeral (DHE)   A Diffie-Hellman key exchange that uses different keys.

diffusion   A means to thwart statistical analysis so that if a single character of plaintext is changed then it should result in multiple characters of the ciphertext changing.

Dig   A Linux command-line alternative to Nslookup.

digital camera   A device that uses internal storage and external SD cards to record photographs and capture video.

digital certificate   A technology used to associate a user's identity to a public key and that has been *digitally signed* by a trusted third party.

digital signature   An electronic verification of the sender.

Digital Signature Algorithm (DSA)   A U.S. federal government standard for digital signatures.

directory service   A database stored on the network itself that contains information about users and network devices.

disabled   Making an account inactive inactive.

disabling default accounts/ passwords   Turning off unnecessary default accounts and passwords.

disabling unnecessary ports and services   Turning off any service that is not being used.

disassociation attack   A wireless attack in which false de-authentication or disassociation frames are sent to an AP that appear to come from another client device, causing the client to disconnect.

disaster recovery plan (DRP)   A written document that details the process for restoring IT resources following an event that causes a significant disruption in service.

Discretionary Access Control (DAC)   The least restrictive access control model in which the owner of the object has total control over it.

dissolvable NAC agent A network access control (NAC) agent that disappears after reporting information to the NAC device.

distance A factor in the location selection of an off-site backup.

Distinguished Encoding Rules (DER) An X.509 encoding format.

distributed denial of service (DDoS) An attack that uses many computers to perform a DoS attack.

distributive allocation Spreading risk.

DLL injection An attack that inserts code into a running process through a Dynamic Link Library.

DNS amplification attack An attack that uses publicly accessible and open DNS servers to flood a system with DNS response traffic.

DNS poisoning An attack that substitutes DNS addresses so that the computer is automatically redirected to an attacker's device.

documented incident definitions An outline that defines in detail what is and is not an incident that requires a response.

domain hijacking An attack that occurs when a domain pointer that links a domain name to a specific web server is changed.

domain name resolution Mapping computer and device names to IP addresses.

Domain Name System Security Extensions (DNSSEC) An extension to DNS that adds additional resource records and message header information, used to verify that DNS data has not been altered in transmission.

domain validation digital certificate Certificate that verifies the identity of the entity that has control over the domain name.

door lock A lock that requires a key or other device to open doors.

downgrade attack An attack in which the system is forced to abandon the current higher security mode of operation and *fall back* to implementing an older and less secure mode.

dumpster diving The act of digging through trash receptacles to find information that can be useful in an attack.

dynamic analysis (fuzzing) Software testing technique that deliberately provides invalid, unexpected, or random data as inputs to a computer program.

E

EAP-FAST An Extensible Authentication Protocol that securely tunnels any credential form for authentication (such as a password or a token) using TLS.

EAP-TLS An Extensible Authentication Protocol that uses digital certificates for authentication.

EAP-TTLS An Extensible Authentication Protocol that securely tunnels client password authentication within Transport Layer Security (TLS) records.

elasticity The ability of an enterprise data center to revert to a former size after expanding.

electromagnetic interference (EMI) Electromagnetic fields emitted from technology devices that can result in interference.

electromagnetic pulse (EMP) A short-duration burst of energy by the source.

Electronic Code Book (ECB) A process in which plaintext is divided into blocks and each block is then encrypted separately.

elliptic curve cryptography (ECC) An algorithm that uses elliptic curves instead of prime numbers to compute keys.

Elliptic Curve Diffie–Hellman (ECDH) A Diffie-Hellman key exchange that uses elliptic curve cryptography instead of prime numbers in its computation.

email digital certificate A certificate that allows a user to digitally sign and encrypt mail messages.

embedded system Computer hardware and software contained within a larger system that is designed for a specific function.

employee offboarding The tasks associated when an employee is released from the enterprise.

employee onboarding The tasks associated when hiring a new employee.

Encapsulating Security Payload (ESP) An IPsec protocol that encrypts packets.

encryption The process of changing plaintext into ciphertext.

end-of-life system   System for which vendors have dropped all support for security updates due to the system's age.

enterprise method   Authentication for the WPA2 Enterprise model.

environmental threat   Threat actions that are related to the surroundings, such as tornados, floods, and hurricanes.

ephemeral key   A temporary key that is used only once before it is discarded.

eradication   An action step in the incident response process that involves finding the cause of the incident and temporarily removing any systems that may be causing damage.

evil twin   An AP set up by an attacker to mimic an authorized AP and capture transmissions, so a user's device will unknowingly connect to this evil twin instead of the authorized AP.

exercises   Simulated attack activities.

exit interview   A "wrap-up" meeting between management representatives and the person leaving an organization.

exploitation framework   A structure of exploits and monitoring tools used to replicate attacks during a vulnerability assessment.

Extended Validation (EV) certificate   Certificate that requires more extensive verification of the legitimacy of the business than does a domain validation digital certificate.

Extensible Authentication Protocol (EAP)   A framework for transporting authentication protocols that defines the format of the messages.

external   The location outside an enterprise in which some threat actors perform.

external threat   Threat from outside an organization.

extranet   A private network that can also be accessed by authorized external customers, vendors, and partners.

F

facial recognition   A biometric authentication that is becoming increasingly popular on smartphones that views the user's face.

failover   Moving data input and output processes from the primary location to the alternative processing site.

false acceptance rate (FAR)   The frequency at which imposters are accepted as genuine when using biometric authentication.

false negative   The failure to raise an alarm when there is abnormal behavior.

false positive   Alarm that is raised when there is no actual abnormal behavior.

false rejection rate (FRR)   The frequency that legitimate users are rejected when using biometric authentication.

familiarity   A social engineering effectiveness principle in which the victim is influenced by the claim that the victim is well-known and well-received.

Faraday cage   A metallic enclosure that prevents the entry or escape of an electromagnetic field.

fat AP   Autonomous AP in which everything is self-contained in a single device.

fault tolerance   A system's ability to deal with malfunctions.

federation   Single sign-on for networks owned by different organizations, *also called* federated identity management (FIM).

fencing   Securing a restricted area by erecting a barrier.

file integrity check (FIC)   A service that can monitor any changes made to computer files.

file system security   Security functions provided by access control lists (ACLs) for protecting files managed by the operating system.

File Transfer Protocol (FTP)   An unsecure TCP/IP protocol that is commonly used for transferring files.

fingerprint scanner   A device that uses fingerprints as a biometric identifier.

fire suppression   Attempts to reduce the impact of a fire.

firewall   Hardware or software that is designed to limit the spread of malware.

firmware OTA updates   Mobile operating system patches and updates that are distributed by the wireless carrier as an over-the-air (OTA) update.

flood guard   A defense against a MAC flooding attack. *See also* port security.

forensics (forensic science)   The application of science to questions that are of interest to the legal profession.

forward proxy   A computer or an application program that intercepts user requests from the internal secure network and then processes those requests on behalf of the users.

FTP Secure (FTPS)   A TCP/IP protocol that uses Secure Sockets Layer or Transport Layer Security to encrypt commands sent over the control port (port 21) in an FTP session.

full backup   The starting point for all backups that copies the entire set of data.

full disk encryption (FDE)   Encryption that protects all data on a hard drive.

full tunnel   A VPN technology in which all traffic is sent to the VPN concentrator and is protected.

funding and resources   An attribute of threat actors that can vary widely.

G

Galois/Counter (GCM)   A process that both encrypts and computes a message authentication code (MAC).

general-purpose guides   Security configuration guides that are generic in scope.

generic account   An account not tied to a specific person.

geofencing   Using the mobile device's GPS to define geographical boundaries where an app can be used.

geolocation   The process of identifying the geographical location of a device.

GNU Privacy Guard (GNuPG)   Free and open-source software that is commonly used to encrypt and decrypt data.

GPS tagging (geo-tagging)   Adding geographical identification data to media such as digital photos taken on a mobile device.

gray box   A penetration test where some limited information has been provided to the tester.

group policy   A preferred approach is to assign privileges by group instead of individually.

group-based access control   Configuring multiple computers by setting a single policy for enforcement.

guest account   An account given to temporary users.

guest network   A separate open network that anyone can access without prior authorization.

H

hactivists   A group of threat actors that is strongly motivated by ideology.

hardware root of trust   The hardware starting point in a chain of trust.

Hardware Security Module (HSM)   A dedicated cryptographic processor that provides protection for cryptographic keys.

hardware security token   A small device (usually one that can be affixed to a keychain) with a window display.

hash   An algorithm that creates a unique digital fingerprint called a "digest."

Hashed Message Authentication Code (HMAC)   A hash function used to authenticate the sender.

heating, ventilation, and air conditioning (HVAC)   Environmental systems that provide and regulate heating and cooling.

heuristic monitoring   A monitoring technique used by an intrusion detection system (IDS) that uses an algorithm to determine if a threat exists.

high availability   A system that can function for an extended period of time with little downtime.

high resiliency   The ability to quickly recover from resource vs. security constraints.

HMAC-based one-time password (HOTP)   A one-time password that changes when a specific event occurs.

hoax   A false warning.

honeynet   A network set up with intentional vulnerabilities to invite attacks and reveal attackers' methods.

honeypot   A computer typically located in an area with limited security and loaded with software and data files that appear to be authentic, but are actually imitations of real data files, to trick attackers into revealing their attack techniques.

host agent health checks   Reports sent by network access control (NAC) "agents" installed on devices to gather information and report back to the NAC device.

host-based firewall   A software firewall that runs as a program on the local computer to block or filter traffic coming into and out of the computer.

host-based intrusion detection system (HIDS)   A software-based application that runs on a local host computer that can detect an attack as it occurs.

host-based intrusion prevention system (HIPS)   A technology that monitors a local system to immediately react to block a malicious attack.

hosted services   A computing model in which servers, storage, and the supporting networking infrastructure are shared by multiple enterprises over a remote network connection.

hot aisle/cold aisle   A layout in a data center that can be used to reduce heat by managing air flow.

hot site   A duplicate of the production site that has all the equipment needed for an organization to continue running, including office space and furniture, telephone jacks, computer equipment, and a live telecommunications link.

hybrid cloud   A combination of public and private clouds.

Hypertext Transport Protocol Secure (HTTPS)   HTTP sent over SSL (Secure Sockets Layer) or TLS (Transport Layer Security).

hypervisor   Software that manages virtual machine operating systems.

identification   Credentials presented by a user accessing a computer system. Also used in forensics as an action step in the incident response process that involves determining whether an event is actually a security incident.

identification of critical systems   Distinguishing important functions that make up the mission-essential functions in an organization.

identify a lack of security controls   A vulnerability scan that looks for missing controls to establish a secure framework.

identify common misconfigurations   A vulnerability scan that looks for misapplied settings in hardware and software.

identify vulnerabilities   A vulnerability scan that looks to identify security weaknesses in a system.

IEEE 802.1x   A standard, originally developed for wired networks, that provides a greater degree of security by implementing port-based authentication.

IMAP (Internet Mail Access Protocol)   A more recent and advanced electronic email system for incoming mail.

immutable systems   Ensuring that once a value or configuration is employed as part of an application, it is not modified.

impact on finance   The impact of a loss of monetary funding on business operations.

impact on life   The impact on human wellbeing.

impact on property   The impact of a loss of tangible assets on business operations.

impact on reputation   The impact of a loss of status on business operations.

impact on safety   The impact of a loss of physical protection on business operations.

impersonation   A social engineering attack that involves masquerading as a real or fictitious character and then playing out the role of that person on a victim.

implicit deny   The principle of being always blocked by default.

improper error handling   Software that does not properly trap an error condition and provides an attacker with underlying access to the system.

improper input handling   Software that allows the user to enter data but does not validate or filter user input to prevent a malicious action.

improperly configured account Account set up for a user that might provide more access than is necessary.

in-band IDS An intrusion detection system (IDS) implemented through the network itself by using network protocols and tools.

incident response plan (IRP) A set of written instructions for reacting to a security incident.

incident response process Action steps to be taken when an incident occurs.

incremental backup A backup that copies any data that has changed since last full backup or last incremental backup.

industrial control systems (ICS) Systems that collect, monitor, and process real-time data to control machines locally or at remote sites.

industry-specific frameworks Frameworks/ architectures that are specific to a particular industry or market sector.

industry-standard frameworks "Supporting structures" for implementing security; also called reference architectures.

infrared Light that is next to visible light on the light spectrum and was once used for data communications.

Infrastructure as a Service (IaaS) A cloud computing model in which customers have the highest level of control and can deploy and run their own software.

infrastructure as code Managing a hardware and software infrastructure using the same principles as developing computer code.

initial exploitation Using information acquired to determine if it provides entry to the secure network.

initialization vector (IV) A nonce that is selected in a non-predictable way.

injection attack An attack that introduces new input to exploit a vulnerability.

inline IDS An intrusion detection system (IDS) that is directly connected to the network and monitors the flow of data as it occurs.

insiders Employees, contractors, and business partners who can be responsible for an attack.

integer overflow attack An attack that occurs when an attacker changes the value of a variable to by using an integer overflow.

integrity Security actions that ensure that the information is correct and no unauthorized person or malicious software has altered the data.

integrity measurement An "attestation mechanism" designed to ensure that an application is running only known and approved executables.

intent and motivation The reasoning behind attacks made by threat actors.

Interconnection Security Agreement (ISA) An agreement between parties intended to minimize security risks for data transmitted across a network.

intermediate certificate authority (CA) An entity that processes the CSR and verifies the authenticity of the user on behalf of a certificate authority (CA).

internal The location within an enterprise in which some threat actors perform.

internal threat Threat that comes from within the organization.

international Information security framework/ architectures that are worldwide.

Internet of Things (IoT) Connecting any device to the Internet for the purpose of sending and receiving data to be acted upon.

Internet Protocol Security (IPsec) A protocol suite for securing Internet Protocol (IP) communications.

intimidation A social engineering effectiveness principle in which the victim is frightened and coerced by threat.

intranet A private network that belongs to an organization that can only be accessed by approved internal users.

intrusion detection system (IDS) A device that detects an attack as it occurs.

intrusive vulnerability scan A scan that attempts to penetrate the system in order to perform a simulated attack.

IP and **Ifconfig** Linux implementations of Ipconfig.

IP spoofing Imitating another computer by means of changing the IP address.

Ipconfig A command-line utility that displays all current TCP/IP network configuration values and refreshes Dynamic Host Configuration Protocol (DHCP) and DNS settings.

iris scanner Using a standard computer webcam to map the unique characteristic of the iris for authentication.

jailbreaking Circumventing the installed built-in limitations on Apple iOS devices.

jamming Intentionally flooding the radio frequency (RF) spectrum with extraneous RF signal "noise" that creates interference and prevents communications from occurring.

job rotation The act of moving individuals from one job responsibility to another.

K

Kerberos An authentication system developed by the Massachusetts Institute of Technology (MIT) and used to verify the identity of networked users.

key escrow A process in which keys are managed by a third party, such as a trusted CA.

key exchange The process of sending and receiving secure cryptographic keys. Also the specific handshake setup between web browser and web server.

key management Procedures to regulate the distribution of door keys.

key strength The resiliency of a key to resist attacks.

key stretching A password hashing algorithm that requires significantly more time than standard hashing algorithms to create the digest.

keylogger Spyware that silently captures and stores each keystroke that a user types on the computer's keyboard.

kiosk OS System and user interface software for an interactive kiosk.

known ciphertext attack Using statistical tools to attempt to discover a pattern in ciphertexts; also called *ciphertext only attack*.

L

lack of vendor support When the company that made a device provides no support for the device.

layered security Creating multiple layers of security defenses through which an attacker must penetrate; *also called* defense-in-depth.

LDAP over SSL (LDAPS) Securing LDAP traffic by using Secure Sockets Layer (SSL) or Transport Layer Security (TLS).

least functionality A principle in which a user is given the minimum set of permissions required to perform necessary tasks.

least privilege Providing only the minimum amount of privileges necessary to perform a job or function.

legal and compliance issues Following the requirements of legislation, prescribed rules and regulations, specified standards, or the terms of a contract.

legal hold A notification sent from the legal team to employees instructing them not to delete electronically stored information or paper documents that may be relevant to an incident.

legal implications Consequences as determined by law of off-site backups.

lessons learned An action step in the incident response process that involves completing incident documentation and performing detailed analysis to increase security and improve future response efforts.

lighting Illuminating an area so that it can be viewed after dark.

Lightweight Directory Access Protocol (LDAP) A protocol for a client application to access an X.500 directory.

live boot media A "lightweight" bootable image on a USB flash drive or optical media.

load balancer A dedicated network device that can direct requests to different servers based on a variety of factors.

location selection A consideration of where an off-site backup should be stored.

location-based policies Policies that establish geographical boundaries where a mobile device can and cannot be used.

log A record of events that occur.

logic bomb Computer code that lies dormant until it is triggered by a specific logical event.

loop prevention A means to mitigate broadcast storms using the IEEE 802.1d standard spanning-tree algorithm (STA).

low latency A small amount of time that occurs between when a byte is input into a cryptographic algorithm and the time the output is obtained.

low power devices Small electronic devices that consume very small amounts of power.

M

MAC spoofing Imitating another computer by means of changing the MAC address.

machine digital certificate Certificate used to verify the identity of a device in a network transaction.

mail gateway A system that monitors emails for unwanted content and prevents these messages from being delivered.

malware Software that enters a computer system without the user's knowledge or consent and then performs an unwanted and usually harmful action.

Mandatory Access Control (MAC) The most restrictive access control model, typically found in military settings in which security is of supreme importance.

mandatory vacations Requiring that all employees take vacations.

man-in-the-browser (MITB) An attack that intercepts communication between a browser and the underlying computer.

man-in-the-middle (MITM) An attack that intercepts legitimate communication and forges a fictitious response to the sender.

manmade threat Threat that is of human origin, such as the vandalism of a wireless antenna.

mantrap A device that monitors and controls two interlocking doors to a small room (a vestibule), designed to separate secure and nonsecure areas.

master image A copy of a properly configured and secured computer software system that can be replicated to other computers.

mean time between failures (MTBF) A statistical value that is the average time until a component fails, cannot be repaired, and must be replaced.

mean time to recovery (MTTR) The average time for a device to recover from a failure that is not a terminal failure.

Media Access Control (MAC) address filtering A method for controlling access to a WLAN based on the device's MAC address.

media gateway A device that converts media data from one format to another.

Memorandum of Understanding (MOU) An agreement between two or more parties to enable them to work together that is not legally enforceable but is more formal than an unwritten agreement.

memory leak A vulnerability that occurs when an application dynamically allocates memory but does not free that memory when finished using it.

Message Digest 5 (MD5) A revision of MD4 that was designed to address MD4's weaknesses.

microSD A smaller form factor type of Secure Digital card commonly used in smaller devices such as smartphones, digital cameras, and tablets.

misconfiguration An incorrectly configured device.

misconfiguration implementation Breaches of cryptography that are the result of incorrect configuration or uses of the cryptography.

mission-essential function The activity that serves as the core purpose of the enterprise.

mitigate Addressing risks by making risks less serious.

mobile OS An operating system for mobile phones, smartphones, tablets, and other handheld devices.

model verification A test used to ensure that the projected application meets all specifications at that point.

motion detection Determining an object's change in position in relation to its surroundings.

MS-CHAP The Microsoft version of Challenge-Handshake Authentication Protocol (CHAP).

multifactor authentication Using more than one type of authentication credential.

multifunctional device (MFD) A device that combines the functions of a printer, copier, scanner, and fax machine.

multimedia messaging service (MMS) Text messages in which pictures, video, or audio can be included.

nation state actors State-sponsored attackers employed by a government for launching computer attacks against foes.

national Information security framework/architectures that are domestic.

near field communication (NFC) A set of standards used to establish communication between devices in very close proximity.

Netcat A command-line alternative to Nmap with additional features scanning for vulnerabilities.

Netstat A command-line utility that can display detailed information about how a device is communicating with other network devices.

network access control (NAC) A technique that examines the current state of a system or network device before it can connect to the network.

network address translation (NAT) A technique that allows private IP addresses to be used on the public Internet.

network intrusion detection system (NIDS) A technology that watches for attacks on the network and reports back to a central device.

network intrusion prevention system (NIPS) A technology that monitors network traffic to immediately react to block a malicious attack.

network mapping scanner A device that combines network device discovery tools and network scanners to find open ports or discover shared folders.

network OS Operating system (OS) software that runs on a network device like a firewall, router, or switch.

network tap (test access point) A separate device that can be installed on the network for monitoring traffic.

network traffic and logs Recorded information about any network activity used in a forensics investigation.

network-based firewall A firewall that functions at the OSI Network layer (Layer 3).

new threat A threat that has not been previously identified.

Nmap A security vulnerability scanner that can determine which devices are connected to the network and the services they are running.

nonce (number used once) A value that must be unique within some specified scope.

non-credentialed vulnerability scan A scan that does not use credentials (user name and password) to conduct an internal vulnerability assessment.

non-disclosure agreement (NDA) A legal contract between parties that specifies how confidential material will be shared between the parties but restricted to others.

non-intrusive vulnerability scan A scan that uses only available information to hypothesize the status of the vulnerability.

non-persistence tools Tools used to ensure that unwanted data is not carried forward but instead a clean image is used.

non-regulatory Information security frameworks/architectures that are not required.

non-repudiation The process of proving that a user performed an action.

normalization Organizing data within a database to minimize redundancy.

Nslookup A command-line utility that can query the Domain Name System (DNS) to obtain a specific domain name or IP address mapping.

NTLM (New Technology LAN Manager) hash A hash used by modern Microsoft Windows operating systems for creating password digests.

O

OAuth An open source federation framework.

obfuscation Making something obscure or unclear.

obfuscation/camouflaged code Writing an application in such a way that its inner functionality is difficult for an outsider to understand.

object identifier (OID)   A designator made up of a series of numbers separated with a dot which names an object or entity.

offline attack   Stealing a message digest database and cracking it offline.

offline CA   A certificate authority that is not directly connected to a network.

off-site backup   A backup should be stored at a different location.

online attack   An attempt to enter different passwords at the login prompt until the right password is guessed.

online CA   A certificate authority that is directly connected to a network.

Online Certificate Status Protocol (OCSP)   A process that performs a real-time lookup of a certificate's status.

on-premises   A computing model in which enterprises purchased all the hardware and software necessary to run the organization.

Open ID Connect   A federation technology that provides user authentication information.

open method   A wireless network mode in which no authentication is required.

open-source intelligence   Freely available automated attack software.

order of restoration   The sequence in which different systems are reinstated.

order of volatility   The sequence in which volatile data must be preserved in a computer forensic investigation.

organized crime   Threat actors that are moving from traditional organized criminal activities to more rewarding and less risky online attacks

out-of-band IDS   An intrusion detection system (IDS) that uses an independent and dedicated channel to reach the device.

owner   A person responsible for the information.

partner on-boarding   The start-up relationship between partners.

pass the hash   An attack in which the user sends the hash to the remote system to then be authenticated on an NTLM system.

passive IDS   An intrusion detection system (IDS) that is connected to a port on a switch in which data is fed to it.

passive reconnaissance   Using searches online for publicly accessible information that can reveal valuable insight about a system.

passive scanner   A vulnerability scanner that can identify the current software operating systems and applications being used on the network, and indicate which devices might have a vulnerability.

passively testing security controls   A vulnerability scan that does not attempt to exploit any weaknesses that it finds but only reports back what it uncovers.

password   A secret combination of letters, numbers, and/or characters that only the user should have knowledge of.

Password Authentication Protocol (PAP)   A weak version of Extensible Authentication Protocol (EAP).

password complexity   An account enforcement policy that determines passwords must meet complexity requirements.

password cracker   Software intended to break the digest of a password to determine its strength.

password expiration   An account enforcement policy that determines how many days a password can be used before the user is required to change it.

password history   An account enforcement policy that determines how many days a new password must be kept before the user can change it.

password length   An account enforcement policy that determines the minimum password length.

password lockout   An account enforcement policy that prevents a logon after a set number of failed logon attempts within a specified period and can also specify the length of time that the lockout is in force.

password recovery   The policies for recovering a password in the event a user forgets a password.

password reuse   An account enforcement policy that determines the number of unique new passwords a user must use before an old password can be reused.

patch A publicly released software security update intended to repair a vulnerability.

patch management tools Tools used to manage security patches.

PBKDF2 A popular key stretching password hash algorithm.

penetration testing A test (pentest) by an outsider that attempts to actually exploit any weaknesses in systems that are vulnerable.

penetration testing authorization Permission to perform a penetration test.

perfect forward secrecy Public key systems that generate random public keys that are different for each session.

permanent NAC agent A network access control (NAC) agent that resides on end devices until uninstalled.

permission auditing and review A review that is intended to examine the permissions that a user has been given to determine if each is still necessary.

persistence The characteristic of endurance to continue to probe for weaknesses and exploit them.

personal email policy A policy that covers using company email to send personal email messages, accessing personal email at a place of employment, and forwarding company emails to a personal email account.

personal identification number (PIN) A passcode made up of numbers only.

Personal Identity Verification (PIV) A U.S. government standard for smart cards that covers all government employees.

Personal Information Exchange (PFX) An X.509 file format that is the preferred file format for creating certificates to authenticate applications or websites.

Personally Identifiable Information (PII) Data that could potentially identify a specific individual.

phishing Sending an email or displaying a web announcement that falsely claims to be from a legitimate enterprise in an attempt to trick the user into surrendering private information.

physical control A control that implements security in a defined structure and location.

physical network segregation Isolating the network so that it is not accessible by outsiders.

Ping A command-line utility to test the connection between two network devices.

pinning Hard-coding a digital certificate within a program that is using the certificate.

pivot Moving around inside the network to other resources.

PKCS#12 An X.509 file format that is one of a numbered set of 15 standards defined by RSA Corporation.

Platform as a Service (PaaS) A cloud service in which consumers can install and run their own specialized applications on the cloud computing network.

pointer deference A pointer with a value of NULL used as if it pointed to a valid memory area.

port mirroring A facility that allows the administrator to configure a switch to copy traffic that occurs on some or all ports to a designated monitoring port on the switch.

port security A flood guard technology that restricts the number of incoming MAC addresses for a port.

Post Office Protocol (POP) An earlier mail system responsible for incoming mail.

preparation An action step in the incident response process that involves equipping IT staff, management, and users to handle potential incidents when they arise.

preservation of the evidence Ensuring that important proof is not destroyed.

preshared key (PSK) The authentication model used in WPA that requires a secret key value to be entered in the AP and all approved wireless devices prior to communicating.

Pretty Good Privacy (PGP) A commercial product that is commonly used to encrypt files and messages.

preventive control A control that attempts to prevent the threat from coming in and reaching contact with the vulnerability.

Privacy Enhancement Mail (PEM) An X.509 file format that uses DER encoding and can have multiple certificates.

privacy The state or condition of being free from public attention to the degree that you determine.

privacy impact assessment Part of a business impact assessment (BIA) that is used to identify and mitigate privacy risks.

privacy officer A manager who oversees data privacy compliance and manages data risk.

privacy threshold assessment Part of a business impact assessment (BIA) that is used to determine if a system contains personally identifiable information (PII), whether a privacy impact assessment is required, and if any other privacy requirements apply to the IT system.

private A data label for restricted data with a medium level of confidentiality.

private cloud A cloud that is created and maintained on a private network.

private key An asymmetric encryption key that does have to be protected.

privilege escalation An attack that exploits a vulnerability in software to gain access to resources that the user normally would be restricted from accessing.

privileged account An account which powerful rights, privileges, and permissions are granted so that a user could perform nearly any action.

production stage An application development stage in which the application is released to be used in its actual setting.

proper error handling Taking the correct steps when an error occurs so that the application does not abort unexpectedly.

proper input validation Accounting for errors such as incorrect user input.

proprietary A data label indicating the data belongs to the enterprise.

protected distribution system (PDS) A system of cable conduits that is used to protect classified information being transmitted between two secure areas.

Protected EAP (PEAP) An EAP method designed to simplify the deployment of 802.1x by using Microsoft Windows logins and passwords.

Protected Health Information (PHI) Data about a person's health status, provision of health care, or payment for health care.

protocol analyzer Hardware or software that captures packets to decode and analyze their contents.

provisioning The enterprise-wide configuration, deployment, and management of multiple types of IT system resources.

proximity card A contactless card that does not require physical contact with the card itself for authentication.

pseudorandom number generator (PRNG) An algorithm for creating a sequence of numbers whose properties approximate those of a random number.

public A data label for the lowest level of data sensitivity.

public cloud A cloud in which the services and infrastructure are offered to all users with access provided remotely through the Internet.

public key An asymmetric encryption key that does not have to be protected.

public key infrastructure (PKI) The underlying infrastructure for the management of public keys used in digital certificates.

pulping Breaking paper back into wood cellulose fibers after the ink is removed.

pulverizing Hammering paper into dust.

purging Erasing data using the operating system "delete" command.

push notification services Sending SMS text messages to selected users or groups of users.

qualitative risk calculation An approach to risk calculation that uses an "educated guess" based on observation.

quantitative risk calculation An approach to risk calculation that attempts to create actual numbers associated with the risk by using historical data.

race condition A software occurrence when two concurrent *threads* of execution access a shared resource simultaneously, resulting in unintended consequences.

RACE Integrity Primitives Evaluation Message Digest (RIPEMD) A hash algorithm that uses two different and independent parallel chains of computation and then combines the result at the end of the process.

radio frequency identification (RFID) A wireless set of standards used to transmit information from paper-based tags to a proximity reader.

RADIUS (Remote Authentication Dial In User Service) An industry standard authentication service with widespread support across nearly all vendors of networking equipment.

RAID (Redundant Array of Independent Drives) A technology that uses multiple hard disk drives for increased reliability and performance.

rainbow tables Large pregenerated data sets of encrypted passwords used in password attacks.

random numbers Numbers for which there is no identifiable pattern or sequence.

ransomware Malware that prevents a user's device from properly and fully functioning until a fee is paid.

RC4 An RC stream cipher that will accept keys up to 128 bits in length.

real-time operating system (RTOS) An operating system that is specifically designed for a system on a chip (SoC) in an embedded system.

recertification The process of periodically revalidating a user's account, access control, and membership role or inclusion in a specific group.

recovery An action step in the incident response process that involves permitting affected systems to return to normal operation.

recovery point objective (RPO) The maximum length of time that an organization can tolerate between backups.

recovery time objective (RTO) The length of time it will take to recover data that has been backed up.

redundancy The use of duplicated equipment to improve the availability of the system.

refactoring Changing the design of existing code.

reference architectures "Supporting structures" for implementing security; also called industry-standard frameworks.

regulatory Information security frameworks/architectures that are required by agencies that regulate the industry.

remote access Trojan (RAT) A Trojan that also gives the threat agent unauthorized remote access to the victim's computer by using specially configured communication protocols.

remote access VPN A user-to-LAN VPN connection used by remote users.

remote wipe A technique used to erase sensitive data stored on the mobile device.

removable media control Tools that can be used to restrict which removable media, such as USB flash drives, can be attached to a system.

replay An attack that makes a copy of the transmission before sending it to the recipient.

reporting requirements/escalation A process for indicating to whom information should be distributed and at what point the security event has escalated to the degree that specific actions should be implemented.

resource exhaustion A situation in which a hardware device with limited resources (CPU, memory, file system storage, etc.) is exploited by an attacker who intentionally tries to consume more resources than intended.

resource vs. security constraint A limitation in providing strong cryptography due to the tug-of-war between the available resources (time and energy) and the security provided by cryptography.

retinal scanner A device that uses the human retina as a biometric identifier.

reverse proxy A proxy that routes requests coming from an external network to the correct internal server.

revert to known state Restoring a device to a previous secure condition.

risk A situation that involves exposure to danger.

risk register A list of potential threats and associated risks.

risk response techniques Different options available when dealing with risks.

rogue AP An unauthorized AP that allows an attacker to bypass many of the network security configurations and opens the network and its users to attacks.

rogue AP system detection   A means for identifying rogue AP devices.

Role-Based Access Control (RBAC)   A "real-world" access control model in which access is based on a user's job function within the organization.

role-based awareness training   Specialized training that is customized to the specific role that an employee holds in the organization.

roles and responsibilities   Clearly designated duties of the members of a cyber-incident response team.

rollback to known configuration   Undo recent changes that cause errors or weaken security.

root digital certificate   A certificate that is created and verified by a CA.

rooting   Circumventing the installed built-in limitations on Android devices.

rootkit   Malware that hides its presence or the presence of other malware.

ROT13   One type of substitution cipher in which the entire alphabet is rotated 13 steps.

round-robin   A scheduling protocol rotation that applies to all devices equally.

router   A device that can forward packets across computer networks.

RSA   The most common asymmetric cryptography algorithm.

Rule-Based Access Control   An access control model that can dynamically assign roles to subjects based on a set of rules defined by a custodian.

runtime code testing   Looking for errors after the program has compiled correctly and is running, such as a pointer deference or memory leak.

safe   A ruggedized steel box with a lock.

salt   A value that can be used to ensure that plaintext, when hashed, will not consistently result in the same digest.

sandbox   A testing environment that isolates untested code from the live production environment.

satellite communications (SATCOM)   A satellite that uses a repeater to send and receive signals from earth.

scalability   The ability to continue to function as the size or volume of the enterprise data center expands.

scarcity   A social engineering effectiveness principle in which the victim is influenced by the idea that something is in short supply.

screen filter   A screen that "blacks out" viewers outside the normal direct viewing angle of a display.

screen lock   A security setting that prevents a mobile device from being accessed until the user enters the correct passcode permitting access.

screenshot   Capturing the current image on the screen in a forensics investigation.

script kiddie   Individual who lacks advanced knowledge of computers and networks and so uses downloaded automated attack software to attack information systems.

secret algorithm   An attempt to hide the existence of an algorithm for enhanced security.

Secure Boot   A standard designed to be used with UEFI to ensure that a computer boots using only software that is trusted by the computer manufacturer.

secure cabinet   A ruggedized steel box with a lock.

secure configuration guides   Guides that are available to help IT security personnel configure hardware devices and software to repel attacks.

secure DevOps   A specific type of software methodology that follows the agile model and heavily incorporates security concepts.

Secure Digital (SD)   One popular type of removable data storage.

Secure FTP (SFTP)   A secure TCP/IP protocol that is used for transporting files by encrypting and compressing all data and commands.

Secure Hash Algorithm (SHA) A secure hash algorithm that creates more secure hash values than Message Digest (MD) algorithms.

Secure Real-time Transport Protocol (SRTP) A protocol for providing protection for Voice over IP (VoIP) communications.

Secure Shell (SSH) An encrypted alternative to the Telnet protocol that is used to access remote computers.

Secure Sockets Layer (SSL) An early and widespread cryptographic transport algorithm; now considered obsolete.

Secure/Multipurpose Internet Mail Extensions (S/MIME) A protocol for securing email messages.

Security and Information Event Management (SIEM) A product that consolidates real-time monitoring and management of security information with analysis and reporting of security events.

Security as a Service (SECaaS) A cloud model in which all security services are delivered from the cloud to the enterprise.

Security Assertion Markup Language (SAML) An Extensible Markup Language (XML) standard that allows secure web domains to exchange user authentication and authorization data.

security automation Tools that test for vulnerabilities.

security control Any device or process that is used to reduce risk.

security guard A human who is an active security element.

security policy A written document that states how an organization plans to protect the company's information technology assets.

security through obscurity A false notion that virtually any system can be made secure so long as outsiders are unaware of it or how it functions.

security token A means of authentication based on a token that the user has.

self-encrypting drives (SEDs) Drives that can automatically encrypt any data stored on it.

self-signed A signed digital certificate that does not depend upon any higher level authority for authentication.

separation of duties The practice of requiring that processes should be divided between two or more individuals.

server OS Operating system software that runs on a network server to provide resources to network users.

server-side execution and validation Input validation that uses the server to perform the validation.

service account A user account that is created explicitly to provide a security context for services running on a server.

Service Level Agreement (SLA) A contract between a vendor and a client that specifies what services will be provided, the responsibilities of each party, and any guarantees of service.

Service Set Identifier (SSID) The alphanumeric user-supplied network name of a WLAN.

session hijacking An attack in which an attacker attempts to impersonate the user by using the user's session token.

session keys Symmetric keys used to encrypt and decrypt information exchanged during the session and to verify its integrity.

shared account An account used by more than one user.

Shibboleth A federation technology open source software package for designing single sign-on (SSO).

shimming Transparently adding a small coding library that intercepts calls made by the device and changes the parameters passed between the device and the device driver.

short message service (SMS) Text messages of a maximum of 160 characters.

shoulder surfing Watching a user enter secret information.

shredding Cutting paper into small strips or particles.

sideloading Downloading unofficial apps.

SIEM aggregation   A SIEM feature that combines data from multiple data sources (network security devices, servers, software applications, etc.) to build a comprehensive picture of attacks.

SIEM automated alerting and triggers   A SIEM feature that can inform security personnel of critical issues that need immediate attention.

SIEM correlation   A SIEM feature that searches the data acquired through SIEM aggregation to look for common characteristics, such as multiple attacks coming from a specific source.

SIEM event duplication   A SIEM feature that can help filter the multiple alerts into a single alarm.

SIEM logs   A SIEM feature that records events to be retained for future analysis and to show that the enterprise has complied with regulations.

SIEM time synchronization   A SIEM feature that can show the order of the events.

sign   A written placard that displays a warning, such as a notice that an area is restricted.

signature-based monitoring   A monitoring technique used by an intrusion detection system (IDS) that examines network traffic to look for well-known patterns and compares the activities against a predefined signature.

Simple Mail Transfer Protocol (SMTP)   An earlier email system that handles outgoing mail.

Simple Network Management Protocol (SNMP)   A TCP/IP protocol that exchanges management information between networked devices. It allows network administrators to remotely monitor, manage, and configure devices on the network.

Single Loss Expectancy (SLE)   The expected monetary loss every time a risk occurs.

single point of failure   A component or entity in a system which, if it no longer functions, would adversely affect the entire system.

single sign-on (SSO)   Using one authentication credential to access multiple accounts or applications.

site-to-site VPN   A VPN connection in which multiple sites can connect to other sites over the Internet.

smart card   A card that contains an integrated circuit chip that can hold information used as part of the authentication process.

snapshot   (1) A backup composed of a series of "reference markers" of the data at a specific point in time; (2) An image of a virtual machine.

SNMPv3   The current version of SNMP that supports authentication and encryption.

social engineering   A means of gathering information for an attack by relying on the weaknesses of individuals.

social media network   Grouping individuals and organizations into clusters or groups based on a like affiliation.

social media policy   A policy that outlines acceptable employee use of social media.

Software as a Service (SaaS)   A model of cloud computing in which the vendor provides access to the vendor's software applications running on a cloud infrastructure.

software defined network (SDN)   Software that virtualizes part of the physical network so that it can be more quickly and easily reconfigured.

software security token   Software stored on a general-purpose device like a laptop computer or smartphone.

something you are   An authentication method based on the features and characteristics of the individual.

something you do   Authentication based on actions that the user is uniquely qualified to perform.

something you have   A type of authentication credential based on the approved user having a specific item in his or her possession.

something you know   Authentication based on something the user knows but no one else knows.

somewhere you are   Authentication based on where the user is located.

sophisticated   Threat actors that have developed a high degree of complexity.

spear phishing   A phishing attack that targets only specific users.

split tunneling   A VPN technology in which only some traffic is sent to the VPN concentrator and is protected while other traffic directly accesses the Internet.

spyware   Tracking software that is deployed without the consent or control of the user.

SSL decryptor   A separate device that decrypts SSL traffic.

SSL/TLS accelerator   A separate hardware card that inserts into a web server that contains one or more co-processors to handle SSL/TLS processing.

staging stage   A stage in application development that performs a quality assurance test to verify that the code functions as intended.

standalone AP   An access point (AP) that does not require another device for management.

standard biometrics   Using fingerprints or other unique physical characteristics of a person's face, hands, or eyes for authentication.

standard naming conventions   Rules for creating account names.

standard operating procedures   Actions and conduct that are considered normal.

stapling   A process for verifying the status of a certificate by sending queries at regular intervals to receive a signed time-stamped response.

stateful packet filtering   A firewall that keeps a record of the state of a connection between an internal computer and an external device and then makes decisions based on the connection as well as the conditions.

stateless packet filtering   A firewall that looks at the incoming packet and permits or denies it based on the conditions that have been set by the administrator.

static program analyzers   Tools that examine software without actually executing the program; instead, the source code is reviewed and analyzed.

steganography   Hiding the existence of data within another type of file, such as an image file.

steganography assessment tools   Tools that can be used to determine if data is hidden well enough in an image, audio, or video file to thwart unauthorized users from finding the data.

storage segmentation   Separating business data from personal data on a mobile device.

stored procedure   A subroutine available to applications that access a relational database.

strategic counterintelligence   An in-depth application of strategic intelligence that involves gaining information about the attacker's intelligence collection capabilities.

strategic intelligence   The collection, processing, analysis, and dissemination of intelligence for forming policy changes.

stream cipher   An algorithm that takes one character and replaces it with one character.

stress testing   Putting an application under a heavier than normal load to determine if the program is robust and can perform all error handling correctly.

Subject Alternative Name (SAN)   Also known as a Unified Communications Certificate (UCC), certificate primarily used for Microsoft Exchange servers or unified communications.

substitution cipher   An encryption algorithm that substitutes one character for another.

supervisory control and data acquisition (SCADA)   A system that controls multiple industrial control systems (ICS).

supply chain   A network that moves a product from the supplier to the customer.

supply chain assessment   Determining the risk to a supply chain network that moves a product from the supplier to the customer.

switch   A device that connects network segments and forwards only frames intended for that specific device or frames sent to all devices.

symmetric cryptographic algorithm   Encryption that uses a single key to encrypt and decrypt a message.

system on a chip (SoC)   A single microprocessor chip on which all the necessary hardware components are contained.

system sprawl   The widespread proliferation of devices across an enterprise.

tabletop exercises   Exercises that simulate an emergency situation but in an informal and stress-free environment.

TACACS+   The current version of the Terminal Access Control Access Control System (TACACS) authentication service.

tailgating   When an unauthorized individual enters a restricted-access building by following an authorized user.

Tcpdump   A Linux command-line protocol analyzer.

technical controls   Using technology that is carried out or managed by devices as a basis for controlling the access to and usage of sensitive data.

template   A type of document in which the standardized content has already been created so that the user needs to enter only specialized and variable components.

Temporal Key Integrity Protocol (TKIP)   The WPA and WPA2 encryption technology.

testing stage   A stage in which an application is tested for any errors that could result in a security vulnerability.

tethering   Using a mobile device with an active Internet connection to share that connection with other mobile devices through Bluetooth or Wi-Fi.

thin AP   An AP that does not contain all the management and configuration functions.

third-party app store   A site from which unofficial apps can be downloaded.

threat   A type of action that has the potential to cause harm.

threat actor   A person or element that has the power to carry out a threat.

threat assessment   Determining what threats an enterprise may be facing.

time offset   The amount of time added to or subtracted from Coordinated Universal Time (UTC) to arrive at the current local time.

time-based one-time password (TOTP)   A one-time password that changes after a set period.

time-of-day restriction   Limitation imposed as to when a user can log in to a system or access resources.

Tracert   A command-line utility that shows the path that a packet takes.

track man hours   Monitoring time in a forensics investigation.

transfer   A response to risk that allows a third party to assume the responsibility of the risk.

transitive trust   A two-way relationship that is automatically created between parent and child domains in a Microsoft Active Directory forest.

transparent proxy   A proxy that does not require any configuration on the user's computer.

Transport Layer Security (TLS)   A widespread cryptographic transport algorithm. Current versions v1.1 and v1.2 are considered secure.

transport mode   An IPsec mode that encrypts only the data portion (payload) of each packet yet leaves the header unencrypted.

Triple Data Encryption Standard (3DES)   A symmetric cipher that was designed to replace DES. No longer considered the most secure symmetric cipher.

Trojan   An executable program that is advertised as performing one activity but which also performs a malicious activity.

troubleshoot common security issues   Identifying security issues that regularly appear and provide an entry point to threat actors.

trust   A social engineering effectiveness principle in which the victim is influenced by confidence.

trust model   The type of trust relationship that can exist between individuals or entities.

trusted OS   An operating system that has been designed through OS hardening.

Trusted Platform Module (TPM)   A chip on the motherboard of the computer that provides cryptographic services.

tunnel mode   An IPsec mode that encrypts both the header and the data portion.

Twofish   A derivation of the Blowfish algorithm that is considered to be strong.

Type I hypervisor   A virtual machine management program that runs directly on the computer's hardware instead of the host operating system.

Type II hypervisor   A virtual machine management program that runs on the host operating system.

typo squatting   *See* URL hijacking.

UEFI (Unified Extensible Firmware Interface)   A newer mechanism that replaces the BIOS for startup.

undocumented assets   Devices that are not formally identified or documented in an enterprise.

Unified Threat Management (UTM)   An integrated device that combines several security functions.

untrained users   Users with little or no instruction in making security decisions.

urgency   A social engineering effectiveness principle in which the victim is influenced by the claim that immediate action is needed.

URL hijacking   Fake sites that are spelled similarly to actual sites (also called *typo squatting*).

usage auditing and review   An audit process that looks at the applications that the user is provided, how frequently they are used, and how they are being used.

USB blocking   A data loss prevention (DLP) technique for blocking the copying of files to a USB flash drive.

USB connections   Universal Serial Bus (USB) connector on mobile devices that is used for data transfer.

USB On-the-Go (OTG)   A specification that allows a mobile device with a USB connection to act as either a host or a peripheral used for external media access.

user digital certificate   The end-point of the certificate chain.

user training   Instructing employees as to the security reasons behind security restrictions.

vendor diversity   Using security products provided by different manufacturers.

vendor-specific guides   Secure configuration guides useful for configuring web servers, operating systems, applications servers, and network infrastructure devices.

version control   Software that allows changes to be automatically recorded and if necessary "rolled back" to a previous version of the software.

video surveillance camera   Video camera used to monitor activity; captured images can be sent to closed circuit TV (CCTV) monitored by a human or recorded for later examination.

Virtual Desktop Infrastructure (VDI)   The process of running a user desktop inside a virtual machine that resides on a server for storing sensitive applications and data on a remote server that is accessed through a smartphone.

Virtual Distributed Ethernet (VDE)   An Ethernet-compliant virtual network that can connect physical computers and/or virtual machines together.

virtual IP (VIP)   An IP address and a specific port number that can be used to reference different physical servers.

virtual LAN (VLAN)   A technology that allows scattered users to be logically grouped together even though they may be attached to different switches.

virtual machine escape protection   A security protection that prevents a virtual machine from directly interacting with the host operating system.

virtual machine sprawl   The widespread proliferation of virtual machines without proper oversight or management.

virtual private network (VPN)   A technology that enables use of an unsecured public network as if it were a secure private network.

virtualization   A means of managing and presenting computer resources by function without regard to their physical layout or location.

virus   Malicious computer code that reproduces itself on the same computer.

vishing A phishing attack that uses telephone calls instead of emails.

voice recognition Using the unique characteristics of a person's voice for authentication.

VPN concentrator A device that aggregates hundreds or thousands of VPN connections.

vulnerability A flaw or weakness that allows a threat agent to bypass security.

vulnerability scan An automated software search through a system for any known security weaknesses that creates a report of those potential exposures.

vulnerability scanner Generic term for a range of products that look for vulnerabilities in networks or systems.

vulnerability testing authorization Permission to perform a vulnerability test.

vulnerable business processes A situation in which an attacker manipulates commonplace actions that are routinely performed; *also called business process compromise.*

W

warm site A remote site that contains computer equipment but does not have active Internet or telecommunication facilities, and does not have backups of data.

waterfall model An application development lifecycle model that uses a sequential design process.

watering hole attack A malicious attack that is directed toward a smaller group of specific individuals by embedding malware in a website frequented by these individuals.

weak configuration Configuration options that provide limited security choices.

web application firewall A firewall that filters by examining the applications using HTTP.

whaling A phishing attack that targets only wealthy individuals.

white box A penetration test where the tester has an in-depth knowledge of the network and systems being tested, including network diagrams,

IP addresses, and even the source code of custom applications.

Wi-Fi Direct The Wi-Fi Alliance implementation of WLAN ad hoc mode.

Wi-Fi enabled microSD card A Secure Digital Input Output (SDIO) card that can wirelessly transmit across a network.

Wi-Fi Protected Access (WPA) The original set of protections from the Wi-Fi Alliance designed to address both encryption and authentication.

Wi-Fi Protected Access 2 (WPA2) The second generation of WPA security from the Wi-Fi Alliance that addresses authentication and encryption on WLANs and is currently the most secure model for Wi-Fi security.

Wi-Fi Protected Setup (WPS) An optional means of configuring security on wireless local area networks primarily intended to help users who have little or no knowledge of security to quickly and easily implement security on their WLANs. Due to design and implementation flaws, WPS is not considered secure.

wildcard digital certificate Certificate used to validate a main domain along with all subdomains.

wiping Overwriting disk space with zeros or random data.

wireless cracker Hardware or software that tests the security of a wireless LAN system by attempting to break its protections of Wi-Fi Protected Access (WPA) or Wi-Fi Protected Access 2 (WPA2).

wireless local area network (WLAN) A wireless network designed to replace or supplement a wired local area network (LAN). Commonly called Wi-Fi.

wireless replay attack A passive attack in which the attacker captures transmitted wireless data, records it, and then sends it on to the original recipient without the attacker's presence being detected.

wireless scanner A device that can discover malicious wireless network activity such as failed login attempts, record these to an event log, and alert an administrator.

witness interviews   Speaking with those present who saw the event or had access to the system in question.

workstation OS   Software that manages hardware and software on a client computer.

worm   A malicious program that uses a computer network to replicate.

X

XOR cipher   An encryption algorithm based on the binary operation e*X*clusive *OR* that compares two bits.

Z

zero day   An attack in which there are no days of warning.

INDEX